Presentation Capture Tool

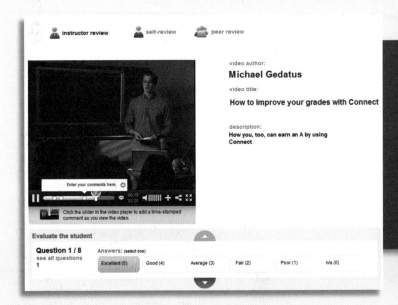

The **presentation capture tool** gives instructors the ability to evaluate presentations and students the freedom to practice their presentations anytime, and anywhere. With its fully customizable rubrics instructors can measure students' uploaded presentations against course outcome and give students specific feedback on where improvement is needed.

Interactive Applications

Interactive Applications for each chapter of the textbook that allow students to practice real business situations, stimulate critical thinking, and reinforce key concepts. Students receive immediate feedback and can track their progress in their own report. Detailed results let instructors see at a glance how each student performs and easily track the progress of every student in their course.

Get Engaged.

Assessment

Connect's easy–to-use assessment tools allow instructors to focus on what's important and ensure there isless time spent on administration and grading, and more time teaching and connecting with students.

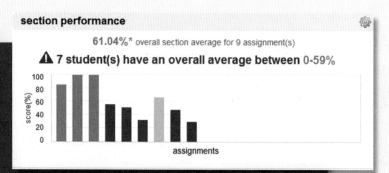

The assignments in Connect are automatically graded, tied to learning objectives and accreditation standards, and feed into instructor reports. Allowing instructors to track student progress, and view reports that assess specific learning outcomes. Instructors can easily generate complete, at-a-glance reports for individual students or the whole class.

Lecture Capture

Make your classes available anytime, anywhere. With simple, one-click recording, students can search for a word or phrase and be taken to the exact place in your lecture that they need to review.

Lesikar's Business Communication

CONNECTING IN A DIGITAL WORLD

THIRTEENTH EDITION

Kathryn Rentz
UNIVERSITY OF CINCINNATI

Paula Lentz
UNIVERSITY OF WISCONSIN–EAU CLAIRE

McGraw-Hill Irwin

LESIKAR'S BUSINESS COMMUNICATION: CONNECTING IN A DIGITAL WORLD,
THIRTEENTH EDITION

Published by McGraw-Hill/Irwin, a business unit of The McGraw-Hill Companies, Inc., 1221 Avenue of the Americas, New York, NY, 10020. Copyright © 2014 by The McGraw-Hill Companies, Inc. All rights reserved. Printed in the United States of America. Previous editions © 2011, 2008, and 2005. No part of this publication may be reproduced or distributed in any form or by any means, or stored in a database or retrieval system, without the prior written consent of The McGraw-Hill Companies, Inc., including, but not limited to, in any network or other electronic storage or transmission, or broadcast for distance learning.

Some ancillaries, including electronic and print components, may not be available to customers outside the United States.

This book is printed on acid-free paper.

2 3 4 5 6 7 8 9 10 QVR/QVR 19 18 17 16 15

ISBN   978-0-07-340321-2
MHID   0-07-340321-0

Senior Vice President, Products & Markets: *Kurt L. Strand*
Vice President, Content Production & Technology Services: *Kimberly Meriwether David*
Managing Director: *Paul Ducham*
Senior Brand Manager: *Anke Braun Weekes*
Executive Director of Development: *Ann Torbert*
Development Editor II: *Kelly I. Pekelder*
Editorial Coordinator: *Heather Darr*
Executive Marketing Manager: *Michael Gedatus*
Lead Project Manager: *Harvey Yep*
Senior Buyer: *Carol A. Bielski*
Cover/Interior Designer: *Cara Hawthorne, cara david DESIGN*
Senior Content Licensing Specialist: *John C. Leland*
Photo Researcher: *Poyee Oster*
Media Project Manager: *Cathy L. Tepper*
Typeface: *10.5/12 Minion Pro*
Compositor: *MPS Limited*
Printer: *Quad/Graphics*

All credits appearing on page or at the end of the book are considered to be an extension of the copyright page.

Library of Congress Cataloging-in-Publication Data

Rentz, Kathryn.
    Lesikar's business communication : connecting in a digital world / Kathryn Rentz, UNIVERSITY OF CINCINNATI, Paula Lentz, UNIVERSITY OF WISCONSIN, EAU CLAIRE. — THIRTEENTH EDITION.
        pages cm
    Includes index.
    ISBN 978-0-07-340321-2 (alk. paper) — ISBN 0-07-340321-0 (alk. paper)
    1. Commercial correspondence. 2. English language—Business English. 3. Business communication.
I. Lentz, Paula. II. Title.
HF5721.L37 2014
651.7—dc23

2012049183

The Internet addresses listed in the text were accurate at the time of publication. The inclusion of a website does not indicate an endorsement by the authors or McGraw-Hill, and McGraw-Hill does not guarantee the accuracy of the information presented at these sites.

www.mhhe.com

Dr. Kathryn Rentz

Dr. Kathryn Rentz is a Professor of English at the University of Cincinnati. She taught her first business writing class as a doctoral student at the University of Illinois at Urbana-Champaign in the early 1980s and has been teaching workplace writing ever since. She helped establish the University of Cincinnati's professional writing program and has served as its coordinator. She has also won the English Department's teaching award, directed the department's graduate program, and helped direct the composition program.

Dr. Rentz's affiliation with the Association for Business Communication goes back to her beginnings as a business writing teacher. She has performed many roles for the ABC, including serving on the board of directors and chairing the publications board. She served two terms as an Associate Editor of the *Journal of Business Communication* and was Interim Editor from 2000–2001, for which she won the Francis W. Weeks Award of Merit. In 2008 she won the ABC's Meada Gibbs Outstanding Teacher Award. In 2011 she was elected Second Vice President for the association, and she will serve as its president in 2013–2014.

Dr. Rentz has published articles on business communication pedagogy and research in such journals as *Business Communication Quarterly,* the *Journal of Business Communication, Technical Communication Quarterly,* and the *Journal of Business and Technical Communication.* She has participated in many professional meetings and seminars over the years and is always learning from her colleagues and her students.

Dr. Paula Lentz

Dr. Paula Lentz is an Assistant Professor and Academic Program Director in the Department of Business Communication at the University of Wisconsin–Eau Claire. She teaches Business Writing, Business Writing II, and Advanced Business Writing. She is also a developer and coordinator of the department's Business Writing Fundamentals Program, which ensures that students have basic writing skills essential for success in their first business writing course. In addition, she chaired the College of Business's Writing Task Force, which developed a college-wide policy for assessing students' writing skills as part of their grade on any writing assignment in any business class.

Dr. Lentz is particularly interested in qualitative research that explores narratives and organizational cultures, genre theory, and writing pedagogy in online environments. She has published in such journals as *Academy of Educational Leadership Journal, Wisconsin Business Education Association Journal, Equal Opportunities International,* and *Qualitative Research in Organizations and Management.* She has also presented her research at several national and regional conferences, including those of the Association for Business Communication and the Academy of Management.

Prior to becoming a full-time academic, she worked as a technical writer and publications editor. She continues to do freelance editing and provides consulting and writing services for several organizations. She received a BA from Coe College, an MA from UW–Eau Claire, and a PhD in Rhetoric and Scientific and Technical Communication from the University of Minnesota.

A Debt of Gratitude

Our deepest respect and appreciation go to **Ray Lesikar,** who wrote the first edition of this book over 35 years ago and led it through 10 revisions. From the beginning, Ray emphasized currency and realism, adaptation to the reader, and straightforward, courteous, correct use of language. A particular strength of his was persuasive writing, to which he brought considerable professional experience. He was a beloved teacher as well as a busy consultant and prolific author, and it is fair to say that, in these roles and as a leader in the Association for Business Communication, he exerted as strong an influence on business communication as anyone else in the field before or since.

In 1991 Ray invited an accomplished business communication and information systems professor at San Diego State University to join him as a coauthor. Thus, with the 6th edition, **Marie Flatley** came on board. Besides doing much of the revision work, Marie added a chapter on communication-related technologies and integrated technology throughout the book. Ever since then, technological currency has been a defining trait of *Business Communication*. An expert on information systems, Marie also put her special stamp on the graphics and research chapters, and she made Lesikar's book one of the first to provide PowerPoint slides, Web-based material, and online activities. Though she has retired from teaching and has officially stepped down as an author for this book, she continues to offer her expertise in other venues.

Ray and Marie made a great team, and they set positive examples for us in ways that are too numerous to list. We're enormously grateful to them and honored to carry on their work.

A lot has changed in the three years since the 12th edition of *Lesikar's Business Communication: Connecting in a Digital World* was published. Twitter and tablets have now become key players on the technology scene, along with Facebook, email marketing, smartphones, and cloud applications. The economies of the United States and many other countries have settled into a recession, creating a tougher job market and changing business and consumer needs. The presence of Gen Yers in the workplace has increased, while Baby Boomers are prolonging their retirement. The boundaries between cultures and countries have become more permeable, making the business world "flatter" and workplaces more diverse. And there's more information overload, making incisive analysis, lucid presentation of data, and development of targeted persuasive strategies more critical.

These changes have necessitated major revisions to the book. Yet its focus on fundamentals remains. Being able to assess a communication situation and audience, determine an appropriate strategy for meeting a business goal, and use words and visuals skillfully is the foundation for all the other skills. The balance between currency and timelessness—a distinguishing trait of this book throughout its 12 previous editions—is one we've worked hard to maintain.

THIS BOOK'S APPROACH AND FEATURES

Each business communication textbook brings a somewhat unique perspective to the subject. This section describes our approach.

The Nature of Business Communication

Our primary assumption about business communication is that it is a *problem-solving activity*. *Lesikar's* was the first book to take this approach, and it is still the only book with this approach at its core. From the first page to the last, this book makes clear that successful business communication requires analysis, judgment, imagination, and effort. Rules of thumb and common patterns are helpful, but preparing an effective document or presentation takes a lot of planning and revision. Students need to be told up front that business communication is not that easy . . . but undertaken with creativity, intelligence, and diligence, it can be extremely rewarding and even fun.

Toward this end, this book includes the most problem-solving cases, by far, of any book on the market—over 150 of them. These realistic scenarios make students consider specific contextual factors as they shape their messages, proposals, and reports. In addition, the cases acquaint students with goals they're likely to encounter on the job, from resolving ethical issues, solving management problems, and crafting company policies to reporting information, selling a product or idea, and managing customer relations. The realistic practice that these cases provide is the key payoff of this book's approach.

Technology

To plan and communicate well, students must know what kinds of communication technologies are available, how their usage differs, and how to use them responsibly. The medium carries its own message, and what medium one uses affects one's communication choices. Plus, familiarity with a wide range of tools enables one to write better, work more efficiently, and produce more professional-looking products. Without overwhelming the students with technical details, we've incorporated dozens of useful communication-related technologies into this book, in every chapter and on almost every topic.

Students must also understand that technology changes. At the foundation of good communication is the ability to do research, to think, to understand other people, to organize one's thoughts logically and tactically, and to use well-chosen verbal and visual elements. We keep our primary emphasis on these skills.

Today's Students

These days, students have a lower tolerance than ever for longwindedness, outdatedness, and irrelevance. We believe that they have a right to expect their business communication book to practice what it preaches. Many of our edits were thus intended to make this edition more reader focused, efficient, engaging, and real.

On the other hand, today's students tend to want clear-cut, quick answers to every question, and this is an unrealistic expectation to bring to business communication. They need to understand what an uncertain enterprise communication is and to be encouraged to solve problems with their own resourceful thinking.

Odd as it may sound, they also need to be encouraged to expand their technological literacy. Research shows that students are expert at using a few applications (e.g., phone apps, email clients, Facebook, and Twitter) but unaware of many other applications useful in business. Further, students tend to be familiar only with such basic software features as "open," "save," "copy," "paste," "print," and "save." Thus, most students can even use some instruction on Word, PowerPoint, and Excel.

Research shows as well that increased use of digital written communication has reduced students' skill with other media (e.g., body language and facial expressions, oral communication). Businesses need employees who can interview others, conduct an effective phone conference, and find information. Many of the exercises and cases in this book require students to practice these skills.

Another fact we've kept in mind is that business communication students' needs and interests can vary greatly, even within the same class. Some students will want to work for major corporations, while others plan to work for small businesses, start their own, or seek work in the nonprofit sector. Some have modest career goals, while others want the fast track to the executive suite. Some will bring strong skills and experience to their coursework, while others will need extra attention to the basics. A comprehensive business communication textbook should accommodate a wide range of student abilities and goals.

This understanding of our students informs the text of the book as well as these special features:

- *Learning Objectives* at the start, at the end, and throughout each chapter that make the main goals of the chapter clear.
- *Introductory Challenges* (formerly "Introductory Situations") that launch each chapter and each form of business communication with a business scenario to draw students quickly into the topic being discussed.
- *Examples of good and bad solutions* for the Introductory Challenges.
- Full-page *Case Illustrations* (real business messages, proposals, and reports), with margin notes, to show how to apply the book's advice.
- *Outlines and checklists* to help students grasp basic organizational patterns and editing guidelines.
- *Communication Matters* boxes that provide expert commentary, interesting facts, and helpful tips.
- *Technology in Brief* boxes illustrating numerous tools and techniques for making the most of technological aids to business communication.
- *Chapter summaries* that distill each chapter's contents into key points.
- *Critical Thinking Questions*, *Skills Building Exercises*, and *Problem-Solving Cases* at the end of the

chapters to promote comprehension, retention, and skillful use of concepts.

- An *Online Learning Center* (OLC) that provides online quizzing, PowerPoint slides, video cases, and *Bizcom Tools & Tips*, a collection of business communication Web resources.
- A *QR code* at the end of every chapter that takes students directly to the book's online resources.

TODAY'S TEACHERS

Business communication teachers face a daunting task: teaching a complex set of concepts and skills in an environment of shrinking resources, increasing class size, and sometimes insufficient support from department administrators. Perhaps the main challenge of the job is that the workload tends to encourage an emphasis on surface features (e.g., correctness and formatting), while effective business communication depends as well on higher-order skills (e.g. critical thinking, adaptation to the audience, and editing one's work). How to do it all—and do it well?

In working to make this edition appealing to students, we hope we've helped with a major part of the battle. The student features listed above also give teachers many excellent talking points and many resources for creating engaging activities and assignments.

In addition, we include the following help for instructors:

- *Annotated PowerPoint slides* for each chapter that include summaries, examples, and interactive slides.
- A downloadable *Instructor's Resource Manual*, which includes sample syllabi and rubrics, sample lectures and classroom activities keyed to the PowerPoint slides, answers to end-of-chapter Critical Thinking Questions and Skills Building Exercises, and sample solutions to selected Problem-Solving Cases.
- *Appendices* on formatting, grading symbols, and documentation of sources.
- A *detailed chapter on correctness*, ending with a diagnostic test for students (with the answers provided in Appendix A).
- A downloadable *Test Bank* for each chapter, along with a computerized test generator for building custom tests.
- An *Online Learning Center* (OLC) that includes resources for every chapter along with video cases and an extensive collection of business communication Web resources, *Bizcom Tools & Tips*.
- A link to *Bcomm Teacher Xchange* (bcommteacherxchange.wordpress.com), our blog for business

communication instructors. As of the end of 2012, we'd posted almost 100 articles, and we post a new one every other week. You can easily keep track of the latest news, tips, and resources in business communication by using the RSS feed or an email subscription.

ORGANIZATION OF THE BOOK

Like the 12 editions before it, this book moves from the more foundational topics to the more specialized ones. The chapters certainly do not have to be taught in the sequence in which they're presented (in fact, a few instructors we know swear by starting with the job-search chapter), but the building-blocks approach represented by this plan tends to work well.

Part I introduces students to the world of business communication. Chapter 1 describes the important role that communication plays in the workplace, current challenges for business communicators, main categories of business communication, and the business communication process. Chapter 2, picking up on a major trend discussed in the previous chapter, discusses the special challenges posed by cross-cultural communication.

Part II reviews the basic techniques of clear, correct, reader-adapted writing. Chapter 3 helps students choose the best wording for their readers, while Chapter 4 focuses on writing effective sentences and paragraphs. Chapter 5 ends this section with advice on managing tone and emphasis.

Part III opens with a chapter on the writing process, the importance of readable formatting, and special considerations for each major medium of business writing, including social media. This section then provides patterns and advice for preparing the most common message types: good-news and neutral messages, bad-news messages, persuasive messages and proposals, and messages related to the job search. These chapters also discuss the choice of direct or indirect structure for the different types of messages.

Part IV concentrates on report writing, beginning with such basics as determining the problem and purpose, gathering and analyzing data, creating a logical structure, writing and formatting the contents, and preparing reports collaboratively. It then discusses four types of short reports and the long, formal report; business research methods, including Internet research; and the use of visuals to enhance reader comprehension.

Part V turns to oral communication, with a chapter on interpersonal communication and meetings and a chapter on oral reports and presentations. The topics range from the basics of speaking and listening to the effective use of different media, including presentation software and Web-conferencing tools.

Part VI provides two chapters—one on writing-related technologies and one on correctness—that can assist students with almost all the other chapters in the book.

Appendices also provide grading checklists, additional guidelines for formatting written documents, and advice and models for documenting sources.

WHAT'S NEW IN THE 13TH EDITION

This edition of *Lesikar's Business Communication* maintains the book's focus on the fundamentals of successful business communication while adapting to the current business and academic environments and incorporating the advice of our helpful reviewers.

Perhaps the most noticeable changes are that

- The cross-cultural communication and research chapters have been moved to earlier locations in the book to better reflect their importance.

- The chapters on good-news and neutral, bad-news, and persuasive messages and proposals no longer have the words "Directness" and "Indirectness" in their titles. These chapters still recommend the more common pattern of organization for each message type, but the change is meant to allow students more latitude in choosing the pattern that best suits the situation.

- The writing style is better adapted to today's students. It is less stuffy, more efficient, and easier to comprehend.

- Just as technology now plays a role in every facet of business, it is everywhere in this book—in the text, in the boxed material, in the examples, in the exercises and cases, and in the visual material. Effective use of communication technologies, which has been a special focus of *Lesikar's* since the 6th edition, has acquired even greater prominence in this edition.

- A QR code at the end of each chapter now makes it easy for students to visit the book's website, where they'll find many more resources.

- Three new executives are featured in the book's six Part Openers: Stuart Crabb, head of learning and development at Facebook; Lynn Marmer, chief communications officer for Kroger Company; and Caroline Molina-Ray, Executive Director of Research and Publications at Apollo Research Institute.

As with each previous new edition, the references, examples, visuals, and exercises have been updated in every chapter. In addition, each chapter has undergone significant revision, as follows:

Chapter 1: Understanding Workplace Communication

- Now opens with an Introductory Challenge (a hypothetical workplace scenario) to generate student interest in the chapter contents.

- Provides the latest statistics on the importance of communication skills in the workplace.

- Updates the "Current Challenges for Business Communicators" section with research on workplace trends from the experts at the Institute for the Future, Apollo Research Institute, and the Aspen Institute.

- Incorporates new media and genres into the discussion of types of workplace communication.

Chapter 2: Communicating Across Cultures

- Now follows Chapter 1 to reflect the increasing importance of communicating well with those in or from other countries and cultures.

- Includes Hofstede's "power distance" factor in the discussion of different cultures' attitudes toward social hierarchy.

- Includes research on the cultural influences on online communication.

- Updates the page of additional resources on cross-cultural communication.

Chapter 3: Adapting Your Words to Your Readers

- Updates the Introductory Challenge as well as the boxed material on annoying business clichés, intergenerational communication, and grammar and style checkers.

- Includes a reference to and definition of *plain language*.

- Uses a more logical, less redundant structure and sharper headings, making the chapter's points clearer and more distinct. (For example, connotation and denotation, often-confused words, and idioms were all discussed in one section. Now they've been separated for better emphasis.)

- Expands and updates the discussion of language referring to those with disabilities.

Chapter 4: Constructing Clear Sentences and Paragraphs

- Opens with an updated Introductory Challenge.

- Trims the prefatory sections to get more quickly to the chapter's advice.

- Adds Communication Matters boxes on limiting the use of "there is/there are" and on avoiding the use of vague "this."

- Includes clearer advice about using short sentences for emphasis and varying sentence structure (e.g., use of coordination and subordination) to manage emphasis.

- Expands the discussion of faulty parallelism.

Chapter 5: Writing for a Positive Effect

- Makes a better case up front for paying attention to the human relations dimension of business writing.

- Shortens the discussion of "the old language of business" since today's students rarely use this language. They do overuse clichés, so the section on this stylistic problem has been expanded.

- Renames the section previously labeled "Resisting the Tendency to Be Formal" to "Choosing the Right Level of Formality" and does a better job of helping students manage the writer–reader relationship through appropriate word choice.

- Renames the section "Tailoring Your Message to Your Reader," which covered points already made in the chapter, to "Avoid Blaming the Reader" and discusses techniques for being tactful. This new section also includes a brief discussion of avoiding anger, replacing the unnecessarily long section on this topic.

- Adds a Technology in Brief box on "Courtesy in the Age of Mobile Devices" based on the latest advice from Emily Post's *Etiquette*.

- Better incorporates the concluding section on managing emphasis by focusing on techniques that contribute to a positive effect.

Chapter 6: Choosing the Best Process and Form

- Updates the audience analysis checklist to address what the audience knows; what the audience needs to know; and what the audience needs to think, feel, do, or believe as a result of the communication.

- Provides current advice on letter writing, particularly on avoiding the use of greetings such as "to whom it may concern" and other outdated expressions.

- Revises the discussion of email to treat it as the established form of business communication it has become rather than as an emerging technology. The sections on email content and structure have also been deleted to make the discussion of email more parallel with that of letters and memos.

- Replaces outdated content on pros and cons of email with advice on current email practices in the workplace and on the role of email in the context of newer communication technologies such as texting and instant messaging.

- Adds a Communication Matters box on the top 10 email mistakes.

- Updates the information on text and instant messaging and social media communication as forms of business messages.

- Adds the content from Chapter 17 regarding print versus online documents, updates this content to reflect the primary differences between the two types, and offers current advice for writing Web content.

Chapter 7: Getting to the Point in Good-News and Neutral Messages

- Shifts the title's focus from directness (an organizational strategy) to the categories of messages being discussed (good-news and neutral).

- Incorporates a running narrative about routine communication at a hypothetical company, White Label Industries, throughout the chapter's Introductory Challenges. This enables instructors to discuss various communication tasks within a single company and provides a consistent scenario for addressing audience, context, and communication goals.

- Updates the good and bad examples to match the new Introductory Challenge scenarios.

- Clarifies the discussion on how to begin a message directly.

- Updates the Case Illustrations.

- Includes a section on direct claims, previously in the chapter on negative messages, with the rationale that routine claims require an approach more like that of neutral messages than that of bad-news messages.

- Adds a Communication Matters box about a company that is doing away with email as a communication channel. This presents an excellent discussion point for instructors.

- Includes 52 revised or new Problem-Solving Cases.

Chapter 8: Maintaining Goodwill in Bad-News Messages

- Shifts the title's focus on indirectness (an organizational strategy) to a focus on the category of messages being discussed (bad-news).

- Cites current research on when to use the direct versus the indirect approach for communicating bad news.

- Addresses the use of apologies in bad-news messages.

- Continues the White Label Industries narrative from Chapter 7 in some of the Introductory Challenges for bad-news messages, which lets instructors continue the simulation in a different rhetorical context.

- Incorporates additional new Introductory Challenges throughout the chapter, with new good and bad sample solutions.

- Adds three new Case Illustrations of bad-news messages written in the indirect approach: a refused request to an external audience, a refused request to an internal audience, and a negative announcement.

- Omits the discussion of direct claims (moved to Chapter 7), keeping the focus in this chapter on preparing claims for an unreceptive audience.

- Adds a Technology in Brief box on using Quick Parts for messages that are sent frequently or routinely.

- Includes 36 revised or new Problem-Solving Cases.

Chapter 9: Making Your Case with Persuasive Messages and Proposals

- Includes "Proposals" in the chapter title to better signal where this topic is covered.

- Updates the "Sales Messages" section with a new Introductory Challenge and new bad and good ways to handle it, new Case Illustrations, and references to the newer sales media (e.g., Facebook pages and Twitter messages).

- Adds a new section, "Enhancing Your Message with Visuals," to highlight the importance of planning compelling visual components for sales messages.

- Adds a Communication Matters box on Web resources for proposal writing.

- Ends with 35 revised or new Problem-Solving Cases for sales and proposal writing.

Chapter 10: Conducting a Winning Job Campaign

- Cites current research on the value employers place on internships.

- Adds a Technology in Brief box on tips for creating an effective LinkedIn profile.

- Includes comments in various parts of the chapter on how employers and job seekers use social networking sites in the hiring or job-search process.

- Distinguishes between features of print résumés and electronic résumés.

- Clarifies the discussion of the various types of electronic résumés (e.g., email, scannable, Web-based).

- Provides an extended discussion of best practices for creating electronic résumés.

- Clarifies when to include references with a résumé.

- Adds a Communication Matters box reporting a study on how much time employers spend reviewing résumés before deciding whether a candidate is a good fit.

- Updates the Case Illustrations for the résumé and cover letter examples.

- Adds a Communication Matters box on the 10 toughest interview questions.

- Adds a Communication Matters box emphasizing the importance of thank-you notes.

Chapter 11: Preparing Informative and Influential Business Reports

- Clarifies the discussion of problem statements by using "problem statement" to mean a description of the situation requiring a solution and "purpose statement" to mean the stated goal of the research conducted to find that solution.

- Adds basic guidelines for conducting research as preparation for Chapter 13 ("Conducting Research for Decision Makers").
- Includes a new Technology in Brief box on report-writing software.
- Reduces the overly long section on writing headings but extends the discussion of making them parallel.

Chapter 12: Choosing the Right Type of Report

- Updates the discussion of problem statements for reports to incorporate the distinction between "problem statement" and "purpose statement."
- Updates and enhances the sample reports.
- Adds a new sample progress report to show students how to prepare one about a course project.
- Removes audit reports since these are too specialized and often too routinized to be useful to most students.
- Ends with 35 revised or new Problem-Solving Cases and 152 additional report topics.

Chapter 13: Conducting Research for Decision Makers

- Is now grouped with the report-writing chapters to signal the importance of research to report writing.
- Opens with a new motivational section, "Why Research Matters," followed by an overview of the main categories of research.
- Gets quickly to resources that students and professionals are likely to use—e.g., the Internet and other Web resources—rather than getting bogged down right away in a list of reference materials.
- Includes a new section on conducting research with social networking tools—Facebook, Twitter, LinkedIn, wikis, blogs, and listservs—and social bookmarking tools.
- Explains what a database (e.g., ABI/Inform) is and how to search it.
- Streamlines the discussion of reference materials by putting these resources into a descriptive table and updates the page-long List of Resources by Research Question.
- Includes more thorough, concrete advice on designing surveys.
- Expands the discussion of ethical guidelines for conducting research.

Chapter 14: Using Visuals to Make Your Point

- Changes "graphics" to "visuals" throughout to better reflect that business communicators have more options than just those that graph raw data.
- Adds a new Introductory Challenge.
- Adds a Communication Matters box on infographics.

- Incorporates many new visuals to illustrate common types of visuals used in business communication.
- Adds a Communication Matters box on avoiding chartjunk.

Chapter 15: Communicating Effectively in Meetings and Conversations

- Incorporates a new Introductory Challenge.
- Adds a Communication Matters box providing specific exercises and tips for improving voice quality.
- Adds a Communication Matters box on negotiation as an interpersonal skill.
- Includes a Technology in Brief box encouraging students to become familiar with online meeting tools such as Skype and to try using these tools for their group meetings.
- Updates the discussion of phone etiquette and organizes the information clearly into categories of initiating calls, answering calls directly, and screening calls for others.
- Deletes the discussion on using speech-recognition software for creating messages and reports. Some of the information is relocated to Chapter 17, "Leveraging Technology for Better Writing."
- Updates the Communication Matters box on using a professional handshake.
- Adds information regarding current research on the relationship between the technology use of "digital natives'" (Gen Xers and Gen Yers) and the potential underdevelopment of their nonverbal communication skills.

Chapter 16: Delivering Oral Reports and Business Speeches

- Enhances and clarifies the section on oral reports.
- Replaces "Making Formal Speeches" with "Giving Speeches and Presentations" to reduce the emphasis on speeches and increase the emphasis on the more common types of talks.
- Adds advice on choosing the best medium/media for the presentation.
- Adds sections on planning for interaction with the audience and choosing the means of audience feedback (e.g., Q&A, Twitter).
- Adds a Communication Matters box on TED talks.
- Gives better advice about planning and using visuals to support a talk.
- Relabels the section "Use of PowerPoint" as "Use of Presentation Software" and presents guidelines for using any presentation tool (e.g., Prezi, Google Docs, SlideRocket).
- Adds a section on using handouts to support a talk.

- Recasts the final section on virtual presentations as "Delivering Web-Based Presentations" and moves it up in the chapter to reflect the increased popularity of webinars.

Chapter 17: Leveraging Technology for Better Writing

- Focuses the chapter specifically on technologies that enhance writing ability rather than on general communication technologies since the latter are discussed throughout the text.
- Eliminates redundancies between this chapter and Chapter 13 ("Conducting Research for Decision Makers") in terms of gathering information electronically.
- Distinguishes between, and discusses separately, the use of technology to organize a project and the use of technology to organize a document.
- Reorganizes content to flow more logically. For example, the discussion of speech-recognition software is moved to the section on technologies for drafting rather than on technologies for revising and editing.
- Updates terminology to reflect current usage (e.g., "electronic calendar" rather than "personal information management tool").
- Discusses RSS feeds and tablet or smartphone apps as information-gathering tools.
- Mentions multimedia tools, document design software, and Web development software as options for creating and presenting information.
- Omits the discussion of print versus electronic documents (moved to Chapter 6).
- Adds visuals of iPad apps to reflect current technology used in business communication.
- Provides a Communication Matters box on knowing one's audience before using texting abbreviations or other "text speak."

Chapter 18: Conveying Professionalism Through Correctness

- Includes 50 new practice sentences to build students' skills in the use of pronoun case, pronoun–antecedent agreement, subject–verb agreement, punctuation, and the apostrophe.
- Provides additional guidelines on pronoun–antecedent agreement.
- Adds a Communication Matters box citing current news articles that discuss the relationship between an employee's use of good grammar and success in the workplace.

In addition, Appendix B ("Physical Presentation of Letters, Memos, and Reports") and Appendix E ("Documentation and the Bibliography") have been updated to reflect current practices and technologies for formatting documents and citing sources.

ACKNOWLEDGMENTS

Many dedicated business communication instructors and business professionals have contributed to this book throughout its long history. We extend our sincere thanks to them for their ideas and inspiration.

We are especially indebted to those who have served as reviewers for this and past editions. They truly deserve much of the credit for improvements in this book.

Reviewers of the 12th edition:

Melissa Bakeman, *California State University—San Bernardino*

Charles D. Baker, *Kent State University*

Donna M. Carlon, *University of Central Oklahoma*

Andrea Deacon, *University of Wisconsin—Stout*

James H. Donelan, *University of California—Santa Barbara*

John S. Donnellan, *The University of Texas at Austin (retired)*

Heather Duvall, *University of Central Oklahoma*

Daniel L. Emery, *University of Oklahoma*

Connie Golden, *Lakeland Community College*

Lawrence W. Hahn, *San Diego Miramar College*

Harold Hellwig, *Idaho State University*

Richard Lacy, *California State University, Fresno*

Nancy Kathryn LeGrand, *Southeast Missouri State University*

Faith McDonald, *The Pennsylvania State University*

Gregory H. Morin, *University of Nebraska—Omaha*

Lauren Paisley, *Genesee Community College*

Richard D. Parker, *High Point University*

Diana Reep, *University of Akron*

Patty Saliba, *Belhaven University*

Terry Sanders, *Macon State College*

Jean Anna Sellers, *Fort Hays State University*

Ida Short, *Schoolcraft College*

Cecil V. Tarrant III, *Western Illinois University*

Deborah Valentine, *Emory University*

Reviewers of previous editions:

Laura Alderson, *University of Memphis*

Carolyn Ashe, *University of Houston—Downtown*

Jean Baird, *Bringham Young University—Idaho*

James J. Balakier, *University of South Dakota*

Lecia Barker, *University of Colorado*

Melissa Barth, *Appalachian State University*

Rathin Basu, *Ferrum College*

Jill M. Batson, *Henderson State University*

Linda Bell, *Reading Area Community College*

Kenneth R. Bellinder, *National–Louis University*

Sandra K. Christianson, *National American University*

Audrey Cohen, *Kingsborough Community College*

Brenda A. Cornelius, *University of Arkansas Community College at Hope*

Sara Cushing, *Piedmont Technical College*

Mary Beth Debs, *University of Cincinnati*

Linda Di Desidero, *University of Maryland University College*

Norma J. Dexter, *Florida State University—Panama City*

Gloria Diemer, *Suffolk County Community College*

Michael E. Durkee, *Miramar Community College*

Carolyn Embree, *The University of Akron*

Donna Everett, *Morehead State University*

Lu Ann Farrell, *Clinton Community College*

Dale Fike, *Redlands Community College*

Alicen Fiosi, *Lamar University*

Sheryl Fitzpatrick, *Waldorf College*

Fernando Ganivet, *Florida International University*

Sean J. Glassberg, *Horry–Georgetown Technical College*

Glenn Good, *Front Range Community College*

Katherine Gotthardt, *National American University*

Diana Green, *Weber State University*

Frances K. Griffin, *Oklahoma State University*

Susan A. Heller, *Reading Area Community College*

Guillermo A. Hernandez, *De Anza College*

Deborah Holder, *Piedmont Technical College*

Robert Insley, *University of North Texas*

Jane Johansen, *University of Southern Indiana*

Jean Kapinsky, *Northcentral Technical College*

Jeanette A. Karjala, *Winona State University*

Brian Keliher, *Grossmont College*

Susan King, *Union County College*

Melinda Knight, *University of Rochester*

Marianna Larsen, *Utah State University*

Anita Leffel, *The University of Texas at San Antonio*

Nancy K. Legrand, *Southeast Missouri State University*

Jere Littlejohn, *University of Mississippi*

John La Lone, *Tarleton State University—Central Texas*

Jeanette S. Martin, *University of Mississippi*

Kenneth R. Mayer, *Cleveland State University*

Robert J. McMahon, *National American University*

Elizabeth Metzger, *University of South Florida*

Richard R. Meza, *Columbia College of Missouri*

Andrea Muldoon, *University of Wisconsin—Stout*

Rebecca Pope-Ruark, *Elon University*

R. Wayne Preslar, *Methodist College*

Zane Quible, *Oklahoma State University*

Windy Rachal, *Nicholls State University*

Pamela L. Ramey, *Kent State University*

Evette W. Richardson, *Norfolk State University*

Lillie A. Robinson, *North Carolina AT&T University*

Heidi Schultz, *University of North Carolina—Chapel Hill*

Janet Sebesy, *Cuyahoga Community College*

Mageya R. Sharp, *Cerritos College*

Stacey Short, *Northern Illinois University*

Julie Simon, *Clarkson College*

Karen J. Smith, *Columbia Southern University*

Lisa Gueldenzoph Snyder, *North Carolina AT&T University*

Eric Soares, *California State University, East Bay*

Jessica Stoudenmire, *El Camino College*

Sandy Thomas, *Kansas City Kansas Community College*

Traci Thompson, *Kilgore College—Longview*

David A. Victor, *Eastern Michigan University*

David Ward, *University of Wisconsin—Madison*

Gary T. Ward, *Reedley College*

Kelly Warren, *Wayland Baptist University*

Karen Schelter Williams, *San Diego Mesa College*

Laura Williams, *Lipscomb University*

Bennie J. Wilson, III, *University of Texas at San Antonio*

Robert Zackowski, *Horry Georgetown Technical College*

In addition, we would particularly like to thank Lora Arduser for her major contributions to the research chapter and Appendix E, Riley Dugan and Emily Elsner Twesme for the problem-solving cases they contributed, and Heather Smith for her excellent work on the PowerPoint slides and Instructor's Manual.

Finally, on our respective home fronts, we acknowledge the support of our loved ones. Kathy acknowledges the support of Dave, Caroline, and Michael Rentz; her sister, Rebecca Horn; and friends in the English Department at the University of Cincinnati. Paula acknowledges her husband John, family members, friends, and colleagues in the College of Business at the University of Wisconsin–Eau Claire. Your support has made this book possible.

Kathryn Rentz
Paula Lentz

LESIKAR'S BUSINESS COMMUNICATION (13th ed.), by Kathryn Rentz and Paula Lentz, brings the contemporary perspective of two experienced teachers to Ray Lesikar's classic textbook. Following the standard set by the 6th edition, this book integrates current technologies and trends throughout while maintaining an emphasis on the fundamentals: careful analysis of the communication problem, development of an audience-focused solution, and clear, correct use of language and visuals. Combined with abundant realistic examples, exercises, and cases, this approach makes *Lesikar's* one of the most pedagogically effective books in the field.

PART OPENERS

The six sections of the book begin with part openers featuring quotes from distinguished business leaders in such well-known companies as Facebook and Berkshire Hathaway. These opening comments attest to the importance of business communication skills in the real world.

PART ONE

Introduction

1 Understanding Workplace Communication
2 Communicating Across Cultures

As head of Learning & Development for Facebook, Stuart Crabb knows what qualities companies look for in a job candidate. He has over 20 years' experience helping companies hire the right people, develop their talent, and become more culturally diverse.

What does it take to succeed at Facebook? According to Crabb, the answers are "critical thinking," "problem solving," "creativity," and "performance." It also takes being "motivated," "individually accountable," and a "good fit" with the company culture.

These happen to be key traits of successful business communicators, too. They understand that communicating well takes analysis, judgment, and even ingenuity. It takes being attuned to people and to each communication situation. And it takes not only verbal skill but also technological and visual literacy.

Like business itself, business communication can be challenging. But the challenge can be fun, and solving communication problems can bring enormous rewards. This book will help prepare you for an exciting future as both a businessperson and a communicator.

Stuart Crabb, Head of Learning & Development for Facebook

PART TWO

Fundamentals of Business Writing

3 Adapting Your Words to Your Readers
4 Constructing Clear Sentences and Paragraphs
5 Writing for a Positive Effect

With a net worth of around $44 billion, Warren Buffett is ranked by *Forbes* magazine as the second-richest person in the world, after Microsoft Cofounder and Chairman Bill Gates. Buffett made his first stock purchase at the age of 11 but sold before the stock skyrocketed. This early lesson taught him to study hard and carefully analyze potential investments. The result was the development of one of the world's largest holding companies, Berkshire Hathaway, Inc.

Although best known for his ability to pick stocks, Buffett was honored in 2006 by the National Commission on Writing for America's Families, Schools, and Colleges for writing Berkshire Hathaway's annual report. Buffett writes, "One way or another, you have to project your ideas to other people. Writing isn't necessarily easy. . . . But you get better and better at it, and I encourage everybody to do that."

Warren E. Buffett, CEO of Berkshire Hathaway, Inc.

at the 13th Edition

- If appropriate, achieve a secondary goal (e.g., reselling or confirming a mutual understanding).
- Close with a goodwill-building comment, adapted to the topic of the message.

Contrasting Acknowledgments

The following two messages show bad and good ways to acknowledge Mr. Lee's order. As you would expect, the good version follows the plan described in the preceding paragraphs.

Slow Route to a Favorable Message. The bad example begins indirectly, emphasizing receipt of the order. Although intended to produce goodwill, the second sentence further delays what the reader wants most to hear. Moreover, the letter is written from the writer's point of view (note the we-emphasis).

This one delays the important news.

> Dear Mr. Lee:
>
> Your April 4 order for $1,743.30 worth of Protect-O paints and supplies has been received. We are pleased to have this nice order and hope that it marks the beginning of a long relationship.
>
> As you instructed, we will bill you for this amount. We are shipping the goods today by Blue Darter Motor Freight.
>
> We look forward to your future orders.
>
> Sincerely,

Fast-Moving Presentation of the Good News. The better message begins directly, telling Mr. Lee that he is getting what he wants. The remainder of the message is a customer welcome and subtle selling. Notice the good use of reader emphasis and positive language. The message closes with a note of appreciation and a friendly, forward look.

This direct message is better.

> Dear Mr. Lee:
>
> Your selection of Protect-O paints and supplies was shipped today by Blue Darter Freight and should reach you by Wednesday. As you requested, we are sending you an invoice for $1,743.30, including sales tax.
>
> Welcome to the Protect-O circle of dealers. Our representative, Ms. ⊙ Wooley, will call from time to time to offer whatever assistance she can. Sh⊙ highly competent technical adviser on paint and painting.
>
> Here in the home plant we also will do what we can to help you profit from Prot⊙ products. We'll do our best to give you the most efficient service. And we'll co⊙ to develop the best possible paints—like our new Chem-Treat line. As you w⊙ from the enclosed brochure, Chem-Treat is a real breakthrough in mildew prote⊙
>
> We genuinely appreciate your order, Mr. Lee. We are determined to serve you⊙ in the years ahead.
>
> Sincerely,

GOOD AND BAD EXAMPLES

Numerous good and bad examples of various business documents—from messages to memos to reports—are featured throughout the text. These writing samples allow students to learn by example. For easy reference, good examples are highlighted with a green bulls-eye and bad examples are denoted by a red missed target.

Contrasting Negative Announcements

Good and bad techniques in negative announcements are illustrated in the following two messages. The bad one is direct, which in some circumstances may be acceptable but clearly is not in this case. The good one follows the pattern just discussed.

Directness Here Alarms the Readers. This bad example clearly will upset the readers with its abrupt announcement in the beginning. The readers aren't prepared to receive the negative message. They probably don't understand the reasons behind the negative news. The explanation comes later, but the readers are not likely to be in a receptive mood when they see it. The message ends with a repetition of the bad news.

Directness here sends a negative message.

> To our employees:
>
> National Window Systems management sincerely regrets that effective February 1 you must begin contributing 25 percent of the cost of your medical insurance. As you know, in the past the company has paid the full amount.
>
> This decision is primarily the result of the rising costs of health insurance, but our profits also have declined the last several quarters. Given this tight financial picture, we needed to find ways to reduce expenses.
>
> We trust that you will understand why we must ask for your help with cutting costs to the company.
>
> Sincerely,

Convincing Explanation Begins a Courteous Message. The better example follows the recommended indirect pattern. Its opening words begin the task of convincing the readers of the appropriateness of the action to be taken. After more convincing explanation, the announcement flows logically. Perhaps it will not be received positively by all recipients, but it represents a reasonable position given the facts presented. After the announcement comes an offer of assistance to help readers deal with their new situation. The last paragraph reminds readers of remaining benefits and reassures them that management understands their interests. It ends on an appreciative, goodwill note.

This indirect example follows the bad-news pattern.

> To All Employees:
>
> Companies all across the United States, no matter how large or small, are struggling to keep up with the rising cost of healthcare. Legislators, healthcare providers, and businesspeople everywhere are working to find a solution to the skyrocketing cost of health insurance.
>
> We are feeling this situation here in our own company. The premiums that we pay to cover our health benefits have increased by 34 percent over the last two years, and they now represent a huge percentage of our expenditures. Meanwhile, as you know, our sales have been lower than usual for the past several quarters.
>
> For the short term, we must find a way to cut overall costs. Your management has considered many options and rejected such measures as cutting salaries and reducing personnel. Of the solutions that will be implemented, the only change that affects you directly concerns your medical insurance. On **March 1** we will begin deducting 25 percent of the cost of the premium.
>
> Jim Taylor in the Personnel Office will soon be announcing an informational meeting about your insurance options. Switching to spousal coverage, choosing a less expensive plan with lighter deductibles, or setting up a flexible spending

THEMATIC BOXES

Each chapter features thematic boxes to highlight and reinforce important topics.

INTRODUCTORY CHALLENGE

Searching for New Regional Headquarters

Introduce yourself to routine inquiries by assuming you are the assistant to the vice president for administration of White Label Industries (WLI). WLI is the manufacturer and distributor of an assortment of high-quality products.

You and your boss were recently chatting about WLI's plans to relocate its regional headquarters. Your boss tells you that she and other top management have chosen the city but have not been able to find the perfect office space. She says that they have not been happy with what realtors have found for them or with what they have found in their own searches of classified ads and realty agencies' websites. When you suggest that they expand their search to something a little less traditional such as craigslist, your boss says, "Great idea! I don't think any of us have used craigslist, though. Could you find some locations and show them to us at our Friday meeting?"

You're a bit intimidated by the prospect, but you know that this is a great chance to demonstrate your professional skills. You visit craigslist and find what you believe would be the perfect office headquarters. You know you could just show the executives the ad at the meeting, but having read the ad and having analyzed your audience, you know the executives will need more information. To present your best professional image at Friday's meeting, you need to write a routine inquiry seeking additional details about the office space.

INTRODUCTORY CHALLENGE

Each box presents a realistic business scenario and provides students with a context for the topics discussed in the chapter.

TECHNOLOGY IN BRIEF

Using a Table of Contents Generator for Speed and Accuracy

The table of contents generator tool in today's word-processing software frees writers from both the physical formatting and the accuracy tasks. Just a few clicks produce and format the table of contents, along with leaders and page numbers. Additionally, today's generators add links so that those reading the report on the screen rather than on paper can easily navigate to a particular section or page by simply clicking it in the table of contents.

The table of contents generator works with Word's built-in styles, which you use as tags to mark the different levels of headings that will be included in the table of contents. If you are using a standard report template, styles are already incorporated in it. If you are creating your own report from a blank document, you could use predefined styles or define your own styles to create titles, headings, and subheads. Styles provide consistency so that headings at certain levels always appear the same, helping the reader see the relationship of the parts of your report.

Furthermore, if you decide to change the material in your report after you have generated the table of contents, you simply regenerate it to update page numbers with only a few clicks.

Shown here is a sample table of contents automatically created in Word 2010.

TECHNOLOGY IN BRIEF

These boxes reflect how current technologies affect business communication, covering such topics as the top 10 email mistakes, courteous use of mobile devices, and tools and technologies that students will encounter in the workplace.

COMMUNICATION MATTERS

The Most Annoying Business Clichés

Blogger and writing expert Mary Cullen surveyed a wide range of clients from various industries to ask them "which overused phrases they would like to see banished." Here are their top replies:

1. At the end of the day
2. 30,000-foot view
3. Give 110%
4. Think outside of the box
5. FYI
6. 800-pound gorilla
7. Throw under the bus
8. My bad
9. Rightsizing
10. Reaching out
11. Low-hanging fruit
12. Paradigm shift
13. Take it offline
14. At this point in time
15. Synergy
16. Action item

Cullen adds one more that particularly bothers her: "Going forward." "Where else would we go?" she asks. "Backward?"

SOURCE: "Top 25 Jargon and Gobbledygook Phrases 2011," *Instructional Solutions*, www.instructionalsolutions.com, 2012. Web, 20 May 2012. From Instructional Solutions, www.instructionalsolutions.com. Reprinted with permission.

COMMUNICATION MATTERS

Communication Matters boxes contain authoritative and anecdotal commentary to emphasize communication concepts from each chapter.

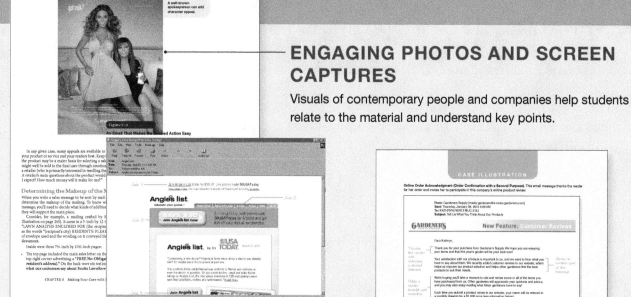

ENGAGING PHOTOS AND SCREEN CAPTURES

Visuals of contemporary people and companies help students relate to the material and understand key points.

NUMEROUS CASE ILLUSTRATIONS

Annotated examples of real business messages, reports, and other documents show how to apply the concepts discussed in the chapters.

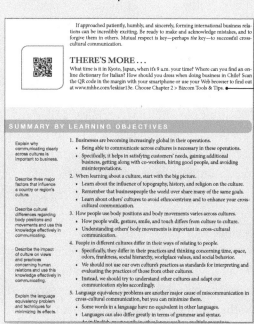

QUICK ACCESS TO ONLINE RESOURCES

A QR code and URL at the end of every chapter will take students directly to the contents of the website's *Bizcom Tools & Tips*. Here they'll find over a hundred Web-based resources—from technology videos to grammar and style tips to advice on proposal writing and other topics.

RELEVANT AND CHALLENGING CASES

An extensive collection of scenario-based cases gives students practice solving communication problems on a wide range of business topics, from Internet use to customer service to marketing research.

A Wealth of Supplements

INSTRUCTOR'S MANUAL

The downloadable Instructor's Manual (IM) shows how to present the book's contents step by step. After an orienting introduction, each IM chapter walks the instructor though the corresponding book chapter, syncing the discussion with the chapter's PowerPoint slides. The IM also provides tips for teaching the first day of class, sample syllabi for the quarter and semester systems, sample answers and talking points for the Critical Thinking Questions and Skills Building Exercises, and sample solutions for the Problem-Solving Cases.

The book's website supplements the IM with teaching notes for the video cases, a wide range of Web-based resources, and a biweekly blog post by the authors. Even a new instructor can get up to speed quickly while having many helpful options to choose from.

TEST BANK AND EZ TEST

The Test Bank includes more than 1,000 multiple-choice, true/false, and short-answer questions. Each question identifies the answer, difficulty level, and Bloom's Taxonomy level coding. Each test question is also tagged to the Learning Objective it covers in the chapter and the AACSB Learning Standard it falls under.

EZ TEST ONLINE

McGraw-Hill's *EZ Test Online* is a flexible and easy-to-use electronic testing program. The program allows instructors to create tests from book-specific items, accommodates a wide range of question types, and enables instructors to add their own questions. Multiple versions of a test can be created, and any test can be exported for use with WebCT, Blackboard, or any other course management system. EZ Test Online is accessible to busy instructors virtually anywhere via the Web, and the program eliminates the need for them to install test software. For more information about EZ Test Online, please see the website at www.eztestonline.com.

PRESENTATION SLIDES

Clear, visually appealing PowerPoint slides support every chapter. In addition to reinforcing the book's key points, the slides provide additional cases to discuss and other forms of interactivity (e.g., questions to answer or blanks to fill in).

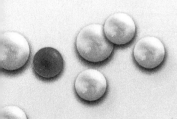

The instructors' version of the slides also contains brief notes to help the teacher emphasize the key points and explain their importance. Instructors can easily add to or revise the slides to adapt them to a particular approach.

MCGRAW-HILL *CONNECT BUSINESS COMMUNICATION*

connect
|BUSINESS COMMUNICATION

LESS MANAGING. MORE TEACHING. GREATER LEARNING.

McGraw-Hill *Connect Business Communication* is an online assignment and assessment solution that connects students with the tools and resources they'll need to understand and apply the book's concepts. *Connect Business Communication* helps prepare students for their future by enabling faster learning, more efficient studying, and higher retention of knowledge.

MCGRAW-HILL *CONNECT BUSINESS COMMUNICATION* FEATURES

Connect Business Communication offers a number of powerful tools and features to make managing assignments easier, so faculty can spend more time teaching. With *Connect Business Communication*, students can engage with their coursework anytime and anywhere, making the learning process more accessible and efficient. *Connect Business Communication* offers you the features described below.

DIAGNOSTIC AND ADAPTIVE LEARNING AND MASTERY OF CONCEPTS

Connect Business Communication provides personalized learning plans to develop or improve students' editing skills, and it empowers students to put responsible writing into practice. This adaptive learning system helps students learn faster, study more efficiently, and retain more knowledge for greater success.

PRACTICE OF PRESENTATION SKILLS INSIDE AND OUTSIDE THE CLASSROOM

The presentation capture tool gives instructors the ability to evaluate presentations and students the freedom to practice their presentations anytime and anywhere.

ONLINE INTERACTIVES

Online Interactives are exercises that enable students to apply key concepts and develop their critical thinking. These Interactives, prepared by the authors, immerse students in experiential learning by engaging them in a variety of realistic interactive scenarios. Students receive immediate feedback at intermediate steps throughout each exercise, as well as comprehensive feedback at the end of the assignment. All Interactives are automatically scored and entered into the instructor gradebook.

STUDENT PROGRESS TRACKING

Connect Business Communication keeps instructors informed about how each student, section, and class is performing, allowing for more productive use of class time and office hours. The progress-tracking function enables you to

- View scored work immediately and track individual or group performance with assignment and grade reports.
- Access an instant view of student or class performance relative to learning objectives.
- Collect data and generate reports required by many accreditation organizations, such as AACSB.

SMART GRADING

When it comes to studying, time is precious. *Connect Business Communication* helps students learn more efficiently by providing feedback and practice material when they need it, where they need it. When it comes to teaching, your time also is precious. The grading function enables you to

- Have assignments scored automatically, giving students immediate feedback on their work and side-by-side comparisons with correct answers.
- Access and review each response, manually change grades, or leave comments for students to review.
- Reinforce classroom concepts with practice tests and instant quizzes.

SIMPLE ASSIGNMENT MANAGEMENT

With *Connect Business Communication*, creating assignments is easier than ever, so you can spend more time teaching and less time managing. The assignment management function enables you to

- Create and deliver assignments easily with selectable end-of-chapter questions and Test Bank items.
- Streamline lesson planning, student progress reporting, and assignment grading to make classroom management more efficient than ever.
- Go paperless with the eBook and online submission and grading of student assignments.

INSTRUCTOR LIBRARY

The *Connect Business Communication* Instructor Library is your repository for additional resources to improve student engagement in and out of class. You can select and use any asset that enhances your lecture. The *Connect Business Communication* Instructor Library includes

- Instructor's Manual
- *Bizcom Tools & Tips*, an extensive collection of Web resources
- PowerPoint files
- Test Bank
- *Bcomm Teacher Xchange*, the authors' blog
- Management Asset Gallery, which contains 23 Self-Assessments and Manager's Hot Seat Videos
- eBook

STUDENT STUDY CENTER

The *Connect Business Communication* Student Study Center is the place for students to access additional resources. The Student Study Center

- Offers students quick access to lectures, practice materials, Web resources, eBooks, and more.
- Provides instant practice material and study questions, easily accessible on the go.
- Gives students access to the personalized learning plan, described above, and more.

LECTURE CAPTURE VIA TEGRITY CAMPUS

Increase the attention paid to lecture discussion by decreasing the attention paid to note taking. For an additional charge Lecture Capture offers new ways for students to focus on the in-class discussion, knowing they can revisit important topics later. See below for further information.

MCGRAW-HILL *CONNECT PLUS BUSINESS COMMUNICATION*

McGraw-Hill reinvents the textbook learning experience for the modern student with *Connect Plus Business Communication*. A seamless integration of an eBook and *Connect Business Communication*, *Connect Plus Business Communication* provides all of the *Connect Business Communication* features plus the following:

- An integrated eBook, allowing for anytime, anywhere access to the textbook.
- Dynamic links between the problems or questions you assign to your students and the location in the eBook where that problem or question is covered.
- A powerful search function to pinpoint and connect key concepts in a snap.

In short, *Connect Business Communication* offers you and your students powerful tools and features that optimize your time and energies, enabling you to focus on course content, teaching, and student learning. *Connect Business Communication* also offers a wealth of content resources for both instructors and students. This state-of-the-art, thoroughly tested system supports you in preparing students for the world that awaits.

For more information about *Connect*, go to www.mcgrawhillconnect.com, or contact your local McGraw-Hill sales representative.

TEGRITY CAMPUS: LECTURES 24/7

Tegrity Campus is a service that makes class time available 24/7 by automatically capturing every lecture in a searchable format for students to review when they study and complete assignments. With a simple one-click start-and-stop process, you capture all computer screens and corresponding audio. Students can replay any part of any class with easy-to-use browser-based viewing on a PC or Mac.

Educators know that the more students can see, hear, and experience class resources, the better they learn. In fact, studies prove it. With Tegrity Campus, students quickly recall key moments by using Tegrity Campus's unique search feature. This search helps students efficiently find what they need, when they need it, across an entire semester of class recordings. Help turn all your students' study time into learning moments immediately supported by your lecture.

Lecture Capture enables you to

- Record and distribute your lecture with a click of a button.
- Record and index PowerPoint presentations and anything shown on your computer so it is easily searchable, frame by frame.
- Offer access to lectures anytime and anywhere by computer, iPod, or mobile device.
- Increase intent listening and class participation by easing students' concerns about note taking. Lecture Capture will make it more likely that you will see students' faces, not the tops of their heads.

To learn more about Tegrity, watch a two minute Flash demo at http://tegritycampus .mhhe.com.

ASSURANCE-OF-LEARNING READY

Many educational institutions today are focused on the notion of *assurance of learning*, an important element of some accreditation standards. *Lesikar's Business Communication* is designed specifically to support your assurance-of-learning initiatives with a simple, yet powerful, solution.

Each Test Bank question for *Lesikar's Business Communication* maps to a specific chapter learning outcome/objective listed in the text. You can use our Test Bank software, EZ Test and EZ Test Online, or *Connect Business Communication* to easily query for learning outcomes/objectives that directly relate to the learning objectives for your course. You can then use the reporting features of EZ Test to aggregate student results in similar fashion, making the collection and presentation of assurance-of-learning data simple and easy.

AACSB STATEMENT

The McGraw-Hill Companies is a proud corporate member of AACSB International. Understanding the importance and value of AACSB accreditation, the authors of *Lesikar's Business Communication, Thirteenth Edition*, recognize the curricula guidelines detailed in the AACSB standards for business accreditation by connecting selected questions in the text and/or the Test Bank to the six general knowledge and skill guidelines in the AACSB standards.

The statements contained in *Lesikar's Business Communication, Thirteenth Edition,* are provided only as a guide for the users of this textbook. The AACSB leaves content coverage and assessment within the purview of individual schools, the mission of the school, and the faculty. While *Lesikar's Business Communication* and the teaching package make no claim of any specific AACSB qualification or evaluation, we have tagged selected questions according to the six general knowledge and skill areas.

McGRAW-HILL AND BLACKBOARD

McGraw-Hill Higher Education and Blackboard have teamed up. What does this mean for you?

1. **Your life, simplified.** Now you and your students can access McGraw-Hill's *Connect* and *Create* right from within your Blackboard course—all with one single sign-on. Say goodbye to the days of logging in to multiple applications.

2. **Deep integration of content and tools.** Not only do you get single sign-on with *Connect* and *Create,* but you also get deep integration of McGraw-Hill content and content engines right in Blackboard. Whether you're choosing a book for your course or building *Connect* assignments, all the tools you need are right where you want them—inside Blackboard.

3. **Seamless gradebooks.** Are you tired of keeping multiple gradebooks and manually synchronizing grades into Blackboard? We thought so. When a student completes an integrated *Connect* assignment, the grade for that assignment automatically (and instantly) feeds into your Blackboard grade center.

4. **A solution for everyone.** Whether your institution is already using Blackboard or you just want to try Blackboard on your own, we have a solution for you. McGraw-Hill and Blackboard can now offer you easy access to industry-leading technology and content, whether your campus hosts it or we do. Be sure to ask your local McGraw-Hill representative for details.

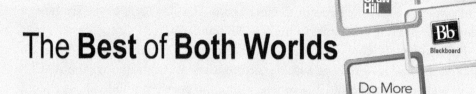

The **Best** of **Both Worlds**

McGRAW-HILL CAMPUS™

McGraw-Hill Campus™ is a new one-stop teaching and learning experience available to users of any learning management system. This institutional service allows faculty and students to enjoy single sign-on (SSO) access to all McGraw-Hill Higher Education materials, including the award-winning McGraw-Hill *Connect* platform, from directly within the institution's website. McGraw-Hill Campus™ provides faculty with instant access to all McGraw-Hill Higher Education teaching materials (e.g., eBooks, Test Banks, PowerPoint slides, animations and learning objects), allowing faculty to browse, search, and use any instructor ancillary content in our vast library at no additional cost to instructor or students. Students enjoy SSO access to a variety of free products (e.g., quizzes, flash cards, narrated presentations) and subscription-based tools (e.g., McGraw-Hill *Connect*). With this program enabled, faculty and students will never need to create another account to access McGraw-Hill products and services. Learn more at www.mhcampus.com.

McGRAW-HILL CUSTOMER CARE CONTACT INFORMATION

At McGraw-Hill, we understand that getting the most from new technology can be challenging. That's why our services don't stop after you purchase our products. You can email our Product Specialists 24 hours a day to get product training online. Or you can search our knowledge bank of Frequently Asked Questions on our support website. For Customer Support, call 800-331-5094, email hmsupport@mcgraw-hill.com, or visit www.mhhe.com/support. One of our Technical Support Analysts will be able to assist you in a timely fashion.

OUTCOMES-BASED ASSESSMENT SOLUTIONS

PERSONALIZED

Connect's presentation capture gives instructors the ability to evaluate presentations and students the freedom to practice their presentations anytime, and anywhere. With its fully customizable rubric, instructors can measure students' uploaded presentations against course outcome and give students specific feedback on where improvement is needed.

ADAPTIVE

Connect provides personalized learning plans to develop or improve editing skills and empowers students to put responsible writing into practice. This adaptive learning system helps students learn faster, study more efficiently, and retain more knowledge for greater success. It pinpoints concepts the student does not understand and maps a personalized study plan for success. With interactive documentation tools, it helps students master the foundations of writing. Developed through hours of ethnographic qualitative and quantitative research, it addresses the needs of today's classrooms, both online and traditional.

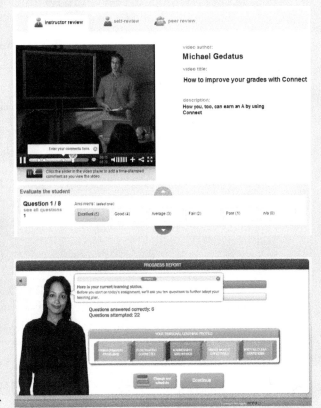

ONLINE LEARNING CENTER (OLC)

www.mhhe.com/rentz13e

Find a variety of online teaching and learning tools that are designed to reinforce and build on the text content. Students will have direct access to the learning tools, while instructor materials are password-protected.

A BLOG FOR BUSINESS COMMUNICATION TEACHERS

Instructors can keep track of the latest business communication news, trends, tips, and tools by following the authors' blog, *Bcomm Teacher Xchange*, at www.bcommteacherxchange.wordpress.com. The articles are searchable by subject, and a new one is posted every other week.

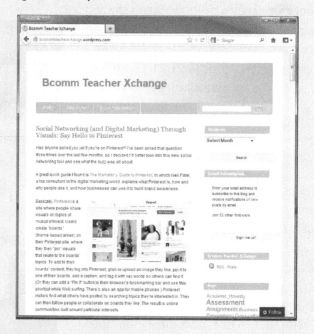

eBOOK OPTIONS

eBooks are an innovative way for students to save money and to "go green." McGraw-Hill's ebooks are typically 40 percent off the bookstore price. Students have the choice between an online and a downloadable CourseSmart eBook.

Through CourseSmart, students have the flexibility to access an exact replica of their textbook from any computer that has Internet service, without plug-ins or special software, via the online version or to create a library of books on their hard drive via the downloadable version. Access to the CourseSmart eBooks lasts for one year.

Features

CourseSmart eBooks allow students to highlight, take notes, organize notes, and share the notes with other CourseSmart users. Students can also search for terms across all eBooks in their purchased CourseSmart library. CourseSmart ebooks can be printed (five pages at a time).

More Info and Purchase

Please visit www.coursesmart.com to learn more and to purchase access to our eBooks. CourseSmart allows students to try one chapter of the eBook, free of charge, before purchase.

Binder-Ready Loose-Leaf Text

This full-featured text is provided as an option to the price-sensitive student. It is a full four-color text that's three-hole punched and made available at a discount to students. It is also available in a package with *Connect Plus*.

 **CREATE**

Craft your teaching resources to match the way you teach! With McGraw-Hill *Create*, www.mcgrawhillcreate.com, you can easily rearrange chapters, combine material from other content sources, and quickly upload content you have written, like your course syllabus or teaching notes. Find the content you need in *Create* by searching through thousands of leading McGraw-Hill textbooks. Arrange your book to fit your teaching style. *Create* even allows you to personalize your book's appearance by selecting the cover and adding your name, school, and course information. Order a *Create* book and you'll receive a complimentary print review copy in three to five business days or a complimentary electronic review copy (eComp) via email in about one hour. Go to www.mcgrawhillcreate.com today and register. Experience how McGraw-Hill Create empowers you to teach *your* students *your* way.

BRIEF CONTENTS

CONTENTS

PART THREE
Basic Patterns of Business Messages 113

CHAPTER SIX
Choosing the Best Process and Form 114

CHAPTER SEVEN
Getting to the Point in Good-News and Neutral Messages 141

CHAPTER NINE
Making Your Case with Persuasive Messages and Proposals 226

CHAPTER SIXTEEN
Delivering Oral Reports and Business Speeches 547

PART SIX
Elements of Professionalism: Technological Proficiency and Correctness 573

CHAPTER SEVENTEEN
Leveraging Technology for Better Writing 574

APPENDIXES

Introduction

As head of Learning & Development for Facebook, Stuart Crabb knows what qualities companies look for in a job candidate. He has over 20 years' experience helping companies hire the right people, develop their talent, and become more culturally diverse.

What does it take to succeed at Facebook? According to Crabb, the answers are "critical thinking," "problem solving," "creativity," and "performance." It also takes being "motivated," "individually accountable," and a "good fit" with the company culture.

These happen to be key traits of successful business communicators, too. They understand that communicating well takes analysis, judgment, and even ingenuity. It takes being attuned to people and to each communication situation. And it takes not only verbal skill but also technological and visual literacy.

Like business itself, business communication can be challenging. But the challenge can be fun, and solving communication problems can bring enormous rewards. This book will help prepare you for an exciting future as both a businessperson and a communicator.

Stuart Crabb, Head of Learning & Development for Facebook

CHAPTER ONE

Understanding Workplace Communication

Learning Objectives

Upon completing this chapter, you will understand the role and nature of communication in business. To achieve this goal, you should be able to

1 Explain the importance of communication to you and to business.

2 Describe the main challenges facing business communicators today.

3 Describe the three main categories of business communication.

4 Describe the formal and informal communication networks of the business organization.

5 Describe factors that affect the types and amount of communicating that a business does.

6 Explain why business communication is a form of problem solving.

7 Describe the various contexts for each act of business communication.

8 Describe the business communication process.

Demonstrating Your Value on a High-Profile Team

You were thrilled to be hired a few months ago as a customer service representative for OrgWare.com, a company that sells management software specially designed for professional associations. The software enables organizations like the American Marketing Association and the Association for Business Communication to manage their finances, keep track of their members, schedule events, and much more.

The company is doing well. In 12 years, it has grown from a five-person business into one that employs 120 people. There are now six regional sales teams located across the U.S., and there's even a development team in Malaysia. But this growth has created a problem: The extensive face-to-face communication that helped make OrgWare.com a thriving business has, in many cases, become difficult or impossible. As a result, the sense of teamwork in the organization is weakening. And it is clear that phone calls, emails, and instant messaging are not sufficient to keep employees engaged and well informed.

The CEO has formed a task force to find an internal communication solution. Will it be an intranet? An electronic newsletter? A secure social networking site? Virtual meetings? A combination? Which would the employees be most likely to read and use? How should the solution be implemented, and what will it cost?

To your surprise, you were asked to help find the answers. The CEO felt that your familiarity with new media could be an asset to the team. You'll also be expected to represent the customer service area and the viewpoints of young employees like yourself.

Everyone on the team will need to research the pros and cons of different media, acquire employees' opinions, write progress reports, share ideas, and ultimately help present the team's recommendation to the top executives.

Are you ready?

THE ROLE OF COMMUNICATION IN BUSINESS

LO1 Explain the importance of communication to you and to business.

Your work in business will involve communication—a lot of it—because communication is a major part of the work of business. The overview that follows will help you prepare for the communication challenges that lie ahead.

The Importance of Communication Skills

Because communication is so important in business, businesses want and need people with good communication skills. Evidence of the importance of communication in business is found in numerous surveys of executives, managers, and recruiters. Without exception, these surveys have found that communication ranks at or near the top of the business skills needed for success.

For example, the 431 managers and executives who participated in a survey about graduates' preparedness for the workforce named "oral communications," "teamwork/collaboration," "professionalism/work ethic," "written communications," and "critical thinking/problem solving" as the top "very important skills" job applicants should have.[1] The employers surveyed for the National Association of Colleges and Employers' *Job Outlook Survey* for 2011 rated "communication" as the most valuable soft skill, with "teamwork skills" and "analytical skills" following closely behind.[2] Why is communication ability so highly valued? As one professional trainer explains, "you will need to

---

[1] The Conference Board, Corporate Voices for Working Families, the Partnership for 21st Century Skills, and the Society for Human Resource Management, *Are They Ready to Work? Employers' Perspectives on the Basic Knowledge and Applied Skills of New Entrants into the 21st Century Workforce*, 21, *Partnership for 21st Century Skills*, Partnership for 21st Century Skills, 2 Oct. 2006, Web, 22 Apr. 2012.

[2] *NACE*, National Association of Colleges and Employers, 2011, Web, 22 Apr. 2012.

Peter Drucker on the Importance of Communication in Business

Peter Drucker, recipient of the Presidential Medal of Freedom and one of the most respected management consultants, educators, speakers, and writers of our time, made these observations about communication:

> Colleges teach the one thing that is perhaps most valuable for the future employee to know. But very few students bother to learn it. This one basic skill is the ability to organize and express ideas in writing and speaking.

> As soon as you move one step from the bottom, your effectiveness depends on your ability to reach others through the spoken or the written word. And the further away your job is from manual work, the larger the organization of which you are an employee, the more important it will be that you know how to convey your thoughts in writing or speaking. In the very large organization . . . this ability to express oneself is perhaps the most important of all the skills a person can possess.

request information, discuss problems, give instructions, work in teams, and interact with colleagues and clients" to achieve cooperation and team efficiency. To advance, you'll also need to be able to "think for yourself," "take initiative," and "solve problems."[3] On the managerial level, you'll find that communication skills are even more essential. In the words of an international business consultant, "nothing puts you in the 'poor leader' category more swiftly than inadequate communication skills."[4]

Unfortunately, businesses' need for employees with strong communication skills is all too often unfulfilled. When NFI Research asked senior executives and managers what areas of their companies they'd most like to see improved, they put "efficiency" and "communication" at the top of the list.[5] According to Solari Communications, "poor communication costs business millions of dollars every single day" in the form of wasted time, misunderstandings, eroded customer loyalty, and lost business.[6] SIS International Research found that poor communication is a problem for small and mid-sized businesses, not just for big corporations. Its data indicated that in 2009 a business with 100 employees spent an average downtime of 17 hours a week on clarifying its communications, which translated into an annual cost of $524,569.[7]

The communication shortcomings of employees and the importance of communication in business explain why you should work to improve your communication skills. Whatever position you have in business, your performance will be judged largely on the basis of your ability to communicate. If you perform and communicate well, you are likely to be rewarded with advancement. And the higher you advance, the more you will need your communication ability. The evidence is clear: Improving your communication skills improves your chances for success in business.

Why Business Depends upon Communication

Every business, even a one-person business, is actually an economic and social system. To produce and sell goods and services, any business must coordinate the activities of many groups of people: employees, suppliers, customers, legal advisors, community

---

[3] Shirley Taylor, "Why Are Communication Skills Important?," *ST Training Solutions*, ST Training Solutions Pte Ltd, n.d., Web, 22 Apr. 2012.

[4] Jonathan Farrington, "The MOST Important Leadership Trait?—It's a 'No-Brainer,'" *Blogit*, Jonathan Farrington, 26 Sept. 2008, Web, 22 Apr. 2012.

[5] Chuck Martin, "NFI Research Result: Wish List," *Forbes.com*, Forbes.com, 4 Feb. 2010, Web, 22 Apr. 2012.

[6] Rich Maggiani, "The Costs of Poor Communication," *Solari*, Solari Communication, 2012, Web, 22 Apr. 2012.

[7] SIS International Research, "SMB Communications Pain Study White Paper: Uncovering the Hidden Cost of Communications Barriers and Latency," *SIS International Research*, SIS International Research, *Market Intelligence Journal*, 10 Mar. 2009, Web, 22 Apr. 2012.

representatives, and government agencies that might be involved. These connections are achieved through communication.

Consider, for example, the communications of a pharmaceutical manufacturer. Throughout the company, employees send and receive information about all aspects of the company's business:

- Salespeople receive instructions and information from the home office and submit orders and regular reports of their contact with customers.

- Executives use written and oral messages to conduct business with customers and other companies, manage company operations, and perform strategic planning.

- Production supervisors receive work orders, issue instructions, receive status reports, and submit production summaries.

- Shop floor supervisors deliver orders to the employees on the production line, communicate and enforce guidelines for safety and efficiency, troubleshoot problems that arise, and bring any concerns or suggestions to management.

- Marketing professionals gather market information, propose new directions for company production and sales efforts, coordinate with the research and development staff, and receive direction from the company's executives.

- Research specialists receive or propose problems to investigate, make detailed records of their research, monitor lab operations for compliance with government regulations, and communicate their findings to management.

- Public relations professionals use various media to build the company's brand and maintain the public's trust.

Numerous communication-related activities occur in every other niche of the company as well: finance and accounting, human resources, legal, information systems, and other departments. Everywhere, employees receive and send information as they conduct their work, and they may be doing so across or between continents as well as between buildings or offices.

Oral communication is a major part of this information flow. So, too, are various types of written communication—instant messaging, text messaging, online postings and comments, email, memos, letters, and reports, as well as forms and records.

All of this communicating goes on in business because communication is essential to the organized effort involved in business. Simply put, communication enables human beings to work together.

Current Challenges for Business Communicators

LO2 Describe the main challenges facing business communicators today.

While communication has always been central to business, the nature of work today presents special communication challenges. Here we discuss four interrelated trends that are likely to influence how you will work and communicate.

The Need for Expanded Media Literacy. When email arrived on the scene in the late 1980s, it created something of a revolution. Instead of being restricted to letters, memos, and printed reports and proposals, business writers could now correspond electronically. As a result, many tasks formerly conducted via the "old" forms—memos in particular—were performed through email instead, and email replaced many phone and face-to-face conversations as well. Email has also had the effect of speeding up communication and of enabling a communicator to reach many more readers simultaneously. It has increased what we can achieve—and are expected to achieve—each day.

Email is still the most heavily used medium in business, but many other media have appeared on the scene. In addition to instant messaging and text messaging, businesses are now using blogs, tweets, podcasts, social networking, virtual meetings, videos, animation, simulations, and even online games. Collectively referred to as **new media**, these forms of communication and the mobile devices with which people access them are causing another revolution.

The impacts of this change are many and far reaching. It is easy now to network with others, even on the other side of the world, and to tap the intelligence of those outside the boundaries of the organization. Obviously, these "new ways for groups to come together and collaborate" will require that employees be "highly conversant with digital networking and virtual collaboration."[8] But new media are also increasing the need for employees who have **social intelligence**—the ability "to quickly assess the emotions of those around them and adapt their words, tone, and gestures accordingly."[9]

With information coming in so fast and from so many sources, organizations are becoming less hierarchical and more brain-like, with each employee acting as a kind of sensor. As a result, front-line employees now have a higher level of decision-making power than ever before.[10] Performing well in such an environment takes "novel and adaptive thinking,"[11] a willingness to "embrace change," and "fierce problem-solving skills."[12] The approach to business communication that this book takes will help you develop these strengths.

Increasing Globalism and Workplace Diversity. Countries and cultures continue to grow more interconnected as businesses expand their reach around the world. According to a panelist for a recent webinar on workplace trends, we are seeing "the emergence of the truly globally integrated enterprise," which means that the likelihood of working on a global team is increasing, as is the importance of "global social networks."[13]

Cross-cultural competency should thus be a part of your skillset.[14] You will need to be aware that your assumptions about business and communication are not shared by everyone everywhere. As the next chapter explains, businesspeople from other countries may have distinctly different attitudes about punctuality and efficiency. They can also differ from you in their preference, or lack thereof, for directness and the show of emotion. And the core features of their culture—such as their preference for individualism or collectivism, their religious beliefs, their political environment, their ideas about social hierarchy, and their attitudes toward work itself—can make their view of how to do business quite different from yours.

You will encounter other kinds of diversity as well. To have adequate retirement income, the so-called Baby Boomers—those born soon after World War II—are extending their careers. This means that organizations are likely to have employees in their twenties, in their sixties and seventies, and every age in between.[15] The influx of women into the workplace has meant increased gender diversity. And according to a diversity officer for a major health-care firm, each generation of U.S. workers has grown more ethnically diverse, with the so-called Generation Y cohort (those born after 1979) having the most ethnic diversity.[16] This trend is making organizations more innovative and productive,[17] and it means that "cultural agility" will need to figure into your workplace communications.[18]

---

[8] David Bollier, *The Future of Work: What It Means for Individuals, Businesses, Markets and Governments*, 15, *The Aspen Institute*, Aspen Institute, 2011, Web, 22 Apr. 2012.

[9] Institute for the Future for Apollo Research Institute, *Future Work Skills 2020*, 8, *Apollo Research Institute*, Apollo Research Institute, 2011, Web, 22 Apr. 2012.

[10] Bollier 19.

[11] Institute for the Future for Apollo Research Institute, *Future of Work Report: Executive Summary*, 4, *Apollo Research Institute*, Apollo Research Institute, Mar. 2012, Web, 22 Apr. 2012.

[12] Bollier 22.

[13] Jim Keane, President, Steelcase Group, *Future of Work Webinar*, *Apollo Research Institute*, Apollo Research Institute, n.d., Web, 7 May 2012.

[14] Institute for the Future for Apollo Research Institute, *Future Work Skills 2020*, 9.

[15] According to Ross C. DeVol, chief research officer for the Milken Institute, one in five Americans will have hit 60 in 2030, and many of these will be staying in the workforce (*Future of Work Webinar*, *Apollo Research Institute*, Apollo Research Institute, n.d., Web, 7 May 2012).

[16] Katherine Haynes Sanstad, Regional Executive Director, Diversity, Kaiser Permanente, *Future of Work Webinar*, *Apollo Research Institute*, Apollo Research Institute, n.d., Web, 7 May 2012.

[17] Institute for the Future for Apollo Research Institute, *Future Work Skills 2020*, 9.

[18] Sanstad.

What One CEO Looks for in Job Candidates

In a *New York Times* interview, Delta CEO Richard Anderson highlighted the importance of communication skills and contextual awareness.

When asked if there had been any change in the qualities he looks for in a job applicant over the last several years, he responded with these comments:

I think this communication point is getting more and more important. People really have to be able to handle the written and spoken word. . . .

The second thing is, I think you've got to have what our pilots call operational awareness. You've got to have your head up . . . and you've got to have situational awareness of everything that's going on around you.

There is so much going on in the world today, you've got to know what's going on globally, what's going on around you, particularly today with what's going on in this economy.

And third, you've got to have not just the business skills, you've got to have the emotional intelligence. It's just not enough to be the best person operating an HP calculator. You have to have the emotional intelligence to understand what's right culturally, both in your company and outside your company.

SOURCE: Adam Bryant, "He Wants Subjects, Verbs and Objects," *The New York Times* 25 Apr. 2009: BU2, *The New York Times*, Web, 30 Apr. 2012.

An Increased Need for Strong Analytical Skills. Adapting to a quickly changing business landscape requires being able to assess information quickly, focus on what's relevant, and interpret information reliably and usefully. As data-gathering devices are built into more objects, there will be more numerical data for us to process. The need for **computational thinking**—the ability "to interact with data, see patterns in data, make data-based decisions, and use data to design for desired outcomes"[19]—will increase. So will the need for **visual literacy**, the ability to create and interpret graphics.[20]

The value of **interpretive skills** extends beyond interpreting numbers. As we've pointed out, being able to understand other people is critical. As "smart machines" automate many workplace tasks, employees will spend more time on tasks that require "sense-making," or "the ability to determine the deeper meaning or significance of what is being expressed."[21] As one expert put it, "We've got to recognize that the real high-value work . . . may actually have an *imaginative* component."[22] This quality is required to discern the key facts, to explore "what if," and to choose the best solution—all central components of successful business communication.

An Increased Focus on Ethics and Social Responsibility One more widespread trend under way in business will likely affect the goals of the organization you work for: an increased focus on ethical and socially responsible behavior.

While ethical scandals have plagued businesses throughout modern history, the Enron and WorldCom scandals of 2002, in which false reports of financial health cheated employees and shareholders alike, seemed to usher in a new era of concern. That concern was well founded: With 2008 came unprecedented discoveries of mismanagement and fraud on the part of some of the United States's largest financial institutions. Accounts of predatory lending, business espionage, and exploitative labor

---

[19] Institute for the Future for Apollo Research Institute, *Future Work Skills 2020*, 4.

[20] Institute for the Future for Apollo Research Institute, *Future Work Skills 2020*, 10.

[21] Institute for the Future for Apollo Research Institute, *Future Work Skills 2020*, 8.

[22] Bollier 8.

SOURCE: CorpWatch, Home page, CorpWatch, n.d., Web, 30 Apr. 2012. From http://www.corpwatch.org.

practices continue to shake the public's confidence in business. On a moral level, doing business in a way that harms others is wrong. On a practical level, doing so undermines trust, which is critical to the success of business. The more an organization builds trust among its employees, its shareholders, its business partners, and its community, the better for the business and for economic prosperity overall. A key way to build trust is through respectful, honest communication backed up by quality goods and services.

Lately, another important dimension of business ethics has developed: **corporate social responsibility**. The Internet has brought a new transparency to companies' business practices, with negative information traveling quickly and widely. Nongovernmental organizations (NGOs) such as CorpWatch, Consumer Federation of America, and Greenpeace can exert a powerful influence on public opinion and even on governments. Businesses now operate in an age of social accountability, and their response has been the development of corporate social responsibility (CSR) departments and initiatives. While the business benefits of CSR have been debated, the public demand for such programs is strong. You may well find that social issues will influence how you do business and communicate in business.

Main Categories of Business Communication

LO3 Describe the three main categories of business communication.

Such newer media as blogs and social networking have weakened the boundary between "inside" and "outside" the organization. One post on a company's blog, for example, could draw comments from employees, from employees in a similar organization or industry, or from potential customers.

Even so, most communication on the job can still be categorized as either internal operational, external operational, or personal. These categories, while not completely distinct, can help you understand your purposes for communicating.

Internal-Operational Communication. All the communication that occurs in conducting work within a business is internal operational. This is the communication among the business's employees that is done to perform the work of the business and track its success.

SOURCE: © Randy Glasbergen/ glasbergen.com

Internal-operational communication takes many forms. It includes the ongoing discussions that senior management undertakes to determine the goals and processes of the business. It includes the orders and instructions that supervisors give employees, as well as written and oral exchanges among employees about work matters. It includes reports that employees prepare concerning sales, production, inventories, finance, maintenance, and so on. It includes the messages that they write and speak in carrying out their assignments and contributing their ideas to the business.

Much of this internal-operational communication is performed on computer networks. Employees send email, chat online, and post information on company portals and blogs for others throughout the business, whether located down the hall, across the street, or in other countries. And today, much of this communication takes place via smartphones and other mobile devices.

External-Operational Communication. The work-related communicating that a business does with people and groups outside the business is **external-operational communication**. This is the business's communication with its publics—suppliers, service companies, customers, government agencies, the general public, and others.

External-operational communication includes all of the business's efforts at selling—from sales letters, emails, and phone calls to Web and television ads, trade-show displays, the company website, and customer visits. Also in this category is all that a business does to gain positive publicity, such as promoting its community-service activities, preparing appealing materials for current and prospective investors, writing press releases for the media, and contributing expert insights at professional meetings and on webinars. In fact, every act of communication with an external audience can be regarded as a public-relations message, conveying a certain image of the company. For this reason, all such acts should be undertaken with careful attention to both content and tone.

The importance of these kinds of external-operational communication hardly needs explaining. Because the success of a business depends on its ability to attract and satisfy customers, it must communicate effectively with those customers.

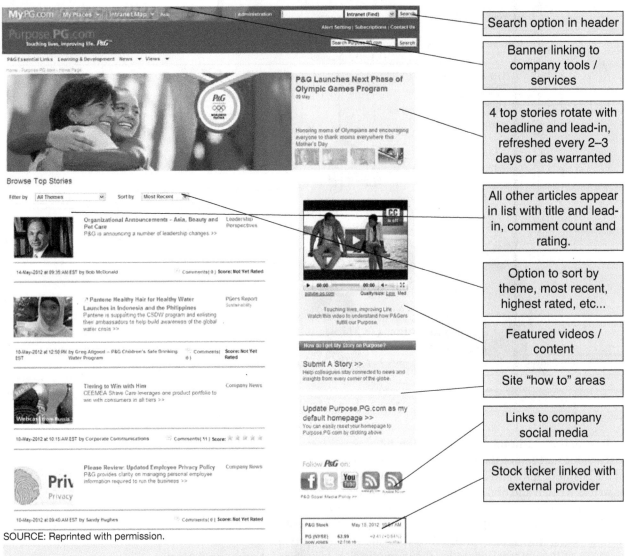

SOURCE: Reprinted with permission.

Search option in header

Banner linking to company tools / services

4 top stories rotate with headline and lead-in, refreshed every 2–3 days or as warranted

All other articles appear in list with title and lead-in, comment count and rating.

Option to sort by theme, most recent, highest rated, etc...

Featured videos / content

Site "how to" areas

Links to company social media

Stock ticker linked with external provider

Companies often use carefully designed portals or intranets, such as this one at Procter & Gamble, to communicate with employees and enable them to communicate with each other.

But businesses also depend on one another in the production and distribution of goods and services. Coordinating with contractors, consultants, and suppliers requires skillful communication. In addition, every business must communicate to some extent with a variety of other external parties, such as government agencies and public-interest groups. Some external audiences for today's businesses are illustrated in Figure 1–1. Like internal communication, external communication is vital to business success.

Personal Communication. Not all the communication that occurs in business is operational. In fact, much of it is without apparent purpose as far as the operating plan of the business is concerned. This type of communication is personal. Do not make the mistake of underestimating its importance. **Personal communication** helps make and sustain the relationships upon which business depends, and it is more important than ever.

Personal communication is the exchange of information and feelings in which we human beings engage whenever we come together—or when we just feel like talking to each other. We are social animals, and we will communicate even when we have little or nothing to say. Although not an official part of the business's operations, personal communication can have a significant effect on their success. This effect is a result of

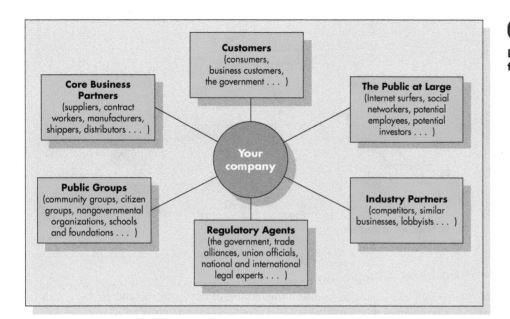

Figure 1–1

Likely External Audiences
for Today's Businesses

Customers
(consumers,
business customers,
the government . . .)

Core Business
Partners
(suppliers, contract
workers, manufacturers,
shippers, distributors . . .)

The Public at Large
(Internet surfers, social
networkers, potential
employees, potential
investors . . .)

Your
company

Public Groups
(community groups, citizen
groups, nongovernmental
organizations, schools
and foundations . . .)

Industry Partners
(competitors, similar
businesses, lobbyists . . .)

Regulatory Agents
(the government, trade
alliances, union officials,
national and international
legal experts . . .)

the influence that personal communication can have on the attitudes of the employees
and those with whom they communicate.

The employees' attitudes toward the business, one another, and their assignments
directly affect their productivity. The nature and amount of personal talk at work affect
those attitudes. In an environment where heated words and flaming tempers are often
present, the employees are not likely to give their best efforts to their jobs. Likewise, a
rollicking, jovial workplace can undermine business goals. Wise managers cultivate the
optimum balance between employees' focus on job-related tasks and their freedom to
engage with others on a personal level. Chat around the water cooler or in the break
room encourages a team attitude and can often be the medium in which actual business
issues get discussed. Even communication that is largely internal-operational will often

Personal
communication in
business is both
inevitable and
important.

Figure 1–2

Formal and Informal Communication Networks in a Division of a Small Business

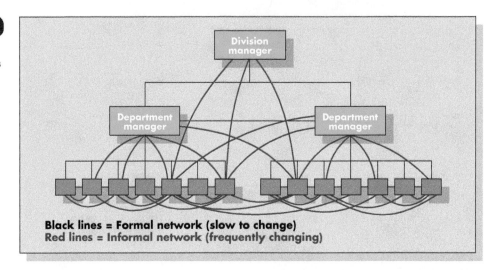

Black lines = Formal network (slow to change)
Red lines = Informal network (frequently changing)

include personal elements that relieve the tedium of daily routine and enable employees to build personal relationships.

Similarly, communication with external parties will naturally include personal remarks at some point. Sometimes you may find yourself writing a wholly personal message to a client, as when he or she has won a major award or experienced a loss of some kind. Other times, you may compose an external-operational message that also includes a brief personal note, perhaps thanking a client for a pleasant lunch or referring to a personal matter that came up in the course of a business meeting.

Using both online and face-to-face networking, you will also cultivate business-related friends. Your relationships with these contacts will not only help you do your current job; they will also be an important resource as you change jobs or even careers. Research shows that "the idea of the steady, permanent job is becoming a relic of another era."[23] Employees are now taking "an entrepreneurial approach" to their lives and skills, considering carefully where to work, what work to do, how much to work, and for how long.[24] The personal connections you make in your current employment will contribute to your future success.

Communication Networks of the Organization

LO4 Describe the formal and informal communication networks of the business organization.

Looking over all of a business's communication (internal, external, and personal), we see an extremely complex system of information flow and human interaction. We see dozens, hundreds, or even thousands of individuals engaging in untold numbers of communication events throughout each workday.

In fact, as Figure 1–2 shows, there are two complex networks of information in virtually any organization—one formal and one informal. Both are critical to the success of the business.

The Formal Network. In simplified form, information flow in a modern business is much like the network of arteries and veins in the body. Just as the body has blood vessels, the business has major, well-established channels for information exchange. This is the **formal network**—the main lines of operational communication. Through these channels flows the bulk of the communication that the business needs to operate. Specifically, the flow includes the upward, lateral, and downward movement of information in the form of reports, memos, email, and other media within the organization; the downward movement of orders, instructions, advisories, and announcements; and the broad dissemination of company information through the organization's newsletter, bulletin boards, email, intranet, or blogs.

---

[23] Bollier 3.

[24] Institute for the Future for Apollo Research Institute, *Future of Work Report* 6.

As we have seen, information routinely flows outward as well. Order acknowledgments, invoices, receipts, correspondence with suppliers and consultants, and other standard external-operational communications can make external audiences part of the formal communication network.

These officially sanctioned lines of communication cause certain forms of communication, or **genres**, to exist within the organization. For example, it may be customary in one company for project leaders to require a weekly report from team members. In another company, the executives may hold monthly staff meetings. Whatever the established form, it will bring with it certain expectations about what can and cannot be said, who may and may not say it, and how the messages should be structured and worded. You will need to understand these expectations in order to use the approved lines of communication to get things done.

The Informal Network. Operating alongside the formal network is the **informal network**. It comprises the thousands upon thousands of personal communications that may or may not support the formal communication network of a business. Such communications follow no set pattern; they form an ever-changing and infinitely complex structure linking the members of the organization to each other and to many different external audiences.

The complexity of this informal network, especially in larger organizations, cannot be overemphasized. Typically, it is really not a single network but a complex relationship of smaller networks consisting of certain groups of people. The relationship is made even more complex by the fact that these people may belong to more than one group and that group memberships and the links between groups are continually changing. The department you belong to, the other employees with whom you come in contact in the course of your workday, and the many connections you make with those outside your organization can cause links in this network to form.

The informal network inside an organization is often referred to as the **grapevine**. This communication network is more valuable to the company's operations than a first impression might indicate. Certainly, it carries much gossip and rumor. Even so, the grapevine usually carries far more information than the formal communication system, and on many matters it is more effective in determining the course of an organization. Skillful managers recognize the presence of the grapevine, and they know that the powerful people in this network are often not those at the top of the formal organizational hierarchy. They find out who the talk leaders are and give them the information that will do the most good for the organization. They also make management decisions that will cultivate positive talk.

Employees' personal relations with external audiences add another dimension to a company's informal network. The widespread use of social media has dramatically increased employees' informal communication with outsiders. Such communication can either help or hurt the company. Here again, wise managers will be sensitive to the informal network and manage in such a way as to encourage talk that is beneficial to the company.

As an employee, you need to be careful about how you participate in the informal network. Unwise remarks can get you known as a troublemaker and even get you fired, whereas representing yourself and your company well can result not only in more pleasant relations but also in professional success.

Variation in Communication Activity by Business

LO5 Describe factors that affect the types and amount of communicating that a business does.

Just how much and what kind of communicating a business does depends on several factors. The nature of the business is one. For example, insurance companies have a great need to communicate with their customers, especially through letters and other mailings, whereas housecleaning service companies have little such need. Another factor is the business's size and complexity. Relatively simple businesses, such as repair services, require far less communication than complex businesses, such as automobile manufacturers.

The business's relation to its environment also influences its communication practices. Businesses in a comparatively stable environment, such as textile manufacturing or food processing, will tend to depend on established types of formal communication in a set organizational hierarchy, whereas those in a volatile environment, such as software development or online commerce, will tend to improvise more in terms of their communications and company structure.

Yet another factor is the geographic dispersion of the operations of a business. Obviously, internal communication in a business with multiple locations differs from that of a one-location business. Enabling employees to work from home, requiring them to travel, or relying on outside contractors can also increase a company's geographical reach and thus affect its communication. Related to this factor is how culturally diverse the company is. The communication of a multicultural organization will require more adaptation to participants' values, perspectives, and language skills than that of a relatively homogeneous organization.

Each business can also be said to possess a certain **organizational culture**, which has a strong effect upon, and is strongly affected by, the company's communication. The concept of organizational or corporate culture was popularized in the early 1980s, and it continues to be a central focus of management consultants and theorists.[25] You can think of a given company's culture as its customary, but often unstated, ways of perceiving and doing things. It is the medium of preferred values and practices in which the company's members do their work.

Recall places you've worked or businesses you've patronized. In some, the employees' demeanor suggests a coherent, healthy culture in which people seem to know what to do and be happy doing it. At the other extreme are companies where employees exhibit little affiliation with the business and may even be sabotaging it through poor customer service or lack of knowledge about their jobs. The content and quality of the company's communication have a great deal to do with employees' attitudes and behavior.

Take care to note that the official culture and the actual culture in a company are not necessarily the same. Officially, the company management may announce and try

---

[25] See Edgar H. Schein, *Organizational Culture and Leadership,* 4th ed. (San Francisco: Jossey-Bass, 2010), print, which reviews the literature on this important concept.

to promote a certain culture through formal communications such as mission statements and mottoes. But the actual culture of a company is a dynamic, living realm of meaning constructed daily through infinite behaviors and communications at all levels of the company. Having your antennae out for the assumptions that actually drive people's conduct in your or your client's workplace will help you become a more effective communicator.

THE BUSINESS COMMUNICATION PROCESS

While business communication involves many different skills, from verbal and visual literacy to technological know-how, none are more important than problem-solving skills and people skills. These are central to the business communication process.

Business Communication as Problem Solving

Virtually every significant communication task that you will face will involve analyzing a unique set of factors that requires at least a somewhat unique solution. For this reason, it makes sense to think of business communication as **problem solving**.

Researchers in many fields—management, medicine, writing, psychology, and others—have studied problem solving. In general, they define *problem* as a gap between where you are now and where you want to be.[26] Within this framework, a problem isn't always something negative; it can also be an opportunity to improve a situation or do things in a better way. As a goal-focused enterprise, business is all about solving problems, and so, therefore, is business communication.

The problem-solving literature divides problems into two main types: *well defined* and *ill defined*. The former can be solved by following a formula, such as when you are computing how much money is left in your department's budget. But most real-world problems, including business communication problems, cannot be solved this way. They do not come to us in neat packages with the path to the best solution clearly implied. Instead, they require research, analysis, creativity, and judgment. One reason why this is the case in business communication is that, as in any communication situation, people are involved—and people are both complex and unique. But the business context itself is often complex, presenting you with multiple options for handling any given situation. For example, if a customer has complained, what will you do about it? Nothing? Apologize? Imply that the customer was at fault? Give a conciliatory discount? Refuse to adjust the bill? Even a "simple" problem like this one requires thinking through the likely short- and long-term effects of several possible solutions.

Solving ill-defined problems involves combining existing resources with innovation and good judgment. Although this book presents basic plans for several common types of business communication messages, you will not be able to solve particular communication problems by just filling in the blanks of these plans. The plans can be thought of as **heuristics**—"rules of thumb" that keep you from reinventing the wheel with each new problem. But the plans do not tell you all you need to do to solve each unique communication problem. You must decide how to adapt each plan to the given situation.

---

[26] For discussions of problem solving, see the following print resources: John R. Hayes, *The Complete Problem Solver*, 2nd ed. (Hillsdale, NJ: Lawrence Erlbaum, 1989); Morgan D. Jones, *The Thinker's Toolkit* (New York: Three Rivers Press, 1998); Janet E. Davidson and Robert J. Sternberg, eds., *The Psychology of Problem Solving* (Cambridge, UK: Cambridge University Press, 2003); Dan Roam, *The Back of the Napkin* (London: Portfolio, 2008); John Adair, *Decision Making and Problem Solving Strategies*, 2nd ed. (London: Kogan Page, 2010).

What this means is that successful business communication is both more challenging and more exciting than you may have thought. You will need to draw on your own powers of interpretation and decision making to succeed with your human communication partners.

Of course, people will handle communication tasks somewhat differently depending on who they are, how they interpret the situation, and who they imagine their recipients to be. Does this mean that all communication solutions are equally valid? Not at all. While there is no perfect solution, there can be many bad ones that have been developed without enough analysis and effort. Focused thinking, research, and planning will not guarantee success in the shifting, complex world of business communication, but they will make your chances of success as high as possible. The next section will help you perform this kind of analysis.

A Model of Business Communication

Figure 1–3 shows the basic elements of a business communication event. Even though people can, and often do, communicate inadvertently, this communication model focuses on what happens when someone deliberately communicates with someone else to achieve particular business-related goals.

You'll notice that the two communicators in the figure are labeled simply Communicator 1 and Communicator 2 instead of Sender and Receiver or Communicator and Audience. Certainly any communication event begins with someone deciding that communication is needed and initiating that communication, with an intended recipient on the other end. But in many situations, especially those involving real-time conversation, the two parties work together to reach a mutual understanding. Even in situations where a communicator is attempting to deliver a complete, carefully prepared message—as in a letter, report, or oral presentation—the intended recipients have already participated in the construction of the message because the writer or presenter has kept them in mind when composing and designing the message. The labels in this model are thus intended to convey the cooperative effort behind every successful communication event.

LO7 Describe the various contexts for each act of business communication.

The Contexts for Communication. Certain features of the communication situation are already in place as the communicators in our model begin to communicate.

Figure 1–3

The Business Communication Process

Communicator 1 ...

1. Senses a communication need
2. Defines the problem
3. Searches for possible solutions
4. Selects a course of action (message type, contents, style, format, channel)
5. Composes the message
6. Delivers the message

The Larger Context
Business-Economic, Sociocultural, Historical

Communicator 1's World
Organizational
Professional
Personal

The Communicators' Relationship

Communicator 2's World
Organizational
Professional
Personal

initial message
chosen channel

1–6

7–10

chosen channel
responding message

Communicator 2 ...

7. Receives the message
8. Interprets the message
9. Decides on a response
10. May send a responding message

The *larger context* includes the general business-economic climate; the language, values, and customs in the surrounding culture; and the historical moment in which the communication is taking place.

Think about how these contexts might influence communication. For example, when the country's economy or a particular industry is flourishing, a communicator's message and the recipient's response may well be different from what they would be during an economic slump. The sociocultural context also affects how individuals communicate. Whether they are communicating in the context of U.S. urban culture, for instance, or the culture of a particular region or another country, or whether they are communicating across cultures, their communication choices will be affected. The particular historical context of their communication can also be a factor. Consider how recent financial scandals in the United States or the increased focus on the environment are influencing the language of business. The skillful communicator is sensitive to these larger contexts, which always exert an influence and, to some extent, are always changing.

The **relationship of the communicators** also forms an important context for communication. Certainly, communication is about moving information from point A to point B, but it is also about interaction between human beings. Your first correspondence with someone begins a relationship between the two of you, whether as individuals, people in certain business roles, or both. All future messages between you will continue to build this relationship.

The communicators' *particular contexts* exert perhaps the strongest influence on the act of communication. These interrelated contexts can be

- **Organizational contexts**. As we've discussed, the type and culture of the organization you represent will shape your communication choices in many ways, and the organizational contexts of your audiences will, in turn, shape their responses. In fact, in every act of business communication, at least one of the parties involved is likely to be representing an organization. What you communicate and how you do so will be strongly shaped by the organization for whom you speak. In turn, the organization to which your audience belongs—its priorities, its current circumstances, even how fast or slow its pace of work—can strongly influence the way your message is received.

- **Professional contexts**. You know from school and experience that different professionals—whether physicians, social workers, managers, accountants, or those involved in other fields—possess different kinds of expertise, speak differently, and have different perspectives. What gets communicated and how can be heavily influenced by the communicators' professional roles. Be aware that internal audiences as well as external ones can occupy different professional roles and therefore favor different kinds of content and language. Employees in management and engineering, for example, have been demonstrated to have quite different priorities, with the former focusing on financial benefit and the latter on technological achievement.[27] Part of successful communication is being alert to your audiences' different professional contexts.

- **Personal contexts**. Who you are as a person comes from many sources: the genes you inherited, your family and upbringing, your life experiences, your schooling, the many people with whom you've come in contact, and the culture in which you were reared. Who you are as a person also depends to some extent on your current circumstances. Successes and failures, current relationships, financial ups and downs, the state of your health, your physical environment—all can affect a particular communicative act. Since much business communication is between individuals occupying organizational roles, personal matters are usually not disclosed. But it is well to keep in mind the effect that these can have on the communicators. If you're

---

[27] See research by Dorothy A. Winsor, especially *Writing Power: Communication in an Engineering Center* (Albany: SUNY Press, 2003), print.

aware, for example, that the intended recipient of your message is under stress or having a bad day, you can adapt your communication accordingly.

LO8 Describe the business communication process.

The Process of Communication. No one can know exactly what occurs inside the minds of communicators when they undertake to create a message, but researchers generally agree that the process includes the following steps:

1. *Sensing a communication need.* A problem has come to your attention, or you have an idea about how to achieve a certain goal. Perhaps someone has written an email of complaint and you must answer it, or perhaps you've noticed that the company could benefit from automating a certain procedure. Whatever the case, you find that an action is in order, and you believe that some form of communication will help you achieve the desired state.

2. *Defining the situation.* To create a successful message or plan a communication event, you need to have a well-informed sense of the situation. For example, if you have received a letter of complaint from a customer, what exactly is the problem here? Does the customer have a legitimate point? What further information might you need to acquire in order to understand the situation? In what ways is this problem like or unlike others you have solved? How might your or your organization's goals be hindered or helped depending on your communication choices?

3. *Considering possible communication strategies.* As your definition of the situation takes shape, you will start considering different options for solving it. What kind of communication event will you initiate, and what will you want to achieve with it? What image of yourself, your company, and your communication partners might you project in your message? To generate a good solution, you will need to think about and research your potential audiences and their contexts, your own goals and contexts, your relationship with each audience, and any relevant larger contexts.

4. *Selecting a course of action.* Considering the situation as you've defined it and looking at your communication options, you will consider the potential costs and benefits of each option and select the optimum one. Your decision will include preliminary choices about the message type, contents, structure, verbal style, and visual format, and about the channel you will use to deliver the message.

5. *Composing the message.* Here is where you either craft your written message or plan your presentation or conversation. If you have decided to convey your message orally, you will make careful notes or perhaps even write out your whole message and also design any visuals you need. If you have decided to write your message, you will draft it and then revise it carefully so that it will get the job done and reflect well on you (see Chapter 6 for helpful writing and revising techniques).

6. *Sending the message.* When your message is prepared or carefully planned, you are ready to deliver it to your intended recipients in the channel you have chosen. You choose a good time to deliver it, realizing, for example, that Monday morning may not be the best time to make an important phone call to a busy executive. You also consider sending auxiliary messages, such as a "heads-up" phone call or email, that could increase your main message's chances of success. You want to do all you can to ensure that your message doesn't get lost amidst all the other stimuli competing for your intended audience's attention.

While these activities tend to form a linear pattern, the communicator often needs to revisit earlier steps while moving through the different activities. In other words, solving a communication problem can be a **recursive** process. This is particularly true for situations that have many possible solutions or heavily involve the audience in the communication process. A communicator may begin a communication event with a certain view of the situation and then find, upon further analysis or the discovery of

Channel Choice Affects Message Success

"Its official, you no longer work for JNI Traffic Control and u have forfided any arrangements made." Can you imagine getting such a text message? The Sydney employer was sued over this inappropriate choice of a communication channel for firing an employee. In settling the matter the commissioner went further in stating that email, text messages, and even answering machines were inappropriate for official business communication. Or what about being notified by text message of an overdue bill? While some might think of that as a service, others would regard it as invasive and inappropriate.

Historically, the importance of channel choice has been disputed, with some arguing that it is simply a means for transmitting words and others arguing that the chosen channel is, in itself, a message. However, today most people realize that the appropriate choice of communication channel contributes significantly, along with the words, to the success of the message. While research has provided guidelines for understanding when to use very lean (printed material) to very rich (face-to-face) channels, new technologies and laws have added new elements to consider. Not only are there no clear-cut rules or guidelines, but the smallest change in context may make one choice better than another.

In selecting a channel, a communicator needs to weigh several factors. These include the message content, the communicators' levels of competency with the channel, the recipient's access to the channel, and the assumptions associated with the channel. Appropriate choice of a communication channel helps people communicate clearly, improving both their productivity and personal relationships.

additional facts, that this view needs to be revised in order to accommodate all the involved parties and their goals.

If all goes as planned, here is what will happen on the recipient's end:

7. *Receiving the message.* Your chosen channel has delivered your message to each intended recipient, who has perceived and decided to read or listen to your message.

8. *Interpreting the message.* Just as you had to interpret the situation that prompted your communication, your recipient now has to interpret the message you sent. This activity will involve not only extracting information from the message but also guessing your communication purpose, forming judgments about you and those you represent, and picking up on cues about the relationship you want to promote between yourself and the recipient. If you have anticipated the recipient's particular contexts and interests successfully, he or she will form the impressions that you intended. The recipient may prompt the initiating communicator for help with this interpretive act, especially if the communication is a live conversation.

9. *Deciding on a response.* Any time you send a message, you hope for a certain response from your recipient, whether it be increased goodwill, increased knowledge, a specific responding action, or a combination of these. If your message has been carefully adapted to the recipient, it has a good chance of achieving the desired response.

10. *Replying to the message.* The recipient's response to your message will often take the form of replying to your message. When this is the case, the receiver is acting as communicator, following the process that you followed to generate your message.

Figure 1–4 lists the main questions to consider when developing a communication strategy. Taking this analytical approach will help you think consciously about each stage of the process and give you the best chance of achieving the desired results.

What is the situation?

- What has happened to make you think you need to communicate?
- What background and prior knowledge can you apply to this situation? How is this situation like or unlike others you have encountered?
- What do you need to find out in order to understand every facet of this situation? Where can you get this information?

What are some possible communication strategies?

- To whom might you communicate? Who might be your primary and secondary audiences? What are their different organizational, professional, and personal contexts? What would each care about or want to know? What, if any, is your prior relationship with them?
- What purpose might you want to achieve with each recipient? What are your organizational, professional, and personal contexts?
- What are some communication strategies that might help you achieve your goals?
- How might the larger business-economic, sociocultural, and historical contexts affect the success of different strategies?

Which is the best course of action?

- Which strategies are impractical, incomplete, or potentially dangerous? Why?
- Which of the remaining strategies looks like the optimum one? Why?
- What will be the best message type, contents, structure, style, and format for your message?
- What channel will you use to deliver it?

What is the best way to design the chosen message?

- Given your goals for each recipient, what information should your message include?
- What logical structure (ordering and grouping of information) should you use?
- What kind of style should you use? How formal or informal should you be? What kinds of associations should your language have? What image of yourself and your audience should you try to project? What kind of relationship with each recipient should your message promote?
- How can you use formatting, graphics, and/or supporting media to make your message easier to comprehend?
- What are your recipients' expectations for the channel you've chosen?

What is the best way to deliver the message?

- Are there any timing considerations related to delivering your message?
- Should you combine the main message with any other messages?
- How can you best ensure that each intended recipient receives and reads or hears your message?

BUSINESS COMMUNICATION: THE BOTTOM LINE

The theme of this chapter might be summed up this way: The goal of business communication is to create a shared understanding of business situations that will enable people to work successfully together.

Timely and clear transfer of information is critical to businesses, now more than ever. But figuring out what kind of information to send, whom to send it to, how to send it, and what form to use requires good decision making. Since every person has his or her own mental "filters"—preconceptions, frames of reference, and verbal worlds—wording the information so that it will be understood can be a challenge. You and your audience may even attach completely different meanings to the same words (a problem that the communication literature calls "bypassing").

Complicating this picture is the fact that communication is not just about information transfer. The creation and maintenance of positive human relations is also essential to business and thus to business communication. Every act of communication conveys an image of you and of the way you regard those to whom you're speaking or writing. Successful business communicators pay careful attention to the human relations dimension of their messages.

Yes, business communication can be challenging. It can also be extremely rewarding because of the results you achieve and the relationships you build. The advice, examples, and exercises in this book will jump-start you toward success. But it will be your ability to analyze and solve specific communication problems that will take you the rest of the way there.

THERE'S MORE . . .

What codes of ethics do major companies and professional organizations use? What are 10 qualities of an effective team member? How can you become a better problem solver? Scan the QR code with your smartphone or use your Web browser to find out at www.mhhe.com/lesikar13e. Choose Chapter 1 > Bizcom Tools & Tips.

SUMMARY BY LEARNING OBJECTIVES

1. Because communication is vital to business operations, businesses need and reward people who can communicate.

   - But good communicators are scarce.
   - So, if you can improve your communication skills, you increase your value to business and advance your own career as well.

   Explain the importance of communication to you and to business.

2. Today's business communicators face special challenges:

   - The need for expanded media literacy.
   - Increasing globalism and workplace diversity.
   - An increased need for strong analytical and interpretive skills.
   - An increased focus on ethics and social responsibility.

   Describe the main challenges facing business communicators today.

3. Communicating in business falls into three main categories:

   - Internal-operational communication is the communication inside a business that enables the business to perform its work and track its success.
   - External-operational communication is the communicating a business does with outsiders (customers, other businesses, the public, government agencies, and others).
   - Personal communication consists of informal exchanges of information not formally related to operations but nevertheless important to an organization's success.

   Describe the three main categories of business communication.

4. The flow of communication in a business organization forms a complex and ever-changing network.

   - The communicating that follows the formal structure of the business comprises the formal network. Operational information flows upward, downward, and laterally through this network, which is sustained by established forms of communication (genres).
   - The flow of personal communication forms the informal network. The internal version of this network is known as the grapevine. But the use of social media is including more outsiders in companies' informal networks.

   Describe the formal and informal communication networks of the business organization.

5. The kind and amount of communicating a business does depend upon such factors as

   - The nature of the business.
   - Its size and complexity.
   - Its environment.
   - The geographic dispersion of its members.

   Describe factors that affect the types and amount of communicating that a business does.

- Its degree of cultural diversity.
- Its organizational culture (an organization's customary, often unstated, ways of perceiving and doing things).

Explain why business communication is a form of problem solving.

6. Business communication can be thought of as a problem-solving activity.
   - Finding communication solutions requires analysis, creativity, and judgment.
   - Heuristics (problem-solving devices such as common communication plans) can help make your communication problem solving more efficient.
   - The common communication plans must still be adapted to each situation.
   - While there is no one perfect solution, a poorly prepared one is likely to fail.

Describe the various contexts for each act of business communication.

7. Business communication takes place in these contexts:
   - The larger business-economic, sociocultural, and historical contexts.
   - The relationship of the communicators.
   - The communicators' own worlds: organizational, professional, and personal.

Describe the communication process.

8. The process of communication involves these activities, which tend to be linear in nature but are often recursive (require revisiting earlier steps):

The initiator
- Senses a communication need.
- Defines the situation.
- Considers possible communication strategies.
- Selects a course of action (message type, contents, style, format, channel).
- Composes the message.
- Sends the message.

The intended recipient
- Receives the message.
- Interprets the message.
- Decides on a response.
- May send a responding message.

KEY TERMS

CRITICAL THINKING QUESTIONS

1 "If there's no definitive solution, then all ways of handling a business communication problem are equally good." Using the discussion of business communication problem solving in this chapter, explain why this statement is false. **LO6**

2 To get a feel for how rapidly information technologies are changing and how significant the impact is on business, list all the information technologies (devices and applications) that you've learned to use over the last five years. Now reflect on how your communication,

work, and life have changed as a result of these technologies. **LO2**

3 "People need to leave their cultures and values at the door when they come to work and just do business." Discuss the possible merits and flaws of this attitude. **LO2**

4 In what ways is imagination important in business? In business communication? **LO2**

5 Times are hard for Robo Solutions, a small local company that creates assembly-line robotics. Lately, the clients have been few and far between. But today the sales staff got encouraging news: James Pritchett, president of a nearby tool and die company, has inquired about the possibility of the company's designing a series of computer-run robots for key processes in the plant. There's a hitch, though; it's Sara McCann's turn to try to snare his business (and the commission)—and Pritchett is known to prefer dealing with men. Do you, as Robo Solutions sales manager, send Sarah anyway, or do you send one of your male salespeople to get Pritchett's business, giving Sarah a shot at the next potential client? How would you solve this communication—and ethics—problem? **LO2**

6 "Never mix business with personal matters—it just leads to damaged relationships, poor business decisions, or both." In what ways might this be a fair statement? In what ways is it unwise advice? **LO3**

7 List the types of companies requiring many kinds of communication. Then make a list of types of companies requiring few kinds. What explains the difference

between these two groups' amount and types of communication? **LO5**

8 In *Images of Organization,* 2nd ed. (Thousand Oaks, CA: Sage, 1997), management scholar Gareth Morgan has analyzed companies using various metaphors. For example, he has looked at those elements of a company that make it appear to run like a machine (with rigidly organized, specific job roles), an organism (with elements that make it dependent upon and responsive to its environment), a brain (with self-managing teams and employees who can do a variety of jobs as needed), and a political system (with employees vying for power and influence). Think of an organization you know well and decide upon its dominant cultural metaphor. Is it one of Morgan's? Or is it a family? A team? A community? A prison? A mixture of several kinds? Once you settle on your metaphor, be prepared to explain how this organization's culture affects, and is affected by, its communication practices. **LO5**

9 As noted in this chapter, companies develop specific forms of communication, or genres, that enable them to get their work done. In a place where you have worked or another organization in which you have been a member, what were the main forms of communication with the employees or members? To what extent were these uniquely adapted to the needs of the organization? **LO5**

10 Using this chapter's discussion of communication, explain how people reading or hearing the same message can disagree on its meaning. **LO7**

SKILLS BUILDING EXERCISES

1 Using the Internet, find a company that has a corporate social responsibility program and study what the company's website says about that program. What kind of image as a corporate citizen is the company trying to project, and how? How convincing is this effort, in your opinion, and why? **LO2**

2 Choose a certain national or regional culture, ethnicity, or generation—one different from your own—and find out what values the people in this demographic are generally known for. How might working or doing business with a person from one of these groups require you to adapt your own values and communication style? **LO2**

3 List the types of external-operational and internal-operational communication that occur in an organization with which you are familiar (school, fraternity, church, etc.). **LO3**

4 Describe the formal network of communication in an organization, division, or department with which you are familiar (preferably a simple one). Discuss why you think the communication network has taken this form

and how successfully it seems to meet the business's needs. **LO4**

5 Find two websites of companies in the same industry—for example, two manufacturers of household products or two wireless service providers. Using the evidence presented on their websites, compare their company cultures. Look at their stated mission (if any), their history (if provided), the gender and qualifications of their personnel (if given), their employee benefits, their information for job applicants, their information for investors, the company image projected by the visual elements on the site—anything that suggests who they are or want you to think they are. Write up your comparison in a well-organized, well-supported message to your instructor. **LO5**

6 Megan Cabot is one of 12 workers in Department X. She has strong leadership qualities, and all her co-workers look up to her. She dominates conversations with them and expresses strong viewpoints on most matters. Although she is a good worker, her dominating personality has caused problems for you, the new manager of Department X.

Today you directed your subordinates to change a certain work procedure. The change is one that has proven superior in the past whenever it has been tried. Soon after giving the directive, you noticed the workers talking in a group, with Megan the obvious leader. In a few minutes she appeared in your office. "We've thought it over," she said. "Your production change won't work." Explain what is happening. How will you handle this situation? **LO4, LO6**

7 After noticing that some workers were starting work late and finishing early, a department head wrote this message to subordinates:

It is apparent that many of you are not giving the company a full day's work. Thus, the following procedures are implemented immediately:

a. After you clock in, you will proceed to your workstations and will be ready to begin work promptly at the start of the work period.

b. You will not take a coffee break or consume coffee on the job at the beginning of the work period. You will wait until your designated break times.

c. You will not participate in social gatherings at any time during the workday except during designated break periods.

d. You will terminate work activities no earlier than 10 minutes prior to the end of the work period. You will use the 10 minutes to put up equipment, clean equipment, and police the work area.

The message was not well received by the workers. In fact, it led to considerable anger and confusion. Using the discussion of communication planning in this chapter, explain where the department head's problem-solving process went awry. What did he or she fail to take into account? **LO6–LO8**

8 Think of a recent transaction you had with a businessperson or with a staff person at your school. Describe the contexts of your communication, from the larger contexts (business-economic, sociocultural, or historical) to the personal (to the extent you know them). How did these influence the outcome of your communication? **LO7**

9 Find an article in the business press or general news about a recent incident involving a company—for example, a merger or acquisition, a scandal or crisis, or the launching of a new product. What kind of communication challenges might this event have posed for the company, both internally and externally? What kinds of messages probably needed to be written, and to whom? **LO1–LO7**

CHAPTER TWO

Communicating Across Cultures

Learning Objectives

Upon completing this chapter, you will be able to describe the major issues in cross-cultural communication and prepare yourself to communicate with international partners. To reach these goals, you should be able to

1 Explain why communicating clearly across cultures is important to business.

2 Describe three major factors that influence a country or region's culture.

3 Describe cultural differences regarding body positions and movements and use this knowledge effectively in communicating.

4 Describe the impact of culture on views and practices concerning human relations and use this knowledge effectively in communicating.

5 Explain the language equivalency problem and techniques for minimizing its effects.

6 Describe what one can do to enhance one's cross-cultural communication skills.

Preparing for Cross-Cultural Communication

To introduce yourself to this chapter, assume that you're a recently hired trainer for a U.S. company that has a new branch office in Sweden. You've been sent to the office to facilitate the training of new employees.

After what seemed a fruitful brainstorming session with the leadership team, you ask the Swedish head manager, Andreas, to appoint a contact person in the group to help you launch the training project. Andreas turns to the HR manager, Prasan, who is from India, and says that he will be your key contact from here on out. You describe the process you want to follow and the documents you'll need in order to go forward. Then you ask Prasan if you can expect the documents by the next day.

Hesitating, Prasan replies, "Yes, I can send everything to you by the end of the day tomorrow." His boss suddenly intervenes: "No, that's not going to happen. You know you have a lot of work right now and won't be able

to meet that deadline." Turning to you, the Swedish manager continues, "You can expect the material you need in two weeks." Prasan looks somewhat embarrassed but nods in agreement.

Back in Andreas's office, you ask, "What just happened? Why did Prasan agree to such an unrealistic deadline?" Andreas explains that the Indian wanted to save face by giving a pleasing answer. Such an answer would keep you from appearing to be demanding and would keep him from appearing to be slow. "He values face-saving more than accuracy," the Swede says—implying that he himself does not. You wonder if such clashes of cultural preference could be handled more gracefully than the one you just witnessed. This chapter will introduce you to cross-cultural communication issues that may arise in business situations and help prepare you to meet them successfully.

LO1 Explain why communicating clearly across cultures is important to business.

THE GROWING IMPORTANCE OF CROSS-CULTURAL COMMUNICATION

As Chapter 1 points out, increasing globalization is one of the major trends in business. The spread of the Internet, social media, and mobile devices has only fueled this trend. And it isn't just for big businesses. According to Laurel Delaney, founder of GlobeTrade.com, "It's the small business owners of the world who are busting borders, discovering unlimited potential for growth and profit, and changing the shape of the world economy."[1]

Both large and small businesses want you to be able to communicate clearly with those from other cultures, for several reasons. A primary reason is that many businesses sell their products and services both domestically and internationally. Being able to communicate cross-culturally will help you be more successful in understanding customers' needs, communicating how your company can meet these needs, and winning their business. Another reason is that you will be a more effective employee within your company. According to the U.S. Bureau of Labor Statistics, the number of nonnative civilians in the U.S. workforce has reached almost 25 million, and this number is on the rise.[2] If you can work harmoniously with those from other cultures, you will help create a more comfortable and productive workplace. Furthermore, if cultural barriers are minimized, your company will be able to hire a wider variety of good people. Also, you will minimize problems stemming from misinterpretations. A final reason is that your attention to communicating clearly with those from other cultures will enrich your business and personal life.

In preparing to communicate with people from other cultures, you might well begin by heeding the advice in the chapters that follow. Adapting your words, sentences,

---

[1] Laurel Delaney, *The World Is Your Market: Small Businesses Gear up for Globalization, Scribd,* Scribd, 2004, Web, 2 May 2012.

[2] *Economic News Release: Table A-7,* Bureau of Labor Statistics, US Department of Labor, 4 May 2012, Web, 6 May 2012.

and overall message to your audience is always important, and never more so than in cross-cultural situations. Clarity, courtesy, and correctness are appreciated everywhere. But how to achieve these goals can vary by culture. In one culture, for example, it might be appropriate to imply the main point, while in another you should state the point directly. Thus, learning about the ways cultures differ is an important foundation for successful business communication. In addition, you must look at the special problems that our language presents to those who use it as a second language. It is around these two topic areas that this review of cross-cultural communication is organized.

DIMENSIONS OF CULTURAL DIFFERENCE

Dutch sociologist Geert Hofstede, probably the most respected expert on cross-cultural differences, defines **culture** as "the collective programming of the mind which distinguishes the members of one category of people from another," and national culture as "that component of our mental programming which we share with more of our compatriots as opposed to most other world citizens."[3] In other words, cultures are "shared ways in which groups of people understand and interpret the world."[4]

Our dominant culture affects almost everything about us—from the way we think and communicate to the way we hold our bodies or establish our personal space. Certainly the spread of capitalism, advances in technology and science, and the explosive growth of electronic media have eroded national differences. The title of a popular book on international business claims that "the world is flat,"[5] and many would agree that we have more in common globally than ever before. But cultural differences are still strong in many places and situations.

Of course, even within one culture there can be many subcultures. With only a moment's reflection on regional, ethnic, and even gender differences within any culture, you will realize that this is true. Plus, the person with whom you are communicating may be completely unrepresentative of his or her culture of origin. National borders are more permeable and workplaces more diverse than they have ever been. Still, an understanding of your communication partner's cultural roots will greatly enhance your interpretive and interaction skills.

Three Major Factors That Affect Culture

LO2 Describe three major factors that influence a country or region's culture.

Following the advice of Canning, a UK-based communication consulting firm, we recommend starting your cross-cultural education with the big picture.[6] Instead of trying to memorize such isolated facts as a culture's typical greeting or attitude toward punctuality, try to gain a holistic understanding, starting with these basic questions:

- What is the *topography* of the country you are studying? In our Internet-influenced age, it may be difficult to believe, but topography still has a profound influence on what types of people live in a certain place. For instance, many natural borders around a country make for a more insular culture than changing, indistinct borders, and life under a broiling sun creates different habits and values than life in a darker, colder environment.

- What is the country's *history*? Have there been certain events or systems of government that have affected the national memory? And what is the country's history with your country?

---

[3] Geert Hofstede, "National Cultures and Corporate Cultures," *Communication Between Cultures,* ed. Larry A. Samovar and Richard E. Porter (Belmont, CA: Wadsworth, 1984) 51, print.

[4] Fons Trompenaars and Peter Woolliams, *Business Across Cultures* (London: Capstone, 2003) 53, print.

[5] Thomas L. Friedman, *The World Is Flat: A Brief History of the Twenty-First Century* (New York: Farrar, Straus, and Giroux, 2005), print.

[6] John Mattock, ed., *Cross-Cultural Communication: The Essential Guide to International Business,* rev. 2nd ed. (London: Kogan Page, 2003) 15–23, print.

Web Tools for Cross-Cultural Communication

The Internet is a rich source of cross-cultural information for business communicators. Not only can you find information about places where you might be doing business, but you can also use some Web-based tools to help you with your communication.

One of these, shown right, is a currency converter, allowing you to convert from one currency to another. In this example, U.S. dollars are converted to Indian rupees. These converters are set up to use regularly updated exchange rates, so you can quote prices in both U.S. dollars and other currency.

The Web also offers free translation tools. Google has a built-in translation feature that lets you easily translate webpages. In the screens shown below, a French website about writing cover letters has been translated into English.

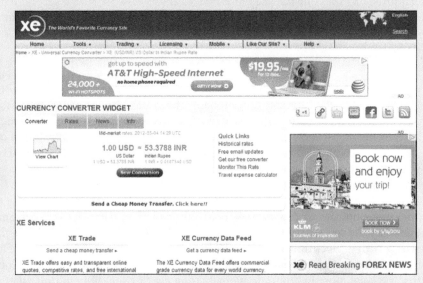

SOURCE: From http://www.xe.com/ucc. The XE.com. Universal Currency Converter, Copyright © 2012 XE Corporation. XE and Universal Currency Converter are registered trademarks of XE Corporation.

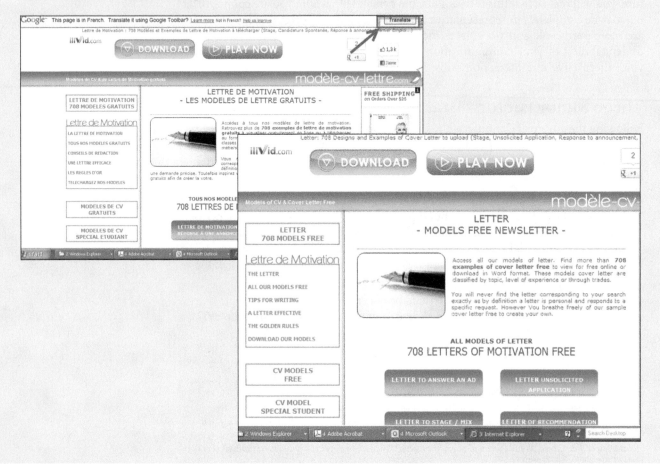

- What role does *religion* play in the culture? Think for a moment about how religious values have shaped the Middle East, different Asian countries, or even the United States. Even when many of a country's people have stopped observing traditional religious practices, the influence of religion can linger, surfacing in certain behaviors and attitudes.

These broad cultural factors can have a major effect on businesspeople's communication practices and preferences. If you know your audience is Islamic, for example, you will be prepared to interpret their behavior when they do not take notes at an important business meeting (they tend to favor oral communication and the use of memory rather than writing) or when they resist detailed planning of a project (since, in Islam, the success of human projects always depends on God's will).

Keep in mind, though, that businesspeople the world over share many goals and problems. All are interested in keeping their businesses financially viable, hiring and retaining good employees, developing marketable products, finding reliable suppliers, and so forth. Your efforts to understand your cross-cultural audience—like those to understand communication partners from your own culture—can lead to many mutually beneficial relationships.

The next two sections will assist you in these efforts by discussing important dimensions of cultural difference, starting with physical differences and then moving to mental and social ones. Sensitivity to these dimensions will help you avoid **ethnocentrism**—the tendency to see only your own cultural programming as "normal"—and make you a better cross-cultural communicator.

Body Positions and Movements

One might think that the positions and movements of the body would be much the same for all people. However, physical behaviors differ by culture, and the differences can affect communication. For example, in the United States most people sit when they wish to remain in one place for some time, but many of the world's people squat when relaxing or even when doing business. Because we do not squat, we tend to view squatting as primitive. This view could adversely affect our communication with people from such countries as Indonesia and Zimbabwe, to whom squatting is a very normal body position.

To take another example, people from the United States who visit certain Asian countries may view the fast, short steps taken by the inhabitants as peculiar and their

LO3 Describe cultural differences regarding body positions and movements and use this knowledge effectively in communicating.

Remember that, despite cultural differences, businesspeople around the world share many of the same goals.

Carefully Present and Receive a Business Card in Japan

In Japan, it is considered bad manners to go to a business meeting without a business card, or *meishi*. There are a number of ways to present the card, but receiving it is an art, too. If you want to make a good impression on the presenter, receive it in both hands, especially when the other party is senior in age or status or a potential customer. Be careful not to fiddle with the card or put it in your rear pocket—that is considered crude. Put it in a distinctive case. Those who do business in both countries often have their business cards translated on the back, as the examples here show.

own longer strides as normal. And when people from those countries encounter U.S. natives who do not bow on meeting and leaving each other, they are likely to interpret the omission as rude. Similarly, people from the United States see standing up as the appropriate thing to do on certain occasions (as when someone enters the room), whereas people from some other cultures do not.

As you know, movements of certain body parts (especially the hands) are a vital form of human communication. Some of these movements have no definite meaning even within a culture. But some have clear meanings, and these meanings may differ by culture. In the United States an up-and-down movement of the head means "yes" and a side-to-side movement of the head means "no." These movements may mean nothing at all or something quite different to people from cultures in which thrusting the head forward, raising the eyebrows, jerking the head to one side, or lifting the chin are used to convey similar meanings.

Hand gestures can have many different meanings. The two-fingered sign that means "victory" or "peace" in the United States is considered vulgar in Australia, and the "OK" sign is insulting in such diverse countries as Russia, Germany, and Brazil.[7] Even the use of fingers to indicate numbers can vary by culture. In the United States, most people indicate "1" by holding up the forefinger, whereas in parts of Europe, "1" is the thumb,

---

[7] Roger E. Axtell, *Gestures: The Do's and Taboos of Body Language around the World* (New York: John Wiley & Sons, 1998) 43, print.

"2" is the forefinger, and so forth. To point to themselves, the Japanese point to their faces, while the Chinese point to their noses and Americans point to their chests.[8] And holding up both hands with the palms facing outwards can mean either "ten," "I surrender," "I'm telling the truth," or "up yours—twice!" depending on where you are.[9]

Even meanings of eye movements vary by culture. In North America, we are taught not to look over the heads of our audience but to maintain eye contact when giving formal speeches. In informal talking, we are encouraged to make eye contact but not to stare. In Indonesia, looking directly at people, especially those who are older or in higher positions, is considered disrespectful. On the other hand, our practices of eye contact are less rigorous than those of the British and Germans. Unless one understands these cultural differences, how one uses eye movement can be interpreted as being impolite on the one hand or being shy on the other.

Touching and particularly handshaking differences are important to understand in cross-cultural communication. Some cultures, like the Chinese, do not like much touching. They will give a handshake that Westerners might perceive as weak. Other cultures that like touching will give greetings ranging from full embraces and kisses to nose rubbing. Here are some additional examples:

Culture	Handshakes
Americans	Firm, three to five pumps
Germans	Brusque, firm, single pump, repeated upon arrival and departure
French	Light, quick, not offered to superiors, repeated upon arrival and departure, may include a double kiss
British	Soft, three to five pumps
Hispanics	Moderate grasp, repeated frequently
Latin Americans	Firm, long-lasting
Middle Easterners	Gentle, repeated frequently
Asians	Gentle; for some, shaking hands is unfamiliar and uncomfortable (an exception to this is the Korean, who generally has a firm handshake)
Arabs	Gentle, longlasting, sometimes with kisses on both cheeks

How people greet each other is a major indicator of their social norms. Instead of critically judging others because of their different greeting styles, seize the opportunity to gain insight into their cultures.

In our culture, smiles are viewed positively in most situations. But in some other cultures (notably African cultures), a smile is regarded as a sign of weakness in certain situations (such as bargaining). Receiving a gift or touching with the left hand is a serious breach of etiquette among Muslims, who view the left hand as unclean, but many cultures attach no such meaning to the left hand. And so it is with other body movements—arching the eyebrows, positioning the fingers, raising the arms, and many more. All cultures use body movements in communicating, but in different ways.

Views and Practices Concerning Factors of Human Relationships

LO4 Describe the impact of culture on views and practices concerning human relations and use this knowledge effectively in communicating.

Probably causing even more miscommunication than differences in body positions and movements are the attitudes of different cultures toward various factors of human relationships. For illustrative purposes, we will review seven of these factors: time, space, odors, frankness, social hierarchy, workplace values, and expression of emotions.

Time. In the United States, people tend to be **monochronic**. They regard time as something that must be planned in order to be used as efficiently as possible. They strive to meet deadlines, to be punctual, to conduct business quickly, and to work on a schedule.

---

[8] Wang De-hua and Li Hui, "Nonverbal Language in Crosscultural Communication," *Sino-US English Teaching* 4.10 (2007): 67, *www.linguist.org.cn*, Web, 5 May 2012.
[9] Allan Pease and Barabara Pease, *The Definitive Book of Body Language* (New York: Bantam, 2006) 111, print.

In some other cultures (especially those of the Middle East and some parts of Asia), people are **polychronic**, viewing time in a more relaxed way. They see extensive planning as unwise and unnecessary. Being late to a meeting or a social function is of little consequence to them. In fact, some of them hold the view that important people should be late to show that they are busy. In business negotiations, the people in these cultures move at a deliberately slow pace, engaging in casual talk before getting to the main issue. It is easy to see how such different views of time can cause people from different cultures to have serious communication problems.

Space. People from different cultures often vary in their attitudes toward space. North Americans tend to prefer about two feet or so of distance between themselves and those with whom they speak. But in some cultures (some Arabian and South American cultures), people stand closer to each other, and not following this practice is considered impolite. To take another example, North Americans view personal space as a right and tend to respect this right of others; thus, they stand in line and wait their turn. People from some other cultures view space as belonging to all. Thus, they jostle for space when boarding trains, standing at ticket counters, or shopping. In encounters between people whose cultures have such different attitudes toward space, actions are likely to be misinterpreted.

Odors. People from different cultures may have different attitudes toward body odors. To illustrate, Americans work hard to neutralize body odors or to cover them up and view those with body odors as unsanitary. On the other hand, in some Asian cultures people view body odors not as something to be hidden but as something that friends should experience. Some of the people from these cultures believe that it is an act of friendship to "breathe the breath" of the person with whom they converse and to feel their presence by smelling. Clearly, encounters between people with such widely differing attitudes could lead to serious miscommunication.

Frankness. North Americans tend to be relatively frank in their relationships with others, quickly getting to the point and perhaps being blunt and sharp in doing so. Germans and Israelis are even more frank than Americans. Asians tend to be far more reticent or implicit and sometimes go to great lengths to save face or not to offend. Americans belong to a **low-context culture**, a culture that explicitly shares all relevant background information when communicating. Asians, on the other hand, belong to a **high-context culture**, which leads them to limit background information and communicate more implicitly.[10] (See the Communication Matters box on the next page for more about these terms.) Thus, Asians may appear evasive, roundabout, and indecisive to North Americans; and North Americans may appear harsh, impolite, and aggressive to Asians. Phone customs may be an exception, especially among the Chinese, who tend to end telephone calls abruptly after their purpose has been accomplished. North Americans, on the other hand, tend to move on to friendly talk and clearly prepare the listener for the end of the call.

Social Hierarchy. In many cultures, strict social classes exist, and class status determines how intimately people are addressed and treated in communication. For this reason, a person from such a culture might quiz a person from another culture to determine that person's class status. Questions concerning occupation, income, title, and origin might be asked. People from cultures that stress human equality are apt to take offense at such questioning about class status. This difference in attitude toward class status is also illustrated by differences in the familiarity of address. Some Americans are quick to use first names. This practice is offensive to people from some other cultures, notably the English and the Germans, who expect such intimate address only from long-standing acquaintances.

---

[10] Iris Varner and Linda Beamer, *Intercultural Communication in the Global Workplace,* 5th ed. (New York: McGraw-Hill/Irwin, 2011) 101–102, print.

High-Context versus Low-Context Cultures: Edward T. Hall

An extremely influential model of cross-cultural differences comes from U.S. anthropologist Edward T. Hall. With *Beyond Culture* (1976), as well as two earlier books (*The Silent Language* [1959], about perceptions of space and time, and *The Hidden Dimension* [1966], focusing on the use of space), Hall essentially launched the field of cross-cultural communication. His most lasting contribution to this field has been his dividing of the cultures of the world into low- and high-context communicators.

Low-context communicators, in Hall's model, tend to express themselves in concrete, direct, and explicit ways. The gist of the message and everything one needs in order to interpret it are all there in the message. American, German, Scandinavian, Swiss, and Finnish people tend to fall into this category. They use and value a straightforward communication style.

High-context communicators use a more multimodal style. Rather than putting everything they mean into words, they use eye movements, body language, tone of voice, and other nonverbal elements to give interpretational cues. Though they communicate implicitly, they expect you to be able to interpret their points by drawing on your knowledge of their cultural context. French, Japanese, Indian, Irish, British, and Arabic people tend to be high-context communicators—though of course their contexts can differ dramatically.

Lately Hall's model has come under fire for being unsupported by formal research. In an extensive review of the topic, Peter Cardon has shown that Hall's generalizations arose from unsystematic observation and have often been contradicted. On the other hand, Cardon's study also shows that Hall's theory about low and high contexts is the most cited theory in cross-cultural communication. The fact that so many researchers, teachers, and consultants have found it useful suggests that, despite its flaws, the model has a certain tried-and-true appeal. So put it into your cross-cultural communication tool box—and apply it with caution.

SOURCE: Peter W. Cardon, "A Critique of Hall's Contexting Model: A Meta-Analysis of Literature on Intercultural Business and Technical Communication," *Journal of Business and Technical Communication* 22.4 (2008): 399–428, print.

Similarly, how people view superior–subordinate relations can vary by culture. Hofstede calls this dimension **power distance**. (See the following Communication Matters box.) The dominant arrangement in Latin America, for example, is a strong boss with weak subordinates doing as the boss directs. In other words, these cultures tend to exhibit "high power distance." In contrast, Israel, New Zealand, and Denmark have "low power

Greetings vary among cultures, as do many other behaviors. Consult authoritative resources, including those with international experience, to learn the preferred ways of interacting in different cultures—and take a cue from your communication partner as well.

COMMUNICATION MATTERS

Five Dimensions of Culture: Geert Hofstede

Between 1967 and 1973, Dutch sociologist Geert Hofstede collected 116,000 questionnaires about business practices and attitudes from IBM employees in over 50 countries. The result was the hugely influential *Culture's Consequences* (1980), one of the most cited works on cross-cultural communication.

The book identified four dimensions of culture, to which a fifth was later added. These have become mainstays in the field of international business. Here they are briefly explained:

- *Power distance.* To what extent do the less powerful members of a culture or organization expect that power will be distributed unevenly? If this is a normal expectation, it means that the company or culture exhibits "high power distance" and values hierarchy and obedience. If not, the company or culture has "low power distance."

- *Individualism vs. collectivism.* An individualistic culture is one in which people are expected to look after themselves and their families, while a collectivist culture promotes strong identification with social groups.

- *Masculinity vs. femininity.* At the feminine end of the spectrum is a "modest, caring" attitude, while at the masculine end is assertiveness and competitiveness.

- *Uncertainty avoidance.* This label refers to the extent to which "a culture programs its members to feel either uncomfortable or comfortable in unstructured situations." Uncertainty-avoiding cultures try to

prevent such situations with strict rules and core values. Uncertainty-accepting cultures tend to be more relaxed, more tolerant of differences, and less rule-bound.

- *Long-term vs. short-term orientation.* This dimension was found in a study conducted by Chinese researchers. People with a long-term orientation are oriented toward the future. They value persistence and thrift. Those with a short-term orientation value the past and present—respecting traditions, fulfilling social obligations, and saving face in social situations.

It is tempting to see whole cultures as falling at one end or the other on these dimensions. But as with other models, one must use this one only as a rough, preliminary guide. As one business executive puts it, "In my own practice, I look upon Hofstede's data as would an airplane passenger looking down upon mountain ranges. . . . These represent country cultures. Smaller ranges represent subcultures within countries. But to understand individuals, you have to land at the nearest airport and meet them at the ground level, taking into account their unique qualities."

SOURCES: Geert Hofstede and Jean-Claude Usunier, "Hoftstede's Dimensions of Culture and Their Influence on International Business Negotiations," 1989, *International Business Negotiations*, ed. Pervez N. Ghauri and Jean-Claude Usunier, 2nd ed. (Amsterdam: Pergamon, 2003) 137–153, print; John W. Bing, "Hofstede's Consequences: The Impact of His Work on Consulting and Business Practices," *Academy of Management Executive* 2004 (18.1): 80–87, print.

distance," which means that authority is widely shared and decisions are often made by consensus. The U.S. falls somewhere in between.[11] These widely differing practices have led to major communication problems in joint business ventures involving people from these cultures.

The role of women varies widely by culture. In North America, we continue to move toward the generally shared goal of gender equality. In some Islamic cultures or subcultures, the allowable behaviors for women are very restricted. To many in our culture, the practices of the people of these other cultures violate basic human rights. In the view of the people of these cultures, their practices are in accord with their heritage and religious convictions. The increasing spread of Western values has made such cultures more hospitable to businesswomen, but they may still encounter serious barriers.

Workplace Values. Also differing by culture are our values regarding work. Americans, for example, have been steeped in the Protestant work ethic. It is the belief that if one puts hard work ahead of pleasure, success will follow. The product of this

---

[11] "Power Distance Index," *ClearlyCultural*, ClearlyCulural.com, n.d., Web, 2 May 2012.

Linear-actives, Multi-actives, and Reactives: Richard D. Lewis

British linguist Richard D. Lewis, founder of a highly successful cross-cultural communication consulting firm, has developed a three-part model for categorizing the world's many cultures. He believes they can be generally described as linear-active, multi-active, or reactive.

Linear-actives are those who tend to follow a linear path toward a desired goal. They "plan, schedule, organize, pursue action chains, do one thing at a time." Lewis cites the Germans and Swiss as exemplars of this group.

Multi-actives are those who have several things going at the same time—and not all of them overtly business related. According to Lewis, they are "lively, loquacious people who do many things at once, planning their priorities not according to a time schedule but according to the relative thrill or importance that each appointment brings

with it." He puts Italians, Latin Americans, and Arabs in this group.

Then there are the *reactives*—those who listen and ponder carefully and move with caution. In Lewis's words, they "prioritize courtesy and respect, listening quietly and calmly to their interlocutors and reacting carefully to the other side's proposals." The Chinese, Japanese, and Finns would be in this group.

Knowing which style your communication partner prefers can help you adjust your expectations and communication style accordingly. But as with all categorizing schemes, use this one only as a general guide, paying careful attention to the actual situation you're in.

SOURCE: Richard D. Lewis, *When Cultures Collide: Leading Across Cultures*, 3rd ed. (Boston: Nicholas Brealey International, 2006), print.

thinking is an emphasis on planning, working efficiently, and maximizing production. Of course, not all of us subscribe to this ethic, but it is a strong force in our culture. The prevailing view in some other cultures is quite different. In Spain, for example, business is more relaxed because of the emphasis placed on interpersonal relationships and the view that planning can be futile.[12]

Views about the relationships of employers and employees also may differ by culture. North American workers expect to move freely from job to job, and they expect employers to hire and fire as their needs change. Expectations are quite different in some other cultures. In Japan, for example, employment tends to be for a lifetime. The company is viewed much like a family, with loyalty expected from employees and employer. Such differences have caused misunderstandings in American–Japanese joint ventures.

Expression of Emotions. From culture to culture, norms for personal expression differ. To illustrate, some Asian cultures strongly frown upon public displays of affection—in fact, they consider them crude and offensive. Westerners, on the other hand, accept at least a moderate display of affection. To Westerners, laughter is a spontaneous display of pleasure, but in some cultures (Japanese, for one), laughter also can be a controlled behavior—to be used in certain social situations. Even such emotional displays as sorrow are influenced by culture. In some Middle Eastern cultures, sorrow is expressed with loud wailing. In similar situations, Westerners typically respond with more controlled emotions, which could be seen as cold and uncaring by Middle Easterners.

A whole culture can tend one way or another regarding the show of emotion. For example, people of the Mediterranean cultures often speak with passion and animation, while Northern Europeans lean toward a more subdued style. Without an understanding of this difference, the first group might see the second as uninterested and lacking in friendliness. The second may see the first as excitable, emotional, and perhaps even unstable.

---

[12] "Business Culture in Spain," *WorldBusinessCulture*, Global Business Culture, 2012, Web, 5 May 2012.

Many more such differences exist. Some cultures combine business and social pleasure; others do not. Some expect to engage in aggressive bargaining in business transactions; others prefer straightforward dealings. Some talk loudly and with emotion; others communicate orally in a subdued manner. Some communicate with emphasis on economy of expression; others communicate with an abundance of verbiage.

There are countless differences between cultures. But it is not necessary that you know them all. What is important is that you recognize their existence, respect them, and study them when necessary. Only then can you adapt your communication style accordingly.

Effects on Business Communication

Because cultural differences will affect communication between people of different cultures, the communication advice presented in the remaining chapters of this book should be modified to fit the cultures involved.

Keep in mind that this book was written largely for U.S. readers. Much of what we say may not apply to other cultures. People in Asian cultures, for example, generally favor a somewhat indirect approach for messages we would treat directly. They begin with an identification of context—that is, a description of the situation the message concerns. They use what appears to us as exaggerated politeness and slowness in moving to the point. In fact, some of our direct messages would be regarded as rude by people in these cultures.[13]

Even the British, whose culture we think of as resembling our own, have communication practices that differ from ours. They especially differ in the treatment of negative situations. They prefer an approach that we would regard as blunt and calloused. They would regard our goodwill strategies as insincere and evasive.

Online communication is also affected by culture. In one study, social networking preferences were found to line up with cultural differences. The U.S. users who were studied formed connections that were much broader and looser than those of their Chinese and South Korean counterparts, who cultivated online relationships more carefully and maintained them longer.[14] Another researcher found that Asians, fearful of overstepping their authority and reluctant to speak to strangers, can be hesitant to offer comments during online conversations.[15]

To be effective in the contemporary workplace, you have no choice but to become a student of culture. Learn the cultures of those with whom you communicate, and don't expect them to understand your culture, although many of them will. With effort and patience, you can develop cross-cultural competency and enjoy its many benefits.

PROBLEMS OF LANGUAGE

The people on earth use more than 3,000 languages. Because few of us can learn more than one or two other languages well, problems of miscommunication are bound to occur in international communication.

LO5 Explain the language equivalency problem and techniques for minimizing its effects.

Lack of Language Equivalency

Unfortunately, wide differences among languages make precisely equivalent translations difficult. One reason for such differences is that languages are based on the concepts, experiences, and views of the particular cultures that developed them. Thus,

---

[13] Richard M. Hodgetts, Fred Luthans, and Jonathan Doh, *International Management: Culture, Strategy, and Behavior* (New York: McGraw-Hill/Irwin, 2006) 190, print.

[14] Sejung Mariana Choi, Shu-Chuan Chu, and Yoojung Kim, "Culture-Laden Social Engagement: A Comparative Study of Social Relationships in Social Networking Sites among American, Chinese and Korean Users," *Computer-Mediated Communication across Cultures*, ed. Kirk St. Amant and Sigrid Kelsey, *IGI Global*, 2012, Web, 2 May 2012.

[15] Kirk St. Amant, "Culture, Context, and Cyberspace: Rethinking Identity and Authority in the Age of the Global Internet," Association for Business Communication Southeast Regional Conference, St. Petersburg, FL, Mar. 2012, conference presentation.

Companies can make blunders in international business through their products, practices, and words. Here are some of those where words were the culprit.

- When Coca-Cola first attempted to market its drink in China, the characters representing it sounded like Coca-Cola but translated to *a wax-flattened mare.* Now the characters that represent it translate to *happiness in the mouth.*

- Olympia tried to introduce a copier in Chile under the name Roto, which is the Spanish word for *broken.*

- American Motor Company's Matador translated into *killer* in Puerto Rico, clearly not a good name in a place with high traffic fatality rates.

- Toyota's MR2 did well in most countries, but in France it is often pronounced *merde,* meaning *human waste.*

- Ford encountered problems when it introduced a low-cost truck it named *Fiera* into Latin American countries. The name translates to *ugly old woman.*

- Bacardi developed and launched a fruity drink, calling it Pavian. In German it means *baboon.*

- When Nike attempted to place a graphic of flames on its shoes, it discovered that the illustration resembled the Arabic script meaning *Allah,* the word for God. The Council on American–Islamic Relations demanded an apology and withdrawal of the shoes from the market.

Selected from David A. Ricks, *Blunders in International Business,* 4th ed. (Malden, MA: Blackwell Publishing, 2006), print.

even a word that seems the same in two languages may have different meanings. For example, we think of a florist as someone who sells flowers and related items in a store. In some cultures, however, flowers are sold by street vendors, mainly women and children. Obviously, our *florist* does not have a precise equivalent in the language of such cultures.

Sometimes a word in one language has no corresponding word in another. For example, *supermarket* has no equivalent in some languages. The French have no word to distinguish between *house* and *home, mind* and *brain,* and *man* and *gentleman.* The Spanish have no word to distinguish between a *chairman* and a *president,* while Italians have no word for *wishful thinking.* And Russians have no words for *efficiency, challenge,* and *having fun.* However, Italians have nearly 500 words for types of pasta. And so it is with words for many other objects, actions, and concepts (for example, *roundup, interview, strike, tough, monopoly, domestic, feminine, responsible, aloof*).

Another explanation for the lack of language equivalency is that there are grammatical and syntactic differences among languages. Some languages (Urdu, for example) have no gerunds, and some have no adverbs and/or adjectives. Not all languages deal with verb mood, voice, and tense in the same way. The obvious result is that even the best translators often cannot find literal equivalents between languages.

Adding to these equivalency problems is the problem of multiple word meanings. Like English, other languages have more than one meaning for many words. Think, for example, of our numerous meanings for the simple word *run* (to move fast, to compete for office, a score in baseball, a break in a stocking, a fading of colors, and many more). The Oxford English Dictionary uses over 15,000 words to define *what.* Unless one knows a language well, it is difficult to know which of the meanings is intended.

Within a culture, certain manners of expression may be used in a way that their dictionary translations and grammatical structures do not explain. Those within the culture understand these expressions; those outside may not. For example, we might say, "Business couldn't be better," meaning business is very good. One from another culture might understand the sentence to mean "Business is bad" (impossible to improve). Or we might say, "We could never be too nice to our customers," meaning that try as we may, we couldn't be overly nice. To one from another culture, the sentence might mean "We cannot be nice to our customers."[16]

Similarly, like-meaning words can be used in different ways in different cultures. One example is the simple word *yes,* a word that has an equivalent in all languages. "The Chinese *yes,* like the Japanese *yes,* can often be understood by Americans and British as their English *yes.* But the Chinese *yes* often means 'I am listening.' Or it may be understood in English as the opposite. For example, when an American says to a Chinese counterpart, 'I see you don't agree with this clause,' the Chinese will usually reply, 'Yes' meaning a polite agreement with the negative question: 'Yes, you are right. I do not agree with the clause.'"[17]

Overcoming such language problems is difficult. The best way, of course, is to know your partner's language well, but the competence required is beyond the reach of many of us. Thus, your best course is first to be aware that translation problems exist and then to ask questions—to probe—to determine what the other person understands. For very important messages, you might consider using a procedure called **back translating**. This procedure involves using two translators, one with first-language skills in one of the languages involved and one with first-language skills in the other language. The first translator translates the message into his or her language, and the second translator then translates the message back into the original. If the translations are good, the second translation matches the original.

Difficulties with English

English is the primary language of international business. This is not to say that other languages are not used. When business executives from different countries have a common language, whatever it may be, they are likely to use it. For example, an executive from Iraq and an executive from Saudi Arabia would communicate with each other in Arabic, while an executive from Venezuela would use Spanish in dealing with an executive from Mexico. However, when executives have no common language, they are likely to use English. The members of the European Free Trade Association conduct all their business in English. In the words of one international authority, "English has emerged as the *lingua franca* of world commerce in much the same way that Greek did in the ancient world of the West and Chinese did in the East."[18]

We must keep in mind, though, that English is not the primary language of many of those who use it. Since many of these users have had to learn English as a second language, they are likely to use it less fluently than native speakers and to experience problems in understanding it. Some of their more troublesome problems are reviewed in the following pages.

Two-Word Verbs. One of the most difficult problems for nonnative speakers of English is the use of two-word verbs. By **two-word verbs** we mean a wording consisting of (1) a verb and (2) a second element that, combined with the verb, produces a meaning that the verb alone does not have. For example, take the verb *break* and the word *up.* When combined, they have a meaning quite different from the meanings the words have alone. And look how the meaning changes when the same verb is combined with other words: *break away, break out, break in, break down.* Figure 2–1 lists some of the more common words that combine with verbs.

Of course, nonnatives studying English learn some of these word combinations, but many of them are not covered in language textbooks or listed in dictionaries. For this reason, we should use these word combinations sparingly when communicating

[16] Jensen J. Zhao, "The Chinese Approach to International Business Negotiation," *Journal of Business Communication* 37 (2000): 225, print.

[17] Zhao 225.

[18] Naoki Kameda, *Business Communication toward Transnationalism: The Significance of Cross-Cultural Business English and Its Role* (Tokyo: Kindaibungeisha Co., 1996) 34, print.

Figure 2–1

Some Two-Word Verbs That Confuse Nonnative Speakers

Verb Plus *Away*	Verb Plus *In*	Verb Plus *Out*	Verb Plus *Up*
give away	cash in	blow out	blow up
keep away	cave in	clean out	build up
lay away	close in	crowd out	call up
pass away	dig in	cut out	catch up
throw away	give in	die out	cover up
Verb Plus *Back*	run in	dry out	dig up
cut back	take in	even out	end up
feed back	throw in	figure out	fill up
keep back		fill out	get up
play back	**Verb Plus *Off***	find out	hang up
read back	break off	give out	hold up
take back	brush off	hold out	keep up
turn back	buy off	lose out	look up
win back	check off	pull out	mix up
Verb Plus *Down*	clear off	rule out	pick up
calm down	cool off	tire out	save up
die down	cut off	wear out	shake up
hand down	finish off	work out	shut up
keep down	let off		slow up
let down	mark off	**Verb Plus *Over***	wrap up
lie down	pay off	check over	**Verb Plus Miscellaneous Words**
mark down	run off	do over	
pin down	send off	hold over	bring about
play down	slow off	pass over	catch on
put down	shut off	put over	get across
run down	sound off	roll over	pass on
shut down	start off	run over	put across
sit down	take off	stop over	put forth
wear down	write off	take over	set forth
		talk over	
		think over	
		win over	

with nonnative speakers of English. Following are some two-word verbs and suggested substitutes:

Two-Word Verbs	Suggested Substitutes
give up	surrender
speed up, hurry up	accelerate
go on, keep on	continue
put off	defer, delay
take off	depart, remove
come down	descend
go in, come in, get in	enter
go out, come out, get out	exit, leave
blow up	explode
think up	imagine
figure out	solve
take out, take away	remove
go back, get back, be back	return

head for home	shoot from the hip	in a rut
seal the deal	over the top	priming the pump
grasp at straws	on the same page	make heads or tails of it
flat-footed	back to the drawing board	tearjerker
on target	start at square one	countdown
out to pasture	a flop (or bust)	shortcut
sitting duck	up the creek without a paddle	educated guess
in the groove	a fish out of water	all ears
nuts (crazy)	a chicken with its head cut off	slower than molasses
circle the wagons	in the ballpark	break the ice

Additional problems result from the fact that some two-word verbs have noun and adjective forms. These also tend to confuse nonnatives using English. Examples of such nouns are *breakthrough, cover-up, drive-in,* and *show-off.* Examples of such adjectives are *going-away* (a going-away gift), *cover-up* (cover-up tactics), *cleanup* (cleanup work), and *turning-off* (turning-off place). Fortunately, some nouns and adjectives of this kind are commonly used and appear in standard dictionaries (words such as *hookup, feedback, breakthrough, lookout,* and *takeover*). In writing to nonnative readers, you will need to use sparingly those that do not appear in standard dictionaries.

Slang and Colloquialisms. As the next chapter points out, slang and colloquialisms can cause problems when your reader or listener is unfamiliar with them. The odds of this being the case are dramatically increased in cross-cultural communication.

For example, will non-U.S. communicators understand the expressions *nerd, couch potato, control freak, 24/7, pumped,* or *basket case*? How about words derived from U.S. sports, such as *kickoff, over the top, out in left field, strike out, touch base,* and *get the ball rolling*? Such expressions are sometimes defined on English as a Second Language (ESL) websites but rarely in dictionaries. They would be risky to use except with those very familiar with U.S. English. (See Figure 2-2 for more colloquialisms to avoid.)

In the United States we tend to use colloquial expressions often in our everyday communicating. They are colorful, and they can communicate clearly to those who understand them. But when you are communicating with nonnative English speakers, try to replace them with words that are clearly defined in the dictionaries that these people are likely to use in translating your message. Following are some examples:

Not This	**But This**
This is just off the top of my head.	Here's a quick idea.
He frequently shoots from the hip.	He frequently acts before he thinks.
We would be up the creek without a paddle.	We would be in a helpless situation.
They couldn't make heads or tails of the report.	They couldn't understand the report.
The sales campaign was a flop.	The sales campaign was a failure.
I'll touch base with you on this problem in August.	I'll talk with you again about this problem in August.
I'll share our research with the committee so they won't have to start from scratch [*or* reinvent the wheel].	I'll share our research with the committee to save them some work.
We will wind down manufacturing operations in November.	We will end manufacturing operations in November.
Your prediction was right on target.	Your prediction was correct.
Don't let him get your goat.	Don't let him upset you.

ADVICE FOR COMMUNICATING ACROSS CULTURES

LO6 Describe what one can do to enhance one's cross-cultural communication skills.

As the preceding sections make clear, cross-cultural communication is fraught with potential barriers and misunderstandings. And even with the best effort on your part, not every act of cross-cultural communication will succeed. Like other kinds of communication, cross-cultural communication involves people—and people are unpredictable. In every culture, some persons are uncooperative, deceitful, prejudiced, or insensitive, while others are respectful, welcoming, sincere, and harmony-seeking. You can only make sure that you are as prepared as possible. Keeping in mind the following advice will help.

Do Your Research

This chapter cites many helpful resources on different cultures and their communication practices, and Figure 2–3 lists additional websites and books. Before any international business encounter, be sure you have done your homework. Learn something about the topography, climate, and location of your potential partners' countries of origin. Learn something about their language—and learn to speak it if you can. Study descriptions of their history, their ways of life, their values, their manners, and even their food and recreation.

Besides doing library and online research, talk with people who have had experience with those in other cultures, and if they have writing samples, ask to see them. Take an intercultural business course or even a course designed for those preparing to do business in a specific country. Pursue opportunities to socialize or do teamwork with nonnatives in your own country. The more effort you make to reach out beyond your own world, the better your cross-cultural relations will be.

Know Yourself and Your Company

As several books by international communication experts point out, a frequent mistake made by those preparing to do business abroad is that they focus all their research on people in the culture they're about to engage with and forget to research themselves. Yet knowing yourself is a good way to anticipate and prevent likely frustrations. For example, if you know you tend to be a "low-context," "low power distance," "individualistic," "masculine," "long-term goals" kind of person, you will be less caught off guard by people at the opposite ends of these spectrums. You can remind yourself to watch and listen carefully for visual and vocal cues, to be patient, to show respect and act with due dignity yourself, and so forth.

It is also very important to understand the business you represent. Is yours a rule-bound, procedure-governed operation or one that is more loose and trusting? Do you solve problems by leaving them to management, by hiring an expert, or by pooling everyone's ideas? Does your company avoid mixing business with pleasure, do employees socialize only with their peers, or does everyone in the company feel free to relax together? Does your company tend to take a straight, efficient route to its goals or learn and adjust as it goes? Just as you will view your international business partner as representative of his or her company, so he or she will view you. Be sure you send accurate signals.

Be Aware—and Wary—of Stereotypes

One of the most sensitive issues in cross-cultural communication is the extent to which generalizing about a culture perpetuates **stereotypes**. We have come to regard stereotyping as negative, with good reason: Stereotyping can prejudice us and blind us to others' true natures. But the reason stereotypes are powerful is that they are based to some degree on observable likenesses within groups of people. They appeal because they are tempting mental shortcuts. But as the international business consultants at Canning point out, that is also their downside. They "are fixed and conventionalized"

Figure 2–3

Additional Resources for Cross-Cultural Communication

Websites:

www.state.gov. The U.S. government's main diplomatic website. The "Countries and Regions" tab on the main menu bar gives you access to the site's Backgound Notes. These provide extensive, frequently updated information on all countries with which the United States has relations.

www.cia.gov/library/publications/the-world-factbook/. Resources from the U.S. Central Intelligence Agency. The site "provides information on the history, people, government, economy, geography, communications, transportation, military, and transnational issues for 267 world entities."

http://trade.gov/index.asp. Website of the International Trade Administration, U.S. Department of Commerce, whose purpose is to promote international trade. Through the "Publications" tab on the main menu bar, you can access the agency's latest publications, including its monthly newsletter, as well as previous articles and reports.

www.export.gov/. Website of the U.S. Commercial Service (under the International Trade Administration), offering assistance of all types on international trade. Of particular value are its Country Commercial Guides, regularly updated for each country (access these through "Find Opportunities" > "Market Research" > "Market Research Library").

www.sba.gov/aboutsba/sbaprograms/internationaltrade/exportlibrary/index.html. Resources from the U.S. government for small businesses interested in doing international trade.

www.oecd.org/home/0,3305,en_2649_201185_1_1_1_1_1,00.html. Website for the Organisation for Economic Co-operation and Development (OECD)—originally the Organisation for European Economic Co-operation (OEEC)—an organization of 34 member countries that share their knowledge and resources on over 200 countries (click the "Countries" tab).

www.uscib.org. Website of the United States Council for International Business, a nongovernmental organization. Can access recent issues of the USCIB's journal *International Business* and news articles for free (must belong to a member company, law firm, or organization to access additional material).

www.fita.org/index.html. Site of the Federation of International Trade Organizations, another nongovernmental organization promoting international trade. Has links to over 8,000 international trade-related websites on such topics as maps and geography, international business terms, trade law, and many more. (A good place to start is "Really Useful Links" in the "Tools of Trade" section of the left-hand main menu bar.) Some links lead to free resources; some are for paying members only.

http://globaledge.msu.edu/. Sponsored by Michigan State University in the United States. Can find extensive resources by country and state, including not only geography, history, and vital statistics but also news, trade, and industry information.

http://timeticker.com. Can find out what time it is in any country or which countries are in any time zone.

www.NationMaster.com. A popular educational website started by an Australian statistics enthusiast. Offers maps, flags, and country profiles, but its greatest strength is statistics on many countries, which the site will graph for you.

www.calliope.be/. An online learning center for international communication at the University of Antwerp. Offers theory, exercises, and cases on intercultural communication in three languages: Dutch, English, and French. You can see what readers in these different cultures prefer to see in such documents as résumés, press releases, and persuasive messages.

www.kwintessential.co.uk/etiquette/doing-business-in.html. Site of a UK consulting firm that offers free guides for doing business in 46 countries.

Selected Books:

Jag Bhalla, *I'm Not Hanging Noodles on Your Ears and Other Intriguing Idioms from Around the* World (Washington, DC: National Geographic, 2009). A compilation of colorful expressions in different languages.

Mary Murray Bosrock, *Asian Business Customs & Manners: A Country-by-Country Guide* (Minnetonka, MN: Meadowbrook, 2007). Other books in this popular series focus on Europe, United States, Mexico/Canada, Russia, and the Middle East.

Martin J. Gannon and Rajnandini Pillai, *Understanding Global Cultures: Metaphorical Journeys Through 30 Nations, Clusters of Nations, Continents, and Diversity,* 5th ed. (Los Angeles: Sage, 2013). An insightful, innovative approach that interprets cultures through their popular metaphors, such as "the Japanese garden" and "the Finnish sauna."

Jeanette S. Martin and Lillian H. Chaney, *Global Business Etiquette: A Guide to International Communication and Customs* (Westport, CT: Praeger, 2012). Comprehensive guide to world business communication and behavior.

Terri Morrison and Wayne A. Conaway, *Kiss, Bow, or Shake Hands: How to Do Business in Sixty Countries*, 2nd ed. (Avon, MA: Adams Media, 2006). An alphabetically arranged country-by-country guide describing the overall culture, behavioral styles, negotiating techniques, protocol, and business practices of each country.

Mustafa F. Ozbilgin and Ahu Tatli, *Global Diversity Management: An Evidence-Based Approach* (London: Palgrave Macmillan, 2008). Case studies and advice concerning many countries and issues.

Kirk St. Amant and Sigrid Kelsey, *Computer-Mediated Communication across Cultures: International Interactions in Online Environments*, IGI Global, 2012, Web, 5 May 2012.

Fons Trompenaars and Charles Hampden-Turner, *Riding the Waves of Culture: Understanding Diversity in Global Business,* 3rd ed. (New York: McGraw-Hill, 2012).

and for that reason "suggest a failure to learn from experience." Well-researched cultural stereotypes can be useful as basic models that you then adjust as you accumulate additional information. The generalizations can be a beginning point of reference, but you should quickly let them go when someone clearly doesn't represent the general type.[19]

---

[19] Mattock 14–15.

Another reason it is important to be aware of stereotypes is that your prospective international business partners are likely to see *you* through the lens of a cultural stereotype. The more familiar you are with the way people from your culture or country are seen by those in another, the better prepared you will be to show them the ways in which you differ from the stereotype.

Adapt Your English to Your Audience

The nonnative English speakers you meet will vary widely in their skill. Some may speak better English than you do, while others may have only the barest grasp of the language. As we have suggested, erring on the side of simplicity is your best bet for clear communication. Write or talk simply and clearly. Talk slowly and enunciate each word. Remember that because most nonnative speakers learned English in school, they are acquainted mainly with primary dictionary meanings and are not likely to understand slang words or shades of difference in the meanings we give words. They will understand you better if you avoid these pitfalls.

You also will communicate better if you carefully word your questions. Be sure your questions are not double questions (for example, avoid a question like "Do you want to go to dinner now or wait until after the rush hour is over?"). Also, avoid the yes/no question that some cultures may have difficulty answering directly. Use more open-ended questions such as "When would you like to go to dinner?" And avoid negative questions such as "Aren't you going to dinner?" If the respondent says "yes," it could mean either "right, I am not going to dinner," or "Yes, I'm going."

Finally, try to confirm that you understand and are being understood correctly. Even in Britain, whose culture is similar to ours in the United States, similar words can have vastly different meanings. For example, we use a billion to mean 1,000,000,000 whereas the British use it to mean 1,000,000,000,000. If a British English speaker asks to *table* an item, an American English speaker will probably interpret that as a request to put it off, when the real request is to bring it to attention.[20] Continually checking for shared meaning can help ensure the accuracy of the communication process.

Be Open to Change

International communication can be a broadening experience if you approach it with openness and tolerance. In addition to learning about new and better ways to do business, you can also grow personally and enlarge your world.

Is adapting to the practices of one's international partners always feasible? No. You may find that the culture of the company you represent will simply not mesh with those of some potential business partners. Is adapting to others' practices always ethical? Here, too, the answer is no. For example, Jean-Claude Usunier lists several practices to avoid in international negotiations, including bribing, buying information, buying influence, giving misleading information, exploiting the other party's ignorance, undermining the competition by buying out their people, and negotiating without intending to keep any promises.[21] Unfortunately, these practices are all fairly widespread, even though some have been made expressly illegal by such acts as the U.S. Foreign Corrupt Practices Act. And other ethical problems—racism, sexism, homophobia, disregard for the environment, exploitation of labor, and so forth—may arise. If put in a situation where you must choose between making a deal or behaving ethically and legally, seek advice from others in your company. You are likely to be advised to do the ethical thing—not only because most businesspeople are honorable but also because, in the Internet age, news about scandalous company dealings travels fast, often with disastrous results.

---

[20] Danielle Medina Walker, Thomas Walker, and Joerg Schmitz, *Doing Business Internationally: The Guide to Cross-Cultural Success*, 2nd ed. (New York: McGraw-Hill/Irwin, 2003) 211, print.
[21] Jean-Claude Usunier, "Ethical Aspects of International Business Negotiations," *International Business Negotiations*, ed. Pervez N. Ghauri and Jean-Claude Usunier, 2nd ed. (Amsterdam: Pergamon, 2003) 437–38, print.

If approached patiently, humbly, and sincerely, forming international business relations can be incredibly exciting. Be ready to make and acknowledge mistakes, and to forgive them in others. Mutual respect is key—perhaps *the* key—to successful cross-cultural communication.

THERE'S MORE . . .

What time is it in Kyoto, Japan, when it's 9 a.m. your time? Where can you find an online dictionary for Italian? How should you dress when doing business in Chile? Scan the QR code in the margin with your smartphone or use your Web browser to find out at www.mhhe.com/leskiar13e. Choose Chapter 2 > Bizcom Tools & Tips.

SUMMARY BY LEARNING OBJECTIVES

Explain why communicating clearly across cultures is important to business.

1. Businesses are becoming increasingly global in their operations.
   - Being able to communicate across cultures is necessary in these operations.
   - Specifically, it helps in satisfying customers' needs, gaining additional business, getting along with co-workers, hiring good people, and avoiding misinterpretations.

Describe three major factors that influence a country or region's culture.

2. When learning about a culture, start with the big picture.
   - Learn about the influence of topography, history, and religion on the culture.
   - Remember that businesspeople the world over share many of the same goals.
   - Learn about others' cultures to avoid ethnocentrism and to enhance your cross-cultural communication.

Describe cultural differences regarding body positions and movements and use this knowledge effectively in communicating.

3. How people use body positions and body movements varies across cultures.
   - How people walk, gesture, smile, and touch differs from culture to culture.
   - Understanding others' body movements is important in cross-cultural communication.

Describe the impact of culture on views and practices concerning human relations and use this knowledge effectively in communicating.

4. People in different cultures differ in their ways of relating to people.
   - Specifically, they differ in their practices and thinking concerning time, space, odors, frankness, social hierarchy, workplace values, and social behavior.
   - We should not use our own culture's practices as standards for interpreting and evaluating the practices of those from other cultures.
   - Instead, we should try to understand other cultures and adapt our communication styles accordingly.

Explain the language equivalency problem and techniques for minimizing its effects.

5. Language equivalency problems are another major cause of miscommunication in cross-cultural communication, but you can minimize them.
   - Some words in a language have no equivalent in other languages.
   - Languages can also differ greatly in terms of grammar and syntax.
   - As in English, most words in other languages have multiple meanings.
   - As a result, accurate translation is difficult.
   - The best advice is to master the language of the nonnative English speakers with whom you communicate.
   - Ask questions carefully to make sure you are understood.
   - Try to avoid two-word verbs and colloquial expressions.
   - Continually check the accuracy of the communication.

6. Keep in mind the following advice about cross-cultural communication:
   - Do your research.
   - Know yourself and your company.
   - Be aware—and wary—of stereotypes.
   - Adapt your English to your audience.
   - Be open to change.

Describe what one can do to enhance one's cross-cultural communication skills.

KEY TERMS

culture, 27

ethnocentrism, 29

monochronic, 31

polychronic, 32

low-context culture, 32

high-context culture, 32

power distance, 33

back translating, 38

two-word verbs, 38

stereotypes, 41

CRITICAL THINKING QUESTIONS

1 Put yourself in the shoes of the trainer described in this chapter's Introductory Challenge. What might have been a better way to handle the situation? Explain why. **LO4**

2 What are the prevailing attitudes in our culture toward the following, and how can those attitudes affect our communication with nonnatives? Discuss. **LO4**

   a. Negotiation methods

   b. Truth in advertising

   c. Company–worker loyalty

   d. Women's appropriate roles in society

   e. The Protestant work ethic

3 Some of our message-writing techniques are said to be unacceptable to people from such cultures as those of Japan and England. Which techniques in particular do you think would be most inappropriate in these cultures? Why? **LO4**

4 Think of English words (other than this chapter's examples) that probably do not have precise equivalents in some other culture. How would you attempt to explain each of these words to a person from that culture? **LO5**

5 Select a word with at least five meanings. List those meanings and consider how you would communicate each of them to a nonnative. **LO5**

6 Is a conversational style appropriate in writing to non-native readers? Discuss. **LO4, LO5**

7 Select a country or region and analyze the likely impact of its topography, history, and religious background on its culture. **LO2**

8 Study a country's culture and then infer its people's likely attitudes toward American values and behaviors. **LO3, LO4**

9 If you were trying to persuade your boss to implement some kind of cross-cultural training in the company, what kind of evidence might help you make a convincing case? **LO1**

10 On a recent trip to India, Mr. Yang, a prominent Chinese executive, dined with his client Himanshu Jain. Mr. Yang commented that the food was spicy, which Mr. Jain interpreted as an opportunity to discuss Indian cuisine. After lengthy explanations, Mr. Yang commented again that the food was spicy.

   What happened here? What barrier is likely getting in the way of clear communication? (Adapted from Danielle Medina Walker, Thomas Walker, and Joerg Schmitz, *Doing Business Internationally: The Guide to Cross-Cultural Success* [New York: McGraw-Hill, 2003] 237, print.) **LO2, LO4**

SKILLS BUILDING EXERCISES

Instructions: Rewrite the following sentences for a nonnative English speaker. **LO5**

1 From newspapers or magazines, find and bring to class 10 sentences containing words and expressions that a nonnative English speaker would not be likely to understand. Rewrite the sentences for this reader. **LO5**

2 Interview a nonnative speaker of English about communication differences between cultures he or she has experienced. Report your findings to the class in a 10-minute presentation. **LO2, LO3, LO4**

3 Research a non-English-speaking country on the Internet or in your library. Look for ways in which the culture of

this country might influence the way its citizens do business. Report your work to the class in a short presentation. **LO2, LO6**

4 Research differences in business etiquette between your country and another one. Report your findings to the class. **LO2, LO4, LO6**

5 Rewrite the following sentences to accommodate a nonnative English speaker. **LO5**

   a. Last year our laboratory made a breakthrough in design that really made our sales skyrocket.

   b. You will need to pin down Mr. Wang to get him to tighten up expenses.

   c. Recent losses have us on the ropes now, but we expect to get out of the hole by the end of the year.

   d. We will kick off the advertising campaign in February, and in April we will bring out the new products.

   e. Maryellen gave us a ballpark figure on the project, but I think she is ready to back down from her estimate.

   f. We will pull the plug on any of our products that are flatlining.

   g. Mr. Maghrabi managed to straighten up and become our star salesperson.

   h. Now that we have cut back on our telemarketing, we will have to build up our radio advertising.

   i. If you want to improve sales, you should stay with your prospects until you win them over.

   j. We should be able to haul in a savings of 8 or 10 grand.

Fundamentals of Business Writing

With a net worth of around $44 billion, Warren Buffett is ranked by *Forbes* magazine as the second-richest person in the world, after Microsoft Cofounder and Chairman Bill Gates. Buffett made his first stock purchase at the age of 11 but sold before the stock skyrocketed. This early lesson taught him to study hard and carefully analyze potential investments. The result was the development of one of the world's largest holding companies, Berkshire Hathaway, Inc.

Although best known for his ability to pick stocks, Buffett was honored in 2006 by the National Commission on Writing for America's Families, Schools, and Colleges for writing Berkshire Hathaway's annual report. Buffett writes, "One way or another, you have to project your ideas to other people. Writing isn't necessarily easy. . . . But you get better and better at it, and I encourage everybody to do that."

Warren E. Buffett, CEO of Berkshire Hathaway, Inc.

CHAPTER THREE

Adapting Your Words to Your Readers

Learning Objectives

Upon completing this chapter, you will be able to adapt your language to specific readers and to select the most effective words for your communication purpose. To reach this goal, you should be able to

1 Explain the role of adaptation in selecting words that communicate.

2 Simplify writing by selecting familiar and short words.

3 Use slang and popular clichés with caution.

4 Use technical words and acronyms appropriately.

5 Use concrete, specific words with the right shades of meaning.

6 Avoid misusing similar words and use idioms correctly.

7 Use active verbs.

8 Use words that do not discriminate.

Choosing the Best Words for Your Message

To consider the importance of choosing words carefully in your business communication, put yourself in this hypothetical scenario. You're fulfilling your business school's co-op requirement by working in the office of a large uniform and career apparel company. Your supervisor tells you that she thinks the company's correspondence with customers seems somewhat stiff and outdated, and she asks if you'll draft a "thank you for your business" form letter for new clients that will "make us sound contemporary but still professional." "Sure," you say.

You sit at your computer and dash off this first draft:

Dear [new customer],

You are welcomed as a new customer and thanked for your business.

It will be seen that we have a lot of wonderful products that have gained us notoriety in our industry. Plus, our CRM is second to none. If you ever have a complaint, our customer-service girls will take care of it ASAP.

We are anxious to serve you further and look forward to a harmonious and mutually profitable collaborative experience.

As you read over what you've written, you're not very pleased. The more you look at the letter, the more you realize that it's not likely to be effective. This chapter will help you understand how to choose your words more wisely.

THE IMPORTANCE OF ADAPTATION

LO1 Explain the role of adaptation in selecting words that communicate.

Clear writing begins with adapting your message to your specific readers. As Chapter 1 explains, readers occupy particular organizational, professional, and personal contexts. They do not all have the same kind or level of vocabulary, knowledge, or values. And as Chapter 2 explains, some may be from cultures very different from yours.

To choose words that communicate clearly and with the appropriate tone, you should learn everything possible about those with whom you wish to communicate. Then you should word your message so that it is easy for them to understand and respond to favorably. Tailoring your message to your readers is not only strategically necessary; it is also a sign of consideration for their time and energy. Everyone benefits when messages are clear and appropriate to the correspondents' situation.

Adaptation Illustrated

The following paragraphs from two company annual reports illustrate the basic principle of **adaptation**. The first was written in such a way that investors without a background in finance could understand it.

Last year your company's total sales were $117,400,000, which was slightly higher than the $109,800,000 total for the year before. After deducting for all expenses, we had $4,593,000 left over for profits, compared with $2,830,000 for 2011. Because of these increased profits, we were able to increase your annual dividend payments per share from the 50 cents paid over the last 10 years.

The second paragraph was adapted to those with financial expertise: stockbrokers, financial managers, financial analysts, and bankers.

The corporation's investments and advances in three unconsolidated subsidiaries (all in the development stage) and in 50 percent-owned companies was $42,200,000 on December 31, 2012, and the excess of the investments in certain companies over net asset value at dates of acquisition was $1,760,000. The corporation's equity in the net assets as of December 31, 2012, was $41,800,000 and in the results of operations for the years ended December 31, 2011 and 2012, was $1,350,000 and

$887,500, respectively. Dividend income was $750,000 and $388,000 for the years 2011 and 2012, respectively.

Which writer was right? Perhaps both. Perhaps neither. The answer depends on what the stockholders of each company were really like. Both examples illustrate the technique of adaptation. They use different words for different audiences, which is one of the most powerful communication strategies.

Adapting to Multiple Readers

Adapting your message to one reader requires considerable care, but what if, as often happens, you need to address your message to several different readers? What if your readers vary widely in terms of their education, knowledge of the subject, and reasons for reading? How can you write your message in such a way that you communicate to everyone? The solution is to write in such a way that your different readers can find and understand the parts of your message that are of value to them.

For example, assume that you are the assistant director of marketing for a telecommunications company, and you need to report some complex marketing data to your boss, to the sales manager, and to the president of the company. How might you design your report so that all three, with their differing levels of familiarity with market research techniques, could understand it?

For the sales manager and the president, the nonexperts, you will need to define any specialized vocabulary you use. You will also spell out the implications of your findings for them. For example, the sales manager in our example will need to know what your findings mean for the sales staff, while the president will want to understand how your findings could enhance the financial health of the company.

Accommodating the nonexperts need not bore the expert readers. They often can benefit from seeing the bigger picture themselves, and they usually are not bothered when definitions and explanations are provided. But it is often helpful to provide clearly worded headings in your message so that readers looking for different things can find those parts, read them carefully, and then skim or skip the rest.

As with every other element of your messages, your choice of words needs to be guided by your audience and purpose. That is the main "rule" for effective wording. The advice that follows should always be considered in light of this overarching principle.

Like good signage that the public can understand, your writing should be adapted to the skills and interests of your readers.

SUGGESTIONS FOR SELECTING WORDS

The recommendations in this section will help you make you writing clear, interesting, correct, and effective.

Use Familiar Words

LO2 Simplify writing by selecting familiar and short words.

To communicate clearly, you must use words that your readers are familiar with. Because words that are familiar to some people may be unfamiliar to others, you will need to decide which ones your readers will understand.

In general, using familiar words means using the language that most of us use in everyday conversation. The U.S. government calls this kind of wording **plain language** and defines it as "communication your audience can understand the first time they read or hear it."[1] To write clearly, avoid the stiff, more difficult words that do not communicate so precisely or quickly. For example, instead of using the less common word *endeavor,* use *try.* Prefer *do* to *perform, begin* to *initiate, find out* to *ascertain, stop* to *discontinue,* and *show* to *demonstrate.*

The suggestion to use familiar words does not rule out some use of more difficult words. You should use them whenever their meanings fit your purpose best and your readers understand them clearly. The mistake that many of us make is to overwork the more difficult words. We use them so much that they interfere with our communication. A good suggestion is to use the simplest words that carry the meaning without offending the readers' intelligence. Often this means using the words you would use in face-to-face communication with your readers.

The following contrasting examples illustrate the communication advantages of familiar words. As you read the examples, consider what it would be like to read an entire message or report written in these styles.

Unfamiliar Words	Familiar Words
This machine has a tendency to develop excessive and unpleasant audio symptoms when operating at elevated temperatures.	This machine tends to get noisy when it runs hot.
Purchase of a new fleet is not actionable at this juncture.	Buying new trucks is not practical now.
We must leverage our core competencies to maximize our competitiveness.	Relying on what we do best will make us the most competitive.
The most operative assembly-line configuration is a unidirectional flow.	The most efficient assembly-line design is a one-way flow.
The conclusion ascertained from a perusal of pertinent data is that a lucrative market exists for the product.	The data studied show that the product is in high demand.
Company operations for the preceding accounting period terminated with a deficit.	The company lost money last year.

A great resource for business writers—and a great model of the advice it gives—is the U.S. Securities and Exchange Commission's *A Plain English Handbook: How to Create Clear SEC Disclosure Documents* (available at www.sec.gov/pdf/handbook.pdf).

Here's what the handbook says about using familiar words:

> Surround complex ideas with short, common words. For example, use *end* instead of *terminate, explain* rather than *elucidate,* and *use* instead of *utilize.* When a shorter, simpler synomym exists, use it.

---

[1]"What Is Plain Language?," *PlainLanguage.gov,* Plain Language Action and Information Network (PLAIN), n.d., Web, 20 May 2012.

The Most Annoying Business Clichés

Blogger and writing expert Mary Cullen surveyed a wide range of clients from various industries to ask them "which overused phrases they would like to see banished." Here are their top replies:

1. At the end of the day
2. 30,000-foot view
3. Give 110%
4. Think outside of the box
5. FYI
6. 800-pound gorilla
7. Throw under the bus
8. My bad
9. Rightsizing
10. Reaching out
11. Low-hanging fruit
12. Paradigm shift
13. Take it offline
14. At this point in time
15. Synergy
16. Action item

Cullen adds one more that particularly bothers her: "Going forward." "Where else would we go?" she asks. "Backward?"

Prefer Short Words

According to studies of readability, short words generally communicate better than long words. Of course, part of the explanation is that short words tend to be familiar words. But there is another explanation: A heavy use of long words—even long words that are understood—leaves an impression of difficulty that hinders communication.

Of course, not all short words are easy, and not all long words are hard. Many exceptions exist. Not everyone knows such one-syllable words as *gybe*, *verd*, and *id*, whereas even children know such long words as *hippopotamus*, *automobile*, and *bicycle*. On the whole, however, word length and word difficulty are related. Thus, you should rely mostly on short words and use long ones with caution.

This point is illustrated by the following examples. Notice how much easier to understand the short-word versions are.

Long Words	Short Words
The *proposed enhancement is under consideration*.	We are *considering your suggestion*.
They *acceded to the proposition to undertake a collaborative venture*.	They agreed to *work with* us.
Prior to *accelerating productive operation*, the supervisor inspected the machinery.	Before *speeding up* production, the supervisor inspected the machinery.
The *unanimity* of current forecasts is not *incontrovertible evidence* of an *impending* business acceleration.	*Agreement* of the forecasts is not *proof* that business *will improve*.
This *antiquated merchandising strategy* is *ineffectual* in *contemporary* business *operations*.	This *old sales* strategy *will not work* with *today's* customers.

Use Slang and Popular Clichés with Caution

LO3 Use slang and popular clichés with caution.

At any given time in any society, some slang words and clichés are in vogue. In the United States, for example, you might currently hear "for real" (or, "for *real*?"), "no worries," and "sweet," while other such expressions—"no way," "get out," and "bodacious"—now sound dated.

Business clichés come and go as well. "State of the art," "cutting edge," and "world class" have given way to "moving forward," "thought leaders," and "best practices." More examples of today's favored clichés are listed in the Communication Matters box on page 52.

It is true that business clichés can sometimes increase your credibility with other businesspeople and make you sound like "one of them." These expressions can also add color to your language and quickly convey a certain idea. But they can also work against you. As Harvard professor Marjorie Garber puts it, "Jargon marks the place where thinking has been."[2] Clichés catch on because they represent popular concepts, but with overuse, they begin to sound like a replacement for thinking. Plus, they run the risk of sounding out of date, and as Chapter 2 explains, they can create problems in cross-cultural communication.

Google "annoying clichés" and you will see that popular expressions can soon become unpopular. Use them sparingly and only in communication with people who will understand and appreciate them.

Use Technical Words and Acronyms Appropriately

LO4 Use technical words and acronyms appropriately.

Every field of business—accounting, information systems, finance, marketing, and management—has its technical language. This language can be so complex that in some cases specialized dictionaries are compiled. Such dictionaries exist for technology, law, finance, and other business specialties. There are even dictionaries for subareas such as databases, ecommerce, and real estate.

As you work in your chosen field, you will learn its technical words and acronyms. In time you will use these terms freely in communicating with people in your field, and you should. Frequently, one such word will communicate a concept that would otherwise take dozens of words to describe. Moreover, specialized language can signal to other specialists that you are qualified to communicate on their level.

However, problems can arise when you use technical terms with people outside your field. Because these words are everyday words to you, you may forget that not everyone knows them. The result is miscommunication. You can avoid such miscommunication by using technical words only when you are sure your readers know them.

Examples of misuse of technical writing are easy to find. To a worker in the Social Security Administration, the words *covered employment* commonly mean employment covered by social security. To some outsiders, however, they could mean working under a roof. *Annuity* has a clear meaning to someone in insurance. A *contract that guarantees an income for a specified period* would have more meaning to uninformed outsiders. Those in the investment field will understand the comment that a company is *too highly leveraged*, but lay investors will need to have it explained that the company has *too much debt*.

Initials (including acronyms) should be used with caution, too. While some initials, such as IBM, are widely recognized, others, such as SEO (search-engine optimization) and CRM (customer relationship management), are not. If you have any doubt that your reader is familiar with the initials, the best practice is to spell out the words the first time you use them and follow them with the initials. You may also need to go one step further and define them.

---

[2]Quoted by Helen Sword, "Yes, Even Professors Can Write Stylishly," *The Wall Street Journal*, Dow Jones & Company, Inc., 6 Apr. 2012, Web, 21 May 2012.

Lost in Translation

Before using slang in messages that might go to an international audience, consider this lesson about how even a seemingly straightforward word can go wrong:

> Some interesting problems can arise when attempts are made to reach what are thought to be single-minded markets supposedly speaking a common language. Spanish is probably the most vivid example of a language that, while it has many commonalities throughout its use in different places, also contains certain words that have marked variations in meaning. As a result, the message that's meant to be conveyed isn't necessarily the message that's received.

To illustrate, according to Philip Cateora in his book *International Marketing*, the word *ball* translates in Spanish as *bola*. *Bola* means ball in several countries and a lie or fabrication in several others, while in yet another, it's a vulgar obscenity. Tropicana brand orange juice, he writes, was advertised as *Jugo de China* in Puerto Rico, but when marketed to the Cuban population of Miami, Florida, it failed to make a dent in the market. To the Puerto Rican, *China* translated into orange, but none of the Cubans in Miami were interested in buying what they perceived to be Chinese juice.

SOURCE: Michael White, *A Short Course in International Marketing Blunders* (Novato, CA: World Trade Press, 2002) 10–11, *Ebrary Online Books*, University of Cincinnati, Web, 20 May 2012.

Your technical language may not be any of the ones mentioned here, but you will have one. You will need to be careful about using it when you write to people who do not understand it.

LO5 Use concrete, specific words with the right shades of meaning.

Use Precise Language

Good business communicators use words that have sharp, clear meanings for their intended readers, as well as the right emotional tone. Choosing such words means being concrete, specific, and sensitive to shades of meaning.

Concrete is the opposite of **abstract**. While abstract words are vague, concrete words stand for things the reader can see, feel, taste, smell, or count.

The most concrete words are those that stand for things that exist in the real world, such as *chair, desk, computer, Bill Gates,* and the *Empire State Building*. Abstract nouns, on the other hand, cover broad, general meanings as in these examples: *administration, negotiation, wealth, inconsistency, loyalty, compatibility, conservation, discrimination, incompetence,* and *communication*. It is difficult to visualize what these words stand for.

Notice how much clearer the concrete words are in the following examples:

Abstract	Concrete
A significant loss	A 53 percent loss
Good attendance record	100 percent attendance record
The leading company	First among 3,212 companies
The majority	62 percent
In the near future	By noon Thursday
Substantial amount	$3,517,000

Grammar and Style Checkers Help Writers with Word Selection

Today, word processors will help writers with grammar and style as well as with spelling. By default, Microsoft Word checks spelling and grammar automatically, using red and green underlines to distinguish between them. But you can tell Word which grammatical issues to look for. In Word 2010, go to File > Options > Proofing and then click the Settings button, highlighted below. That will open an extensive list of options in the Grammar Settings box. Word will look for whatever options you check.

Although grammar and style checkers are not as accurate as spelling checkers, they will identify words, phrases, and sentences that could be improved. In fact, they often suggest a way to fix the problem and provide an explanation of correct usage.

In the example shown here, the writer told Word to look for instances of passive voice. Then, when she had written the first part of a document, she clicked Review > Spelling and Grammar to have Word check it. The review identified an instance of passive voice. To see how to correct it, she clicked the "Explain . . ." button, and an explanation appeared. Now she will need to decide if she wants to keep the sentence as is or change it to active voice.

If you use your word processor to help you identify potential problems, just remember that no computer application can tell you if your wording is appropriate; only you can determine that.

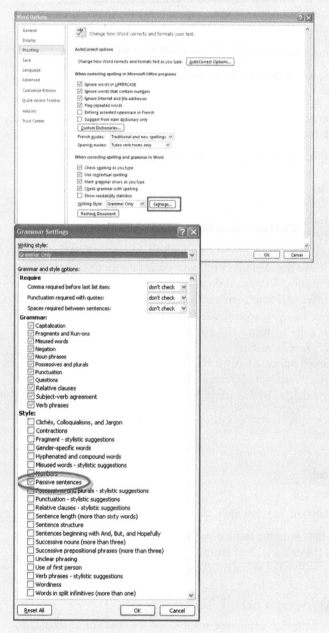

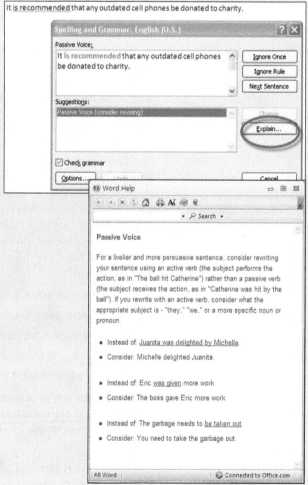

Closely related to being concrete is being **specific**. Even if you are talking about something intangible, you can still make your wording as precise as possible. These examples show what we mean:

Vague	Specific
We have a great company.	We've been voted one of the *Business Courier's* "Best Places to Work" for the last five years.
Our batteries are better.	Our batteries cost less and last longer.
Please respond soon.	Will you let me know by June 1?

Concrete, specific wording can make a dramatic difference in longer passages. Try to understand this paragraph written in abstract language:

> It is imperative that the firm practice extreme conservatism in operating expenditures during the coming biennium. The firm's past operating performance has been ineffectual for the reason that a preponderance of administrative assignments has been delegated to personnel who were ill equipped to perform in these capacities. Recently instituted administrative changes stressing experience in operating economies have rectified this condition.

Written for concreteness and specificity, this message might read as follows:

> We must reduce operating expenses at least $2 million during 2013–14. Our $1,350,000 deficit for 2012-13 was caused by poor investment decisions authorized by Mr. Sartan and Mr. Ross. We have hired Ms. Janice Pharr, a CPA with over 25 years of managerial experience, to restructure the finance department and establish better investment guidelines.

As you can see, concrete, specific wording is not only easier to understand; it is also more informative and interesting.

But being specific isn't your only concern. You also need to elicit the right emotional response from your reader. Good writers possess a sensitivity to words' shades of meaning. Some words are forceful and some timid; some are positive and some negative; some are formal and some informal. Any given word can occupy a place on many different scales of tone and meaning. To achieve your communcation goals, you need to choose the words that will achieve the desired effect with your intended readers.

Consider the differences among *tycoon, industry giant, successful entrepreneur,* and *prominent business executive.* All four terms indicate a person who has acquired wealth and power in business, but you would use these terms in different circumstances. For example, *tycoon* calls to mind the robber barons of the late 19th and early 20th centuries, whereas *prominent business executive* suggests a less flashy, less greedy person who has achieved success within the context of a corporation. Similarly, *fired, dismissed, downsized, separated, terminated,* and *discharged* refer to the same action but have different shades of meaning. So it is with each of the following groups of words:

> sell, market, advertise, promote
>
> money, funds, cash, finances
>
> improve, enhance, fix, correct
>
> concern, issue, problem, incident
>
> secretary, administrative assistant, support staff, coordinator

Though the words in each list share the same **denotation** (basic meaning), they vary widely in their **connotations** (their social and emotional associations). Being attentive to what different words imply will make you a more skillful and effective writer.

Select Words for Appropriate Usage

LO6 Avoid misusing similar words and use idioms correctly.

Certain pairs of words in our language can cause trouble for writers. For example, do you know the difference between *fewer* and *less*? *Fewer* is used with items that can be counted (e.g., customers), while *less* is used to refer to an overall quantity of something that can't be counted (e.g., traffic). *Affect* and *effect* are often used as synonyms. But *affect* is a verb meaning "to influence," whereas *effect* is most often used as a noun that means "a result" of something (in its verb form, *effect* means "to bring about"). Similarly, careful writers use *continual* to mean "repeated regularly and frequently" and *continuous* to mean "repeated without interruption." They write *farther* to express geographic distance and *further* to indicate "more, in addition."

You'll find more examples of often misused words in the "Wrong Word" section of Chapter 18. Watch out for these, as well as for different words that sound alike or nearly alike. Here are some common examples:

Incorrect	Correct
The company needs to improve *it's* website.	The company needs to improve *its* website.
The company needs to improve *its'* website.	*It's* time for the company to improve *its* website.
After we *choose* the winner, we celebrated.	After we *chose* the winner, we celebrated.
They're isn't any reason to delay.	*There* isn't any reason to delay.
The employees have received *they're* bonus checks.	The employees have received *their* bonus checks.
Their not going to be happy.	*They're* not going to be happy.
Please give me your *advise*.	Please give me your *advice*.
	Please *advise* me on this matter.

In your effort to be a skillful writer, you should also use **idioms** correctly. Idioms are word combinations that have become standard in a language. Many of these seem arbitrary, but to avoid unclear or distracting writing, you need to use the word combinations that people expect. For example, there is really no logic behind using the word *up* in the sentence "Look up her name in the directory," but leaving it out would make the sentence nonsensical. Other idiomatic errors just sound bad. "Independent of" is good idiomatic usage; "independent from" is not. Similarly, you "agree to" a proposal, but you "agree with" a person. You are "careful about" a sensitive situation, but you are "careful with" your money. Here are some additional illustrations:

Faulty Idiom	Correct Idiom
authority about	authority on
comply to	comply with
different than	different from
enamored with	enamored of
equally as bad	equally bad
in accordance to	in accordance with
in search for	in search of
listen at	listen to
seldom or ever	seldom if ever
based off of	based on

As you can see, some word choices are unwise, some are awkward, and some are just plain wrong. If you are unsure which word you need or would have the best effect, consult a dictionary.

Prefer Active Verbs

LO7 Use active verbs.

Of all parts of speech, verbs do the most to make your writing interesting and lively, and for good reason: They contain the action of the sentence.

But not all verbs add vigor to your writing. Overuse of the verb "to be" and passive voice can sap the energy from your sentences. To see the difference between

The Trouble with Idioms

Nonnative speakers have particular trouble with idiomatic expressions in foreign languages.

Consider the English verbal phrase "put up with." If you're a native English speaker, it makes clear sense to you—but imagine how nonsensical it might sound to a nonnative speaker hearing or reading it for the first time.

On the other hand, choosing the appropriate preposition to describe going "to" a certain place can be challenging for a nonnative French speaker. The preposition changes depending on whether you are using it with the name of a city or island ("á Paris"), with the feminine name of a country ("au Japon" [Japan]), with the masculine name of a country ("en Belgique" [Belgium]), with the name of a continent ("en Amerique du Sud [South America]"), with the masculine name of a state or region ("dans le Nevada"), or with the feminine name of a state or region ("en Californie" [California])!

When communicating with an inexperienced user of your language, try to keep idiomatic expressions to a minimum and to be tolerant of errors in idiom that he or she may make. And when attempting to use the language of another culture, be careful to check your wording against a good phrase dictionary or some other expert source.

---

writing that relies heavily on forms of "to be" and writing that uses active verbs, compare the following two passages (the forms of "to be" and their replacements are italicized):

> There *are* over 300 customers served by our help desk each day. The help desk personnel's main tasks *are* to answer questions, solve problems, and educate the callers about the software. Without their expert work, our customer satisfaction ratings *would be* much lower than they *are*.

> Our help desk personnel *serve* over 300 customers each day. They *answer* questions, *solve* problems, and *educate* the users about the software. Without their expert work, our customer satisfaction ratings *would drop* significantly.

As these examples show, using active verbs adds impact to your writing, and it usually saves words as well.

In addition to minimizing your use of "to be" verbs, you can make your verbs more active by using what grammarians refer to as **active voice**. A sentence with a verb that can take a direct object (the recipient of the action) can be written either in a direct (active) pattern or an indirect (passive) pattern. For example, the sentence "the auditor inspected the books" is in active voice. In **passive voice,** the sentence would read: "The books were inspected by the auditor." For further support of the advantages of active over passive voice, compare the following sentences:

Passive	Active
The results were reported in our July 9 letter.	We reported the results in our July 9 letter.
This policy has been supported by our union.	Our union supported this policy.
The new process is believed to be superior by the investigators.	The investigators believe that the new process is superior.
The policy was enforced by the committee.	The committee enforced the policy.
The office will be inspected by Mr. Hall.	Mr. Hall will inspect the office.
It is desired by the director that this problem be brought before the board.	The director wants the secretary to bring this problem before the board.
A complete reorganization of the administration was effected by the president.	The president completely reorganized the administration.

Everything You Wanted to Know about Active and Passive Voice

Students are often confused by the terms *active voice* and *passive voice*. Here's the lowdown:

Broadly speaking, there are two main categories of verbs in English: those that can take direct objects and those that can't. To illustrate, the verb *repair* can take a direct object (that is, you can repair something), while the verb *happen* cannot (you can't happen anything).

Sentences with verbs that can take direct objects are the ones that can be written in either active or passive voice. When you write in active voice, the sentence is in "who + does/did what + to what/whom" order, as in this example:

An authorized technician repaired the new laser printer.

   [who]   [did what]   [to what]

When you write the same idea in passive voice, the direct object moves to the start of the sentence and bumps the real subject to a phrase at the end of it (or out of it altogether). With this move, you now have

The new laser printer was repaired

  [what]   [had something done to it]

by an authorized technician.

  [by whom]

Or even just

The new laser printer was repaired. [real subject removed]

As you can see, inverting the word order this way makes the sentence less energetic, more roundabout, and sometimes less informative.

You can find instances of passive voice in your own writing by looking for two- and three-word verbs that consist of

- a form of the verb to be (for example, *is, was, has been, will be*) and
- a verb in past-tense form (for example, *installed, reduced, chosen, sent*).

When you find such verbs—*was installed, has been reduced, will be chosen*—see if your meaning would be clearer and sharper if you wrote in the active voice instead.

The suggestion that active voice be preferred does not mean passive voice is incorrect or you should never use it. Sometimes passive voice is preferable.

For example, when the doer of the action is unimportant to the message, passive voice properly de-emphasizes the doer.

Advertising is often criticized for its effect on price.

The copier has now been repaired.

Passive voice may enable you to avoid accusing your reader of an action:

The damage was caused by exposing the material to sunlight.

The color desired was not specified in your order.

Passive voice also may be preferable when the performer is unknown, as in this example:

During the past year, the equipment has been sabotaged seven times.

Yet another situation in which passive voice may be preferable is one in which the writer does not want to name the performer:

The interviews were conducted on weekdays between noon and 6 p.m.

Two complaints have been made about you.

Your writing will be clearest and liveliest, though, when you favor the active voice.

Give your writing impact by using strong verbs.

Avoid Overuse of Camouflaged Verbs

An awkward construction that should be avoided is the **camouflaged verb**. When a verb is camouflaged, the verb describing the action in a sentence takes the form of a noun. Then other words have to be added. For example, suppose you want to write a sentence in which *eliminate* is the action to be expressed. If you change *eliminate* into its noun form, *elimination*, you must add more words to have a sentence. Your sentence might then be "The staff *effected an elimination of* the surplus." The sentence is wordy and hard to understand. You could have avoided the camouflaged construction with a sentence using the verb *eliminate*: "The staff eliminated the surplus."

Here are two more examples. If we take the action word *cancel* and make it into a noun, *cancellation*, we would have to say something like "to effect a cancellation" to communicate the action. If we change *consider* to *consideration*, we would have to say "give consideration to." So it would be with the following examples:

Action Verb	Noun Form	Wording of Camouflaged Verb
acquire	acquisition	make an acquisition
appear	appearance	make an appearance
apply	application	make an application
appraise	appraisal	make an appraisal
assist	assistance	give assistance to
cancel	cancellation	make a cancellation
commit	commitment	make a commitment
discuss	discussion	have a discussion
investigate	investigation	make an investigation
judge	judgment	make a judgment
liquidate	liquidation	effect a liquidation
reconcile	reconciliation	make a reconciliation
record	recording	make a recording

Note the differences in overall effect in these contrasting sentences:

Camouflaged Verb	Clear Verb Form
An *arrangement was made* to meet for breakfast.	We *arranged* to meet for breakfast.
Amortization of the account *was effected* by the staff.	The staff *amortized* the account.
Control of the water *was not possible*.	They *could not control* the water.
The new policy *involved the standardization* of the procedures.	The new policy *standardized* the procedures.
Application of the mixture *was accomplished*.	They *applied* the mixture.
We must *bring about a reconciliation of our* differences.	We must *reconcile* our differences.
The *establishment* of a wellness center *has been accomplished* by the company.	The company has *established* a wellness center.

From these illustrations you can see that our suggestion to avoid camouflaged verbs overlaps with two of our preceding suggestions. First, camouflaged verbs are abstract nouns, and we suggested that you prefer concrete words over abstract words. Second, camouflaged verbs frequently require passive voice, and we advised using active voice.

You can apply these related suggestions by following two helpful writing hints. The first is to make the subjects of most sentences either persons or things. For example, rather than write "consideration was given to . . . ," you should write "we considered. . . ." The second is to write most sentences in normal order (subject, verb, object), with the doer of the action as the subject. Involved, strained, passive structures often result from attempts at other orders.

SUGGESTIONS FOR NONDISCRIMINATORY WRITING

LO8 Use words that do not discriminate.

As the workforce has grown more diverse, it has become increasingly important to avoid discriminatory words. By **discriminatory words** we mean words that do not treat all people with equal respect. More specifically, they are words that refer negatively to groups of people, such as by gender, race, nationality, sexual orientation, age, or disability. Such words do not promote good business ethics or good business and thus have no place in business communication.

Many discriminatory words are a part of the vocabularies we have acquired from our environments. We often use them innocently, not realizing how they affect others. We can eliminate discriminatory words from our vocabularies by examining them carefully and placing ourselves in the shoes of those to whom they refer. The following review of the major forms of discriminatory words should help you achieve this goal.

Use Gender-Neutral Words

Take care not to use words that discriminate by gender ("sexist" words). Although this form of discrimination can be directed against men, most instances discriminate against women. Our language developed in a society in which it was customary for women to work in the home and for men to be the breadwinners and decision makers. But times have changed, and the language you use in business needs to acknowledge the gender-diverse nature of most workplaces today. Suggestions for doing this follow.

Masculine Pronouns for Both Sexes. Perhaps the most troublesome sexist words are the masculine pronouns (*he, his, him*) when they are used to refer to both sexes, as in this example: "The typical State University student eats *his* lunch at the student center." Assuming that State is coeducational, the use of *his* excludes the female students. Historically, of course, the word *his* has been classified as generic—that is, able to refer to both sexes. But many modern-day businesspeople do not agree and are offended by the use of the masculine pronoun in this way.

You can avoid the use of masculine pronouns in such cases in three ways. First, you can reword the sentence to eliminate the offending word. Thus, the illustration above could be reworded as follows: "The typical State University student eats lunch at the student center." Here are other examples:

Sexist	Gender-Neutral
If a customer pays promptly, *he* is placed on our preferred list.	A customer who pays promptly is placed on our preferred list.
When an unauthorized employee enters the security area, *he* is subject to dismissal.	An unauthorized employee who enters the security area is subject to dismissal.
A supervisor is not responsible for such losses if *he* is not negligent.	A supervisor who is not negligent is not responsible for such losses.
When a customer needs service, it is *his* right to ask for it.	A customer who needs service has the right to ask for it.

A second way to avoid sexist use of the masculine pronoun is to make the reference plural. Fortunately, the English language has plural pronouns (*their, them, they*) that refer to both sexes. Making the references plural in the examples given above, we have these nonsexist revisions:

If customers pay promptly, *they* are placed on our preferred list.

When unauthorized employees enter the security area, *they* are subject to dismissal.

Supervisors are not responsible for such losses if *they* are not negligent.

When customers need service, *they* have the right to ask for it.

A third way to avoid sexist use of *he*, *his*, or *him* is to substitute any of a number of gender-neutral expressions. The most common are *he or she*, *he/she*, *s/he*, *you*, *one*, and *person*. Using neutral expressions in the problem sentences, we have these revisions:

If a customer pays promptly, *he or she* is placed on our preferred list.

When an unauthorized employee enters the security area, *he/she* is subject to dismissal.

A supervisor is not responsible for such losses if *s/he* is not negligent.

When *one* needs service, *he/she* has the right to ask for it.

You should use such expressions with caution, however. They tend to be somewhat awkward, particularly if they are used often. For this reason, many skilled writers avoid them. If you use them, you should pay attention to their effect on the flow of your words. Certainly, you should avoid sentences like this one: "To make an employee feel he/she is doing well by complimenting her/him insincerely confuses her/him later when he/she sees his/her co-workers promoted ahead of him/her."

Words Derived from Masculine Words. As we have noted, our culture was male dominated when our language developed. Because of this, many of our words are masculine even though they do not refer exclusively to men. Take *chairman*, for example. This word can refer to both sexes, yet it does not sound that way. More appropriate and less offensive substitutes are *chair, presiding officer, moderator,* and *chairperson*.

In today's diverse workplaces, mutual respect between genders and across generations is key.

How Diverse Is Too Diverse?

Can your employer tell you what to wear, outlaw decorated fingernails, or forbid the display of such body art as tattoos and piercings?

According to EmployeeIssues.com, a website about employee rights, the answer is *yes*—as long as the appearance policies are clearly stated in writing and are applied fairly to all employees.

Just as employers can require the use of uniforms, they can delineate what kinds of personal clothing will be acceptable on the job. For example, they might define "business casual" in a way that explicitly excludes T-shirts, shorts, and flip-flops. And as long as tattoos and body piercings aren't required by your religion, they can be grounds for being disciplined or even fired—as long as the rules have been clearly laid out and communicated.

Looking professional need not mean selling out your cultural or ethnic heritage, argues Kali Evans-Raoul, founder of an image consultancy for minorities. Everyone must "balance self-expression with workplace realities," she asserts. Just as one doesn't wear a uniform at home, one shouldn't expect to bring one's entire personal look to work.

To avoid conflicts over your on-the-job identity, your best bet is to try to choose an employer whose values align with your own. Then find and abide by that company's appearance policy.

SOURCES: "Dress Cody Policy," *EmployeeIssues.com,* EmployeeIssues.com, 2003–2012, Web, 23 May 2012, and Dan Woog, "Your Professional Image: Balance Self-Expression with Workplace Expectations," *Monster.com,* Monster.com, 2009, Web, 23 May 2012.

Similarly, *salesman* suggests a man, but many women work in sales. *Salesperson, salesclerk,* or *sales representative* would be better. Other sexist words and gender-neutral substitutes are as follows:

Sexist	Gender-Neutral
man-made	manufactured
manpower	personnel, workers
congressman	representative, member of Congress
businessman	business executive, businessperson
mailman	letter carrier, mail carrier
policeman	police officer
fireman	firefighter
repairman	repair technician
cameraman	camera operator
freshman	first-year student

Many words with *man* and *his* in them have nonsexist origins. Among such words are *manufacture, management, history,* and *manipulate.* Also, some sexist words are hard to avoid (*manhole,* for example), and some companies still use *chairman* to refer to an executive of either gender. Whenever possible, though, use the more inclusive term.

Other Words That Lower Status by Gender. In addition to avoiding "man" words, watch out for other wording that might imply a lower status for women. For example, male executives sometimes refer to their female employees by first name only, while using first and last names or titles and last names ("Mr. Cross") for male employees. Then there are the many female forms for words that refer to work roles. In this group are *lady lawyer, authoress, sculptress,* and *poetess.* You should refer to women in these work roles by the same words that you would use for men: *lawyer, author, sculptor, poet.* Using words such as *male nurse* or *male teacher* can be demeaning as well.

In deciding which words to avoid and which to use, you will have to rely on your best judgment. Remember that your goal should be to use words that are fair and that do not offend.

Avoid Words That Stereotype by Race, Nationality, or Sexual Orientation

Words that characterize all members of a group based on their race, nationality, or sexual orientation can be especially harmful because they frequently reinforce negative stereotypes about this group. Members of any minority vary widely in all characteristics. Thus, it is unfair to suggest that Jews are miserly, that Italians are Mafia members, that Hispanics are lazy, African Americans can do only menial jobs, that gays are perfectionists, and so on. Unfair references to minorities are sometimes subtle and not intended, as in this example: "We conducted the first marketing tests in the low-income areas of the city. Using a sample of 200 African-American families, we . . . ." These words unfairly suggest that only African Americans live in low-income areas.

Also unfair are words suggesting that a minority member has struggled to achieve something that is taken for granted in the majority group. Usually well intended, words of this kind can carry subtle discriminatory messages. For example, a reference to a "neatly dressed Hispanic man" may suggest that he is an exception to the rule—that most Hispanics are not neatly dressed, but here is one who is.

Eliminating unfair references to minority groups from your communication requires two basic steps. First, you must consciously treat all people equally, without regard to their minority status. You should refer to minority membership only in those rare cases in which it is a vital part of the message to be communicated. Second, you must be sensitive to the effects of your words. Specifically, you should ask yourself how those words would affect you if you were a member of the minorities to which they refer. You should evaluate your word choices from the viewpoints of others.

Avoid Words That Stereotype by Age

Your avoidance of discriminatory wording should be extended to include age discrimination—against both the old and the young. While those over 65 might be retired from their first jobs, many lead lives that are far from the sedentary roles in which they are sometimes depicted. They also are not necessarily feeble, forgetful, or slow. While some do not mind being called *senior citizens*, others do. Be sensitive with terms such as *mature* and *elderly* as well; perhaps *retired, experienced,* or *veteran* would be better received. Likewise, when tempted to refer to someone as *young* (*young accountant, accomplished young woman*), be sure that calling attention to the person's age is defensible.

Also be careful when using one of the popular generational labels in your writing. While it makes sense for the popular management literature to use such labels as *Baby Boomer* and *Millennial* as short-hand references to different generations, the same labels can seem discriminatory in business messages. Your co-worker Frank probably does not want to be referred to as the "Baby Boomer in the group," and your manager Courtney probably will not appreciate your saying that she holds the opinions she does because she's a "Generation Xer." Use such labels only when relevant and appropriate.

Understanding the Different Generations in the Workplace

According to *Generations, Inc.,* five generations now comprise the U.S. workforce: the Traditional Generation (born between 1918 and 1945), the Baby Boomers (born right after World War II), Generation X (born between 1960 and 1979), Generation Y or the Millennials (born after 1979), and the Linkster Generation (born after 1995). Different social and historical forces have shaped these generations, with the result that their values and work habits are quite different

The three main groups—Boomers, Gen Xers, and Gen Yers—have these major traits and preferences:

- The *Boomers* "have the wisdom of experience that can provide historical perspective," have a "tenacity" that can help the organization meet new challenges, and "are team players who can enhance any group in which they participate." But they "need to be engaged," need to feel that they are still valuable, and need to feel free to use their knowledge to make decisions within reasonable limits (they shouldn't be "micromanaged").

- *Gen Xers* "are happy working MTV style, meaning they like activities that require intense bursts of energy and

that challenge them to think quickly." They don't like "stupid rules," they do like "individual recognition," and they want to move ahead based on merit, not on schmoozing or seniority. They value work–life balance more than the Boomers did and are thus unwilling to work as hard, but they do value professional development. They want to be free to bring their own style to work but also want clear, fair, quick feedback on their performance.

- *Gen Yers* like to work in supportive environments like the ones that most of them grew up in. Thus, they react better to "coaching" than to being told what to do, and they like frequent reassurance that they are on the right track. Like Gen Xers, they are willing to work hard but not overly hard, they want to understand the value of the work, and they like creativity. They tend to be more fun-loving and less anxious than Gen Xers, though. They are also even more comfortable with communication technologies than Gen Xers are, so much so that they may need to be encouraged to use other forms of communication (e.g., face-to-face and phone conversations).

SOURCE: Meagan Johnson and Larry Johnson, *Generations, Inc.* (New York: AMACOM, 2010), print.

Avoid Words That Typecast Those with Disabilities

People with disabilities are likely to be sensitive to discriminatory words. Like those in other minority groups, they run the risk of having others exclude them, treat them as strange, or minimize their abilities. But they are the largest minority group in the world; in the U.S., 19% of the noninstitutionalized population has a disability.[1] Plus, all of us have different levels of ability in different areas. It is important to keep these facts in mind when choosing your words.

For example, negative descriptions such as *crippled, confined to a wheelchair, wheelchair bound, handicapped,* and *retarded* should be avoided. Instead, use *wheelchair user, developmentally disabled,* or whatever term the people with the disability prefer. In general, that also means saying "those with disabilities" rather than "the disabled" to avoid suggesting that the disability is the only noteworthy trait of people in this group.

Work to develop a nonbiased attitude, and show it through carefully chosen words.

Some Final Words about Words

There's a lot to keep in mind when selecting the most appropriate words. Under time pressure, it can be tempting to take a shortcut and settle—as Mark Twain once put

---

[1]"Disability in America Infographic," *Disabled World,* Disabled World™ disabledworld.com, 1 Dec. 2011, Web, 23 May 2012. The graphic is based on U.S. census information.

it—for the best word's "second cousin." But remember: Business and business relationships can be won or lost with one word choice. The effort to say what you mean as clearly, readably, and appropriately as you can is effort well spent.

THERE'S MORE...

How can you find the word with the right connotation? What is "corporate speak" and why should you avoid it? What are 5 common business writing mistakes? Scan the QR code with your smartphone or use your Web browser to find out at www.mhhe.com/lesikar13e. Choose Chapter 3 > Bizcom Tools & Tips.

SUMMARY BY LEARNING OBJECTIVES

Explain the role of adaptation in selecting words that communicate.

1. To communicate clearly, you must adapt your words to your reader.
   - Adaptation means using words the reader understands.
   - It therefore involves using all your knowledge of your reader.

Simplify writing by selecting familiar and short words.

2. Select words that your reader will understand.
   - These are the familiar words (words like *old* instead of *antiquated*).
   - They are also the short words (*agreed to quit* rather than *acceded to the proposition to terminate*).

Use slang and popular clichés with caution.

3. Use slang and popular clichés with caution.
   - They may make your writing sound stale and make you sound superficial.
   - They may also cause miscommunication.

Use technical words and acronyms appropriately.

4. Use technical words and acronyms appropriately.
   - Technical words are appropriate when your reader will understand them. When writing to nonexperts, explain these terms or use more accessible ones.
   - Spell out and define acronyms as needed.

Use concrete, specific words with the right shades of meaning.

5. Use precise language.
   - Prefer concrete, specific words to abstract, general ones. For example, *57 percent majority* is more concrete than *majority*, and *June 1* is more specific than *soon*.
   - Choose words with the appropriate connotations (shades of meaning).

Avoid misusing similar words and use idioms correctly.

6. Avoid misusing similar words and use idioms correctly.
   - Don't confuse similar words (e.g., *fewer* and *less, it's* and *its*).
   - Follow the conventions for idioms (two-word expressions, such as *comply with* and *different from*).

Prefer active verbs.

7. Prefer active verbs.
   - Action verbs are more vigorous and interesting than forms of "to be."
   - In active voice, the subject acts; in passive voice, it receives the action. Prefer the active voice (e.g., *we reported the results* rather than *the results were reported by us*).
   - Active voice is stronger, more vigorous, and more interesting. But passive voice can be preferable in some situations.
   - Avoid overuse of camouflaged verbs—making the verb a noun and then having to add words (e.g., use *appear* rather than *make an appearance*).

Use words that do not discriminate.

8. Avoid discriminatory words.
   - Do not use words that discriminate against women (for example, using *he, him,* or *his* to refer to both sexes and words such as *fireman, postman, lady lawyer,* and *authoress*).

- Do not use words that suggest stereotyped roles of race, nationality, or sexual orientation (African Americans and menial jobs, Italians and the Mafia, gays and perfectionists).
- Do not use words that discriminate against certain age groups or those with disabilities.

KEY TERMS

adaptation, 49

plain language, 51

concrete, 54

abstract, 54

specific, 56

denotation, 56

connotation, 56

idioms, 57

active voice, 58

passive voice, 58

camouflaged verb, 60

discriminatory words, 61

CRITICAL THINKING QUESTIONS

1 Explain how you would apply the basic principle of adaptation to your choice of words for each of the following writing tasks. **LO1**

   a. An article in a company newsletter.
   b. A message to company executives requesting approval to purchase new computer hardware.
   c. A progress report to the chief engineer explaining how the development of a new safety device is going.
   d. A message to employees explaining a change in pension benefits.
   e. A letter to company stockholders explaining a change in company reporting dates.

2 Evaluate this comment: "I'm not going to simplify my writing for my readers. That would be talking down to them. Plus, if they can't understand English, that's their problem." **LO2**

3 "Using short words makes the writing sound too simple and not very professional." Discuss. **LO2**

4 "It's important to use business clichés like *cutting edge* and *state of the art* to sound professional." Discuss. **LO3**

5 "Acronyms and long, hard words contribute to miscommunication. Thus, they should be avoided in all business communication." Discuss. **LO4**

6 Using examples other than those in the book, identify some technical terms that would communicate effectively to others in the field but would need to be clarified for those outside the field. **LO4**

7 Style experts advise against monotonous-sounding writing—that is, writing that has a droning, "blah-blah" effect when read aloud. What advice in this chapter might help you avoid a monotonous style? **LO2, LO5**

8 List synonyms (words with similar meanings) for each of the following words. Then explain the differences in shades of meaning as you see them. **LO5**

   a. salesperson
   b. co-worker
   c. old
   d. tell
   e. happiness
   f. customer
   g. boss
   h. misfortune
   i. inquire
   j. stop
   k. lie
   l. mistake

9 Explain what's wrong with this sentence: "This procedure is different than the one we use." How would you correct it? Can you think of other examples of this kind of error? **LO6**

10 Define and give examples of active and passive voice. Explain when each should be used. **LO7**

11 Do you know of a situation in which a female secretary or staff person is referred to by her first name only (e.g. "See Joan at the front desk and she'll take care of you") but the higher-ranking employees are referred to by their first and last names (e.g., "Jim Smith can answer your question")? What do you think of this practice? Is it ever acceptable? **LO8**

Using Familiar Words (LO2)

Instructions, Sentences 1–20: Assume that your readers are at about the 10th-grade level in education. Revise these sentences for easy communication to this audience.

1 We must terminate all deficit financing.

2 We must endeavor to correct this problem by expediting delivery.

3 A proportionate tax consumes a determinate apportionment of one's monetary flow.

4 Business has an inordinate influence on governmental operations.

5 It is imperative that consumers be unrestrained in determining their preferences.

6 Mr. Sanchez terminated Kevin's employment as a consequence of his ineffectual performance.

7 Our expectations are that there will be increments in commodity value.

8 Can we ascertain the types of customers that have a predisposition to utilize our instant-credit offer?

9 The preponderance of the businesspeople we consulted envisions signs of improvement from the current siege of economic stagnation.

10 If liquidation becomes mandatory, we shall dispose of these assets first.

11 Recent stock acquisitions have accentuated the company's current financial crisis.

12 Mr. Coward will serve as intermediary in the pending labor–management parley.

13 Ms. Smith's idiosyncrasies supply adequate justification for terminating her employment.

14 Requisites for employment by this company have been enhanced.

15 The unanimity of current forecasts is not incontrovertible evidence of an impending business acceleration.

16 People's propensity to consume is insatiable.

17 The company must desist from its deficit financing immediately.

18 This antiquated merchandising strategy is ineffectual in contemporary business operations.

19 Percentage return on common stockholders' equity averaged 23.1 for the year.

20 The company's retained earnings last year exceeded $2,500,000.

Using Technical Words Appropriately (LO4)

21 From a scholarly business journal, select a paragraph (at least 150 words long) that would be difficult for a student less advanced in the subject than you. Rewrite the paragraph so that this student can understand it easily.

Selecting Concrete Words (LO5)

Instructions, Sentences 22–30: Revise these sentences to make them conform to the writing suggestions discussed in the book.

22 We have found that young men are best for this work.

23 She makes good grades.

24 John lost a fortune in Las Vegas.

25 If we don't receive the goods soon, we will cancel.

26 Some years ago she made good money.

27 His grade on the aptitude test was not high.

28 Here is a product with very little markup.

29 The cost of the online subscription was reasonable.

30 There is only a little time left on our copier's warranty.

Avoid Misusing Similar Words (LO6)

Instructions, Sentences 31–42: Some of the following are correct and some incorrect. Indicate which is which and correct the problem sentences.

31 We have less than 25 registrants so far.

32 I did not mean to infer that you had made a mistake.

33 If you turn in you're report by Friday, you can have Monday off.

34 He is not adverse to your suggestion; he simply wants more information.

35 You may have whichever computer you choose.

36 The handbook offers advise on professional behavior.

37 Please except my apologies.

38 It's time to remodel the break room.

39 A complementary breakfast is included.

40 Write in such a way that you elicit the response you want.

41 This car needs its' battery replaced.

42 There is no reason why we should refund their money.

Using Proper Idiom (LO6)

Instructions, Sentences 43–50: These sentences use faulty idioms. Make the changes you think are necessary.

43 The purchasing officer has gone in search for a substitute product.

44 Our office has become independent from the Dallas office.

45 This strike was different than the one in 2000.

46 This letter is equally as bad.

47 She is an authority about mutual funds.

48 When the sale is over with, we will restock.

49 Our truck collided against the wall.

50 We have been in search for a qualified supervisor since August.

Limiting Use of Passive Voice (LO7)

Instructions, Sentences 51–57: Revise the following sentences to eliminate passive voice.

51 Our action is based on the assumption that the competition will be taken by surprise.

52 It is believed by the typical union member that his or her welfare is not considered to be important by management.

53 You were directed by your supervisor to complete this assignment by noon.

54 It is believed by the writer that this company policy is wrong.

55 The union was represented by Cecil Chambers.

56 These reports are prepared by the salespeople every Friday.

57 If more information is desired, the customer service department can be contacted.

Avoiding Camouflaged Verbs (LO7)

Instructions, Sentences 58–68: Revise the following to eliminate camouflaged verbs.

58 It was my duty to make a determination of the damages.

59 Harold made a recommendation that we fire Mr. Schultz.

60 We will ask him to bring about a change in his work routine.

61 This new equipment will result in a savings in maintenance.

62 Will you please make an adjustment on this invoice?

63 Implementation of the plan was effected by the crew.

64 Approval of all orders must be made by the chief.

65 A committee performs the function of determining the award winner.

66 Adaptation to the new policy was performed easily by the staff.

67 Verification of the amount is made daily by the auditor.

68 The president tried to effect a reconciliation of the two groups.

Avoiding Discriminatory Language (LO8)

Instructions, Sentences 69–80: Change these sentences to avoid discriminatory language.

69 Any worker who ignores this rule will have his salary reduced.

70 The typical postman rarely makes mistakes in delivering his mail.

71 A good executive plans his daily activities.

72 The committee consisted of a businessman, a banker, and a lady lawyer.

73 A good secretary screens all telephone calls for her boss and arranges his schedule.

74 An efficient salesman organizes his calls and manages his time.

75 Two representatives of our company attended the conference: a Hispanic engineer and one of our younger managers.

76 Three people applied for the job, including two well-educated black women.

77 These parking spaces are strictly for use by the handicapped.

78 He is one of the best gay designers in the city.

79 We recommend Mr. Sanchez, one of our oldest managers.

80 As a GenXer, she is very computer savvy.

CHAPTER FOUR

Constructing Clear Sentences and Paragraphs

Learning Objectives

Upon completing this chapter, you will be able to construct sentences and paragraphs that are adapted to your readers and easy to understand. To reach this goal, you should be able to

1 Explain the role of adaptation in writing clear sentences.

2 Write short, clear sentences by limiting sentence content and economizing on words.

3 Design sentences that give the right emphasis to content.

4 Employ unity and good logic in writing effective sentences.

5 Compose paragraphs that are short and unified, use topic sentences effectively, and communicate coherently.

Writing Sentences and Paragraphs That Communicate

This summer you're making some college money by working as a groundskeeper at a local hotel. Recently, you and the other hotel staff—including the rest of the maintenance crew and the housekeepers—received this written message from the new assistant manager:

> It has come to my attention that certain standards of quality are not being met by personnel in service positions. For successful operations, it is imperative that we adhere to the service guidelines for staff in each functional area, as set forth by corporate in the training materials that were reviewed during your orientation and onboarding. Be advised that there will be two mandatory training sessions on May 1, one at 4:00 p.m. for daytime employees and the other at 3:00 for the late shift, to reinforce your understanding of performance standards. Just as a machine cannot work properly if the pistons are all firing at different times, we cannot achieve our goals if individuals are setting their own criteria for how to serve our guests. I assume that I will see each and every one of you at a training session so that we may move forward with better comprehension of our roles and responsibilities.

You're no management pro, but you're sure this is a faulty message. In addition to being impersonal and insulting, it is difficult to understand, and the key point—that everyone will need to attend a training session—is buried in the middle of the paragraph. How can you avoid writing like this? The advice in this chapter will help.

THE IMPORTANCE OF ADAPTATION

LO1 Explain the role of adaptation in writing clear sentences.

As you have seen, choosing the right words is essential for clear communication. Equally basic is the task of arranging those words into clear sentences and the sentences into clear paragraphs. Like choosing words, constructing clear sentences and paragraphs involves adaptation to the intended readers.

Fitting your writing to your readers requires the reader analysis we discuss in Chapter 1 and Chapter 6. You should study your readers to find out what they are like—what they know, how they think, and what their contexts are. Then write in a way that will communicate with and appeal to them.

In general, this procedure involves using the simpler sentence structures to reach people with lower communication abilities and people not knowledgeable about the subject. It involves using the more complex sentence structures only when communicating with more verbal, knowledgeable people. However, as we will see, even advanced readers tend to prefer simplicity.

Writing effectively also requires managing the emphasis in your sentences in such a way that your key points stand out. Making each sentence express a main idea and ordering the sentence elements according to accepted rules of grammar and logic will help you achieve your goals as well as convey a professional image.

The final section of this chapter offers advice about how to turn your well-constructed sentences into well-constructed paragraphs—paragraphs that are united, efficient, forward moving, and coherent. Delivering your contents in easy-to-digest chunks is one of your most powerful strategies for engaging and informing your busy readers.

CARE IN SENTENCE DESIGN

The following rules of thumb will help you write sentences that communicate clearly and correctly.

Limit Sentence Content

LO2 Write short, clear sentences by limiting sentence content and economizing on words.

Business audiences tend to prefer simple, efficient sentences over long, complex ones. Having too much to do in too little time is a chronic problem in business. Type "time management" or "information overload" into your Web browser's search box and see how many hits you get. No one, whether executive or first-level employee, wants to read writing that wastes time.

Readability Statistics Help Writers Evaluate Document Length and Difficulty

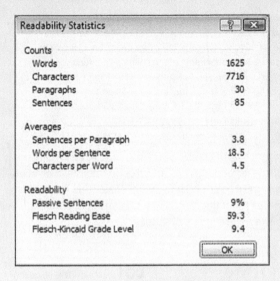

Grammar and style checkers give writers the option of viewing readability statistics. These statistics report the number of words, characters, paragraphs, and sentences in a document along with averages of characters per word, words per sentence, and sentences per paragraph.

The report you see here was generated for a scholarly manuscript. It reports an average of 18.5 words per sentence, a bit high for a business document but probably at an acceptable level for a scholarly document's readers. The Flesch-Kincaid score confirms that the reading grade level is 9.4, too high for business documents but likely appropriate for a scholarly audience. However, the Flesch Reading Ease score should give the writer cause to review the document for accessibility, even for its targeted audience. The 59.3 score is slightly below the 60–70 range that Microsoft recommends.

Favoring short sentences can save your readers time. It can also prevent miscommunication. According to readability studies, the more words and ideas there are in a sentence, the greater the likelihood of misunderstanding. This finding suggests that the mind can hold only so much information at one time. Thus, to give it too much information in your sentences is to risk falling short of your communication purpose.

Compare these two versions of the same content:

Long, Difficult Sentences	Shorter, Clearer Sentences
This letter is being distributed with enrollment confirmation sheets, which are to serve as a final check on the correctness of the registration of students and are to be used later when obtaining semester grades from the regline system, which are to be available two weeks after the term officially ends.	This letter is being distributed with enrollment confirmation sheets. These sheets will serve now as a final check on student registration. Later, the codes on them will be used to access course grades through the regline system; the grades will be available two weeks after the term officially ends.
Some authorities in human resources object to expanding normal salary ranges to include a trainee rate because they fear that through oversight or prejudice probationers may be kept at the minimum rate longer than is warranted and because they fear that it would encourage the spread from the minimum to maximum rate range.	Some authorities in human resources object to expanding the normal salary range to include a trainee rate, for two reasons. First, they fear that through oversight or prejudice probationers may be kept at the minimum rate longer than is warranted. Second, they fear that expansion would increase the spread between the minimum and the maximum rate range.
Regardless of their seniority or union affiliation, all employees who hope to be promoted are expected to continue their education either by enrolling in the special courses to be offered by the company, which are scheduled to be given after working hours beginning next Wednesday, or by taking approved online courses selected from a list, which can be found on the company portal.	Regardless of their seniority or union affiliation, all employees who hope to be promoted are expected to continue their education in either of two ways. (1) They may enroll in special courses to be given by the company. (2) They may take approved online courses selected from the list on the company portal.

Avoiding Stringy and See-Saw Sentences

If you try to pack too much information into a sentence, you can wind up with a stringy sentence like this:

While we welcome all applications, we are particularly interested in candidates who have at least three years' experience, although we will consider those with less experience who have a degree in the field or who have earned a certificate from an industry-certified trainer, and we will also consider fluency in Italian a plus.

A see-saw sentence is one that goes back and forth between two points, like this:

A blog can add visibility to a business, although it can be labor intensive to maintain, but the time spent on the blog could be worthwhile if it generates a buzz among our potential customers.

In these cases, edit the sentences down to readable size, use helpful transitional phrases (*in addition, on the other hand*) between them, and don't switch directions too often.

Here, for example, are more readable versions of the problem sentences:

While we welcome all applications, we are particularly interested in candidates who (1) have at least three years' experience or (2) have less experience but have earned a degree or certificate in the field. Fluency in Italian is also a plus.

A blog can add visibility to a business. True, maintaining a blog takes time, but if the blog generates a buzz among our potential customers, the time will be well spent.

The long sentences on the left require much more effort to understand than the shorter sentences on the right.

Bear in mind, though, that what constitutes a short, readable sentence is related to the reader's ability. Readability studies suggest that writing intended to communicate with the middle-level adult reader should average 16 to 18 words per sentence. For more advanced readers, the average may be higher. For less advanced readers, it should be lower.

Moreover, preferring short sentences does not mean making all sentences equally short. The overuse of short sentences results in a choppy, elementary-sounding effect. You should use moderately long sentences occasionally. They help you de-emphasize less important content and increase interest by adding variety. And sometimes the information needed to convey a thought requires a long sentence. Even so, you should take care not to make the long sentences excessively long.

The following examples illustrate the point. The paragraph below is an excerpt from an employee handbook. Obviously the use of one long sentence to convey the information was a poor decision.

When an employee has changed from one job to another job, the new corresponding coverages will be effective as of the date the change occurs, unless, however, if due to a physical disability or infirmity as a result of advanced age, an employee is changed from one job to another job and such change results in the employee's new job rate coming within a lower hourly job-rate bracket in the table, in which case the employee may, at the discretion of the company, continue the amount of group term life insurance and the amount of accidental death and dismemberment insurance that the employee had prior to such change.

So many words and relationships are in the sentence that they cause confusion. The result is vague communication at best—complete miscommunication at worst.

Now look at the message written in all short sentences. The meanings may be clear, but the choppy effect is distracting and irritating. Imagine reading a long document written in this style.

An employee may change jobs. The change may result in a lower pay bracket. The new coverage is effective when this happens. The job change should be because

Too many simple sentences create an elementary-sounding style, so combine ideas where appropriate for your adult readers.

of physical disability. It can also be because of infirmity. Old age may be another cause. The company has some discretion in the matter. It can permit continuing the accidental death insurance. It can permit continuing the dismemberment insurance.

The following paragraph takes a course between these two extremes. Generally, it emphasizes short sentences, but it combines content items where appropriate.

The new insurance coverage becomes effective when because of disability, infirmity, or age an employee's job change results in lower pay. But at its discretion, the company may permit the old insurance coverage to continue.

The upcoming sections on conciseness, management of emphasis, and sentence unity can help you decide how much content each sentence should carry.

Economize on Words

A second basic technique for shortening sentences is to use words economically. Anything you write can be expressed in many ways, some shorter than others. In general, the shorter wordings save the reader time and are clearer and more interesting.

To help you recognize instances of uneconomical wording, we cover the most common types below.

Cluttering Phrases. An often-used uneconomical wording is the **cluttering phrase**. This is a phrase that can be replaced by shorter wording without loss of meaning. The little savings achieved in this way add up.

Here is an example of a cluttering phrase:

In the event that payment is not made by January, operations will cease.

The phrase *in the event that* is uneconomical. The little word *if* can substitute for it without loss of meaning:

If payment is not made by January, operations will cease.

Similarly, the phrase that begins the following sentence adds unnecessary length:

In spite of the fact that they received help, they failed to exceed the quota.

Although is an economical substitute:

Although they received help, they failed to exceed their quota.

Is *That* a Surplus Word?

How easy is it to read the following sentence without making a misstep?

> We found the reason for our poor performance was stiff competition from a local supplier.

In such a sentence, adding the word *that* where it is implied would help:

> We found *that* the reason for our poor performance was stiff competition from a local supplier.

On the other hand, sometimes *that* can be omitted, as in this example:

> Check all the items *that* you wish to order.

How do you know whether to include *that*? You'll have to judge by pretending to be the reader. If *that* prevents misreading, keep it. If it seems unnecessary or distracting, leave it out.

The following partial list of cluttering phrases (with suggested substitutions) should help you avoid them:

Cluttering Phrase	Shorter Substitution
Along the lines of	Like
At the present time	Now
For the purpose of	For
For the reason that	Because, since
In accordance with	By
In the amount of	For
In the meantime	Meanwhile
In the near future	Soon
In the neighborhood of	About
In very few cases	Seldom, rarely
In view of the fact that	Since, because
With regard to, with reference to	About

Surplus Words. To write economically, eliminate words that add nothing to sentence meaning. As with cluttering phrases, we often use meaningless extra words as a matter of habit. Eliminating these **surplus words** sometimes requires recasting a sentence, but often they can just be left out.

The following is an example of surplus wording from a business report:

It will be noted that the records for the past years show a steady increase in special appropriations.

The beginning words add nothing to the meaning of the sentence. Notice how dropping them makes the sentence stronger—and without loss of meaning:

The records for the past years show a steady increase in special appropriations.

Here is a second example:

His performance was good enough to *enable him* to qualify for the promotion.

The words *to enable* add nothing and can be dropped:

His performance was good enough to qualify him for the promotion.

Don't write like a faceless bureaucrat. Avoid an impersonal "blah-blah" effect by writing concise, clear sentences.

The following sentences further illustrate the use of surplus words. In each case, the surplus words can be eliminated without changing the meaning.

Contains Surplus Words	Eliminates Surplus Words
He ordered desks *that are* for executives.	He ordered executive desks.
There are four rules *that* should be observed.	Four rules should be observed.
In addition to these defects, numerous other defects mar the operating procedure.	Numerous other defects mar the operating procedure.
The machines *that were* damaged by the fire were repaired.	The machines damaged by the fire were repaired.
By *the examining of* production records, they found the error.	By examining production records, they found the error.
In the period between April and June, we detected the problem.	Between April and June we detected the problem.
I am prepared to report *to the effect* that sales increased.	I am prepared to report that sales increased.

Roundabout Constructions. As we have noted, you can write anything in many ways. Some of the ways are direct, while some cover the same ground in a roundabout way. Usually the direct ways are shorter and communicate better.

This sentence illustrates **roundabout constructions**:

The department budget *can be observed to be decreasing* each *new* year.

Do the words *can be observed to be decreasing* get to the point? Is the idea of *observing* essential? Is *new* needed? A more direct and better sentence is this one:

The department budget decreases each year.

Here is another roundabout sentence:

The union *is involved in the task of reviewing* the seniority provision of the contract.

There Is, There Are . . . Do You Really Need Them?

There is/There are sentences are sometimes justified, as in these examples:

> *There is* simply no reason why we cannot achieve our goals this quarter.
> When *there are* more than 14 attendees, we use the larger computer lab.

But sometimes *there is* and *there are* just add extra words, as these pairs of sentences illustrate:

> **Wordy:** If *there is* a problem with the copier, the service agreement will cover it.
> **Better:** If the copier has a problem, the service agreement will cover it.

> **Wordy:** *There are* three ways in which the Princess Resort is superior to the Breezemont Hotel.
> **Better:** The Princess Resort is superior to the Breezemont Hotel in three ways.

> **Wordy:** *There are* varying opinions on the plan depending on whether you are a manager or a staff person.
> **Better:** The managers and the staff people have different opinions about the plan.

When tempted to write *there is* or *there are*, see if you can say what you want to say more concisely and directly.

If the union is *involved in the task of reviewing*, it is really *reviewing*. The sentence should be written in these direct words:

> The union *is reviewing* the seniority provision of the contract.

The following sentence pairs further illustrate the advantages of short, direct wording over roundabout wording:

Roundabout	Direct
The president *is of the opinion that* the tax was paid.	The president *believes* the tax was paid.
It is essential that the income be used to retire the debt.	The income *must* be used to retire the debt.
Reference is made to your May 10 report *in which you concluded* that the warranty does not apply.	Your May 10 report *concluded* that the warranty does not apply.
The supervisors *should take appropriate action to determine* whether the absentee reports are being verified.	The supervisors *should determine* whether the absentee reports are being verified.
The price increase *will afford* the company *an opportunity* to retire the debt.	The price *will enable* the company to retire the debt.
During the time she was employed by this company, Ms. Carr was absent once.	*While* employed by this company, Ms. Carr was absent once.
He criticized everyone he *came in contact with*.	He criticized everyone he *met*.

Unnecessary Repetition of Words or Ideas. Repeating words obviously adds to sentence length. Such repetition sometimes serves a purpose, as when it is used for emphasis or special effect. But all too often it is without purpose, as this sentence illustrates:

> We have not received your payment covering invoices covering June and July purchases.

It would be better to write the sentence like this:

> We have not received your payment covering invoices for June and July purchases.

Another example is this one:

> He stated that he believes that we are responsible.

The following sentence eliminates one of the *thats*:

> He stated that he believes we are responsible. [See the Communication Matters box on page 75 for more advice about *that*.]

Repetitions of ideas through the use of different words that mean the same thing (*free gift, true fact, past history*) also add to sentence length. Known as **redundancies**, such repetitions are rarely needed. Note the redundancy in this sentence:

> The beginning of the speech will open with a welcome.

The beginning and *will open* are two ways to say the same thing. The following sentence is better:

> The speech will open with a welcome.

Here are other examples of redundancies and ways to eliminate them:

Needless Repetition	Repetition Eliminated
Please *endorse your name on the back* of this check.	Please *endorse* this check.
We must *assemble together* at 10:30 AM *in the morning*.	We must *assemble* at 10:30 AM.
Our new model *is longer in length* than the old one.	Our new model *is longer* than the old one.
If you are not satisfied, *return it back* to us.	If you are not satisfied, *return* it to us.
Tod Wilson is the present *incumbent*.	Tod Wilson is the *incumbent*.
One should know the *basic fundamentals* of clear writing.	One should know the *fundamentals* of clear writing.
The *consensus of opinion* is that the tax is unfair.	The *consensus* is that the tax is unfair.
By acting now, we can finish *sooner than if we wait until a later date*.	By acting now, we can finish *sooner*.
At the present time, we *are* conducting two clinics.	We *are* conducting two clinics.
As a matter of interest, I would like to learn more about your procedure.	I am *interested* in learning more about your procedure.
We should *plan in advance for the future*.	We should *plan*.

Manage Emphasis in Sentence Design

Any written business communication contains a number of items of information, not all of which are equally important. Some are very important, such as a conclusion in a report or the objective in a message. Others are relatively unimportant. One of your tasks as a writer is to form your sentences to communicate the importance of each item. The following advice will help you do so.

Use Short Sentences for Emphasis. Sentence length affects emphasis. **Short sentences** carry more emphasis than long, involved ones. They call attention to their contents by conveying a single message without the interference of related or supporting information.

For example, notice the impact of the concluding sentence in the following excerpt from a fundraising letter:

> Alumni like you have started a transformation that has increased our academic achievements, increased our enrollment, and created an internationally recognized campus landscape. But we have more to do.

Beginnings and endings of business messages are often good places for short sentences. A short opening enables you to get to the point quickly, and a short closing leaves the reader with an important final thought. Here are some examples:

Openings:

Yes, your insurance is still in effect.

Will you please send me your latest catalog?

Closings:

Thank you again for your generous contribution.

I'm looking forward to your presentation.

Use Independent and Dependent Clauses Deliberately. When a sentence contains two or more ideas, the ideas share emphasis. How they share it depends on how the sentence is constructed. If two ideas are presented equally, or **coordinated** (in two independent clauses, for example), they get about equal emphasis. But if one idea is **subordinated** to the other (for example, in one independent clause and one dependent clause), one gets more emphasis than the other.

To illustrate the varying emphasis you can give information, consider this example. You have two items of information to write. One is that the company lost money last year. The other is that its sales volume reached a record high. You could present the information in at least three ways. First, you could give both items equal emphasis by placing them in separate short sentences or by joining them with "and":

> The company lost money last year. The loss occurred despite record sales.

> The company lost money last year, and the loss occurred despite record sales.

Second, you could present the two items in the same sentence with emphasis on the lost money.

> Although the company enjoyed record sales last year, it lost money.

Third, you could present the two items in one sentence with emphasis on the sales increase:

> The company enjoyed record sales last year, although it lost money.

Which way would you choose? The answer would depend on what you want to emphasize. You should think the matter through and follow your best judgment, using coordination and subordination to help you achieve your communication goal.

Think Logically to Determine Emphasis. The following paragraphs illustrate the importance of thinking logically when managing emphasis. In the first, each item of information gets the emphasis of a short sentence and none stand out. However, the

items are not equally important and do not deserve equal emphasis. Notice, also, the choppy effect that the succession of short sentences produces.

> The main building was inspected on October 1. Mr. George Wills inspected the building. Mr. Wills is a vice president of the company. He found that the building has 6,500 square feet of floor space. He also found that it has 2,400 square feet of storage space. The new store must have a minimum of 6,000 square feet of floor space. It must have 2,000 square feet of storage space. Thus, the main building exceeds the space requirements for the new store. Therefore, Mr. Wills concluded that the main building is adequate for the company's needs.

In the next paragraph, some of the items are subordinated, but not logically. The really important information does not receive the emphasis it deserves. Logically, these two points should stand out: (1) the building is large enough and (2) storage space exceeds minimum requirements. But they do not stand out in this version:

> Mr. George Wills, who inspected the main building on October 1, is a vice president of the company. His inspection, which supports the conclusion that the building is large enough for the proposed store, uncovered these facts. The building has 6,500 square feet of floor space and 2,400 square feet of storage space, which is more than the minimum requirement of 6,000 and 2,000 square feet, respectively, of floor and storage space.

The third version manages the emphasis more logically. The short beginning sentence emphasizes the conclusion. The supporting facts—that the building exceeds the minimum floor and storage space requirements—receive main-clause emphasis. The less important facts, such as the reference to George Wills, are treated subordinately. Also, the most important facts are placed at the points of emphasis—the beginning and ending.

> The main building is large enough for the new store. According to Vice President George Wills, who inspected the building on October 1, the building's 6,500 square feet of floor space exceed the minimum requirement by 500 square feet, and the 2,400 square feet of storage space exceed the minimum requirement by 400 square feet.

The preceding illustrations show how sentence construction can determine emphasis. You can make items stand out, you can treat them equally, or you can deemphasize them.

The choices are yours. But what you do must be the result of good, sound thinking and not simply a matter of chance.

Give Sentences Unity

LO4 Employ unity and good logic in writing effective sentences.

Good sentences have **unity**. This means that all the parts of the sentence work together to create one clear point.

Lack of unity in sentences is usually caused by one of two problems: (1) unrelated ideas or (2) excessive detail.

Unrelated Ideas. Combining unrelated ideas in a sentence is the most obvious violation of unity. Putting two or more ideas in a sentence is not grammatically wrong, but the ideas must have a reason for being together and clearly convey one overall point.

You can give unity to sentences that contain unrelated ideas in three ways: You can (1) put the ideas in separate sentences, (2) subordinate one of the ideas to the other, or (3) add words that show how the ideas are related. The first two of these techniques are illustrated by the revisions of the following sentence:

Mr. Jordan is our sales manager, and he has a degree in law.

Perhaps the two ideas are related, but the words do not tell how. One solution would be simply to put each in a separate sentence:

Mr. Jordan is our sales manager. He has a law degree.

Now the sentences are unified, but they're choppy. A better solution would be to keep the ideas together but to subordinate one to the other, as in this example:

Mr. Jordan, our sales manager, has a law degree.

Adding words to show the relationship of the ideas can also correct an unfocused sentence, as illustrated in the revision of the following example:

Our production increased in January, and our equipment is wearing out.

The sentence has two ideas that seem unrelated. One way of improving it is to make a separate sentence of each idea. A closer look reveals, however, that the two ideas really are related—the words just do not show how. The sentence could be revised to show the connection:

Even though our equipment is wearing out, our production increased in January.

The following contrasting pairs of sentences further illustrate the technique:

Unrelated	Improved
Our territory is the southern half of the state, and our salespeople cannot cover it thoroughly.	Our territory is the southern half of the state, and it is too large for our salespeople to cover thoroughly.
Using the cost-of-living calculator is simple, but no tool will work well unless it is explained clearly.	Using the cost-of-living calculator is simple, but, like any tool, it will not work well unless it is explained clearly.
We concentrate on energy-saving products, and 70 percent of our business comes from them.	Because we concentrate on energy-saving products, 70 percent of our business comes from them.

Excessive Detail. Putting too much detail into one sentence tends to hide the central thought, and it also makes the sentence too long.

If the detail isn't necessary, remove it. If it is important, keep it, but divide the sentence into two or more sentences, as in the following examples:

Excessive Detail	Improved
Because our New York offices, which were considered plush in the 1990s, are now badly in need of renovation, as is the case with most offices that have not been maintained, we recommend closing them and finding a new location.	Our New York offices, which were furnished in the 1990s, have not been maintained properly. As they badly need repair, we recommend closing them and finding a new location.
We have attempted to trace the Plytec insulation you ordered from us October 1, and about which you inquired in your October 10 message, but we have not yet been able to locate it, although we are sending you a rush shipment immediately.	We are sending you a rush shipment of Plytec insulation immediately. Following your October 10 inquiry, we attempted to trace your October 1 order, but we were unable to locate it.
In 2009, when I, a small-town girl from a middle-class family, began my studies at Bradley University, which is widely recognized for its business administration program, I set my goal as a career with a large public company.	A small-town girl from a middle-class family, I entered Bradley University in 2009. I selected Bradley because of its widely recognized business administration program. From the beginning, my goal was a career with a large public company.

Word Sentences Logically

At some point, you've probably had a teacher write "awkward" beside one or more of your sentences. Often, the cause of such a problem is illogical wording. The paragraphs that follow will help you avoid some of the most common types of illogical sentences. But keep in mind that many awkward sentences defy efforts to label them. The only guards against letting these kinds of sentences slip past you are your own good ear and careful editing.

Mixed Constructions. Sometimes illogical sentences occur when writers mix two different kinds of sentences together. This problem is called a **mixed construction**.

For example, can you describe what's wrong with the following sentence about cutting costs?

First we found less expensive material, and then a more economical means of production was developed.

If you said that the first half of the sentence used active voice but the second half switched to passive voice, you're right. Shifts of this kind make a sentence hard to follow. Notice how much easier it is to understand this version:

First we found less expensive material, and then we developed a more economical means of production.

There's a similar problem in the following sentence:

The consumer should read the nutrition label, but you often don't take the time to do so.

Did you notice that the point of view changed from third person (*consumer*) to second (*you*) in this sentence? The following revision would be much easier to follow:

Consumers should read nutrition labels, but they often don't take the time to do so.

Sometimes we start writing one kind of sentence and then change it before we get to the end, illogically putting parts of two different sentences together. Here's an example:

Because our salespeople are inexperienced caused us to miss our quota.

Rewriting the sentence in one of the following ways (by changing either the subject or the predicate) would eliminate the awkwardness:

Because our salespeople are inexperienced, we missed our quota.

Our inexperienced salespeople caused us to miss our quota.

Don't Make Me Laugh

Misplaced modifiers can have unintentionally humorous effects, as these examples show:

My mother told me that I would have gray hair when I was ten.

The company created a new toy for children made of plastic.

We saw several monkeys on vacation in Mexico.

Many people watched the Fourth of July fireworks in their cars.

To keep the joke from being on you, put the modifier next to what it modifies.

SOURCE: "Misplaced Modifiers," *JamesBaquet.com*, James Baquet, 15 Jan. 2012, Web, 1 June 2012.

These sentences further illustrate the point:

Mixed Construction	Improved
Some activities that the company participates in are affordable housing, conservation of parks, and litter control.	Some causes the company supports are affordable housing, conservation of parks, and litter control.
Job rotation is when you train people by moving them from job to job.	Job rotation is a training method in which people are moved from job to job.
Knowing that she objected to the price was the reason we permitted her to return the goods.	Because we knew she objected to the price, we permitted her to return the goods.
My education was completed in 2009, and then I began work as a manager for Home Depot.	I completed my education in 2009 and then began work as a manager for Home Depot.
The cost of these desks is cheaper.	These desks cost less. (*or* These desks are cheaper.)

Incomplete Constructions. Certain words used early in a sentence signal that the rest of the sentence will provide a certain kind of content. Be careful to fulfill your reader's expectations. Otherwise, you will have written an **incomplete construction**.

For example, the following sentence, while technically a sentence, is incomplete:

She was so happy with the retirement party we gave her.

She was so happy . . . that what? That she sent everyone a thank-you note? That she made a donation to the library in the company's name? In a sentence like this, either complete the construction or leave "so" out.

Or consider the incomplete opening phrase of this sentence:

As far as time management, he is a master of multitasking.

You can rectify the problem in one of two ways:

As far as time management goes [*or* is concerned], he is a master of multitasking.

As for time management, he is a master of multitasking.

Dangling/Misplaced Modifiers. Putting modifiers in the wrong place or giving them nothing to modify in the sentence is another common way that sentence logic can go awry. Consider this sentence:

Believing the price would drop, the purchasing agents were instructed not to buy.

CHAPTER 4   Constructing Clear Sentences and Paragraphs

The sentence seems grammatically correct … but it doesn't make sense. It looks as though the purchasing agents believed the price would drop—but if they did, why did someone else have to tell them not to buy? The problem is that the people whom the opening phrase is supposed to modify have been left out, making the opening phrase a **dangling modifier**.

You can correct this problem by putting the right agents after the opening phrase:

Believing the price would drop, we instructed our purchasing agents not to buy.

What makes this sentence hard to follow?

We have compiled a list of likely prospects using the information we gathered at the trade show.

Surely the "prospects" aren't really the ones using the information. The sentence would be clearer if the final phrase, a **misplaced modifier**, were more logically placed, as in

Using the information we gathered at the trade show, we have compiled a list of likely prospects.

Faulty Parallelism. Readers expect the same kinds of content in a sentence to be worded in the same way. **Faulty parallelism** violates this logical expectation.

How might you make the similar items in this sentence more parallel in wording?

They show their community spirit through yearly donations to the United Way, giving free materials to Habitat for Humanity, and their employees volunteer at local schools.

Here's one way:

They show their community spirit by donating yearly to the United Way, giving free materials to Habitat for Humanity, and volunteering at local schools.

Can you spot the faulty parallelism in this sentence?

To create a more appealing website, we can gather personal stories, create a new logo, as well as making the layout more readable.

Here's a corrected version:

To create a more appealing website, we can gather personal stories, create a new logo, and make the layout more readable.

Note that if you format your series as a bulleted list, you still need to keep the items parallel. This example has faulty parallelism:

The branding standards include

- The approved logos
- A style guide
- Using the approved color palette
- How to redesign existing materials

This bulleted list has much better parallelism:

The branding standards include

- The approved logos
- A style guide
- The approved color palette
- Instructions for redesigning existing materials

Other rules of grammar besides those mentioned here can help you avoid illogical constructions and write clear sentences. See Chapter 18 for more examples and advice.

CARE IN PARAGRAPH DESIGN

Skillful paragraphing is also important to clear communication. Paragraphs show the reader where topics begin and end, thus helping the reader mentally organize the information. Strategic paragraphing also helps you make certain ideas stand out and achieve the desired response to your message.

The following advice will help you use paragraphing to your best advantage.

Give Paragraphs Unity

Like sentences, paragraphs should have **unity.** When applied to paragraph structure, unity means that a paragraph sticks to a single topic or idea, with everything in the paragraph developing this topic or idea. When you have finished the paragraph, you should be able to say, "Everything in this paragraph belongs together because every part concerns every other part."

A violation of unity is illustrated in the following paragraph from an application letter. Because the goal of the paragraph is to summarize the applicant's coursework, all the sentences should pertain to coursework. By shifting to personal qualities, the third sentence (in *italics*) violates paragraph unity. Taking this sentence out would correct the problem.

> At the university I studied all the basic accounting courses as well as specialized courses in taxation, international accounting, and computer security. I also took specialized coursework in the behavioral areas, with emphasis on human relations. *Realizing the value of human relations in business, I also actively participated in organizations, such as Sigma Nu (social fraternity), Alpha Kappa Psi (professional fraternity), intramural soccer, and A Cappella.* I selected my elective coursework to round out my general business education. Among my electives were courses in investments, advanced business report writing, financial policy, and management information systems. The enclosed résumé provides a complete list of my business-related coursework.

LO5 Compose paragraphs that are short and unified, use topic sentences effectively, and communicate coherently.

Give every paragraph a clear focus.

Keep Paragraphs Short

As a general rule, you should keep your paragraphs short. This suggestion will help with paragraph unity because unified paragraphs tend to be short.

Using short paragraphs also aids comprehension by helping your reader see the structure of your ideas. In addition, such writing is inviting to the eye. People simply prefer to read writing with frequent paragraph breaks.

How long a paragraph should be depends on its contents—on what must be included to achieve unity. Readability research has suggested an average length of eight lines for longer papers such as reports. Shorter paragraphs are appropriate for messages.

Keep in mind that these suggestions concern only an average. Some good paragraphs may be quite long—well over the average. Some paragraphs can be very short—as short as one line. One-line paragraphs are an especially appropriate means of emphasizing major points in business messages. As noted earlier, a one-line paragraph may be all that is needed for a goodwill closing comment or an attention-grabbing opening.

A good rule to follow is to question the unity of all long paragraphs—say, those longer than eight lines. If, after looking over such a paragraph, you conclude that it has unity, leave it as it is. But you will sometimes find more than one topic. When you do, make each topic into a separate paragraph.

Make Good Use of Topic Sentences

One good way of organizing paragraphs is to use topic sentences. The **topic sentence** expresses the main idea of a paragraph, and the remaining sentences build around and support it. In a sense, the topic sentence serves as a headline for the paragraph, and all the other sentences supply the story.

Not every paragraph must have a topic sentence. Some paragraphs, for example, introduce ideas, continue the point of the preceding paragraph, or present an assortment of facts that lead to no conclusion. The central thought of such paragraphs is difficult to put into a single sentence. Even so, you should use topic sentences whenever you can. They force you to determine the central idea of each paragraph and help you check for paragraph unity.

Where the topic sentence should be in the paragraph depends on the subject matter and the writer's plan, but you basically have three choices: the beginning, end, or middle.

Topic Sentence First. The most common paragraph arrangement begins with the topic sentence and continues with the supporting material. In fact, the arrangement is so appropriate for business information that one company's writing manual suggests that it be used for virtually all paragraphs.

To illustrate the writing of a paragraph in which the topic sentence comes first, take a paragraph reporting on economists' replies to a survey question asking their view of business activity for the coming year. The facts to be presented are these: 13 percent of the economists expected an increase; 28 percent expected little or no change; 59 percent expected a downturn; 87 percent of those who expected a downturn thought it would come in the first quarter. The obvious conclusion—and the subject for the topic sentence—is that the majority expected a decline in the first quarter. Following this reasoning, we would develop a paragraph like this:

> *A majority of the economists consulted think that business activity will drop during the first quarter of next year.* Of the 185 economists interviewed, 13 percent looked for continued increases in business activity, and 28 percent anticipated little or no change from the present high level. The remaining 59 percent looked for a recession. Of this group, nearly all (87 percent) believed that the downturn would occur during the first quarter of the year.

Topic Sentence at the End. The second most common paragraph arrangement places the topic sentence at the end. Paragraphs of this kind usually present the supporting details first, and from these details they lead readers to the conclusion, as in this example:

Beware the Vague or Illogical "*This*"

When using *this* to add coherence to your writing, be careful to make the reference both clear and logical.

What does *this* refer to in the following example?

> I do not think the donors should be listed on the website. *This* may make some viewers feel uncomfortable or pressured to donate.

This almost refers to something clearly, but not quite. We can make the meaning sharp by revising the example in one of these ways:

> I do not think the donors should be listed on the website. *Naming the donors* could make some viewers feel uncomfortable or pressured to donate.

> I think we should avoid naming the donors on the website. *This practice* could make some viewers feel uncomfortable or pressured to donate.

Here's another example:

> We need exposure to other markets. One of the easiest ways to do *this* is to advertise strategically.

"One of the easiest ways" to do what? There is nothing in the previous sentence that *this* can refer to. Here's a possible correction:

> We need to gain exposure to other markets. One of the easiest ways to do this is to advertise strategically.

Now *do this* has something it can refer to: "gain exposure."

Any time you use the word *this* to refer to previous content, be sure the reference is clear. If it isn't, reword the content or write "this [something]" (e.g., "this practice").

> The significant role of inventories in the economic picture should not be overlooked. At present, inventories represent 3.8 months' supply, and their dollar value is the highest in history. If considered in relation to increased sales, however, they are not excessive. In fact, they are well within the range generally believed to be safe. *Thus, inventories are not likely to cause a downward swing in the economy.*

Topic Sentence within the Paragraph. A third arrangement places the topic sentence somewhere within the paragraph. This arrangement is rarely used, and for good reason: It does not emphasize the topic sentence, which contains the main point. Still, you can sometimes justify using this arrangement for a special effect, as in this example:

> Numerous materials have been used in manufacturing this part. And many have shown quite satisfactory results. *Material 329, however, is superior to them all.* When built with Material 329, the part is almost twice as strong as when built with the next best material. It is also three ounces lighter. Most important, it is cheaper than any of the other products.

Leave Out Unnecessary Detail

You should include in your paragraphs only the information needed to achieve your purpose.

What you need, of course, is a matter of judgment. You can judge best by putting yourself in your reader's place. Ask yourself questions such as these: How will the information be used? What information will be used? What will not be used? Then make your decisions. If you follow this procedure, you will probably leave out much that you originally intended to use.

The following paragraph from a message to an employee presents excessive information.

> In reviewing the personnel records in our company database, I found that several items in your file were incomplete. The section titled "Work History" has blanks for three items of information. The first is for dates employed. The second is for company name. And the third is for type of work performed. On your record only

company name was entered, leaving two items blank. Years employed or your duties were not indicated. This information is important. It is reviewed by your supervisors every time you are considered for promotion or for a pay increase. Therefore, it must be completed. I request that you log into the company portal and update your personnel record at your earliest convenience.

The message says much more than the reader needs to know. The goal is to have the reader update the personnel record, and everything else is of questionable value. This revised message is better:

A recent review of the personnel records showed that your record is incomplete. Please log into the company portal at your earliest convenience to update it. This information will enable your supervisors to see all your qualifications when considering you for a promotion or a pay increase.

Make Paragraphs Coherent

Like well-made sentences, well-made paragraphs move the reader logically and smoothly from point to point. They clearly indicate how the different bits of information are related to each other in terms of logic and the writer's apparent purpose. This quality of enabling readers to proceed easily through your message, without side trips and backward shifts, is called **coherence**.

The best way to give your message coherence is to arrange its information in a logical order—an order appropriate for the situation. So important are such decisions to message writing that we devote whole chapters to different patterns of organization. But logical organization is not enough. Various techniques are needed to tie the information together. These techniques are known as **transitional devices**. Here we will discuss three major ones: repetition of key words and ideas, use of pronouns, and the use of transitional words.

Repetition of Key Words and Ideas. By repeating key words and ideas from one sentence to the next, you can smoothly connect successive ideas. The following sentences illustrate this transitional device (key words in *italics*):

I am a certified financial planner (CFP) and a member of the Financial Planning Association (FPA). Roughly 70 percent of the *FPA's* 23,800 *members* are *CFPs*. To earn this designation, we had to study for and pass a difficult exam. In addition, about half the *members* have been in business at least 15 years. As an *organization*, we want to establish *planning* as a true profession, one seen in the same light as medicine, the law, and accounting.

Use of Pronouns. Because pronouns refer to words previously used, they make good transitions between ideas. The demonstrative pronouns (*this, that, these, those*) can be especially helpful. The following sentences (with the demonstrative pronouns in *italics*) illustrate this technique.

Ever since the introduction of our Model V nine years ago, consumers have suggested only one possible improvement—voice controls. During all *this* time, making *this* improvement has been the objective of Atkins research personnel. Now we proudly report that *these* efforts have been successful.

A word of caution, though: When using *this* or another demonstrative pronoun to refer to an earlier sentence, try to use it with a noun—for example, *this plan*—to make the reference clear (see the Communication Matters box on page 87).

Transitional Words. When you talk in everyday conversation, you connect many of your thoughts with transitional words. But when you write, you may not use them enough. So be alert for places where providing such words will help move your readers through your paragraphs.

Among the commonly used transitional words are *in addition, besides, in spite of, in contrast, however, likewise, thus, therefore, for example*, and *also*. A more extensive list appears in Chapter 11, where we review transitions in report writing. These words bridge thoughts by indicating the nature of the connection between what has been said and what will be said next. *In addition*, for example, tells the reader that what is to be discussed next builds on what has been discussed. *However* clearly signals that a contrasting idea is coming. *Likewise* indicates that what will be said resembles what has just been said.

Notice how the transitional expressions (in *italics*) in the following paragraph show the relations among the parts and move the reader steadily forward through the ideas:

> Three reasons justify moving from the Crowton site. *First*, the building rock in the Crowton area is questionable. The failure of recent geologic explorations in the area appears to confirm suspicions that the Crowton deposits are nearly exhausted. *Second*, the distances from the Crowton site to major markets make transportation costs unusually high. Obviously, any savings in transportation costs will add to company profits. *Third*, the out-of-date equipment at the Crowton plant makes this an ideal time for relocation. The old equipment at the Crowton plant could be scrapped.

The transition words *first, second*, and *third* bring out the paragraph's pattern of organization and make it easy for the reader to follow along.

Keep in mind that transitional devices can also be used between paragraphs—to tie thoughts together, to keep the focus of the message sharp, and to move the reader smoothly from point to point. Strive for coherence on both the paragraph and the document level.

THERE'S MORE . . .

Where can you find an online exercise on faulty parallelism? On redundancy? On wordiness? How about more advice on combining ideas in sentences or on writing clear paragraphs? Scan the QR code with your smartphone or use your Web browser to find out at www.mhhe.com/lesikar13e. Choose Chapter 4 > Bizcom Tools & Tips.

SUMMARY BY LEARNING OBJECTIVES

1. Writing that communicates uses words that the reader understands and sentence structures that convey a clear meaning. It is writing that is adapted to the reader.

   Explain the role of adaptation in writing clear sentences.

2. In general, you should use short sentences, especially when adapting to readers with low reading ability. Do this in two ways:

   Write short, clear sentences by limiting sentence content and economizing on words.

   - Limit sentence content by breaking up sentences that are too long.
   - Use words economically by following these specific suggestions:
     - Avoid cluttering phrases (*if* rather than *in the event that*).
     - Eliminate surplus words—words that contribute nothing (*It will be noted that*).
     - Avoid roundabout constructions (use *decreases* rather than *can be observed to be decreasing*).
     - Avoid unnecessary repetition, also known as redundancy (*In my opinion, I think*).

3. Give every item you communicate the emphasis it deserves by following these suggestions:

   Design sentences that give the right emphasis to content.

   - Use short sentences to emphasize points.
   - Be aware that how you combine points (with coordination or subordination) determines the emphasis given.
   - Think logically to manage emphasis. Subordinate less important information and put more important information in positions of emphasis.

Employ unity and good logic in writing effective sentences.

4. Strive for unity and clear logic in your sentences.
   - Make certain that all the information in a sentence belongs together—that it forms a unit. These suggestions help:
     — Combine only related thoughts.
     — Eliminate excessive detail.
   - Take care to use logical wording. Watch for these problems:
     — Mixed constructions.
     — Incomplete constructions.
     — Dangling/misplaced modifiers.
     — Faulty parallelism.

Compose paragraphs that are short and unified, use topic sentences effectively, and communicate coherently.

5. Design your paragraphs for clear communication by following these standards:
   - Give the paragraphs unity.
   - Keep the paragraphs short.
   - Use topic sentences effectively, usually at the beginning but sometimes within or at the end of the paragraph.
   - Leave out unnecessary details.
   - Use these transitional devices for coherence:
     — Repetition of key words and ideas.
     — Pronouns that refer back to previous content.
     — Transitional words (e.g., *moreover, in other words*).

KEY TERMS

cluttering phrase, 74

surplus words, 75

roundabout constructions, 76

redundancies, 78

short sentences, 79

coordinated, 79

subordinated, 79

sentence unity, 81

mixed construction, 82

incomplete construction, 83

dangling modifier, 84

misplaced modifier, 84

faulty parallelism, 84

paragraph unity, 85

topic sentence, 86

coherence, 88

transitional devices, 88

CRITICAL THINKING QUESTIONS

1 How are sentence length and sentence design related to adaptation? **LO1**

2 Discuss this comment: "Long, involved sentences tend to be difficult to understand. Therefore, the shorter the sentence, the better." **LO1, LO2**

3 Discuss ways to give ideas more or less emphasis in your sentences. Illustrate with examples. **LO3**

4 Explain how unity can apply equally well to a sentence, to a paragraph, and to longer units of writing. **LO4, LO5**

5 What are the principal causes of lack of unity in sentences? **LO4**

6 This chapter discusses several kinds of illogical wording in sentences. Give an example of each, explain the problem, and correct it. **LO4**

7 Analyze several types of business writing (e.g., a sales letter, a blog post, a report, a business article). Be ready to explain how paragraphing in business writing is influenced by genre or medium. **LO5**

8 How can you tell when paragraphs in business writing are *too* short? What determines how long they should be? **LO5**

9 "Topic sentences are useful for reports and letters, but email messages don't need them." Discuss. **LO5**

10 Discuss and illustrate the three main transitional devices. Find a section of a business letter or article that uses transitional devices. Identify these devices and be ready to explain how they add coherence to the excerpt. **LO5**

Managing Sentence Content LO2, LO3, LO4

Instructions, Sentences 1–7: Break up these sentences into shorter, more readable sentences. You may need to reorganize and reword some of the content.

1 Records were set Wednesday by both the New York Stock Exchange Composite Index, which closed at 8,001.40 up 27.08 points, topping its previous high of 7,986.50, and Standard & Poor's 500 Index, which finished at 1,264.03, up 6.90, moving up significantly and also setting a five-day high.

2 Reserving this property requires a $500 security deposit, which will be refunded unless there is damage to the property or evidence that there has been smoking in the cottage or a pet on the premises or if the reservation is canceled within one month prior to the rental period.

3 The Consumer Education Committee is assigned the duties of keeping informed of the qualities of all consumer goods and services, especially of their strengths and shortcomings, of gathering all pertinent information on dealers' sales practices, with emphasis on practices involving honest and reasonable fairness, and of publicizing any of the information collected that may be helpful in educating the consumer.

4 The upswing in business activity in 2012 is expected to continue and possibly accelerate in 2013, and gross domestic product should rise by $542 billion, representing a 4 percent increase, which is significantly higher than the modest 1 percent increase of 2011.

5 As you will not get this part of Medicare automatically, even if you are covered by Social Security, you must sign up for it and pay $88.50 per month, which the government will match, if you want your physician's bills to be covered.

6 Given our discussion yesterday, I have decided that you may choose either to take the final exam or to have the paper for which you received your highest grade count as an additional 15 percent of your course grade, but you must let me know in writing by May 15 which option you prefer.

7 Although we have not definitely determined the causes for the decline in sales volume for the month, we know that during this period construction on the street adjacent to the store severely limited traffic flow and that because of resignations in the advertising department promotion efforts dropped well below normal.

8 Instructions: Assume that you are the assistant manager of a hotel and are describing your hotel's meeting room to a prospective customer who is thinking of holding a seminar there. Turn the following pieces of information into coherent writing, inserting paragraph breaks where you think appropriate. Be ready to explain why you grouped the information and managed the emphasis the way you did. You may need to add some words or information to make the facts flow smoothly. **LO3, LO4, LO5**

We have a meeting room.

It will be available on the date you requested.

It can seat 100 people.

The seating can be arranged to your specifications.

It is quiet.

It is on the ground floor.

It is not near the guest rooms.

The lounge has live music on occasion.

The lounge is at the opposite end of the hotel from the meeting room.

The meeting room has a lectern.

It has a projector.

It has a screen.

It has a laptop hookup and Wi-Fi.

We can rent additional equipment.

We can rent it at no charge to you.

The charge for the room is $300.

This is the charge for one day.

Making Sentences Economical LO2

Instructions, Sentences 9–36: Revise the following sentences for more economical wording.

9 In view of the fact that we financed the experiment, we were entitled to some of the profit.

10 We should see the prime lending rate increase in the near future.

11 I will talk to him with regard to the new policy.

12 The candidates who were the wealthiest won the election.

13 There are many obligations that we must meet.

14 We purchased gloves that are lined with wool.

15 Mary is of the conviction that service has improved.

16 Sales can be detected to have improved over last year.

17 It is essential that we take the actions that are necessary to correct the problem.

18 The chairperson is engaged in the activities of preparing the program.

19 Martin is engaged in the process of revising the application.

20 You should study all new innovations in your field.

21 In all probability, we are likely to suffer a loss this quarter.

22 The job requires a minimum of at least three years of experience.

23 In spite of the fact that they hadn't paid their previous bill, they placed another order.

24 We expect to deliver the goods in the event that we receive the money.

25 In accordance with their plans, company officials sold the machinery.

26 This policy exists for the purpose of preventing dishonesty.

27 The salespeople who were the most successful received the best rewards.

28 The reader will note that this area ranks in the top 5 percent in per capita income.

29 Our new coats are made of a fabric that is wrinkle resistant.

30 Our office is charged with the task of counting supplies not used in production.

31 Losses caused by the strike exceeded the amount of $640,000.

32 This condition can be assumed to be critical.

33 Our goal is to effect a change concerning the overtime pay rate.

34 Mr. Wilson replaced the old antiquated machinery with new machinery.

35 We must keep this confidential information from being shared with others.

36 The consensus of opinion of this group is that Wellington was wrong.

Wording Sentences Logically LO4

Instructions, Sentences 37–58: Revise the following to eliminate illogical and awkward wording.

37 Because the Swift Company has a service-oriented culture is the reason it supports all forms of volunteerism.

38 On the night of your party, we experienced a rare occurrence with our seafood supplier canceling at the last minute.

39 Our staff is among the best as we strive for the highest level of customer service.

40 Thank you for your feedback that will help us continue to improve.

41 The meeting room you have reserved has a projector, Internet access, and will enable your attendees to hear the trainer easily.

42 As a five-star hotel, our guests' satisfaction is our top priority.

43 Upon review of the facts, the problem was a short in the wiring.

44 This streamlined process will save us so much money.

45 Depending on how you make your request will determine how the reader will respond.

46 On behalf of the management team, I appreciate your extra work on the project.

47 We need to know how many will attend, and please indicate their choice of entrée.

48 During tomorrow's staff meeting we will discuss our progress on the new ad campaign and how well the installation of the new software is going.

49 As far as phone call monitoring, I believe we should try other methods first.

50 Through our research of three local charities we feel that each would make a good one for our company to sponsor.

51 Each department will now be able to update your section of the website.

52 It is such a worthy cause, but I fear this nonprofit's website will not attract many donations.

53 After reviewing the organization's bylaws, I found that they need to be revised and updated.

54 This is an important message, but by placing it in a long paragraph, it is unlikely that many people will read it.

55 As a 501(c)(3) organization, donations are tax deductible.

56 The main reason his report was late was because his email account was hacked yesterday.

57 After talking to our user testers, it is clear that we need to revise the device.

58 You can volunteer to help with publicity, set up, clean up, or you can bring refreshments.

Managing Paragraph Focus LO5

Instructions, Paragraphs 59–63: Write a topic sentence as needed for each of the following, and reword any of the other sentences to create a smooth, clear paragraph. Be ready to defend your placement of the topic sentence.

59 Jennifer has a good knowledge of office procedures. She works hard. She has performed her job well. She is pleasant most of the time, but she has a bad temper, which has led to many personal problems with the work group. I cannot recommend her for promotion. I approve a 5 percent raise for her.

60 Last year our sales increased 7 percent in California and 9 percent in Arizona. Nevada had the highest increase, with 14 percent. All states in the western region enjoyed increases. Oregon recorded only a 2 percent gain. Sales in Washington increased 3 percent.

61 I majored in marketing at Darden University and received a B.S. degree in 2009. Among the marketing courses I took were marketing strategy, promotion, marketing research, marketing management, and consumer behavior. Included, also, was a one-semester internship in retailing with Macy's Department Stores.

62 Our records show that Penn motors cost more than Oslo motors. The Penns have less breakdown time. They cost more to repair. The longer working life offsets Penn's cost disadvantage. So does its better record for breakdown.

63 Recently China ordered a large quantity of wheat from the United States. Likewise, Germany ordered a large quantity. Increased demand by Eastern European countries also contributed to the improved outlook for wheat farming.

CHAPTER FIVE

Writing for a Positive Effect

Learning Objectives

Upon completing this chapter, you will be able to write business communications that have a positive effect on human relations. To reach this goal, you should be able to

1 Explain the need for a positive effect in business messages.

2 Use a conversational style that has the appropriate level of formality and eliminates "rubber stamps."

3 Use the you-viewpoint to build goodwill.

4 Employ positive language to achieve goodwill and other desired effects.

5 Explain and use the elements of courtesy.

6 Use the three major techniques for emphasizing the positive and de-emphasizing the negative.

Affecting Human Relations through Writing

To prepare yourself for this chapter, play the role of Customer Service Director at a large office-supply company. You asked your latest hire, a new college graduate named Jason, to draft a reply to a complaint you received about one of your products. To the right is the message he wrote.

If this message were to go out, it would be a customer relations disaster. Jason's words are blunt, tactless, and unfriendly, and they show no consideration for the reader. Overall, they leave a bad impression—the impression of a writer and a business unconcerned about others' feelings. This chapter will show you how to avoid such an impression.

Dear Mr. Morley:

Your December 3rd complaint was received and contents noted. After reviewing the facts, I regret to report that I must refuse your claim. If you will read the warranty brochure, you will see that the shelving you bought is designed for light loads—a maximum of 800 pounds. You should have bought the heavy-duty product.

I regret the damage this mistake caused you and trust that you will see our position.

Hoping to be of service to you in the future,

Jason Abbott

Customer Service

THE IMPORTANCE OF A POSITIVE EFFECT

LO1 Explain the need for a positive effect in business messages.

As the previous two chapters explain, getting your point across efficiently and accurately is essential to successful business communication. Unclear writing can not only waste people's time but also create costly misunderstandings. You will take a giant step toward a successful career if you learn to write clearly.

But as Chapter 1 points out, clarity is not your only communication goal. Writing involves a human relations dimension, and if you neglect it, you will lose customers, alienate your co-workers, and lose the support of your superiors. The "people" content of your messages often needs as much attention as the informational content—and in some cases, it will be your primary consideration.

Sure, it's easier to fire off a curt email to a complaining customer or an annoying co-worker than to slow down and take that person's feelings into account. But messages written in haste have a way of coming back to haunt you. Think of a time you felt mistreated by someone in business. Perhaps you got an insensitive reply from an insurance company or an impersonal rejection letter from a company you were hoping to work for. Such interactions leave you with negative feelings about the company that will probably last a long time. Plus, you may spread those feelings to other potential customers or employees—or even go onto the Internet to broadcast your displeasure.

This chapter will help you see how to write in a way that elicits positive responses. In other words, it will help you build **goodwill** with your business associates and customers. Businesses cannot survive without goodwill, and you will not last long in business if you do not value it. Courteous, pleasant behavior is part of being a professional. Read on to see how to make your writing meet this professional standard.

Business Etiquette—It Depends on Where You Are

Most people are aware that certain unwritten rules for professionalism govern people's business interactions. Those with whom we do business expect us to show respect through our actions, words, and even appearance.

But what is considered appropriate will vary from situation to situation, industry to industry, and country to country. For example, in a small informal company, relatively casual clothing and relaxed behavior would be expected, and anyone behaving too formally would be considered stiff and rude. In a more formal setting, such as a bank or the executive offices of a large organization, what one should wear, say, or even laugh at would be more constrained.

Doing business with those in or from another country requires additional considerations. For example, according to a website researched by MBA students at the University of Texas–Dallas, it is considered rude in China for women to wear high heels or wear short-sleeved clothing while doing business, or for men to wear anything besides a conservative business suit. The Chinese are also offended by large hand movements, being pointed at while spoken to, and any actions involving touching the mouth.

To learn good business etiquette, consult such sources as Judith Bowman's *Don't Take the Last Donut: New Rules of Business Etiquette* (Pompton Plains, NJ: Career Press, 2009) and Jeanette S. Martin and Lillian H. Chaney's *Global Business Etiquette: A Guide to International Communication and Customs* (Westport, CT: Praeger, 2012). And then adapt their advice to your specific situation.

SOURCE: "China," *InternationalBusinessCenter.org*, International Business Center, 1998–2012, Web, 7 June 2012.

LO2 Use a conversational style that has the appropriate level of formality and eliminates "rubber stamps."

USING A CONVERSATIONAL STYLE

One technique that helps build goodwill is to write in **conversational language**. Conversational language is warm, natural, and personable. It leaves an impression that people like, and it is also the language that is most easily understood.

In business, a conversational style does not always mean being colloquial. It does mean tailoring your language to your reader and avoiding stiff, impersonal wording.

Choosing the Right Level of Formality

Business relationships are much more casual than they used to be. As recently as the early 20th century, routine business letters would contain such expressions as "beg to advise," "enclosed herewith," and "thanking you in advance, I remain. . . ." But companies have flatter organizational structures now, and as social distinctions have broken down, the business world in general has acquired a friendlier tone. Many top executives promote a relaxed company culture, and some even wear t-shirts and blue jeans to work.

Still, a certain formality is expected in many business situations, just as many businesspeople still wear suits. When to be formal and when to be casual will depend on whom you're writing to, what genre you're using, and what you're saying. If you choose the wrong level of formality for the situation, you run the risk of offending your reader. A too-formal style can sound impersonal and parental, while a too-informal style can make you sound as though you aren't taking the reader seriously.

The more formal style is appropriate when you are

- Communicating with someone you don't know.
- Communicating with someone at a higher level than you.

- Using a relatively formal genre, such as a letter, long report, or external proposal.
- Writing a ceremonial message, such as a commendation or inspirational announcement.
- Writing an extremely serious message, such as a crisis response or official reprimand.

When you are writing in less formal situations, you can bring your formality down a notch. Co-workers and other associates who know each other well and are using an informal medium, such as texting, often joke and use emoticons (e.g., a smiley face) and initialisms (e.g., BTW) in their correspondence. When appropriate, such touches add goodwill.

Adjusting your level of formality can sometimes be as simple as substituting one word or phrase for another. Compare these examples of more and less formal wording:

More Formal	Less Formal
Studied, investigated, analyzed	Looked into
Rearranged	Juggled
Ensure	Make sure
Exceptional, superior	Great, terrific
As a result, therefore	So
Confirm	Double check
Consult with	Check with
Correct, appropriate	Right
Thank you	Thanks
We will	We'll
I am	I'm
Let me know	Keep me posted
By June 3	ASAP

A message using the wording on the left would convey the more formal image but would still sound like a person speaking naturally. In your effort to sound more formal, do not make the mistake of using stilted and unnecessarily difficult words. You can sound conversational while also being respectful and clear, as these contrasting examples illustrate:

Stiff and Dull	Conversational
Enclosed please find the brochure about which you inquired.	Enclosed is the brochure you requested.
In reply to your July 11 letter, please be advised that your adherence to the following instructions will facilitate the processing of your return.	Here are the procedures for returning your purchase and obtaining a refund.
This is in reply to your letter of December 1, expressing concern that you do not have a high school diploma and asking if a GED would suffice as prerequisite for the TAA Training Program.	The GED you mention in your December 1 letter qualifies you for the TAA Training Program.
This is to acknowledge receipt of your letter dated 5 May 2013.	We received your May 5 letter and have forwarded it to the claims department for immediate attention.

See Chapter 6 for more advice about choosing the right level of formality for different message types.

Cutting Out "Rubber Stamps"

Rubber stamps are expressions used by habit every time a certain type of situation occurs. They are used without thought and are not adapted to the specific situation. As the term indicates, they are used much as you would use a rubber stamp.

Because they are used routinely, rubber stamps communicate the effect of routine treatment, which is not likely to impress readers favorably. Such treatment tells readers that the writer has no special concern for them—that the present case is being handled in the same way as any other. In contrast, words specially selected for this case show the writer's concern for and interest in the readers.

Chapter 2 discusses the problems that slang and popular clichés can cause. Here, we focus on the type of business clichés that are more routine and less colorful than those—the kind of wording that makes a message sound like a form letter. One common example is the "thank you for your letter" opening. Its intent may be sincere, but its overuse make it a rubber stamp. Another is the closing sentence "if I can be of any further assistance, do not hesitate to call on me." Other examples of rubber stamps in this category are the following:

I am happy to be able to answer your message.

I have received your message.

This will acknowledge receipt of . . .

This is to inform you that . . .

In accordance with your instructions . . .

I will appreciate your cooperation on this matter.

Thank you for your time.

Please let me know if you have any questions.

Thank you in advance for . . .

Perhaps you are asking yourself, "What's wrong with thanking the reader for his or her time or with offering to answer questions?" The answer is that such rubber stamps are not specific enough. They signal that you have quit thinking about the reader and his or her situation. A better ending is one that thanks the reader for something in particular or that offers to answer questions about a particular topic.

You do not need to know all the rubber stamps to stop using them. You only need to write in the language of good conversation, addressing your comments to a real person in a specific situation.

LO3 Use the you-viewpoint to build goodwill.

USING THE YOU-VIEWPOINT

Writing from the **you-viewpoint** (also called **you-attitude**) is another technique for building goodwill in written messages. As you will see in following chapters, it means focusing on the reader's interests, no matter what type of message you are preparing. It is fundamental to the practice of good business communication.

In the broadest sense, you-viewpoint writing emphasizes the reader's perspective. Yes, it emphasizes *you* and *your* and de-emphasizes *we* and *our*, but it is more than a matter of just using second-person pronouns. *You* and *your* can appear prominently in sentences that emphasize the we-viewpoint, as in this example: "If you do not pay by the 15th, you must pay a penalty." Likewise, *we* and *mine* can appear in sentences that emphasize the you-viewpoint, as in this example: "We will do whatever we can to protect your investment."

In face-to-face communication, words, voice, facial expressions, and gestures combine to create the desired communication effect. In writing, the printed word alone must do the job.

The point is that the you-viewpoint is an attitude of mind that places the reader at the center of the message. Sometimes it just involves being friendly and treating people the way they like to be treated. Sometimes it involves skillfully managing people's response with carefully chosen words in a carefully designed order. How you apply it will depend on each situation and your own judgment.

Sample Uses of the You-Viewpoint

Although the you-viewpoint involves much more than word selection, examples of contrasting wording help illustrate the principle. First, take the case of a person writing to present good news. This person could write from a self-centered point of view, beginning with such words as "I am happy to report. . . ." Or he or she could begin with news the reader cares about—for example, "Your proposal has been accepted." The messages are much the same, but the effects are likely to be different.

Or consider the case of a writer who must inform the reader that a request for credit has been approved. A we-viewpoint beginning could take this form: "We are pleased to have your new account." Some readers might view these words favorably. But some would sense a self-centered writer concerned primarily with making money. A you-viewpoint beginning would go something like this: "Your new charge account is now open for your convenience."

The you-viewpoint is especially important in bad-news messages. For example, take the case of an executive who must say no to a professor's request for help on a research project. The bad news is made especially bad when it is presented in we-viewpoint words: "We cannot comply with your request to use our staff on your project because they are too busy doing their jobs." A skilled writer using the you-viewpoint would look at the situation from the reader's point of view, find an explanation or alternative likely to satisfy this reader, and present the response in you-viewpoint language. The you-viewpoint response might take this form: "While we do not have the available staff to assist you with your project, we would be glad to share sample documents with you. If you will tell me. . . ."

The following additional examples demonstrate the different effects that changes in viewpoint are likely to produce.

We-Viewpoint	**You-Viewpoint**
We are happy to have your order for Hewlett-Packard products, which we are sending today by UPS.	Your Hewlett-Packard printers were shipped by UPS today and should reach you by noon tomorrow.
We sell the Chicago Cutlery set for the low price of $24.00 each and suggest a retail price of $36.50.	With a cost of only $24.00, each Chicago Cutlery set you sell at $36.50 will bring you a $12.50 profit.
Our policy prohibits us from permitting outside groups to use our facilities except on a cash-rental basis.	Our policy of renting our facilities to outside groups ensures that our full range of services will be available to your guests.
We have been quite tolerant of your past-due account and must now demand payment.	If you are to continue to enjoy the benefits of credit buying, you must clear your account now.
We have received your report of May 1.	Thank you for your report of May 1.
So that we may complete our file records on you, we ask that you submit to us your January report.	So that your file records may be completed, please send us your January report.
We require that you sign the sales slip before we will charge your account.	For your protection, you are charged only after you have signed the sales slip.

Ethical Use of the You-Viewpoint

The you-viewpoint has been a matter of some controversy. Its critics argue that it can be insincere and manipulative. For this reason, they say, it is more ethical just to "tell it like it is."

These arguments have some merit. Without question, the you-viewpoint can be abused. But those who favor its use argue that it need not—in fact, should not—be just a self-serving technique. The objective is to treat people courteously because that is the way we all like to be treated. The you-viewpoint also helps readers see quickly in what ways a given message applies to them. This "translation" work supports both clarity and courtesy.

You do not have to use the you-viewpoint exclusively or overdo it. You can use it when it is friendly and sincere and when your desired effects are ethical. In such cases, using the you-viewpoint is "telling it as it is"—or at least as it should be. With this position in mind, we advocate its use as an important element of good business communication.

LO4 Employ positive language to achieve goodwill and other desired effects.

ACCENTUATING THE POSITIVE

As you know, one can say anything in many ways, and each way conveys a different meaning. Whether your written message achieves its goal often will depend on the types of words you choose. In most cases, positive or neutral wording will succeed better than negative wording.

Use Positive Words

As Chapter 3 points out, all words have certain emotional associations. Because people generally prefer positive to negative feelings, positive words are usually best for achieving your message goals. This is not to say that negative words have no place in business writing. Such words are powerful, and you will sometimes want to use them. But you will usually need the more positive words. They tend to put the reader in the right frame of mind, and they emphasize the pleasant aspects of the goal. They also create the goodwill that helps build good relations.

Negative words tend to produce the opposite effects. They may stir up your reader's resistance to your goals, and they are likely to be highly destructive of goodwill. Carefully consider the negativeness and positiveness of your words in order to select the ones that are most appropriate in each case.

Be particularly wary of strongly negative words. These words have unhappy and unpleasant associations that usually detract from your goal. They include such words as *mistake, problem, error, damage, loss*, and *failure*. There are also words that deny—words such as *no, do not, refuse*, and *stop*. And there are words whose sounds or meanings have unpleasant effects: *guts, scratch, grime, sloppy*, and *nauseous*. As you think about these words, notice their effect on your feelings. If possible, use more positive alternatives.

Focus on What You *Can* Do

Often times when we have to convey negative news, the fact that we must say "no" dominates our thinking. This reaction leads us to write in a style that is more negative and selfish than it actually has to be. In many cases, you will be able to help solve the reader's problem even if you cannot do exactly what he or she wants.

Let's consider the case of a company executive who had to deny a local civic group's request to use the company's meeting facilities. To soften the refusal, the executive could let the group use a conference room, which might be somewhat small for its purpose. The executive came up with this totally negative response:

> We *regret* to inform you that we *cannot* permit you to use our auditorium for your meeting, as the Sun City Investment Club asked for it first. We can, however, let you use our conference room, but it seats *only* 60.

The negative words are italicized. First, the positively intended opening, "We *regret* to inform you," is an unmistakable sign of coming bad news. "*Cannot* permit" is unnecessarily harsh. And notice how the good-news part of the message is hindered by the limiting word *only*. The writer focused only on the negative aspects of the situation. As a result, that is what the reader is being asked to focus on as well.

Had the executive considered the situation more positively, he or she might have written

> Although the SunCity Investment Club has reserved the auditorium for Saturday, we can offer you our conference room, which seats 60.

Not a single negative word appears in this version. Both approaches achieve the primary objective of denying a request, but their emphasis is quite different. Clearly the second approach would do a better job of building goodwill.

Copyright © 2011 Ted Goff.

"You'll be happy to know that we've redefined the word impossible, and it no longer applies to what you have to do."

Parent, Child, or Adult?

In the 1950s, psychologist Eric Berne developed a model of relationships that he called Transactional Analysis. It has proven to be so useful that it is still popular today.

At the core of this model is the idea that, in all our transactions with others (and even within ourselves), people occupy one of three positions: parent, child, or adult.

- A *parent* is patronizing, spoiling, nurturing, blaming, criticizing, and/or punishing.
- A *child* is uninhibited, freely emotional, obedient, whining, irresponsible, and/or selfish.

- An *adult* is reasonable, responsible, considerate, and flexible.

Significantly, the "self" that one projects invites others to occupy the complementary position. Thus, acting "parental" leads others to act "childish" and vice versa, while acting "adult" invites others to be adults.

In both internal and external business messages, strive for "adult–adult" interactions. Your courtesy and professionalism will be likely to elicit the same from your readers.

Or take the case of a writer granting the claim of a woman for cosmetics damaged in transit. Granting the claim is the most positive outcome that such a situation can have. Even though this customer has had a somewhat unhappy experience, she is receiving what she wants. The negative language of an unskilled writer, however, can so vividly recall the unhappy aspects of the problem that the happy solution is moved to the background, as in this negative response:

> We received your claim in which you contend that we were responsible for *damage* to three cases of Estée Lauder lotion. We assure you that we sincerely *regret* the *problems* this has caused you. Even though we feel in all sincerity that your receiving clerks may have been *negligent*, we will assume the *blame* and replace the *damaged* merchandise.

Clearly, this grudging, accusatory, and negative approach would not be conducive to goodwill.

In the following version of the same message, the writer focuses on what can be done to settle the problem. The job is done without using a negative word and without mentioning the situation being corrected or suspicions concerning the honesty of the claim. The goodwill effect of this approach is likely to keep the reader as a customer:

> Three cases of Estée Lauder lotion are on their way to you by FedEx and should be on your sales floor by Saturday.

Here are a few more contrasting examples (the negative words are in *italics*):

Negative	Positive
Smoking is *not* permitted anywhere except in the lobby.	Smoking is permitted in the lobby only.
We *cannot* deliver until Friday.	We can deliver the goods on Friday.
We *regret* that we *overlooked* your coverage on this equipment and apologize for the *trouble* and *concern* it must have caused you.	You were quite right in believing that you have coverage on the equipment. We have now credited your account for. . .
We *regret* to inform you that the guest room is not available on the date you requested.	The guest room is already booked for the evening of August 7. Would August 8 be a possibility? We would be able to accommodate your party at any time on that date.

BEING COURTEOUS

LO5 Explain and use the elements of courtesy.

A major contributor to goodwill in business documents is courtesy. By **courtesy** we mean treating people with respect and consideration. Courtesy produces friendly relations between people, and the result is a better human climate for solving business problems and doing business.

As with every other facet of your communications, how to be courteous ultimately depends on the given situation. Including "please," "thank you," "we're sorry," and other standard expressions of politeness do not necessarily make a message courteous. Rather than focusing on stock phrases, consider what will make your reader feel most comfortable, understood, and appreciated. A message with no overtly polite expressions whatsoever can still demonstrate great courtesy by being easy to read, focusing on the reader's interests, and conveying the writer's feelings of goodwill.

Still, courtesy generally is enhanced by using certain techniques. We have already discussed three of them: writing in conversational language, employing the you-viewpoint, and choosing positive words. More follow.

Avoid Blaming the Reader

Customers, co-workers, bosses, and other businesspeople you work with are going to make mistakes—just as you will. When they do, your first reaction is likely to be disappointment, frustration, or even anger. After all, their mistakes will cost you time, energy, and possibly even money.

But you must avoid the temptation to blame the reader when you are resolving a problem. No one likes being accused of negligence, wrongdoing, or faulty thinking. It is better to objectively explain the facts and then move on to a solution.

The following examples illustrate:

Blaming Language	**More Positive Language**
You failed to indicate which fabric you wanted on the chair you ordered.	To complete your order, please check your choice of fabric on the enclosed card.
If you had read the instructions that came with your cookware, *you would have known* not to submerge it in water.	The instructions explain why the cookware should not be submerged in water.
Your claim that we did not properly maintain the copier *is false*.	Listed below are the dates the copier was serviced and the type of service it received.
Your request for coverage is denied because *you did not follow* the correct appeals procedure.	We need additional information to be able to process your appeal. Please supply [the needed information] and resubmit your request to. . . .

Notice two helpful, related strategies in the better language above. One is to avoid using *you* when doing so would blame the reader. In these situations, you will actually have better you-viewpoint if you do not use *you*. The second strategy is to keep the focus on the facts rather than on the people. So instead of writing "*you should not submerge* the cookware in water," write "the cookware *should not be* submerged in water." Notice that the preferred wording in this example uses passive voice, a type of writing you learned about in Chapter 3. As that chapter notes, passive voice (omitting the doer of the action) is not only acceptable but desirable in cases where it will keep you from assigning blame.

A more general strategy that can help you maintain good relations, even when you feel that *you* have been unfairly blamed, is to blow off steam before you write your message. Try never to send a message written in anger. Tempting as it can be to do so, you will almost always regret it. Take the time to calm down and write in a reasonable tone. A good relationship with your reader is worth much more than a moment's self-indulgence.

Refrain from Preaching

You can help give your documents a courteous effect by not preaching—that is, by avoiding the tone of a lecture or a sermon. Most people like to be treated as equals; they do not want to be bossed or talked down to. Writing that suggests unequal writer–reader relations is likely to hinder your goals.

Preaching is usually not intended. It often occurs when the writer is trying to convince the reader of something, as in this example:

> You must take advantage of savings like this if you are to be successful. The pennies you save pile up. In time they will turn into dollars.

It is insulting to tell the reader an elementary fact as if he or she did not know it. Such obvious information should be omitted.

Likewise, flat statements of the obvious fall into the preachy category. Statements such as "Rapid inventory turnover means greater profits" are obvious to the experienced retailer and would probably produce negative reactions. So would most statements that include such phrases as "you need," "you want," "you should," and "you must."

Another form of preachiness is to tell the reader how to react, as in this example: "Would you like to make a deal that would make you a 38 percent profit? Of course you would!" This parental-sounding language would surely offend. Less extreme examples, such as "You'll be happy to know," can have a similar negative effect.

Do More Than Is Expected

One sure way to gain goodwill is to do a little more than you have to do for your reader. We are all aware of how helpful little acts of support can be in other areas of our personal relationships. Too many of us, however, stop short of these in our messages. Perhaps in

The first step toward creating goodwill with your readers is to put yourself in their shoes.

TECHNOLOGY IN BRIEF

Courtesy in the Age of Mobile Devices

In the U.S., the name Emily Post has been synonymous with good manners for decades. With the publication of *Etiquette in Society, in Business, in Politics, and at Home* in 1922, Post became the undisputed authority on the topic, and she continued to be so the rest of her life. Her children, grandchildren, and great-grandchildren have carried on her tradition. *Emily Post's Etiquette* is now in its 18th edition, and it now includes a chapter on Personal Communication Devices. Here are some excerpts from the chapter:

Cell Phones

- Without exception, turn your device off in a house of worship, restaurant, or theater; during a meeting or presentation; or anytime its use is likely to disturb others.

- If you must be alerted to a call, put your device on silent ring or vibrate, and check your caller ID or voice mail later. (Put it in your pocket; a vibrating phone, skittering across a tabletop, is just as disruptive as a ring.)

- Wherever you are, if you must make or take a call, move to a private space and speak as quietly as you can.

- Keep calls as short as possible; the longer the call, the greater the irritation to those who have no choice but to listen.

- On airplanes, it's a courtesy to everyone on board to quickly wrap up your call when the flight crew instructs passengers to turn off all electronic devices before takeoff. When cell phone use is permitted after landing, keep your calls short, limiting them to information about your arrival. Save any longer calls for a private spot in the terminal.

- Think about what your ring tone says about you. Is your frat boy hip-hop tone the right ring for your new job as a trainee at an accounting firm?

Text Messaging

- Text messaging is a strictly casual communication. You shouldn't use text messaging when informing someone of sad news, business matters, or urgent meetings unless it's to set up a phone call on the subject.

- Be aware of where you are. The backlight will disturb others if you text in a theater or house of worship.

- Keep your message brief. If it's going to be more than a couple of lines, make a call and have a conversation.

- Don't be a pest. Bombarding someone with texts is annoying and assumes they have nothing better to do than read your messages.

- Be very careful when choosing a recipient from your phone book; a slip of the thumb could send a text intended for a friend to your boss.

- Whenever you have a chance, respond to text messages, either by texting back or with a phone call.

- Don't text anything confidential, private, or potentially embarrassing. You never know when your message might get sent to the wrong person or forwarded.

SOURCE: Based on Peggy Post, Anna Post, Lizzie Post and Daniel Post Senning, Emily Post's Etiquette: Manners for a New World 18E, 2001, pp. 240–248.

---

an effort to be concise, we include only the bare essentials. But the result can be brusque, hurried treatment, which is inconsistent with the effort to build goodwill.

The writer of a message refusing a request to use company equipment, for example, needs only to say "no" to accomplish the primary goal. But this blunt response would destroy goodwill. To maintain positive relations, the writer should explain and justify the refusal and then suggest alternative steps that the reader might take. A wholesaler's brief extra sentence to wish a retailer good luck on a coming promotion is worth the effort. So are an insurance agent's few words of congratulations in a message to a policyholder who has earned some kind of distinction.

Likewise, a writer uses good judgment in an acknowledgment message that includes helpful suggestions about using the goods ordered. And in messages to customers a writer for a sales organization can justifiably include a few words about new merchandise, new services, price reductions, or any other topic likely to be of interest.

Remember that your goal is both to communicate *and* to build positive human relations, so go the extra mile for your readers.

Be Sincere

Courteous treatment is sincere treatment. If your messages are to be effective, people must believe you. You must convince them that you mean what you say and that your courtesy and friendliness are authentic.

The best way of getting sincerity into your writing is actually to be sincere. If you honestly want to be courteous, if you honestly believe that you-viewpoint treatment leads to harmonious relations, and if you honestly think that tactful treatment spares your reader's feelings, you are likely to apply these techniques sincerely, and this sincerity will show in your writing.

Don't Overdo the Goodwill Techniques. Being sincere will help you avoid two problems. The first is the overdoing of your goodwill techniques. The effort to be positive and to display the you-viewpoint can be taken to such an extreme that readers will be put off. For example, referring too often to your reader by name can seem manipulative, as in this example:

> If you will help these children, Ms. Collins, you will become a heroine in their eyes.

The following example, included in a form letter from the company president to a new charge customer, has a touch of unbelievability:

> I was delighted today to see your name listed among Macy's new charge customers.

Or how about this one, taken from an adjustment message of a large department store?

> We are extremely pleased to be able to help you and want you to know that your satisfaction means more than anything to us.

Don't Exaggerate. The second danger that you should avoid is exaggerating the positive. It is easy to see through most exaggerated statements, and when that happens, you have damaged the reader's trust in you. Exaggerations are overstatements of facts. Although some hype is conventional in sales writing, even here boundaries exist. The following examples clearly overstep these boundaries:

> Already thousands of new customers are beating paths to the doors of Martin dealers.

> Never has there been, nor will there be, a fan as smooth running and whispering quiet as the North Wind.

> Everywhere coffee drinkers meet, they are talking about the amazing whiteness Rembrandt gives their teeth.

Many exaggerated statements involve the use of superlatives. All of us use them, but only rarely are they actually warranted. Words like *greatest, most amazing, finest, healthiest,* and *strongest* are seldom appropriate. Other strong words may have similar effects—for example, *extraordinary, incredible, delicious, more than happy, sensational, terrific, revolutionary, world-class,* and *perfection.* Such words cause us to doubt rather than believe.

LO6 Use the three major techniques for emphasizing the positive and de-emphasizing the negative.

MANAGING EMPHASIS FOR A POSITIVE EFFECT

Getting the desired effect in writing often involves giving proper emphasis to the items in the message. As the previous chapter discussed, every message contains a number of facts and ideas that must be presented. Some of these items are more important than others, and some will be received more positively than others. A part of your job as a writer is to determine which items to emphasize in your message.

The three most useful ways to manage emphasis for a positive effect are to use position, sentence structure, and space. The following paragraphs explain each.

Emphasis by Position

The beginnings and endings of a writing unit carry more emphasis than the center parts. This rule of emphasis applies whether the unit is the message, a paragraph of the message, or a sentence within the paragraph (see Figure 5–1). Some authorities think that the reader's fresh mental energy explains beginning emphasis. Some say that the last parts stand out because they are the most recent in the reader's mind. Whatever the explanation, research has suggested that this emphasis technique works.

In light of this fact, you should put your more positive points in beginnings and endings and, if possible, avoid putting negative points in these positions. If we were to use this technique in a paragraph turning down a suggestion, we might write it like this (the key point is in *italics*):

> In light of the current budget crunch, we approved those suggestions that would save money while not costing much to implement. While *your plan is not feasible at this time*, we hope you will submit it again next year when we should have more resources for implementing it.

As you can see, putting information in the middle tends to de-emphasize it. Consider position carefully when organizing your positive and negative contents.

Sentence Structure and Emphasis

Closely related to the concept of emphasis by position is the concept of managing emphasis through sentence structure. As noted in Chapter 4, short, simple sentences and main clauses call attention to their content. In applying this emphasis technique to your writing, carefully consider the possible arrangements of your information. Place the more positive information in short, simple sentences or main clauses. Put the less important information in subordinate structures such as dependent clauses and modifying phrases. This sentence from the previous example illustrates the technique (the negative point is in a dependent clause):

> While *your plan is not feasible at this time*, we encourage you to submit it again next year when we are likely to have more resources for implementing it.

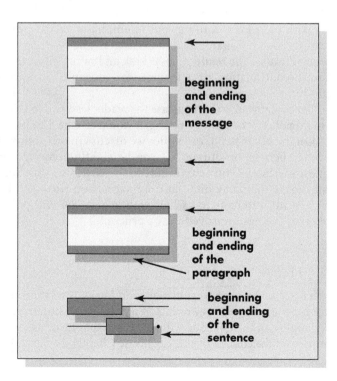

Figure 5–1

Emphasis by Position

Here's another example:

> Your budget will be approved *if you can reduce your planned operating expenses by $2000.*

Space and Emphasis

As a general rule, the more space you devote to a topic, the more you emphasize it. Therefore, deemphazing the negative means spending as little space on it as possible and giving the positive contents more space.

When we say not to spend much space on negative news, we mean the actual negative point. As Chapter 8 will show, you will often need to preface such news with explanatory, cushioning words in order to prepare your readers to receive it as positively as possible. For this reason, it often takes longer to say "no" than to say "yes," as in these contrasting openings of a message responding to a request:

A Message That Says "Yes"

> Your new A-level parking sticker is enclosed.

A Message That Says "No"

> Your new University Hospital parking sticker is enclosed. As always, we had many more applicants for A-level passes than we had spaces. Your B-level sticker will enable you to park in the Eden Garage, which is connected to the hospital by a covered skywalk. If you would like to discuss additional options, please contact Ann Barnett, Director of Parking Services, at 555-6666 or ann.barnett@uh.com.

The "no" version certainly took longer. But notice that the space actually devoted to the negative news is minimal. In fact, the negative news isn't even stated; it is only implied in the positive second sentence ("Your B-level sticker ..."). Look how much of the paragraph focuses on more positive things. That is the allocation of space you should strive for when minimizing the negative and emphasizing the positive.

THE ETHICS OF POSITIVE EMPHASIS

As with use of the you-viewpoint, emphasis on the positive, when overdone, can lead to fake and manipulative messages. The technique is especially questionable when it causes the reader to overlook an important negative point in the message—the discontinuation of a service, for example, or information about an unsafe product.

Do not let your effort to please the reader lead you to be dishonest or insincere. That would not only be morally wrong; it would also be a bad way to do business.

On the other hand, the topics we discuss in our communication—whether data, events, people, or situations—can be rightly perceived in multiple ways. In your quest to achieve your communication purpose, think before you let negative feelings make their way into your messages. You will often be able to depict the glass as half full rather than as half empty, and you will probably find that your own perspective has improved in the process.

THERE'S MORE ...

What are seven ways to cultivate good business relationships? How can you improve your use of the you-viewpoint? What are some negative words to avoid in business writing? Scan the QR code with your smartphone or use your Web browser to find out at www.mhhe.com/Lesikar13e. Choose Chapter 5 > Bizcom Tools & Tips.

1. Although clarity is a major goal of business writing, you should also strive to create positive effects.

   - Specifically, you should seek to build goodwill, which sustains good human relations in business.
   - Lost goodwill can result in lost business, alienated co-workers, and lost support from your superiors.

   Explain the need for a positive effect in business messages.

2. Write messages in a conversational style (language that sounds like people talking).

   - Such a style requires that you choose the appropriate level of formality for the situation.
   - It requires that you avoid unnecessary formality and stiffness (*thanking you in advance, please be advised*).
   - It requires that you avoid the so-called rubber stamps—words used routinely and without thought (*this is to inform, in accordance with*).

   Use a conversational style that has the appropriate level of formality and eliminates "rubber stamps."

3. In your messages, you will need to emphasize the you-viewpoint (*your refund is enclosed . . . rather than I am happy to report . . .*).

   - But be careful not to be or appear to be insincere.
   - And do not use the you-viewpoint to manipulate the reader.

   Use the you-viewpoint to build goodwill.

4. You should prefer positive to negative words.

   - Negative words have unpleasant meanings (*We cannot deliver until Friday*).
   - Positive words have pleasant meanings (*We can deliver Friday*).
   - Select those negative and positive words that achieve the best effects for your goal.

   Employ positive language to achieve goodwill and other desired effects.

5. You should strive for courtesy in your messages by doing the following:

   - Practice the goodwill techniques discussed in the chapter.
   - Avoid blaming the reader.
   - Refrain from preaching or talking down to your reader.
   - Do more than is expected.
   - Be sincere (avoid exaggeration and overdoing the goodwill techniques).

   Explain and use the elements of courtesy.

6. Use the three major techniques for positive emphasis in writing.

   - Determine the items of information the message will contain.
   - Give each item the emphasis it deserves.
   - Show emphasis in these ways:
     — By position (beginnings and endings receive prime emphasis).
     — By sentence structure (short sentences and main clauses emphasize more than long sentences and subordinated ideas).
     — By space (the greater the space devoted to a topic, the greater the emphasis).

   Use the three major techniques for emphasizing the positive and de-emphasizing the negative.

KEY TERMS

goodwill, 95	rubber stamps, 98	courtesy, 103
conversational language, 96	you-viewpoint (*or* you-attitude), 98	

CRITICAL THINKING QUESTIONS

1. Discuss this comment: "Getting the goodwill effect requires extra effort and time, and time costs money." **LO1**

2. "If a company really wants to impress the readers of its messages, the messages should be as formal as possible." Discuss. **LO2**

3. "If you can find words, sentences, or phrases that cover a common situation, why not use them every time that situation comes about? They're not offensive, and they sound businesslike." Discuss. **LO2**

4. Discuss this comment: "The you-viewpoint is insincere and deceitful." **LO3**

5. Evaluate this comment: "It's hard to argue against courtesy. But businesspeople don't have time to spend extra effort on it. Anyway, they want their documents to go straight to the point—without wasting words and without sugar coating." **LO5**

6. "I like writers who shoot straight. When they are happy, you know it. When they are angry, they let you know." Discuss. **LO3–LO5**

7. "It is never acceptable to show anger in a business message." Discuss. **LO5**

8. A writer wants to include a certain negative point in a message and to give it little emphasis. Discuss each of the three basic emphasis techniques as they relate to what can be done. **LO6**

9. Imagine that a customer has written to complain about the lack of attention that she received when visiting a paint store. The manager's responding letter explains why the sales staff were so busy, offers to make a special appointment with the customer to discuss her decorating needs, and then ends with the following paragraph: "We do apologize again for any inconvenience that this situation caused you. We thank you for your understanding. Please do not hesitate to contact us again if we ever fall short of the superior service that you have come to expect from us." If the manager asked for your feedback on this letter, what would you say? It's full of polite expressions. Is it a good concluding paragraph? Discuss. **LO2–LO6**

SKILLS BUILDING EXERCISES

Using a Conversational Style (LO2)

Instructions, Sentences 1–10: Rewrite in conversational style.

1. I hereby acknowledge receipt of your July 7 letter.

2. Please be so kind as to reply at your earliest possible convenience.

3. Attached please find the receipt requested in your May 1st inquiry.

4. You are hereby advised to endorse the enclosed proposal and return same to the undersigned.

5. This is to advise that henceforth all invoices will be submitted in duplicate.

6. Kindly be advised that this book has been requested by another patron and will therefore be due on 10 May 2012.

7. In reply to your letter of July 13, permission to quote from our report is hereby granted.

8. Please be advised that, with regard to above invoice, a payment of $312 has been credited to your account.

9. I am submitting under separate cover the report you requested.

10. Kindly advise the director as to your availability for participation in the program.

Using the You-Viewpoint (LO3)

Instructions, Sentences 11–25: Rewrite the following using you-viewpoint. You may need to add additional material.

11. Company policy requires that you submit the warranty agreement within two weeks of sale.

12. We will be pleased to deliver your order by the 12th.

13. We have worked for 37 years to build the best lawn mowers for our customers.

14. Today we are shipping the goods you ordered February 3.

15. (From an application letter) I have seven years of successful experience selling office supplies.

16. (From an email to employees) We take pleasure in announcing that, effective today, the Company will give a 20 percent discount on all purchases made by employees.

17. We are happy to report approval of your application for membership.

18. Items desired should be checked on the enclosed order form.

19. Our long experience in the book business has enabled us to provide the best customer service possible.

20 So that we can sell at discount prices, we cannot permit returns of sale merchandise.

21 We invite you to buy from the enclosed catalog.

22 Tony's Red Beans have an exciting spicy taste.

23 We give a 2 percent discount when payment is made within 10 days.

24 I am pleased to inform you that I can grant your request for payment of travel expenses.

25 We cannot permit you to attend classes on company time unless the course is related to your work assignment.

Accentuating the Positive (LO4)

Instructions, Sentences 26–40: Underscore all negative words in these sentences. Then rewrite the sentences for a more positive effect. Use your imagination to envision the situation for each.

26 Your misunderstanding of our January 7 email caused you to make this mistake.

27 We hope this delay has not inconvenienced you. If you will be patient, we will get the order to you as soon as our supply is replenished.

28 We regret that we must call your attention to our policy of prohibiting refunds for merchandise bought at discount.

29 Your negligence in this matter caused the damage to the equipment.

30 You cannot visit the plant except on Saturdays.

31 We were disappointed to learn from your July 7 email that you are having trouble with our Model 7 motor.

32 Tuff-Boy work clothing is not made from cloth that shrinks or fades.

33 Our Stone-skin material is less weak than the fabric used by other brands.

34 Even though you were late in paying the bill, we still allowed the discount.

35 We were sorry to learn of the disappointing service you have had from our sales force, but we feel we have corrected all mistakes with recent personnel changes.

36 We have received your complaint of the 7th in which you claim that our product was defective and have thoroughly investigated the matter.

37 I regret the necessity of calling your attention to our letter of May 1.

38 We have received your undated letter, which you sent to the wrong office.

39 I regret to have to say that I will be unable to speak at your conference, as I have a prior commitment.

40 Do not walk on the grass.

Basic Patterns of Business Messages

What are the key traits of effective communication on the job?

Lynn Marmer, VP of Corporate Affairs for the Kroger company, has something to say about that. When she was appointed the chief communications officer of the Fortune 25 Company in 1997, she became the first female officer of this leading grocery retailer. Her responsibilities include external communications and media, corporate social responsibility and sustainability, customer relations, philanthropy and community engagement, government relations, and crisis communications. And she has made Kroger an innovator in the use of multimedia for internal communication.

But "whatever the medium (traditional, social, speeches, or television interviews) or audience (employees, external, investors, policymakers)," she says, "I always strive to honor my own four cardinal rules:

- Tailor the medium and message to the interests/needs of the audience.
- Make the writing clear, unambiguous, and easy to understand; use active voice.
- Be honest, transparent, and authentic.
- Strive to connect with the audience in a way that supports and reinforces the company's brand promise."

Kroger is one of the largest retailers in the world, with 2,400 grocery stores in 31 different states, $90 billion in sales, and more than 330,000 employees. But wherever you work (or apply to work) and whatever you write, following Marmer's advice will set you apart as a skillful professional who enhances a company's success.

CHAPTER SIX

Choosing the Best Process and Form

Learning Objectives

Upon completing this chapter, you will understand the process for writing business messages and the purpose and forms of the main types of business messages. To reach this goal, you should be able to

1 Describe the writing process and effective writing strategies.

2 Explain the importance of readable formatting.

3 Describe the development and current usage of the business letter.

4 Describe the purpose and form of memorandums (memos).

5 Describe the purpose and form of email.

6 Understand the nature and business uses of text messaging and instant messaging.

7 Understand the nature and business uses of social media.

8 Understand the inverted pyramid structure for organizing and writing Web documents.

The Nature of Business Messages

Introduce yourself to this chapter by shifting to the role of Julie Evans, a recent college graduate in her first job as an accounts manager at a small company that manufactures windows. You are amazed (and sometimes overwhelmed) by the types of messages you send each day. Every day you process dozens of internal email messages. Occasionally you write and receive memorandums. Then there are the more formal communications you exchange with people outside the company—both email and letters. You also write messages for social media sites and daily rely on text and instant messaging for quick communication. With so many audiences and so many ways to send messages, you often wonder if you're making good choices. This chapter will help you understand the writing process and the types of business messages so that you are sure to meet your audience's needs.

THE IMPORTANCE OF SKILLFUL WRITING

Much of this book focuses on writing in business. Is skillful oral communication important? Absolutely. How about skillful use of graphics? It's critical. Then why the emphasis on writing?

First, experienced businesspeople tend to place writing skills ahead of other communication skills when asked what they seek in job applicants. And they seek strong writing skills in particular when considering whom to promote. For example, in one study, a majority of the 305 executives surveyed commented that fewer than half their job applicants were well-versed enough in "global knowledge, self-direction, and writing skills" to be able to advance in their companies.[1] As people move up, their jobs involve handling more information, and this work often requires the written forms of communication.

Another reason for our strong focus on writing is that writing is in some ways more difficult to do well than other kinds of communication. Writers essentially have no safety net; they can't rely on their facial expressions, body language, or tone of voice to make up for wording that isn't quite what they mean. The symbols on the page or screen must do the whole communication job. Plus, the symbols used in writing—the alphabet, words, punctuation, and so forth—share no characteristics with the object or concept they represent (unless you count words that sound like the sounds they name, such as "buzz"). Representing something with a photograph is relatively easy. Representing that same thing in words is much harder. Capturing a complex reality by putting one word after another requires ingenuity, discipline, and the ability to anticipate how readers will likely react as they read.

The first major section of this chapter will help you achieve this impressive but commonplace feat in the workplace by showing you how to break the writing process into parts and skillfully manage each part. The remainder of the chapter will discuss the main forms of business messages, which bring with them certain features and conventions of use. These discussions provide the foundation for subsequent chapters on writing different kinds of business messages.

---

[1] Paula Wasley, "Tests Aren't Best Way to Evaluate Graduates' Skills, Business Leaders Say in Survey," *The Chronicle of Higher Education*, The Chronicle of Higher Education, Jan. 2008, Web, 08 June 2012.

Figure 6–1

**Message Planning
Checklist**

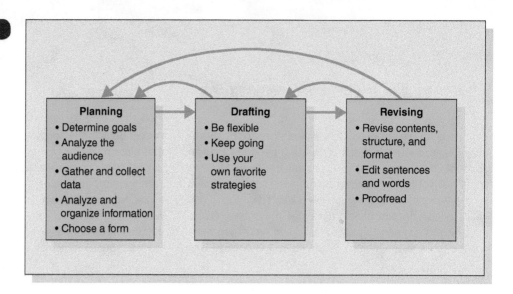

Planning	Drafting	Revising
• Determine goals • Analyze the audience • Gather and collect data • Analyze and organize information • Choose a form	• Be flexible • Keep going • Use your own favorite strategies	• Revise contents, structure, and format • Edit sentences and words • Proofread

LO1 Describe the writing process and effective writing strategies.

THE PROCESS OF WRITING

Writing researchers have been studying the composing process since the 1970s. They have found, not surprisingly, that each person's way of developing a piece of writing for a given situation is unique. On the other hand, they have also drawn several conclusions about the nature of the process and about strategies that can help it. Familiarizing yourself with these findings will help make you a more deliberate, effective writer.

As Figure 6–1 shows, preparing any piece of writing involves three stages: **planning**, **drafting**, and **revising**. These stages can be defined roughly as figuring out what you want to say, saying it, and then saying it better. Each of these stages can be divided into various specific activities, which the rest of this section describes. However, as the arrows in the figure suggest, business writers should not think of the three stages as strictly chronological or separate. In practice, the stages are interrelated. Like the steps for solving business communication problems described in Chapter 1, they are **recursive**. For example, a writer in the planning stage may start writing pieces of the draft. Or he or she may find when drafting that gathering more information is necessary. Or he or she may decide that it's necessary to revise a piece of the document carefully before continuing with the drafting. An undue emphasis on keeping the stages separate and chronological will hinder the success of your messages. Allow yourself to blend these stages as necessary.

A good rule of thumb for student writers is to spend roughly a third of their writing time in each of the three stages. A common mistake that writers make is to spend too much time on drafting and too little on the other two stages, planning and revising. Preparing to write and improving what you have written are as critical to success as the drafting stage, and careful attention to all three stages can actually make your writing process more efficient. Once you have become an experienced business writer, you will be able to write many routine messages without as much planning and revising. Even so, some planning and revising will still be essential to getting the best results with your messages.

Planning the Message

Chapter 1 presents a problem-solving approach to business communication. As Figure 1–4 indicates, you need to develop a definition of the problem that you are trying to solve. Once you have defined your problem, you can plan your message by answering several questions regarding your context and audience. As you plan written documents in particular, you can make the planning process more manageable by thinking about it in five smaller steps: determining goals; analyzing your audience; gathering and collecting information; analyzing and organizing the information; and choosing the form, channel, and format the document will take.

Planning a good message takes time. The reason is that you have a lot to consider when writing to an audience you may not know all that well. The investment of your time pays

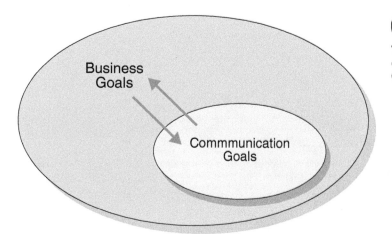

Figure 6–2

dividends when you are able not only to achieve the goal of your message but also to enhance your professional image by writing a coherent, concise, and thorough document.

Determining Goals. Because business writing is largely performed in response to a certain situation, one of your main planning tasks is to figure out what you want to do about that situation. Bear in mind that in business communication, "what to do" means not only what you want your communication to achieve but also any action related to the larger business problem. Let's say, for example, that you manage a hotel where the air conditioning has stopped functioning. You will need to decide what, if anything, to communicate to your guests about this problem. But this decision is related to other decisions. How and when will you get the air conditioning problem solved? In the meantime, will you simply apologize? Make arrangements for each guest to have a free continental breakfast or complimentary beverages? Rent fans for meeting rooms and any guest rooms occupied by people with health problems? As Figure 6–2 shows, solving the business problem and solving the communication problem are closely related. You will need to bring your **business goals** to bear on your **writing goals**—though sometimes, clarifying your writing goals will help you generate business solutions.

Analyzing Your Audience. Once you know your purpose—what you want your message to do—you need to think about the audience who will read your message. Who will be affected by what you write? What organizational, professional, and personal issues or qualities will affect the audience's response to your message? What organizational, professional, and personal issues or qualities do you have that affect how you will write your message? What is your relationship with your reader? Are you writing to your superior? Your colleagues? Your subordinates? Clients? Answers to these questions and others (see Figure 6–3) will influence your channel of communication, tone, style, content, organization, and format.

In the hotel manager scenario we discussed, for instance, how might your approach in an announcement to guests who are currently at the hotel differ from your approach in a response to a guest's complaint letter a week after the incident? Though you should take time to **analyze your audience** early in the planning process, you should continue to think of your audience as you proceed through the rest of the planning stage and through the drafting and revising stages, too. Always be thinking about what kind of information will matter most to your audience and adapt your message accordingly. If you fail to meet your audience's needs, your message fails as well, and your professional image is compromised.

Gathering Information. Once you have a sense of what you want your message to achieve and what your audience needs to know, you may need to do some research. In many cases this research can be informal—finding past correspondence; consulting with other employees or with outside advisors; or reviewing sales records, warranties, and product descriptions. In other cases you will do formal research such as conducting

Figure 6–3

**Audience Analysis
Checklist**

What is my relationship *to* my audience?

☐ Subordinate
☐ Colleague
☐ Superior
☐ Client/Customer
☐ Other: _____

What is my relationship *with* my audience?

☐ Friendly and informal. I know my audience well. We communicate often and have a social business relationship.
☐ Friendly and formal. We've met and have a cordial, business-like relationship.
☐ Neutral or no relationship. I don't know my audience personally.
☐ Unfriendly or hostile.
☐ Other: _____

What will my audience's reaction to my message be?

☐ Positive
☐ Negative
☐ Neutral

What factors in my company culture or other background information should I take into account?

☐ _____
☐ _____
☐ _____

What factors in my audience's culture or background should I take into account?

☐ _____
☐ _____
☐ _____

What does my audience need to know?

☐ _____
☐ _____
☐ _____

What does my audience already know?

☐ _____
☐ _____
☐ _____

What do I want my audience to think, feel, do, or believe as a result of my message?

☐ _____
☐ _____
☐ _____

_____ would be the best channel for delivering the message because _____.

surveys or reviewing the literature on a certain subject. Chapter 13 discusses various methods and sources at your disposal for this kind of research. In general, you will collect any information that can help you decide what to do and what to say in your message.

Gathering information by using your memory, imagination, and creativity is also important. Visualizing your readers and bearing their interests in mind is an excellent planning technique. Making a list of pertinent facts is helpful. Brainstorming (generating possible solutions without censoring them) will allow you to develop creative solutions. Drawing a diagram of your ideas can also enable you to collect your thoughts. Use any strategy that shows promise of contributing to a solution.

Analyzing and Organizing the Information. Once you have a number of ideas, you can start to **analyze** them. If your data are numerical, you will do the calculations that enable you to see patterns and meaning in the numbers. You will put other kinds of data together as well to see what course of action they might indicate, weighing what the parties involved stand to gain or lose from each possible solution.

As you ponder what to do and say with your message, you will, of course, keep your readers in mind. What kind of information will most matter to them? In the scenario described above, will the hotel guests want information about what caused the air conditioning problem or about when it will be fixed and what they can do to stay comfortable in the meantime? As always, your intended readers are your best guide to what information to include.

They are also your guide for **organizing** the information. Whatever order will draw the most positive reaction from your readers is the best order to use. If you have information that your readers will consider routine, neutral, or positive, put it first. This plan, called using the *direct order*, is discussed in the next chapter. On the other hand, if you think your information could run the risk of evoking a negative response, you will use an *indirect order*, using your message's opening to prepare the reader to receive the news as positively as possible. As you will see in Chapter 8, such a message usually requires a more skillful use of organization and word choice than one written in direct order. Regardless of the situation, all readers appreciate a logical pattern for the information.

Choosing a Form, Channel, and Format. Writers in school typically produce writing of two types: essays or research papers. But on the job you have a wide range of established **forms of communication** (genres) to choose from. Which one you use has a huge impact on your planning. For instance, if you want to advertise your company's services, how will you do it? Write potential customers a letter? Email them? Send a brochure? Create a website? Post a message on your company's social media sites? Use some combination of these? Each form has its own formatting and stylistic conventions and even conventions about content. Business writers do not launch into writing a document without some sense of what kind of document it will be. The medium itself helps them know what to say and how to say it. On the job, choosing the type of document to be written is an important part of planning.

Specific decisions about a document's format or visual design can be made at any point in the writing process, but usually the planning stage involves preliminary decisions along these lines. How can you make the information easily readable and accessible to your audience? Will you be dividing up the contents with headings? How about with a bulleted or numbered list? How long or short will the paragraphs be? Will there be any visual elements such as a logo or picture or diagram? Anticipating the format can help you plan an inviting and readable message.

Formatting devices have such a large impact on readers' reactions that we will discuss them separately in the next section. But decisions about formatting are an integral part of the business writer's writing process, even in the planning stage.

Drafting

Writing experts' main advice about drafting boils down to these words: "**Be flexible**." Writers often hinder themselves by thinking that they have to write a finished document on the first attempt with the parts in their correct order and with perfect results. Writing is such a cognitively difficult task that it is better to concentrate only on one thing at a time. The following suggestions can help you draft your messages as painlessly and effectively as possible.

Avoid Perfectionism When Drafting. Trying to make your first draft a perfect draft causes two problems. First, spending too much energy perfecting the early parts can make you forget important pieces and purposes of the later parts. Second, premature perfectionism can make drafting frustrating and slow and thus keep you from wanting to revise your message when you're done. You will be much more inclined to review your message and improve it if you have not agonized over your first draft.

Keep Going. When turning your planning into a draft, don't let minor problems with wording or grammar distract you from your main goal—to generate your first version of the document. Have an understanding with yourself that you will draft relatively quickly to get the ideas down on paper or onto the screen and then go back and carefully revise. Expressing your points in a somewhat coherent, complete, and orderly fashion is hard enough. Allow yourself to save close reexamination and evaluation of what you've written for the revision stage.

Use Any Other Strategies That Will Keep You Working Productively. The idea with drafting is to keep moving forward at a reasonably steady pace with as little stalling as possible. Do anything you can think of that will make your drafting relatively free and easy. For example, write at your most productive time of day, write in chunks, start with a favorite part, talk aloud or write to yourself to clarify your thoughts, take breaks, let the project sit for a while, create a setting conducive to writing—even promise yourself a little reward for getting a certain amount accomplished. Your goal is to get the first orderly expression of your planned contents written just well enough so that you can go back and work with it.

Revising

Getting your draft ready for your reader requires going back over it carefully—again and again. Do you say what you mean? Could someone misunderstand or take offense at what you have written? Is your organization best for the situation? Is each word the right one for your goals? Are there better, more concise ways of structuring your sentences? Can you move the reader more smoothly from point to point? Does each element of format enhance readability and highlight the structure of the contents? When revising, you turn into your own critic. You challenge what you have written and look for better alternatives. Careful attention to each level will result in a polished, effective message.

Any given message has so many facets that using what professional writers call "levels of edit" may be helpful. The levels this term refers to are *revising, editing,* and *proofreading.*

When **revising**, you look at top-level concerns: whether or not you included all necessary information, if the pattern of organization is logical and as effective as possible, if the overall meaning of the message comes through, and if the formatting is appropriate and helpful.

You then move to the **editing** level, focusing on your style. You examine your sentences to see if they pace the information in such a way that the reader can easily follow it, if they emphasize the right things, and if they combine pieces of information coherently. You also look at your word choices to see if they best serve your purpose.

Successful writers often seek others' perspectives on important documents.

Finally, you **proofread**, looking at mechanical and grammatical elements—spelling, typography, punctuation, and any grammar problems that tend to give you trouble. Editing functions in your word-processing program can help you with this task.

One last word about revision: Get feedback from others. As you may well know, it is difficult to find weaknesses or errors in your own work.

Seek assistance from willing colleagues, and if they give you criticism, receive it with an open mind. It is better to hear this feedback from them than from your intended readers when costly mistakes may have already been made.

THE IMPORTANCE OF READABLE FORMATTING

LO2 Explain the importance of readable formatting.

Have you ever opened a letter or a reading for a class, seen long, unbroken blocks of text, and dreaded jumping into the piece? Business readers are even more likely to have this reaction. They are far too bombarded with messages to have patience with this kind of document. If you want your readers to actually read what you write and get your ideas and information, you must pay attention to an important element of any message: its **physical format**.

Decades ago, you might well have been able to rely on a secretary or typist to format your documents for you. But widespread use of the personal computer with its full-featured publishing capabilities has placed the responsibility for readable formatting much more on the writer. Except for projects that involve a graphic designer, you will make the key formatting decisions for your messages. What kind and size of type will you use? What kind of headings? Will you use any means of typographical emphasis? How about numbered or bulleted lists? Should the document include such visual elements as logos, textboxes, pictures, or diagrams? Smart decisions on such matters will not only increase your readers' motivation to read but also enable them to quickly comprehend the main points and structure of the message.

For example, below is the starting text of a memo (sent by email) from a university registrar to the faculty with the subject line "'X' and 'WX' Grades Effective for Autumn '13 Grading." How inviting do you find the format, and how easy is it to extract the information about the two new grades?

At its October 20, 2013, meeting, the Faculty Senate, having received a favorable recommendation from the Academic Affairs Committee, voted to approve the creation and Autumn Quarter implementation of two new grades: "X" and "WX." Instructors will record an "X" on the final grade roster for students who never attended any classes and did not submit any assigned work. The "X" will appear on the transcript and will carry zero (0.00) quality points, thus computed into the GPA like the grades of "F" and "UW." Instructors will record a "WX" for those students who officially withdrew from the class (as denoted on the grade roster by either "EW" or "W") but who never attended any classes and did not submit any assigned work. The "WX" may be entered to overwrite a "W" appearing on the grade roster. An assignment of "WX" has no impact on the student's GPA. A "W" will appear on the student's online grade report and on the transcript. The "WX" recognizes the student's official withdrawal from the class and only records the fact of nonparticipation. The need to record nonparticipation is defined in "Rationale" below. With the introduction of the "X" and "WX" grades to denote nonparticipation, by definition all other grades can only be awarded to students who had participated in the class in some way. Instructors will record a "UW" (unofficial withdrawal) only for students who cease to attend a class following some participation. Previously, instructors utilized the "UW" both for those students who had never attended classes and for those who had attended and participated initially but had ceased to attend at some point during the term. In cases of official withdrawal, instructors have three options available at the time of grading: "W," "WX," and "F." If the student has officially withdrawn from the class, a "W" (withdrawal) or "EW" (electronic withdrawal) will appear on the grade roster. If the student participated in the class and the withdrawal was in accordance with the instructor's withdrawal policy as communicated by the syllabus, the instructor may retain the student's "W" grade by making no alteration to the grade roster. . . .

Now look at the first part of the actual message that was sent out. What formatting decisions on the part of the writer made this document much more readable?

At its October 20, 2013, meeting, the Faculty Senate, having received a favorable recommendation from the Academic Affairs Committee, voted to approve the creation and Autumn Quarter implementation of two new grades: "X" and "WX."

Definition of "X" and "WX" Grades, Effective Autumn Quarter 2013

- "X" (nonattendance):

   Instructors will record an "X" on the final grade roster for students who never attended any classes and did not submit any assigned work.

   The "X" will appear on the transcript and will carry zero (0.00) quality points, thus computed into the GPA like the grades of "F" and "UW."

- "WX" (official withdrawal, nonattending):

   Instructors will record a "WX" for those students who officially withdrew from the class (as denoted on the grade roster by either "EW" or "W") but who never attended any classes and did not submit any assigned work.

   The "WX" may be entered to overwrite a "W" appearing on the grade roster. An assignment of "WX" has no impact on the student's GPA. A "W" will appear on the student's online grade report and on the transcript. The "WX" recognizes the student's official withdrawal from the class and only records the fact of nonparticipation. The need to record nonparticipation is defined in "Rationale" below.

Participation and Nonparticipation Grades

With the introduction of the "X" and "WX" grades to denote nonparticipation, by definition all other grades can only be awarded to students who had participated in the class in some way.

Instructors will record a "UW" (unofficial withdrawal) only for students who cease to attend a class following some participation. Previously, instructors utilized the "UW" both for those students who had never attended classes and for those who had attended and participated initially but had ceased to attend at some point during the term.

Official Withdrawals

In cases of official withdrawal, instructors have three options available at the time of grading: "W," "WX," and "F."

1. *If the student has officially withdrawn from the class,* a "W" (withdrawal) or "EW" (electronic withdrawal) will appear on the grade roster. If the student participated in the class and the withdrawal was in accordance with the instructor's withdrawal policy as communicated by the syllabus, the instructor may retain the student's "W" grade by making no alteration to the grade roster. . . .

Reprinted with permission from Dr. Douglas Burgess, Registrar, University of Cincinnati.

The remaining sections of this chapter describe specific purposes and traits of different message types. Appendix B provides in-depth advice about their physical design. No matter what you're writing, taking time to make careful formatting decisions during your writing process will significantly enhance your chances of achieving your communication goals.

LETTERS

LO3 Describe the development and current usage of the business letter.

Letters are the oldest form of business messages. The ancient Chinese wrote letters, as did the early Egyptians, Romans, and Greeks. In fact, American businesspeople used letters as early as 1698 to correspond about sales, collections, and other business matters.[2]

From these early days letters have continued to be used in business. Although their use and purpose have evolved as other business communication genres have developed, they are still the best choice for many communication tasks.

Letters Defined

The general purpose of a letter is to represent the writer and his or her topic rather formally to the recipient. For this reason, **letters** are used primarily for corresponding with people outside your organization. When you write to internal readers, they are often familiar to you—and even if they are not, you all share the connection of being in the same company. Your messages to such audiences tend to use less formal media. But when you write to customers, to suppliers, to citizens and community leaders, and to other **external audiences**, you will often want to present a professional, polished image of your company by choosing the letter format, complete with an attractive company letterhead and the elements of courtesy built into this traditional format. Your readers will expect this gesture of respect. Once you have established friendly relations with them, you may well conduct your business through emails, phone calls, instant or text messaging, and social media. But especially when corresponding with an external party whom you do not know well, a letter is often the most appropriate form to use.

Letter Form

The format of the business letter is probably already familiar to you. Although some variations in format are generally acceptable, typically these information items are included: date, inside address, salutation (Dear Ms. Smith), body, and complimentary close (Sincerely yours). Other items sometimes needed are attention line, subject line, return address (when letterhead is not used), and enclosure information. Figure 6–4 presents one option for formatting a letter. More options are presented in Appendix B.

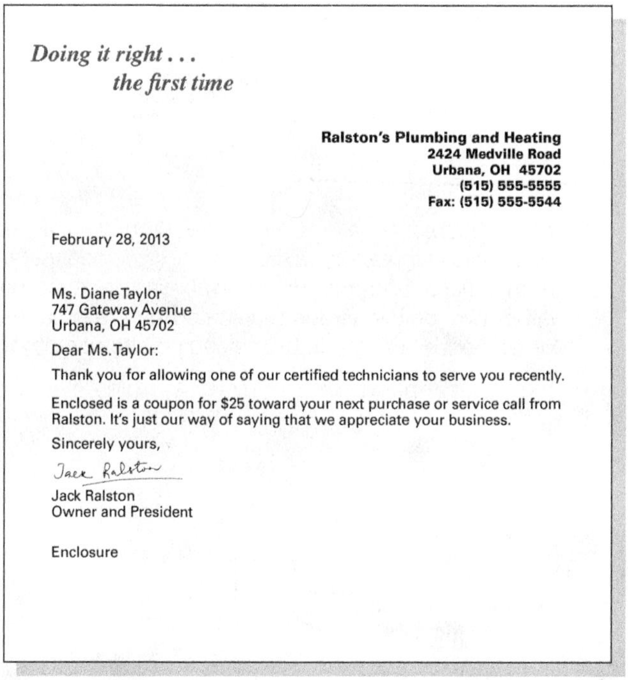

Doing it right . . .
the first time

Ralston's Plumbing and Heating
2424 Medville Road
Urbana, OH 45702
(515) 555-5555
Fax: (515) 555-5544

February 28, 2013

Ms. Diane Taylor
747 Gateway Avenue
Urbana, OH 45702

Dear Ms. Taylor:

Thank you for allowing one of our certified technicians to serve you recently.

Enclosed is a coupon for $25 toward your next purchase or service call from Ralston. It's just our way of saying that we appreciate your business.

Sincerely yours,

Jack Ralston

Jack Ralston
Owner and President

Enclosure

Figure 6–4

Illustration of a Letter in Full Block Format (Mixed Punctuation)

[2] JoAnne Yates, *Control through Communication: The Rise of System in American Management* (Baltimore: The Johns Hopkins UP, 1989) 95, print.

Letter Formality

As formal as letters can be, they are not nearly as formal as they used to be. Chapter 5 points out that business messages have grown more conversational. This is true of letters as well as of other forms of correspondence.

For instance, in the past, if writers did not know the reader's name, wrote to a mass audience, or wrote to someone whose gender could not be determined by the reader's name (e.g., Pat Smith), they might have used a salutation such as "To Whom It May Concern," "Dear Sir/Madame," or "Dear Ladies and Gentlemen." These expressions are now considered stiff and old fashioned. More modern options include "Dear Human Resources" or "Dear Pat Smith." Writers can also omit the salutation, perhaps adding a subject line (a brief phrase stating the writer's main point) instead. Some business writers also consider the use of the terms "Dear," "Sincerely Yours," and even "Sincerely," outdated or excessively formal. These writers will omit "Dear," replace "Sincerely yours" with "Sincerely," omit the complimentary close, or use "Best regards" or some other cordial phrase. Your audience and company culture will determine what is appropriate for you.

Regardless of its formality, the letter should always be regarded as an exchange between real people as well as a strategic means for accomplishing business goals.

LO4 Describe the purpose and form of memorandums (memos).

MEMORANDUMS (MEMOS)
Memorandums Defined

Memorandums, or **memos**, are a form of letter written inside the business. Though in rare cases they may be used to communicate with those outside the business, they are usually exchanged **internally** by employees as they conduct their work. Originally,

Businesses with multiple locations send many of their internal messages by email as well as instant and text messaging.

memos were used only in hard copy, but their function of communicating within a business has been largely replaced by email. Even so, they still are a part of many companies' communications. They are especially useful for communicating with employees who do not use computers in their work.

Memos can be used for a wide range of communication tasks. For example, as Chapter 12 points out, some memos communicate factual, problem-related information and can be classified as reports. As with the letter, the purpose and use of the memo have evolved as other business communication genres have emerged, but the memo is still an important means for communicating in many organizations.

Memorandum Form

Memorandums can be distinguished from other messages primarily by their form. Some companies have stationery printed especially for memos, while many use standard or customized templates in word processors. Sometimes the word *memorandum* appears at the top. But some companies prefer other titles, such as *Interoffice Memo* or *Interoffice Communication*. Below this main heading come the specific headings common to all memos: *Date, To, From, Subject* (though not necessarily in this order). This simple arrangement is displayed in Figure 6–5. As the figure indicates, hard-copy memos are initialed by the writer rather than signed.

Large organizations, especially those with a number of locations and departments, often include additional information on their memorandum stationery. *Department, Plant, Location, Territory, Store Number*, and *Copies to* are examples (see Figure 6–6). Since in some companies memos are often addressed to more than one reader, the heading *To* may be followed by enough space to list a number of names.

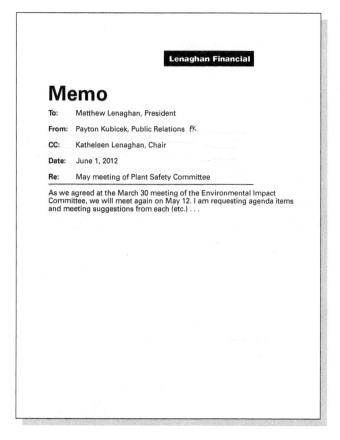

Figure 6–5

Illustration of Memo Form Using the MS Word Professional Template

Penny-Wise Stores, Inc.

MEMORANDUM

To: **Date:**

                                          From:

Store: **Store:**

At: **At:**

Territory: **Territory:**

Copies to:

Subject: Form for In-house Letters (Memos)

This is an illustration of our memorandum stationery. It should be used for written communications within the organization.

Notice that the memorandum uses no form of salutation. Neither does it have any form of complimentary close. The writer does not need to sign the message. He or she needs only to initial after the typed name in the heading.

Notice also that the message is single-spaced with double-spacing between paragraphs.

Memorandum Formality

Because memos usually are messages sent and received by people who work with and know one another, they tend to use casual or informal language. Even so, some memos use highly formal language. As in any business communication, you will use the level of formality appropriate to your audience and writing goals.

EMAIL

Although businesspeople routinely communicate via social media, text messaging, and instant messaging, email remains the most widely used means of written communication in the workplace. In fact, even among those businesspeople who use tablets, email is the most frequently used app.[3]

Email Defined

According to one estimate, 92 percent of Americans use **email**—a number that has remained constant even with the advent and popular use of text messaging, instant messaging, and social media.[4] It's easy to see why email remains popular. Email addresses are readily available, and anyone can send a message to any email address (or multiple addresses simultaneously), regardless of who provides the email account. The speed at which readers receive a message can also make email more attractive than a letter or a memo. Consequently, businesses continue to use email as a low-cost, quick, and efficient means of communicating with both **internal and external audiences**

---

[3] PRWeb, "Tablets Make Their Way into the Workplace: Email and Note Taking are the Most Popular Business Uses, Says NPD In-Stat," *PRWeb*, Vocus, Inc., 14 Feb. 2012, Web, 22 May 2012.

[4] Kristen Purcell, "Search and Email Still Top the List of Most Popular Online Activities," *Pew Internet & American Life Project*, Pew Research Center, 9 Aug. 2011, Web, 24 May 2012.

either formally or informally. Furthermore, email provides HTML and other formatting options that text messaging, instant messaging, and social media may not, and it does not limit the writer to any number of characters or amount of text. In addition, emails can be archived and filed for easy access to a written record of correspondence.

Email, however, also presents communication challenges. Sometimes people use email to avoid having difficult face-to-face or phone conversations, which is not a good way to accomplish communication goals or cultivate the audience's goodwill. Emails are also easily forwarded and therefore can never be considered confidential. Additionally, many businesspeople deal with spam—unsolicited messages or mass emails that are not relevant to their work. Moreover, some writers may assume that an informal email message is not held to the same standards of professionalism, clarity, or correctness as a more formal message might be. Finally, when not used properly, email can be costly. According to one source, "In 2010 organizations lost about $1,250 per user a year in productivity due to spam and up to $4,100 per year due to emails [that] were written poorly."[5] It is important, then, that business writers ensure their emails communicate clearly, cultivate goodwill, and promote a professional image.

Email Form

When you look at an email, you likely notice that its form contains elements of both memos and letters. For example, emails generally contain a *Date, To, From, Subject* heading structure similar to that of a memo. They may also contain salutations and complimentary closes similar to those found in letters.

Although the various email systems differ somewhat, email format includes the following:

- **To:** This is where you include the email address of the recipients. Be sure the address is accurate.

- **Cc:** If someone other than the primary recipient is to receive a *courtesy copy,* his or her address goes here. Before people used computers, *cc:* was called a *carbon copy* to reflect the practice of making copies on carbon paper.

- **Bcc:** This line stands for *blind courtesy copy.* The recipient's message will not show this information; that is, he or she will not know who else is receiving a copy of the message.

- **Subject:** This line describes the message as precisely as the situation permits. The reader should get from it a clear idea of what the message is about. Always include a subject line to get your reader's attention and indicate the topic of the message. In the absence of a subject line, a reader may think your message is junk mail or unimportant and delete it.

- **Attachments:** In this area you can enter a file that you desire to send along with the message. Attach only files the reader needs so that you do not take up unneeded space in his or her inbox.

- **The message:** The information you are sending goes here. Typically, email messages begin with the recipient's name. If the writer and reader are acquainted, you can use the reader's first name. If you would normally address the reader by using a title (Ms., Dr., Mr.), address him or her this way in an initial email. You can change the salutation in subsequent messages if the person indicates that informality is desired. The salutations commonly used in letters (Dear Mr. Dayle, Dear Jane) are sometimes used, but something less formal ("Hi, Ron") or no salutation at all is more common. A friendly generic greeting such as "Greetings" is appropriate for a group of people with whom you communicate. As we discussed in the section on letters, you'll want to avoid outdated expressions such as "To Whom It May Concern." Like a letter, an email message often ends with a complimentary close followed by a signature block containing the writer's name,

---

[5]Govloop, "Does Email Help or Hinder Your Professional Productivity?" *AOL Government*, AolGov, 24 Apr. 2012, Web, 24 May 2012.

Figure 6–7

**Illustration of Email Form
Using Microsoft Outlook**

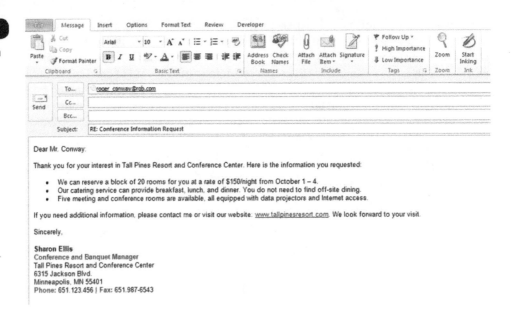

job title, company, and contact information. Some writers also use the signature block as an opportunity to promote a sale, product, or service. Figure 6–7 shows a standard email format.

Email Formality

A discussion of email formality is complicated by the fact that email messages are extremely diverse. They run the range from highly informal to formal. The informal messages often resemble face-to-face oral communication; some even sound like chitchat that occurs between acquaintances and friends. Others, as we have noted, have the increased formality of reports.

A helpful approach is to view email language in terms of three general classifications: **casual**, **informal**, and **formal**.[6] Your audience should determine which type of language you choose, regardless of your personal style or preference.

Casual. By casual language we mean the language we use in talking with close friends in everyday situations. It includes slang, colloquialisms (informal expressions), contractions, and personal pronouns. Its sentences are short—sometimes incomplete—and it may use mechanical emphasis devices and initialisms (e.g., LOL, BTW) freely. Casual language is best limited to your communications with close friends. Following is an example of casual language:

Hey, Cindy,

Props for me! Just back from reps meeting. We totally nailed it . . . plan due ASAP. Meet, my office, 10 AM, Wed?

Brandon

Use casual language only when you know your readers well—when you know they expect and prefer casual communication. You should also avoid slang, initialisms, emphasis devices, or other casual elements if you are not certain that they will communicate clearly.

Informal. Informal language retains some of the qualities of casual writing. It makes some use of personal pronouns and contractions. It occasionally may use colloquialisms but more selectively than in casual writing. It has the effect of conversation, but it

---

[6]Heidi Schultz, *The Elements of Electronic Communication* (Boston: Allyn and Bacon, 2000) 43–47, print.

Using Good Email Etiquette Helps Writers Achieve Their Goals

Using proper email etiquette is as easy as applying a bit of empathy to your messages: Send only what you would want to receive. The following additional etiquette guides will help you consider a variety of issues when using email.

- Is your message really needed by the recipient(s)?

- Is your message for routine rather than sensitive messages?

- Are you sure your message is not spam (an annoying message sent repeatedly) or a chain letter?

- Have you carefully checked that your message is going where you want it to go?

- Has your wording avoided defamatory or libelous language?

- Have you complied with copyright laws and cited sources accurately?

- Have you avoided humor and sarcasm that your reader may not understand as intended?

- Have you proofread your message carefully?

- Is this a message you would not mind having distributed widely?

- Does your signature avoid offensive quotes or illustrations, especially those that are religious, political, or sexual?

- Is your recipient willing or able to accept attached files?

- Are attached files a size that your recipient's system can handle?

- Are the files you are attaching virus free?

---

is polished conversation—not chitchat. Its sentences are short, but they are well structured and organized. They have varied patterns that produce an interesting style. In general, it is the writing that you will find in most of the illustrations in Chapters 7–9, and it is the language that this book uses. You should use it in most of your business email messages, especially when writing to people you know only on a business basis. An example of an email message in informal language is the following:

Cindy:

The management team has approved our marketing plan. They were very complimentary. As you predicted, they want a special plan for the large accounts. They want it as soon as possible, so let's get together to work on it. Can we meet Wednesday, 10 A.M., my office?

Brandon

> PS. Dear Boss. I know you are reading this
> email as I type so I am writing to you to say
> STOP SPYING ON ME AND GET BACK
> TO WORK THIS MINUTE!

SOURCE: From www.sangreat.net.

Composing an Email: The Top 10 Mistakes

Writing an effective email takes careful thought and planning. The top 10 mistakes managers make when composing email include (1) using vague subject lines such as "meeting"; (2) hiding the main point; (3) using the "BCC" field to be sneaky in their communication; (4) not deleting strings of replies and forwards the reader does not need to see; (5) ignoring grammar and mechanics; (6) avoiding long emails—though sometimes long messages are necessary; (7) creating long, poorly organized paragraphs; (8) avoiding emotion or using an inappropriate tone and style; (9) using email when it's not the best communication channel; and (10) forgetting that email creates a permanent record of their decisions and behavior.

SOURCE: Tim Flood, "Top Ten Mistakes Managers Make with Email," *WSJ.com, The Wall Street Journal*, 4 Feb. 2010, Web, 8 June 2012.

Formal. A formal style of writing maintains a greater distance between writer and reader than an informal style. It avoids personal references and contractions, and its sentences are well structured and organized. Formal style is well illustrated in the examples of the more formal reports in Chapter 12. It is appropriate to use in email messages resembling formal reports, in messages to people of higher status, and to people not known to the writer.

As with any business message, formal or informal, your emails should achieve your communication goal, promote goodwill, and present a professional image. To do this, follow the advice in Chapters 2–5 for writing clear, courteous messages. You will also want to follow the guides in Chapter 18 to ensure your messages are expressed correctly.

THE NEWER MEDIA IN BUSINESS WRITING

Sometimes writers in today's fast-paced, global business world need to communicate more immediately and quickly than a letter, a memo, or an email will allow. Technology provides business writers with many more channels for immediate, quick communication including text messaging, instant messaging, and social networking.

However, as with more traditional business writing media such as letters, memos, and emails, the use of these more immediate channels should be driven by audience needs and expectations as well as the writer's goals and purposes.

LO6 Understand the nature and business uses of text messaging and instant messaging.

Text Messaging

Text messaging, also called short message service (SMS), is, as its name suggests, used for sending short messages generally from a mobile phone. Because the purpose of a text message is to convey a quick message, the writing in text messages is quite different from that in the more traditional message forms. Because mobile phone service providers may limit the number of characters in a text message, the emphasis is on brevity. You include only the essentials.

The need for brevity has led to the use of many abbreviations. So many of these abbreviations have developed that one might say a new language has developed. In fact, a dictionary of over 1,100 text messaging abbreviations has been compiled at Webopedia, an online computer technology encyclopedia (www.webopedia.com /quick_ref/textmessageabbreviations.asp). Some examples are the following:

b4 (before)   u (you)

gr8 (great)   BTW (by the way)

CU (see you)   NP (no problem)

COMMUNICATION MATTERS

"Twitiquette": New Technologies, New Expectations

As new communication genres and technologies become mainstream, so do acceptable practices for using them. Now that Twitter and "tweeting" are part of our everyday business communication, many writers use Twitter for routine messages. Standards for their professional use are emerging—referred to as *twitiquette*. It's tempting to think that messages limited to 140 characters would be easy to construct, but though tweets are short and direct, a lot can go wrong in a very short time. *PCWorld* offers these tips for ensuring that your audience gets your intended message:

- Use a blog instead of Twitter for long commentary rather than send numerous tweets. Your followers may be overwhelmed by "running commentary" on a topic, especially if you do not usually post several tweets in succession.

- Consider which type of message—a private message (D message) or a public message (@ message)—is appropriate for your audience and purpose.

- Check spelling and avoid excessive acronyms. Because smart phones have QWERTY keyboards, *PCWorld* advises users to avoid "abbrevo-speak" unless you really need space. Further, "No matter how many people fail to take it seriously, spelling still counts on Twitter."

- Try to get tweets into one sentence.

- If you are retweeting and exceed 140 characters, shorten or edit the retweet, though you should try to preserve the original meaning and language.

- Remember that Twitter is public. Don't post anything you wouldn't want everyone to know.

SOURCE: Christopher Null, "Twitter Etiquette: How to Tweet Politely," *PC World*, PCWorld Communications, Inc., 28 July 2009, Web, 8 June 2012.

FBM (fine by me)	HRY (how are you)
TC (take care)	TYT (take your time)

In addition to abbreviations, writers use typed symbols to convey emotions (emoticons), which can also be found at Webopedia:

:-) standard smiley	:-! foot in mouth
;) winking smile	:-(sad or frown
:-0 yell	(((H))) hugs

Whether and when these abbreviations and emoticons are used depends on the writer's relationship with the audience.

Good business writers will compose text messages that not only convey the writer's message but also allow for brief responses from the receiver. Let's say, for example, that you've learned that an important visiting customer is a vegetarian and you have reservations for lunch at Ruth's Chris Steakhouse. You need to let your boss know—before the lunch meeting. However, the boss is leading an important meeting in which a phone call would be disruptive and inappropriate, so you decide to send a text message.

Your immediate thought might be to send the following: *Marina Smith is a vegetarian. Where should we take her for lunch today? Zeke.*

Many businesspeople use their phones to send and receive emails and text messages. With such a small display screen, conciseness and clarity are especially important.

Although your message does convey the major fact and is only 77 characters counting spaces, it forces the recipient to enter a long response—the name of another place. It might also result in more message exchanges about availability and time.

A better version might be this: *Marina Smith is a vegetarian. Shall we go to 1) Fish House, 2) Souplantation, 3) Mandarin House? All are available at noon. Zeke*

This version conveys the major fact in 130 characters and allows the recipient to respond simply with 1, 2, or 3. As the writer, you took the initiative to anticipate your reader's needs, identify appropriate alternatives, and then gather information—steps that are as important with text messaging as they are with other messages. If your text messages are clear, complete, and concise and have a professional and pleasant tone, you will find them a valuable tool for business use.

Instant Messaging

Instant messaging, commonly referred to as IM-ing or online chatting, is much like telephone conversation in that parties communicate in real time (instantly). It differs primarily in that it is text-based (typed) rather than voice-based communication, though voice-based instant messaging is possible. Many writers will use the same abbreviations and emoticons in instant messages that they use in text messages. Here again, the use of these devices depends on your audience and purpose.

Because instant messages are similar to phone conversations, you should write **instant messages** much as you would talk in conversation with another person. If the person is a friend, your language should reflect this friendship. If the person is the president of your company, a business associate, or fellow worker, the relationship should guide you. The message bits presented in instant messaging are determined largely by the flow of the conversation. Responses often are impromptu. Even so, in business situations you should consciously direct the flow toward your objective and keep your language and content professional.

LO7 Understand the nature and business uses of social media.

Social Media

You are probably familiar with such **social media** sites as Facebook, Twitter, or LinkedIn. Perhaps you have a blog (a "Web log") where you keep an online diary or journal that you share publicly. Although you may use these sites to connect with friends, family, or classmates, many business writers also use them to connect with clients, customers, colleagues, and supervisors, as they answer questions, promote products, network with other professionals, or interact briefly with co-workers. Business professionals, then, are using social networking sites for purposes that are likely very different from your purpose in using them (see the corporate blog in Figure 6–8).

Generally, the messages on social networking sites are brief, with some sites, such as Twitter, restricting messages to 140 characters. As with text messaging, messages must not only be brief but concise and clear. If you have only so much space for your message, you need to make sure your reader immediately knows your point and has enough detail to act on your message. Therefore, messages on social media sites should begin with your main point (what you need your reader to do, think, feel, or believe as a result of reading your message) and then follow with details in order of importance.

In addition, because the messages on these sites are public, you never want to use language or a tone or writing style that you would be embarrassed to have your boss see, that may have legal implications, or that might get you fired. In fact, if you currently have a page on a social networking site where family and friends are your audience, you will want to remove any pictures or language that you wouldn't want a prospective employer, current employer, co-worker, customer, or client to see. No matter how private you believe your page to be, you can never know what your friends and family are sharing with other people. Mashable.com cites a study by Reppler, a social media monitoring service, that found "more than 90 percent of recruiters and hiring managers have visited a potential candidate's profile on a social network." Interestingly, the study found that employers are just as likely to reject a candidate (69 percent) as

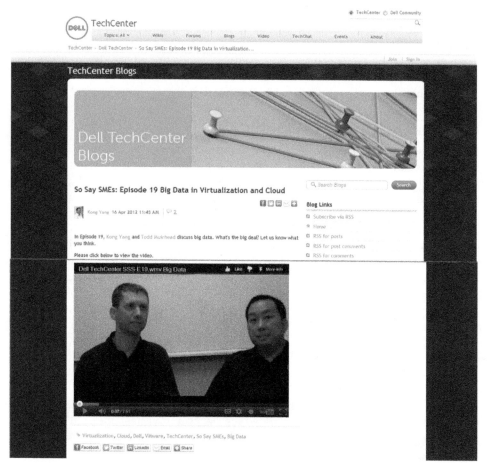

Figure 6–8

Example of a Corporate Blog
SOURCE: Copyright © Dell Inc. All Rights Reserved.

they are to hire a candidate (68 percent) based on what is on someone's social networking site.[7]

Regardless of the type of business messages you send, remember that on the job, companies often monitor employees' computer activity. They can detect excessive use, inappropriate or unethical behavior, disclosure of proprietary information, use of sexually explicit language, and attachments with viruses. Companies' monitoring systems also have features that protect the company from legal liabilities. As a business professional, you must know your company's computer use policy and avoid writing anything that would reflect poorly on you or your company or put you or your company at risk.

PRINT VERSUS ONLINE DOCUMENTS

LO8 Understand the inverted pyramid structure for organizing and writing Web documents.

As we have discussed, business professionals use a variety of print and electronic genres for business writing. The basic principles of business writing apply to both print and electronic text; that is, your text must be *reader-centered, accessible, complete, concise, and accurate.* Though electronic documents often provide the opportunity for more creative and interactive features than print documents, these features are useless if your reader does not have the technology to access them. Furthermore, no matter how great your blog or your website looks, if your message is unclear or incomplete, your blog or site serves no purpose. Business writers also have to realize that many audiences may be

[7]Erica Swallow, "How Recruiters Use Social Networks to Screen Candidates," *Mashable.com*, Mashable, Inc., 23 Oct. 2011, Web, 26 May 2012.

viewing a company's website on a mobile device with a small viewing area. In fact, Janice Redish, an expert in Web writing says, "Understanding your site visitors and their needs is critical to deciding what to write, how much to write, the vocabulary to use, and how to organize the content on your website." While this advice also applies when writing print documents, writing for online delivery presents special considerations.[8] The following are the main ones to keep in mind.

Comparing Print and Online Text

Jakob Nielsen, noted usability expert, has found that Web readers read an average of 20 percent of the words on a page.[9] He says that print text can be distinguished from Web text in that print text tends to be linear, while Web text is nonlinear. That is, when people read print documents, they often start at the beginning and continue reading until they reach the end. By contrast, online readers scan for relevant information and may be diverted by links or other features of the display in their search. In addition, he says that when people look for information in electronic documents, particularly on the Web, they do so not necessarily to read what an author has to say about an issue but to accomplish a specific task (e.g., locate a statistic, fill out a form). Online text, then, needs to facilitate the reader's ability to find and use information.

Furthermore, online text can produce comprehensive data more concisely than a print document. Because technology allows writers to embed links to relevant or related information rather than include that information in a paragraph or on a page, electronic documents can incorporate a lot of information in a relatively small space. Print documents, though, could become quite long and unwieldy if an author were to try to include every fact, statistic, or resource related to the topic at hand.

Lastly, print documents generally require that thoughts be expressed in complete sentences, with occasional bulleted lists added for clarity and visual appeal. In electronic documents, writers tend to rely much more on bulleted lists and other terse forms of text. Depending on the medium, they may use fragments and frequent abbreviations.

Organizing Content

Redish notes that most people visit Web pages because they need to *do* something. Consequently, they do not read as much as they scan for information, and they want what they need quickly, which means that writers should "think 'information,' not 'document.'"[10] As with print documents, online information must be organized well. Redish advocates organizing Web pages in the **inverted pyramid style**, where the main point is presented first, followed by supporting information and then by any historical or background information (see Figure 6–9).

Figure 6–9

Illustration of the "Inverted Pyramid" Structure
SOURCE: "Inverted Pyramid Writing," *Google Images*, Google, 2009, Web, 30 May 2012.

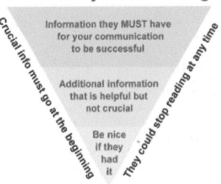

Other kinds of electronic documents can benefit from this advice as well. If readers are merely scanning for information, they may not scroll for information, which means that the main point must stand out. Similar to information in printed business documents, information in electronic documents should be chunked in short paragraphs and contain headings and lists that emphasize a logical structure and presentation of the information. Figure 6–10 provides an example of writing in the inverted pyramid style.

---

[8]Janice Redish, *Letting Go of the Words: Writing Web Content That Works* (San Francisco: Elsevier, 2012) 20, print.
[9]Jakob Nielsen, "Writing Style for Print vs. Web," *Alert Box*, Jakob Nielsen, 7 June 2008, Web, 12 July 2009.
[10]Redish 102.

News

SAP to pay $4.3B for cloud B2B vendor Ariba

By Chris Kanaracus
June 4, 2012 06:00 AM ET   ⬭ Add a comment    + Briefcase   What's this?

Computerworld - SAP has agreed to purchase cloud-based e-commerce vendor Ariba for $4.3 billion.

The deal has been unanimously approved by Ariba's board and is expected to close by Sept. 30.

The addition of Ariba's business-to-business commerce platform will expand SAP's cloud software lineup, which got an earlier boost from the ERP vendor's recent $3.4 billion acquisition of SuccessFactors, a provider of human resources services.

SAP's cloud computing strategy is aimed at enabling the company to compete against traditional rivals such as Oracle, as well as pure cloud vendors like Workday and NetSuite.

Ariba reported $444 million in 2011 revenue and said its trading network is involved with more than $319 billion in "commerce transactions, collaborations, and intelligence among more than 730,000 companies," according to a statement.

SAP said it will consolidate all "cloud-related supplier assets" under the auspices of Ariba, which will operate as an independent subsidiary.

The company plans to keep Ariba's platform open, allowing it to accept data from "any source," according to SAP co-CEO Bill McDermott. SAP also plans to use the platform it bought last year from Crossgate, which has some of the same features as Ariba's.

Figure 6–10

Example of an Online Article Written in the Inverted Pyramid Structure.
SOURCE: Used with permission of Computerworld Online. Copyright © 2012. All rights reserved.

Presenting the Content

Your choice of design elements (font, color, and graphics) depends on your audience. Redish notes that one of the important differences between print and electronic documents is that the resolution (sharpness of the letters and images) is lower on a screen than in print. Thus, while you can use a variety of serif and sans serif fonts in a variety of sizes in print documents, you will want to choose sans serif fonts (those without tails at the ends of the letters) in at least a 12-point size for most online documents so that the serifs do not obscure the text. In addition, readers usually see printed documents on 8½ × 11 paper, but online readers may see electronic documents in windows of varying sizes. For this reason, Redish recommends a line length of 50 to 70 characters or 8 to 10 words. Short lines are also more quickly and easily read, though you do not want lines so short that your text does not capture the main point.

Likewise, text formatting conventions differ in print and electronic environments. In both environments, writers can use emphasis devices such as bullets, headings, bold text, or italics. However, because underlining also represents links in electronic environments, writers should favor italics or bold text in that context.

In addition, as with printed text, writers should use colors that are appropriate for an audience's culture and visually appealing. For most readers, this will be a dark text on a light background.

Making Your Web Writing Accessible

Many businesses have seen the wisdom of ensuring that their websites are accessible by people with disabilities; in fact, accessibility is generally required by law. Many features of the Web that we take for granted may present difficulties for those with disabilities. For instance, how do people with hearing impairments access audio content on a website? How do people with visual disabilities access text? How does a person with a motor impairment use a mouse? Incorporating text along with audio files gives people who have hearing impairments access to a site, while incorporating text with visuals enables the screen readers of those with visual impairments to "read" the visual for the user. People with motor disabilities can be helped with voice-activated features or key commands rather than mouse-controlled navigation.

THERE'S MORE . . .

Would you like to learn more about the writing process? Are you curious about uses of social media in business? Do you need additional advice on writing for the Web? Scan the QR code with your smartphone or use your Web browser to find out at www.mhhe.com/lesikar13e. Choose Chapter 6 > Bizcom Tools & Tips.

SUMMARY BY LEARNING OBJECTIVES

Describe the writing process and effective writing strategies.

1. The writing process consists of five main stages:
   - Planning includes the following activities:
     — Determining goals.
     — Analyzing the audience.
     — Gathering and collecting information.
     — Analyzing and organizing the information.
     — Choosing a form, channel, and format.
   - Drafting needs to be flexible.
     — Avoid perfectionism when drafting.
     — Keep going—don't stop for excessive tinkering.
     — Pursue any strategy that will help you make progress on the draft.
   - Revising involves three main levels of edit:
     — Revising for content, organization, and format.
     — Editing sentences and words.
     — Proofreading to catch mechanical and grammatical errors.
   - The five stages are recursive—you can revisit earlier stages at any time.

Explain the importance of readable formatting.

2. Making good formatting decisions is critical to your messages' success.
   - Good formatting makes your messages inviting.
   - Good formatting makes your information easier to find and follow.

3. These are the highlights of the development of business letters:

- The early civilizations (Chinese, Greek, Roman, Egyptian) used them.

- They are now used largely in more formal situations, especially with external audiences.

- Letter formats are standardized (see Appendix B).

- Early business letters used a stilted language.

- Strategic organization and humanized language characterize today's letters.

Describe the development and current usage of the business letter.

4. The memorandum (memo) is a form of letter written inside the business.

- Hard-copy memorandums usually are processed on special stationery (*Memorandum* at the top; *Date, To, From,* and *Subject* follow).

- Large organizations often include more information (*Department, Plant, Location, Copies to, Store Number,* etc.)

- Memos vary widely in formality, but most are relatively informal.

- Most memos are written in the direct order, though sometimes strategic indirectness is needed.

Describe the purpose and form of memorandums (memos).

5. Email is a popular communication channel in business.

- Emails are written to internal and external audiences.

- Emails can communicate quickly to one person or to many.

- Email is convenient because messages can be sent to anyone with an email address, regardless of where the email account is located.

- Email provides HTML or other editing tools for text formatting.

- Email provides a convenient means of archiving, filing, and retrieving messages.

- Emails can have a tone that is casual, informal, or formal depending on the audience.

- Email form has some characteristics of memos (e.g., *Date, To, From, Subject* lines) and some characteristics of letters (e.g., a salutation and a complimentary close).

- Email should never be considered confidential.

- Email should not be used as a means of avoiding face-to-face or phone interaction.

Describe the purpose and form of email.

6. Text messaging and instant messaging (IM-ing) are important newer types of business messages.

- Text messaging is widely used today.

- The writing stresses brevity and uses shortcuts—but never at the expense of clarity.

- Instant messaging is like a telephone conversation, but it uses type rather than voice.

- Write your instant messages as though you were talking to the other person.

Understand the nature and business uses of text messaging and instant messaging.

7. Social networking sites are becoming increasingly popular.

- Business writers use them to connect with professional colleagues, co-workers, clients, and customers.

- Be sure that content for any social networking site presents a positive professional image.

Understand the nature and business uses of social media.

8. Many business writers will find themselves creating documents that are read online. To write effective accessible online documents, you should do the following:

— Analyze your audience.

— Organize your message in the inverted pyramid style.

— Use a sans serif font in at least 12-point type.

— Keep lines of text and paragraphs short.

— Use emphasis devices such as bold text, italics, bullets, and headings; avoid underlining.

— Ensure that your site can be accessed by those who have disabilities.

Understand the inverted pyramid structure for organizing and writing Web documents.

planning, 116

drafting, 116

revising, 116

recursive, 116

business goals, 117

writing goals, 117

analyze your audience, 117

gathering information, 118

analyze, 119

organizing, 119

forms of communication, 119

be flexible, 119

revising, 120

editing, 120

proofreading, 120

physical format, 121

letters, 123

external audiences, 123

memorandoms, *or* memos, 124

internally, 124

email, 126

internal and external
  audiences, 126

casual, 128

informal, 128

formal, 128

text messaging, 130

instant message, 132

social media, 132

inverted pyramid style, 134

CRITICAL THINKING QUESTIONS

1 Identify and explain the steps in the writing process. **LO1**

2 Think about a writing project that you recently completed. Using the terminology in this chapter, describe the process that you used. How might using different strategies have made the project more pleasant and productive? What helpful strategies did you use, if any, that were not mentioned in this chapter? **LO1**

3 Think about a letter you received or wrote recently, and explain why it was appropriate to use a letter in this situation. **LO3**

4 Will hard-copy letters and memos diminish in importance given the prevalence of email in the workplace? Become obsolete? Vanish? **LO3**

5 a. Discuss the reasons for social networking's phenomenal growth.

   b. Do you use social media for business purposes? If so, how? Describe what works well and what does not. **LO8**

6 Why should business writers be concerned about grammar and spelling in their email communication, even with audiences they know? **LO5**

7 Some authorities say that shortcuts in text messaging and instant messaging will lead to users' inability to spell properly in more formal contexts. Do you agree? **LO7**

8 Letters, memorandums, and email messages can differ more than in their physical makeup. Explain and discuss. **LO3–LO5**

9 Discuss and justify the wide range of formality used in memos and email messages. **LO4, LO5**

10 What factors might determine whether or not instant messaging would be an appropriate medium to use in a given situation? **LO6**

SKILLS BUILDING EXERCISES

1 Interview a working professional about his or her writing process. In addition to asking about general strategies for different kinds of writing, ask how he or she tackled a particularly difficult writing situation. Write the results of your findings in a brief memo report to your instructor. **LO1**

2 Find a sample of business writing and evaluate its use of formatting elements. If they are effective, say why; if not, explain what you would do differently. **LO2**

3 Using various formatting devices, turn the following contents into a readable, attractive flyer, brochure, or email announcing a health club's new rates for employees of a nearby hospital. (You may want to consult Appendix B's advice on formatting.) **LO2, LO5**

New Special Rates for Metropolitan Hospital Staff! The Health Club is now offering special rates for all Metropolitan Hospital employees. The Club is a full-service exercise club located at 42 Adams

Street, just across from the hospital. Our facilities may be a good option for Metropolitan employees to explore. We offer the following membership types for Metropolitan employees or retirees: Single Standard, 1 year prepaid ($200/year); Single Standard, by the month ($15/month plus a one-time $50 enrollment fee); Single Deluxe, 1 year prepaid ($300/year). Single Deluxe includes your personal locker and a towel service. Metropolitan employees' spouses or domestic partners are eligible for a 20 percent discount on the Club's normal rates. You can take a tour, join the Club, or ask any questions by calling 555-5555. We have a large free-weight room; new Cybex (Nautilus-style) machines; ellipticals, treadmills, bikes, steppers, and rowers; an Olympic-size swimming pool; aerobics, Pilates, and yoga classes; racquetball and handball courts; a large gym/basketball court; a whirlpool; a steam room and saunas; shower and locker room facilities; and free parking. A small fee for some classes may apply. Our hours are Monday through Friday, 5 AM to 10 PM; Saturday, 7 AM to 8 PM; and Sunday, 7 AM to 6 PM. Our website address is www.healthclubin.org.

4 Instructions: Write a text message shorter than 160 characters for each of the cases below. Be sure your message is both clear and complete. **LO6**

a. You own three coffee shops around your area. Although you have a loyal base of regular customers, you realize that there is both room to grow this base and a real need to compete with the growing presence of Starbucks and other competitors. Your coffee is good and reasonably priced, but seasonal fruit and muffins have long been your specialties. In fact, since the local television station included your shop in a healthy eating segment, your low-fat muffins have been selling out every day even though you have been increasing production. When some of your loyal customers started grumbling about not always being able to get them, you knew you wanted to serve your customers better.

Because most of them have mobile phones, text messaging seems like an obvious solution. You have decided to offer an opt-in polling service that would ask their preference for a particular low-fat muffin or fresh fruit. Your customers could select the days of the week they would be interested in getting the poll. Although they would not be placing an order, they would be helping you plan. You'll also be spending well-targeted promotion dollars while creating goodwill with your loyal customers. Now you need to write this poll question.

b. You are on your way to the airport for a trip to a week-long conference when you remember a file you were supposed to send to a customer. So many last-minute details came up that you really don't remember if you sent it. Unfortunately, you cannot access your work computer from outside the company firewall, but you have a colleague, Chris VanLerBerghe, who would be able to check your email outbox to confirm whether or not you sent it. Chris could also send the file, if necessary. However, you cannot reach her by phone now because she is in an important planning meeting, so you decide to send a text message with the exact information she will need to help you out. Be sure your message is both clear and complete.

c. As you are in the morning sales meeting, your mobile phone vibrates, indicating that you have an incoming call. You recognize the source—Yesaya Chan, the high school student you are mentoring/tutoring in math. When you are finally able to listen to the call, you learn that Yesaya needs your help tonight because his teacher moved a test up a couple of days. He wants to know if you can meet him at the local library at 5 PM, noting that it will be open late tonight. You will say yes, but the earliest you can be there on such short notice is 6 PM. Suggest that he still go to the library at 5 PM and work as many of the review problems on his own as he can. You will help him with the others when you get there. Because he is probably in class now, you will send your response as a text message so it won't interrupt his class.

5 Assume the role of the hotel manager we discussed in the "Planning the Message" section of this chapter. The air conditioning has stopped functioning on one of the busiest and hottest weekends of the year. You need to explain the situation and what you are going to do (or have done) about it to three audiences: your guests, your co-workers who will be helping you solve the problem, and your boss, who will not be at the hotel until Monday. Develop a plan for the message you will send to each of these audiences in which you follow the five steps discussed in this chapter for planning a message. (You may find Figure 1–4 useful as well.) Be sure you consider your goal in communicating with each audience, the format/channel your communication will take, the content each audience will need, and the tone and style that will be appropriate for each audience. **LO1**

6 You work as a marketing director for a national chain of clothing stores specializing in professional wear for men and women. You think it would be a great idea to run daily specials and advertise them on Twitter, Facebook, and email. However, when you take your idea to the weekly management meeting, some question what these advertisements would look like. Using what you've learned about planning messages, writing email, and communicating through social media, write a sample message for each medium. How long will your messages be? What type of content will you include? What will you say in one medium that you might not say in another? What might be the advantages of one medium over another? **LO1, LO2, LO5, LO7**

7 You work as a developer for a software company. You're writing an announcement to all company employees reminding everyone of an all-hands meeting tomorrow. The announcement will be posted on the company intranet, which employees know to check multiple times per day, as that's your company's preferred mode of internal communication. The purpose of the meeting is to make sure everyone is ready for the go-live of your software at a local clinic. It's really important that everyone knows how to document any support calls from the clinic and the protocol for prioritizing calls for service—not that you're expecting difficulties; you just want to make sure your support for the clinic is organized and orderly. Use the inverted pyramid approach to organize your message. **LO1, LO2, LO5, LO8**

CHAPTER SEVEN

Getting to the Point in Good-News and Neutral Messages

Learning Objectives

Upon completing this chapter, you will be able to write good-news and neutral messages effectively. To reach this goal, you should be able to

1 Properly assess the reader's likely reaction to your message.

2 Describe the general plan for direct-order messages.

3 Write clear, well-structured routine inquiries.

4 Write direct, orderly, and favorable answers to inquiries.

5 Write order acknowledgments and other thank-you messages that build goodwill.

6 Write direct claims in situations where an adjustment will likely be granted.

7 Compose adjustment grants that regain any lost confidence.

8 Write clear and effective internal-operational communications.

THE PREVALENCE OF GOOD-NEWS AND NEUTRAL MESSAGES IN BUSINESS

Most business messages are those that solve everyday business problems—requesting information, providing information, announcing good news, or communicating about matters that are a routine part of a company's culture and work. As a result, audiences receive these messages as good-news or neutral communication. Chapter 1 explains why most messages are about routine matters: Communication is central to organized human activity. Especially in business, people need to know what to do, why, and how. They undertake any job knowing they have a certain function to perform, and they need information to be able to perform it well. When external audiences interact with companies, they also expect and need information presented as clearly and concisely as possible.

For this reason, many **good-news** and **neutral messages** are written in what is called the **direct order**. There are, of course, unlimited kinds of good-news and neutral messages. Each business is unique and will have developed its preferred style for communicating these messages based on its audiences and communication goals. However, regardless of the type of message, the direct order is usually best because it gets your reader to your main point immediately.

This chapter first describes a general plan for writing good-news and neutral messages in a direct order. Then we adapt this general plan to some of the more common business situations where it is appropriate. We show why each of these situations requires somewhat special treatment. We believe that this review of common direct plans will enable you to adapt them to any related situation.

LO1 Properly assess the reader's likely reaction to your message.

PRELIMINARY ASSESSMENT

As discussed in Chapter 6, writing any messages other than those for the most mechanical, routine circumstances requires careful thinking about the situation, your readers, and your goals. When determining your message's basic plan, a good beginning is to assess your reader's probable reaction to what you have to say. If the reaction is likely to be positive or even neutral, your best approach is likely to be a direct one—that is, one that gets to the objective right away without delay. If your reader's reaction is likely to be negative, you may need to use the indirect plan, discussed in Chapter 8. The general plan for the direct approach in positive and neutral situations follows.

LO2 Describe the general plan for direct-order messages.

THE GENERAL DIRECT PLAN

Beginning with the Objective

Begin with your **objective**. If you are seeking information, start by asking for it. If you are giving information, start giving it. Whatever your key point is, lead with it.

In some cases, you might need to open with a brief orienting phrase, clause, or even sentence. Especially if your reader is not expecting to hear from you or is not familiar with you or your company, you may need to preface your main point with a few words of background, but keep any prefatory remarks brief and get to the real message. Then stop the first paragraph. Let the rest of the message fill in the details.

Covering the Remaining Part of the Objective

Whatever else must be covered to complete your objective makes up the bulk of the remainder of the message. If you cover all of your objective in the beginning (as in an inquiry in which a single question is asked), nothing else is needed. If you have to ask or answer additional questions or provide information, do so in the body of your message. Cover your information systematically—perhaps listing the details or arranging them by paragraphs. If these parts have their own explanations or commentary, include them.

Ending with Goodwill

End the message with some appropriate friendly comment as you would end a face-to-face communication with the reader.

Include a closing that is relevant to the topic of your message. General closings such as "Thank you" or "If you need further information, please don't hesitate to ask" are polite, but they are cliches. You will build more goodwill with a closing that is tailored to your message—for example: "If you will answer these questions about Ms. Hill right away, we can fill the accounting position before our busy tax season."

Be aware, though, that phrases such as "as soon as possible" or "at your convenience" may have very different meanings for you and your reader. If you need your response by a specific date or time, give your reader that information as well as a reason for the deadline so that your reader understands the importance of a timely response. You may say, for example, "Your answers to these questions by July 1 will help Ms. Hill and us as we meet our deadline for filling the accounting position."

Now let us see how you can adapt this general plan to fit the more common direct message situations.

ROUTINE INQUIRIES

INTRODUCTORY CHALLENGE

Searching for New Regional Headquarters

Introduce yourself to routine inquiries by assuming you are the assistant to the vice president for administration of White Label Industries (WLI). WLI is the manufacturer and distributor of an assortment of high-quality products.

You and your boss were recently chatting about WLI's plans to relocate its regional headquarters. Your boss tells you that she and other top management have chosen the city but have not been able to find the perfect office space. She says that they have not been happy with what realtors have found for them or with what they have found in their own searches of classified ads and realty agencies' websites. When you suggest that they expand their search to something a little less traditional such as

craigslist, your boss says, "Great idea! I don't think any of us have used craigslist, though. Could you find some locations and show them to us at our Friday meeting?"

You're a bit intimidated by the prospect, but you know that this is a great chance to demonstrate your professional skills. You visit craigslist and find what you believe would be the perfect office headquarters. You know you could just show the executives the ad at the meeting, but having read the ad and having analyzed your audience, you know the executives will need more information. To present your best professional image at Friday's meeting, you need to write a routine inquiry seeking additional details about the office space.

Choosing from Two Types of Beginnings

LO3 Write clear, well-structured routine inquiries.

The opening of the **routine inquiry** should focus on the main objective. Routine inquiries usually open in one of two ways: (1) with a direct question or request or (2) with a brief statement to orient the reader, followed by the request or question.

If you begin with a direct question or request, you can ask one broad question that sets up other questions you'll ask in the body of the message. For example, if your objective is to get more information about the office space described in the Introductory Challenge, you might begin with a general question:

Could you please send me additional information about the Riverdale office space you advertised on craigslist on May 24?

The body of your message would then present a list of the specific information you are seeking.

On the other hand, if you have only one piece of information you are seeking, you could begin with your specific question:

> Could you please send me the dimensions of the first- and second-floor corner offices of the Riverdale office space you advertised on craigslist on May 24?

You might then offer some explanation of what you're looking for, or you might conclude your message.

If you think your reader would need or appreciate some background information or an orienting statement, provide one. This information helps reduce any startling effect that a direct opening question might have and can help soften the tone if the direct opening question sounds demanding or blunt.

> The 3200-square-foot Riverdale office space you advertised on May 24 on craigslist seems like a great fit for our regional headquarters. To help us decide on a new office space, could you please answer a few questions about the Riverdale offices?

Regardless of how you begin, be sure your reader has a clear sense of your message's purpose.

Informing and Explaining Adequately

To help your reader answer your questions, you may need to include explanation or information. If you do not explain enough or if you misjudge the reader's knowledge, you make the reader's task difficult. For example, answers to your questions about office space for WLI may depend on characteristics or specific needs of the company. Without knowing how WLI will use the space, even the best realtor or property manager may not know how to answer your questions or perhaps direct you to other office space that better meets your needs.

Where and how you include the necessary explanatory information depend on the nature of your message. Usually, a good place for general explanatory material is before or after the direct request in the opening paragraph. In messages that ask more than one question, include any necessary explanatory material with the questions. Such messages may alternate questions and explanations in the body of the message.

Structuring the Questions

After you ask your initial question and provide any relevant background information, your message will take one of two directions. If your inquiry involves only one question, you have achieved your objective, and you may move to a goodwill ending to finish your message. If you have to ask several questions, develop an organized, logical list in the body of your message.

First, if you have two or more questions, make them stand out. Combining two or more questions in a sentence de-emphasizes each and invites the reader to overlook some. You can call attention to your questions in a number of ways. First, you can make each question a separate sentence with a **bullet** (for example, ●, ○, ■) to call attention to it.

Second, you can give each question a separate paragraph whenever your explanation and other comments about each question justify a paragraph.

Third, you can order or rank your questions with numbers. By using words (*first, second, third,* etc.), numerals (*1, 2, 3,* etc.), or letters (*a, b, c,* etc.), you make the questions stand out. Also, you provide the reader with a convenient checklist for answering.

Fourth, you can structure your questions in **true question form**. Sentences that merely hint at a need for information do not attract much attention. The statements "It would be nice if you would tell me . . ." and "I would like to know . . ." are really not questions. They do not ask—they merely suggest. The questions that stand out are those written in question form: "Will you please tell me . . .?" "How much would one be able to save . . .?" "How many contract problems have you had . . .?"

Avoid questions that can be answered with a simple *yes* or *no* unless you really want a simple *yes* or *no* answer. For example, the question "Is the chair available in blue?" may not be what you really want to know. Better wording might be "In what colors is the chair available?" Often, combining a yes/no question with its explanation yields a better, more concise question. To illustrate, the wording "Would your software let us deliver our training modules in any format? We need to deliver them in HTML5" could be improved by asking "Would your software let us deliver our training modules in HTML5?"

Ending with Goodwill

The goodwill ending described in the general plan is appropriate here, just as it is in most business messages. Remember that the closing does the most toward creating goodwill when it fits the topic of the message and includes important deadlines and reasons for them.

Reviewing the Order

In summary, the plan recommended for the routine inquiry message is as follows:

- Focus directly on the objective, with either a specific question that sets up the entire message or a general request for information.
- Include any necessary explanation, wherever it best fits.
- If two or more questions are involved, make them stand out with bullets, numbering, paragraphing, and/or question form.
- End with goodwill words adapted to the topic of the message.

Contrasting Examples

The following two routine inquiry messages illustrate bad and good approaches to requesting information about office space for a new WLI regional headquarters (recall the Introductory Challenge). The first example follows the indirect pattern. The second is direct and more appropriate for this neutral message. You can also study the Case Illustrations on pages 148 and 149. The margin comments help you see how these sample inquiries follow the advice in this chapter.

As you read the first example, note that it is marked by a " 🎯 " icon in the side panel. We use this icon throughout the book wherever we show bad examples. The good examples will be indicated by a " 🎯 " icon.

The Indirect Message. The less effective message begins slowly and gives obvious information. Even if the writer thinks that this information needs to be communicated, it does not deserve the emphasis of the opening sentence. The writer gets to the point of the message in the second paragraph. There are no questions here—just hints for information. The items of information the writer wants do not stand out but are listed in rapid succession in one sentence. The close is selfish and stiff.

Choosing the Right Font

Of all the issues a writer considers when writing an effective business message, the type of font to use may be at the bottom of the list (if it is on the list at all). However, choosing the right font can make your documents look as professional as they sound.

- *What are my choices?* The main choice is either a serif or sans serif font. Letters in serif fonts such as Book Antiqua (shown in the box) have "tails" (serifs). Letters in sans serif fonts such as Verdana (also shown in the box) do not. You can see that the "T" in Times New Roman has the "tails" that the "T" in Tahoma does not. What do serifs do? Serifs connect letters, which makes the space between words more distinguishable and the text therefore more readable—at least in printed documents. In electronic documents, the serifs may actually hinder readability depending on the font size and monitor resolution. Sans serif fonts, however, allow for more white space, which makes letters and words stand out. A possible choice, then, is to use a sans serif font for headings and a serif font for body text.

- *How many fonts can I use?* Limit yourself to not more than two fonts. It's fine to use only one font. However, if you use more than two, you will have a document that looks cluttered and visually confusing. If you do choose two fonts, be sure that one is a serif font and one is a sans serif font. This way the fonts complement rather than compete with each other. Remember that excessive formatting of your fonts (bold, italics, underlining) will also undermine the professional look of your document.

- *How big should my fonts be?* This depends on the font. Start with the body text at 9–12 points. Make your headings two points larger than your body text. Whatever size you choose, be sure the text is readable and looks professional. Fonts that are too small are hard to read. Fonts that are too big look amateurish and visually attack the reader.

- *What style should I choose?* That will depend on what kind of document you're writing and to whom. Look at the sample fonts below. Which would be more appropriate in a print ad for party supplies? In an annual report to investors? In an invitation to a formal event? As you can see, each typeface has its own personality. Choose yours carefully to match your situation.

This font is 12-point Verdana.

This typeface is 12-point Script MT Bold.

This typeface is 12-point Book Antiqua.

THIS TYPEFACE IS 12-POINT GOUDY STOUT.

This message's indirect and vague beginning slows reading.

Dear Mr. Piper:

We saw the advertisement for 3,200 square feet of Riverdale office space that you posted a couple of weeks ago on craigslist. As we are interested, we would like additional information.

Specifically, we would like to know the interior layout, annual cost, availability of transportation, length of lease agreement, escalation provisions, and any other information you think pertinent.

If the information you give us is favorable, we will inspect the property. Please send your reply as soon as possible.

Sincerely,

The Direct and Effective Message. The second example begins directly by asking for information. The explanation is brief but complete. The questions are made to stand out; thus, they help make answering easy. The message closes with a courteous and appropriate request for quick action.

TECHNOLOGY IN BRIEF

Shortcut Tools Help Writers Improve Productivity and Quality

Shortcuts help writers save time and improve quality. One of the easiest to use is the AutoCorrect tool in Word (shown here). This tool will automatically replace a word you enter with another word you enter to replace that particular word. The default setting is generally set to correct common misspellings and typos. However, it also can be used to expand acronyms or phrases used repeatedly.

If you worked frequently with the Association for Business Communication, you might set up the AutoCorrect tool to replace the acronym ABC with the full name. Not only will this shortcut enable you to save time, but it also will improve the quality of your work by inserting a correctly spelled and typed replacement every time.

Dear Mr. Piper:

Will you please answer the following questions about the 3,200-square-foot Riverdale office suite advertised May 24 on craigslist? This space may be suitable for the new regional headquarters we are opening in your city in August.

- Is the layout of these offices suitable for a work force of two administrators, a receptionist, and seven office employees? (If possible, please send us a diagram of the space.)
- What are the dimensions of the corner offices on the first and second floors?
- What is the annual rental charge?
- Are housekeeping, maintenance, and utilities included?
- What type of flooring and walls does the office space have?
- Does the location provide easy access to mass transportation and the airport?
- What is the length of the lease agreement?
- What escalation provisions are included in the lease agreement?

We look forward to learning more about your property. We hope to secure a space that meets our needs by July 21.

Sincerely,

This direct and orderly message is better.

Routine Inquiries (Getting Information about a Training Program). This email message is from a company training director to the director of a management-training program. The company training director has received literature on the program but needs additional information. The message seeks this information.

Direct—a general request sets up the specific question

To... sgarbett@sedonagroup.com

Cc...

Subject: Questions on Management Courses

Ms. Garbett:

Please send me the additional information we need to determine whether to enroll some of our executives in your online management courses. We have the general information and the schedule that are posted on your website. Specifically, we need answers to these questions:

Reference to a website tells what the writer knows and helps the reader in responding

Numbered questions stand out to help the reader respond

1. What are your quantity discount rates? We could enroll about six executives for each course.

2. To what background level is your program geared? We have engineers, accountants, scientists, and business executives. Most have college degrees. Some do not.

Explanations are worked into the questions where needed

3. Can we make arrangements for the attendees to receive college credit for the course? Some of our executives are working on degrees and would want credit.

4. May we have the names and email addresses of training directors of companies that have enrolled their executives in your management courses?

I would appreciate having this information in time for our October 3 staff meeting, and I look forward to learning more about your courses.

A favorable forward look creates a goodwill close

Ronald Dupree
Director of Training
Sorbet Inc.
Phone: 619.594.6942
Fax: 801.309.2411
www.sorbet.com

Routine Inquiry (An Inquiry about Hotel Accommodations). This letter to a hotel inquires about accommodations for a company's annual meeting. In selecting a hotel, the company's managers need answers to specific questions. The message covers these questions.

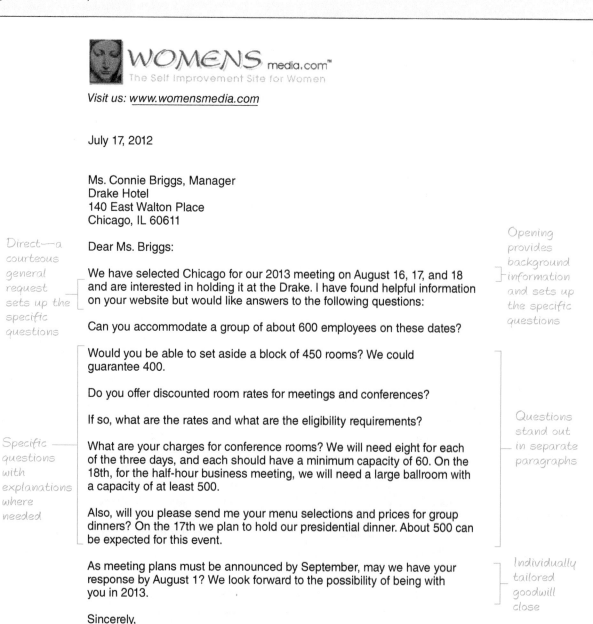

WOMENS media.com™
The Self Improvement Site for Women

Visit us: www.womensmedia.com

July 17, 2012

Ms. Connie Briggs, Manager
Drake Hotel
140 East Walton Place
Chicago, IL 60611

Dear Ms. Briggs:

Direct—a courteous general request sets up the specific questions

Opening provides background information and sets up the specific questions

We have selected Chicago for our 2013 meeting on August 16, 17, and 18 and are interested in holding it at the Drake. I have found helpful information on your website but would like answers to the following questions:

Can you accommodate a group of about 600 employees on these dates?

Would you be able to set aside a block of 450 rooms? We could guarantee 400.

Do you offer discounted room rates for meetings and conferences?

If so, what are the rates and what are the eligibility requirements?

Specific questions with explanations where needed

Questions stand out in separate paragraphs

What are your charges for conference rooms? We will need eight for each of the three days, and each should have a minimum capacity of 60. On the 18th, for the half-hour business meeting, we will need a large ballroom with a capacity of at least 500.

Also, will you please send me your menu selections and prices for group dinners? On the 17th we plan to hold our presidential dinner. About 500 can be expected for this event.

As meeting plans must be announced by September, may we have your response by August 1? We look forward to the possibility of being with you in 2013.

Individually tailored goodwill close

Sincerely,

Patti Wolff

Patti Wolff
Site Selection Committee Chair

FAVORABLE RESPONSES

Answering a Potential Customer's Question

Continue in your role as assistant to the vice president for operations of White Label Industries (WLI). This time, your task is to respond to a customer's message.

In your email inbox this morning, you have an inquiry from a veterinarian, a Dr. Motley, who wants to know more about WLI's Chem-Treat paint. In response to an advertisement, this prospective customer asks a number of specific questions about Chem-Treat. Foremost, she wants to know whether the paint is safe to use around the animals (and their owners) who visit her clinic. Do you have supporting evidence? Do you guarantee the results? Does the paint resist dirt and stains? How much does a gallon cost? Will one coat do the job?

You can answer all but one of the questions positively. Of course, you will report this one negative point (that two coats are needed to do most jobs), but you will take care to de-emphasize it. The response will be primarily a good-news message. Because the reader is a potential customer, you will work to create the best goodwill effect.

LO4 Write direct, orderly, and favorable answers to inquiries.

When you answer inquiries positive, your primary goal is to tell your readers what they want to know. Because your message will be a **favorable response**, directness is appropriate.

Identifying the Message Being Answered

Because this message is a response to another message, you should identify the message you are answering. Such identification helps the reader recall or find the message being answered. If you are writing an email response, the original message is appended to your message. Of course, in an email message, your subject line will identify the message you are answering, but in hard copy messages, you may also use a subject line (Subject: Your April 2 Inquiry about Chem-Treat), as illustrated in Appendix B. Or you can refer to the message incidentally in the text ("as requested in your April 2 inquiry"). Preferably you should identify the message early in your message

Beginning with the Answer

Directness here means giving the readers what they want at the beginning. Thus you *begin by answering*. When a response involves answering a single question, you begin by answering that question. When it involves answering two or more questions, one good plan is to begin by answering one of them—preferably the most important. In the Chem-Treat case, this opening would get the response off to a fast start:

Yes, WLI's Chem-Treat acrylic latex paint is among the safest on the market.

An alternative is to begin by stating that you are giving the reader what he or she wants—that you are complying with the request. This example illustrates this type of beginning.

Here are the answers to your questions about Chem-Treat.

Logically Arranging the Answers

If you are answering just one question, you have little to do after handling that question in the opening. You answer it as completely as the situation requires, and you present whatever explanation or other information is needed. Then you are ready to close the message.

If, on the other hand, you are answering two or more questions, the body of your message becomes a series of answers. You should order them logically, perhaps answering the questions in the order your reader used in asking them. You may even number your answers, especially if your reader numbered the questions. Or you may decide to arrange your answers by paragraphs so that each stands out clearly.

Skillfully Handling the Negatives

When your response will include some bad news along with the good news, you will need to handle the bad news with care. Unless you are careful, it is likely to receive more emphasis than it deserves.

In giving proper emphasis to the good- and bad-news parts, you should use the techniques discussed in Chapter 5, especially positioning. That is, you should place the good news in positions of high emphasis—at paragraph beginnings and endings and at the beginning and ending of the message as a whole. You should place the bad news in secondary positions. In addition, you should use space emphasis to your advantage. This means giving less space to bad-news parts and more space to good-news parts. You also should select words and build sentences that communicate the effect you want. Generally, this means using positive words and avoiding negative words and putting bad news in modifying phrases or clauses rather than in main clauses. Your overall goal should be to present the information in your response so that your readers feel good about you and your company.

Considering Extras

To create goodwill, as well as future business, you should consider including extras with your answers, as recommended in Chapter 5. These are the things you say and do that are not actually required. Examples are a comment or question showing an interest in the reader's situation, some additional information that may prove valuable, and a suggestion for use of the information supplied. In fact, extras can be anything that presents more than the routine response. A business executive answering a college professor's request for information on company operations could supplement the requested information with suggestions of other sources. A technical writer could explain highly technical information in simpler language. In the Chem-Treat problem, additional information (e.g., how much surface area a gallon covers) would be helpful. Such extras encourage readers to build a business relationship with you.

Closing Cordially

As in the other types of direct messages, your ending should be cordial, friendly words that fit the case. For example, you might close the Chem-Treat message with these words:

> If I can help you further in deciding whether Chem-Treat will meet your needs, please let me know.

Reviewing the Plan

To write a favorable response message, you should use the following plan:

- Identify, either incidentally or in the subject line, the message being answered.
- Begin with the answer or state that you are complying with the request.
- Continue to respond in a way that is logical and orderly.
- De-emphasize any negative information.
- Consider including extras.
- End with a friendly comment adapted to your reader.

Contrasting Illustrations

The following contrasting email messages in answer to the Chem-Treat inquiry illustrate two strategies for answering routine inquiries. The first message violates much of the advice in this and earlier chapters. The second meets the requirements of a good business message. It accounts for the reader's needs and the writer's business goals.

An Indirect and Hurried Response. The not-so-good message begins indirectly with an obvious statement referring to receipt of the inquiry. Though well intended, the second sentence continues to delay the answers. The second paragraph begins to respond to the reader's request, but it emphasizes the most negative answer by position and by wording. This answer is followed by hurried and routine answers to the other questions asked. Only the barest information is presented. There is no goodwill close.

This email is indirect and ineffective.

Subject: Your Inquiry of April 3

Dr. Motley,

I have received your April 3 message, in which you inquire about our Chem-Treat paint. I want you to know that we appreciate your interest and will welcome your business.

In response to your question about how many coats are needed to cover new surfaces, I regret to report that two are usually required. The paint has been well tested in our laboratories and is safe to use as directed.

Ray Lindner

Customer Service Representative

An Effective Direct Response. The better message begins directly with the most favorable answer. Then it presents the other answers, giving each the emphasis and positive language it deserves. It subordinates the one negative answer by position, volume of treatment, and structure. More pleasant information follows the negative answer. The close is goodwill talk with some subtle selling strategy included.

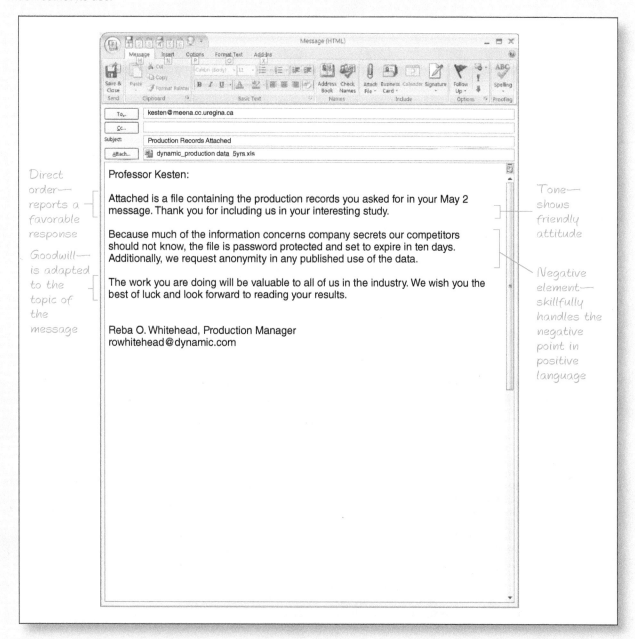

Routine Response (Favorable Response to a Professor's Request). This email message responds to a professor's request for production records that will be used in a research project. The writer is giving the information wanted but must restrict its use.

Direct order— reports a favorable response

Goodwill— is adapted to the topic of the message

Tone— shows friendly attitude

Negative element— skillfully handles the negative point in positive language

---

Message (HTML)

To..: kesten@meena.cc.uregina.ca

Cc...:

Subject: Production Records Attached

Attach..: dynamic_production data 5yrs.xls

Professor Kesten:

Attached is a file containing the production records you asked for in your May 2 message. Thank you for including us in your interesting study.

Because much of the information concerns company secrets our competitors should not know, the file is password protected and set to expire in ten days. Additionally, we request anonymity in any published use of the data.

The work you are doing will be valuable to all of us in the industry. We wish you the best of luck and look forward to reading your results.

Reba O. Whitehead, Production Manager
rowhitehead@dynamic.com

Routine Response (A Request for Detailed Information). Answering an inquiry about a company's experience with executive suites, this letter numbers the answers as the questions were numbered in the inquiry. The opening appropriately sets up the numbered answers with a statement that indicates a favorable response.

Merck & Co., Inc.
One Merck Drive
P.O. Box 100, WS1A-46
Whitehouse Station NJ 08889

 MERCK

August 7, 2013

Ms. Ida Casey, Sales Manager
Liberty Insurance Company
1165 Second Ave.
Des Moines, IA 50318-9631

Dear Ms. Casey:

Direct—makes the purpose clear

Here is the information about our use of temporary executive suites that you requested in your August 3 fax.

Orderly listing of answers

Complete yet concise answers

1. Our executives have mixed feelings about the effectiveness of the suites. At the beginning, the majority opinion was negative, but it appears now that most believe the suites meet our needs.

2. The suites option definitely has saved us money. Rental costs in the suburbs are much lower than downtown costs; annual savings are estimated at nearly 30 percent.

3. We began using executive suites at the request of several sales representatives who had read about other companies using them. We pilot tested the program in one territory for a year using volunteers before we implemented it companywide.

4. We are quite willing to share with you the list of facilities we plan to use again. Additionally, I am enclosing a copy of our corporate policy, which describes our guidelines for using executive suites.

Friendly—adapted to the one case

This extra builds goodwill

If after reviewing this information you have any other questions, please write me again. If you want to contact our sales representatives for firsthand information, please do so. I wish you the best of luck in using these suites in your operations.

Sincerely,

David M. Earp

David M. Earp
Office Manager

Enclosure

Subject: Your April 3 Inquiry about Chem-Treat

Dr. Motley:

Yes, Chem-Treat's low-odor, low-VOC acrylic latex paint is among the safest, most environmentally friendly paints on the market. Several hospitals and clinics have used Chem-Treat successfully and have reported no reactions to it.

Chem-Treat's latex formula also makes it ideal for high-traffic areas. Cleaning usually requires nothing more than a little soap and water.

One gallon of Chem-Treat is usually enough for one-coat coverage of 500 square feet of previously painted surface. For the best results on new surfaces, you will want to apply two coats. For such surfaces, you should figure about 200 square feet per gallon for a long-lasting coating.

We appreciate your interest in Chem-Treat, Dr. Motley. You can view Chem-Treat's safety ratings and customer reviews on our website: www.wli.com/chemtreat/features.

Ray Lindner

Customer Service Representative

This direct mail does a better job.

ORDER ACKNOWLEDGMENTS AND OTHER THANK-YOU MESSAGES

INTRODUCTORY CHALLENGE

Building Goodwill with a "Thank-You" Message

The next work you take from your inbox is an order for paints and painting supplies. It is from Mr. Tony Lee of Central City Paint Company, a new customer whom White Label Industries (WLI) has been trying to attract for months. You usually acknowledge orders with routine messages, but this case is different. You feel the need to welcome this new customer and to cultivate him for future sales.

After checking your current inventory and making certain that the goods will be on the way to Mr. Lee today, you are ready to write him a special acknowledgment and thank him for his business.

In the course of your professional career, you will find yourself in situations where business and social etiquette require thank-you messages. Such messages may be long or short, formal or informal. They may be also combined with other purposes such as confirming an order. In this section we focus on one specific kind of thank-you message—the **order acknowledgment**—as well as more general thank-you messages for other business occasions.

LO5 Write order acknowledgments and other thank-you messages that build goodwill.

Order Acknowledgments

Acknowledgments are sent to let people who order goods know the status of their orders. Most acknowledgments are routine. They simply tell when the goods are being shipped. Many companies use form or computer-generated messages for such situations. Some use printed, standard notes with check-off or write-in blanks. But individually written acknowledgments are sometimes justified, especially with new accounts or large orders.

Skillfully composed acknowledgments can do more than acknowledge orders, though this task remains their primary goal. These messages can also build goodwill through their warm, personal, human tone. They can make the reader feel good about doing business with a company that cares and want to continue doing business with

Tables Help Writers Organize Data for Easy Reading

Setting up tables within a document is an easy task thanks to tools in today's word-processing programs. This feature allows writers to create tables as well as import spreadsheet and database files. In both instances, information can be arranged in columns and rows with detail in the cells. Headings can be formatted, and formulas can be entered in the cells. The table you see here could be one the writer created for use in a favorable response to an inquiry about possible locations for a meeting in Chicago.

Organizing information with tables makes it easier for both the writer and the reader. A careful writer will include column and row labels as needed, helping the reader extract information both quickly and accurately.

Hotel Name	Address	Convention Room Rate for Standard Rooms	Guest Rating
Chicago Marriott Downtown	540 North Michigan Avenue, Chicago, IL 60611-3869	$409	4.2
Drake Hotel	140 East Walton Street, Chicago, IL 60611-1545	$309	4.3
Palmer House Hilton	17 East Monroe Street, Chicago, IL 60603-5605	$252	4.4

that company. To maintain this goodwill for repeat customers, you will want to revise your form acknowledgments regularly.

Directness and Goodwill Building in Order Acknowledgments

Like the preceding direct message types, the acknowledgment message appropriately begins with its good news—that the goods are being shipped—and it ends on a goodwill note. Except when some of the goods ordered must be delayed, the remainder of the message is devoted to goodwill building. This goodwill building can begin in the opening by emphasizing receipt of the goods rather than merely the shipment of the goods:

> The Protect-O paints and supplies you ordered April 4 should reach you by Wednesday. They are leaving our Walden warehouse today by Arrow Freight.

It can also include a warm expression of thanks for the order, especially when a first order is involved. Anything else you can say that will be helpful to the reader is appropriate—information about new products, services, or opportunities for the reader. A forward look to continued business relations is logical gesture in the close.

Tact in Order Acknowledgments

Sometimes the task of acknowledging is complicated by your inability to send the goods requested right away. You could be out of them, or perhaps the reader did not give you all the information you need to send them. In either case, a delay is involved. In some cases, delays are routine and expected and do not pose a serious problem. In these situations, you can use the direct approach. However, you will still want to minimize any negative news so that your routine message does not become a negative-news message. You can do this by using positive language that focuses on what *can* or *will* happen rather than what didn't or won't happen.

In the case of a vague order, for example, you should request the information you need without appearing to accuse the reader of giving insufficient information. To illustrate, you risk offending the reader by writing "You failed to specify the color of phones you want." But you gain goodwill by writing "So that we can send you precisely the phones you want, please check your choice of colors on the space below." This sentence handles the matter positively and makes the action easy to take. It also shows a courteous attitude.

Similarly, you can handle back-order information tactfully by emphasizing the positive part of the message. For example, instead of writing "We can't ship the ink jet cartridges until the 9th," you can write "We will rush the ink jet cartridges to you as soon as our stock is replenished by a shipment due May 9." If the back-order period is longer than the customer expects or longer than the 30 days allowed by law, you may choose to give your customer an alternative, such as a substitute product or service. Giving the customer a choice builds goodwill.

In some cases delays will lead to major disappointments, which means you will have to write a bad-news message. A more complete discussion of how to handle such negative news is provided in Chapter 8.

Strategies for Other Thank-You Messages

One of the first **thank-you messages** you write will be the one for a job interview, which is discussed in Chapter 10. Once you are employed, you may send thank-you messages after a meeting or when someone does a favor for you or gives you a gift, when you want to acknowledge others' efforts that have somehow benefited you, when you want to thank customers for their business, or perhaps when someone has donated time or money to your organization or a cause it supports. The possibilities for situations when you might send thank-you notes are many, and sending a message of sincere thanks is a great way to promote goodwill and build your and your company's professional image.

Thank-you messages are often brief, and because they are positive messages, they are written directly. You can begin with a specific statement of thanks:

> Thank you for attending the American Cancer Society fundraiser lunch for Relay for Life last week and for donating money to the cause.

Follow with a personalized comment relevant to the reader:

> With your support, the 2013 Relay for Life will be our most successful yet … [details follow].

Conclude with a forward-looking statement:

> I look forward to joining you on June 12 for this worthy cause.

Your tone should be informal and friendly. If you are on a first-name basis with the reader, you may omit a salutation or use the reader's first name, but if your relationship with the reader is a formal one, do not use the reader's first name to create a contrived sense of closeness.

Whether you hand write the thank-you, send an email, or use company stationery depends on the audience. If you have poor handwriting or believe your handwriting does not convey a professional image, you may choose to type your message. Though you should always check your own spelling, grammar, and punctuation before sending any message, doing so is especially important in handwritten notes when you have no computer software to alert you to possible errors.

Summarizing the Structure of Order Acknowledgments and Other Thank-You Messages

To write an order acknowledgment or thank-you message,

- Use the direct order: Begin by thanking the reader for something specific (e.g., an order).
- Continue with your thanks or with further information.
- Use positive, tactful language to address vague or delayed orders.

- If appropriate, achieve a secondary goal (e.g., reselling or confirming a mutual understanding).
- Close with a goodwill-building comment, adapted to the topic of the message.

Contrasting Acknowledgments

The following two messages show bad and good ways to acknowledge Mr. Lee's order. As you would expect, the good version follows the plan described in the preceding paragraphs.

Slow Route to a Favorable Message. The bad example begins indirectly, emphasizing receipt of the order. Although intended to produce goodwill, the second sentence further delays what the reader wants most to hear. Moreover, the letter is written from the writer's point of view (note the we-emphasis).

This one delays the important news.

Dear Mr. Lee:

Your April 4 order for $1,743.30 worth of Protect-O paints and supplies has been received. We are pleased to have this nice order and hope that it marks the beginning of a long relationship.

As you instructed, we will bill you for this amount. We are shipping the goods today by Blue Darter Motor Freight.

We look forward to your future orders.

Sincerely,

Fast-Moving Presentation of the Good News. The better message begins directly, telling Mr. Lee that he is getting what he wants. The remainder of the message is a customer welcome and subtle selling. Notice the good use of reader emphasis and positive language. The message closes with a note of appreciation and a friendly, forward look.

This direct message is better.

Dear Mr. Lee:

Your selection of Protect-O paints and supplies was shipped today by Blue Darter Freight and should reach you by Wednesday. As you requested, we are sending you an invoice for $1,743.30, including sales tax.

Welcome to the Protect-O circle of dealers. Our representative, Ms. Cindy Wooley, will call from time to time to offer whatever assistance she can. She is a highly competent technical adviser on paint and painting.

Here in the home plant we also will do what we can to help you profit from Protect-O products. We'll do our best to give you the most efficient service. And we'll continue to develop the best possible paints—like our new Chem-Treat line. As you will see from the enclosed brochure, Chem-Treat is a real breakthrough in mildew protection.

We genuinely appreciate your order, Mr. Lee. We are determined to serve you well in the years ahead.

Sincerely,

Online Order Acknowledgment (Order Confirmation with a Second Purpose). This email message thanks the reader for her order and invites her to participate in this company's online product review.

From: Gardeners Supply [mailto:gardeners@e-news.gardeners.com]
Sent: Thursday, January 08, 2013 9:08 AM
To: KATHRYN.RENTZ@UC.EDU
Subject: Tell Us What You Think About Our Products

GARDENER'S SUPPLY COMPANY

New Feature: Customer Reviews

Dear Kathryn,

Thanks the reader and indicates a shared interest

Thank you for your purchase from Gardener's Supply. We hope you are enjoying your items and that this year's garden will be your best ever!

Your satisfaction with our products is important to us, and we want to hear what you have to say about them. We recently added customer reviews to our website, which helps us improve our product selection and helps other gardeners find the best products to suit their needs.

Moves to another goal of the message

Adds a reader benefit and incentive

We're hoping you'll take a moment to rate and review some or all of the items you have purchased from us. Other gardeners will appreciate your opinions and advice, and you may also enjoy reading what fellow gardeners have to say!

Each time you submit a product review to our website, your name will be entered in a monthly drawing for a $1,000 prize (see information below).

Here are the item(s) you recently purchased. Just click on an item to write a review.

Pictures provide a quick visual confirmation of the order

Men's Waterproof Gloves
⭐ Rate and review it

Glove Set, 3 Pairs
⭐ Rate and review it

Links make participation easy

Forward-looking ending builds goodwill

Thank you again for shopping with us.

The Employee-Owners at Gardener's Supply

Copyright @2008 America's Gardening Resource, Inc.

Order Acknowledgment (Acknowledgment with a Problem). This email letter concerns an order that cannot be handled exactly as the customer would like. Some items are being sent, but one must be placed on back order and another cannot be shipped because the customer did not give the information needed. The message skillfully handles the negative points.

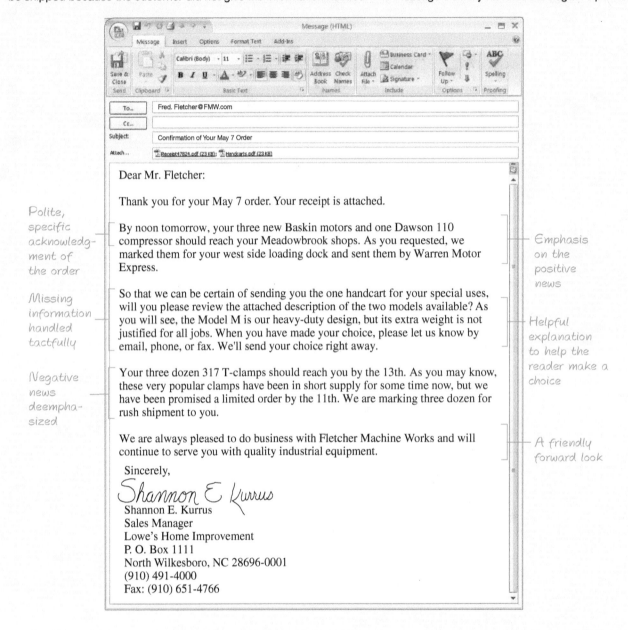

Polite, specific acknowledgment of the order

Missing information handled tactfully

Negative news deemphasized

Emphasis on the positive news

Helpful explanation to help the reader make a choice

A friendly forward look

To... Fred.Fletcher@FMW.com

Subject: Confirmation of Your May 7 Order

Attach... Receipt47824.pdf (23 KB); Handcarts.pdf (23 KB)

Dear Mr. Fletcher:

Thank you for your May 7 order. Your receipt is attached.

By noon tomorrow, your three new Baskin motors and one Dawson 110 compressor should reach your Meadowbrook shops. As you requested, we marked them for your west side loading dock and sent them by Warren Motor Express.

So that we can be certain of sending you the one handcart for your special uses, will you please review the attached description of the two models available? As you will see, the Model M is our heavy-duty design, but its extra weight is not justified for all jobs. When you have made your choice, please let us know by email, phone, or fax. We'll send your choice right away.

Your three dozen 317 T-clamps should reach you by the 13th. As you may know, these very popular clamps have been in short supply for some time now, but we have been promised a limited order by the 11th. We are marking three dozen for rush shipment to you.

We are always pleased to do business with Fletcher Machine Works and will continue to serve you with quality industrial equipment.

Sincerely,

Shannon E Kurrus

Shannon E. Kurrus
Sales Manager
Lowe's Home Improvement
P. O. Box 1111
North Wilkesboro, NC 28696-0001
(910) 491-4000
Fax: (910) 651-4766

Thank-You Message (A Follow-Up to a Meeting). This email from a representative of a telecommunications equipment company thanks a potential customer in Germany for a recent meeting.

Hello, Herman:

Meeting you and the other members of the product selection team last Friday was a pleasure. We are honored not only that you took the time to explain the current dynamics and structure at General Telekom but also that you gave us your entire day. Thank you for your generosity.

I understand that you have graciously offered to share some of United Plorcon's key product qualities with other executives in your company. We are extremely appreciative that you have offered to help in this way. Based on our discussions at the meeting, we will summarize the main points of interest and send them to you.

To make the cost-benefit charts more self-explanatory, I will slightly condense the material and add some notes. They will not be confidential, so please share them if you wish. I will send those condensed charts to you before the end of the week. After we send them, I will follow up with you to make sure that you have all the material you need to explain who we are and what we offer.

Finally, thank you for your hospitality. Staying in an ideally located hotel, having coffee at a beautiful castle, viewing some of the world's best art, and sharing an exquisite meal made my first visit to Stuttgart a most memorable one. I hope that between our two companies, we can create many opportunities for our United Plorcon team to return to your beautiful city.

I look forward to talking with you again soon.

Respectfully yours,

Uses the reader's first name, which indicates a close business relationship

Specifics add sincerity

Politely thanks the reader for something specific (while also reminding him of his promise)

Prepares for future communications between the two parties

Ends on a positive note; looks to the future

A Workplace without Email? One Company's Strategy

French tech company Atos discovered that its 80,000 employees were spending 15–20 hours per week on email but finding only 15 percent of the email actually necessary.

The company's solution to making communication more productive is to phase out email as an internal communication tool, with the goal of eliminating it altogether by 2014. Instead, employees will use social media, instant messaging, and collaboration tools such as Microsoft's Live Meeting for their internal communication. In addition to eliminating unnecessary communication in the office, the company says moving to communication technologies such as instant messaging means that people will better balance their work and personal lives, as they cannot check for messages outside the office as easily as they could if they were using email.

Comments on the article range from enthusiasm and support for the idea to skepticism, the latter belief being that people will just substitute time spent on instant messaging and social media for the time they would have spent on email. Many note (rightly so) that email, like instant messaging and social media, is just the technology—ultimately the users control how productively it is used.

SOURCE: "IT Firm Phasing Out Email to Boost Productivity," *CBC News Technology* and *Science*, CBS News, 16 Dec. 2011, Web, 15 May 2012.

DIRECT CLAIMS

INTRODUCTORY CHALLENGE

Requesting a Correct Shipment and Revised Invoice

Continue in your role with White Label Industries (WLI). As the assistant to the vice president of operations, you manage the supervisors on the paint production line. Today, one of the team leaders came to you for some feedback on his writing. Last week, he ordered some safety equipment (goggles and face masks) for employees on the production line; however, he received gloves instead of goggles and only half the masks he ordered, as well as an invoice for $100 more than his order should have cost. He is fairly certain he received someone else's order. He just wants the correct order shipped and his bill adjusted accordingly.

He called his sales representative but got her voice mail. He left her a quick message to call him about the order, but he also wants to send her an email explaining the situation. He asks for your feedback on the email, and you are surprised at the indirect language and unnecessarily negative and harsh tone. You need to use what you know about writing a direct claim to help him write a message that not only resolves the issue but also builds goodwill.

LO6 Write direct claims in situations where an adjustment will likely be granted.

Occasionally things go wrong between a business and its customers (e.g., merchandise is lost or broken during shipment, customers are inaccurately billed for goods or services). Such situations are not routine for a business; for most businesses, the routine practice is to fulfill their customers' expectations. Because claim messages are not about routine circumstances and because they involve unhappy news, many are written in the indirect approach discussed in Chapter 8. Nevertheless, there are some instances where directness in writing a claim is appropriate, and for this reason we discuss the direct claim in this chapter.

Using Directness for Claims

Most businesses want to know when something is wrong with their products or services so they can correct the matter and satisfy their customers. Many times the easiest and quickest way for you to address these claims is simply to call the company directly to settle the matter. Sometimes, though, you may want to write a claim if you need a written record of the request. Or, depending on a company's phone options for accessing customer service, a written claim sent via email or the company website may be more efficient than a phone call.

When writing a claim in cases where you anticipate that the reader will grant an adjustment of your claim, you may use the direct approach (e.g., adjusting an incorrect charge to an invoice). Be sure that when you write the claim, you keep your tone objective and professional so that you preserve your reader's goodwill. If you use words such as *complaint* or *disappointment*, you will compromise your chances of receiving an adjustment quickly.

Organizing the Direct Claim

Because you anticipate that the reader will willingly grant your request, a direct claim begins with the claim, moves to an explanation, and ends with a goodwill closing.

Beginning a Direct Claim. The direct claim should open with just that—the direct claim. This should be a polite but direct statement of what you need. If the statement sounds too direct, you may soften it with a little bit of explanation, but the direct claim should be at the beginning of your message, as in this example:

> Please adjust the invoice (# 6379) for our May 10 order to remove the $7.50 shipping charge.

Explaining the Issue. The body of the direct claim should provide the reader with any information he or she might need to understand your claim. To continue with the same example, we might write the following brief middle paragraph:

> Because our order totaled $73.50, we were able to take advantage of your offer for free shipping on orders of $50 or more and should not have been charged a shipping fee.

Providing a Goodwill Closing. Your close should end with an expression of goodwill. A simple ending like the following can suffice:

> Please send a corrected copy of the invoice to me at jsmith@americanmortgage.com. We look forward to continued business with National Office Supplies.

Reviewing the Plan

To write a direct claim message, you should use the following plan:

- Begin with a polite direct statement of your claim.
- In the body of the message, give the reader information he or she needs to adjust the claim.
- Close with an expression of goodwill.

Contrasting Examples of Claim Messages

The following two email messages show contrasting ways of handling the erroneous shipment described in the Introductory Challenge. The first is slow and harsh. The second is courteous, yet to the point and firm.

An Indirect and Harsh Message. The first message starts slowly with a long explanation of the situation. Some of the details in the beginning sentence are helpful, but they do not deserve the emphasis that this position gives them. The problem is not described until the second paragraph. The wording here is clear but much too strong. The words are angry and insulting, and the writer talks down to the reader. Such words are more likely to produce resistance than acceptance. The negative writing continues into the close, leaving a bad final impression.

This claim is insulting, too indirect, and too long.

Subject: Problem with Our Order #2478

Beth,

As you know, White Label Industries has been ordering our safety supplies from you for over 15 years. We have always depended on you for quick and accurate service, which, unfortunately, looks like it didn't happen this time. When our orders are not accurate and our safety gear is not what we ordered, you put our employees in jeopardy, and WLI loses money if employees don't have safety gear and can't work.

You can imagine how shocked I was when I opened the order expecting face masks and goggles but found gloves and half the face masks I ordered. I was also surprised to see a bill that was $100 more than I planned.

I tried to call you, but you didn't answer, so I left a voice message. I'm guessing you want to fix this quickly, so please call me or email me and let me know what you are going do. If my employees do not have the masks and goggles by tomorrow, employees can't work, and we will have to shut down our production line, which will cost us a lot of money. This was really disappointing service, but I'm sure it won't happen again, as you have always been accurate in the past. We would hate to think that we need to go with a different supplier. Thank you.

Ken

A Firm yet Courteous Message. The second message follows the plan suggested in the preceding paragraphs. A subject line quickly and neutrally identifies the situation. The message begins with a clear statement of the claim. Next, it uses objective language to tell what went wrong. The ending is rational and shows that the writer is interested in resolving the issue, not placing blame.

This direct claim is clear and efficient while also maintaining goodwill.

Subject: Need Correct Order Shipped (Invoice 6750)

Beth,

Please send 50 safety goggles and 100 face masks, as well as a new invoice, to replace the incorrect order that arrived this morning.

On Monday, I placed the order for the safety goggles and face masks, but today I received only 50 face masks and 15 boxes of safety gloves. The invoice indicated that this order was supposed to go to J&M Medical Supplies.

If you send the order today, we should receive it tomorrow. Our employees will need the safety equipment in order for us to keep the production line running.

Please let me know how you want to handle the return of J&M's order.

Thanks,

Ken

ADJUSTMENT GRANTS

Dealing with the Unexpected

Continuing in your role with White Label Industries (WLI), this time you find on your computer an email message from an unhappy customer. It seems that Ms. Bernice Watson, owner of Tri-Cities Hardware, is upset because some of the 30 Old London lampposts she ordered from WLI arrived in damaged condition. "The glass is broken in 17 of the units," she writes, "obviously because of poor packing." She had ordered the lights for a special sale. In fact, she had even featured them in her advertising. The sale begins next Friday. She wants a fast adjustment—either the lamps by sale time or her money back.

Of course, you will grant Ms. Watson's request. You will send her an email message saying that the goods are on the way. And because you want to keep this good customer, you will try to regain any lost confidence with an honest explanation of the problem. This message is classified as an adjustment grant.

When you can grant an adjustment, the situation is a happy one for your customer. You are correcting an error. You are doing what you were asked to do. As in other positive situations, a message written in the direct order is appropriate.

LO7 Compose adjustment grants that regain any lost confidence.

In most face-to-face business relations, people communicate with courteous directness. You should write most business messages this way.

Considering Special Needs

The adjustment-grant message has much in common with the message types previously discussed. You begin directly with the most important point—here, the good news that you are granting the adjustment. You refer to the message you are answering, and you close on a friendly note. Because the situation stems from an unhappy experience, you have two special needs. One is the need to overcome any negative impressions caused by the experience. The other is the need to regain any confidence in your company, its products, or its service that the reader may have lost.

Need to Overcome Negative Impressions. To understand the first need, just place yourself in the reader's shoes. As the reader sees it, something bad has happened—goods have been damaged, equipment has failed, or sales have been lost. The experience has not been pleasant. Granting the claim will take care of much of the problem, but some negative thoughts may remain. You need to work to overcome any such thoughts.

You can attempt to do this using words that produce positive effects. For example, in the opening you can do more than just give the affirmative answer. You can add goodwill, as in this example:

> The enclosed check for $89.77 is our way of showing you that your satisfaction is our top priority.

Throughout the message you should avoid words that unnecessarily recall the bad situation you are correcting. You especially want to avoid the negative words that could be used to describe what went wrong—words such as *mistake, trouble, damage, broken*, and *loss*. Even general words such as *problem, difficulty*, and *misunderstanding* can create unpleasant effects. Negative language makes the customer's complaint the focus of your message. Your goal is to move the customer beyond the problem and to the solution—that the customer is going to have his or her claim granted. You can only do this if you use positive, reader-centered language.

Also negative are the apologies often included in these messages. Even though well intended, the somewhat conventional "we sincerely regret the inconvenience …" type of comment is of questionable value because it emphasizes the negative happenings for which the apology is made. If you sincerely believe that you owe an apology or that one is expected, you can apologize and risk the negative effect. But do it early and move on, and don't repeat it at the end. In most instances, however, your efforts to correct the problem will show adequate concern for your reader's interests.

Need to Regain Lost Confidence. Except in cases in which the cause of the difficulty is routine or incidental, you also will need to regain the reader's lost confidence. Just what you must do and how you must do it depend on the situation. If something can be done to correct a bad procedure or a product defect, you should do it. Then you should tell your reader what has been done as convincingly and positively as you can. If what went wrong was a rare, unavoidable event, you should explain this. Sometimes you will need to explain how a product should be used or cared for. Sometimes you will need to resell the product. Whatever you say should be truthful, professional, and reader focused.

Reviewing the Plan

To organize a message granting an adjustment, writers should use the following plan:

- Begin directly—with the good news.
- Incidentally identify the correspondence that you are answering.
- Avoid negatives that recall the problem.
- Regain lost confidence through explanation or corrective action.
- End with a friendly, positive comment.

Adjustment Grant Messages (Explaining a Human Error). This email message grants the action requested in the claim of a customer who received a leather computer case that was monogrammed incorrectly. The writer has no excuse because human error was to blame. His explanation is positive and convincing.

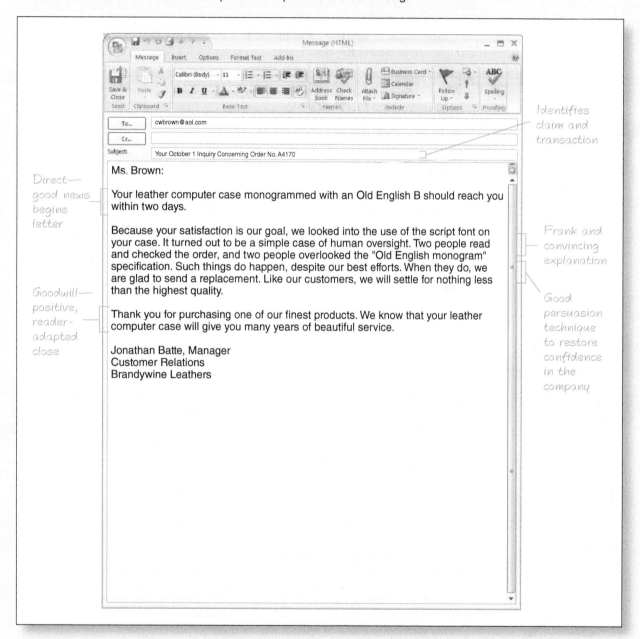

Identifies claim and transaction

Direct—good news begins letter

Ms. Brown:

Your leather computer case monogrammed with an Old English B should reach you within two days.

Frank and convincing explanation

Because your satisfaction is our goal, we looked into the use of the script font on your case. It turned out to be a simple case of human oversight. Two people read and checked the order, and two people overlooked the "Old English monogram" specification. Such things do happen, despite our best efforts. When they do, we are glad to send a replacement. Like our customers, we will settle for nothing less than the highest quality.

Goodwill—positive, reader-adapted close

Thank you for purchasing one of our finest products. We know that your leather computer case will give you many years of beautiful service.

Jonathan Batte, Manager
Customer Relations
Brandywine Leathers

Good persuasion technique to restore confidence in the company

To... cwbrown@aol.com

Subject: Your October 1 Inquiry Concerning Order No. A4170

167

Contrasting Adjustments

The two messages below illustrate an ineffective and effective way to write adjustment messages. The first, with its indirect order and grudging tone, is ineffective. The directness and positiveness of the second clearly make it the better message.

A Slow and Negative Approach. The ineffective message begins with an obvious comment about receiving the claim. It recalls vividly what went wrong and then painfully explains what happened. As a result, the good news is delayed for an additional paragraph. Finally, after two delaying paragraphs, the message gets to the good news. Though well intended, the close leaves the reader with a reminder of the trouble.

This email is indirect and negative.

Subject: Your Broken Old London Lights

Ms. Watson,

We have received your May 1 claim reporting that our shipment of Old London lamppost lights reached you with 17 broken units. We regret the inconvenience and can understand your unhappiness.

Following our standard practice, we investigated the situation thoroughly. Apparently the fault is the result of an inexperienced temporary employee's negligence. We have taken corrective measures to assure that future shipments will be packed more carefully.

I am pleased to report that we are sending replacements today. They should reach you before your sale begins. Our driver will pick up the broken units when he makes delivery.

Again, we regret all the trouble caused you.

Stephanie King

The Direct and Positive Technique. The better message uses the subject line to identify the transaction. The opening words tell the reader what she most wants to hear in a positive way that adds to the goodwill tone of the message. With a you-viewpoint explanation, the message then reviews what happened. Without a single negative word, it makes clear what caused the problem and what has been done to prevent its recurrence. After handling the essential matter of picking up the broken lamps, the message closes with positive talk.

This message is direct and positive.

Subject: Your May 1 Report on Invoice 1248

Ms. Watson:

Seventeen carefully packed Old London lamppost lamps should reach your sales floor in time for your Saturday promotion. Our driver left our warehouse today with instructions to special deliver them to you on Friday.

Because your satisfaction with our service and products is important, we have thoroughly checked our shipping procedures. It appears that the shipment to you was packed by a temporary employee who was filling in for a hospitalized veteran packer. We now have our veteran packer back at work and have taken measures to ensure better performance by our temporary staff.

As you know, the Old London lamppost lights have become one of the hottest products in the lighting field. We are confident they will contribute to the success of your sale.

Stephanie King

INTERNAL-OPERATIONAL MESSAGES

Reminding Employees of the Shipping Policy

As the administrative assistant for the vice president of operations at White Label Industries (WLI), you have been asked by your boss to send a note on her behalf to all employees reminding them of the company's shipping policy. Whether customers pay shipping charges depends on the products they order. However, some customers who repeatedly order the same product are sometimes charged for shipping and sometimes are not, which, of course, leads to unhappy customers and is costly for WLI.

As Chapter 1 explained, **internal-operational communications** are those messages that stay within a business. They are messages to and from employees that get the work of the organization done. The memorandums discussed in Chapter 6 are one form of operational communication. Internal email messages are another, and so are the various documents posted on bulletin boards, mailed to employees, uploaded on intranets, or distributed as handouts.

LO8 Write clear and effective internal-operational communications.

The formality of such messages ranges widely. At one extreme are the casual memorandum and email exchanges between employees concerning work matters. At the other are formal documents communicating company policies, directives, and procedures. Then, of course, there are the various stages of formality in between.

Casual Operational Messages

The documents at the bottom of the formality range typically resemble casual conversation. Usually they are quick responses to work needs. Rarely is there time or need for careful construction and wording. The goal is simply to exchange the information needed to conduct the company's work.

Frankness describes the tone of these casual operational messages as well as many of the messages at more formal levels. The participants exchange information, views, and recommendations forthrightly. They write with the understanding that all participants are working for a common goal—what is best for the company—and that people working together in business situations want and need straightforward communication.

Still, remember that being frank doesn't mean being impolite. Even in quick messages, you should build goodwill with a positive, courteous tone.

Moderately Formal Messages

Moderately formal messages tend to resemble the messages discussed earlier in this chapter. Usually they require more care in construction, and usually they follow a direct pattern. The most common arrangement begins with the most important point and works down. Thus, a typical beginning sentence is a topic (theme) statement. In messages in memorandum form, the opening repeats the subject-line information and includes the additional information needed to identify the situation. The remainder of the message consists of a logical, orderly arrangement of the information covered. When the message consists of items in sequence, the items can be numbered and presented in this sequence.

Suggestions for writing **moderately formal internal messages** are much the same as those for writing the messages covered previously. Clarity, correctness, and courtesy should guide your efforts. The following example of a hard-copy memorandum illustrates these qualities. It is moderately formal, yet it is conversational. It is organized in the direct order, beginning with the objective and then systematically and clearly covering the vital bits of information. It is straightforward yet courteous.

DATE: April 1, 2013
TO: Remigo Ruiz
FROM: Becky Pharr
SUBJECT: Request for Cost Information Concerning Meeting at Timber Creek Lodge

As we discussed in my office today, please get the necessary cost information for conducting our annual sales meeting at the Timber Creek Lodge, Timber Creek Village, Colorado. Our meeting will begin on the morning of Monday, June 5; we should arrange to arrive on the 4th. We will leave after a brief morning session on June 9.

Specifically, we'll need the following information:

- Travel costs for all 43 participants, including air travel to Denver and ground travel between the airport and the lodge. I have listed the names and home stations of the 43 participants on the attached sheet.
- Room and board costs for the five-day period, including cost with and without dinner at the lodge. As you know, we are considering the possibility of allowing participants to purchase dinners at nearby restaurants.
- Costs for recreational facilities at the lodge.
- Costs for meeting rooms and meeting equipment (e.g., laptops, projectors). We will need a room large enough to accommodate our 43 participants.

I'd like to have the information by April 15. If you need additional information, please let me know.

Formal Messages

The most **formal operational** messages are those presenting policies, directives, and procedures. Usually written by executives for their subordinates, these administrative messages are often compiled in manuals, perhaps kept in loose-leaf form and updated as new material is developed. Their official status accounts for their formal tone.

Formal operational messages usually follow a direct order, although the nature of their contents can require variations. The goal should be to arrange the information in the most logical order for quick understanding. Since the information frequently involves a sequence of information bits, numbering these bits can be helpful. And since these documents must be clearly understood and followed, the writing must be clear to all, including those with low verbal skills. The following example illustrates these qualities:

DATE: June 10, 2013
TO: All Employees
FROM: Terry Boedeker, President
SUBJECT: Energy Conservation

To help keep costs low, the following conservation measures are effective immediately:

- Thermostats will be set to maintain temperatures of 72 degrees Fahrenheit throughout the air-conditioning season.
- Air conditioners will be shut off in all buildings at 4 PM Monday through Friday.
- Air conditioners will be started as late as possible each morning so as to have the buildings at the appropriate temperature within 30 minutes after the start of the workday.
- Lighting levels will be reduced to approximately 80 to 100 watts in all work areas. Corridor lighting will be reduced to 50 watts.
- Outside lighting levels will be reduced as much as possible without compromising safety and security.

In addition, will each of you help with this conservation effort? Specifically, I ask that you do the following:

- Turn off lights not required in performing your work.
- Keep windows closed when the cooling system is operating.
- Turn off all computer monitors and printers at the end of the day.

I am confident that these measures will reduce our energy use significantly. Your efforts to follow them will be greatly appreciated.

Even though this message is straightforward, note the writer's courtesy and his use of *us* and *our*. When writing direct messages, skillful managers make use of such strategies for maintaining good relations with employees. Remembering this goal becomes especially important in situations where managers have news to convey or requests to make that employees may not be ready to accept. In fact, in these situations an indirect order will be more appropriate, as Chapters 8 and 9 will discuss. For most internal-operational communication, however, the direct order will be both expected and appreciated.

Summarizing the Structure of Internal-Operational Messages

To write an internal-operational message, writers should do the following:

- Organize in the direct order.
- Choose the appropriate tone (casual, moderately formal, or formal).
- Be clear and courteous.
- Order the information logically.
- Close in a way that builds goodwill.

Contrasting Examples of Internal-Operational Messages

The following two messages show contrasting ways in which the operational message regarding WLI's inconsistent shipping policies (see the Introductory Challenge at the beginning of this section) may be addressed.

A Wordy, Confusing, and Indirect Message. The reader really has to search for the writer's purpose and intent in this message. In addition, it is wordy, long, and disorganized and lacks visual appeal.

Subject: Inconsistent Shipping Policies

WLI has been incurring increasing freight expenses and a decline in freight revenue over the last two years, impacting our ability to achieve our financial goals. The warehouse team has done a lot of research into the reasons behind this increase, and it has come to our attention that a very considerable number of shipments are going out of Cedar Rapids (1) as unbillable to the customer and/or (2) as overnight shipments rather than ground.

WLI has only one product for which shipping is not billed to the customer—the Chem-Treat paint. In all other cases, product shipments are supposed to be billed to the customer. ***Therefore, effective immediately, except for Chem-Treat shipments, which by contract provide for free overnight (weekday delivery) shipping, WLI will bill the customer for all shipments of products. Finance will screen all orders to ensure that they indicate billable shipping terms.***

WLI's overnight shipping falls into a few categories, including shipments of products to customers and shipments of marketing materials to prospects and customers. There are no customer programs or marketing programs for which WLI offers overnight shipping (except Chem-Treat). ***Therefore, effective***

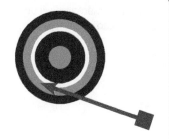

This indirect message wastes time and dwells on the negative.

immediately, except for Chem-Treat shipments, which by contract provide for overnight (weekday delivery) shipping, WLI will not ship products overnight to customers unless the overnight shipping is billed to the customer. Also effective immediately, shipments of sales/marketing materials are to be shipped ground, not overnight.

This policy change will impact some of your work processes, requiring you to be more planful in getting products shipped to customers in a businesslike and timely manner, and challenging you to prevent last-minute rush situations. I suspect that much of the freight performance situation, from a financial point of view, is an awareness issue for our Cedar Rapids team. I thank each of you in advance for adherence to this policy. We are fortunate to have an excellent distribution team in Cedar Rapids. That team needs all of our help so that their high-quality shipping and inventory control performance becomes matched by strong financial performance.

Exceptions to the billable shipping-only and no overnight shipping policies must be brought to me for approval prior to entering the order.

Dean Yourg

VP Operations

A Direct, Concise, and Visually Appealing Message. This message is written directly and is more accurate because it communicates correctly the main point that this is a reminder of an existing policy, not an announcement of a new policy. This message is also more concise and gives the reader only the information he or she needs to know to comply. In addition, headings and bulleted lists make for much easier reading.

This direct message will be easy to read and reference. Its tone is straightforward but courteous.

Subject: Refresher on Our Shipping Policy

Please remember that our shipping policy is as follows:

Shipping Charges:

- *Chem-Treat paint* is the only product for which shipping is **not** billed to the customer.
- *All other product shipments* (including sales/marketing materials) **are** billed to the customer.

Overnight Shipping:

- Sales/marketing materials are to be shipped ground, not overnight.
- *Chem-Treat paint* may be shipped overnight at **no charge** to the customer, as provided by contract.
- *All other overnight product shipments* **are billed** to the customer.

Billing our customers accurately and consistently for shipping improves customer satisfaction with our service. In addition, the increased freight revenue will help us achieve our financial goals and control our shipping and inventory costs.

To ensure that your customers receive their products quickly, refer to the shipping and mailing timeline on WLI's intranet.

The Finance Department will be screening all shipment invoices to make sure that shipments are billed accurately. If you have questions regarding the shipping policy or require an exception, please contact me at Ext. 555.

Dean Young

VP Operations

OTHER DIRECT MESSAGE SITUATIONS

In the preceding pages, we have covered the most common direct message situations. Others occur, of course. You should be able to handle them with the techniques that have been explained and illustrated.

In handling such situations, remember that, whenever possible, you should get to the goal of the message right away. You should cover any other information needed in good logical order. You should carefully choose words that convey just the right meaning. More specifically, you should consider the value of using the you-viewpoint, and you should weigh carefully the differences in meaning conveyed by the positiveness or negativeness of your words. As in the good examples discussed in this chapter, you should end your message with appropriate and friendly goodwill words.

THERE'S MORE . . .

Would you like to learn more about the various types of direct messages, building relationships with your reader, or developing your professional writing style? Scan the QR code with your smartphone or use your Web browser to learn more at www.mhhe .com/lesikar13e. Choose Chapter 7 > Bizcom Tools & Tips.

SUMMARY BY LEARNING OBJECTIVES

1. Properly assess the reader's likely reaction to your message.
   - If the reaction is likely to be negative, indirect order is your likely choice.
   - If it is likely to be positive or neutral, you probably want directness.

   Properly assess the reader's likely reaction to your message.

2. Describe the general plan for direct-order messages.
   - Begin with the objective.
   - Cover any necessary explanation.
   - Systematically present any remaining parts of the objective.
   - End with adapted goodwill.

   Describe the general plan for direct-order messages.

3. The routine inquiry is a basic direct-order message.
   - Begin it with a request—either (1) a request for specific information wanted or (2) a general request for information.
   - Somewhere in the message, explain enough to enable the reader to answer.
   - If the inquiry involves more than one question, make each stand out—perhaps as separate sentences or separate paragraphs.
   - Consider numbering the questions.
   - Word them as questions.
   - End with an appropriate friendly comment.

   Write clear, well-structured routine inquiries.

4. When responding to inquiries favorably, you should begin directly.
   - If the response contains only one answer, begin with it.
   - If it contains more than one answer, begin with a major one or a general statement indicating you are answering.
   - Identify the message being answered early, perhaps in a subject line.
   - Arrange your answers (if more than one) logically.
   - Make them stand out.

   Write direct, orderly, and favorable answers to inquiries.

- If both good- and bad-news answers are involved, give each answer the emphasis it deserves, perhaps by subordinating the negative.
- For extra goodwill effect, consider doing more than was asked.
- End with appropriate cordiality.

Write order acknowledgments and other thank-you messages that build goodwill.	5. Write order acknowledgments and other thank-you messages in the form of a favorable response.

5. Write order acknowledgments and other thank-you messages in the form of a favorable response.
   - Personalized order acknowledgments can build goodwill.
   - Good business and social etiquette often require that you write other kinds of thank-you messages.
   - Use the direct order: Begin by thanking the reader with specific wording.
   - Continue with your thanks or with further information.
   - Use positive, tactful language to address vague or delayed orders.
   - If appropriate, achieve a secondary goal (e.g., reselling or confirming a mutual understanding).
   - Close with a goodwill-building comment adapted to the topic of the message.

Write direct claims in situations where an adjustment will likely be granted.

6. Direct claims are routine messages that are written when a company has clearly not met your expectations for a product or service.
   - Direct claims differ from indirect claims, which are written when you are not sure the company will grant your claim.
   - Direct claims are written when a company clearly has made an error that it will want the opportunity to correct.
   - You write most direct claims as follows:
     — Begin a direct claim by stating the claim.
     — Provide sufficient detail in the message so that the reader knows what happened and what issues he or she needs to address.
     — End with a goodwill statement.

Compose adjustment grants that regain any lost confidence.

7. Because messages granting adjustments are positive responses, write them in the direct order.
   - They differ from other direct-order messages in that they involve a negative situation, so you will need to overcome any negative impressions the situation has created.
   - Open with the good news—what you are doing to correct the wrong.
   - In the opening and throughout, emphasize the positive.
   - Avoid the negative—words like *trouble, damage,* and *broken.*
   - Try to regain the reader's lost confidence, maybe with an explanation or with assurance of corrective measures taken.
   - End with a goodwill comment, avoiding words that recall what went wrong.

Write clear and effective internal-operational communications.

8. Internal-operational communications must also be clear and effective.
   - Organize most of them in the direct order.
   - Choose the appropriate tone (casual, moderately formal, formal).
   - Make them clear and courteous.
   - Give administrative communications (policies, directives, procedures) the careful attention they deserve.
   - Organize them logically; strive for clarity.
   - Close with a goodwill statement.

good news messages, 142

neutral messages, 142

direct order, 142

objective, 142

routine inquiry, 143

true question form, 145

order acknowledgment, 155

thank-you messages, 157

direct claim, 163

adjustment grant, 166

internal-operational
communications, 169

CRITICAL THINKING QUESTIONS

1 When is the direct order appropriate in inquiries? When would you use the indirect order? Give examples. **LO1**

2 "Explanations in inquiries merely add length and should be eliminated." Discuss. **LO3**

3 Discuss why just reporting truthfully may not be a sufficient strategy for handling negative information in messages answering inquiries. **LO4**

4 Defend a policy of doing more than asked in answering routine inquiries. Can the policy be carried too far? **LO4**

5 What can acknowledgment messages do to build goodwill? **LO5**

6 Discuss situations where the following email forms of an order acknowledgment would be preferred: form message and a special message. **LO5**

7 Discuss how problems (vague orders, back orders) should be handled in messages acknowledging orders. **LO5**

8 Why is it usually advisable to do more than just grant the claim in an adjustment-grant message? **LO7**

9 Discuss the use of directness in internal-operational communications. Why is it desirable? Can it be overdone? When might indirectness be appropriate? **LO8**

SKILLS BUILDING EXERCISES

1 Point out the shortcomings in this email response to an inquiry about a short course in business communication that Casey Webster's company offered to its employees. The course was taught by a local college professor. Mr. Braden's initial inquiry included five questions: (1) How did the professor perform? (2) What was the course format (length, meeting structure)? (3) What was the employee evaluation of the instruction? (4) Was the course adapted to the company and its technical employees? (5) Was homework assigned? **LO1, LO2, LO4**

Subject: Course evaluation

Mr. Braden:

Your January 17 inquiry addressed to the Training Director has been referred to me for attention since we have no one with that title. I do have some training responsibilities and was the one who organized the in-house course on clear writing. You asked five questions about our course.

Concerning your question about the instructor, Professor Alonzo Britt, I can report that he did an acceptable job in the classroom.

Some of the students, including this writer, felt that the emphasis was too much on grammar and punctuation, however. He did assign homework, but it was not excessive.

We had class two hours a day from 3:00 to 5:00 PM every Thursday for eight weeks. Usually the professor lectured the first hour. He was a good lecturer but sometimes talked over the heads of the students. This was the main complaint in the evaluations the students made at the end of the course, but they had many good comments to make also. Some did not like the content, which they said was not adapted to the needs of a technical worker. Overall, the professor got a rating of B- on a scale of A to F.

We think the course was good, but it could have been better adapted to our needs and our people. I also think it was too long—about 10 hours (five meetings) would have been enough. Also, we think the professor spent too much time lecturing and not enough on application work in class.

Please be informed that the information about Professor Britt must be held in confidence.

Casey Webster

2 Point out the shortcomings in this message granting a claim for a fax machine received in damaged condition. Inspection of the package revealed that the damage did not occur in transit. **LO7**

Dear Ms. Orsag:

Your May 3 letter in which you claim that the Rigo FAX391 was received in damaged condition has been carefully considered. We inspect all our machines carefully before packing them, and we pack them carefully in strong boxes with Styrofoam supports that hold them snugly. Thus we cannot understand how the damage could have occurred.

Even so, we stand behind our product and will replace any that are damaged. However, we must ask that first you send us the defective one so we can inspect it. After your claim of damage has been verified, we will send you a new one.

We regret any inconvenience this situation may have caused you and assure you that problems like this rarely occur in our shipping department.

Scott Hilderbran

3 List your criticisms of this email message inquiring about a convenience store advertised for sale: LO3

Subject: Store details needed

Mr. Meeks:

This is in response to your advertisement in the May 17 *Daily Bulletin* in which you describe a convenience store in Clark City that you want to sell. I am very much interested since I would like to relocate in that area. Before I drive down to see the property, I need some preliminary information. Most important is the question of financing. I am wondering whether you would be willing to finance up to $50,000 of the total if I could come up with the rest, and how much interest you would

charge and for how long. I also would like to have the figures for your operations for the past two or three years, including gross sales, expenses, and profits. I also need to know the condition of the building, including such information as when built, improvements made, repairs needed, and so on.

Hoping that you can get these answers to me soon so we can do business.

4 Criticize the following thank-you message from a college student to a professor who has sent her a job lead. **LO5**

Subject: Thanks

Dear Prof. Smith,

Thanks for the hot tip on the job! I'm interviewing there tomorrow!

Sarah

5 Critique the following direct claim message: **LO6**

I wonder if you would consider reducing the bill I recently received for repair work that Tom, one of your men, performed last week. I did not realize that he would charge me for the time he spent going to Home Depot to get the parts he needed. If I'd known this, I probably wouldn't have chosen your company to do the work.

Please let me know your reply as soon as possible.

Kim Keeley

6 Criticize the following operational message from a restaurant manager: **(LO8)**

Wait staff:

It has come to my attention that our customer service is substandard. We will therefore hold mandatory training sessions over the next three weeks. See your shift supervisor to plan your work schedule so that you can attend.

PROBLEM-SOLVING CASES

Routine Inquiries

1 You recently learned about a service organization on your campus, Mentors for Majors. The Mentors are alumni and other working professionals who have agreed to field student inquiries about the nature of their jobs, about strategies for career success, and so forth.

You've been thinking about a certain kind of career, and you'd like to get more information about it from an experienced professional. Checking over the list, you find

that there's a mentor in this very area. Write an email to the person in which you ask your questions. Find out the main things you'd like to know about this field of employment in a way that shows consideration for the reader and demonstrates your own serious interest in that type of job. (If your instructor directs, use either someone you know or someone you've researched on the Internet and through other resources. Turn in a one-paragraph profile of this person along with your email of inquiry.)

2 You are a sales manager in a company (you choose what kind), and you just attended a professional meeting where the featured speaker extolled the virtues of using Google+ (a social networking space for collaboration and communication)

in her organization. Intrigued, you'd like to learn more about how Google+ might enhance collaboration and "collective intelligence" among your sales staff or in your company in general.

First, do some Internet research on Google+. You might also set up a Google+ account of your own to explore the Google+ features more thoroughly.

Then email the speaker you heard—who welcomed follow-up questions—and ask her what you most want to know about setting up and using Google+ in your type of company or department. Whether or not you will pursue this idea further will depend on her answers, so think carefully about what to ask.

---

3 You are a new assistant to a marketing manager at Home Hardware, a national chain of hardware stores. Your boss has been studying the stores' sales data from the last 10 years, and it appears that the post-Baby Boomer generations have somewhat different hardware needs and preferences than their elders did. For one thing, fewer younger adults are buying homes than the Boomers did at their age; instead, the younger generations tend to be renters longer. But even young homeowners seem to want different products, and different qualities in their products, than their predecessors did.

"We need to get into the minds of these buyers and find out what their world is like," your boss says. "I think it's time we did some focus group research to learn more about this demographic. Look into having one of our local marketing research firms conduct a couple of focus groups for us. See what process they'd recommend to help us understand our younger customers. Find out what strategies they use, how much they'd charge—you know, everything that would be involved in having them conduct some focus groups for us."

You do an Internet search to identify some potential firms. To be methodical about your research and have a written record of what you learn, you decide to submit your inquiries in writing. Your first one will go to Burke, Inc. The company's website provides an email address for "general inquiries," and that looks like your best bet. After thinking carefully about what you need to find out and what would make one research firm better than another for Home Hardware's needs, write your inquiry. (You may need to learn more about market research firms in general to figure out what to ask).

---

4 You're part of the management team at a home healthcare company. You have a staff of about 12 registered nurses (RNs), 13 licensed practical nurses (LPNs), and 18 personal care aides (PCAs), who provide services to the chronically ill, those involved in lengthy rehabilitation programs, and senior citizens. Your company has been in business a long time and is well regarded. But you've got a big problem: This year, your PCAs had a whopping 60 percent turnover rate.

This problem is costing the company a great deal of money. Each PCA you hire has not only been through several interviews and a testing procedure but has also undergone two days of training. When the PCAs leave, all that time spent on them is wasted—and some even disappear with the cell phones you issued them. Plus, the PCAs who have to fill in for the ones who suddenly leave have to be paid overtime or else *they* will grow dissatisfied and possibly leave.

What you pay your PCAs is well within the industry standard, so you're not inclined to raise their wages. But you do wonder if your hiring process could be improved. Specifically, you've decided to look into personality testing as a way of hiring only those candidates who are really suited to the work.

You've done a bit of informal research on personality testing, and you've learned that there are several different kinds, that there may be legal issues involved, and of course that it comes with a cost. To test the waters, you decide to call RightFit, a local HR management group, to discuss the possibilities. The receptionist puts you through to Sheila Smith, apparently the owner of the business, but you get her voice mail. Thinking quickly, you simply leave the message that you're calling to discuss the possibility of contracting their personality-testing services but that you'll follow up with an email providing the details.

Now write that email to Ms. Smith. Tell her enough about your situation and ask her enough on-target questions to help her prepare a helpful response for you.

---

5 You're part of the management team at Mazor's Deli, a local restaurant chain with five locations in the city. Each month, the management—everyone from the five store managers up to the president/owner—has a luncheon meeting in which they discuss any issues that have arisen, the financial health of the business, progress on current initiatives, any ideas for creating new business, and various other topics. You think such meetings are a great idea, and you understand the advantages of face-to-face communication (especially in this company's culture, which is close knit and family oriented)—but you wonder if these meetings are really worth the time and expense involved.

You recently attended a Restaurant Managers Association meeting where you learned that many of your peers are conducting business meetings online. One online meeting technology you kept hearing about was _____ (WebEx, GoToMeeting, MeetingBurner, or some other one—you choose). Curious, you checked out the product's website, viewed the demo, and studied the fact sheet. You are thinking that this product just might be a viable alternative to Mazor's monthly management meetings.

To gather more facts before sharing your idea with your superiors, you decide to consult a person you met at the RMA meeting who seemed to know a lot about online conferencing and about the particular tool you're interested in. Thinking carefully about what you'd like to learn about using this technology for meetings, prepare your questions in the form of an email of inquiry.

---

6 Parking is tight at your urban university, especially near certain buildings. The campus has two large parking garages, and both of them are far away and downhill from the business building where you have most of your classes as an MBA student. Normally you don't mind since you enjoy the trek from the garage to the business building. But as the president of your local chapter of Delta Pi Epsilon, the national business honor society for graduate students, you find yourself needing to reserve one of the few surface spaces close to the building. You have invited a local businessperson to come speak at the chapter meeting on May 3 from 4:00 to 5:30 p.m.

This guest will be rushing to the meeting from work and will be carrying a laptop as well as various print materials to distribute. You think it would be impractical as well as rude to force this guest to park in a garage and then trudge up a long hill to get to your building.

The parking services website at your school informs you that any special parking requests must be made in writing and sent via email to Ms. Barbara Stallmeyer. Write Ms. Stallmeyer and get permission for the reserved parking space you need. Be sure you make your request at least two weeks in advance as the website directs you to do.

---

7 You've been given an important assignment from your boss, the VP at a real estate firm in Philadelphia: to arrange a retreat for the sales staff where they can relax, recharge, and restrategize. The boss wants to hold the retreat in or near Cape May, NJ. He has specifically instructed you to find a large cottage, not a hotel or resort, because he wants the event to have the feel of a getaway, not a business meeting. But the retreat will serve important business purposes, so employees' families will not be invited.

After a good bit of Internet searching, you think you've found the perfect place: a large cottage overlooking Delaware Bay. You learn a lot about the property from the website—such as how many the cottage will sleep and what kind of beds are provided, how it is equipped (it has a large modern kitchen, a game room with air hockey and ping pong tables, and several large-screen TVs with cable service), what it will cost, and how much money is due by when. You also learn that linen service is provided and that minimal cleaning will be required at the end of your group's stay.

But you need to know more. For example, is there an area inside the cottage or on the porch, with enough seats, where the guests can comfortably meet and talk? The pictures on the website don't make that clear. Is there Wi-Fi and cell phone service? What attractions nearby might your co-workers enjoy? And then there are the smaller things. Are charcoal and lighter fluid included with the grill, or is it a gas grill? Are there paper towels? Salt and pepper? Kitchen linens and soap? What if the group wants to go out for drinks or food during the retreat? Are there suitable places nearby? Is the cottage in a nice area? You've never been there.

You wanted to ask the realtor these and other questions by phone, but you and she have been playing phone tag. Plus, you want a written record of her answers. So you'll craft a well-organized email message to get the information you need to ensure that this important company event goes well—and reflects well on you. Be sure to tell her what she needs to know about your event in order to give you helpful answers. (With your instructor's permission, you may change the venue and other details as appropriate.)

---

8 You work for a large credit union that is upgrading the software it uses to manage and maintain members' account and personal information. Everyone who works with or has access to members' information (tellers, customer service representatives, financial officers, loan representatives, department supervisors and managers, employee trainers, technical writers, marketing specialists, clerical staff, and information systems specialists) will need training on the upgraded software. Your boss has asked you, as the lead corporate trainer, to coordinate training sessions.

You discover that the makers of the software (Financial Software Systems, Inc.) can provide training on site or at its corporate headquarters, which happen to be in your town. You need to know which of these options is not only the most feasible and practical but also the most cost effective.

You have 500 employees who will need training. You have a corporate training room with 20 computers, a reliable Internet connection, and a data projector. The software will be installed in six months. Ideally, you would like to train all of your employees in the two months before the installation. That way they can continue to practice on the software installed in the corporate training room if they would like.

Although you have thought about calling for the information, you decide to write so that you have a permanent record of the answers to your questions. Write to Ms. Whitley Freeman, training coordinator, to inquire about Financial Software Inc.'s availability to provide training and for information that will help you decide whether to train on site or at company headquarters.

---

9   You are a recently hired associate at Van Fleet Analytics, a medium-sized marketing research firm. In addition to being a well-respected industry leader in marketing research, the firm prides itself on its work within the community. One specific community service project is the company's annual "bowl-a-thon" to raise money for the local Humane Society. Your supervisor asks you to coordinate this year's bowl-a-thon. In the past, the bowl-a-thon has been held at different bowling alleys throughout the city, so your supervisor leaves it up to you to find the best deal. In conducting research on the Internet, you come across Marcotti Lanes, which bills itself as "one of the premier bowling and entertainment centers in the region." Intrigued, you decide to find out more.

In an email of inquiry, come up with realistic details about the event (e.g., date, time, number of lanes needed, food and beverage requirements) that you will need to let Marcotti Lanes know about. In addition, devise a list of questions that will determine if Marcotti Lanes is suitable for your event. These questions may be related to cost, non-bowling entertainment options, or anything else of importance. Write the questions in such a way that you'll be sure to receive a thorough, detailed response.

---

10   As Komal Gupta, the person in charge of the opening ceremonies buffet for the university's World Village celebration next month, you need to order food appropriate for the celebration. Your town has a great Middle Eastern restaurant (Zorah's) that you think you want to feature. You visit the restaurant's website and are happy to learn that you would be able to order enough tabouli, hummus, pita bread, rice flavored with almonds and pine nuts, slow-roasted chicken (Zorah's specialty!), and baklava for 120 people.

What you aren't sure of, though, is the cost. In addition, the website says the items can be ordered by the half tray or the whole tray, and you're not sure how many people a half tray or whole tray will serve.

You're hoping that because the event is for a worthy cause and because the event would generate publicity for Zorah's, you might get a bit of a price break on the order. You would even be willing to pick up the order by 11 a.m. on the Saturday of the event. Using the email address provided on Zorah's website, write a request for the information you need to decide whether you will serve Zorah's food at the World Village celebration.

---

11   You took out your car loan with Community Bank because of its low interest rates. However, your regular checking and savings accounts are at Ocean State Credit Union. You can already tell that sending in a payment coupon and check each month will be neither convenient nor easy to remember. You wonder if you can just have your car payment for Community Bank automatically deducted from your Ocean State account and sent to Community Bank. You go to Community Bank's website and learn that this is possible, but no details are provided regarding the process, so you decide to click the link to "Contact Us" and ask your questions in the text box that appears. Though you'll want to think of more questions, you will at least want to know if there is a fee for this service and how long it takes to set up this payment option.

---

12   You are an intern for Canon City's recently formed Downtown Area Development Commission. The commission promotes downtown businesses, markets the downtown area as a great place for businesses to locate, and encourages citizens to shop downtown stores and enjoy local entertainment and dining. To build community spirit, the commission has decided to hold a contest to find its logo. Artists who are Canon City residents are encouraged to submit their designs for the commission to use on all of its work. The artists agree to be photographed and have their names used in the commission's publicity. The winning artist will receive $2,500 and a year of free advertising in the commission's monthly newsletter and on the commission's website.

All the artists need to do is submit a logo in .jpg format, proof of residency (think of what this might be as you write your document), and the legal agreement relinquishing rights to royalties or profit from their work if the commission chooses their logo. The logo can be sent by email or in the mail on a DVD, but it's not your fault if the DVD is damaged in the mail. The other forms can be completed online or downloaded and sent in the mail. Add any other details you think would be helpful.

Your job is to write a request to local artists asking that they submit a design. The announcement will be posted on the commission's website. You can format it in Microsoft Word as you want it to appear on the site. Your company's webmaster will take care of the online formatting; he just needs to know how you want it to look. It's important for artists to know that if they violate any of the steps in submitting their logo, they will be immediately disqualified from the contest.

13 You and a friend have decided to move off campus next year into an apartment. Together, you have narrowed down your list of requirements: The apartment needs to be within a 15-minute walk of campus, have two bedrooms, allow pets, have on-site laundry facilities, and cost no more than $550 per month including rent and utilities.

After scouring your campus resources with no luck, you come across a posting on craigslist that sounds like it might be perfect: "2-bedroom apartment within walking distance of campus. Laundry nearby. Cost: $535/month. Available August 1. Contact Casey at cvenit@ecrealestate.com for more information." Taking into account your needs, write an email to Casey to find out if this apartment will meet all of your requirements.

Remember, this correspondence could be the start of a year-long professional relationship.

Favorable Responses

14 You are an alum of _____ (your school). You currently work as the director for a local nonprofit organization (you pick the organization). Recently, your school's Center for Career Services contacted you asking if you would be willing to provide an internship for current students at your school. These students would be juniors and seniors majoring in accounting, finance, management, or marketing, though the Center for Career Services thinks marketing and management majors would be most interested.

You are willing to provide the internship. You can offer 15 hours a week to someone who would be willing to help with marketing, public relations, social media advertising, and general office tasks. The intern would assist in writing grant proposals and perhaps presenting reports orally and in writing to the organization's board of directors. What you cannot offer, though, is financial compensation. You're a nonprofit organization that is not, nor is ever likely to be, in a position to pay an intern.

Write a response to the Center for Career Services explaining what you can do and minimizing any negative news.

---

15 You're a junior financial analyst at the Wrigley Company in Chicago, and you've just received an email from a student at the local university asking if she can shadow you for a day to learn more about what the work in her major will be like. Write the student and tell her she can shadow you; tell her which day of the ones she suggested is best for you and when she should arrive; tell her where to park and how to enter the building and where/how to meet you; and cover any additional questions she's likely to have. Drawing upon your knowledge of the job you're pretending to have and the kind of company it's in, write a cordial, clear, well-organized, and thorough email that gets the visit set up and prepares the student to have an educational, enjoyable day.

---

16 You assist the operations manager at a manufacturing company, and one of your jobs is to ensure that you always have enough staff to maintain your production schedule.

In the last week, you've heard from several of your supervisors that your newer employees, as well as some of the more experienced ones, are asking about how to request vacation time during the summer. They want to know when they can take vacation, how soon they need to let you know, where they can go to use the online vacation leave forms (which are new since last summer when employees had to print forms and fill them out), and how they can check online to see how much vacation they've accrued (also new since last summer when they had to contact their supervisors directly).

Summer is a slow time for your company except for the first two weeks in June, the last week in July, and the first week in August, when no one is allowed to take vacation.

Creating realistic details as needed, write a response to these employees explaining the vacation request policy and process.

---

17 You are an intern for Kaya Asher, director of corporate communications at Argus, a management consulting firm. Kaya has been asked to lead a seminar to help the sales representatives use more persuasive oral communication, including formal presentations. Because she wants to do more than just tell her audience about oral communication skills, she plans to use YouTube videos to make her presentation more interesting and engaging. She has asked you to find four YouTube videos, two that illustrate effective oral communication and two that illustrate poor oral communication. You find four videos that you think will work for her as well as some alternatives. Write a response to her request. Provide links to the videos as well as a brief summary of what each video contains and why you think it is appropriate for Kaya's presentation.

18 You're an assistant manager at the Hilton Hotel, St. Petersburg, FL. You've just fielded a phone call from Mark Freshley, who was a guest at your hotel last week. He had breakfast in the hotel café the morning he checked out, so the printed bill you prepared for him was missing this last expense. He'd like for you to email him a new final bill showing this expense so that his company can reimburse him for it.

Write the email to Mr. Freshley and send him the bill as an attachment. While you're at it, you'll thank him for his business, of course. You'll also take advantage of this opportunity to invite him to join Hilton's rewards program, HHonors. Study the program at hhonors.hilton.com and select the details that you believe will be most appealing to him.

19 As director of corporate communications at the headquarters of a large consumer-goods manufacturer, you've just received an email from Jan Tofar—one of the company's newest, youngest hires—proposing that you discuss "mindfulness" in one of your weekly feature articles for the company intranet. Jan has been reading research and Web posts about the negative effects of multitasking and the benefits of a focused approach to one's work. She believes that the employees should be educated on this topic and taught how to minimize distractions that create stress and hamper productivity. Specifically, you will use her ideas and some

research of your own to write a feature article about the benefits of reducing multitasking and increasing mindfulness at work. Before coming to this decision, you made sure to get the approval of Human Resources, since employee productivity and welfare is their area of expertise and authority. In your favorable response to Jan, be sure you show that you appreciate her idea, that you will do a good job on the article, and that she'll get credit for her suggestion.

20 Recently, you received a letter from Jana Perkins, president of Midway University's Beta Upsilon Sigma (BUS) business fraternity. BUS is holding a silent auction to raise money for LIVESTRONG, a foundation to help cancer survivors and fight cancer, and has contacted you to see if your company, Backwoods Outfitters, could supply some items for the auction. Your company sells camping gear, hunting and fishing equipment, biking gear, skis, snowshoes, clothing, nonperishable food and dry goods, canoes, kayaks—anything anyone would need for an outdoor venture no

matter how large or how small. In addition, Backwoods Outfitters offers weekend rental packages that include a tent, canoe, backpacks, and supplies for $200 per weekend. The store also rents canoes, kayaks, bikes, skis, snowshoes, and additional camping gear separately.

As the manager for Backwoods Outfitters, you are happy to grant Jana's request and see this as a great opportunity to advertise your company and do something for the students and community. Respond to Jana's letter, telling her which item or items you will provide for the auction.

21 Great news: As president of your school's Rowing Club, you've just received an offer from Michael Selzer, the manager of a local grocery store and an alum of your school, to pay your student organization $500 to staff his store's table at the city marathon and half-marathon. Considering that your student organization is currently fundraising to pay for a cross-country trip to attend a competition, the timing of this offer couldn't be better.

The water and sports drinks will be provided by the marathon, and Selzer will handle the setup of the table and promotional banner. Your club is being asked to provide the

person power—a minimum of seven people to staff the table from 7:00 a.m. to 3:00 p.m. This time commitment may be an issue for some of your members, given that the race is being held the weekend before finals week.

Write an email to Selzer thanking him for the opportunity and agreeing to participate. Find out how many people have to be at the table at any given time, and ask any other questions you may have. Be sure you make him feel good about choosing your organization for this fundraising opportunity.

Order Acknowledgments and Other Thank-You Messages

22 You're a student who just shadowed a professional in your area of study. You had a great day with _____ at the _____ company. Sure, there was some down time when she was answering email and doing paperwork, but

she made an effort to tell you what she was doing and why. (Plus, for those down times, she'd given you some good reading material about the company and its industry.) She also included you in a meeting with her team and in chats with other employees on her breaks. She treated you to lunch and had gone to the trouble to invite a couple of entry-level employees—with jobs like the one you hope to get after you graduate—to join you. All in all, she really outdid herself. Thank her in a way that befits the effort she went to for you.

(Fill in the realistic details that your message will need in order to be effective.)

---

23 You've just been hired as a marketing intern for a large online auto parts dealership, AutoGeek.com. Your boss drops by your desk and asks you to look at the order-acknowledgment email message that the company currently uses. Here's what it says:

> This email was sent from a notification-only email address. Please do not reply to this message.

> **Dear [Customer]:**

> You have received this message because you have ordered a product from AutoGeek.com. If you'd like to be removed from our mailing list, reply with a blank message to sales@AutoGeek.com.

> Please be advised that you may not change or cancel your order, as we begin processing orders as soon as they are placed.

> We are currently checking your credit information and inventory availability. You will receive a

> Sales Invoice once your order has been assembled and packaged. If you do not receive a Sales Invoice within 24 hours, please contact us.

> Your invoice number is: 11-38520.

> All orders are shipped no signature required. Please be aware that orders only ship on business days, we do not offer weekend or holiday delivery. All orders placed after 5 p.m. EST will ship the following business day. A tracking number will be emailed to you within 1–2 business days.

> Frequently asked questions: Visit our website and click on Customer Service.

> Thank you for buying from AutoGeek.com.

"Think you can do better?" your boss asks. "Absolutely," you answer. Go for it. (If your instructor permits, you may choose another type of business for this case.)

---

24 A few years ago you and your spouse bought a lake cottage near Saugatuck, MI, to rent out until you retire there. It's an attractive, nicely furnished cottage, and it rents reasonably well during the short summer season (this far north, the warm weeks don't last very long).

You've been fielding inquiries from one Deb Sloan, who has been considering renting your cottage for the week of July 4. Today you got her rental deposit in the mail and her

confirmation that she and her family do want to rent the cottage.

Send her a receipt for her deposit and thank her for choosing your property. Make her feel good about her choice and provide any additional information she might need. You could build some extra goodwill—and perhaps turn her into a repeat renter—by suggesting things to do and places to visit while she's in the area.

---

25 As part-owner of your parents' restaurant, Zorah's, you responded to Komal Gupta's request for information about serving 120 people at the World Village Celebration (See case #10). You said in response to the request for a price break that you would put a little extra food on all the trays and include a full order of olives (priced at $20) at no charge. You also agreed to waive the $100 deposit that is usually required for large orders.

Komal was impressed by your response and placed an order. Because each tray serves about 40 people, Komal

placed an order for three trays of each of the following items: tabouli ($60), hummus and pita bread ($50), flavored rice ($60). Because the slow-roasted chicken must cook all day and is only available for dinner customers, grape leaves stuffed with lamb ($0.75 each, two per person) were ordered instead.

Write a note to Komal Gupta acknowledging the order and expressing your gratitude. Make Komal feel that selecting your cuisine for the event was a great choice.

---

26 As the assistant to the executive director of the Association for Business Communication, write the "welcome" message that you will send to new members. The message will include a receipt for their first-year dues, their member number (with which they can access members-only webpages), and of course contact information for the organization. Highlight any other benefits of membership you think

new members would enjoy. Add any other opportunities for members to become active in the ABC. Just as importantly, though, make readers feel good about the investment they've just made in their professional development. Remember that the more they take advantage of what the organization has to offer, the more likely they'll be to renew their membership next year.

---

27 Recently, you met with Dan Arojo, marketing manager with DeZine, a major architectural and construction firm. His company released an RFP (request for proposal) for someone to design, host, and maintain his company's website. Your company, Web2Go, specializes in Web design and plans to submit a proposal. Fortunately, Mr. Arojo was kind enough to meet with you to answer some questions regarding the proposal. He emphasized that DeZine is looking for a creative site that uses modern Web technologies but is user friendly, easily navigated, and visually appealing.

You learned that DeZine's signature architectural style is edgy and "hip" while being environmentally conscious. You learned that you will need to include a list of all fees you will charge for designing, creating, and hosting the site; if there are fees that DeZine will incur that are not part of the proposal, you must list them, as the company wants no surprises. In addition, if you plan to subcontract any of the work (e.g., use freelance designers, artists, writers), you must list the subcontractors in the proposal as well. Furthermore, any work you create would become the property of DeZine, not Web2Go. After your talk with Mr. Arojo, you are confident that your company's proposal will meet his needs and are excited about submitting it. Write a thank-you note to Mr. Arojo for meeting with you and providing you with the information for your proposal.

---

28 As the general manager of Riverview Golf Club, you are responsible for the club's facilities, accounting, and event planning. The club's 400 members are very pleased with the job you are doing. Last year, you received a special commendation from the club's membership for your role in securing and hosting a big golf tournament called the Midwestern Open. Things are going quite well for both you and the club.

Recently, you received the following email:

> Hello, my name is Michael Jones, and I am an assistant for Senator Katherine Rettig. The senator will be in town this weekend to meet with some of her constituents. As you may know, the senator is an avid golfer. Ever since she watched last year's Midwestern Open on television, she has been very interested in playing a round of golf at your club. We understand that your club is private, so please don't feel obligated to permit the senator to play at your club if you believe it would upset your membership. However, she would really like to play your course, and would require no special attention other than allowing three members of her legislative team to play alongside her. Ideally, the senator would like to play on Saturday afternoon.
>
> Thank you for your consideration.

You are very excited about the possibility of Senator Rettig's playing at Riverview! It would generate great publicity for the club. And since she is very popular with your membership, you don't foresee any problems with allowing her to play on Saturday afternoon. In fact, you believe that many of the members would be interested in meeting the senator to hear her opinions on the recent tax bill that was introduced into the Senate.

Respond to Michael Jones's email granting permission for the senator to play at Riverview. Provide directions and state what time the senator should arrive at the club. Also, ask Mr. Jones if the senator would be willing to meet informally with some interested members for a half-hour discussion of the new tax bill either before or after her golf round.

---

29 You are the community liaison for a nonprofit organization of your choice. Your organization participates in a program where donors can give to your program through an automatic credit or debit card deduction. Write a letter to these donors to thank them for their donations and update them on the organization's accomplishments during the past year and plans for the coming year. *Tip*: Think about how you might use technology to help you include a personalized salutation rather than simply "Dear Donor."

---

30 Recently, your student organization attended a national conference and competition in Anaheim, California. You did a considerable amount of fundraising from both campus departments and businesses in the local community prior to the trip to defray costs for your members.

After a lot of hard work and determination, your group placed fourth out of 25 teams from all over the United States. It was a great experience—and clearly it would not have been possible without the financial help from your supporters.

Now that the competition is over and you are back on campus, write a thank-you letter to your supporters. Let them know how thankful you are for their contributions. Make sure that your letter is professional so that you can keep them on your donor list for the future.

---

31 You are currently completing your senior year of college and are in the process of applying to jobs for after graduation. One of the companies you would love to work for is Grant Thornton. At the moment, It does not have any job openings in your area, so you emailed their human resources manager, Janet Robino, to request an informational interview.

She must have liked your message because she invited you to visit the firm. You did so yesterday, and Janet was very generous. She showed you around the office and patiently answered your questions. In addition, she introduced you to other employees at the firm, who described the projects that they were currently working on. When the visit was over, Ms. Robino gave you a Thornton coffee mug. It was a very good experience, and you learned a great deal! Write a thank-you note to Ms. Robino expressing your appreciation for all that she and her colleagues did during your visit.

Direct Claims

32 You're a clerk in the accounting office of Hocking Hills Resort and Spa, which recently placed a 2/3-page advertisement in *Travel Ohio* magazine. Today's email brought a notice from the magazine that Hocking Hills' account had been charged $3,700—the amount that a full-page ad costs.

You check with Lizzie Adams, the assistant director of sales and marketing for the resort, and she informs you that this amount is wrong. She proves it by showing you a list of the magazine's advertising rates and a copy of the purchase order, which clearly states the amount for a 2/3-page ad. Obviously, the accounting office for *Travel Ohio* has made an error.

Write *Travel Ohio* to request a credit to Hocking Hills's account. Use the medium and any supporting evidence that you think will do the best job of getting the results you seek.

33 You open the box of monogrammed shirts you ordered online for the servers at your new restaurant, and your face falls: The shirts are the right color, style, and sizes, but the monogrammed name on the shirts, "Mama Mia's," is misspelled.

You call the company from whom you purchased the shirts, Rite Uniforms, and talk with a customer service representative, Suzanne Miller. When you explain the situation, she first offers her sincere apologies. She then tells you what to do to get the shirts replaced. First, you need to fax her a letter on company letterhead that explains the error and requests replacement shirts. Once she receives this letter (which she will need in order to process your request), she will send you return shipping instructions and get the company working on your replacement shirts.

As you prepare to do as she asks, you think about anything else you might add to your message that will help Rite Uniforms solve the problem to your liking and get your relationship with them off on the right foot. Prepare your fax for Suzanne.

34 Remington Textiles is hosting a welcome dinner for a delegation of German executives who are interested in learning about Remington's products and possibly pursuing some contracts. You really want to make a good impression, so you have paid close attention to the details for the dinner. You even contracted with a local design company, Ridge Water Designs, to make an elegant, tasteful welcome banner to place above the doorway of the private room at the restaurant where the dinner will take place.

When you ordered the banner, Robin Heinze, the designer, told you that Ridge Water Designs could do the banner but could not deliver it until the afternoon of the dinner. Though you were nervous about getting the banner so close to the time of the dinner, you agreed after you were assured that everything would be fine. The banner arrived two hours before the dinner. It looked great, but Ridge Water Designs had spelled the German company's name incorrectly. Obviously, you could not use the banner, which cost $225, and you were incredibly disappointed, as you had sent Ridge Water Designs an email with the spelling of the company's name and even spelled it over the phone when you ordered the banner. On the day of the dinner, Ridge Water Designs had sent you a quick email to confirm that the banner was sent but had indicated that no one would be in the office for the rest of the day.

Write to Robin Heinze and request that you not be charged $225 for a sign that you obviously could not use.

35 You are the production supervisor for Pearl River Growers, a greenhouse and nursery. You ordered 200 trays of dahlia "plugs" (plants that start growing in small pots and are transferred to larger pots or gardens once they've matured). One of the trays arrived frozen, which means that all of the plugs are dead. Choose an effective communication channel and create a message requesting a replacement tray.

36 You are the building manager for Schneider Enterprises. After a recent construction project at the company, you contracted Custom Cleaning Services, a commercial cleaning company, to clean the office. According to the contract, you would pay $3,000 once the job was completed. When you drew up the contract for the cleaning, you and Beth Menendez, manager of Custom Cleaning Services, developed a checklist of cleaning jobs that needed to be done. The cleaning crew worked throughout the weekend. Though you let them in the building on Saturday morning and Sunday morning, you only checked in the evening that the building was locked after the crew left. You did not check the crew's work.

When you arrive for work on Monday morning, you notice that the cleaning crew missed some of the items on the checklist, and the cleaning job is sloppy. There are streaks on the windows. The walls also have streaks of dust, dirt, and fingerprints. Some of the light fixtures have not been cleaned or dusted, and the floor seems to have a film of some kind on it—like the cleaner did not quite cut through all of the dirt. You know that Beth would not find this cleaning job acceptable and would want you to be a satisfied customer.

Contact Beth and request what you think is reasonable for addressing this situation.

---

37 You are a musician who has ordered books of sheet music for a wedding reception that you and the other three members of your quartet will play for in two weeks. Unfortunately, when the books arrive, they are not what you ordered. You can return the music, but you still do not have what you need for the wedding in two weeks. You feel that because this is the company's fault, the company should overnight the right music at no charge to you. You'll gladly return the music you can't use, but you won't be paying the $7.95 shipping charge—that would be unreasonable since the mistake was not your fault. You called to talk with a customer service representative but got a message saying that all phone lines were busy and that for faster service, you should go to the company's customer support webpage. You go to the page and learn that you can type your message into a Web form and receive a response within two hours. Write a direct claim that gets you what you need.

---

38 You are the owner of a small bakery, Lakewood Confectioners. Your business is expanding, and you decide to order three new display cases from Wolburg Furniture, a company based 200 miles away with whom you have not previously done business. However, you have heard positive reviews about the quality of its products from a friend and fellow small-business owner. When the display cases arrive, you are surprised to find four sitting on the loading dock, not the three that you ordered. You double-check with your bookkeeper, Sam Ross, and verify that the purchase order clearly specified three display cases. Normally, you would simply put the extra item in a box and return it to the sender. However, these display cases are large, and shipping one would be both time consuming and expensive. In addition, the large extra case is taking up the limited space on your loading dock. Send an email to Wolburg Furniture's shipping department requesting that someone come pick up the extra display case as soon as possible.

Adjustment Grants

39 You're a customer service representative at CarParts.com, and you recently received a request, posted to your website, that you correct an error your company made (see Chapter 8, case #14). The customer makes a good case, and the purchase records confirm his account of what happened: The website does list the wrong number for the part (a problem that you have the webmaster correct immediately). The purchase records also show that this customer buys from you quite often.

You'll be glad to pay the return shipping for the wrong part (you will send him a prepaid UPS label) and will credit his account once you receive it. You will also be glad to send the replacement part directly to the car repair shop, as he requested. He does need to understand, though, that it's just not economically feasible for you to send this part via overnight shipping. The best you can do is get it to the shop within two business days. He'll need to let you know if, under these circumstances, he still wants the part delivered there. You'll of course extend your apologies for the trouble caused by the error on your website. Overall, you'll do your best to restore any goodwill that the incident may have cost you and make the customer feel good about ordering from you again.

---

40 You work in member services for a local credit union. Today you received a phone call from Sue Wong, a very upset credit union member. Every month, her paycheck is deposited in her savings account, with $1,000 automatically transferred to her checking account so that she can pay her bills. The automatic transfer has been occurring for three years and has never failed before. Last month, however, the funds were not transferred. Not realizing the funds had not transferred, Ms. Wong wrote several checks against the checking account. The account, of course, had insufficient funds to cover the checks, and Ms. Wong incurred service charges of $250.

Although Ms. Wong should have checked her account balance before writing the checks, the error is clearly the credit union's fault. When you spoke with Ms. Wong on the phone, you told her you would transfer the funds and reverse the service charges.

Credit union policy requires that you follow up these types of phone calls with a letter verifying that you have resolved the issue and explaining to the member what you did. Write the letter to Ms. Wong. You might remind her that if she would use the automatic payment option offered by the power company, most credit card companies, and many other services, she wouldn't have to worry about what is in her checking account or about even having to transfer money to her account each month.

---

41 Play the role of Suzanne Miller at Rite Uniforms and respond to case #33 in this chapter. The customer has faxed his request for replacement shirts to you as you requested, and you're now emailing him to provide instructions for returning the shirts. Include in your message any information that will answer his likely questions, and be sure to do your best to restore any lost goodwill.

---

42 You have just received a claim letter from Candace at Handel and Schmidt Holdings (see Chapter 8, case #16). As Bob Sawyer's trusty office assistant at Sawyer Steakhouse, you must handle her request for a partial refund on her bill. Sawyer's is the most popular steakhouse in the city—and it just so happened that, on short notice, the mayor decided to bring some visiting dignitaries to dinner on the night when the complaining customer held his company outing. That would account for the seating delay that the customer's party experienced. As for the unpleasant server and mixed-up orders . . . you're not sure what happened there. Perhaps the surprise VIPs threw the staff into something of a tizzy. Regardless, you are disappointed that Handel and Schmidt's experience did not reflect your usually stellar service.

At any rate, you understand the customer's point and are genuinely sorry that his special occasion was flawed. You'll definitely adjust the bill and do any other reasonable thing you can to regain his confidence and earn his repeat business.

---

43 Rarely do your professional cleaners make a mistake, but it looks like this time is an exception. Ms. Julie Todd just brought in an Eileen Fisher knit jacket that your cleaners managed to shrink so badly that it isn't even an adult size anymore. She also brought in a printed webpage showing that the jacket, which is no longer available, had sold for $250. You asked her how long she'd had the jacket, and she said two years. You promised to have your cleaners see what they could do with the jacket and then get back to her.

Now you must write her a letter offering her an adjustment. The jacket was so hopelessly shrunk that it could not be restored to anything near its original size. You have an adjustment chart that you use in cases like this one, and it indicates that you should pay her half of the clothing article's original value. So you'll offer to void the cleaning charge for the jacket and credit her account for $125 (if she wants the jacket back, though, you cannot adjust the bill; you keep the article of clothing in such circumstances so that customers won't feel encouraged to make other such claims and then keep the clothing).

---

44 Oops—it looks like one of the mowing teams at your company (Beauty Lawn) made a mistake (see case #12 in Chapter 8). Your customer's request for an adjustment is reasonable, so you'll grant it. You're just happy the damage wasn't any worse. What else might make this new customer feel that he chose the right lawn care company and that such errors will not be likely in the future? Say whatever you think appropriate to retain his loyalty and restore his confidence in Beauty Lawn's expertise.

Internal-Operational Messages

45 Revise the following poorly written message so that the message is clear and direct and has an appropriate tone and style. You may add information if you need to for the message to make sense. Be sure to fix any grammar, mechanics, punctuation, or word choice errors.

From:	Jim Hannigan
Sent:	Tuesday, June 2, 2013
To:	All Employees
Subject:	Security System

As many of you have noticed the security system is not working at this time, we are aware of this problem and are awaiting repair parts to correct the issue.

In response, the outer doors are unlocked and you will not need to use your badge until we are repaired.

Later this evening we will be falling back to keyed door locks for the evening.

If you are going out the front door, you will need to use the handle to get out the exterior doors after 5 PM.

Thank you for your patients,

Jim Hannigan
Building Supervisor
Ext. 5555

---

46 Revise the following poorly written message so that the message is clear and direct and has an appropriate tone and style. You may add information if you need to for the message to make sense. Be sure to fix any grammar, mechanics, punctuation, or word choice errors.

> Employees are taking too long of breaks. This must stop immediately so that we don't lose productivity. If we lose productivity, we could lose customers, and you could lose your job.
>
> Remember that you get 15 minutes in the morning and 15 in the afternoon. You get 30 minutes for lunch. This means you don't leave early, and it doesn't mean you take 30 minutes to eat and then take another 5 or 10 to get back to work. This means you get back to work after 30 minutes. Also, this means that when you are working, you are not allowed to be on Facebook or email for personal reasons. This has lead to alot of waste time, to.
>
> I know all of you care about your jobs. If their is any questions, please do not hesitate to contact me. Thank you for all of your hard work. It is appreciated.

---

47 As a company that has more than 50 employees living in or near the city where it is located, your company is covered by the U.S. Family Medical Leave Act (FMLA). This means that employees who meet certain criteria, as outlined by the U.S. Department of Labor (www.dol.gov/esa/whd/regs/compliance/whdfs28.pdf), may take up to 12 weeks of unpaid leave if they have a baby, an extended illness, or an impaired relative to take care of.

Many companies have started "leave donation" programs that enable employees to donate some of their accumulated sick leave or vacation time to fellow employees who have taken unpaid leaves. As office manager for your company, you periodically remind employees of this opportunity to help their colleagues. You think the time has come around again for this reminder, especially since you're aware of at least two employees who might need their co-workers' donations.

Write the employees, some of whom have never heard of this program, about the leave donation program. You will direct them to the FMLA website and to your own company's intranet for the full, official details; however, you will include the basics in your message: how much leave employees need to have accumulated in order to donate, the minimum and maximum amount of hours they can donate, the irreversibility of the donation, what recipients may use it for, how to donate, the fact that donating is strictly voluntary, and whatever else you think readers need to know in order to decide whether to pursue the matter further. (To generate such details, you can visit the FMLA website and the website at your school or business that describes this kind of policy.)

---

48 You are the facilities and grounds supervisor for AVG Enterprises. It's now April 1. Every summer you clean the office carpeting and polish and wax the floors. Employees can also request that their offices be painted, but their supervisors need to justify and approve the request. Those who have had their offices painted in the last five years can forget having them painted again, as you do not have the time or the budget. You do the floors one department at a time. You have to schedule cleaning for accounting, human resources, education and training, facilities and grounds, communications, sales, marketing, and information systems departments. Usually, it takes a week to do one department, as you have to do this early in the evening so that the floors are dry by the time employees arrive the next morning. If any offices need to be painted, the job needs to be done before the floors are done; you need three weeks' notice so that you can pick colors, order paint, and schedule the work. The floor maintenance will begin June 1. Develop a cleaning schedule that you'll send to all employees and department supervisors. Remind employees of the approval process for getting their offices painted. Because not everyone in the building has access to email, you'll write this as a memo.

---

49 You are the human resources manager for a public relations company. Your company employs people in many types of positions (e.g., communication, marketing and sales, creative services, accounting, customer service and support, clerical). You were talking with a colleague at a recent Society for Human Resource Management meeting and learned that your colleague's company offers professional development activities for its employees. These activities are generally workshops in which an expert shares his or her knowledge on a particular topic such as conflict resolution or email etiquette. Workshops are held on site. Most are only an hour or so and are held once a month during the workday. Of course, employees are paid to attend these sessions and are not required to attend all of them—only the ones that interest them.

You think this kind of professional development program is just what your company needs. You present such a program to your CEO and receive permission to try the program for six months, so you develop a list of topics, set a schedule, and contact experts who agree to lead the workshops.

Send a message to the employees of your company in which you describe the program, present a schedule, invite them to attend, and include a brief list of the topics the program offers in the next six months. Be sure you think about what information might motivate readers to participate in this program.

---

50 Over the last 10 years, you and four friends have grown your little technology consulting business, IT Doctors, into an 80-person company. The time has finally come to hire a human resources professional rather than contracting out the payroll and benefits services. So you hire Lauren Kiser, who brings extensive knowledge and experience to the position. After working there a couple of months, Lauren comes to you with a concern. "IT Doctors doesn't have a sexual harassment policy," she says. "I see a lot of friendly teasing going on between the male and female employees, but sometimes the females seem a bit offended. To have a welcoming company culture and to ensure that you don't run into legal trouble, I think you really need a sexual harassment policy. It doesn't have to accuse anyone of anything. But it should make clear what constitutes sexual harassment and emphasize that any such forms of behavior are grounds for reprimand or even dismissal."

To help you develop such a policy for IT Doctors, she sends you some Web links to other companies' policies and also directs you to the U.S. Equal Employment Opportunity Commission's (EEOC's) website. Thinking carefully about the information you've gathered and the kind of response you want from your employees, send out a memo in which you announce IT Doctors' new sexual harassment policy.

---

51 Continue on as the executive in case #50 above. The new sexual harassment policy you announced two months ago seems to have been well received, but recently you had to use it as grounds for a written warning to an employee whom two employees had complained about. This warning went into the offending employee's personnel file.

Perhaps as a result of this action, news of which no doubt made its way around the company grapevine, other employees seem to have become curious about exactly what goes into a personnel file and how that information can be used. After doing some research on this topic, send the employees an email in which you enlighten them. In preparing your email, consider the kinds of questions they're likely to have. For example, what kinds of documents get put into a personnel file? Which, if any, of these can be shared, and with whom? Are the contents of personnel files ever shared with those who are considering hiring IT Doctors' former employees? Can employees read their own personnel files? You may well think of additional questions that you should address.

---

52 Each year your company organizes a team to participate in your city's Making Strides Against Breast Cancer walk, one of a series of walks sponsored by the American Cancer Society. This year you are the coordinator of your company's team. Your first task is to invite all employees to an informational meeting. Send a message to everyone in the company regarding the meeting and include an agenda for the meeting. A little research on the Making Strides Against Breast Cancer website will help you decide what to include in your message. Of course you want your message to start generating enthusiasm for the cause right away—but be sure you make clear that coming to the meeting won't obligate anyone to participate in the walk. You just want to spread the word about it and be sure that anyone looking for a worthy cause to support (and an inspiring team experience) knows about this opportunity. Those who want to be on the team can sign up at the end of the meeting or let you know by August 3.

CHAPTER EIGHT

Maintaining Goodwill in Bad-News Messages

Learning Objectives

Upon completing this chapter, you will be able to write indirect messages to convey bad news. To reach this goal, you should be able to

1 Determine which situations require using the indirect order for the most effective response.

2 Write indirect-order messages following the general plan.

3 Use tact and courtesy in refusals of requests.

4 Compose tactful, yet clear, claim messages using an indirect approach.

5 Write adjustment refusals that minimize the negative and overcome bad impressions.

6 Write negative announcements that maintain goodwill.

LO1 Determine which situations require using the indirect order for the most effective response.

APPROACHES TO WRITING BAD-NEWS MESSAGES

As explained in Chapter 7, the indirect order is especially effective when you must say "no" or convey other disappointing news. Several research studies indicate that negative news is received more positively when an explanation precedes it.[1] An explanation can convince the reader that the writer's position is correct or at least that the writer is taking a logical and reasonable position, even if the news is bad for the reader. In addition, an explanation cushions the shock of bad news. Not cushioning the shock makes the message unnecessarily harsh, and harshness destroys goodwill.

However, research also indicates that the direct approach is warranted for communicating negative news in some contexts.[2] In one study of "data breach notification letters" (letters a company uses to alert readers when the security of their personal information has been compromised), the researcher concluded that when "writers must convince readers that a potential problem exists and encourage them to act," a direct approach may be more appropriate.[3] In addition, if you think that your negative news will be accepted routinely, you might choose directness. For example, in many buyer–seller relationships in business, both parties expect back orders and order errors to occur now and then. Thus, messages reporting this negative information would not really require indirectness. You also might choose directness if you know your reader well and feel that he or she will appreciate frankness. Although such instances are less common than those in which indirectness is the preferable strategy, you should always analyze your audience and business goals to choose the most appropriate organizational approach to delivering negative news.

As in the preceding chapter, we first describe a general plan. Then we adapt this plan to specific business situations—four in this case. First is the refusal of a request, a common task in business. Next we cover two related types of negative messages: indirect claims and adjustment refusals. Finally, we cover negative announcements, which are bad-news messages with unique characteristics.

LO2 Write indirect-order messages following the general plan.

THE GENERAL INDIRECT PLAN

The following plan will be helpful for most negative-news situations.

Using a Strategic Buffer

Indirect messages presenting bad news often begin with a strategic buffer. By **buffer** we mean an opening that identifies the subject of the message but does not indicate that negative news is coming. That is, the buffer is relevant to the topic of the message but does not state what the rest of the message will say about it.

A buffer can be neutral or positive. A neutral buffer might simply acknowledge your receipt of the reader's earlier message and indicate your awareness of what it said. A positive buffer might thank the reader for bringing a situation to your attention or for being a valued customer or employee. You do need to use care when opening on a positive note. You do not in any way want to raise the reader's hopes that you are about to deliver the news that he or she may be hoping for. That would only make your task of maintaining good relations more difficult.

Some may argue that not starting with the good news is, for savvy readers, a clear tip-off that bad news is coming. If this is the case, then why not just start with the bad

---

[1] Valerie Creelman, "The Case for 'Living' Models," *Business Communication Quarterly* 75:2 (2012): 176–191, print.

[2] Jennifer R. Veltsos, "An Analysis of Data Breach Notifications as Negative News," *Business Communication Quarterly*, 75:2 (2012): 203, print; Creelman.

[3] Veltsos.

news? The answer is that most readers appreciate a more gradual introduction to the message's main negative point even when they know it is coming. A buffer gives them a chance to prepare for the news—and even if they suspect that it will be negative, the use of a buffer indicates consideration for their feelings.

Setting Up the Negative News

For each case, you will have thought through the facts involved and decided that you will have to say "no" or present some other kind of negative news. You then have to figure out how you will present your reasons in such a way that your reader will accept the news as positively as possible. Your strategy might be to explain the fairness of a certain action. It might be to present facts that clearly make the decision necessary. Or you might cite the expert opinion of authorities whom both you and your reader respect. It might even be possible to show that your reasons for the negative decision will benefit the reader in the long run.

Whatever explanatory strategy you choose, these reasons should follow your buffer and precede the negative news itself. In other words, the paragraph after the buffer should start explaining the situation in such a way that by the time the negative news comes, the reader is prepared to receive it in the most favorable light possible.

Presenting the Bad News Positively

Next, you present the bad news. If you have developed your reasoning convincingly, this bad news should appear as a logical outcome. You should present it as positively as the situation will permit. In doing so, you must make certain that the negative message is clear—that your approach has not given the wrong impression.

One useful technique is to present your reasoning in first and third person, avoiding second person. To illustrate, in a message refusing a request for a refund for a returned product, you could write these negative words: "Since you have broken the seal, state law prohibits us from returning the product to stock." Or you could write these words emphasizing first and third person: "State law prohibits us from returning to stock all products with broken seals."

It is sometimes possible to take the sting out of negative news by linking it to a reader benefit. For example, if you preface a company policy with "in the interest of fairness" or "for the safety of our guests," you are indicating that all of your patrons, including the reader, get an important benefit from your policy.

Your efforts to present this part of the message positively should employ the positive word emphasis described in Chapter 5. In using positive words, however, you must make certain your words truthfully and accurately convey your message. Your goal is to present the facts in a positive way, not to confuse or mislead.

Offering an Alternative Solution

For almost any negative-news situation that you can think of, there is something you can do to help the reader with his or her problem.

If someone seeks to hold an event on your company grounds and you must say "no", you may be able to suggest other sites. If someone wants information that you do not have, you might know of another way that he or she could get similar information. If you cannot volunteer your time and services, perhaps you know someone who might, or perhaps you could invite the reader to make the request again at a later, better time. If you have to announce a cutback on an employee benefit, you might be able to suggest ways that employees can supplement this benefit on their own. Taking the time to help the readers in this way is a sincere show of concern for their situation. For this reason, it is one of your most powerful strategies for maintaining goodwill.

Ending on a Positive Note

Since even a skillfully handled bad-news message can be disappointing to the reader, you should end the message on a *forward-looking note*. Your goal here is to shift the reader's thoughts to happier things—perhaps what you would say if you were in face-to-face conversation with the person. Preferably your comments should fit the topic of your message, and they should not recall the negative message. They should make clear that you value your relationship with the reader and still regard it as a positive one.

Apologizing

Many times when a writer must deliver bad news, the first thought is to apologize. After all, if a customer or co-worker is unhappy—for any reason—somehow apologizing seems a good strategy for making a situation better. Sometimes an apology can make a bad situation better, but other times it can make a bad situation worse. For example, if a customer incurs finance charges because you forgot to credit a payment to the customer's account, an apology, along with a credit to the account and removal of the finance charge, may help restore goodwill. On the other hand, if the bad news is something you had no control over (e.g., a customer didn't follow instructions for using a product and the item broke), apologizing can make you appear in the wrong even when you're not. A reader may also wonder why, if you're so sorry, you cannot do what the reader wants you to do. Apologies may even have legal implications if they can be construed as admissions of guilt.

If you do apologize in a bad-news message, do so early in the message as you explain the reasons and deliver the bad news. Then move beyond the apology just as you move beyond the bad news and toward your forward-looking conclusion. If you think your apology may have legal implications, you can have your message reviewed by a supervisor or your company's legal department before sending it.

Following are adaptations of this general plan to four of the more common negative business message situations. From these applications you should be able to see how to adapt this general plan to almost any other situation requiring you to convey bad news.

REFUSED REQUESTS

INTRODUCTORY CHALLENGE

Denying a Request for a Donation

As in Chapter 7, assume the role of assistant to the White Label Industries (WLI) vice president. Today your boss assigned you the task of responding to a request from the local chapter of the National Association of Peace Officers. This worthy organization has asked WLI to contribute to a scholarship fund for certain needy children.

The request is persuasive. It points out that the scholarship fund is terribly short. As a result, the association is not able to take care of all the needy children. Many of them are the children of officers who were killed in the line of duty. You have been moved by the persuasion and would like to comply, but you cannot.

You cannot contribute now because WLI policy does not permit it. Even though you do not like the effects of the

policy in this case, you think the policy is good. Each year WLI earmarks a fixed amount—all it can afford—for contributions. Then it donates this amount to the causes that a committee of its executives considers the most worthy. Unfortunately, all the money earmarked for this year has already been given away. You will have to say no to the request, at least for now. You can offer to consider the association's cause next year.

Your response must report the bad news, though it can hold out hope for the future. Because you like the association and because you want it to like WLI, you will try to handle the situation delicately. The task will require your best strategy and your best writing skills.

The **refusal of a request** is definitely bad news. Your reader has asked for something, and you must say no. Your **primary goal**, of course, is to present this bad news. You could do this easily with a direct refusal; however, opening with the bad news that you are refusing the reader's request could make you and your company appear insensitive. As a courteous and caring businessperson, you have the secondary goal of maintaining goodwill. To achieve this second goal, you must convince your reader that the refusal is fair and reasonable before you break the bad news.

LO3 Use tact and courtesy in refusals of requests.

Developing the Strategy

Finding a fair and reasonable explanation involves carefully thinking through the facts of the situation. First, consider why you are refusing. Then, assuming that your reasons are just, try to find the best way of explaining them to your reader. To do so, you might well place yourself in your reader's shoes. Try to imagine how the explanation will be received. What comes out of this thinking is the strategy you should use in your message.

One often-used explanation is that company policy forbids compliance. This explanation may work but only if the company policy is defensible and clearly explained. Often you must refuse simply because the facts of the case justify a refusal—that is, you are right and the reader is wrong. In such cases, your best course is to review the facts and to appeal to the reader's sense of fair play.

In any situation, you may have multiple ways to offer a fair and reasonable explanation. Your job is to analyze your audience and communication goals and select the one that best fits your case.

Setting Up the Explanation in the Opening

Having determined the explanation, you begin the message with a buffer that sets up the discussion. For example, in the case of WLI's refusal to donate to the National Association of Peace Officers' worthy cause, the following opening meets this case's requirements well:

> Your organization is doing a commendable job of educating needy children. Like many other worthy efforts, it well deserves the support of our community.

This beginning, on-subject comment clearly marks the message as a response to the inquiry. It implies neither a yes nor a no answer. The second statement sets up the explanation, which will point out that the company has already given its allotted donation money to other worthy organizations. This buffer puts the reader in an agreeable or open frame of mind—ready to accept the explanation that follows.

Presenting the Explanation Convincingly

As with the general plan, you next present your reasoning. To do this you use your best persuasion techniques: positive wording, proper emphasis, sound logic, and supporting detail to convince your reader.

Handling the Refusal Positively

Your handling of *the refusal follows logically* from your reasoning. If you have built the groundwork of explanation and fact convincingly, the refusal comes as a logical conclusion and as no surprise. If you have done your job well, your reader may even support the refusal. Even so, because the refusal is the most negative part of your message, you should not give it much emphasis. You should state it quickly, clearly, and positively; and you should keep it away from positions of emphasis, such as paragraph endings.

You might even be able to make the message clear without stating the negative news explicitly. For example, if you are refusing a community member's request to use your company's retreat facility for a fundraiser, you will convey "no" clearly if you say that

you must restrict the use of the facility to employees only and then go on to offer alternative locations. You must be sure, though, that your message leaves no doubt about your answer. Being unclear the first time will leave you in the position of writing an even more difficult, more negative message later.

To state the refusal positively, you should carefully study the effects of your words. Such harsh words as *I refuse, will not,* and *cannot* stand out. So do such apologies as "I deeply regret to inform you . . ." and "I am sorry to say. . . ." You can usually phrase your refusal in terms of a positive statement of policy. For example, instead of writing "your insurance does not cover damage to buildings not connected to the house," write "your insurance covers damage to the house only." Or instead of writing "We must refuse," a wholesaler could deny a discount by writing "We can grant discounts only when. . . ." In some cases, your job may be to educate the reader. Not only will this be your explanation for the refusal, but it will also build goodwill.

Using a Compromise When Practical

If the situation justifies a **compromise**, you can use it in making the refusal positive. More specifically, by saying what you can do (the compromise), you can clearly imply what you cannot do. For example, if you write "What we can do is to (the compromise), . . ." you clearly imply that you cannot do what the reader requested. Such statements contain no negative words and usually are as positive as the situation will permit.

Closing with Goodwill

Even a skillfully handled refusal is the most negative part of your message. Because the news is disappointing, it is likely to put your reader in an unhappy frame of mind. That frame of mind works against your goodwill goal. To leave your reader with a feeling of goodwill, you must shift his or her thoughts to more pleasant matters.

The best closing subject matter depends on the facts of the case, but it should be positive talk that fits the one situation. For example, if your refusal involves a counterproposal, you could say more about the counterproposal. Or you could make some friendly remark about the subject of the request as long as it does not remind the reader of the bad news. In fact, your closing subject matter could be almost any friendly remark that would be appropriate if you were handling the case face to face. The major requirement is that your ending words have a goodwill effect.

Ruled out are negative apologies, such as "Again, may I say that I regret that we must refuse". Also ruled out are the equally timeworn appeals for understanding, such as "I sincerely hope that you understand why we must make this decision." Such words sound selfish and emphasize the bad news.

Fitting the General Plan to Refused Requests

Adapting the preceding analysis to the general plan, we arrive at the following outline for the refused request:

- Begin with words that indicate a response to the request, are neutral about the answer, and set up the strategy.
- Present your justification or explanation, using positive language and you-viewpoint.
- Refuse clearly and positively.
- Include a counterproposal or compromise when appropriate.
- End with an adapted goodwill comment.

Contrasting Refusals

The advantage of the indirect order in refusal messages is illustrated by the following contrasting examples of WLI's possible response to the request from the National Association of Peace Officers. Both refuse clearly. But only the one that uses the indirect order is likely to regain the reader's goodwill.

Harshness in the Direct Refusal. The first example states the bad news right away. This blunt treatment puts the reader in an unreceptive frame of mind. The result is that the reader is less likely to accept the explanation that follows. The explanation is clear, but note the unnecessary use of negative words (*exhausted, regret, cannot consider*). Note also how the closing words leave the reader with a strong reminder of the bad news.

Subject: Your request for a donation

Ms. Cangelosi:

We regret to inform you that we cannot grant your request for a donation to the association's scholarship fund.

So many requests for contributions are made of us that we have found it necessary to budget a definite amount each year for this purpose. Unfortunately, our budgeted funds for this year have been exhausted, so we simply cannot consider additional requests. We won't be able to consider your request until next year.

We deeply regret our inability to help you now and trust that you understand our position.

Mark Stephens

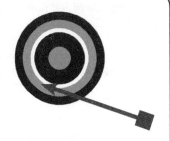

This bad email is harsh because of its directness and negative language.

Tact and Courtesy in an Indirect Refusal. The second example skillfully handles the negative message. Its opening words are on subject and neutral. They set up the explanation that follows. The clear and logical explanation ties in with the opening. Using no negative words, the explanation leads smoothly to the refusal. Note that the refusal is also handled without negative words and yet is clear. The friendly close fits the one case.

This email using the indirect approach is better.

Subject: Your Scholarship Fund Request

Ms. Cangelosi:

Your efforts to build the scholarship fund for the association's needy children are commendable.

White Label Industries assists worthy causes whenever we can. That is why every January we budget in the upcoming year the maximum amount we believe we are able to contribute to such causes. Then we distribute that amount among the various deserving groups as far as it will go. Since our budgeted contributions for this year have already been made, we are placing your organization on our list for consideration next year.

We wish you success in your efforts to improve the lives of the children in our city.

Mark Stephens

INDIRECT CLAIMS

INTRODUCTORY CHALLENGE

Seeking an Adjustment for a Subpar Experience

Play the role of Jeff Sutton, owner and president of Sutton Creative Services. You've just received a bill from Regal Banquet Center for the winter-holiday party that your company held there last week. It's for $1,410, which you had agreed to pay for an elegant three-course meal, plus drinks, for your 27 employees.

The food was as good as its reputation, but there were two problems. First, the room for the party was much too warm. You complained to the servers but to no avail. You would have opened windows to correct the problem yourself, but the room you were given did not have any windows (something you weren't happy about either). Second, there was apparently a shortage of servers on the night of your event. Some of your employees had to wait a long time for their food, while those who had their food first either had to start eating before the others or let their food get cold while waiting for all to be served. This ragged timing ruined the dinner, and it also threw off the timing of the program you had planned.

You were embarrassed by these problems. They reflected poorly on you and your efforts to thank your employees for their work. While you understand that unexpected problems can arise, you just don't think you should have to pay the full amount for a subpar experience. You'll need to write a claim message asking for an adjustment to your bill.

When something goes wrong between a business and its customers, usually someone begins an effort to correct the situation. Typically, the offended party calls the matter to the attention of those responsible. This claim can be made in person, by phone, or by written message (email or letter).

LO4 Compose tactful, yet clear, claim messages using an indirect approach.

Our concern here is how to make it in a written message. You would likely choose a written medium if you wanted a record of the interchange, were not on personal terms with the recipient, or knew that writing to the recipient would be quicker and more efficient than contacting the reader by phone. While some claim messages are written directly (see Chapter 7), many are also written indirectly when the writer anticipates resistance or a strong negative reaction on the part of the reader. In this chapter, we examine an approach for writing **indirect claims**.

Choosing the Right Tone

Your goal in a claim message is to convince your recipient that you deserve some kind of compensation or remedy for a situation that has occurred. But even if you are completely in the right, you will not advance your cause with accusatory, one-sided language. When writing this kind of message, project an image of yourself as a reasonable person. Just as importantly, project an image of the reader as a reasonable person. Give him or her a chance to show that, if presented with the facts, he or she will do the right thing. Do not give in to the temptation to blame or whine. Keep your tone as objective as you can while also making sure that the reader understands the problems caused by the situation. Focus as much as possible on facts, not feelings.

Leading into the Problem in the Beginning

A claim message needs to identify the transactions involved. This you can do early in the message as a part of the beginning. One way is to put the identification in the subject head in an email message or in the subject line of a letter, as in this example:

Subject: Fire Extinguishers: Your Invoice C13144

Another way is just to include a neutral but relevant buffer:

Today we received via FedEx Ground the fire extinguishers we ordered on 5 May 2009 (invoice # C13144).

Whether you use a subject line and your first paragraph or the first paragraph alone to *introduce the problem*, choose your words with care. Such negatively charged words as complaint or disappointment can put your readers on the defensive before you've even had a chance to make your case.

Describing the Problem Clearly

In the body of your message, explain what happened. The words describing the problem should be courteous yet firm. They should cover the problem completely, giving enough information to permit the reader to judge the matter. Present your case using facts and logic. If there were consequences to what happened, include them. This beginning sentence illustrates the point:

When we purchased a Quick Time microwave (Serial No. 713129), we were told that because of our light use and the quality of the microwave, we needed only the six-month warranty rather than the three-year extended warranty. We have had the microwave for only seven months, but it suddenly quit working.

Notice that this example uses the passive voice ("were told") to avoid accusing or blaming language. You should follow these statements with any other evidence that supports your eventual request to replace the microwave.

Since unanticipated problems occur in business, writing a clear, complete, and fairminded claim will usually solve them.

Requesting the Correction

The facts you present should prove your claim, so your next step is to follow logically with making the claim. How you handle the claim, however, is a matter for you to decide. You have two choices: You can state what you want (money back, replacement), or you can leave the decision to the reader. You choose which, based on the situation.

Building Goodwill with a Fair-Minded Close

Your final friendly words should leave no doubt that you are trying to maintain a positive relationship. You could express appreciation for what you seek. However, you want to avoid the cliché "Thanking you in advance." Instead, say something like "I would be grateful if you could get the new merchandise to me in time for my Friday sale." Whatever final words you choose, they should clearly show that yours is a firm yet cordial and fair request.

Outlining the Indirect Claim Message

Summarizing the preceding points, we arrive at this outline for the indirect claim message:

- Identify the situation (invoice number, product information, etc.) and lead into the problem.
- Present enough facts to be convincing.

- Seek corrective action.
- End positively—friendly but firm.

Contrasting Examples of Indirect Claim Messages

The following two messages show contrasting ways of handling Jeff Sutton's problem with the Regal Banquet Center. The first is blunt and harsh. The second is courteous, yet clear and firm.

A Blunt and Harsh Message. From the very beginning, the first message—a letter that the reader is returning along with his reduced payment—is insulting. "To whom it may concern" is impersonal, generic, and outdated. The opening paragraph is a further affront, blurting out the writer's stance in angry language. The middle of the message continues in this negative vein, accusing the reader with *you* and *your* and using emotional language. The negative writing continues into the close, leaving a bad final impression. Such wording is more likely to produce resistance than acceptance.

Subject: Bill Adjustment

To Whom It May Concern:

I just received a bill for $1,410 for the winter party that I held for my employees at the Regal Banquet Center. I absolutely refuse to pay this amount for the subpar job you did of hosting this event.

First, you put us in an unpleasant room with no windows even though we had made our reservations weeks in advance. The room was also much too warm. I asked your staff to adjust the temperature, but apparently they never did. Since the room didn't have any windows, we just had to sit there and swelter in our dress clothes. As if this weren't bad enough, it took the servers so long to bring all our food out that some people had finished eating before others were even served. This made a complete mess of the nice dinner and the scheduled program.

I had heard good things about your center but now regret that I chose it for this important company event. The uncomfortable and chaotic experience reflected poorly on me and on my appreciation for my employees. Enclosed is my payment for $1,000, which I feel is more than fair.

Sincerely,

Jeff Sutton, Owner and President

Sutton Creative Services

This blunt and accusing letter is unlikely to lead to a cooperative reply or further business with the reader.

A Firm Yet Courteous Message. The second message (page 202) follows the plan suggested in preceding paragraphs. A subject line quickly identifies the situation. The first paragraph leads into the problem. Next, in a tone that shows firmness without anger, it tells what went wrong. Then it requests a specific remedy. The ending uses subtle persuasion by implying confidence in the reader. The words used here leave no doubt about the writer's interest in a continued relationship.

Refused Request Message to an External Audience (Denying an Artist's Request). A regional medical facility displays local artists' work at its various satellite locations. Artists submit applications to have their work displayed. This message shows a good strategy for denying a request to an artist who applied to have her work displayed in the Lake Superior Family Medicine Clinic's reception area.

Lake Superior
Family Medicine Clinic

Visit us: Web: https://www.lsfm.org

Lake Superior Family Medicine Clinic
4546 Burger Lane
North Concord, WI 54746
Web: www.lsfm.org
phone: 715-987-4958
fax: 715-567-7684

June 15, 2012

Ms. Jane Burroughs
2942 County Highway J
North Concord, WI 54746

Dear Jane:

Relevant, neutral buffer—gains the reader's favor by thanking her

Thank you for submitting your artwork for consideration at Lake Superior Family Medicine Clinic. The jury's deliberation process took more time than expected due to the number of submissions. Such a delay is a rare occurrence, so your patience was appreciated.

Provides a reasonable, convincing explanation supported by a fact

The Medical Center's art wall and case is a free service open to local artists like you. This exhibit area has been embraced by not only artists but also community members because of the beauty it showcases. In fact, it's so popular that we had 75 requests from local artists last month. Due to the limited wall space available and the large number of art submissions, your artwork was not chosen for display at this time.

Offers an alternative

The jury enjoyed your pieces and noted that your art "personified light." We encourage you to submit up to 10 pieces from your collection once again in 120 days. As outlined in the initial request letter dated May 22, 2012, artists can submit up to 10 submissions every 120 days.

Provides a relevant, forward-looking conclusion that builds goodwill

If you have any questions, please contact me. Again, thank you for submitting your artwork. We look forward to your next submission.

Sincerely,

Samantha Kennedy

Director, Marketing/Community Relations
Lake Superior Family Medicine Clinic
Email: sakennedy@lsfmc.org
Phone: 715-456-7890

Refused Request Message to an Internal Audience (Saying "No" to an Employee). This message shows a good strategy for denying a hard-working employee's vacation request because of CEO Kelsey Riley's directive.

Positive, relevant buffer highlights points the reader and writer can agree upon—presents the writer as a reasonable person

Logically explains the reasons for rejecting the reader's request

Provides good news and a positive alternative for the reader

Offers a goodwill close and moves beyond the bad news

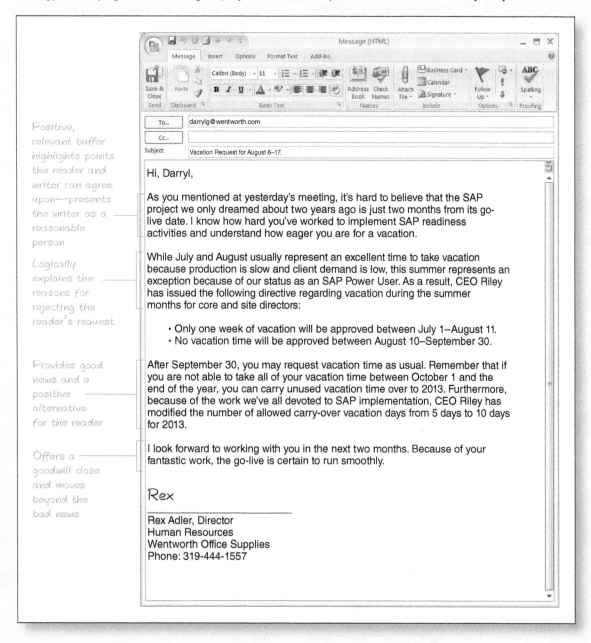

To... darrylg@wentworth.com

Cc...

Subject: Vacation Request for August 6–17.

Hi, Darryl,

As you mentioned at yesterday's meeting, it's hard to believe that the SAP project we only dreamed about two years ago is just two months from its go-live date. I know how hard you've worked to implement SAP readiness activities and understand how eager you are for a vacation.

While July and August usually represent an excellent time to take vacation because production is slow and client demand is low, this summer represents an exception because of our status as an SAP Power User. As a result, CEO Riley has issued the following directive regarding vacation during the summer months for core and site directors:

- Only one week of vacation will be approved between July 1–August 11.
- No vacation time will be approved between August 10–September 30.

After September 30, you may request vacation time as usual. Remember that if you are not able to take all of your vacation time between October 1 and the end of the year, you can carry unused vacation time over to 2013. Furthermore, because of the work we've all devoted to SAP implementation, CEO Riley has modified the number of allowed carry-over vacation days from 5 days to 10 days for 2013.

I look forward to working with you in the next two months. Because of your fantastic work, the go-live is certain to run smoothly.

Rex

_____

Rex Adler, Director
Human Resources
Wentworth Office Supplies
Phone: 319-444-1557

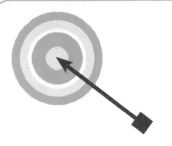

This more tactful but honest email invites the reader to do what is fair and retains goodwill.

Subject: Invoice #3712 (for Sutton Party on December 12, 2013)

Dear Ms. Sanchez:

As you know, Sutton Creative Services held its winter-holiday party at Regal Banquet Center on December 12. While the food was exceptional, I have some concerns regarding our experience.

When I booked the party last August, I requested that we have the party in Salon A because of its size and view of the city. The room we were given for the event was Salon C. As you know, the room is small and has no windows. In addition, the location also had the drawback of making the temperature hard to control. The servers were sympathetic but were unable to keep the room from getting too warm for my 27 employees. I know that you book many parties during the holiday season; however, as the attached copy of our contract shows, we agreed that Sutton Creative Services would be in Salon A.

It also appeared that more servers were needed for our party. The fare was elegant, but with only two servers, some guests had finished eating before others had even started. As a result, we had to start the after-dinner program in the middle of the meal, requiring the speaker to talk while people were eating. This made it difficult for people to hear and pay attention to his presentation.

Overall, the event was not the impressive "thank-you" to my hard-working employees I had in mind when we drew up the contract. In light of these circumstances, I am requesting a revised invoice of $1,000. I believe this is a fair amount for an experience that I am sure did not represent the Regal's typical level of customer service.

I would be grateful for your response by the end of the month so that I can forward the adjusted bill to my accountant for payment.

Sincerely yours,

Jeff Sutton, President and Owner

Sutton Creative Services

ADJUSTMENT REFUSALS

INTRODUCTORY CHALLENGE

Denying a Customer's Claim

Sometimes your job at White Label Industries (WLI) involves handling a complaint. Today that is one of your tasks because the morning email has brought a strong claim for adjustment on an order for WLI's Do-Craft fabrics. The claim writer, Ms. Arlene Sanderson, explains that a Do-Craft fabric her upholstering company used on some outdoor furniture has faded badly in less than 10 months. She even includes photographs of the fabric to prove her point. She contends that the product is defective, and she wants her money back—all $2,517 of it.

Inspection of the photographs reveals that the fabric has been subjected to strong sunlight for long periods. Do-Craft fabrics are for indoor use only. Both the WLI brochures on the product and the catalog description stress this point. In fact, you have difficulty understanding how Ms. Sanderson missed it when she ordered from the catalog. Anyway, as you see it, WLI is not responsible and should not refund the money. At the same time, it wants to keep Ms. Sanderson as a repeat customer. Now you must write the message that will do just that. The following discussion tells you how.

Adjustment refusals are a special type of refused request. Your reader has made a claim asking for a remedy. Usually you grant these claims. Most are legitimate, and you want to correct any error for which you are responsible. But such is not the case in Ms. Sanderson's situation. The facts require that you say no. The following section shows you how to handle this type of message.

LO5 Write adjustment refusals that minimize the negative and overcome bad impressions.

Determining the Strategy

The primary difference between this and other refusal messages is that in these situations, as we are defining them, your company will probably have clear, reasonable guidelines for what should and should not be regarded as legitimate requests for adjustment. You will, therefore, not have to spend much time figuring out why you cannot grant the reader's request. You will have good reasons to refuse. The challenge will be to do so while still making possible an ongoing, positive relationship with the reader.

Setting Up Your Reasoning

With your strategy in mind, you begin with words that set it up. Since this message is a response to one the reader has sent, you also acknowledge this message. You can do this by a date reference early in the message. Or you can do it with words that clearly show you are writing about the specific situation.

One good way of setting up your strategy is to begin on a **point of common agreement** and then to explain how the case at hand is an exception. To illustrate, a case involving a claim for adjustment for failure of an air conditioner to perform properly might begin this way:

> You are correct in believing that an 18,000 BTU Whirlpool window unit should cool the ordinary three-room apartment.

The explanation that follows this sentence will show that the apartment in question is not an ordinary apartment.

Another strategy is to build the case that the claim for adjustment goes beyond what can reasonably be expected. A beginning such as this one sets it up:

> Assisting families to enjoy beautifully decorated homes at budget prices is one of our most satisfying goals. We do all we reasonably can to reach it.

The explanation that follows this sentence will show that the requested adjustment goes beyond what can be reasonably expected.

Making Your Case

In presenting your reasons for refusal, explain your company's relevant policy or practice. Without accusing the reader, call attention to facts that bear on the case—for example,

© 2008 Ted Goff

"Sorry, we believe that the customer is only right some of the time under certain circumstances, and none of them apply to you."

SOURCE: Copyright © 2008 Ted Goff.

Outlook Quick Parts Tool Allows Writers to Reuse Content

If you use Outlook and have content that frequently appears in your email messages, you may want to consider using the Quick Parts tool.

Let's say, for example, that you send reminders every two weeks to employees regarding their time sheets. After you've created your content and formatted it the way you always want it to appear in your reminder messages, select the text. Once the text is selected, from the Insert ribbon, click the Quick Parts dropdown arrow, click "Auto Text," and then click "Save Selection to AutoText Gallery." From there, you can use the "Create New Building Block"

dialog box to customize your Quick Parts selection. Over time, you can build, categorize, and organize a list of Quick Parts selections.

The next time you need to send your message, you just open a new message, go to the Insert ribbon, click Quick Parts, and choose your text from the list that appears. The content will be inserted into your email just as you originally saved it in Quick Parts. You save time, and you know that your reminders will be consistent in their look and their content.

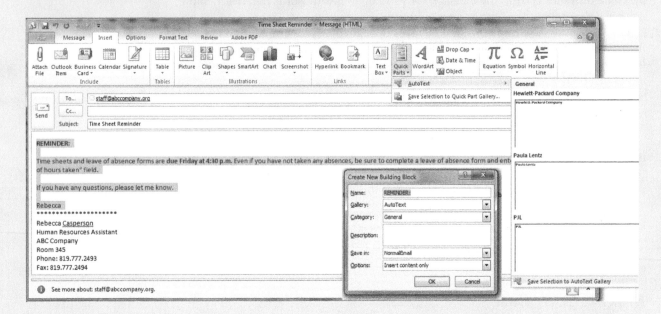

that the item in question has been submerged in water, that the printed material warned against certain uses, or that the warranty has expired. Putting together the policy and the facts should lead logically to the conclusion that the adjustment cannot be granted.

Refusing Positively and Closing Courteously

As in other refusal messages, your refusal derives from your explanation. It is the logical result. You word it clearly, and you make it as positive as the circumstances permit. For example, this one is clear, and it contains no negative words:

> For these reasons, we can pay only when our employees pack the goods.

If a compromise is in order, you might present it in positive language like this:

> In view of these facts, we can repair the equipment at cost.

As in all bad-news messages, you should end this one with some appropriate, *positive comment*. You could reinforce the message that you care about the reader's business or the quality of your products. In cases where it would not seem selfish, you could write about new products or services that the reader might be interested in. Neither negative apologies nor words that recall the problem are appropriate here.

Adapting the General Plan

When we apply these special considerations to the general plan, we come up with the following specific plan for adjustment refusals:

- Begin with words that are on subject, are neutral about the decision, and set up your strategy.
- Present the strategy that explains or justifies, being factual and positive.
- Refuse clearly and positively, perhaps including a counterproposal.
- End with positive, forward-looking, friendly words.

Contrasting Adjustment Refusal Messages

Bad and good treatment of WLI's refusal to refund the money for the faded fabric are illustrated by the following two messages. The bad one, which is blunt and insulting, destroys goodwill. The good one, which uses the techniques described in the preceding paragraphs, stands a fair chance of keeping goodwill.

Bluntness in a Direct Refusal. The bad email begins bluntly with a direct statement of the refusal. The language is negative (*regret, must reject, claim, refuse, damage, inconvenience*). The explanation is equally blunt. In addition, it is insulting ("It is difficult to understand how you failed . . ."). It uses little tact, little you-viewpoint. Because the close is negative, it recalls the bad news.

Subject: Your May 3 claim for damages

Ms. Sanderson,

I regret to report that we must reject your request for money back on the faded Do-Craft fabric.

We must refuse because Do-Craft fabrics are not made for outside use. It is difficult for me to understand how you failed to notice this limitation. It was clearly stated in the catalog from which you ordered. It was even stamped on the back of every yard of fabric. Since we have been more than reasonable in trying to inform you, we cannot possibly be responsible.

We trust that you will understand our position. We regret very much having to deny your request.

Marilyn Cox, Customer Relations

The bad email shows little concern for the reader's feelings.

Tact and Indirect Order in a Courteous Refusal. The good message (page 207) begins with friendly talk on a point of agreement that also sets up the explanation. Without accusations, anger, or negative words, it reviews the facts of the case, which free the company from blame. The refusal is clear, even though it is implied rather than stated. It is skillfully handled. It uses no negatives, and it does not receive undue emphasis. The close shifts to helpful suggestions that fit the one case—suggestions that may actually result in a future sale.

Adjustment Refusal Letter (Refusing a Refund). An out-of-town customer bought an expensive dress from the writer and mailed it back three weeks later asking for a refund. The customer explained that the dress was not a good fit and that she did not like it anymore. But perspiration stains on the dress proved that she had worn it. This letter skillfully presents the refusal.

103 BREAKER RD. HOUSTON, TX 77015 713-454-6778 Fax: 713-454-6771

On-subject opening

February 19, 2012

Ms. Cherie Ranney
117 Kyle Avenue E
College Station, TX 77840-2415

Dear Ms. Ranney:

Review of the facts—supports the writer's position

We understand your concern about the elegant St. John's dress you returned February 15. As always, we are willing to do as much as we reasonably can to make things right.

Set-up for the explanation

Negative language minimized in the refusal

What we can do in each instance is determined by the circumstances. With returned clothing, we generally give refunds. Of course, to meet our obligations to our customers for quality merchandise, all returned clothing must be unquestionably new. As you know, our customers expect only the best from us, and we insist that they get it. Thus, because the perspiration stains on your dress would prevent its resale, we must consider the sale final. We are returning the dress to you. With the proper alterations, it can be an elegant addition to your wardrobe.

Good restraint—no accusations, no anger

Friendly goodwill close

Please visit us again when you are in the Houston area. It would be our pleasure to serve you.

Emphasis on what can be done—helps restore goodwill

Sincerely,

Marie O. Mitchell
President

dm

Subject: Your May 3 Message about Do-Craft Fabric

Ms. Sanderson:

Certainly, you have a right to expect the best possible service from Do-Craft fabrics. Every Do-Craft product is the result of years of experimentation. And we manufacture each yard under the most careful controls. We are determined that our products will do for you what we say they will do.

Because we do want our fabrics to please, we carefully inspected the photos of Do-Craft Fabric 103 that you sent us. It appears that each sample has been subjected to long periods in extreme sunlight. Because Do-Craft fabrics cannot withstand exposure to sunlight, all our advertising, the catalog, and a stamped reminder on the back of every yard of the fabric advise customers that the fabric is meant for indoor use only.

As you can see from our catalog, the fabrics in the 200 series are recommended for outdoor use. You may also be interested in the new Duck Back cotton fabrics listed in our 500 series. These plastic-coated cotton fabrics are economical, and they resist sun and rain remarkably well.

If we can help you further in your selection, please contact us at service@wli.com.

Marilyn Cox, Consumer Relations

This better email is indirect, tactful, and helpful.

NEGATIVE ANNOUNCEMENTS

INTRODUCTORY CHALLENGE

Announcing a Medical Coverage Cut

As the assistant to the human resources director at National Window Systems, you have been given the difficult assignment of writing a bad-news message for your boss. She has just returned from a meeting of the company's top executives in which the decision was made to deduct 25 percent of the employees' medical insurance premiums from their paychecks. Until now, National Window Systems has paid it all. But the rising cost of health coverage is forcing the company to cut back on these benefits, especially since profits have declined for the past several quarters. Something has to give if National Window Systems is to remain competitive while also avoiding lay-offs. The administrators decided on a number of cost-cutting measures including this reduction in the company's payment for medical insurance. The message you will write to National Window Systems employees is a negative announcement.

Occasionally, businesses must announce bad news to their customers or employees. For example, a company might need to announce that prices are going up, that a service or product line is being discontinued, or that a branch of the business is closing. Or a company might need to tell its employees that the company is in some kind of trouble,

LO6 Write negative announcements that maintain goodwill.

When making a negative announcement, remember that an indirect, tactful approach is usually better than a blunt "loud" approach.

that people will need to be laid off, or, as in the Introductory Challenge, that employee benefits must be reduced. Such **negative announcements** generally follow the instructions previously given in this chapter.

Determining the Strategy

When faced with the problem of making a negative announcement, your first step should be to determine your overall strategy. Will you use direct or indirect organization?

In most cases the *indirect arrangement* will be better. This route is especially recommended when it is reasonable to expect that the readers would be surprised, particularly disappointed, or even angered by a direct presentation. When planning an indirect announcement, you will need to think about what kind of buffer opening to use, what kind of explanation to give, how to word the news itself, and how to leave your readers feeling that you have considered their interests.

Setting Up the Bad News

As with the preceding negative message types, you should plan your indirect beginning (buffer) carefully. You should think through the situation and select a strategy that will set up or begin the explanation that justifies the announcement. Perhaps you will begin by presenting justifying information. Or maybe you will start with complimentary or cordial talk focusing on the good relationship that you and your readers have developed. Choose the option that will most likely prepare your reader to accept the coming bad news.

Positively Presenting the Bad News

In most cases, the opening paragraph will enable you to *continue with* background reasons or explanations in the next paragraph, before you present the negative news. Such explaining will help you put the negative news in the middle of the paragraph rather than at the beginning where it would be emphasized.

As in other negative situations, you should use positive words and avoid unnecessary negative comments when presenting the news itself. Since this is an

Like all human resources professionals, Joan McCarthy, director of human resources communication for Comcast Cable, sometimes has to deliver negative news to employees, whether it's about healthcare coverage, organizational change, or other issues. Her advice? "Balance, not spin, is the key. Frequent, candid communication that balances the good with the bad will go much further toward restoring and maintaining employee trust than the most creative 'spin.'"

Sometimes McCarthy will state negative news directly, while other times she takes a more gradual approach. Whichever pattern you use, "it's important to communicate openly and honestly," she advises. But you should also balance out the negative by "reinforcing the positive, putting the news in perspective, and showing what the organization is doing to help." In these ways you can "communicate bad news in a way that preserves your company's credibility and keeps employee trust and morale intact."

announcement, however, you must make certain that you cover all the factual details involved. People may not be expecting this news. They will therefore want to know the whys and whats of the situation. And if you want them to believe that you have done all you can to prevent the negative situation, you will need to provide evidence that this is true. If there are actions the readers must take, these should be covered clearly as well. All questions that may come to the readers' minds should be anticipated and covered.

Focusing on Next Steps or Remaining Benefits

In many cases negative news will mean that things have changed. Customers may no longer be able to get a product that they have relied upon, or employees may have to find a way to pay for something that they have been getting for free. For this reason, a skillful handling of a negative announcement will often need to include an effort to help people solve the problem that your news just created for them. In situations where you have no further help to offer—for example, when announcing certain price increases—you can still help people feel better about your news by calling attention to the benefits that they will continue to enjoy. You can focus on the good things that have not changed and perhaps even look ahead to something positive or exciting on the horizon.

Closing on a Positive or Encouraging Note

The ending words should cement your effort to cover the matter positively. They can be whatever is appropriate for this one situation—a positive look forward, a sincere expression of gratitude, or an affirmation of your positive relationship with your readers.

Reviewing the Plan

Applying the preceding instructions to the general plan, we arrive at this specific plan for negative announcements written in indirect order:

- Start with a buffer that begins or sets up justification for the bad news.
- Present the justification material.
- Give the bad news positively but clearly.
- Help solve the problem that the news may have created for the reader.
- End with appropriate goodwill talk.

Negative Announcement (Decreasing Work Hours). Shop employees are told of the effects a slow economy will have on their work hours. The message is friendly and empathetic but clearly conveys the negative news. The goodwill close looks forward to better economic times.

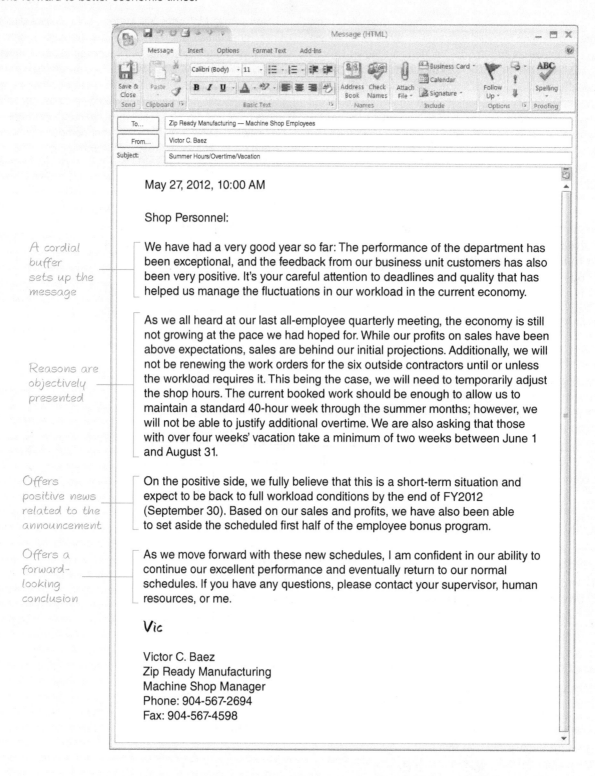

A cordial buffer sets up the message

Reasons are objectively presented

Offers positive news related to the announcement

Offers a forward-looking conclusion

May 27, 2012, 10:00 AM

Shop Personnel:

We have had a very good year so far: The performance of the department has been exceptional, and the feedback from our business unit customers has also been very positive. It's your careful attention to deadlines and quality that has helped us manage the fluctuations in our workload in the current economy.

As we all heard at our last all-employee quarterly meeting, the economy is still not growing at the pace we had hoped for. While our profits on sales have been above expectations, sales are behind our initial projections. Additionally, we will not be renewing the work orders for the six outside contractors until or unless the workload requires it. This being the case, we will need to temporarily adjust the shop hours. The current booked work should be enough to allow us to maintain a standard 40-hour week through the summer months; however, we will not be able to justify additional overtime. We are also asking that those with over four weeks' vacation take a minimum of two weeks between June 1 and August 31.

On the positive side, we fully believe that this is a short-term situation and expect to be back to full workload conditions by the end of FY2012 (September 30). Based on our sales and profits, we have also been able to set aside the scheduled first half of the employee bonus program.

As we move forward with these new schedules, I am confident in our ability to continue our excellent performance and eventually return to our normal schedules. If you have any questions, please contact your supervisor, human resources, or me.

Vic

Victor C. Baez
Zip Ready Manufacturing
Machine Shop Manager
Phone: 904-567-2694
Fax: 904-567-4598

Contrasting Negative Announcements

Good and bad techniques in negative announcements are illustrated in the following two messages. The bad one is direct, which in some circumstances may be acceptable but clearly is not in this case. The good one follows the pattern just discussed.

Directness Here Alarms the Readers. This bad example clearly will upset the readers with its abrupt announcement in the beginning. The readers aren't prepared to receive the negative message. They probably don't understand the reasons behind the negative news. The explanation comes later, but the readers are not likely to be in a receptive mood when they see it. The message ends with a repetition of the bad news.

To our employees:

National Window Systems management sincerely regrets that effective February 1 you must begin contributing 25 percent of the cost of your medical insurance. As you know, in the past the company has paid the full amount.

This decision is primarily the result of the rising costs of health insurance, but our profits also have declined the last several quarters. Given this tight financial picture, we needed to find ways to reduce expenses.

We trust that you will understand why we must ask for your help with cutting costs to the company.

Sincerely,

Directness here sends a negative message.

Convincing Explanation Begins a Courteous Message. The better example follows the recommended indirect pattern. Its opening words begin the task of convincing the readers of the appropriateness of the action to be taken. After more convincing explanation, the announcement flows logically. Perhaps it will not be received positively by all recipients, but it represents a reasonable position given the facts presented. After the announcement comes an offer of assistance to help readers deal with their new situation. The last paragraph reminds readers of remaining benefits and reassures them that management understands their interests. It ends on an appreciative, goodwill note.

To All Employees:

Companies all across the United States, no matter how large or small, are struggling to keep up with the rising cost of healthcare. Legislators, healthcare providers, and businesspeople everywhere are working to find a solution to the skyrocketing cost of health insurance.

We are feeling this situation here in our own company. The premiums that we pay to cover our health benefits have increased by 34 percent over the last two years, and they now represent a huge percentage of our expenditures. Meanwhile, as you know, our sales have been lower than usual for the past several quarters.

For the short term, we must find a way to cut overall costs. Your management has considered many options and rejected such measures as cutting salaries and reducing personnel. Of the solutions that will be implemented, the only change that affects you directly concerns your medical insurance. On **March 1** we will begin deducting 25 percent of the cost of the premium.

Jim Taylor in the Personnel Office will soon be announcing an informational meeting about your insurance options. Switching to spousal coverage, choosing a less expensive plan with lighter deductibles, or setting up a flexible spending

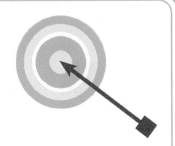

This indirect example follows the bad-news pattern.

account may be right for you. You can also see Jim after the meeting to arrange a personal consultation. He is well versed in the many solutions available and can give you expert advice for your situation.

Our healthcare benefits are some of the best in our city and in our industry, and those who continue with the current plan will not see any change in their medical coverage or their co-pays. Your management regards a strong benefits program as critical to the company's success, and we will do all we can to maintain these benefits while keeping your company financially viable. We appreciate your cooperation and understanding.

Sincerely,

Using Directness in Some Cases

As we mentioned at the beginning of this chapter, in some cases it is likely that the reader will react favorably to a direct presentation of the bad news. If, for example, the negative news is expected (as when the news media have already revealed it), its impact may be viewed as negligible. There is also a good case for directness when the company's announcement will contain a remedy or announce new benefits that are designed to offset the effects of the bad news. As in all announcements with some negative element, this part must be worded as positively as possible. Also, the message should end on a goodwill note. The following example of a store's announcement about discontinuing a customer reward program illustrates this situation.

Dear Ms. Cato:

Effective January 1 Frontier Designs is discontinuing our Preferred Customer program so that we may offer several new promotions.

Your accumulated points will be converted to a savings coupon worth as much as or more than your points total. Your new points total is on the coupon enclosed with this letter. You may apply this coupon in these ways:

- When shopping in our stores, present your coupon at the register.
- When shopping from our catalogs, give the coupon number to the telephone service agent, enclose your coupon with your mail order, or enter it with your online order at www.frontierdesigns.com/catalog.

In all these cases we will deduct your coupon value from your purchase total. If you have any questions, please call us at 1-800-343-4111.

We thank you very much for your loyalty. You'll soon hear about exciting new opportunities to shop and save with us.

Sincerely,

THERE'S MORE . . .

Would you like to learn more about breaking bad news? Would you like to learn tips for maintaining goodwill in bad-news situations? Could your tone and style in bad-news messages be improved? Scan the QR code with your smartphone or use your Web browser to visit www.mhhe.com/lesikar13e. Choose Chapter 8 > Bizcom Tools & Tips.

1. When the main point of your message is bad news, use the indirect order.

   - But exceptions exist, as when you believe that the news will be received routinely.
   - Make exceptions also when you think the reader will appreciate directness.

   Determine which situations require using the indirect order for the most effective response.

2. In general, bad-news messages follow this general plan.

   - Begin with a buffer that sets up the strategy.
   - Develop the strategy.
   - Present the bad news as a logical result of the strategy and as positively as possible.
   - Try to offer an alternative solution.
   - End on a positive note.
   - Determine whether to apologize

   Write indirect-order messages following the general plan.

3. The refusal of a request is one bad-news situation that you will probably choose to treat indirectly.

   - In such situations, strive to achieve two main goals:
     — To refuse.
     — To maintain goodwill.
   - Begin by thinking through the problem, looking for a logical explanation (or reasoning).
   - Write an opening that sets up this explanation.
   - Then present your explanation (reasoning), taking care to use convincing and positive language.
   - Refuse clearly yet positively.
   - Use a compromise when practical.
   - Close with appropriate, friendly talk that does not recall the bad news.

   Use tact and courtesy in refusals of requests.

4. Indirect claim messages are written when the writer anticipates resistance or a strong negative reaction on the part of the reader.

   - Plan to write neutrally and reasonably.
   - Lead into the problem with your beginning.
   - Then describe the problem clearly, thoroughly, and tactfully.
   - Either ask for what you seek or invite your reader to decide what is fair.
   - End on a positive but firm note that leaves open the possibility for future business.

   Compose tactful, yet clear, claim messages using an indirect approach.

5. Indirectness is usually best for refusals of adjustments.

   - First, determine your explanation (reasoning) for refusing.
   - Begin with neutral words that set up your reasoning and do not give away the refusal.
   - Then present your reasoning, building your case convincingly.
   - Refuse clearly and positively.
   - Close with appropriate friendly talk that does not recall the refusal.

   Write adjustment refusals that minimize the negative and overcome bad impressions.

6. Sometimes businesses must announce bad news to their customers or employees.

   - Indirect organization usually is better for these announcements.
   - Precede the bad news with a convincing explanation.
   - Use positive words when possible to cover the bad news.
   - Use directness when appropriate. This is the case when the news is expected or will have little negative impact.
   - Even so, handle the negative with positive wording.

   Write negative announcements that maintain goodwill.

buffer, 190

refusal of a request, 193

compromise, 194

primary goal, 193

indirect claims, 197

adjustment refusals, 203

point of common agreement, 203

Negative announcements, 208

CRITICAL THINKING QUESTIONS

1 Give examples of times (or situations) when direct-ness would be appropriate for responses giving negative information. **LO1**

2 Writing in the indirect order usually requires more words than does writing in the direct order. Since conciseness is a virtue in writing, how can the indirect order be justified? **LO1**

3 What strategy is best in a message refusing a request when the reasons for the refusal are strictly in the writer's best interests? **LO3**

4 "Apologies in refusals are negative because they call attention to what you are refusing. Thus, you should avoid using them." Discuss. **LO3**

5 Explain how a claim message can be either direct or indirect. **LO4**

6 "If I'm not emotional in my claim messages, the readers won't understand how upset I am." Respond to this statement. **LO4**

7 Some business writers explain an adjustment refusal simply by saying that company policy did not permit granting claims in such cases. Is this explanation adequate? Discuss. **LO5**

8 Negative announcements usually need to include much more than the announcement. Explain. **LO6**

9 Give examples of negative announcements that would be appropriately written in the direct order. **LO6**

SKILLS BUILDING EXERCISES

1 Point out the shortcomings in the following email message from a sports celebrity declining an invitation to speak at the kickoff meeting for workers in a fund-raising campaign for a charity. **LO3**

Subject: Your request for free lecture

Ms. Chung:

As much as I would like to, I must decline your request that I give your membership a free lecture next month. I receive many requests to give free lectures. I grant some of them, but I simply cannot do them all. Unfortunately, yours is one that I must decline.

I regret that I cannot serve you this time. If I can be of further service in the future, please call on me.

Sincerely yours,

2 Criticize the following message refusing the claim for a defective riding lawn mower. The mower was purchased 15 months earlier. The purchaser has had difficulties with it for some time and submitted with the claim a statement from a local repair service verifying the difficulties. The writer's reason for refusing is stated in the email. **LO5**

Subject: Your May 12 claim

Mr. Skinner:

Your May 12 claim of defective workmanship in your Model 227 Dandy Klipper riding mower has been reviewed. After considering the information received, I regret to report that we cannot refund the purchase price.

You have had the mower for 15 months, which is well beyond our one-year guarantee. Even though your repair person says that you had problems earlier, he is not one of our authorized repair people. If you will read the warranty you refer to in your letter, you will see that we honor the warranty only when our authorized repair people find defects. I think you will understand why we must follow this procedure.

If you will take the machine to the authorized service center in your area (La Rue Lawn and Garden Center), I am confident they can correct the defect at a reasonable charge.

If I can be of additional service, please contact me.

Sincerely,

3 You work for an online mail-order company, Nonsensi-cals, that sells such novelty items as T-shirts with clever sayings, unique toys and games, and such household accessories as framed posters and retro table lamps. Most of the employees are young, somewhat quirky, and very Internet savvy. Now consider the following email sent to everyone from the company president: **LO6**

Subject: No More Social Networking during Work Hours

It has become obvious to me that people are spending too much time doing social networking and not enough time actually working while on the job. From now on, you must do your networking (whether on MySpace, Facebook, LinkedIn, or any other such network) on breaks or during other personal time. Anyone found using these websites on company time will receive an official reprimand.

Considering the advice in this chapter, what would be the main ways to improve this negative announcement?

4 You own a small new- and used-book store and café with free wireless Internet access. You enjoy the calm, quiet atmosphere of your store and like that your customers choose your store to conduct business, socialize with friends, or just enjoy a good book and a cup of coffee. Increasingly, many customers are talking on their cell phones—very loudly and in places where they shouldn't be. They hold up the order line by talking on the phone when they should be talking to the cashier. They disrupt others who are enjoying the quiet atmosphere to work or read. Sure, customers who are working on the computer may need to talk on the phone, but must these customers be so loud and disruptive that those across the room who are trying to read can hear their conversations?

Many customers have actually complained. You want to make these customers happy but not at the expense of making your cell phone users unhappy. Write a cell phone use policy to post in your store. **LO6**

PROBLEM-SOLVING CASES

Refused Requests

1 You were recently invited to serve on the board of the Eastman Health Foundation, a nonprofit organization that provides various funds and services to area health agencies and hospitals. At this point in your career, serving on the board of a high-profile organization like this one would be a great career enhancer, so you readily accepted the invitation.

But now the foundation's executives want you to organize and lead their major fundraiser for the year, a silent auction. When the board discussed fundraising ideas, you enthusiastically supported this one—but you have neither the time nor inclination to be in charge of it.

Figure out how to say no while also showing that your support for the organization is genuine. Maybe some kind of counteroffer will help.

2 As the HR director at Hader Building Supply, you couldn't be happier with how your efforts to establish an employee-volunteer program have worked out. Thanks to the employees' donations of their time and expertise to the Hader Helps program, the community where you live has been improved, and the company has gained a more positive public profile. But there are still some bumps in the road, and today you're dealing with one of them.

Part of the program you set up is a database of company-approved schools, foundations, and other nonprofit organizations for which employees may volunteer. In order to get approved time off work for their contributions, employees must choose one of these organizations. There are over 30 organizations on the list, and more are added each month as employees propose new causes for the company to support.

Beth Atkinson, one of the office staff, has just sent you an email requesting that the local chapter of the Center for Family Values be approved as one of Hader's nonprofit partners.

You check out the organization's website, and what you suspected is confirmed: The organization supports political action that is pro-life and opposed to same-sex unions. And even though the center isn't affiliated with any particular denomination, it has strong ties with Christian churches, as its Pastors for Family Values webpage indicates.

You simply cannot grant Beth's request. The guidelines for proposing an addition to the list of supported organizations state that the organization can have no religious or political affiliations. While the Center for Family Values is not an official political organization, it is an advocacy group with an explicit political agenda, which the website encourages visitors to support through volunteering, donating, voting, and writing legislators.

You worked very hard to get the employees behind the new volunteer program, and you don't want Beth to start any negative talk about it. Refuse her request in such a way that you do not lose her support for the program.

3 Today you've received a solicitation from a well-meaning service organization, People Working Together (PWT). PWT is inviting your company, Handymen for Hire, to be a featured sponsor of its annual Repair Affair. This event, the major fundraiser and publicity effort, has volunteers from all over the city contributing one day's labor to helping their less fortunate neighbors with yard work, home repairs, and other tasks. Your contribution of $1,000 will help pay for the volunteers'

T-shirts (on which your company's name will appear), the supplies, and the picnic that will follow the day's work.

While this amount doesn't sound like much for a successful business, you're a small organization that can afford to make only a limited number of charitable contributions. You've given over $5,000 to such causes this year, and that's all you can afford right now. But, truthfully, you're not sure that the publicity opportunity PWT offers would be the best use of your money. Those helped by PWT aren't likely to become your customers since one reason they're being helped is that they can't afford to pay for services like yours. True, the volunteers might be potential customers—but the fact that they're volunteering suggests that they're able to do their own repairs. It looks very unlikely that you'll ever be willing to be a sponsor of PWT's event.

Write the PWT chair a letter turning down the request for a sponsorship while maintaining a positive company image. Perhaps you can think of something you can offer that will help soften the "no." (Or, play the role of office manager and assume that your boss has asked you to write the letter for his or her signature.)

4 As executive director of the Northwest Human Resources Institute, you have been gathering information to help the organization's board of directors decide where to hold its annual meeting three years from now. Specifically, the board has asked you to investigate two possible sites: Seattle, Washington, and Portland, Oregon. In both cities you received good help from representatives of the chamber of commerce, but Collin Mallard of Seattle was particularly helpful. He went out of his way to show you the city and give you insider information on its attractions and restaurants. He also took you to the hotels with appropriate facilities for your event and introduced you to the managers. Overall, he was a delightful tour guide. You were hoping to send your organization's business his way.

Unfortunately, the board has decided on Portland for the meeting. Now it is your job to inform Mr. Mallard that Seattle's bid has been turned down. Certainly, you will express your thanks for his help. You can also report that the decision was a close one and that Seattle will be considered for later years. Send your message to Mr. Mallard via letter. Remember that the board will see a copy of it. (If your instructor directs, research the two cities and come up with plausible reasons why Portland was chosen.)

5 As a new college graduate, you're delighted that not one but two companies have offered you a position in their _____ (you decide which) department. You met representatives of both companies at your university's job fair. From this first contact came an invitation for an on-site job interview with each company. You really enjoyed learning more about the operations of both companies and meeting their friendly employees. Both companies have great employee benefits, and the salaries they're offering are comparable.

After careful thought, you've decided to go with Company B. You sense a little better match between their values and yours, and you think the opportunity for advancement might be better there as well.

Write the recruiter at Company A to reject its offer. Of course you will convey your appreciation for the company's consideration, and the things you learned on your visit will enable you to give some well-deserved compliments. What will be stickiest is figuring out how to explain why you're choosing another offer. The explanation won't need to be long, but the company does deserve one. You certainly don't want to close the door on future employment or business relations with this company, so the time you spend crafting this letter will be time well spent. (If your instructor directs, research two companies to use for this assignment.)

6 You're responsible for marketing communications at MyBiz.com, a mid-sized company that makes software specially designed for managing small businesses. Today you've received an email from Rachel Lundemeyer, who works for the Association for Small Business Owners, asking if your company would like to purchase an ad to run in the association's quarterly magazine, *Small Business Today*. She informs you that the magazine has a circulation of around 3,500, and she has included the prices for 1/4-, 1/2-, and full-page ads.

You've actually been cutting back on print ads. They're expensive, and you believe that your promotional webinars are a much more effective way to generate sales leads. Plus, your advertising money has already been earmarked for other purposes for this year.

It's possible that you'd be interested in purchasing an ad next year. You'd need more information, though. Do readers pay for this magazine (e.g., with their membership dues), or is it distributed free to prospects on a mailing list? You'd be more inclined to advertise in the magazine if readers paid for it since that would indicate a certain level of interest on their part. And are there other promotional opportunities available in the magazine—for example, could you publish a promotional article about your company, or is there a "highlighted vendors" section that you could be listed in? Does the magazine include QR codes so readers can easily visit the advertisers' websites?

Respond to Rachel to refuse her request for now and to gather the additional information you'll need to be able to consider future requests from her.

7 The professional development program at MediTech has been restructured (see "Negative Announcements," case #26). However, you, the budget director, have received a proposal from Victor Ramos, one of your four senior sales managers, to attend the annual United Professional Sales Association's annual conference. Mr. Ramos knows that the conference, which is in a city 330 miles away, does not fall within the new guidelines for reimbursement, but he has an idea. As a senior sales manager, he (along with all employees in the sales department) earns a bonus when the sales department exceeds corporate sales goals. These bonuses have not been cut because MediTech sees these bonuses as an incentive for the sales staff and senior management to work harder to attract new customers, and during these tough economic times, MediTech needs all of the customers it can get. Mr. Ramos proposes, though, that instead of paying him the money for his sales bonus, the company use the money to pay for his trip to the annual sales conference.

Initially, you think this is a great idea. As long as an employee is motivated to do well, you don't think it should matter to the company what the incentive is. Granted, the company could just pay Mr. Ramos the bonus money and let him use it as he wishes, but then Mr. Ramos would have to pay income tax. It seems like a win-win situation, especially given that Mr. Ramos has agreed to take vacation time to attend the conference.

You take Mr. Ramos's proposal to the others on your executive management team (the president, CEO, and vice president) and are surprised when they reject Mr. Ramos's proposal. How could they? It seems like a no-brainer. But the executive management has some valid reasons. If Mr. Ramos is allowed to do this, then all of the other 25 senior managers will be allowed also, which would create an administrative nightmare for the people in your accounting department. Furthermore, even though Mr. Ramos is willing to take vacation time to attend the conference, the company must pay him if he is on company business—which he seemingly would be if the company pays him his sales bonus to attend the conference—and there is no way you can just let him have the time off. The other senior managers may be angry and think Mr. Ramos is getting special treatment.

Your job is to write a response to Mr. Ramos on behalf of the executive management team refusing his request. You think his initiative and creative thinking in finding another funding source for professional development are commendable. Be sure you retain his goodwill so that he is motivated to continue doing such a wonderful job for MediTech.

---

8 You are a supervisor in the Marketing Department at Plytec Plastics. You and four others have been working on a campaign for a company product that will be released in three months. Today is Wednesday. Because your boss, the manager of the Marketing Department, needs a week to prepare the presentation of the campaign to the board of directors, she has asked for the campaign materials by Monday of next week. You and the rest of your team have known about the deadline for three months. This morning you received a message from Mary, the graphic artist, saying that there is no way she can finish her portion of the project by Monday. She says she can have the project finished by Thursday and is requesting an extension. In her message she says she has been swamped with work for two other projects. In addition, her children have been sick this week with colds, so she has had to take time off to care for them, and she is hosting a birthday party for one of her children on Sunday, so she cannot work over the weekend to finish her part of the project.

You talk to your boss, who says she cannot wait until Thursday for Mary's work. To be honest, neither can you, as it reflects poorly on your leadership and supervisory abilities if you cannot deliver a team project on time. Your boss's calendar is so busy that she really needs a full week to get her presentation ready for the board, and if her presentation is not excellent, the entire department appears incompetent. Mary has had three months to get her work done, and many times—just yesterday, as a matter of fact—you have seen her on Facebook or on personal phone calls when she should have been working on the project. She was also late with her work for the last project you worked on together, and you are a bit annoyed that this is happening again.

You are thinking that since you have two other graphic artists in the department, you will ask one of them to work with you on future projects. You know for sure that if Mary does not have her material ready by Monday, you will be talking about Mary's inability to meet deadlines in her performance and salary review next month. Though you plan to talk with Mary in person, you also want a permanent record of your decision, so you decide to write a message to Mary denying her request for an extension and offering at least one suggestion for what she might do to meet her deadline.

---

9 You have worked for three months at TAM International, a marketing analysis firm. You have quite a problem on your hands. Recently, Masooma Lahiri-Larson of Kohl's Corporation requested 25 printed copies of your company's latest state retail-market analysis report. After listening to the phone message, you promptly mailed the reports (you had the Kohl's Corp. contact information and shipping address on file from a previous order). Per your company policy, you included an invoice for the printed copies totaling $625.

However, you just received an email from an irate Masooma. She distinctly remembers ordering one electronic PDF copy of the report, costing a one-time flat fee of $250. Masooma indicates that she is not only refusing to pay the

$625 for the 25 printed copies of the report but is also going to write an editorial to *Retail Marketers Monthly* to expose the treatment she has received. Her memory is not accurate. You have a copy of the order that she submitted online. It does not say anything about a $250 flat fee for 25 copies. In fact, it clearly says she ordered 25 copies at $24 each plus tax and shipping. You have no idea where she got the idea she would pay only $250. Maybe she just didn't read the receipt that was emailed to her.

Obviously, though, your company and your boss will not be pleased about the bad press! Write a message to Masooma refusing her request to honor a $250 fee. See what you can do to mend the relationship between your two companies as well so that you can avoid the bad press.

---

10 Brian Kerry is the public relations director for Billings Industries, a company that has a large campus with beautiful gardens and a park-like setting. Falling Water Sounds, a local arts organization, wants to host a summer concert series on the company's campus where people can bring their friends and families, enjoy a picnic, and listen to a variety of music groups. Falling Water Sounds wanted to have the concert series in city parks, but people cannot bring alcohol into city parks, and Falling Water Sounds wants people to be able to enjoy whatever food and drink they want to bring to the concert and does not anticipate a rowdy crowd or illegal activity. The goal is to get families and friends together for an evening of music.

Brian envisions families enjoying a concert on the company's campus; he thinks this is a great opportunity for the company to be a good citizen and to promote the company's presence in the community. However, Brian decides to deny the request. Think of at least three reasons why Brian might deny the request. Then, assume the role of Brian and write a letter to Falling Water Sounds denying the request to hold the summer concert series on your company's property.

Indirect Claims

11 The small company that you work for, InFocus Solutions of Washington, DC, is busy prepping for its annual board meeting. As the junior member of the team, you were asked to order lunch from Breadline and to pick up the order on the day of the meeting. Abiding by Breadline's catering policy, you paid for half of the lunch when ordering and will pay the rest of the bill upon pickup.

Sandwiches and salads for 20 people, plus chips, drinks, and dessert came to a total of $235.84. You paid $117.92 over the phone with your company credit card when you placed the order.

After weeks of preparation, the day of the meeting is finally here. As you board the Metro on your way into the office, you receive an "Urgent Alert" on your cell phone from the city. An unidentified package has been spotted on the White House grounds; consequently, until further notice, no one except emergency personnel are allowed within a 5-block radius of the White House. Your office is outside of the locked down area . . . but then you remember that Breadline is only a block away from the White House!

Thankfully, you are able to make other lunch reservations, and the board meeting is an all-around success. However, Breadline still owes InFocus Solutions $117.92 for the lunch you were unable to pick up. You're worried because of a clause in the contract saying "deposits are nonrefundable except in extreme cases (e.g., a natural disaster)." You may not get your deposit back. You understand that Breadline likely purchased the food for your lunch before you cancelled it and would lose money if it returned your deposit; but you also think that especially in Washington, DC, a suspicious package is the equivalent of a natural disaster. Send the manager a message requesting an adjustment to your account.

---

12 Your yard is big and hilly, and you just don't have the time and energy right now to maintain it yourself. You finally sprang for a professional lawn-mowing service, but the first visit from BeautyLawn did not go well (see also case #44 in Chapter 7). Yes, the grass looks nice, and the crew trimmed nicely around the edges—but they also mowed over the very area you asked them not to mow, the hill where your daffodils were just starting to come up. The crew chief, while respectful and hard-working, did not seem to understand English very well. You suspect that even though he wanted to be accommodating, he simply didn't understand the instructions you gave him.

Write BeautyLawn a persuasive claim in which you explain what happened and request that this first yard service be at no charge. You think that's a pretty fair request, given that you won't be enjoying your daffodils this year.

---

13 Assume the role of Carla Reyes. You arrived at the airport last Saturday only to find that Cross Country Airlines canceled your 1:00 p.m. flight because of a severe thunderstorm. You thought about renting a car and driving the seven hours to your home, but several other stranded passengers with canceled flights had the same idea, so no cars were available for one-way rental.

While you were at a major airport, you live in a small town where there are only two flights to your hometown each day. You were rebooked on the only later flight available that day, at 9:50 p.m. You waited all day in the airport and were just 25 minutes from boarding your flight when you were told that your 9:50 flight had been canceled because a flight crew was unavailable. The agent at the Cross Country Airlines service counter said

---

that the 1:00 p.m. flight the following day was already booked and that you had been assigned to Sunday's 9:50 p.m. flight.

The airline offered to put you up in a hotel for the evening and transport you to the airport on Sunday. This was unacceptable. First, you were flying home to attend your grandfather's 80th birthday celebration on Sunday. You would have missed the party if you had taken that 9:50 p.m. Sunday flight. Second, the hotel checkout is at 11:00 a.m., which means you would have had to spend almost 12 hours at the airport on Sunday.

Fortunately, by 10:00 p.m. on Saturday, you were able to secure a one-way car rental to your hometown, so you decided to cancel your seat on the Sunday, 9:50 p.m. flight. The car rental cost $96. As you made the seven-hour drive to your home, you decided that you should be refunded the $112 cost of the ticket that you were not able to use through no fault of your own. In addition, to compensate for the seven hours you had to spend driving through the night to reach your grandfather's party, you believe the airline should pay for your rental as well.

Write to Cross Country Airlines and request that the company pay for your rental and refund the money for your ticket. Be sure to provide details the reader needs to know to act quickly on your request.

---

14 On a recent road trip, you noticed that your 2001 Dodge Caravan shimmied every time you accelerated. You thought the problem might be an underinflated tire, but even after you stopped to put air in the tires, your car still shook whenever you pressed the accelerator. You resolved to take it to the repair shop when you got home.

When you had the car checked out, you learned that it had a broken front right axle. You've had good experiences ordering parts from CarParts.com, so you convinced the owner of the repair shop to let you order the part yourself, which would be cheaper than having the shop order it. Then you'd have the shop install the part.

You searched CarParts's website and found the exact part for your make and model of Caravan, which you bought. When the part arrived, you took it to the repair shop. Later that day, Duane, the repair technician, called to tell you that the part was too long—in other words, you had ordered the wrong part for your car. You went back to CarParts's website to see what might have happened. You entered your car information, and the part that you'd ordered still came up as the appropriate one. There was only one possible explanation: The website had assigned the wrong part number to the axle. Now you'll have to go back to the shop to pick up the erroneous part, ship it back to CarParts, and get them to send a replacement part right away.

Using the "Contact us" link on the company's website, email CarParts.com to request that it send you a prepaid shipping label to return the wrong part and that it send the correct part by overnight shipping directly to the repair shop. Whether you do business with this company in the future will probably depend on its reply.

---

15 When Ultimate Fitness Gym opened in your town, you were thrilled. You took advantage of the grand opening deal of a lifetime membership fee of $25 per month. That was three years ago. The gym is building a new facility. You are a little surprised when you receive a letter four months before the new gym's grand opening offering you a new lifetime membership of $39.99 per month. The letter says that previous lifetime memberships will not be valid once the new facility opens and encourages you to take advantage of this great deal. You're thinking that $39.99 per month is definitely not as great a deal as your current lifetime membership of $25 per month, and you wonder why you would pay the increased price when you've already bought what is supposed to be a lifetime membership.

You called the gym and were told, "The 'lifetime' in 'lifetime membership' refers only to the life of your membership in this building. A new building means a new membership, and our new lifetime memberships are $39.99 per month."

Your brother, who is an attorney, reads the contract and says that even though it does not specify that "lifetime" means the life of the membership in a particular building, it is worded in such a way that the gym can change the terms. This seems like a flimsy explanation for raising your membership. In fact, it seems as though the gym is desperate for a way to raise revenue to cover the cost of the new building and is targeting lifetime memberships. You also feel you were misled about the terms of your contract when you were told you had purchased a "lifetime" membership for $25 per month.

You have talked with the employees at the front desk and to the gym's manager, but they refuse to waive the new lifetime membership fee for current lifetime members. Frustrated with the employees' lack of sympathy, understanding, and action, you decide to write a letter to the gym's owner asking that he reconsider the new lifetime membership fee and allow yours to remain at $25 per month.

---

16 You are a manager at a local financial services firm, Handel and Schmidt Holdings. Your administrative assistant, Candace, is retiring after 35 years with the firm. To celebrate her years of service, you've organized a lunch outing to Sawyer's, a local steakhouse, and invited the entire staff of 25 (See case #42 in Chapter 7.) Everyone in the office is looking forward to the outing, as the last two months have been very busy, and your whole staff could use a break. When you get to Sawyer's, you are told by the hostess that your tables are not ready, and you wait 30 minutes before being seated. Once your party is seated, the outing turns into a disaster. Your server is rude, and some of the orders get mixed up. You feel bad for Candace and also embarrassed because it was your idea to choose Sawyer's. At the very least, you feel that you deserve a partial refund of your money. You decide to write to the owner, Bob Sawyer, to express your displeasure.

17 You are the executive director of a community regional arts center. You recently contracted a local firm, WJF Designs, to design and print 500 promotional posters for the events and concerts in the upcoming season. You wrote the content and sent it to the firm's graphic designer and copy editor who sent copies to you for proofreading.

Today the firm delivered your posters and an invoice for $1,500. For whatever reason, when you proofed the flyers, you failed to notice that the dates for the following season were not changed from 2013 to 2014. You will need to have the posters reprinted.

You cannot leave these posters as they are, and it would look tacky to cross out the wrong date and write in the new one. While you realize you should have found the error when you were proofreading the final copy, you also feel WJF should have noticed the error and corrected it—after all, you paid a lot of money for the copy editor's work, which included proofing the content. Write a message to Jordan Peters at WJF. Explain the error and request that the posters be reprinted. In addition, build your case for having WJF cover half the cost of reprinting the posters.

---

18 You and your family have just returned from five days (four nights) at SunFun Resort at Wrightsville Beach, NC. Your room was nice, the staff was friendly, and the beach was great. What was disappointing was that the pool was closed during your whole stay because of "mechanical problems." When you expressed your disappointment to the young people staffing the front desk, they clearly hadn't been advised on how to handle the situation and simply said, with apologies, that there was nothing they could do. You didn't want to make an angry fuss about it since you were there to relax, so you let the matter drop.

But now that you're back home, you think you'll write the management of the resort to request a partial refund. After all, the room rate was over $370 per night, plus tax, and the big, beautiful swimming pool was one reason you chose SunFun instead of another resort. You live in Michigan, and it's not likely that you'll return to Wrightsville any time soon, so you definitely want a refund, not a coupon for a discounted future stay. (You may make up additional details as long as they are realistic and do not change the basic facts of the case.)

Adjustment Refusals

19 You work in the customer service department for Trombley Kitchen Works, makers of high-quality kitchen utensils. You receive a phone call from a longtime customer, Tom Dahrman, who complains about the quality of your Trombley Pro 3000 knife set and asks for a refund. Mr. Dahrman claims that he had been using his knife according to how it was demonstrated on your television commercials but that the blade broke from the handle. When you ask him to elaborate, he mentions that on one of your television commercials, a man in a chef's outfit uses a Trombley Pro 3000 knife to cut through a variety of objects, including chicken bones and even a steel pipe. After watching the commercial, Mr. Dahrman had broken the knife by attempting to cut through his rusty kitchen faucet, which was in need of repair.

This commercial is supposed to demonstrate the quality and sharpness of your knives but is very clearly a dramatization. In fact, there is an obvious disclaimer at the bottom of the television screen stating that the knife is not to be used to cut through pipe. Further, instructions that are included with the knife sets clearly specify how the knives are to be used and mention that they are intended solely for routine cooking tasks. In this case, you do not feel that Mr. Dahrman is entitled to the refund that he is demanding, as he did not use the knife the way it was intended to be used. When you tell him so, though, he grows angrier and insists on an adjustment. You assure him that you will speak with a manager about the situation and email him the resolution.

Your manager sometimes grants adjustments in complaint cases where a refund is not strictly warranted, but in this case he says "absolutely not." Inform Mr. Dahrman that Trombley cannot give him a refund and explain the manager's decision. At the same time, attempt to come up with a creative, realistic solution that will keep Mr. Dahrman a loyal and happy customer.

---

20 As a customer service representative for a manufacturer of upscale kitchen appliances, you're going to have to say no to Janet Hay's request for a refund. According to the handwritten note she included with the food processor that she just shipped back to you via UPS, she had mail ordered the item almost three months ago, when it was on sale. She had then stored it until her niece's wedding. But when the niece got around to using the food processor, it made a weird sound and gave off an electrical smell. So Ms. Hay has sent it back and is asking for a refund to her credit card.

The problem is that Ms. Hay has waited too late to make this return. As the packing slip said, any defective products need to be returned within 60 days of purchase. After that, there is nothing you can do except recommend an authorized repair center.

Write to Ms. Hay to give her the bad news. See if you can figure out how to keep her goodwill and her future business. You'll also need to resolve what to do with the defective food processor she returned.

21 What a complicated complaint from Carla Reyes! (See case #13.) You certainly see how the situation must look from her point of view. For reasons beyond her control, she missed the outbound flight that she'd paid for, and then, because the airline didn't have a crew, she missed her second flight and had to pay for a rental car—all of this after waiting nearly nine hours in an airport for her second flight.

Unfortunately, your hands are tied. The ticket receipt does clearly state that tickets are not refundable because air travel is sometimes affected by factors beyond the control of Cross Country Airlines. Cross Country Travel reimburses the cost of a missed flight only if the airline has made an error it could have avoided, if the passenger has a documented medical emergency, or if the passenger has paid a $150 flight insurance fee. And you never reimburse a rental vehicle— renting a vehicle is the customer's choice. Though you can understand Carla's desire to get home for her grandfather's birthday, the truth is that Cross Country Airlines did all it could to get people on flights. You simply are not allowed to give refunds in such cases. However, you are allowed to give a coupon toward the customer's next flight with you.

Respond to Ms. Reyes's complaint, trying to the best of your ability to restore good relations with her.

---

22 You are a branch manager for a large bank. On July 1 the bank began assessing a $15 surcharge to all debit cards that had not been used in six months. The $15 fee was deducted from cardholders' checking or savings accounts. Eight weeks before the July 1 deadline, the bank's customer service department sent letters to all debit cardholders whose cards had been inactive telling them that if they didn't use their cards by July 1, they would be assessed the $15 fee. Customers were also told that if they no longer wished to have the card, they were to call an 800 number to deactivate it. In addition, all cardholders were reminded that after July 1, they had to use their cards at least once every six months to avoid the fee. The notice was also placed on cardholders' monthly statements, posted on the bank's website, included in the bank's quarterly newsletter, and advertised in branch office lobbies.

After July 1 customers with unused cards were assessed the $15 fee. Many customers who somehow missed the notices of the policy change called customer service to express their anger and disappointment. Once the customer service representatives reminded these customers of the multiple notices regarding the fee, most grudgingly accepted that they should have paid more attention. One particularly angry customer, though, was not satisfied with this explanation. After her phone call to customer service, Laura Nelson wrote a letter to you, the branch manager, saying that the bank had done an insufficient job in informing customers of the fee. She said a phone call would have been the best way to let her and others know, and she wants the $15 fee returned to her account. She says that if you don't give her the $15, she will take her accounts elsewhere.

You believe that the bank did all it could do to inform the customers. Making phone calls to all of them would have been unreasonable and inefficient. Besides, in a society where phone scams and financial fraud are becoming common, would she have thought a voice message about a $15 fee on a debit card was credible? Write a response to Ms. Nelson denying her request to return the $15 to her account. Retain her goodwill so that she does not take her accounts to another bank.

---

23 You are a manager for Renata's, a large, upscale bar and grill. During the summer months, you sponsor a 10K charity fun run. Each year you donate the proceeds to a different charity. This year the proceeds go to the United Way and to the Waite City Free Clinic. Runners pay a $50 registration fee to participate in the event. The fee covers Renata's costs: insurance, liability, security, water, and promotional materials. Though you'll let people register for the run at any time, including the day of the event, you do not refund the registration fee after March 15 for any reason. You need to know your budget, and adjusting credit card charges or handling cash for anyone who wanted a refund would be too time consuming.

Today (May 5) you received an email from Oliver Shand. He paid the $50 registration fee on February 2. He broke his ankle on February 24. He thought he would be healed in time to participate, but he just has not had time to do the rehabilitation and training he will need to participate in the run. He wants his card credited for $50. You're a runner, and you empathize with him, but he should have requested the refund when he broke his ankle. Besides, you think it's pretty cheap and a little tacky that he would want a refund for what is essentially a charitable donation (which, by the way, he will still get a receipt for so that he can claim a tax deduction). You are going to deny his request, using critical thinking and problem-solving skills to explain why the fee is nonrefundable after March 15 and to help him feel more positive about your keeping his money.

---

24 You work in customer service at the headquarters of Petro company, a large chain of gas stations. Today you must answer a complaint that you received from a customer whose car was damaged by the automatic car wash at one of your stations. When the car went through the wash, the whirling brush on the driver's side broke the mirror. The customer says that when he complained to the manager on duty at the station, she called his attention to the sign at the entry to the car wash stating that Petro would not be responsible for any damage to the cars. She also noted that the sign says to fold in the mirrors of the car before entering the car wash. When the customer explained that his mirrors do not fold in, the manager said she was sorry but that there was nothing she could do. Using a link on your company's website, the customer has written the company an email message. He feels that your car washes should be safe for cars like his, and he wants you to pay $100 toward repairing the damaged mirror.

Write a response in which you refuse his request. The best you can do in cases like this is attach a coupon good for $10 at any of your stations' stores.

---

25 As the manager of SunFun Resort at Wrightsville Beach, NC, you're going to have to say no to a customer's request for a partial refund (see case #18 under "Indirect Claims"). Under corporate policy, you're allowed to give refunds at your discretion if the hotel has made a mistake or a mishap has occurred, but not if the pool goes out. As an outdoor facility, the pool is not considered a core service, and you can't guarantee that it will be open during any given guest's stay, just as you can't promise that the weather will be pleasant. Also, when something goes wrong in a guest room, your repair staff can correct it or the guest can be moved to a different room; but when the pool goes out, you're at the mercy of the pool contractor and the supplier of the parts. Thus, while you do your best to keep the pool open, you can't take responsibility when it has to be closed for a period of time, and giving refunds for such periods would be costly to your business.

Write the customer to say that you can give a $100 discount on his next stay of two nights or more at one of your properties. Fortunately, there is a SunFun Resort in Traverse City, MI. While it's unlikely the customer will return to Wrightsville Beach any time soon, the resort in Michigan would be relatively near anywhere he lives.

Negative Announcements

26 Your company, MediTech, is an industry leader in manufacturing cardiac medical devices. MediTech lets its 20 senior management staff attend one professional development activity a year (e.g., an annual professional conference, continuing education) anywhere in the United States for up to five days. The senior managers really enjoy this program because it provides a break in their routine and lets them travel, network, and build their knowledge of the latest industry trends and products.

However, business has not been good this past year, so the company has decided to save money by limiting travel for these activities to within 150 miles of the office. The company also will not pay for hotel stays or any registration fees over $100. When the alternatives are layoffs, increased employee contributions toward health insurance, switching to an employee health insurance plan with less coverage, or eliminating sales performance bonuses, cutting this policy seems like one way to save money without affecting everyone in the company. If senior managers want to take vacation time or pay for activities beyond what the company covers, they certainly may.

As MediTech's budget director, you know senior managers will be upset. The policy has been around so long that some even see this policy as a right and a status symbol rather than a privilege. Some others may wonder how they will maintain their skills or network with others in their fields. They certainly won't want to pay for these activities themselves. Write a message to your senior management staff explaining why the new professional development restrictions are in place. Appeal to their management expertise so that they see this as a good business decision. Provide alternatives for networking and developing their skills.

---

27 You're a regional manager for Arch Insurance, Inc., whose specialty is corporate travel and personal accident policies. Most of your company's revenue comes from selling policies to businesses and other organizations that need to cover their employees when they're at work or traveling. Just now you were "called on the carpet" by your boss for excessive expenditures for wining and dining clients. She says that the seven agents who work for you spent over $9,000 last quarter taking representatives of companies, hospitals, and other organizations out to lunch and dinner, either to thank them for their business or attract them as customers. Sure, landing even one good contract with a large organization can mean thousands of dollars for the company, and representatives of a company that caters to businesses can't afford to look "cheap." But you have to agree that things have gotten out of hand. Your boss says that many of the receipts are for the most expensive restaurants in the area and for such extravagant purchases as $150 bottles of wine. This has got to stop. There are plenty of elegant ways to say "thank you" or to appeal to a client besides spending money hand over fist.

Using your good problem-solving skills, think about how to advise your employees. Then write the negative announcement that will change their behavior but also maintain their goodwill and their drive to succeed.

---

28 Assume that you are the ___ (you choose the supervisory position) of a small ___ (you choose the type) company or department. More and more, you've noticed, when walking past employees' cubicles and offices, that a social networking site such as Facebook, MySpace, or LinkedIn is up on the screen. You've read some articles pointing out that social networking on the job can be quite a drain on employees' productivity, and you worry that this is happening in your company (have you noticed any lapse in performance lately?). You think the time has come to send an email to the employees advising them to limit their use of social networking on the job.

The thing is, you know that social networking does also bring certain company benefits. You don't want to have the IT person block or monitor the use of social networking sites, nor do you want a strict policy that will actually be counterproductive. So you're going to try to get people to monitor themselves.

Think carefully about what you want the employees to do and why (for example, instead of doing social networking, what should they be doing?). Then write the message that will get them to change their behavior.

---

29 Your company, AET Manufacturing, finds itself in a tough position. The company needs to update its software and tracking systems to remain competitive in the industry. If the company updates the software, employees will need extensive training in how to use it. However, because of its small size, the company would have to lay off three employees for the summer if it paid everyone for attending the eight-hour technology training session.

You have been given the task of informing employees of the technology upgrades and the necessity to come in for an eight-hour training session on a Saturday without pay. Think of ways to make this change sound as positive and appealing to employees as possible. Because you cannot afford to actually pay the employees for this training, think of how you might otherwise compensate them.

---

30 Play the role of assistant to Bill Hannigan, owner of a chain of hair and nail salons in the tri-state area. (With your instructor's permission, choose a different business or organization that serves its customers through scheduled appointments.) The business's policy is "three strikes and you're out": that is, if a customer breaks three appointments within 12 months and without advance notice, that client is not allowed to make any further appointments.

Until now, the managers at the different salons have dealt with this issue informally as it has arisen. When customers who've reached their limit have called to schedule another appointment, the managers have just handled the situation by

phone. But Mr. Hannigan wants to ensure that customers in this category are treated uniformly and tactfully. He's asked you to write a form letter that can be sent to customers who have broken their third appointment to tell them that, in the future, the salon will be able to serve them on a walk-in basis only.

In your letter, leave blanks where information specific to each case will be included and indicate in brackets what kind of information that will be. Think carefully about the facts you'll need to include in order to justify your position. And do what you can to maintain the customer's goodwill. You do not want to alienate the customer or his or her family and friends, some of whom may also be your customers.

---

31 You are the owner of a small company called Marvel Technology Solutions. The company has been in business for eight years and has done well financially. In addition, you believe that your company enjoys one of the most positive working environments in the industry. Your employees get along very well with one another, work well as a team, and express their genuine appreciation for how you run your company.

Despite your company's history of success, this last year has been very difficult. The downturn in the economy has made it tough for many small businesses, and Marvel is no exception. It has been a struggle the last few months just to meet payroll, which has had a noticeable effect on the workplace environment, as many of your employees wonder if they will be laid off. You have pondered the possibility of laying employees off, but every time this thought crosses your mind, you quickly dismiss it. Your 14 employees are all outstanding, hardworking, and loyal. You would feel terrible if

you had to lay any of them off. However, your financial situation necessitates that you do something.

After much thought, you have decided that the best way to improve the financial situation would be to have everyone—including yourself—take a temporary 15 percent pay cut. Obviously, this will not be a very popular move, as some of your co-workers have spouses who have recently lost their jobs at other companies, so any reduction in salary will make it hard for these families to pay their bills. However, it is better to have a job at reduced pay than no job at all.

Write a memo to your employees announcing and explaining your decision to have everyone take a temporary pay cut. Mention that industry experts predict that the economy will improve in 8 to 10 months—which, if true, will put an end to the need for the pay cut. You may also wish to emphasize the historically positive work environment at your company and appeal to your employees' sense of camaraderie and loyalty.

---

32 You work as an administrative intern for Peck and Briggs, a small but well-respected public accounting firm located in Cleveland, OH. Traditionally, Peck and Briggs has replaced its employees' computers on a rotating schedule every three years. But the recession has required some cost-cutting measures, and those who are waiting for replacement computers will now need to wait another year before

receiving their upgraded computers. In addition, everyone in the firm will need to be advised that computers will now be replaced on a four-year, not three-year, schedule. This means that they will need to make do with the Microsoft Office suite that is on their current computers, since that software is upgraded only when the computers are replaced. (This issue will not affect the accounting software, since the firm uses

Intacct.com, a cloud-based software service, rather than software on their own computers.)

Your task is to draft a message for Mr. Peck, senior partner, to send to all employees informing them of the new policy.

---

33 You are the facilities supervisor at Iverness Form and Function, LLC, an architecture firm. The custodians report that the break room is so trashed, the amount of time needed to clean it has increased from 15 to 30 minutes each day. Employees who take late lunches and afternoon breaks have no clean space to use. People are not wiping the tables after they eat, used napkins remain on the tables or on the floor, and dirty dishes are left in the sink. People will heat food that overflows or explodes in the microwave and just leave without cleaning it up. Some of the food in the refrigerator is over a month past its due date. Given all the complaining you have heard about the break room, you would think that people would be more diligent in cleaning up after themselves.

In fact, someone left the message "CLEAN UP AFTER YOURSELF!!!!!!! YOUR MOTHER DOESN'T WORK HERE!!!!!!!!!!!!!!!!!!!!!!!!!!" on the microwave last week. As the office manager, you realize that while the custodians are responsible for cleaning every room in the building, the employees' messes are excessive and unbecoming of people in professional positions. Send an email to employees to encourage them to clean up after themselves. Just last week you were giving a tour to a member of your town's chamber of commerce and were thoroughly embarrassed when you took him through the break room. Keep in mind that even though you are sending the email to all employees, it's not likely that every employee contributes to the mess.

---

34 You're a communications intern at J. J. Brown's, a mail-order clothing and camping gear store, and you've been asked to revise the messages the company sends to customers whose orders have had to be delayed or canceled. When a customer calls to place an order, the call-center representative checks to see that each item being ordered is available, but if other customers are requesting the same item at around the same time, the computer shows the items to be in stock even though an item is sold out. Sometimes when this happens, you can tell customers that more of the desired item is being ordered and give them an estimated delivery date. Other times, when the item is

gone, it's permanently gone, which is especially likely with clearance items.

Your boss feels that the current form emails informing customers of canceled or delayed orders are too stiff and impersonal. After all, the goods your company sells are associated with fun and adventure. The revised messages shouldn't be too cheerful (after all, they are bad-news messages), but they should convey a more positive image.

Write the two messages that are needed, one for canceled orders and one for delayed orders. In your messages, leave blanks where information specific to each order will be included and indicate in brackets what kind of information that will be.

---

35 Next week auditors from company headquarters will be visiting your branch office, observing and interviewing employees to ensure that your company follows corporate policies and procedures. You see this as a routine activity, so you are surprised at the hostility and resistance your employees are showing toward the auditors and their visit. Many are threatening to take vacation or call in sick during the week of the visit. You worry that the auditors will sense the negativity of those who are here, especially given employees' comments such as "Well, they better not expect to set up their desks and computers in *my* department."

You simply will not tolerate this negativity. Auditors visit the company every three years, and employees know this. Plus, if they are doing their jobs correctly, employees have nothing to worry about. They just need to show up for work, be mature, and treat the auditors with respect.

Write an announcement to employees letting them know what week the auditors will arrive. Tell the employees in the Accounting Department that temporary workspaces will be set up in the department for the auditors. Yes, this may be inconvenient, but it's the most centrally located and spacious area in the building. In addition, tell the employees that they will not be allowed to take vacation during this time unless they already received vacation approval prior to the sending of this message. You should also remind employees of the company policy stating that if an employee calls in sick and the supervisor thinks the employee is lying, the employee may be required to provide a doctor's note. No, the policy is not often used, but you have no problem enforcing it if employees use sick days to avoid the auditors. Be sure your message leaves your readers feeling better about the auditors' visit.

---

36 Revise the following negative announcement to improve the organization, content, tone, grammar, punctuation, and mechanics.

Dear Valued Quality Food Mart Customers; Due to the fact that some customers have recently abused our

coupon policy, effective immediately we are prohibiting the use of double coupons, this includes any use of any coupon with another coupon or using any coupon with sale items that do not require a coupon.

What this does mean is you using only one coupon on an item or getting only the sale price for you're grocery items. Not using more than one coupon or using a coupon with an item already on sale. We will still take all manufacturers coupons and store coupons. Just not more than one at a time and not for an item on sale.

We are doing this because people use coupons in a manor for which they are not intended. Due to the popularity of reality shows such as "Coupon Frenzy" where people compete using coupons to see how much groceries they can get for free or not alot of cost. We can not do this and remain in business, we must manage how we and customers use coupons so that we can serve you better.

Thank you for your understanding. Please feel free to contact us if you have any questions. We apologize for any inconvenience this may cause you.

CHAPTER NINE

Making Your Case with Persuasive Messages and Proposals

Learning Objectives

Upon completing this chapter, you will be able to use persuasion effectively, especially when making requests, composing sales messages, and writing proposals. To reach this goal, you should be able to

1 Describe important strategies for writing any persuasive message.

2 Write skillful persuasive requests that begin indirectly, develop convincing reasoning, make a call to action, and close with goodwill.

3 Discuss ethical concerns regarding sales messages.

4 Describe the planning steps for direct mail or email sales messages.

5 Compose sales messages that gain attention, present persuasive appeals, use appropriate visual elements, and effectively drive for action.

6 Write well-organized and persuasive proposals.

THE PREDOMINANCE OF INDIRECTNESS IN PERSUASIVE MESSAGES

Everything you write on the job will have some kind of persuasive purpose—to convince the reader of your professionalism, convey an appealing company image, promote good relations, or all of these. But in some situations, persuasion will be your central goal. In these cases, your readers will hold a certain position, and your task will be to move them from this position to another one that is more favorable to you or your company. Meeting this challenge requires careful analysis, strategic thinking, and skillful writing.

Because you will be proposing something that your reader probably does not already agree with or want to do, it is often best to organize persuasive messages in an **indirect order**. Preparing the reader to accept your idea is a much better strategy than announcing the idea from the start and then having to argue uphill through the rest of the message. Ideally, you should organize each persuasive message so that, from the title or subject line to the end, your readers will agree with you. If you try to have them on your side from start to finish, you'll have your best chance of success.

Although indirectness works for most persuasive messages, sometimes you will want to use a **direct approach**. For example, if you know your reader prefers directness or if you believe your readers will discard your message unless you get to the point early, then directness is in order. As we discuss later in this chapter, proposals in response to specific requests may also use directness.

In the following pages we first provide some general advice for effective persuasion using the indirect approach. We then explain how the indirect order is used in two kinds of persuasive messages: the persuasive request and the sales message. Finally, we cover another important category of persuasive writing: proposals. These, as you will see, can use either the direct or indirect pattern, depending on whether they are invited or uninvited.

GENERAL ADVICE ABOUT PERSUASION

LO1 Describe important strategies for writing any persuasive message.

All our previous advice about adapting your messages to your readers comes into play with persuasive messages—only more so. Moving your reader from an uninterested or even resistant position to an interested, cooperative one is a major accomplishment. To achieve it, keep the following advice in mind.

Know Your Readers

For any kind of persuasive message, thinking about your subject from your readers' point of view is critical. To know what kind of appeals will succeed with your readers, you need to know as much as you can about their values, interests, and needs. Companies specializing in email and direct-mail campaigns spend a great deal of money to acquire this kind of information. Using a variety of research techniques, they gather **demographic information** (such as age, gender, income, and geographic location) and **psychographic information** (such as social, political, and personal preferences) about their target audience. They also develop mailing lists based on prior shows of interest from consumers and purchase mailing lists from other organizations that have had success with certain audiences.

If you don't have these resources, you can use other means to learn as much as possible about the intended readers. You can talk with customer service about the kinds of calls they're getting, study the company's customer database, chat with people around the water cooler or online, and run ideas past colleagues. Good persuasion depends on knowledge as well as on imagination and logic.

Choose and Develop Targeted Reader Benefits

No one is persuaded to do something for no reason. Sometimes their reasons for acting are related to **tangible** or measurable rewards. For example, they will save money, save time, or acquire some kind of desired object. But often, the rewards that persuade are **intangible**. People may want to make their lives easier, gain prestige, or have more freedom. Or perhaps they want to identify with a larger cause, feel that they are helping others, or do the right thing. In your quest for the appeals that will win your readers over, do not underestimate the power of intangible benefits, especially when you can pair them with tangible rewards.

When selecting the **reader benefits** to feature in your persuasive messages, bear in mind that such benefits can be intrinsic, extrinsic, or a combination. **Intrinsic benefits** are benefits that readers will get automatically by complying with your request. For example, if you are trying to persuade people to attend your company's awards dinner, the pleasure of sharing in their colleagues' successes will be intrinsic to the event. Door prizes would be an **extrinsic benefit**. We might classify the meal itself as a combination—not really the main feature of the event but definitely central to it. Intrinsic benefits are tightly linked to what you're asking people to do, while extrinsic ones are added on and more short-lived. Let intrinsic benefits do the main work of your persuasive effort. Focusing too much on extrinsic benefits can actually cheapen your product or service in the readers' eyes.

When presenting your reader benefits, be sure the readers can see exactly how the benefits will help them. The literature on selling makes a useful distinction between **product features** and reader benefits. If you say that a wireless service uses a certain kind of technology, you're describing a feature. If you say that the technology results in fewer missed or dropped calls, you're describing a benefit. Benefits persuade by enabling readers to envision the features of the recommended product or action in their own worlds.

One common technique for achieving this goal is to use what we call **scenario painting**—a description that pictures the reader in a sample situation enjoying the promised benefits. Here is an example of scenario painting from the Carnival Cruise Lines website:

> Think your schedule is too tight to take a fun-filled vacation? Our Baja Mexico sailings are just the cruises to change your mind. You can experience the tropical beauty of Baja with a 3-day weekend cruise to Ensenada. Relax in the privacy of Ensenada's private beaches before hitting the fashionable shops of Avenida Primera for new jewelry—duty-free, of course.
>
> Have an extra day to spare? Our 4-day Baja cruises visit Catalina Island. Who knows? You may spot some of Hollywood's elite while sunning on the golden beaches of California's Emerald Island.

Scenario painting is common in sales messages, but you can also use it to good advantage in other persuasive messages, even internal ones. Whatever your persuasive situation or strategy, be sure to provide enough detail for readers to see how they will benefit from what you are asking them to do.

Make Good Use of Three Kinds of Appeals

The first acknowledged expert on persuasion, the Greek philosopher Aristotle, lived almost 2,500 years ago, but many of his core concepts are still widely taught and used. Of particular value is his famous categorizing of persuasive appeals into three kinds: those based on **logic (logos)**, those based on **emotion (pathos)**, and those based on the **character** of the speaker (**ethos**). All three kinds come into play in every persuasive message—in fact, one might say, in every kind of message. But as the writer of a persuasive message, you will need to think especially carefully about how to manage these appeals and which ones to emphasize given your intended audience.

As you plan your message, consider what kind of logical appeals you might use. Saved money? Saved time? A more dependable or effective product? How about emotional appeals? Higher status? More sex appeal? Increased popularity? And don't neglect appeals based on character. What kind of image of yourself and your company will resonate with the reader? Should you get a celebrity or expert to endorse your product or to serve as the spokesperson? Not only when planning but also when revising your persuasive message, assess your appeals. Be sure to choose and develop the ones most likely to persuade your audience.

Make It Easy for Your Readers to Comply

Sometimes writers focus so much on creating persuasive appeals that they put insufficient thought into making the requested action as clear and easy to perform as possible.

If you want people to give money or buy your product, tell them where and how to do it, and supply a preaddressed mailing envelope or a Web address if applicable. If you want employees to give suggestions for improving products or operations, tell them exactly where and how to submit their ideas, and make it easy for them to do so. If you want people to remember to work more safely or conserve on supplies, give them specific techniques for achieving these goals and include reminders at the actual locations where they need to remember what to do. Making the desired action specific and easy to perform is a key part of moving your readers from resistance to compliance with your request.

With this general advice in mind, we now turn to the three main types of persuasive writing in business: persuasive requests, sales messages, and proposals.

PERSUASIVE REQUESTS

INTRODUCTORY CHALLENGE

Raising Funds for a Worthy Cause

You're a mid-level manager for Arslan, one of the largest custodial services companies in your city. Like many others in the company, you devote some of your personal time to serving the community. Arslan wants you to do this volunteer work for the sake of good public relations. You want to do it because it is personally and professionally rewarding.

Currently, as chair of the fundraising committee of the city's Junior Achievement program, you head all efforts to get financial support for the program from local businesspeople. The committee can contact some of these potential donors by phone, but there are too many for you to be able to reach all of them this way.

At its meeting today, the Junior Achievement board of directors discussed various solutions. One director suggested using a fundraising letter. The board accepted the idea with enthusiasm. With just as much enthusiasm, it gave you the assignment of writing the letter.

As you view the assignment, it is not a routine letter-writing problem. Although the local businesspeople are probably generous, they are not likely to part with money without good reason. In fact, their first reaction to a request for money is likely to be negative. So you will need to overcome their resistance in order to persuade them. Your task is indeed challenging.

At many points in your career—starting with your job search—you will need to make **persuasive requests**. Perhaps, as in the scenario above, you will be asked to write a fundraising message. Perhaps you will need to ask your management for another staff position or for special equipment. You may need to persuade a potential client to join you in a meeting so that you can demonstrate the benefits of your products. Or maybe you will be trying to persuade your employees to change their behavior in some way.

Whether written to internal or external readers, requests that are likely to be resisted require a slow, deliberate approach. In essence, you must persuade the reader that he or she should grant your request before you actually state it. Such an achievement requires that you carefully plan your persuasive strategy.

LO2 Write skillful persuasive requests that begin indirectly, develop convincing reasoning, make a call to action, and close with goodwill.

Determining Your Strategy

Figuring out the best persuasive approach involves three interrelated tasks: determining what you want, figuring out your readers' likely reactions, and deciding upon a persuasive strategy that will overcome reader objections and evoke a positive response.

Think carefully about your actual goals for your persuasive request. A request for a one-time-only donation might be written very differently from a request that is intended to create a long-time, multiple donor. If you were convincing employees to leave the parking places next to the building for customers' use, you would write a very different message if it were the third rather than the first request. Your goals, considered in the context of your organization's goals and your relationship with your readers, are key shapers of your persuasive message.

To anticipate how your readers will react to your request, consider everything you know about them and then put yourself in their shoes. Look at the request as they are likely to see it. Figure out what's in it for them and how to overcome any objections they may have. From this thinking and imagining, your plan should emerge.

The specific plan you develop will depend on the facts of the case. You may be able to show that your reader stands to gain in time, money, or other tangible benefits. Or you may be able to show that your reader will benefit in goodwill or prestige. In some cases, you may persuade readers by appealing to their love of beauty, excitement, serenity, or other emotions. In different cases, you may be able to persuade readers by appealing to the pleasant feeling that comes from doing a good turn. You decide on the benefits that will be most likely to win over your readers.

A special kind of persuasive request is one that casts the request as a problem–solution message. With this strategy, you first present a problem that you and the readers share—called the **common-ground persuasion technique**—and then show how doing as you propose will solve the problem for all concerned. Many fundraising letters use this technique, giving us striking facts about the current economic climate, the environment, or living conditions in a certain area of the world. But this strategy can also be a powerful one for internal audiences who might not be receptive to a straightforward proposal for action but who share your opinion that something needs to be done.

A persuasive request situation is a special opportunity for analysis, creativity, and judgment. With careful use of all three, you can plan messages that will change your readers' minds and move them to action.

Many persuasive messages arrive uninvited, and they compete with many other messages. Unless they gain the reader's attention at the beginning, they are likely to end up in the recycle bin.

Gaining Attention in the Opening

In the indirect messages discussed in Chapter 8, the goal of the opening is to set up the explanation for the negative news. The opening of a persuasive request has a similar goal: to lead into your central strategy. But the opening of a persuasive request has an additional goal: to gain attention.

You need to draw your reader in with the opening of your persuasive message because you are writing to a person who has not invited your message and may not agree with your goal. An interesting beginning is a good step toward getting this person in a receptive mood.

Determine what your reader will find compelling. It might be some statement that arouses curiosity, or it might be a statement offering or implying a reader benefit. Because questions get people thinking, they are often effective openings. The following examples indicate the possibilities.

From the cover letter of a questionnaire seeking the opinions of medical doctors:

What, in your opinion as a medical doctor, is the future of the private practice of medicine?

From a message requesting contributions for orphaned children:

While you and I dined heartily last night, 31 orphans at San Pablo Mission had only dried beans to eat.

From a message seeking the cooperation of business leaders in promoting a fair:

What would your profits be if 300,000 free-spending visitors came to our town during a single week?

If writing your request in the form of a problem–solution message, you should start with a goal that you and the readers share. For example, let's say that a project manager in your company has retired and that you want to recommend his capable administrative assistant as his replacement. Since no member of the support staff has ever broken into the managerial ranks, any direct proposal to promote your candidate will be likely to be met with resistance. To get readers on your side from the beginning, you could start your message with facts that everyone can agree upon: that someone has retired, that his or her duties are important, and that someone capable needs to be found quickly. Your subject line for an email along these lines might be something like, "Reassigning Jim Martin's Duties" (which everyone supports), not "Promoting Kathy Pearson" (which your readers will resist).

Whatever the case, the form of indirectness that you choose for your opening should engage your readers right away and get them thinking along the lines that will lead to their approval of your request.

Developing the Appeal

Following the opening, you should proceed with your goal of persuading. Your task here is a logical and orderly presentation of the reasoning you have selected.

As with any argument intended to convince, you should do more than merely list points. You should help convey the points with convincing details. Since you are trying to penetrate a neutral or resistant mind, you need to make good use of the you-viewpoint. You need to pay careful attention to the meanings of your words and the clarity of your expression. You need to use logic and emotion appropriately and project an appealing image. And because your reader may become impatient if your appeal is not clear, you need to make every word count.

Making the Request Clearly and Positively

After you have done your persuading, move to the action you seek. You have tried to prepare the reader for what you want. If you have done that well, the reader should be ready to accept your request.

As with negative messages, your request requires careful word choice. You should avoid words that detract from the request. You also should avoid words that bring to

The Ingredients of Successful Fundraising

Expert fundraiser Jerold Panas conducted several focus groups to find out what makes fundraising successful. The answers boiled down to "three Es"—plus one "I":

- Empathy—the ability to understand the audience's values and interests
- Energy—the determination to put sufficient work into the fundraising effort
- Enthusiasm—the fundraiser's obvious commitment to the cause
- Integrity—the fundraiser's sincerity and truthfulness

SOURCE: *Asking: A 59-Minute Guide to Everything Board Members, Volunteers, and Staff Must Know to Secure the Gift*, rev. ed. (Medfield, MA: Emerson& Church, 2009) 17–20, print.

mind images and ideas that might work against you. Words that bring to mind reasons for refusing are especially harmful, as in this example:

> I am aware that businesspeople in your position have little free time to give, but will you please consider accepting an assignment to the board of directors of the Children's Fund?

The following positive tie-in with a major point in the persuasion strategy does a much better job:

> Your organizing skills and stature in the community would make you an ideal board member for the Children's Fund.

Whether your request should end your message will depend on the situation. In some cases, you will profit by following the request with additional persuasive material. This procedure is especially effective when your reader needs a lot of convincing. In cases where your request is relatively simple, won't cost the reader much, and isn't likely to be resisted, you can end your message with the request. Even here, though, you combine or follow the request with wording that makes the reader feel good about doing as you ask (see the sample messages on pages 234–236).

Summarizing the Plan for Requests

From the preceding discussion, the general plan for persuasive requests can be summarized as follows:

- Open with words that (1) gain attention and (2) set up the strategy.
- Develop the strategy using persuasive language and the you-viewpoint.
- Make the request clearly and without negatives (1) either at the end of the message or (2) followed by words that continue the persuasive appeal.

Contrasting Persuasive Requests

The persuasive request is illustrated by contrasting letters that ask businesspeople to donate to Junior Achievement. The first message is direct and bland. The second message, which follows the indirect approach and provides convincing details, is much more likely to succeed.

A Selfish Blunt Approach. The weaker letter begins with the request. Because the requested action is something the reader probably doesn't want to do, the direct beginning is likely to get a negative reaction. In addition, the comments about how much to give tend to lecture rather than suggest. Some explanation follows, but it is weak and scant. In general, the letter is poorly written. It makes little use of the you-viewpoint. Perhaps its greatest fault is that the persuasion comes too late. The selfish close is a weak reminder of the action requested.

Dear Mr. Williams:

Will you please donate to the local Junior Achievement program? We have set $50 as a fair minimum for businesses to give. But larger amounts would be appreciated.

The organization badly needs your support. Currently, about 900 young people will not get to participate in Junior Achievement activities unless more money is raised.

If you do not already know about Junior Achievement, let me explain. Junior Achievement is an organization for high school students. They work with local business executives to form small businesses and then operate the businesses. In the process, they learn about our economic system. This is a good thing, and it deserves our help.

Hoping to receive your generous donation,

This direct, bland approach is not likely to persuade.

Skillful Persuasion Using the Indirect Order. The next message follows the recommended indirect pattern. Its opening generates interest and sets up the persuasive strategy. Notice the effective use of the you-viewpoint throughout. Not until the reader has been sold on the merits of the request does the message ask the question. It does this clearly and directly. The final words leave the reader thinking about the benefits that a *yes* answer will give.

Dear Mr. Williams:

Right now—right here in our city—620 teenagers are running 37 corporations. The kids run the whole show; their only adult help comes from business professionals who work with them.

Last September these young people applied for charters and elected officers. They created plans for business operations. For example, one group planned to build websites for local small businesses. Another elected to conduct a rock concert. Yet another planned to publish electronic newsletters for area corporations. After determining their plans, the kids issued stock—and sold it, too. With the proceeds from stock sales, they began their operations. This May they will liquidate their companies and account to their stockholders for their profits or losses.

What's behind these impressive accomplishments? As you've probably guessed, it's Junior Achievement. Since 1919, this nonprofit organization has been teaching school kids of all ages about business, economics, and entrepreneurship. Thanks to partnerships between volunteers and teachers, these students gain hands-on experience with real business operations while learning the fundamentals of economics and financial responsibility. They also learn cooperation and problem solving. It's a win–win situation for all involved.

To continue to succeed, Junior Achievement needs all of us behind it. During the 13 years the program has been in our city, it has had enthusiastic support from local business leaders. But with over 900 students on the waiting list, our plans for next year call for expansion. That's why, as a volunteer myself, I ask that you help make the program available to more youngsters by contributing $50 (it's deductible). By helping to cover the cost of materials, special events, and scholarships, you'll be preparing more students for a bright future in business.

Please make your donation now by completing our online contribution form at www.juniorachievement.org. You will be doing a good service—for our kids, for our schools, and for our community.

Sincerely,

This indirect, interesting letter has a much greater chance of success.

A Persuasive External Request (Asking for Information about Employment Applicants). In this letter a trade publication editor seeks information from an executive for an article on desirable traits of job applications. Granting the request will require time and effort from the executive. Thus, indirect persuasion is appropriate.

FastTrack
Jumpstarting Your Business Career

November 20, 2014

Ms. Adelade O. Romano
Director of Human Resources
Chalmers-DeLouche, Inc.
17117 Proden Road
St. Paul, MN 55108

Dear Ms. Romano:

Opening question arouses interest and sets up what's coming.

What clues have you found in employment applications that help you estimate a person's character and desirability to your firm?

The explanation for the opening question logically follows.

Young people entering business are eager for any clue that will put them on the other side of the fence. They want to know what goes on in your mind when you are judging the people behind the letters and résumés. In our column, "Applications That Talk," we want to send a message especially to those people. To make the article as practical as possible, we are drawing our information from people in the field who really know.

Persuasive strategy appeals to her ego and her desire to help others.

A mutual friend of ours, Max Mullins, told me of your recent problem of finding the most desirable person behind 250 applications. What specific points did you look for in these applications? What clues distinguished some people from the others? When the going got hard, what fine points enabled you to make your final choice? The young professionals of today are eager for answers to such questions.

Request evolves logically from the preceding paragraphs.

You can help solve their problem if you will jot down your personal comments on a diverse sample of these applications and then allow me to interview you about your judgments. All applicant information would of course be kept confidential.

Request is clearly stated.

Final words recall the central appeal

Will you share your insights with me and with hundreds of young professionals? If so, please call or email me to set up an interview time that is convenient for you. It is just possible that, through this article, you will contribute to the success of a future leader in your own company. At the least, you will be of service to the many young people who are trying to get "that" job that is so important to them right now.

Sincerely,

Charlotte C. Clayton

Charlotte C. Clayton
Associate Editor

enclosures

405 Perrin Ave.
Austin, TX 78716
512-437-7080
FAX: 512-437-7081
Clayton@fasttrack.com

A Persuasive Internal Request (Using a Central Emotional Appeal Supported by Logical and Character-Based Appeals). The writer wants employees to participate in the company's annual blood drive. He needs to convince them of the importance of the drive and overcome their likely objections. This message will be distributed to employees' mailboxes.

C AMBERLY
Engineering & Construction

Department of Community Relations
Mail Location 12
123 Jackson Street
Edison, Colorado 80864
(719) 777-4444
CommunityRelations@Amberly.com

February 27, 2014

Opens with an attention-getting, you-focused question

Did you help save Brad Meyer's life?

Uses a character-based appeal; invites the reader to identify with these "lifesavers"

A few years ago, an employee of Amberly was driving to a friend's wedding when an oncoming car, operated by a drunk driver, swerved across the center line. Brad doesn't remember the crash. But he does remember two months spent in the hospital, two months of surgery and therapy.

Tells an engaging story with specific details

Without the help of people like us, Brad would not have lived. Some Amberly employees save lives regularly. We're blood donors. Please be a lifesaver and join us on Friday, March 19, for Amberly's annual blood drive.

Your help is needed for a successful drive.

Avoids words such as "draw blood" or "needle" that would bring unpleasant thoughts to mind

Giving blood is simple. The entire process will take less than 45 minutes.

Giving blood is safe. Experienced health professionals from the Steinmetz Blood Center will be on site to conduct the procedure exactly as they would in a clinical setting.

Giving blood is convenient. The Steinmetz staff will be in Room 401, Building B, between 9:00 a.m. and 3:00 p.m. To save time, make an appointment to donate. Call the Steinmetz Blood Center at 569-1170.

Addresses likely reader objections

Giving blood is important. Nobody knows who will need blood next, but one thing is certain—it will be available only if healthy, caring people take time to give it. Brad's accident required 110 units—more than 12 gallons—of blood. Because 110 people set aside 45 minutes, Brad Meyer has a lifetime of minutes to be grateful.

Recalls the emotion-based opening and links it to a logical appeal: You or someone in your family might benefit

Take a few moments now to make your pledge on the reverse side of this letter. Then return it to the Community Relations department, Mail Location 12, by March 15.

Makes the requested action clear and easy

From Brad and from other families—like yours and mine—who might need it in the days to come,

Thank you,

John M. Piper

John M. Piper
Director, Community Relations

A Persuasive Email to Members of a Professional Organization. The writer of this message, the president of the American Society for Training and Development (ASTD), uses character appeal as well as logic and emotion to persuade readers to participate in a survey.

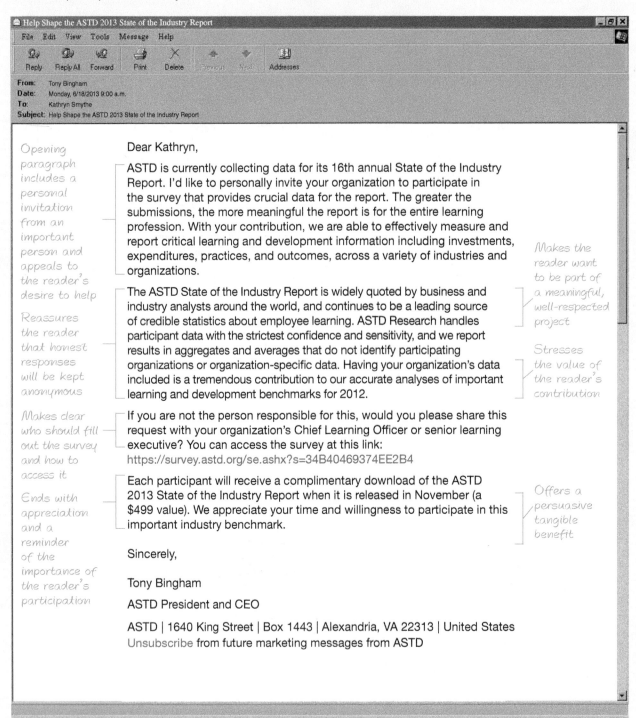

Opening paragraph includes a personal invitation from an important person and appeals to the reader's desire to help

Dear Kathryn,

ASTD is currently collecting data for its 16th annual State of the Industry Report. I'd like to personally invite your organization to participate in the survey that provides crucial data for the report. The greater the submissions, the more meaningful the report is for the entire learning profession. With your contribution, we are able to effectively measure and report critical learning and development information including investments, expenditures, practices, and outcomes, across a variety of industries and organizations.

Makes the reader want to be part of a meaningful, well-respected project

Reassures the reader that honest responses will be kept anonymous

The ASTD State of the Industry Report is widely quoted by business and industry analysts around the world, and continues to be a leading source of credible statistics about employee learning. ASTD Research handles participant data with the strictest confidence and sensitivity, and we report results in aggregates and averages that do not identify participating organizations or organization-specific data. Having your organization's data included is a tremendous contribution to our accurate analyses of important learning and development benchmarks for 2012.

Stresses the value of the reader's contribution

Makes clear who should fill out the survey and how to access it

If you are not the person responsible for this, would you please share this request with your organization's Chief Learning Officer or senior learning executive? You can access the survey at this link:
https://survey.astd.org/se.ashx?s=34B40469374EE2B4

Ends with appreciation and a reminder of the importance of the reader's participation

Each participant will receive a complimentary download of the ASTD 2013 State of the Industry Report when it is released in November (a $499 value). We appreciate your time and willingness to participate in this important industry benchmark.

Offers a persuasive tangible benefit

Sincerely,

Tony Bingham

ASTD President and CEO

ASTD | 1640 King Street | Box 1443 | Alexandria, VA 22313 | United States
Unsubscribe from future marketing messages from ASTD

SALES MESSAGES

Generating More Customers for Your Business

Play the role of Zach Miller, a student in your university's college of business. You've had your own house-painting business ever since you started college. So far, you've gained your customers through word of mouth only, but you think it's time to expand.

You've got two buddies willing to come on board if you can generate enough business for them to work full time in the summer months and part time in the spring and fall. You've decided that your first step in growing the business will be to advertise your services to the faculty and staff of your school. After getting permission to post your message to the listservs of several offices and academic departments, you sit down to think through what you want to say.

Considering your audience, you decide to reveal to them that you're a student. Given the line of work they're in, your readers obviously like the feeling of helping young people succeed. On the other hand, you'll need to overcome any concern that the job you'll do will be less than professional. As you start figuring out your persuasive details, you realize that it may be a good idea to include links to other information. Hmmm . . . this message is going to take some careful planning in order to be effective. The following sections will help you think through your options.

One of the most widely disseminated forms of business communication is the **sales message**. It is such an important component of most businesses' sales strategies that it has become an elaborate, highly professionalized genre, shaped by extensive consumer research. Think about the typical sales letter that you receive. Careful attention has been paid to the message on the envelope, to the kinds of pieces inside, and to the visual

Face-to-face selling is only part of the picture. Many sales occur through mail, email, Web-based media, and mobile messaging.

appeal of those pieces, as well as to the text of the letter itself. Clearly, advertising professionals produce many of these mailings, as well as much of the fundraising literature that we receive. You can also see a professional's hand in many of the sales emails that appear in your in-box, as well as in other sales communications, such as blogs, Facebook pages, and white papers. Why, then, should you study sales writing?

As a businessperson, you will often find yourself in the position of helping to shape a major sales campaign or contribute to its success through social networking. You may have valuable insight into your product's benefits and your potential customers. You need to be familiar with the conventions for sales messages and to be able to offer your own good ideas for their success.

In addition, knowledge of selling techniques can help you in many of your other activities, especially the writing of other kinds of business messages. As we've said, most of them involve selling something—an idea, a line of reasoning, your company, yourself. Sales techniques are more valuable to you than you might think. After you have studied the remainder of this chapter, you should see why.

Questioning the Acceptability of Sales Messages

LO3 Discuss ethical concerns regarding sales messages.

Sales messages are a controversial area of business communication, for two main reasons: They are often unwanted, and they sometimes use ethically dubious persuasive tactics. You probably know from your own experience that sales letters are not always received happily. Called "junk" mail, these mailings often go into the wastebasket or recycle bin without being read. They must be profitable, though, because they are still heavily used.

Sales messages sent by email may create even more hostility among intended customers. Angrily referred to as "spam," unsolicited email sales messages have generated strong resistance among email users. Perhaps it is because these messages clutter in-boxes. Maybe it is because mass mailings place a heavy burden on Internet providers, driving up costs to the users. Or perhaps the fact that they invade the reader's privacy is to blame. Whatever the explanation, the resistance is real. You will need to consider these objections any time you use this sales medium.

Fortunately, a more acceptable form of email selling has developed. Called **permission-based email**, it permits potential customers to sign up for email promotions on a company's website or provide their email addresses to an email or phone marketer. The potential customers may be asked to indicate the products, services, and specific topics of their interest, or the company may be able to track those interests based on what the customer has searched for or ordered in the past. The marketers can then tailor their messages to the customer, and the customer will receive only what he or she wants. According to a recent report by *eMarketer,* 93 percent of U.S. online consumers have at least one email subscription, and it is by far their preferred method for hearing about sales or promotions (64 percent of those surveyed ranked this method first, as opposed to 25 percent for postal mail and 8 percent for social media sites). Permission-based email is thus a powerful sales practice, and it has helped address the problem of unwanted sales messages.[1]

As for the charge that persuasive messages use unfair persuasive tactics, this is, unfortunately, sometimes the case. The unfair tactics could range from deceptive wording and visuals to the omission of important information to the use of emotional elements that impair good judgment. In a Missouri court case, Publishers Clearing House was found guilty of deception for direct mail stating that the recipients were already winners, when in fact they were not.[2] To consider a different example, one linen supply company sent a letter to parents of first-year students at a university telling them that the students would need to purchase extra-long sheets, offered by

---

[1] *10 Best Practices for Email Marketing,* 2, eMarketer, eMarketer, May 2011, Web, 20 June 2012.
[2] See Helen Rothschild Ewald and Roberta Vann, "'You're a Guaranteed Winner': Composing 'You' in a Consumer Culture," *Journal of Business Communication* 40 (2003): 98–117, print.

this company, to fit the extra-long beds on campus—but omitted the fact that only one dorm out of four had such beds. And it is well documented that images, because they work on an emotional level, persuade in ways that tend to bypass the viewers' reasoned judgment, leading some to question the ethics of such elements.[3] Certain kinds of online sales messages are particularly obnoxious, such as giant pop-ups that obscure the screen. Some of these trap readers in a loop that they can't exit without restarting their computers or, in extreme cases, having to remove spyware or viruses.

Any persuasive message is, by its very nature, biased. The writer has a favored point of view and wants to persuade the reader to adopt it. Therefore, considering the ethical dimension of your communication, while important for all types of messages, is especially critical for persuasive messages. Let your conscience and your ability to put yourself in the readers' shoes guide you as you consider how to represent your subject and win others to your cause.

Preparing to Write a Sales Message

LO4 Describe the planning steps for direct mail or email sales messages.

Before you can begin writing a sales message, you must know all you can about the product or service you are selling. You simply cannot sell most goods and services unless you know them well and can tell the prospects what they need to know. Before prospects buy a product, they may want to know how it is made, how it works, what it will do, and what it will not do. Clearly, a first step in sales writing is careful study of your product or service.

As we have stressed, you must also study your readers. You should gather demographic, psychographic, and any other kind of information that will help you understand why they might want or need your product. The more you know about your readers, the better you will be able to adapt your sales message to them.

In large businesses, a marketing research department or agency typically gathers information about prospective customers. If you do not have such help, you will need to gather this information on your own. If time does not permit you to do the necessary research, you may have to use logic and imagination. For example, the nature of a product can tell you something about its likely buyers. Industrial equipment would probably be bought by people with technical backgrounds. Expensive French perfumes and cosmetics would probably be bought by people in high-income brackets. Long-term care insurance would appeal to older people in middle-income brackets.

To be able to choose the most persuasive channel for your message, you should familiarize yourself with all the sales media that are now available. Often times, several media will need to work together to have the best effect. These days, sales emails are often linked to websites, and websites often provide links to social networking sites. You may even decide that the best approach is to start with an email and follow up with a phone call, or speak face to face with a prospect and then hand him or her some sales literature. There have never been so many media available, and the more you know about them, the better your selling can be.

Determining the Central Appeal

With your product or service, your prospects, and your medium or media in mind, you are ready to create the sales message. This involves selecting and presenting your persuasive appeals, whether emotional, logical, character based, or a combination. But for most sales messages, one appeal should stand out as the main one—mentioned in the beginning, recalled in the middle, and reiterated at the end. While other benefits can be brought in as appropriate, the message should emphasize your central, best appeal.

---

[3] Charles A. Hill, "The Psychology of Rhetorical Images," *Defining Visual Rhetorics*, ed. Charles A. Hill and Marguerite Helmers (Mahwah, NJ: Lawrence Erlbaum, 2004) 30–38, print.

Sophisticated Selling in White Papers

A kind of sales writing that many companies now use is the white paper. Originally, it was intended to brief government officials on affairs of state, but it has become a popular form of indirect selling.

A business white paper typically opens with a description of a situation, usually some kind of problem that the recipient's company faces or soon will face, or a need that it has. This section, which often cites numerous respected sources, can go on for several paragraphs or pages without even mentioning the seller's product. At some point, though, the white paper will offer the seller's products or services as a solution to the problem or answer to the need. The document thus has the look and feel of a research report but is ultimately a sales document.

For example, a white paper written by a software developer might discuss the difficulty of finding an appropriate tool for internal communication—a problem many companies share—and then focus on its own product as a solution. Many white papers are written business to business, informing one's partners in the industry of new technology or other kinds of products that can benefit all concerned.

White papers are often beautifully formatted and illustrated, as if produced by the staff of a professional print or online magazine. In fact, they are similar in nature to the subtly promotional articles in trade magazines. For guidelines and examples, subscribe to the WhitePaperSource newsletter at www.whitepapersource.com.

Emotional appeals—those based on our senses and emotions—can be found in almost any sales message, but they predominate in messages for goods and services that do not perform any discernable rational function. The following example illustrates:

Linger in castle corridors on court nights in London. Dance on a Budapest balcony high above the blue Danube. Seek romance and youth and laughter in charming capitals on five continents. And there you'll find the beguiling perfume that is fragrance Jamais.

Logical appeals are useful for selling products that help readers save money, do a better job, or get better use from a product. Illustrating a rational appeal (saving money) are these words from a message selling magazine subscriptions:

We're slashing the regular rate of $36 a year down to only $28, saving you a full 22 percent. That means you get 12 information-filled new issues of *Science Digest* for only $2.33 a copy. You save even more by subscribing for 2 or 3 years.

Character-based appeals can enhance any kind of sales message. They persuade by stating or implying "I use this product, so you should, too" or "I am an authority, so you should do what I recommend." Ads that employ sports figures, film stars, or experts to sell their products are relying heavily on character-based appeals. Companies themselves often project an appealing "character" in their sales campaigns. Note how the following excerpt from a sales letter for *Consumer Reports* magazine uses the company's identity to persuade:

Consumer Reports is on your side. We're a nonprofit consumer protection organization with no commercial interests whatsoever. To put it bluntly, we don't sell out to big companies and private interest groups—we're accountable to no one except to consumers. And when you're not beholden to advertisers (like other so-called consumer protection publications), you can tell it like it is.

People may also buy a certain product because they want to identify with, and be identified with, a certain successful, socially responsible, or "cool" company as projected in the company's sales messages.

In any given case, many appeals are available to you. You should use those that fit your product or service and your readers best. Keep in mind that how the buyer will use the product may be a major basis for selecting a sales strategy. For example, cosmetics might well be sold to the final user through emotional appeals, but selling cosmetics to a retailer (who is primarily interested in reselling them) would require rational appeals. A retailer's main questions about the product would be "Will it sell? What turnover can I expect? How much money will it make for me?"

Determining the Makeup of the Mailing

When you write a sales message to be sent by mail or email, a part of your effort is to determine the makeup of the mailing. To know what you want to say in your main message, you'll need to decide what kinds of additional pieces will be included and how they will support the main piece.

Consider, for example, a mailing crafted by Scotts LawnService (see the Case Illustration on page 245). It came in a 9-inch by 12-inch white envelope with the words "LAWN ANALYSIS ENCLOSED FOR (the recipient's address)" on the front, as well as the words "(recipient's city) RESIDENTS: PLEASE TAKE NOTICE." Both the kind of envelope used and the wording on it conveyed the image of an official, personalized document.

Inside were three 7½-inch by 10½-inch pages:

- The top page included the main sales letter on the front, with bold letters in the top right corner advertising a **"FREE No-Obligation Lawn Analysis for (the resident's address)."** On the back were six testimonials under the heading **"Here's what our customers say about Scotts LawnService."**

Direct-mail messages can include many extras beyond the main message.

- The second page, on glossy paper, had "before" and "after" pictures of a lawn under the heading **"Now you can enjoy a thick, green, beautiful lawn . . . *and Scotts LawnService will do the work!"* On the back were various character appeals for the company under the heading **"Here's why you can expect more from Scotts LawnService than any other lawn service."**

- The third sheet was a replica of a "FREE LAWN ANALYSIS" form "TO BE COMPLETED FOR (the recipient's) FAMILY at (the recipient's address)," with "SAMPLE" stamped (or appearing to be stamped) across the form.

The last piece was a return envelope with a detachable form to fill out and return. Both parts advertised again the "FREE No-Obligation Lawn Analysis."

The envelope often begins the persuasive effort.

The author of this elaborate mailing determined that the free lawn analysis would be the immediate selling point, with the main reader benefit being the beautiful lawn that the analysis would lead to. With these decisions made, the writer could then decide what to place in the foreground of the letter, what other pieces to include, and how to coordinate the letter with the other pieces. Even if someone else, such as a graphic artist or desktop publishing expert, will be designing the pieces of your mailing, you will need to be able to explain what you want and plan how all parts of the sales package will work together, especially for a complex mailing like the one described here.

Email sales messages can use all the publishing features available on the computer. The message can be presented creatively with color, font variations, box arrangements, artwork, and more. It may include links to the seller's website as well as to other supporting material and to the ordering procedure. And it may have attachments. Just as with a direct-mail package, the email sales package can use many elements to persuade and to provide all the information a reader will need in order to make a purchase.

Gaining Attention Before the Message Begins

LO5 Compose sales messages that gain attention, present persuasive appeals, use appropriate visual elements, and effectively drive for action.

Sales messages must gain the reader's attention right away. Otherwise, they won't be read. For this reason, the sales effort often begins before the actual message does.

Many mailed messages have an attention getter on the envelope. It may be the offer of a gift ("Your gift is enclosed"). It may present a brief sales message ("12 months of *Time* at 60 percent off the newsstand price"). It may present a picture and a message (a picture of a cruise ship and "Tahiti and more at 2-for-1 prices"). An official-appearing envelope sometimes is used. So are brief and simple messages such as "Personal" or "Sensitive material enclosed."

With email, of course, there is no envelope. The attention begins with the *From, To,* and *Subject* fields. To avoid having your message regarded as **spam** (promotional email sent indiscriminately to a huge number of readers), you should clearly tell who you are and identify your company. You should also address the reader by name. Though some readers will delete the message even with this clear identification, the specificity will induce some to read on.

The subject line in email messages is the main place for getting attention. Here honesty and simplicity should be your guide. The subject line should tell clearly what your message is about, and it should be short. It should avoid sensational wording, such as "How to earn $60,000 the first month." In addition, avoiding sensationalism involves limiting the use of solid caps, exclamation points, dollar signs, and "free" offers. In fact, you risk having spam filters block your message or send it to the junk folder of your readers' computers if you use "free" or other words and phrases commonly used in spam. An email with the subject line "Making your restaurant more profitable" that is sent to a researched list of restaurant managers and owners is much more likely to be opened and read than a message with the subject line "You have to read this!" that is sent to thousands of readers.

Gaining Attention in the Opening of the Message

The first words of your message must also gain attention and motivate the reader to keep reading. What you do here can be creative, but the method you use should help set up your strategy. It should not just gain attention for attention's sake. Attention is easy to gain if nothing else is needed. In a sales letter, a sensational statement such as "You can be a millionaire!" or "Free chocolate for the rest of your life!" would gain attention, but it wouldn't be likely to help sell most products or services, which can't live up to such extravagant claims.

Gaining—and Keeping—Readers' Attention on Facebook and Twitter

Messages on Facebook and Twitter don't use envelopes or subject lines, so how do you gain attention in these media? Monica Clarke of The Wakeman Agency, a New York-based public relations firm serving nonprofits and small to medium-sized businesses, has some advice.

If you can afford it, hire a celebrity spokesperson; "co-branding or collaborating with a 'star' may give your cause the spark it needs." But if that's not feasible, use television ads, magazine ads, your website, and other outlets to start a buzz.

Once you have people logged in, "the major effort must be focused on not losing their attention." Keep the feeds coming, and provide content "that will get people talking to their friends about your social media marketing campaign." Find an interesting angle "and work it—don't just provide information about your organization, but provide information about the bigger picture." Just setting up a Facebook or Twitter account and hoping for followers is a surefire way to become "just another '@' symbol in the crowd."

SOURCE: "Standing Out Amongst Millions—How to Get Attention on Twitter and Facebook," *The Wakeman Agency*, The Wakeman Agency, n.d., Web, 20 June 2012.

One of the most effective attention-gaining openings is a statement or question that introduces a need that the product will satisfy. For example, this rational-appeal opening would be likely to tap into a retailer's main need:

Here is a proven best-seller—and with a 12 percent greater profit.

This paragraph of a message selling a fishing vacation at a lake resort illustrates a need-fulfilling beginning of an emotional-appeal approach:

Your line hums as it whirs through the air. Your line splashes and dances across the smooth surface of the clear water as you reel. From the depth you see the silver streak of a striking bass. You feel a sharp tug. The battle is on!

A different tack is illustrated by the following example. It attracts interest by telling a story and using character-based appeal:

In 1984 three enterprising women met to do something about the lack of accessible health information for women.

Whatever opening strategy you choose, it should introduce or lead into your central selling point.

Building a Persuasive Case

With the reader's attention gained, you proceed with the sales strategy that you have planned. In general, you establish a need. Then you present your product or service as fulfilling that need.

The plan of your sales message will vary with each case. But it is likely to follow certain general patterns determined by your choice of appeals. If your main appeal is emotional, for example, your opening has probably established an emotional atmosphere that you will continue to develop. Thus, you will sell your product based on its effects on your reader's senses. You will describe the appearance, texture, aroma, and taste of your product so vividly that your reader will mentally see it, feel it—and want it. In general, you will seek to create an emotional need for your product.

A Direct-Mail Message (Selling a Lawn Care Service). This sales letter used all three types of appeals (logical, emotional, and character based). It also came with several other pieces—including "before" and "after" pictures, customer testimonials, and a sample "free lawn analysis" form with the customer's name and address printed on it.

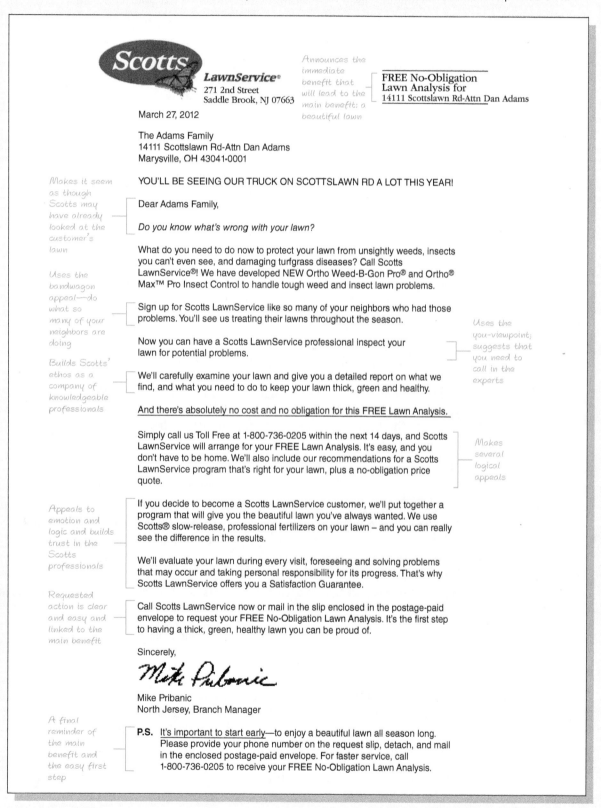

Announces the immediate benefit that will lead to the main benefit: a beautiful lawn

Scotts *LawnService®*
271 2nd Street
Saddle Brook, NJ 07663

FREE No-Obligation
Lawn Analysis for
14111 Scottslawn Rd-Attn Dan Adams

March 27, 2012

The Adams Family
14111 Scottslawn Rd-Attn Dan Adams
Marysville, OH 43041-0001

YOU'LL BE SEEING OUR TRUCK ON SCOTTSLAWN RD A LOT THIS YEAR!

Makes it seem as though Scotts may have already looked at the customer's lawn

Dear Adams Family,

Do you know what's wrong with your lawn?

What do you need to do now to protect your lawn from unsightly weeds, insects you can't even see, and damaging turfgrass diseases? Call Scotts LawnService®! We have developed NEW Ortho Weed-B-Gon Pro® and Ortho® Max™ Pro Insect Control to handle tough weed and insect lawn problems.

Uses the bandwagon appeal—do what so many of your neighbors are doing

Sign up for Scotts LawnService like so many of your neighbors who had those problems. You'll see us treating their lawns throughout the season.

Now you can have a Scotts LawnService professional inspect your lawn for potential problems.

Uses the you-viewpoint; suggests that you need to call in the experts

Builds Scotts' ethos as a company of knowledgeable professionals

We'll carefully examine your lawn and give you a detailed report on what we find, and what you need to do to keep your lawn thick, green and healthy.

And there's absolutely no cost and no obligation for this FREE Lawn Analysis.

Simply call us Toll Free at 1-800-736-0205 within the next 14 days, and Scotts LawnService will arrange for your FREE Lawn Analysis. It's easy, and you don't have to be home. We'll also include our recommendations for a Scotts LawnService program that's right for your lawn, plus a no-obligation price quote.

Makes several logical appeals

Appeals to emotion and logic and builds trust in the Scotts professionals

If you decide to become a Scotts LawnService customer, we'll put together a program that will give you the beautiful lawn you've always wanted. We use Scotts® slow-release, professional fertilizers on your lawn – and you can really see the difference in the results.

We'll evaluate your lawn during every visit, foreseeing and solving problems that may occur and taking personal responsibility for its progress. That's why Scotts LawnService offers you a Satisfaction Guarantee.

Requested action is clear and easy and linked to the main benefit

Call Scotts LawnService now or mail in the slip enclosed in the postage-paid envelope to request your FREE No-Obligation Lawn Analysis. It's the first step to having a thick, green, healthy lawn you can be proud of.

Sincerely,

Mike Pribanic

Mike Pribanic
North Jersey, Branch Manager

A final reminder of the main benefit and the easy first step

P.S. It's important to start early—to enjoy a beautiful lawn all season long. Please provide your phone number on the request slip, detach, and mail in the enclosed postage-paid envelope. For faster service, call 1-800-736-0205 to receive your FREE No-Obligation Lawn Analysis.

If you select a rational appeal as your central theme, your sales description is likely to be based on factual material. You should describe your product based on what it can do for your reader rather than how it appeals to the senses. You should write matter-of-factly about such qualities as durability, savings, profits, and ease of operation.

When using character-based appeals, you will emphasize comments from a well-known, carefully selected spokesperson. Or, if the character being promoted is that of the company itself, you will provide evidence that your company is expert and dependable, understands customers like "you," and stands behind its service or product.

The writing that carries your sales message can be quite different from your normal business writing. Sales writing usually is highly conversational, fast moving, and aggressive. It even uses techniques that are incorrect or inappropriate in other forms of business writing, such as sentence fragments or catchy slang. As the Case Illustrations show, it also uses visual emphasis devices (underscore, capitalization, boldface, italics, exclamation marks, color) and a variety of type sizes and fonts. And its paragraphing often appears choppy. Any sales message is competing with many other messages for the intended reader's attention. In this environment of information overload, punchy writing and visual effects that enable quick processing of the message's main points have become the norm in professional sales writing.

Stressing the You-Viewpoint

In no area of business communication is the use of the you-viewpoint more important than in sales writing. A successful sales message bases its sales points on reader interest. You should liberally use and imply the pronoun *you* throughout the sales message as you present your well-chosen reader benefits.

For example, assume you are writing a sales message to a retailer and that one point you want to make is that the manufacturer will help sell the product with an advertising campaign. You could write this information in a matter-of-fact way: "Home-Health products will be advertised in *Self* magazine for the next three issues." Or you could write it based on what the advertising means to the reader: "Your customers will read about HomeHealth products in the next three issues of *Self* magazine." As you can see, viewing things from the reader's perspective strengthens your persuasiveness. The following examples further illustrate the value of presenting facts as reader benefits:

Facts	You-Viewpoint Statements
We make Aristocrat hosiery in three colors.	You may choose from three lovely shades.
The Regal weighs only a few ounces.	The Regal's featherlight touch makes vacuuming easier than ever.
Lime-Fizz is a lime-flavored carbonated beverage.	Your customers will keep coming back for the refreshing citrus taste of Lime-Fizz.
Baker's Dozen is packaged in a rectangular box with a bright bull's-eye design.	Baker's Dozen's new rectangular package fits compactly on your shelf, and its bright bull's-eye design is sure to catch the eyes of your customers.

You may also want to make use of scenario painting, putting the reader in a simulated context that brings out the product's appeal. The J. Peterman company is famous for this technique, exemplified in the following excerpt from an advertisement for a picnic backpack:

It's a 7-mile hike to Snowmass Lake.

Best do it in late spring, early summer.

The Importance of Vividness in Sales Messages

In reviewing the research on visual persuasion, Charles A. Hill identifies *vividness* as a key element in persuasive messages, whether verbal or visual.

Research has shown that readers are more persuaded by one vivid picture or story than they are by statistics. For example, the picture of a hungry child or a detailed story about the child can persuade more successfully than the statistic that thousands of children are hungry. This finding seems illogical because many cases should logically outweigh one case. But as Hill points out, reactions to vividness are not logic based. They tend to elicit immediate, emotional responses, not reasoned ones, and emotion often persuades more powerfully than reason.

Hill offers the following hierarchy of vividness, with the most vivid information at the top and the least at the bottom:

Actual experience

Moving images with sound

Static photograph

Realistic painting

Line drawing

Narrative, descriptive account

Abstract, impersonal analysis

Statistics

Look for ways to include vivid, attractive detail—whether in the form of words or graphics—at key points in your persuasive message. But be sure to do so ethically.

SOURCE: "The Psychology of Rhetorical Images," *Defining Visual Rhetorics*, ed. Charles A. Hill and Marguerite Helmers (Mahwah, NJ: Lawrence Erlbaum, 2004) 25–40, print.

At sunset, the orange hues of Snowmass Mountain reflect off this glassy, ripple free water. Many stop here to rest before a summit run.

Audrey and I are here for a picnic. No further quest required, less equipment, too. I have the overnight gear. She, this perfectly equipped lightweight picnic backpack.

Choosing Words Carefully

In persuasive messages, every word can influence whether the reader will act on your request. Try putting yourself in your reader's place as you select words for your message. Some words, while closely related in meaning, have different emotional effects. For example, the word *selection* implies a choice, while the word *preference* implies a first choice. Consider how changing a single adjective changes the effect of these sentences:

The NuPhone's *small* size . . .

The NuPhone's *compact* size . . .

The NuPhone's *sleek* size . . .

Framing your requests in the positive is also a proven persuasive technique. Readers will tend to opt for solutions to problems that avoid negatives. Here are some examples:

Original Wording	Positive Wording
Tastee ice cream has nine grams of fat per serving.	Tastee ice cream is 95 percent fat free.
Our new laser paper keeps the wasted paper from smudged copies to less than 2 percent.	Our new laser paper ensures smudge-free copies over 98 percent of the time.

Enhancing Your Message with Visuals

The Web has made today's readers more visually oriented than any before in history. When preparing any kind of sales message, be sure to consider whether photos, tables, boxes, word art, borders, or other graphical elements would enhance your message's appeal.

As pointed out in our discussion of the Scotts LawnService mailing, sales letters can contain elaborately designed materials. Often, the envelope will contain artful text and images. Inside, you'll find visual elements ranging from logos and creatively chosen fonts to photos of products and customers.

Email sales messages have become just as visually appealing, if not more so. Many that sell products, such as the Wolferman's message on the left in Figure 9–1, are almost all pictures. Some are at the oppositive end of the spectrum, such as some email messages designed to be read on mobile devices (the message on the right in Figure 9–1). Probably most fall somewhere in between these two extremes, such as the Case Illustration on page 249.

The *visual literacy* you read about in Chapter 1 definitely comes into play when designing sales messages. You need to understand, for example, that a photo is not just a literal representation of a person or a product; it conveys a mood, a set of values, and even an experience. Where to put the visual elements is also an important decision, requiring that you imagine the readers' likely response to the screen or page design. Whatever visual elements you choose and wherever you put them, be sure that they project the desired message and complement the textual content.

Figure 9–1

Many sales emails today are designed to be displayed in two formats, one for a computer screen and one for a mobile device. As you see here, the large-screen version can be graphically rich, but the mobile version might include text and links only.

SOURCE: Reprinted with permission of Harry & David Operations, Inc.

An Email Sales Message (Persuading Readers Who Used a Trial Version of an Application to Purchase It). This message uses logical appeals and a variety of visual elements to make the product's benefits stand out.

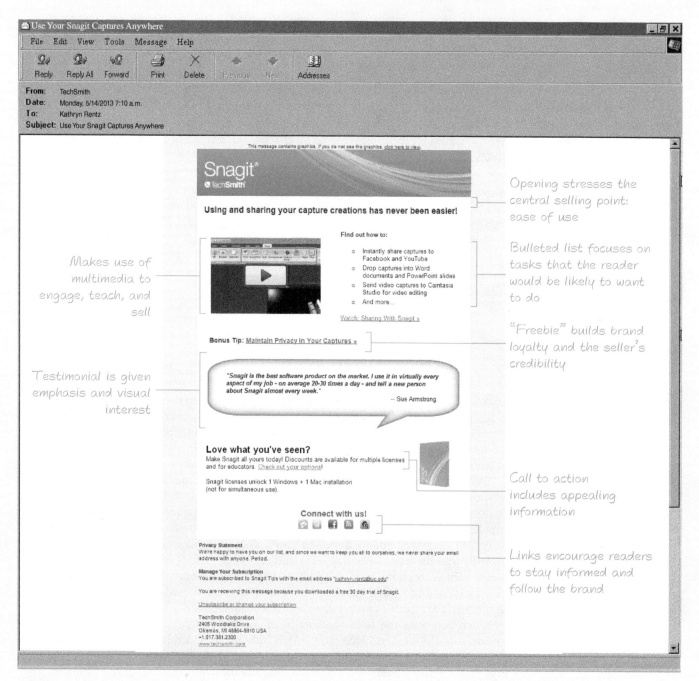

SOURCE: Reprinted with permission.

Persuasive Strategies Vary across Cultures

When writing persuasive messages, be especially careful to adapt them to the culture of the intended readers.

For example, while sales letters in English and Chinese use many of the same core elements, there are also these crucial differences:

- English sales letters often use attention-getting headlines and postscripts that pressure readers to act, while Chinese sales letters do not use these aggressive strategies.

- Both types of letters contain a salutation, but it is more formal in Chinese letters (for example, "Honored Company" instead of "Dear Mr. Smith"). Furthermore, Chinese letters follow the salutation with polite words of greeting, whereas English letters go directly into sales talk.

- English letters tend to describe the product's benefits by using "you," whereas the Chinese, finding the use of "you" disrespectful, tend to use "we" (as in "Our consistent goal is to produce comfortable luxury cars of high standard and good quality").

- Both types of letters extol the benefits of the product, but Chinese letters use fewer details, especially about price.

- When making the actual request, Chinese letters are less pushy than English letters, favoring such mild language as "If you are interested in our products, please contact us."

- Both types of letters use a complimentary close, but instead of "Sincerely yours," the Chinese attempt to promote cooperation and mutual respect with such closings as "Wishing good health."

SOURCE: Zhu Yunxia, "Building Knowledge Structures in Teaching Cross-Cultural Sales Genres," *Business Communication Quarterly* 63.4 (2000): 49–69, print.

Including All Necessary Information

Of course, the information you present and how you present it are matters for your best judgment. But you must make sure that you present enough information to complete the sale. You should leave none of your readers' questions unanswered. Nor should you fail to overcome any likely objections. You must work to include all such information in your message, and you should make it clear and convincing.

You will also need to decide how to apportion your information across all the pieces in your mailing or the layout of a screen. With direct mail, you should use your letter to do most of the persuading, with any enclosures, attachments, or links providing supplementary information. These supplements might provide in-depth descriptions, price lists, diagrams, and pictures—in short, all the helpful information that does not fit easily into the letter. You may want to direct your readers' attention to these other pieces with such comments as "you'll find comments from your satisfied neighbors in the enclosed brochure," "as shown on page 7 of the enclosed catalog," or "you'll see testimonials of satisfied customers in the blue shaded boxes."

When you send the sales message by email, the supporting information can be worked into the message, accessed via Web links, or provided in attachments that you invite the reader to view. Because people skim email quickly, be sure to keep the message itself relatively short. Skillfully chunking the message visually (see the Case Illustration on page 249) also helps reduce the impression of excessive length.

Driving for the Sale

After you have developed your reader's interest in your product or service, the next logical step is to drive for the sale. After all, this is what you have been working for all along. It is the natural conclusion to the previous paragraphs.

How to word your drive for the sale depends on your strategy. If your selling effort is strong, your drive for action also may be strong. It may even be worded as a command

Figure 9-2

An Email That Makes the Desired Action Easy

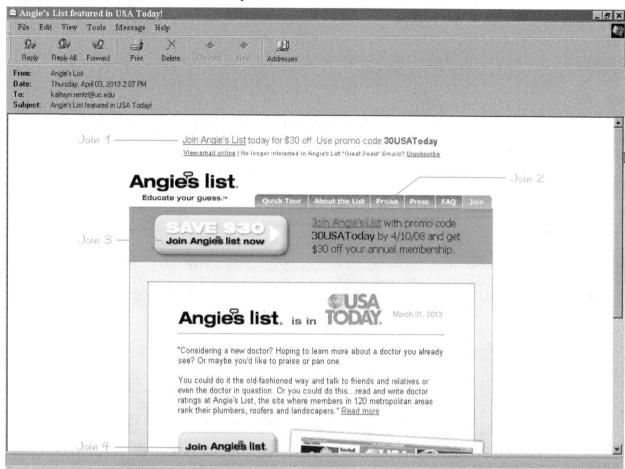

SOURCE: Reprinted with permission.

("Order your copy today—while it's on your mind."). If you use a milder selling effort, you could use a direct question ("May we send you your copy today?"). In any event, the drive for action should be specific and clear. For best effect, it should take the reader through the motions of whatever he or she must do. Here are some examples:

Just check your preferences on the enclosed order card and drop it in the mail today.

To start enjoying *House and Garden*, just call 1-888-755-5265. Be sure to have promo code 3626 handy to receive your 40 percent discount.

Similarly, in email selling you will need to make the action easy. Make it a simple click—a click to an order form or to the first part of the ordering process. For example, you might say "Just click the button below to order your customized iPhone case now!" or "You can download our free new catalog of business gifts at http://thankyoutoo. com." Many sales emails, such as the one shown in Figure 9–2, make the desired action easy by including multiple places for readers to perform it.

Because readers who have been persuaded sometimes put things off, you should urge immediate action. "Do it now" and "Act today" are versions of this technique, although some people dislike the commanding tone of such words. A milder and generally more acceptable way of urging action is to tie it in with a good reason for acting now. Here are some examples:

. . . to take advantage of this three-day offer.

. . . so that you can be ready for the Christmas rush.

. . . so that you can immediately begin enjoying. . . .

Another effective technique for the close of a sales message is to use a few words that recall the main appeal. Associating the action with the benefits that the reader will gain by taking it adds strength to your sales effort. Illustrating this technique is a message selling a fishing resort vacation that follows its action words with a reminder of the joys described earlier:

It's your reservation for a week of battle with the fightingest bass in the Southland.

Adding a Postscript

Unlike other business messages where a postscript (P.S.) appears to be an afterthought, a sales message can use a postscript as a part of its design. It can be used effectively in a number of ways: to urge the reader to act, to emphasize the major appeal, to invite attention to other enclosures, or to suggest that the reader pass along the sales message. Postscripts effectively used by professionals include the following:

PS: Remember—if ever you think that *Action* is not for you, we'll give you every cent of your money back. We are that confident that *Action* will become one of your favorite magazines.

PS: Hurry! Save while this special money-saving offer lasts.

PS: Our little magazine makes a distinctive and appreciated gift. Know someone who's having a birthday soon?

PS: Click now to order and you'll automatically be entered into a contest for a 4G Android smartphone.

Offering Name Removal to Email Readers

Until January 1, 2004, it was a courtesy to offer the recipients of commercial email the option of receiving no further emails from the sender. Now, thanks to the so-called CAN-SPAM Act, it is a legal requirement as well.[4] Consider placing this invitation in a prominent place—perhaps even before the main message (see Figure 9–2). Wherever it is, the link should be easy to identify.

Ideally, it should also take only one or two clicks to work. Unfortunately, a 2010 report indicated that this trend was going in the wrong direction: The unsubscribe function of nearly half of the retail emails studied required three or more clicks, which was an increase from the year before.[5] On the other hand, providing readers the option of being emailed less frequently, of receiving emails about certain products only, or of following the brand through another channel (e.g., Facebook) seems to be regarded favorably by both consumers and businesses.[6]

Reviewing the General Sales Plan

From the preceding discussion, a general plan for the sales message emerges. This plan is similar to the classic AIDA (attention, interest, desire, action) model developed almost a century ago. It should be noted, however, that in actual practice, sales messages vary widely. Creativity and imagination are continually leading to innovative techniques. Even so, the most common plan is the following:

- Gain favorable attention.
- Create desire by presenting the appeals, emphasizing supporting facts, emphasizing the reader's viewpoint, and enhancing the message with appropriate visual elements.
- Include all necessary information—using a coordinated sales package (brochures, leaflets, links, and other appended parts).
- Drive for the sale by urging action now and recalling the main appeal.

---

[4] For further information, consult the Federal Trade Commission's publication *The CAN-SPAM Act: A Compliance Guide for Business* at http://business.ftc.gov/documents/bus61-can-spam-act-compliance-guide-business.

[5] "Room for Improvement in Email Opt-Outs," *eMarketer*, eMarketer, 5 Apr. 2010, Web, 21 June 2012.

[6] "Room for Improvement."

- Possibly add a postscript.
- In email writing, offer to remove the reader from your email list to comply with legal requirements.

Evaluating Contrasting Examples

The following two email sales messages show bad and good efforts to promote Zach Miller's painting business (described in the Introductory Challenge on page 237).

A Weak, Self-Centered Message. The ineffective example begins with a dull, vague subject line. The first sentence talks only about the writer and delays answering the reader's obvious question, "What's the offer?" The second sentence begins to hint at the topic, but it is still writer focused. The middle paragraph contains some potentially good logical points, but the general, bland language won't generate much enthusiasm. Also, the character appeal is weak. Zach comes across as just another struggling student trying to pay his way through school; he does not make a convincing case that he and his friends would actually do a good job. The final sentence doesn't tell the reader what information to include in a response—and no final selling ends the message.

Subject: Offer from a Student

Hello,

My name is Zach Miller, and I'm a business student here at North Rapids University. I've been learning about business not only in the classroom but on the job, by running my own house-painting operation.

If you'd like to have your house painted this summer, I can do it for considerably less than what you'd pay a professional service. I would carefully prepare your house for painting, and I use good-quality paint. My two friends and I will also guarantee to complete the job within three days (weather permitting).

Please email me if you'd like an estimate.

Sincerely,

Zach Miller

This me-focused message is short on appealing reader benefits.

Skillful Use of Character and Rational Appeals. The better message follows the advice presented in the preceding pages. The subject line contains concrete reader benefits and states right away that the job will be professionally done. The opening sentence is an engaging question and is again focused on key benefits. The second paragraph builds confidence in the writer and his co-workers, and it ends by allaying any worries that the homeowner will be held liable if one of the students is injured. The third paragraph provides convincing logical details about the job. In the final paragraph, the writer uses a Web link to make it easy for readers to submit an estimate request, and he directs them to an attachment that contains further information and one last reader benefit.

Subject: A Professional-Quality Paint Job for Less

Would you like a great deal on having your house painted this summer while supporting NKU students?

My name is Zach Miller, and I'm a junior business major here at NKU, in the Honors Plus program. I'm a graduate of St. Xavier High School and have been running my own house-painting business for three years. I employ two other NKU students, Jeff Barnes and Alex Wilson, who are also business students. We are all fully licensed and insured.

We use only 100% acrylic paints from top manufacturers like Benjamin Moore, Porter, and Sherwin Williams. Our specialty is careful preparation. We will scrape or power wash all surfaces of your house and do any needed minor repairs before we paint. The work comes with a two-year guarantee and, combined with our low rates, is an excellent value.

If you'd like a free estimate, just fill out the online estimate request form. The attached flyer tells more about me and also includes a coupon for 10% off if you schedule your paint job the day you receive your estimate.

Zach Miller
millerzs@mail.nku.edu
cellular: (431) 445-5560

The you-viewpoint and better details give this message strong appeal.

PROPOSALS

INTRODUCTORY CHALLENGE

Selling Your Services through Proposal Writing

Play the role of Evan Lockley, vice president of account management at Whitfield Organizational Research. Your company collects internal information for businesses that want to improve their management techniques, information flow, employee morale, work processes, or other parts of their operations. To keep a steady stream of clients coming in, Whitfield must write numerous proposals for performing this kind of research.

As the manager of client accounts and the lead proposal writer at Whitfield, you now sit down to write a proposal to submit to RT Industries. This company is about to implement an enterprise resource planning (ERP) system. This implementation will require employees in every functional area of the business—from purchasing to inventory to design, manufacturing, and shipping—to learn the system and enter the data for their area. If the implementation is successful, the management at RT Industries will be able to tell, with the click of a few buttons, exactly how every facet of the business is doing. But implementing such a system is a major and potentially disastrous organizational change, and RT knows it. That's why they want to pay an organizational research firm to track the implementation and make sure it's as successful as possible. RT has invited Whitfield, along with other firms, to bid on this job.

You and one of your principal researchers have visited with the implementation team at RT Industries to learn more about the system they've chosen and their particular concerns. Whitfield has experience tracking such organizational changes, so you feel your odds of winning this client are good. But now you need to make your case. How can you craft a proposal that will make as positive an impression as possible? How can you make sure the readers at RT Industries will choose you over the competition? Read on to see how to write a persuasive proposal.

LO6 Write well-organized and persuasive proposals.

Proposals share certain characteristics with reports. Both genres require that information be carefully gathered and presented. Visually, they can seem quite similar; at their most formal, they use the same kinds of prefatory material (e.g., title page, letter of transmittal, table of contents). And proposals frequently use the direct pattern that most reports use. But proposals differ from reports in one essential way: Proposals are intentionally *persuasive*. Proposal writers are not just providing information in an orderly, useful form. They are writing to get a particular result, and they have a vested

Web Resources for Proposal Writing

You can find excellent free advice about proposal writing—along with examples and templates—on the Internet. Here are just a few useful sites to check out:

- CapturePlanning at **CapturePlanning.com** is perhaps the best all-around site for learning about proposal writing. The site is full of freebies—from examples to articles to templates—that you can access just by registering.

- The team at **learntowriteproposals.com** offers such useful articles as "Our Top Ten Proposal Writing Tips," "10 Ways to Make Your Proposal Easier to Understand," and "11 Things Not to Do When You Write a Business Proposal."

- Debra Klug, author of **ProposalWriter.com**, discusses a wide range of relatively specific topics, such as getting a government grant to start a business, and provides a huge assortment of links to proposal-related resources.

- At **fedmarket.com**, Richard White provides links to his free webinars and publications about how to win government contracts.

- The **YouTube.com** videos by Julia King Tamang ("How to Write a Winning Proposal") and Doug Stern ("Six Keys to Writing a Great Proposal") offer sound, specific advice that supplements the advice in this chapter.

interest in that result. Whether they use the direct or indirect approach, their purpose is to persuade. The following sections provide an introduction to the main types of proposals and offer guidelines for preparing them.

Types of Proposals

Proposals can vary widely in purpose, length, and format. Their purpose can be anything from acquiring a major client to getting a new copier for your department. They can range from one page to hundreds of pages. They can take the form of an email, a memo, a letter, or a report. They are usually written, but they can be presented orally or delivered in both oral and written form. As with other kinds of business communication, the context will determine the specific traits of a given proposal. But all proposals can be categorized as either internal or external and either solicited or unsolicited. It is with the unsolicited type that indirect organization most often comes into play.

Internal or External. Proposals can be either **internal** or **external**. That is, they may be written for others within your organization or for readers outside your organization.

The reasons for internal proposals differ, but you will almost surely find yourself having to write them. They are a major means by which you will get what you need in order to do your job better or change your organization. Whether you want a computer upgrade, an improved physical environment, specialized training, travel money, or additional staff members, you will usually need to make your case to management. Of course, much of what you need as an employee will already be provided by your company. But when resources are tight, as they almost always are, you will have to persuade your superiors to give you the money rather than allocating it to another employee or department. Even if your idea is to enhance company operations in some way—for example, to make a procedure more efficient or cost effective—you may find yourself having to persuade. Companies tend to be conservative in terms of change. The management wants good evidence that the trouble and expense of making a change will pay off.

Whether solicited or unsolicited, proposals must do an effective job of presenting what is being proposed. You must work hard to meet the needs of your audience to win their business.

In addition, as the practice of outsourcing has grown, many companies have adopted a system in which departments have to compete with external vendors for projects. As the director of technical publications for a company, for example, you may find yourself bidding against a technical-writing consulting firm for the opportunity, and the funding, to write the company's online documentation. If you are not persuasive, you may find yourself with a smaller and smaller staff and, eventually, no job yourself. Clearly, the ability to write a persuasive internal proposal is an important skill.

External proposals are also written for a variety of reasons, but the most common purpose is to acquire business for a company or money from a grant-awarding organization. Every consulting firm—whether in training, financial services, information technology, or virtually any other business specialty—depends upon external proposals for its livelihood. If such firms cannot persuade companies to choose their services, they will not be in business for long. Companies that supply other companies with goods they need, such as uniforms, computers, or raw materials, may also need to prepare proposals to win clients. Business-to-business selling is a major arena for external proposals.

But external proposals are also central to other efforts. A company might propose to merge with another company; a city government might propose that a major department store choose the city for its new location; a university professor might write a proposal to acquire research funding. Many nonprofit and community organizations depend upon proposals for grant money to support their work. They might write such proposals to philanthropic foundations, to wealthy individuals, to businesses, or to government funding agencies. Depending on the nature of the organization that you work for, proficiency in external proposal writing could be critical.

Solicited or Unsolicited. Another way to categorize proposals is **solicited** versus **unsolicited**. A solicited proposal is written in response to an explicit invitation offered by a company, foundation, or government agency that has certain needs to meet or goals to fulfill. An unsolicited proposal, as you can probably guess, is one that you submit without an official invitation to do so.

The primary means by which organizations solicit proposals is the **request for proposals,** or **RFP** (variations are requests for quotes—RFQs—and invitations for/to bid—IFBs or ITBs—both of which tend to focus only on price). These can range from brief announcements to documents of 50, 100, or more pages, depending upon the scope and complexity of the given project. As you might expect, their contents can also vary. But a lot of thought and research go into a good RFP. In fact, some RFPs—for instance, a company's request for proposals from IT firms to design and implement its technology infrastructure—need to be just as elaborately researched as the proposals being requested. Whatever its topic or purpose, the RFP needs to include a clear statement of the organization's need, the proposal guidelines (due date and time, submission process, and proposal format and contents), and the approval process, in addition to such helpful information as background about the organization.

When responding to an RFP, you should be careful to heed its guidelines. With some firms, your proposal gets eliminated if it arrives even one minute late or omits a required section. This is particularly true for proposals to the federal government, whose proposal guidelines are notoriously, and perhaps understandably, regimented (see Figure 9–3). On the other hand, most RFPs give you some latitude to craft your proposal in such a way that your organization can put its best foot forward. You will want to take advantage of this maneuvering room to make your proposal the most persuasive of those submitted. Of course, you will decide in the first place to respond only to those RFPs that give your organization (or, if it is an internal RFP, your department) a good chance to win.

In business situations, solicited proposals usually follow preliminary meetings between the parties involved. For example, if a business has a need for certain production equipment, its buyers might first identify likely suppliers by considering those they already know, by looking at industry material, or by asking around in their professional networks. Next they would initiate meetings with these potential suppliers to discuss the business's needs. Some or all of these suppliers would then be invited to submit a proposal for filling the need with its particular equipment. As you can see, the more relationships you have with companies that might use your goods or services, the more likely it is that they will invite you to a preliminary meeting and then invite you to bid. One expert, in fact, asserts that "winning starts with pre-RFP relationships," which "provide the intelligence you need to design and execute a winning plan."[7] Another advises that "proposals can be won (or lost) before the RFP hits the streets."[8]

Even if you are preparing a proposal for a government or foundation grant, it is wise—unless the RFP specifically forbids it—to call the funding source's office and discuss your ideas with a representative.

When writing unsolicited proposals, your job is harder than with solicited proposals. After all, in these scenarios, the intended reader has not asked for your ideas or services. For this reason, your proposal should resemble a sales message. It should quickly get the readers' attention and bring a need of theirs vividly to mind. It should then show how your product or services will answer the need. And from beginning to end, it should build your credibility. For example, if you want to provide training for a company's workforce or persuade a company to replace its current insurance provider with your company, you will need to target your readers' need in the opening, use further details to prepare them to receive your plan, lay out the benefits of your proposal quickly and clearly, and get the readers to believe that yours is the best company for the job. Careful and strategic preparation of unsolicited proposals can result in much success.

As with solicited proposals, you should try, if at all possible, to make prior contact with a person in the organization who has some power to initiate your plan. All other

---

[7] "What It Takes to Win," *CapturePlannning.com*, CapturePlanning.com, 2012, Web, 21 June 2012.

[8] Carl Dickson, "What a Private Sector Company Can Learn From Government Proposals," *Captureplanning.com*, CapturePlanning.com, 2012, Web, 21 June 2012.

Figure 9–3

First Page of a Government RFP

This first page of an RFP posted on Vermont's "Buildings and General Services" website (www.bgs.vermont.gov) shows the beginning of a long list of vendor requirements. The complete proposal for this relatively simple project is 23 pages long. To have a chance of winning the contract, you would need to study all 23 pages carefully and follow the instructions to the letter.

STATE OF VERMONT
OFFICE OF PURCHASING & CONTRACTING
RFP – BGS SNOW REMOVAL SERVICES 2012
PAGE 1

1. **OVERVIEW:**

 1.1. **SCOPE AND BACKGROUND:** The Office of Purchasing & Contracting is seeking to establish purchasing agreements with one or more companies that can provide BGS Snow Removal Services in the Burlington Area, Burlington, Vermont.

 1.2. **CONTRACT PERIOD:** Contracts arising from this request for proposal will be for a period of **12 months** with an option to renew for two (2) additional 12-**month** periods. Proposed start date will be **October 1, 2012.**

 1.3. **CONTRACT VALUE/QUANTITY:** The estimated annual value of this contract is $80,000.00. The annual value and quantities are estimated only based on prior usage; actual purchases may be higher or lower depending on the state's needs.

 1.4. **SINGLE POINT OF CONTACT:** All communications concerning this Request for Proposal (RFP) are to be addressed in writing to the attention of: **Robert Pierce**, Purchasing Agent, State of Vermont, Office of Purchasing & Contracting, 10 Baldwin St - Montpelier, Montpelier, VT 05633-7501. **Robert Pierce**, Purchasing Agent is the sole contact for this proposal. Actual contact with any other party or attempts by bidders to contact any other party could result in the rejection of their proposal.

 1.5. **BIDDERS' CONFERENCE:** A bidder's conference will be held on **July 23, 2012 at 11:00 AM**. Meeting will start at the BGS maintenance shop at 1705 Hedgeman Avenue in Colchester, Vermont.

 1.6. **QUESTION AND ANSWER PERIOD:** Any vendor requiring clarification of any section of this proposal or wishing to comment or take exception to any requirements or other portion of the RFP must submit specific questions in writing no later than **July 30, 2012 4:30PM**. Questions may be e-mailed to robert.pierce@state.vt.us . Any objection to the RFP or to any provision of the RFP, that is not raised in writing on or before the last day of the question period is waived. At the close of the question period a copy of all questions or comments and the State's responses will be posted on the State's web site http://bgs.vermont.gov/purchasing/bids . Every effort will be made to have these available as soon after the question period ends, contingent on the number and complexity of the questions.

 1.7. **INSTRUCTIONS FOR BIDDERS**: see sections 5 and 6.

2. **DETAILED REQUIREMENTS:**

 1.0 Without notification from the State, the Contractor will plow all snowfall of two inches or more, or at the end of each snow fall.

 2.0 Snow removal services for this site will be (24) hours a day, (7) days a week.

 3.0 Contractor shall take care not to damage buildings, guardrails, curbs and automobiles, Contractor will make repairs to material damaged during performing these services. Determination of the need for and extent of repair is the sole discretion of the State of Vermont Contract Coordinator.

 4.0 Contractor shall be responsible for incidental and emergency calls for removing snow that may interfere with State operations in the complex.

 5.0 Where applicable, driver/operator must be CDL certified.

 6.0 The contractor shall at all times provide adequate supervision of his/her employees to ensure complete and satisfactory performance of all work in accordance with the terms of the contract. The contractor will have a responsible supervisor on the job at all times when the work of the contract is being carried out.

 7.0 The contractor and his/her employees will be subject to all applicable State and Federal regulations for the conduct of personnel.

 8.0 Contractor's employees shall not utilize or operate State owned equipment of any type without specific authorization of the contract coordinator.

 9.0 The contractor will screen all personnel to assure the State that all employees are capable of performing the services in accordance with the RFP. A background check will be required to perform services as part of this contract.

Wise Words from a Professional Proposal Writer

A proposal or grant is the beginning of a relationship. Essentially, the readers are interviewing your company or organization, trying to determine whether a basis for a positive, constructive alliance exists. Your proposal is the face you are presenting to the client or funding source.

If they feel comfortable with your proposal, they will feel comfortable with your company or organization.

SOURCE: Richard Johnson-Sheehan, *Writing Proposals*, 2nd ed. (New York: Pearson/Longman, 2008) 232–33, print.

things being equal, a proposal to someone you know is preferable to a "cold" proposal. It is best to view the unsolicited proposal as part of a larger relationship that you are trying to create or maintain.

Proposal Format and Contents

Every proposal is unique, but some generalizations can be made. To succeed, proposals must be designed with the key decision makers in mind, emphasize the most persuasive elements, and present the contents in a readable format and style.

Format and Formality. The simplest proposals are often email messages. Internal proposals (those written for and by people in the same organization) usually fall into this category. The more complex proposals may take the form of long reports, including prefatory pages (title pages, letter of transmittal, table of contents, executive summary), text, and an assortment of appended parts. Most proposals have arrangements that fall somewhere between these extremes.

Because of the wide variations in the makeup of proposals, you need to investigate the situation carefully before designing a particular proposal. Try to find out what format the readers will expect and what other proposal writers have submitted in similar situations. In the case of an invited proposal, review the request thoroughly, looking for clues concerning the preferences of the inviting organization. If you are unable to follow any of these courses, design a format based on your analysis of the audience and your knowledge of formatting strategies. Your design should be the one that you think is best for the one situation.

The same advice applies to your decisions about formality. Let your reader and the circumstances be your guide. Internal proposals tend to be less formal than external ones because the parties are often familiar with each other and because internal documents, in general, are less formal than external ones. If you are proposing a major initiative or change, however, using a formal presentation—whether oral, written, or both—may be in order. Likewise, external proposals, while they tend to be formal, can be quite informal if they are short and the two parties know each other well. Many successful business proposals are pitched in letter format. As with every other kind of message, knowledge of and adaptation to your reader are key.

Content. Whether you are writing an external or internal proposal or a solicited or unsolicited one, your primary goal is the same: to make a persuasive argument. Every element of your proposal—from the title to the cover letter to the headings and organization of your content to the way you say things—needs to contribute to your central argument.

To be able to design your proposal according to this principle, you need to know your readers and their needs (which may be represented in an RFP). You also need to

The Seven Deadly Sins of Proposal Writing

Expert proposal writer Tom Sant warns against seven ways to put your proposal on the fast track to the trash can or delete folder:

1. Failing to qualify the deal (i.e., bidding on jobs that you can't win).

2. Not focusing on what the customer cares about.

3. Not structuring the document persuasively.

4. Not differentiating your offer and your company.

5. Not offering a compelling value proposition.

6. Not making it easy to understand and use.

7. Not editing carefully to remove mistakes and credibility killers.

SOURCE: *The Seven Deadly Sins of Proposal Writing: How to Write Proposals that Help Win Deals*, Qvidian, Qvidian, 2011, Web, 21 June 2012.

know how you can meet those needs. From these two sets of facts, you can develop your central argument. What is your competitive edge? Value for the money? Convenience? Reliability? Fit of your reader's needs or mission with what you have to offer? Some or all of the above? How you frame your argument will depend on how you think your proposal will be evaluated.

The reader of a business proposal will bring three basic criteria to the evaluation process:

- Desirability of the solution (Do we need this? Will it solve our problem?)
- Qualifications of the proposer (Can the author of the proposal, whether an individual or company, really deliver, and on time and on budget?)
- Return on investment (Is the expense, whether time or money, justified?)

If you can answer these questions affirmatively from the point of view of your intended recipient, you have a good chance of winning the contract or your management's approval.

When you have figured out what to propose and why, you need to figure out how to propose it. If the RFP provides strict guidelines for contents and organization, follow them. Otherwise, you have considerable latitude when determining your proposal's components. Your reader is likely to expect some version of the eight topics listed below, but you should adapt them as needed to fit the facts of your case. (See page 261 and pages 262–267 for two very different examples.)

1. *The writer's purpose and the reader's need.* An appropriate beginning is a statement of your purpose (to present a proposal) and the reader's need (such as reducing the turnover of sales staff). If the report is in response to an invitation, that statement should tie in with the invitation (for example, "as described in your July 10 announcement"). The problem and your purpose should be stated clearly, in the way described in Chapter 11. This proposal beginning illustrates these recommendations:

   As requested at the July 10 meeting with Alice Burton, Thomas Cheny, and Victor Petrui in your Calgary office, Murchison and Associates present the following proposal for studying the high rate of turnover among your field representatives. We will assess the job satisfaction of the current sales force, analyze exit interview records, and compare company compensation and human resource practices with industry norms to identify the causes of this drain on your resources.

An Internal, Unsolicited Proposal. This email proposal asks a company to sponsor an employee's membership in a professional organization. Starting with the subject line, the writer tries to avoid saying anything that the reader—in this case, the head of a corporate communications department—would disagree with. When enough background and benefits are given, the writer states the request and then describes the cost in the most positive terms. Offering to try the membership for one year helps the proposal seem relatively modest.

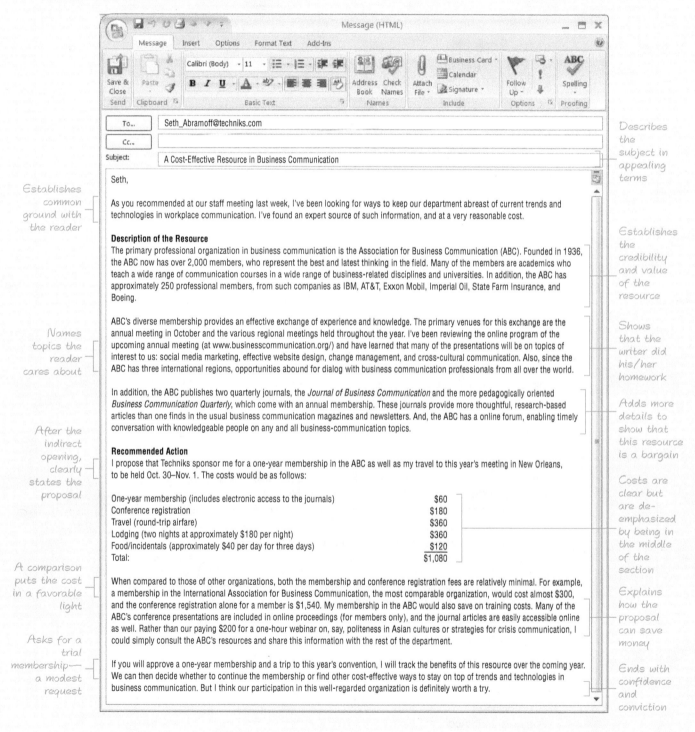

Describes the subject in appealing terms

Establishes common ground with the reader

Establishes the credibility and value of the resource

Names topics the reader cares about

Shows that the writer did his/her homework

Adds more details to show that this resource is a bargain

After the indirect opening, clearly states the proposal

Costs are clear but are de-emphasized by being in the middle of the section

A comparison puts the cost in a favorable light

Explains how the proposal can save money

Asks for a trial membership—a modest request

Ends with confidence and conviction

To... Seth_Abramoff@techniks.com

Cc...

Subject: A Cost-Effective Resource in Business Communication

Seth,

As you recommended at our staff meeting last week, I've been looking for ways to keep our department abreast of current trends and technologies in workplace communication. I've found an expert source of such information, and at a very reasonable cost.

Description of the Resource
The primary professional organization in business communication is the Association for Business Communication (ABC). Founded in 1936, the ABC now has over 2,000 members, who represent the best and latest thinking in the field. Many of the members are academics who teach a wide range of communication courses in a wide range of business-related disciplines and universities. In addition, the ABC has approximately 250 professional members, from such companies as IBM, AT&T, Exxon Mobil, Imperial Oil, State Farm Insurance, and Boeing.

ABC's diverse membership provides an effective exchange of experience and knowledge. The primary venues for this exchange are the annual meeting in October and the various regional meetings held throughout the year. I've been reviewing the online program of the upcoming annual meeting (at www.businesscommunication.org/) and have learned that many of the presentations will be on topics of interest to us: social media marketing, effective website design, change management, and cross-cultural communication. Also, since the ABC has three international regions, opportunities abound for dialog with business communication professionals from all over the world.

In addition, the ABC publishes two quarterly journals, the *Journal of Business Communication* and the more pedagogically oriented *Business Communication Quarterly*, which come with an annual membership. These journals provide more thoughtful, research-based articles than one finds in the usual business communication magazines and newsletters. And, the ABC has a online forum, enabling timely conversation with knowledgeable people on any and all business-communication topics.

Recommended Action
I propose that Techniks sponsor me for a one-year membership in the ABC as well as my travel to this year's meeting in New Orleans, to be held Oct. 30–Nov. 1. The costs would be as follows:

One-year membership (includes electronic access to the journals)	$60
Conference registration	$180
Travel (round-trip airfare)	$360
Lodging (two nights at approximately $180 per night)	$360
Food/incidentals (approximately $40 per day for three days)	$120
Total:	$1,080

When compared to those of other organizations, both the membership and conference registration fees are relatively minimal. For example, a membership in the International Association for Business Communication, the most comparable organization, would cost almost $300, and the conference registration alone for a member is $1,540. My membership in the ABC would also save on training costs. Many of the ABC's conference presentations are included in online proceedings (for members only), and the journal articles are easily accessible online as well. Rather than our paying $200 for a one-hour webinar on, say, politeness in Asian cultures or strategies for crisis communication, I could simply consult the ABC's resources and share this information with the rest of the department.

If you will approve a one-year membership and a trip to this year's convention, I will track the benefits of this resource over the coming year. We can then decide whether to continue the membership or find other cost-effective ways to stay on top of trends and technologies in business communication. But I think our participation in this well-regarded organization is definitely worth a try.

A Solicited External Proposal. A design and manufacturing company has invited research firms to propose plans for tracking its implementation of an enterprise resource planning (ERP) system—information technology that integrates all functions of the company, from job orders to delivery and from accounting to customer management. The midlevel formality of this proposal responding to the RFP is appropriate given the proposal's relative brevity and the two parties' prior meeting.

WHITFIELD
Organizational Research

7 Research Parkway, Columbus, OH 45319 614-772-4000 Fax: 614-772-4001

February 3, 2014

Ms. Janice Spears
Chief Operations Officer
RT Industries
200 Midland Highway
Columbus, OH 45327

Identifies the context for the proposal and shows appreciation for being invited to submit

Dear Janice:

Thank you for inviting Whitfield Organizational Research to bid on RFP 046, "Study of InfoStream Implementation at RT Industries." Attached is our response.

Reminds the reader of the previous, pleasant meeting

Reinforces the need for the study

We enjoyed meeting with you to learn about your goals for this research. All expert advice supports the wisdom of your decision to track InfoStream's implementation. As you know, the road of ERP adoption is littered with failed, chaotic, or financially bloated implementations. Accurate and timely research will help make yours a success story.

Whitfield Organizational Research is well qualified to assist you with this project. Our experienced staff can draw upon a variety of minimally invasive, cost-effective research techniques to acquire reliable information on your employees' reception and use of InfoStream. We are also well acquainted with ERP systems and can get a fast start on collecting the data you need. And because Whitfield is a local firm, we will save you travel and lodging costs.

Summarizes the proposing company's advantages

Compliments the receiving company, shows the writer's knowledge of the company, and states the benefits of choosing the writer's company

RT's culture of employee involvement has earned you a place on *Business Ohio's* list of the Best Ohio Workplaces for the last five years. The research we propose, performed by Whitfield's knowledgeable and respectful researchers, will help you maintain your productive culture through this period of dramatic change. It will also help you reap the full benefits of your investment.

Indirectly asks the reader for the desired action

We would welcome the opportunity to work with RT Industries on this exciting initiative.

Sincerely yours,

Evan Lockley

Evan Lockley
Vice President, Account Management

enclosure

(continued)

Response to RFP 046:
Study of InfoStream Implementation at RT Industries

Proposed by
Whitfield Organizational Research
February 3, 2014

Executive Summary

Provides a clear overview of the problem, purpose, and benefits

RT Industries has begun a major organizational change with its purchase of InfoStream enterprise resource planning (ERP) software. To track the effect of this change on personnel attitudes and work processes in the company, RT seeks the assistance of a research firm with expertise in organizational studies. Whitfield Organizational Research has extensive experience with personnel-based research, as well as familiarity with ERP software. We propose a four-part plan that will help ensure the success of your implementation.

Our methodology will be multifaceted, minimally disruptive, and cost effective. The results will yield a reliable picture of how InfoStream is being received and used among RT's workforce. With this information, RT's change leaders can intervene appropriately to effectively manage this companywide innovation.

Project Goals

Shows knowledge of the company; reminds readers of the investment they want to protect

RT Industries has so far invested over $1.6 million and over 1,000 employee hours in the purchase of and management's training on InfoStream's ERP system. As RT integrates the system fully into its company of 800+ employees over the next 12 months, it will invest many additional dollars and hours in the project, with the total investment likely to top $2 million. Adopting such a system is one of the most wide-ranging and expensive changes a company can make.

Reinforces the need for the study

As Jeri Dunn, Chief Information Officer of Nestle USA, commented in *CIO Magazine* about her company's troubles with its ERP adoption, "No major software implementation is really about the software. It's about change management." An ERP system affects the daily work of everyone in the company. The most common theme in ERP-adoption failure stories—of which there are many—is lack of attention to the employees' experience of the transition. Keeping a finger on the pulse of the organization during this profound organizational change is critical to maximizing the return on your investment.

Our research will determine

- How well employees are integrating InfoStream into their jobs.
- How the new system is changing employees' work processes.
- How the system is affecting the general environment or "culture" in the company.

States the benefits, supported by clear logic

Whitfield has designed a four-part, multimethod research plan to gather these data. Through our periodic reports, you will be able to see how InfoStream is being integrated into the working life of the company. As a result, you will be able to make, and budget for, such interventions as strategic communications and additional training. You will also find out where employee work processes need to be adjusted to accommodate the new system.

Whitfield Organizational Research 2

Instituting a change of this magnitude *will* generate feedback, whether it is employee grumbling or constructive criticism. Whitfield associates will gather this feedback in a positive, orderly way and compile it into a usable format. The findings will enable RT's management to address initial problems and ward off future problems. The research itself will also contribute to the change management efforts of the company by giving RT's employee stakeholders a voice in the process and allowing their feedback to contribute to the initiative's success.

Deliverables

The information you need will be delivered as shown below. All dates assume a project start date of July 1, 2014.

Readers can see the products of the proposed research up front

Approximate Date:	Deliverable:
October 1, 2014	Written report on an **initial** study of 12–14 employees' work processes and attitudes and on a companywide survey.
February 1, 2015	Written report at **midyear** on the same employees' work processes and attitudes and on a second companywide survey.
June 30, 2015	**Year-end** report (written and oral) on employees' work processes and attitudes and on a final companywide survey.

Anticipated Schedule/Methods

The research will take place from July 1, 2014, the anticipated go-live date for InfoStream at RT, to approximately June 30, 2015, a year later. As shown below, there will be four main components to this research, with Part III forming the major part of the project.

Gives details of the project in a readable format

Research Part and Time Frame	Purpose	Methods
Part I (July '14)	Gather background information; recruit research participants	Gather data on RT (history, products/ mission, organizational structure/ culture, etc.). Interview personnel at RT and at InfoStream about why RT is adopting an ERP system, why RT bought InfoStream, and how employees at RT have been informed about InfoStream. During this period we will also work with the COO's staff to recruit participants for the main part of the study (Part III).

(continued)

Whitfield Organizational Research   3

Research Part and Time Frame	Purpose	Methods
Part II (July '14):	Obtain the perspective of the InfoStream launch team	Conduct a focus group with the launch team, with emphasis on their goals for and concerns about the implementation. Anticipated duration of this interview would be one hour, with participants invited to share any additional feedback afterward in person or by email.
Part III (July–Sept. '14; Nov. '14–Jan. '15; Mar.–June '15):	Assess the impact of InfoStream on employee work processes and attitudes	Conduct three rounds of 1–2 hour interviews with approximately 12–14 RT employees to track their use of InfoStream. Ideally, we will have one or two participants from each functional area of the company, with multiple levels of the company represented.
Part IV (September '14, January '15, May '15)	Assess companywide reception of InfoStream	Conduct three Web-based surveys during the year to track general attitudes about the implementation of InfoStream.

This plan yields the following time line:

	7/14	8/14	9/14	10/14	11/14	12/14	1/15	2/15	3/15	4/15	5/15	6/15
Initial research	▒											
Focus group	▒											
1st round of interviews	▒	▒	▒									
1st Web survey			▒									
Initial report				▒								
2nd round of interviews					▒	▒	▒					
2nd Web survey							▒					
Midyear report								▒				
3rd round of interviews									▒	▒	▒	
3rd Web survey											▒	
Year-end report												▒

Timeline makes it easy to see what will happen at each point

(continued)

Interview Structure and Benefits

While Parts I, II, and IV will provide essential information about the project and its reception, the most valuable data will come from Part III, the onsite interviews with selected RT employees. Gathering data in and about the subject's own work context is the only reliable way to learn what is really happening in terms of the employees' daily experience. Following is a description of our methodology for gathering these kinds of data:

Initial interview:

- Gather background information about the participants (how long they have worked at RT, what their jobs consist of, what kind of computer experience they've had, how they were trained on InfoStream).
- Ask them to show us, by walking us through sample tasks, how they use InfoStream.
- Ask them to fill out a questionnaire pertaining to their use of InfoStream.
- Go back over their answers, asking them to explain why they chose the answers they did.
- Ask them either to keep notes on or email us about any notable experiences they have with InfoStream.
- Take notes on any interruption, interactions, and other activities that occur during the interview.

From data gained in these interviews, we will assess how well the participants' current work processes are meshing with InfoStream. We will also document how use of InfoStream is affecting the participants' attitudes and their interactions with other employees and departments. We will check our findings with the participants for accuracy before including these data in the initial report.

Midyear interview:

- Ask the participants if they have any notable experiences to relate about InfoStream and/or if any changes have occurred in the tasks they perform using InfoStream.
- Have the participants fill out the same questionnaire as in the first interviews.
- Discuss with participants the reasons for any changes in their answers since the first questionnaire.
- Observe any interactions or other activities that occur during the interview.
- Check our findings with the participants for accuracy before including these data in the midyear report.

Year-end interviews:

- Will be conducted in the same fashion as the second interviews.
- Will also include questions allowing participants to debrief about the project and about InfoStream in general.

Benefits of this interview method:

- Because researchers will be physically present in the employees' work contexts, they **can gather a great deal of information**, whether observed or reported by the employee, **in a short amount of time**.
- Because employees will be asked to elaborate on their written answers, the researcher **can learn the true meaning of the employee's responses**.

Special section elaborates on the company's unique methodology; helps justify the most expensive part of the plan

Whitfield Organizational Research 5

- Asking employees to verify the researcher's findings **will add another validity check and encourage honest, thorough answers**.

Specific Knowledge Goals

We will design the interviews and the companywide surveys to find out the extent to which

- InfoStream is making participants' jobs easier or harder, or easier in some ways and harder in others.

- InfoStream is making their work more or less efficient.

- InfoStream is making their work more or less effective.

- They believe InfoStream is helping the company overall.

- They are satisfied with the instruction they have received about the system.

- InfoStream is changing their interactions with other employees.

- InfoStream is changing their relations with their supervisors.

- InfoStream is affecting their overall attitude toward their work.

The result will be a detailed, reliable picture of how InfoStream is playing out at multiple levels and in every functional area of RT Industries, enabling timely intervention by RT management.

A tantalizing list of what the readers most want to know whets their desire to hire the proposing company

Cost

Because we are a local firm, no travel or lodging expenses will be involved.

Research Component	Estimated Hours	Cost
Part I (background fact finding)	6 hours	$300
Part II (focus group with launch team)	3 hours (includes preparation and analysis)	$300
Part III (3 rounds of on-site interviews)	474 hours	$18,960
Part IV (3 rounds of Web-based surveys)	48 hours	$1,920
Preparation of Reports	90 hours	$3,600
		Total: $25,080

Cost breakdown justifies the expense but is not so detailed that the readers can nitpick specific items

Credentials

Whitfield Organizational Research has been recognized by the American Society for Training and Development as a regional leader in organizational consulting. We have extensive education and experience in change management, organizational psychology, quantitative and qualitative research methods, and team building. Our familiarity with ERP software, developed through projects with such clients as Orsys and PRX Manufacturing, makes us well suited to serve RT's needs. Résumés and references will be mailed upon request or can be downloaded from www .whitfieldorganizationalresearch.com.

Efficient credentials section focuses only on relevant qualifications

If a proposal is submitted without invitation, its beginning must gain attention in order to motivate the recipient to read the proposal. An effective way of doing this is to begin by briefly summarizing the highlights of the proposal with emphasis on its benefits. This technique is illustrated by the beginning of an unsolicited proposal that a consultant sent to prospective clients:

Is your social marketing strategy working?

Twitter, blogs, Facebook, LinkedIn—such tools have become essential to building your brand. Are you making the best use of them?

Using a three-step social media audit, Mattox and Associates can find out. With access to your media and just one day of on-site interviews, our experts will tell you . . . [the rest of the proposal follows].

Your clear statement of the purpose and problem may be the most important aspect of the proposal. If you do not show right away that you understand what needs to be done and have a good plan for doing it, you may well have written the rest of your proposal in vain.

2. *The background.* A review of background information promotes an understanding of the problem. Thus, a college's proposal for an educational grant might benefit from a review of the relevant parts of the college's history. A company's proposal of a merger with another company might review industry developments that make the merger desirable. Or a chief executive officer's proposal to the board of directors that a company be reorganized might discuss related industry trends.

3. *The need.* Closely related to the background information is the need for what is being proposed. In fact, background information may well be used to establish need. Your goal in this important section is to paint a picture of the problem or goal in such a way that the reader feels a keen need for what you are proposing.

   You might wonder if this section applies in situations where an RFP has been issued. In such cases, won't readers already know what they need? In many cases the answer is no, not exactly. They may think they know, but you may see factors that they've overlooked. Plus, restating their problem in ways that lead to your proposed solution helps your persuasive effort. And whatever the situation, elaborating on the receiving organization's needs enables your readers to see that *you* understand those needs.

4. *The description of your plan.* The heart of a proposal is the description of what the writer proposes to do. This is the primary message of the proposal. It should be concisely presented in a clear and orderly manner, with headings and subheadings as needed. It should give sufficient detail to convince the reader of the plan's logic, feasibility, and appropriateness. It should also identify the "deliverables," or tangible products, of the proposal.

5. *The benefits of the proposal.* Your proposal should make it easy for your readers to see how your proposed action will benefit them. A brief statement of the benefits should appear at the front of your proposal, whether in the letter of transmittal, executive summary, opening paragraph, or all of the above. But you should elaborate on those benefits in the body of your proposal. You might do so in the section describing your plan, showing how each part will yield a benefit. Or, you might have a separate section detailing the benefits. As with sales writing, the greater the need to persuade, the more you should stress the benefits.

   As an example of benefits logically covered in proposals, a college's request for funding to establish a program for retraining the older worker could point to the profitability that such funding would give local businesses. A proposal offering a consulting service to restaurants could stress such benefits as improved efficiency, reduced employee theft, savings in food costs, and increased profits.

© 2005 Ted Goff

new & Improved

"We need something to come after this part. Any ideas?"

SOURCE: Copyright © 2005 Ted Goff.

6. *Cost and other particulars.* Once you have pitched your plan, you need to state clearly what it will cost. You may also need to cover such other particulars as time schedules, performance standards, means of appraising performance, and equipment and supplies needed. Remember that a proposal is essentially a contract. Anticipate and address any issues that may arise, and present your requirements in the most positive light.

7. *Evidence of your ability to deliver.* The proposing organization must sometimes establish its ability to perform. This means presenting information on such matters as the qualifications of personnel, success in similar cases, the adequacy of equipment and facilities, operating procedures, and environmental consciousness. With an external proposal, resist the temptation to include long, generic résumés. The best approach is to select only the most persuasive details about your personnel. If you do include résumés, tailor them to the situation.

8. *Concluding comments.* In most proposals you should urge or suggest the desired action. This statement often occurs in a letter to the readers, but if there is no cover letter or the proposal itself is not a letter, it can form the conclusion of your proposal. You might also include a summary of your proposal's highlights or provide one final persuasive push in a concluding section.

Whatever you're writing—whether a proposal, request, sales message, or some other kind of message—the art of persuasion can be one of your most valuable assets. Adding the tips in this chapter to your general problem-solving approach will help you prepare for all those times in your career when you will need others' cooperation and support.

THERE'S MORE . . .

What are six principles for ethical persuasion? How can you increase the effectiveness of your sales letters? How should you format your proposal? Scan the QR code with your smartphone or use your Web browser to find out at www.mhhe.com/lesikar13e. Choose Chapter 9 > Bizcom Tools & Tips.

Describe important strategies for writing any persuasive message.

1. Certain advice applies to all persuasive messages:
   - Know your readers—well.
   - Choose and develop targeted reader benefits.
     — Both tangible and intangible benefits can be persuasive.
     — Favor intrinsic over extrinsic benefits.
     — Express product features as reader benefits.
     — Use scenario painting to help your readers experience the product's appeal.
   - Make good use of three kinds of appeals.
     — Emotional appeals play on our senses (e.g., taste, hearing) and our feelings (e.g., love, anger).
     — Rational appeals appeal to logic (e.g., thrift, durability, efficiency).
     — Character-based appeals use an appealing spokesperson or an attractive image of the company to help sell the product.
   - Make it easy for your readers to comply.

Write skillful persuasive requests that begin indirectly, develop convincing reasoning, make a call to action, and close with goodwill.

2. Requests that are likely to be resisted require an indirect, persuasive approach.
   - Such an approach involves developing a strategy—a plan for persuading.
   - Your opening words should set up this strategy and gain attention.
   - Follow with convincing persuasion.
   - Then make the request—clearly yet positively.
   - The request can end the message, or more persuasion can follow (whichever you think is appropriate).

Discuss ethical concerns regarding sales messages.

3. Sales messages are a controversial area of business communication.
   - Many sales messages are unwanted.
     — "Junk" mail clutters people's mailboxes.
     — "Spam" clutters their in-boxes.
   - Some sales messages use unethical tactics.
     — They may make deceptive claims.
     — They may omit important information.
     — They may rely heavily on visuals that trigger an emotional response.
     — They may interfere with or even sabotage the reader's computer.
   - Use your conscience and your ability to put yourself in the readers' shoes to create ethical persuasive messages.

Describe the planning steps for direct mail or email sales messages.

4. A sales message requires special planning.
   - Learn all you can about your service or product and your intended readers.
   - Then select an appropriate central appeal and supporting appeals.
   - Determine the makeup of the mailing.
     — Decide what you will include in the main message and what you will put in auxiliary pieces.
     — Consider a creative approach to the sales letter format.
     — Email sales messages can also have auxiliary pieces and innovative format.

Compose sales messages that gain attention, present persuasive appeals, use appropriate visual elements, and effectively drive for action.

5. Although variations often occur, the sales message generally follows this traditional plan:
   - The opening gains attention and sets up the sales strategy.

- The body builds your persuasive case.
  - It develops the appeals you have chosen.
  - It uses punchy writing and techniques for visual emphasis (typography, white space, color, and other visual elements).
- In emotional selling, the words establish an emotional atmosphere and build an emotional need for the product or service.
- Rational selling appeals to reason by using facts and logic.
- Character-based appeals build trust and invite identification with the company.
- The message uses appealing language and the you-viewpoint throughout.
- Appropriate visual elements support the persuasive text.
- All the information necessary for the sale (e.g., prices, terms, choices) is included, with the main message conveying the key points and any auxiliary pieces providing supporting information.
- Next comes the drive for the sale.
  - It may be a strong drive, even a command, if a strong sales effort is used.
  - It may be a direct question if a milder effort is desired.
  - In either case, the action words are specific and clear, frequently urging action *now*.
  - Taking the action should be associated with the benefits to be gained.
  - Postscripts often are included to convey a final sales message.
  - In email messages, opt-out links should be provided as a professional courtesy and to comply with the law.

6. Proposals resemble reports but differ in their fundamental purpose.
   - They are intentionally persuasive.
   - They can be categorized in two ways:
     - Internal or external.
     - Solicited or unsolicited.
   - They vary widely in terms of format and formality.
     - As with reports, proposal formats can range from short emails to long, elaborate documents.
     - Their levels of formality vary as well.
   - The goal for your content is to make a persuasive argument.
     - Review your readers' needs and your ability to address them.
     - Then develop your central argument.
     - Bear in mind the main criteria that evaluators use.
   - The contents of proposals vary with need, but you should consider these topics:
     - The writer's purpose and the reader's need.
     - The background.
     - The need.
     - The description of the plan.
     - The benefits.
     - The particulars (e.g., methods, schedule, costs, performance standards).
     - Your ability to deliver.
     - Concluding comments.

Write well-organized and persuasive proposals.

KEY TERMS

indirect order, 227

direct approach, 227

demographic information, 227

psychographic information, 227

tangible rewards, 227

intangible rewards, 227

reader benefits, 228

intrinsic benefits, 228

extrinsic benefits, 228

product features, 228

scenario painting, 228

logic (logos), 228

emotion (pathos), 228

character (ethos), 228

persuasive requests, 229

sales messages, 229

proposals, 229

common-ground persuasion technique, 230

permission-based email, 238

spam, 243

internal proposal, 255

external proposal, 255

solicited proposals, 256

unsolicited proposals, 256

requests for proposals (RFPs), 257

CRITICAL THINKING QUESTIONS

1 Explain why a persuasive request is usually written in the indirect order. Could the direct order ever be used for such messages? Discuss. **LO2**

2 What does it mean to use the you-viewpoint in persuasive requests? **LO2**

3 Compare persuasive requests and sales messages. What traits do they share? How are they different? **LO2, LO5**

4 Consider ads that you have seen on television. Which ones rely heavily on emotional appeals? Which on logical appeals? Which on character-based appeals? Do the chosen appeals seem appropriate given the product, service, or cause that is being promoted? **LO1, LO5**

5 Think of a television, radio, print, email, or Internet sales message or persuasive request that you regard as especially effective. Explain why you think it was well designed. **LO2, LO5**

6 What appeals would be appropriate for the following products when they are being sold to consumers? **LO1, LO4**

  a. Shaving cream

  b. Home repair tools

  c. Frozen vegetables

  d. Software

  e. Lubricating oil

  f. Perfume

  g. Tires

  h. Women's jeans

  i. Fancy candy

  j. Video games

7 Assume that you're preparing a sales mailing that won't use the reader's name. Would you still use a salutation (e.g., "Dear Occupant")? If so, what would you use? If not, how would the message begin? **LO5**

8 "Any request or sales message that is longer than a page will just bore the reader." Discuss this statement. **LO5**

9 If you were helping to design an email message to sell solar panels, would you include visual elements? If so, what kind? If not, why not? **LO5**

10 Discuss the relationship between the sales message and its accompanying support information in an example you've seen. What was the purpose of each piece? **LO4, LO5**

11 Examine the call for action in a sales message you've received. Do you think it is effective? Why or why not? **LO5**

12 Think of a sample persuasive request or sales message that you regard as ethically questionable. Discuss the nature of the ethical problems. **LO3**

13 In what ways does its persuasive purpose make a proposal different from a short report? **LO6**

14 Discuss the differences between solicited and unsolicited proposals. **LO6**

15 For what kinds of situations might you select email format for your proposal? Letter format? A longer, report-like format? **LO6**

16 "I don't need to discuss my readers' needs in my proposal. They know what their needs are and don't want to waste time reading about them." Discuss. **LO6**

1   Assume that, as a volunteer for a nonprofit organization in your town, you have been asked to write the next fundraising letter for the organization. In what ways might you gather enough information about the intended readers to write a successful message? **LO1**

2   List the tangible and intangible benefits that you might describe when promoting the following items or services: **LO1**

     a. Membership in a health club.

     b. High-speed Internet service or digital cable service.

     c. A certain line of clothing.

     d. Car insurance.

3   List some extrinsic benefits you might use as an extra push if you were promoting the items in exercise 2. **LO1**

4   For each item in exercise 2, list two likely product features and then turn them into reader benefits. **LO1**

5   Choose one of the items in exercise 2 and write a paragraph that uses scenario painting to promote the item. **LO1**

6   Criticize the persuasive request message below. It was written by the membership chairperson of a chapter of the Service Corps of Retired Executives (SCORE), a service organization whose members donate their managerial talents to small businesses in the area. The recipients of the message are recently retired executives. **LO2**

Dear Ms. Petersen:

As membership chair it is my privilege to invite you to join the Bay City chapter of the Service Corps of Retired Executives. We need you, and you need us.

We are a volunteer, not-for-profit organization. We are retired business executives who give free advice and assistance to struggling small businesses. There is a great demand for our services in Bay City, which is why we are conducting this special membership drive. As I said before, we need you. The work is hard and the hours can be long, but it is satisfying.

Enclosed is a self-addressed envelope and a membership card. Please join us by filling out the card and returning it to me. We meet the first Monday of every month (8:30 at the Chamber of Commerce office). This is the fun part—strictly social. A lot of nice people belong.

I'll see you there Monday!

Sincerely yours,

7   Evaluate the following sales message. It was written to people on a mailing list of fishing enthusiasts. The writer, a professional game fisher, is selling his book by direct mail. **LO5**

Have you ever wondered
why the pros catch fish
and you can't?

They have secrets. I am a pro, and I know these secrets. I have written them and published them in my book, *The Bible of Fishing*.

This 240-page book sells for only $29.95, including shipping costs, and it is worth every penny of the price. It tells where to fish in all kinds of weather and how the seasons affect fishing. It tells about which lures to use under every condition. I describe how to improve casting and how to set the hook and reel them in. There is even a chapter on night fishing.

I have personally fished just about every lake and stream in this area for over forty years and I tell the secrets of each. I have one chapter on how to find fish without expensive fish-finding equipment. In the book I also explain how to determine how deep to fish and how water temperature affects where the fish are. I also have a chapter on selecting the contents of your tackle box.

The book also has an extensive appendix. Included in it is a description of all the game fish in the area—with color photographs. Also in the appendix is a glossary that covers the most common lures, rods, reels, and other fishing equipment.

The book lives up to its name. It is a bible for fishing. To receive your copy, fill out the enclosed card and send it to me in the enclosed stamped and addressed envelope. Include your check for $29.95 (no cash or credit cards, please). Do it today!

Sincerely yours,

8   Critique each of the following parts of sales messages. **LO5**

Email Subject Lines

     a. Earn BIG profits NOW!!!

     b. Reduce expenses with an experienced consultant's help.

     c. Free trial offer ends this week!

     d. Your coupons are about to expire.

     e. This week's travel deals

     f. Tell us about your experience with us.

     g. Evaluate our service.

     h. The best electric razor on the market!

     i. Your opinion needed.

     j. Your account needs to be updated now.

     k. Inquiry

Openings

Product or Service: A Credit Card That Gives Bonus Points toward Multiple Airlines

a. Where would you like to go? How would you like to get there?

b. With a Blue Horizons credit card, you'll get 5,000 sky points just for opening an acount.

c. How does "no annual fee" sound?

Product or Service: A Financial Consulting Service

d. Would you hire yourself to manage your portfolio?

e. Are you satisfied with the income your portfolio earned last year?

f. Dimmitt-Hawes Financial Services has helped its clients make money for over a half century.

Parts of Sales Presentations

Product or Service: A Pest-Control Company

a. If your home gets hit by termites while you're covered by our plan, you won't pay a dime for any future treatments or repairs—guaranteed.

b. Our guarantee covers all future treatments and any needed repairs.

c. Once you purchase our guarantee, all treatments and repairs will be covered for as long as your plan is active.

Product or Service: A Mail-Order Food Company

d. Our pasta assortment makes a great gift for your family, friends, and colleagues.

e. Treat your friends and business associates to a true taste of Italy with this elegant and affordable gift.

f. The aroma will remind you of walking into a neighborhood ristorante in Milano or Rome.

Product or Service: Vermont Smoked Ham

g. You won't find a better-tasting ham than the old-fashioned Corncob Smoked Ham we make here on our Vermont farm.

h. Our Corncob Smoked Ham is tender and delicious.

i. You'll love this smoky-delicious Corncob Smoked Ham.

Product or Service: A Unique Mattress

j. Control Comfort's unique air support system lets you control the feel and firmness of your bed simply by pushing a button.

k. The button control adjusts the feel and firmness of Control Comfort's air support system.

l. Just by pushing a button you can get your choice of feel and firmness in Control Comfort's air support system.

Action Endings

Product or Service: An Alumni Directory

a. To receive your personal copy, just sign and return the enclosed order form along with your check, money order, or credit card information.

b. To find out what your classmates are doing now, just fill out and return the enclosed card.

c. Don't put it off! Now, while it's on your mind, sign and return the enclosed card.

Product or Service: A News Magazine

d. To begin receiving your copies of *Today's World*, simply fill out and return the enclosed card.

e. For your convenience, a subscription card is enclosed. It is your ticket to receiving *Today's World*.

f. If you agree that *Today's World* is the best of the news magazines, just sign and return the enclosed card.

Postscripts

a. You can also monogram items you order before November 1.

b. All orders placed before November 1 are eligible for monogramming.

c. If you order before November 1, you can have your items monogrammed.

9 Find and study the online RFP for an Entrepreneurial Student-Community Parnership Stipend Award, sponsored by the Prima Civitas Foundation. What are the criteria (both explicit and implied) for a successful proposal? When reviewing a set of proposals that all meet these criteria, what kinds of facts might lead the selection committee to fund certain projects and not others? **LO6**

10 Pretend you are writing an unsolicited internal proposal requesting funding for traveling to a major professional meeting in your area of expertise. What kinds of information will you need to include? What arguments might your supervisors or management find convincing? What kinds of objections might you need to overcome? **LO6**

PROBLEM-SOLVING CASES

Persuasive Requests

1 As a student employee in your school's human resources department, you've attracted positive attention for the ways you've improved the writing on the department's website. As a result, the assistant director has asked you on several occasions to critique other written material, such as news releases and university announcements from this office. That business communication course you took last semester must have really paid off!

Today your boss drops by your desk with a printout of an email that he's frowning over. "We're not getting the participation we want in our yearly Take Our Daughters and Sons to Work Day," he complains. Handing you the email, he says, "Here's what we sent out this year. I think this invitation may be part of the problem." You read what it says:

Subject: Take Our Daughters and Sons to Work Day—April 23

In accordance with the national "Take Our Daughters and Sons to Work Day," university faculty and staff are invited to bring their children who are between 8–18 to work with them on April 23. This day will expose children to activities that occur on a typical day at Heartland University. It will include departmental tours, financial awareness workshops, Public Safety fingerprinting and mug shots, visiting a residence hall, athlete autographs, recreation center activities, and dining discounts. Faculty and staff who would like to participate should reply to Amber Bradley at the email address above or call 572-3384 by April 21. Please include the following information:

Your name, department, and phone number

Number of children

Age of each child

To learn more about the national program, please visit www.daughtersandsonstowork.org/wmspage.cfm?parm1=485. If you would like to provide a different learning activity for the children, please contact me immediately.

Amber Bradley

Human Resources

572-3382

You agree that the invitation is not very appealing, nor does it answer some of the readers' likely questions. Using your best problem-solving strategies for persuasive requests, rewrite it for your boss. (Your instructor may substitute a different campus event.)

2 As an entry-level employee for a business research firm, RetailData.com, you've been assigned the task of recruiting survey participants for a report on best practices in sales-associate management. The survey will gather such information as the companies' key performance indicators (KPIs)—that is, such quantitative data as sales per labor hour, downtime per associate, wages/sales ratio, and units sold per transaction—as well as information on such additional topics as hiring and training practices, turnover management, performance incentives, and the use of labor management software. In short, your company hopes to create a report that companies can use in order to "benchmark" their retail management practices against those of others in their industry. The report will be sold, along with many other industry reports, on RetailData.com.

Write a persuasive email that will get store managers and executives to participate in your survey. Your email will contain a link to the Web-based survey, so the message you are writing will not need to discuss the contents of the survey in great detail. Instead, use the email to get readers to appreciate the importance of the information they will be helping to generate. You can offer them a free copy of the resulting report, and five of the participants will be selected at random to receive one free additional report on a different business topic. The individual responses will be shared with no one, and the data will be presented in aggregated form so that no particular companies will be identified in the report. The survey will run from May 6 to May 24, 2013. The report will be finished by June 30, 2013. Add any additional material that you believe is warranted. Remember: The more successful your invitation, the better the report (and the better you and your company will look).

3 Assume that your business communication instructor is requiring you to "shadow" a professional in your field for half a day so that you can use your observations as the basis of a short report. Find someone in your field whose job you want to learn more about and write him or her a persuasive email requesting that you be allowed to tag along for a morning or afternoon. Do not choose someone you know. Think carefully about the reader's possible objections and include the information that will make your request successful.

4 As a respected businessperson in your neighborhood, you've been elected to its community council, the group that officially represents the neighborhood to the city council. Like other community councils, yours promotes the economic viability of the community and its quality of life in such ways as organizing community events, deterring crime, blocking any undesirable development projects, and raising funds to enhance the neighborhood.

At last night's council meeting you volunteered to use your persuasive writing skills to get more residents to use their recycling bins. Currently, only about 80 percent of the community recycles (the council got this figure from the city, which, thanks to microchips in each city-provided bin and cart, can keep track of the number of households that recycle in each neighborhood). The community council wants to increase that percentage, not only to help the environment and the city (which makes money by selling the recyclables it collects) but also to benefit the community; for a limited time, the council will receive $100 from the city for every 10 households it adds to their recycling total. As you think about how to persuade more of your neighbors to recycle, you consider the various reasons why they may not be recycling. Maybe there's a way the council can help remove those stumbling blocks.

But there's more: The council also wants residents to sign up for the RecycleBank Rewards Program, which rewards individuals based on how many pounds of recyclables they produce for each pickup period. When people register for the program at www.RecycleBank.com, the city will weigh how much those households are recycling and then submit that information to RecycleBank, which will award each household the appropriate reward points. The points are good for discounts at many local stores and restaurants and at such national chains as Dick's Sporting Goods, CVS Pharmacy, and Bed Bath & Beyond. To get the discounts, members go to RecycleBank.com and either print the coupons they want or use the electronic versions when making online purchases. RecycleBank has been proven to dramatically increase the amount of recycling that people do, which helps keep garbage out of expensive landfills.

After creating a detailed profile of your neighborhood (real or imagined), prepare the message or messages that will help the council achieve its recycling goals.

---

5 As an employee of the _____ Company (you decide what kind), you're in charge of this year's fundraising for the United Performing Arts Fund (UPAF) of southeast Wisconsin (or for the Fine Arts Fund of Cincinnati, or for a comparable fund in another city or region). Your company is a proud contributor to this organization's yearly campaign, and you want to do your best to help the company achieve its goal of $_____ (you decide how much) for this year.

Employees will make their contributions via the fund's website. They should log in using their company email address and use the password that has been assigned to their company (you can decide what it is). This way, the company's total contribution can be tracked. Depending on the actual organization you choose for this assignment, there may be different payment options available, including automatic payroll deduction. Donors will not only be eligible for the perks that the fund gives for each donation level; they will also be entered into a company-sponsored drawing for prizes (you decide what would be realistic and appealing). But of course it's the intrinsic benefits that you'll use for your main persuasive effort.

---

6 You work as a marketing co-op student in the office of Community Relations and Marketing at your school. This office promotes and oversees all university-wide charitable events. One such event is the yearly book drive on behalf of the city's public schools (from kindergarten/elementary schools through high schools).

Your job is to write a persuasive message to send to all students, faculty, and staff soliciting their contributions. You'll need to tell them when, where, and how to donate their books. You'll also need to tell them what kinds of books you want and what kind of shape these books need to be in (you're willing to take used books if they're in good condition; those that aren't good enough will be taken to a recycling center). Think about your readers' likely questions and about the kinds of details that might prompt them to go to the trouble to donate. Once you've worked out the logistics and your persuasive strategy, write the message.

---

7 You work for the state of North Dakota as the director of the Job Service Office in your town. You help the unemployed search for work, take required employment exams or software competency tests, write résumés and application letters, fill out applications, prepare for interviews, and practice interview skills. You've read about similar agencies in other states where local offices have a business advisory board made up of businesspeople in the community. You think this is just what you need—an advisory board that informs you of trends in various industries, gives advice on skills employers are looking for in their employees, and provides general input regarding jobs in your community. You decide that you are going to create such a board. You envision that the Business Advisory Board will meet formally twice a year. Two or three times a year, you may survey them to learn about employment trends in your community or gather other employment information. You also would like board members to be available informally to provide input regarding the services you offer and how you might improve your work. You're guessing that being a board member would require 10–15 hours per year, and you'd like for each member to agree to a two-year term.

Your first step in recruiting members is to think about the types of businesses in your community: manufacturing, industry, technology, law, medicine, finance, retail, food service, and hospitality. You'll also need to think about why these businesses might benefit from having a member of their staff on your Business Advisory Board.

Prepare a letter of invitation to send to the human resources directors at these businesses. Persuade them to recruit a representative from their company to serve on your Business Advisory Board.

---

8 You work at the company headquarters for Wholesome Foods, a grocery-store chain with over 50 stores located throughout the United States. One of your jobs is to recruit customers for your Email Advisory Panel. Customers who join this panel receive approximately eight surveys a year on such topics as product selection, customer service, and the general shopping experience. Essentially, the panel is a group of loyal Wholesome Foods customers who make it easy for you to get feedback that helps your stores remain competitive. For each survey they complete, the panel members are automatically entered into a drawing for $1,000. They do need to complete every survey in order to continue to be panel members.

Your first step in recruiting members is to include on customers' receipts an invitation for them to visit the company website, take a survey, and have their names entered into a drawing for $1,000. Anyone who takes this first step then receives an email inviting him or her to join the panel.

Write the email invitation, persuading those who have already shown interest in the store to join the panel and become regular survey respondents.

---

9 The nonprofit organization you direct coordinates an annual health and wellness fair for residents of your city. Each year, professionals from the community (e.g., physicians, dentists, cosmetologists, mechanics, lawyers, and social workers) volunteer their time, services, and supplies to help the underserved in your community. For example, dentists offer free cleanings. Physicians and nurses offer blood pressure, immunization, and diabetes screenings and refer patients to the town's free clinic as needed. A social worker might provide resources to someone in danger of losing his or her home. Someone who cannot afford car repairs can get them at your fair and then be able to get to his or her job. The fair provides much needed services for around 400 people each year. It's really heartwarming to see a community come together in this way.

As your instructor directs, write to one professional audience (e.g., a physician, a mechanic) and persuade him or her to volunteer for this year's fair.

---

10 You are an intern in the human resources department at a financial services firm. Your boss has instructed you to send an announcement to all staff letting them know that the staff photo will be at 5 p.m. next Wednesday after you've closed for the day. The office takes a staff photo once a year. The pictures are used in promotional material (e.g., brochures, the company webpage, Facebook). Unfortunately, in recent years fewer people have shown up for the picture. Last year only a quarter of the firm's 100 employees attended. Excuses included "I'm too busy," "What's in it for me?," "I have to pick my kids up from dance lessons," "I have to go to the gym," "I only work until 3:00, and I'm not staying or coming back," and "No way. Make me." Your boss is counting on you to write a persuasive announcement to the employees requesting that they take the time to show up for the photo; she hopes that everyone will be there. They don't have to do anything special. All they have to do is take five minutes to be part of the picture. As you write, think about why taking such a photo might be important to the firm and to its clients.

---

11 Your campus organization (you choose the organization) participates in several community service projects each year. This year, the group has chosen to support the Global Soap Project as one of its service activities. Your members will collect used soap from local hotels to donate to the Project, which turns the leftover soap into new bars of soap that are distributed to the underprivileged around the world. Write a letter to local hotel owners to solicit their help in collecting used bar soap. Be sure to include details about the project and who will benefit (check out www.globalsoap.org for details). Of course, you'll also include information about the organization you represent.

---

12 You are a student assistant at your university's business college. You have numerous responsibilities, including updating your college's Facebook page. Recently, the Dean announced the creation of a new student committee that will provide suggestions on how to enhance the facilities, increase participation in college events, and improve morale around the college. In fact, you have heard a lot of grumbling from students about many things related to the college, and you are sure that once this committee is formed, there will be no shortage of ideas from students on how to improve the college! The Dean asks you to create a Facebook post describing the new committee and soliciting student volunteers. The committee will have 5–7 members and will meet every other Friday at noon. Write a Facebook post of no more than 150 words persuading students to join the new committee.

---

13 You were afraid of this: Your health insurance company has refused to cover the visit you made to a hospital emergency room two weeks ago. You are covered under the company's HMO plan, meaning that, except in emergencies, your healthcare is covered only if you receive it from an approved provider. While the hospital you went to does accept your insurance, the insurance company is claiming that your situation was not an emergency and that you should have gone to one of their doctors' offices instead—which would have been much less expensive. You call the insurance company to explain the facts, and the representative advises you to state your case in a letter to the company's claims department. She says to be sure to include your policy number and the number of the claim. She also advises that you request coverage for both the hospital fee and the emergency-room doctor's fee, since these are two different expenses.

Write the letter that will persuade the company to cover the fees of almost $900. You'll explain that around 8 p.m. of the day you went to the hospital, you had come down with a terrible stomach virus—one that had been going around and had even caused some schools to be closed (it was in the local news). The nausea and diarrhea had been so extreme that you began to get severely dehydrated. At almost midnight, you decided you'd better get to the hospital, so you got your housemate to drive you there. The desk people took one look at you and, after you threw up in the bucket you'd brought with you, had a nurse take you to the treatment area. There you got an antinausea injection and two liters of fluid. The doctor told you that he'd treated several cases like yours and that you were right to come in. You were released at about 6 a.m., still feeling terrible but out of danger. You also had a prescription for antinausea medicine that would see you through the rest of the illness. In light of the circumstances, you don't see what other course you could have taken. Get the insurance company to see it your way.

---

14 Your school has a Center for Community Engagement that recruits organizations who have service opportunities for students and recruits students to volunteer at those places. Until now, the participating organizations, along with their Web addresses (if they have websites), have simply been listed on a page on the center's website. But your supervisor at the center has something more persuasive, attractive, and uniform in mind: He wants to replace the list of organizations with an Online Volunteer Directory that will provide links to Web-based profiles of the organizations. He asks you, his trusty student assistant, to prepare the directory. Each profile should include the name of and contact information for the organization, its purpose/mission/key activities, an appealing photo or two, and any additional information that students would need in order to understand what the organization does and why they should volunteer for it.

Prepare the first entry for the online directory to show to your boss. If he likes it, you'll use it as a model for all the other profiles in the directory. So find a local organization that uses student volunteers on a regular basis, gather all the information you can about the purpose and activities of the organization (you may need to speak with someone at the organization), figure out why students should volunteer (what exactly are the volunteer opportunities, and what are the benefits of volunteering?), and prepare a nicely formatted, nicely written profile of the organization that will persuade students to volunteer.

Keep in mind that you're writing this message as something of a spokesperson for the organization and also that your entry will appear on the website of a university office. So avoid attention-getters like "Do you like free beer?" Some levity may be appropriate, but your entry should still be professional in its contents and appearance.

---

15 You were recently hired in the training and development department for an accounting firm with offices throughout the country. As in all professions, accountants must communicate clearly, concisely, and correctly with their audiences. Recently, though, the manager for your local office has been receiving complaints about emails your accountants and other staff are sending. Emails appear to be written quickly and are often incomplete, making a number of exchanges necessary for the audience to understand the message. In addition, they appear poorly edited. One client received an email where the accountant typed "principle" rather than "principal"! All staff in your office have been made aware of the issue, but no one seems inclined to do anything about it. Many cite a lack of time as a reason for not writing well, but because you know these people to be extremely professional, you also wonder if individuals think they communicate better than they do or do not know how to write any better than they already are. The complaints are still coming.

Your boss suggested you develop some training opportunities to encourage good business writing. You developed a series of four workshops on business writing for employees at your local office, and now you need to sell the employees on the need to attend them. Create a flyer promoting the series. Think about the times and days you'll offer the workshops and the topics you'll cover. While the flyer is certainly informative, remember that these are very busy people who might not think they need to attend. You need to persuade them to attend using positive and encouraging language in your flyer and focusing on reader benefits.

Sales

16 As a member of the management team of the Summerdale Swim and Tennis Club, you've just attended a strategizing session in which the team generated ideas for increasing memberships. Your boss presented data about current memberships broken down by demographic categories. One group that stood out for its low number of memberships was older adults. "We're doing well attracting young adults with kids," your boss says, "but we're not attracting enough senior citizens. In fact, our data show that many members let their memberships lapse once their kids reach their teenage years."

The team decides that one strategy to remedy this problem will be to send a letter to those aged 50 and over who have let their club membership lapse. You've been assigned the task of creating this mailing. Studying the websites of several swim and tennis clubs and using realistic facts as well as your imagination, write the letter that will persuade these former members to rejoin. Consider carefully how to turn features of the club into benefits for your readers. (Your instructor may require you to create certain additional pieces for this mailing, or may change the organization.) Alternative assignment: Write the letter for prospects aged 50 and over who have never been members of the club. Assume that you're using a list of AARP (American Association of Retired Persons) members in your area to identify these prospects.

17 You're the secretary of a service organization on campus. To raise money for your activities, your members put together and sell exam-week care packages for parents to buy for their kids at the end of the term. When exams begin, your organization delivers the packages. It's time to write this year's sales letter for these packages. Inventing reasonable details about the organization and the packages, considering what would appeal to the parents, and anticipating the information you will need from them, write the letter (and order form) that will get them to purchase a care package. The student needs to live in a residence hall in order to be eligible.

18 You are the director of social media and online marketing for Fit-ology, a company that designs online fitness and nutrition plans for customers. As part of customers' online fitness programs, you encourage (but don't require) them to purchase your nutritional shakes. With 210 calories, 2 grams of fat, 21 grams of carbs, 29 grams of protein, and 25 flavors, they are a great meal substitute or postworkout snack. The problem is that sales of the shakes have declined each month for the last six months. In truth, you haven't really promoted them because you have been rolling out new fitness plans and redeveloping your interactive website.

To encourage Fit-ology customers to purchase the shakes, you'll email them an offer of 20 percent off their next shake order with a minimum purchase of a 30-serving supply (current price: $120 or $4/shake; you do the math to figure out the sale price) and throw in four free shake packets. To get the discount, they'll need to use the promotional code Fit-Shake when they submit their online order. Tell them where/how they can make their purchase, reacquaint them with the shake, and give them a reason to act now. (You can assume that legal language about not combining this offer with any other offer, not using the offer to pay for taxes and processing/shipping charges, and a few other caveats will be typed in small print at the bottom of the letter. You can also assume a disclaimer regarding food allergies and weight-loss guarantees.)

19 Like other large restaurant chains, Tasty Treats has a customer rewards club. Customers who join the Tasty Treats Tasters' Club can take advantage of the company's deal of the day just by signing up on the company's website and having a coupon sent to their email inbox. Customers can print the coupon or just present the coupon and bar code on their phone when they pay for their food. In addition, club members receive special coupons to use at any time, and twice a year they are eligible for drawings for large prizes (e.g., trips, electronics). Throughout the year, club members are also eligible for random prize drawings for free meals or company merchandise.

Lately, some of the chain's franchisees have been grumbling that they are not getting enough business through this program. So your boss, marketing director of Tasty Treats Corporation, directs you to write two messages—one for the company website and one for Facebook—persuading readers to go to your website and become members of the Tasty Treats Tasters' Club. To encourage them to sign up, you may want to provide an incentive.

Carefully consider the persuasive, logistical, and visual elements to include and then write the message.

20 Choose a type of catalog- and online-based company that sells products you're familiar with—for example, home furnishings, medical/herbal products, auto parts/accessories—and write a sales letter to past customers who haven't bought from you in a while. You'll offer them 20 percent off their next order, with no minimum purchase required. (To get the discount, they'll need to use the promotional code 16652A.) Tell them where/how they can make their purchase, reacquaint them with your appealing products, and give them a reason to act now. (You can assume that legal language about not combining this offer with any other offer, not using the offer to pay for taxes and processing/shipping charges, and a few other caveats will be typed in small print at the bottom of the letter.)

21 You work in the Employee Relations Department at Mayfaire Clinic. Two years ago, the clinic was dealing with such a high volume of patient communication that it couldn't keep up. Some of the communication was, of course, essential (e.g., a patient talking to a nurse about symptoms), but other communication (e.g., reordering contact lenses for patients, sending bills in the mail and processing payments, or checking on a patient's test results) was causing a backlog and taking employees' time away from patients who needed them. The clinic's solution was to develop MyMayfaire.com, a website where patients could order contacts, pay bills, check test results, schedule appointments, update their contact information, update insurance information, and receive their health profiles from their annual exams. It seemed like an ideal solution except for one thing—few people signed up for it.

You think the patient response is slow for a few reasons: People are wary of having their health information available online, they think the process for signing up will take too much time, or they may have missed previous letters informing them of the MyMayfaire.com option.

You've looked at previous mailings sent to patients and determined that they were not very persuasive (you didn't write them). You decide you will create a well-written persuasive message to get people to sign up. Write a persuasive letter to patients, selling them on the idea of using MyMayfaire.com.

22 Finding housing in your university town is complicated. There are so many landlords and rental opportunities that it's hard for students to know their best options. In addition, many students have never signed a lease or may not know their rights as tenants. You and three other students decide to start a business. You are going to create an ad-supported online service listing the rental options and providing advice on signing leases, security deposits, and other issues tenants may face. Not only will you be listing properties, you'll also let students rate properties and give feedback on landlords, rental agencies, and the rental units themselves. You'll sell ads for $25 per month and automatically bill the advertiser's account unless he or she cancels the ad.

You will target advertisers from businesses throughout your community that serve the student population, but you also think that landlords and rental agencies might benefit from buying ad space. Even though you know some landlords and properties are likely to get poor ratings (student rentals are notorious for their poor condition), you want to send a sales letter or email to area landlords and rental agencies persuading them to purchase ad space on your site. In your message, you will need to think carefully about why landlords and rental agencies would still want to advertise on your site if your readers may give them bad ratings.

23 Your upscale clothing store—part of a national chain—recently moved from a location downtown to one in an affluent suburb north of town. You'd like for those customers who patronized your store in its previous location to continue to shop with you. Write all the local customers for whom you have mailing addresses and invite them to visit you at your new location. You can offer them a limited-time-only coupon to sweeten the invitation—but your message should also remind them of why they like to shop at your store. Plus, your new location has some benefits: The store is bigger, and it's in a nicer area with other appealing businesses around. Think of the verbal and visual contents that will entice your customers to continue to shop with you and prepare this persuasive mailing. (Your instructor may allow you to choose a different kind of store.)

24 You're part of the management team of a business that manufactures and sells ceiling fans. Even though your operation is small, your fans are popular, and you sell them online to customers across the United States.

Unfortunately, the tight economy has taken its toll on your business; sales are down considerably even though it's summer. In response, the management team has decided that they will purchase a promising email distribution list and send an email sales message to all those on the list. You've been put in charge of drafting a sample message, which the team will discuss at its next meeting.

Create an email message to sell your company's fans. What is distinctive about your products? Why should readers spend their limited discretionary money on a ceiling fan? Study the websites of various fan sellers to generate the details that will make your message persuasive. Should you use any visuals in your message? Links to additional information? Carefully think through the whole selling effort. You think you'll design the message in Word and save it as a PDF to show how the email will actually look once your IT person prepares it for delivery. (Your instructor may allow you to use a different product for this case.)

25 You're part of the marketing communications team for US Airways, a major airline that flies to airports all over the world. Periodically, you send the members of your frequent-flyers program "upselling" emails that are intended to get these people to enroll or re-enroll in your more exclusive, costly programs. You've been assigned the task of designing the latest message intended to promote the Airways Crowne Club, a for-fee service (involving both an initial fee and a monthly fee) whose subscribers are allowed access to a comfortable, quiet lounge at over 50 airports around the world.

This sales campaign will offer an extra month at no charge to those who purchase or renew a one-year Crowne Club membership within a certain period and use the designated promo code. In addition, 10 percent of their purchase will be donated to a worthy foundation.

Study the websites of various airlines and various foundations to generate the contents for your message. Think carefully about what information to include in the message and what links to provide. (At your instructor's discretion, you may plan an upselling sales message for a different company's current customers.)

Proposals

26 Find the call for nominations for a campus-wide faculty award at your school and, thinking of it as a type of RFP, respond with your "proposal": a letter persuading the selection committee to choose your nominee as the winner. Be careful to study the criteria for the award and to provide convincing evidence that your nominee meets these criteria. In addition to collecting your memories of the nominee, be sure to learn all you can about his or her accomplishments from the school or faculty member's own website or from other Internet resources.

27 You are a store manager at a discount clothing retailer in the southern United States. The clothing retailer, Stacey's, has a corporate office in each state where there are satellite retail locations: North Carolina, South Carolina, Georgia, Alabama, Mississippi, Tennessee, and Kentucky. Each month store managers are required to attend a store managers' meeting at the Stacey's corporate offices in their state. Most managers drive an average of 100 miles to reach the monthly store meetings; some drive as many as 175 miles.

The meetings are important to Stacey's because they allow managers from different stores to interact, share ideas, and build community. Additionally, the monthly meetings allow the corporate team to show store managers new products and highlight features of the inventory that will be arriving in the next month. Unfortunately, you've noticed that while you are away at the managers' meetings, sales in your store are down an average of 10 percent each day of your absence. You feel that traveling to the meetings not only cuts into your own productivity but also costs the company a significant amount of money.

Since you recognize the importance of meeting with other managers and having a good connection to corporate, you would like the company to implement a monthly managers' video Web conference and biannual meetings at each state's headquarters in place of the monthly face-to-face meetings. You decide to research three viable options for video Web conferencing and submit a proposal for your idea to your boss in Birmingham, AL.

---

28 As the lead communications specialist at Littleton Advertising and Creative Services, you and your team are tired of the amount of editing you need to do whenever someone submits material to your department for publication in the company newsletter, press releases, annual report, and website. You're pretty sure that the routine correspondence that doesn't come through your department for editing could use some help as well. There is no consistency in formatting, punctuation, and mechanics. You've seen as many variations in capitalization, number use, and abbreviations as there are people in the company. And it's not only the writing that is not consistent. People use several variations of the company's logo in their work.

To employees outside your department, these issues may seem trivial, but you recognize the importance of writing and formatting standards to communicating and promoting your company's brand. This means that your clients should have a reasonable expectation that every document they receive from your company, from routine correspondence to material on the website, will look and sound as though it came from the same company.

You know that it's your and your staff's job to edit written materials before publishing them, but you also think that the employees who write them could be more consistent. After all, how hard is it for someone to use a round bullet instead of a square bullet? Furthermore, it is reasonable to expect that everyone in your department have some consistency in their initial drafts so that your final editing and revising are not so time consuming. Plus, you worry that the documents you don't see (e.g., letters, emails) may not be written or edited as well as they could be and want employees to be empowered to write well independently of your editing.

You think an online corporate style guide housed on Littleton's intranet is your answer and decide to propose to your CEO that Littleton have one. You and your team will develop it and implement it. Because this is summer, it's your slow time anyway, so you have the time to create it. In your proposal, make the case for creating and using a style guide, include a timeline for developing it, and propose a plan for implementing the style guide at your company. An Internet search for corporate style guides will help you gather information for your proposal.

---

29 Due to staffing changes, the morale at your company has dropped to an all-time low. Employees are not excited about going to work, and it's beginning to show in productivity rates: As a whole, sales are down 9 percent from last quarter.

You serve on the company's Quality Circle, which recently met to brainstorm ideas for improving morale. The group agreed that everyone needs a little more fun. Toward that end, they decided that the company should sponsor a team-building activity each quarter for the next three quarters. Taking your suggestion, they also decided that the first such activity should be a poker tournament, to be hosted onsite after hours for employees and their significant others.

You were chosen to draft a proposal that would sell the team-building idea, and the idea of a poker tournament in particular, to your boss/company owner. You have a lot of logistics to work out. You'll first need to see what kinds of rules govern gambling in your state; those will determine what form the "betting" will take. In light of the company's financial situation, you'll also figure out how to keep the costs under control. The Quality Circle proposed soliciting donations from local businesses (gift cards, coupons, and products) to use as prizes, with the company buying a top prize to go to the overall winner of the evening. Do the additional research you need to do to plan the event. You'll also want to find creditable sources about the benefits of team-building activities in general. When you've got all the information you need, write up your ideas in a well-written, persuasive proposal that the Quality Circle—and your boss—will like. (With your instructor's permission, choose a different kind of teambuilding event.)

---

30 You work as an instructional designer at Britten Dental, a large dental franchise with 30 locations and over 500 full- and part-time employees in five states. Your job is to develop and create online learning, training, and continuing education opportunities for Britten's employees.

You love almost everything about your job—your fun co-workers, the interesting work, using your creative and technical abilities . . . everything! What you do not love, though, is that because of your highly social office and the number of meetings you attend to work with content experts in developing training materials, it's sometimes difficult to get your work done. Some days all you need is to carve out some quiet time and space to work, but that is not likely to happen in your busy office. Someone always needs you, and it's convenient for them to stop by your desk for help or for a quick chat. It's also hard to be working intently on a project and then leave at your most inspired moment to attend a meeting.

Upon visiting the Instructional Design Professionals group on LinkedIn, you notice how many instructional designers work full or part time from home; you think this might just be what you need. You could structure your work week to be at the office two days a week for meetings and other face-to-face contact and then spend three days a week working from home to do your instructional design work. Of course, you would be available by phone or email at home, but you would have more control over interruptions with phone and email than you would with interruptions at the office.

Before you take your idea to your supervisor, you prepare a proposal. To write the proposal, you research the advantages and disadvantages of working from home; figure out the equipment you would need; estimate the cost of setting up a work office in your home and convince Britten to pay for it; and determine any other costs your employer might incur. Address why this is a good idea not just for you but for Britten Dental as well. Be sure your proposal adequately addresses any resistance your supervisor might have.

---

31 You were recently hired to be the assistant manager for True Springs Bakery, a provider of 100 percent organic baked goods. You are in charge of making the schedule, ordering supplies, and keeping the shop in good running order when the manager is not there. Business is doing very well, but you have noticed that some of the bakery's practices are a little "old fashioned." For example, the cash register is one of the few that you have seen that is not electronic, and many customers have complained that you do not accept credit cards.

You have mentioned your concerns to the manager, but she quickly dismisses the idea of upgrading the technology because she believes it would be too expensive. However, you were recently looking through a consumer technology magazine and saw an advertisement for a product called "Square" (www.squareup.com). Square allows you to accept credit cards by attaching a small swipe device to your smartphone. The device is affordable, and you can accept credit cards wherever you take your smartphone. Most of the bakery's employees own smart phones and are technologically savvy. This sounds like an excellent opportunity to upgrade the technology at the bakery without making a major financial investment.

Write a proposal to your manager outlining why you think investing in 5–6 Square devices would be beneficial for the bakery. Use information from the website to strengthen your proposal.

---

32 You were recently hired as assistant manager at one of the four branch offices of a regional, privately owned insurance company. As you get to know the business's operations, you realize that the company has no sexual harassment policy. You mention this fact to your boss, the branch manager, and she agrees that this is a problem. The company was an all-male operation (except for secretaries) for many years, but several female agents—and even one female manager, your boss—have been hired over the last 10 years or so, and the company is now about 12 percent female. An official sexual harassment policy is overdue.

"Our founder, Sam Jenkins, is a pretty old-fashioned businessman, though," she says. "He likes to think that we're one big happy family, and he may worry that adopting a sexual harassment policy will offend some of the employees and hint that there are problems where there are none." Together, she and you decide to write a carefully prepared proposal to Jenkins and his HR director that will convince them to adopt a sexual harassment policy. You'll do sufficient research on the topic to be able to provide convincing reasons for this move. You'll also prepare the policy that you want the company to adopt and offer suggestions for its implementation.

---

33 As director of corporate communications and public relations for C. J. Erlanger, a popular plumbing and heating company in a large metropolitan area, you think the time has come to create a more formal, robust corporate philanthropy program. Your company is a good community citizen; it already gives time, money, and supplies on a random basis to charities that request help. But that's the problem: These donations are random, and it's hard to use random acts of kindness as a basis for compelling publicity for your company.

You decide to write a proposal in which you (1) convince the owners of the benefits of a better organized corporate philanthropy program and (2) propose the type of program that you think the company should create.

Research the benefits of corporate philanthropy programs, think carefully about the logistics of your plan, and do any additional planning that will enable you to decide exactly what you want to propose and why. Then write the proposal. Send it as an email attachment to VP Jean Carpenter, who is interested in your idea and has agreed to share it with the other four company executives. Invent any additional details that will not significantly alter the challenge before you. Be sure your readers can see the connections between what you are proposing and its potential company benefits.

34 You have just returned from a national sales professionals conference where you learned that many companies are using Facebook in innovative ways to attract readers and generate fans. In addition to having appealing profiles and ads, the most popular sites host chats (interactive commenting that takes place within a designated time period), conduct polls, hold events, and provide other extras that engage readers and get them to spread the good word about the site to their friends.

In contrast, your company, an up-and-coming seller of athletic wear, currently has only a simple Facebook profile page that it updates now and then with news of special offers.

You described to the sales VP, your boss, what you learned at the conference, and he's definitely interested. Research the possibilities that make sense for your company and write a proposal to your boss in which you recommend additional ways to leverage your company's Facebook page. Your boss wants the full argument spelled out so that he'll clearly understand what you're proposing, the reasons why, and the effort it will take to implement and maintain your proposed strategies. He also wants to be able to explain your ideas to the other executives and sales staff as needed.

35 You work for the _____ company (you decide what kind) as a (you decide what position). You want to take an online course on _____ (you decide what topic) and have the company cover the cost. You've run the idea past your supervisor, who is basically supportive but will need to get the OK from his/her boss. For this you'll need to make your case persuasively and in writing. Write an email proposal to your supervisor requesting that the company cover the cost of the course. Convince the decision maker that the course is worth the money. Be sure to tie it to your current or likely future job responsibilities and explain how the company will benefit. Remember to think of the major objections your readers might have and be sure to account for these as you build your argument. To ensure that your proposal has a sufficient level of detail, you may want to do some research on a few colleges' online course offerings for relevant classes.

CHAPTER TEN

Conducting a Winning Job Campaign

Learning Objectives

Upon completing this chapter, you will be able to conduct an effective job search; compose effective cover messages, résumés, and follow-ups; and prepare for interviews. To reach these goals, you should be able to

1 Develop and use a network of contacts in your job search.

2 Assemble and evaluate information that will help you select a job.

3 Identify the sources that can lead you to an employer.

4 Compile résumés for print and electronic environments that are strong, complete, and organized.

5 Write targeted cover messages that skillfully sell your abilities.

6 Explain how you can participate effectively in an interview.

7 Write application follow-up messages that are appropriate, friendly, and positive.

8 Maintain your job-search activities.

Finding Your First Post-College Job

Introduce yourself to this chapter by assuming a role similar to one you are now playing. You are Julia Alvarez, a student at Wilmont University. In a few months, you will complete your studies for work in human resources management.

You believe that it is time to begin seeking the job for which those studies have been preparing you. But how do you do this? Where do you look? What does the search involve?

How should you present yourself for the best results? Once you get an interview, how should you prepare for it? After the interview, what should you say in a thank-you note to the employer? And what about other correspondence you might have to write to accept a position, decline a position, or perhaps resign from your current job? The answers to these and related questions are reviewed in the following pages.

THE JOB SEARCH

Of all the things you do in life, one of the most important is getting a job. Whether it involves your first job or one further down your career path, job seeking is directly related to your success and your happiness. Therefore, you must be careful and diligent in your **job search**. The following review of job-search strategies should help you succeed.

Building a Network of Contacts

You can begin the job search long before you are ready to find employment. In fact, you can do it now by building a **network of contacts**. More specifically, you can build relationships with people who can help you find work when you need it. Such people include classmates, professors, and businesspeople.

Right now, your classmates are not likely to be holding positions in which they make or influence hiring decisions, but some of them may know people who can help you. In the future, when you want to make a career change, they may hold such positions. The wider your circle of friends and acquaintances, the more likely you are to make employment contacts.

Knowing your professors and making sure that they know you can also lead to employment contacts. Because professors often consult for business, they may know key executives and be able to help you contact them. Professors sometimes hear of position openings and can refer you to the hiring executives. Demonstrating your work ethic and your ability in the classroom is a great way to get your professors to know you and help you. Take advantage of opportunities to meet your professors outside the classroom, especially the professors in your major field.

Obviously, meeting business professionals can also lead to employment contacts. You may already know some through family and friends. But broadening your relationships among businesspeople would be helpful. You can do this in various ways, especially through college professional groups such as the Association for Information Technology Professionals, Delta Sigma Pi, and the Society for the Advancement of Management. By taking an active role in the organizations in your field of study, especially by working on program committees and by becoming an officer, you can get to know the executives who serve as guest speakers. You also might meet businesspeople online. If you share a particular interest on a blog or are known as one who contributes valuable comments to others' blogs, you may get some good job leads there. Likewise, you can network on social media sites such as LinkedIn by starting a group or actively contributing to one.

In addition to these more common ways of making contacts, you can use some less common ones. By working in community organizations (charities, community improvement groups, fundraising groups), you can meet community leaders. By attending meetings of professional associations (every field has them), you can meet the leaders in your field. In fact, participation in virtually any activity that provides contacts with businesspeople can be mutually beneficial, both now and in the future.

LO1 Develop and use a network of contacts in your job search.

Obtaining an Internship

Internships are a wonderful way to network with people in your field, gain professional knowledge and experience, or simply learn whether your current field is where you want to build a career.

One source estimates that as many as 75% of employers look for internships on students' résumés.[1] According to a recent survey by the National Association of Colleges and Employers, "graduates who took part in a paid internship were more likely to get a job offer, have a job in hand by the time they graduated, and receive a higher starting salary offer than their peers who undertook an unpaid internship or no internship at all."[2] While many students may find paid internships more desirable, unpaid internships can also be valuable. Many students can earn college credits toward their degree (and perhaps get tuition for these credits waived or reduced) or receive a stipend, and the U.S. Department of Labor has laws governing the fair use of unpaid interns' work.[3] The key is to make sure that an unpaid internship provides the opportunity to gain real-world, marketable skills and to make sure the employer does not unfairly take advantage of an intern's unpaid time, expertise, and labor.

Though a quick Web search for internships will net several links to internship types, the first step in finding an internship simply may be to contact your school's career services office. You may also want to use many of the networking strategies discussed in the previous section.

Identifying Appropriate Jobs

LO2 Assemble and evaluate information that will help you select a job.

To find the right job (or internship), you need to investigate both internal and external factors. The best fit occurs when you have carefully looked at yourself: your education, personal qualities, experience, and any special qualifications. However, to be realistic, these internal qualities need to be analyzed in light of the external factors. Some of these factors may include the current and projected job market, economic needs, location preferences, and family needs.

Analyzing Yourself. When you are ready to search for a job, you should begin the effort by analyzing yourself. In a sense, you should look at yourself much as you would look at a product or service that is for sale. After all, when you seek employment, you are really selling your ability to work—to do things for an employer. A job is more than something that brings you money. It is something that gives equal benefits to both parties—you and your employer. Thus, you should think about the **personal qualities** you have that enable you to be an accountable and productive worker that an employer needs. This self-analysis should cover the following categories.

Education. The analysis might well begin with education. Perhaps you have already selected your career area such as accounting, organizational or technical communication economics, finance, information systems, international business, management, or marketing. If you have, your task is simplified, because your specialized curriculum has prepared you for your goal. Even so, you may be able to note special points—for example, electives that have given you additional skills or that show something special about you (such as psychology courses that have improved your human relations skills, communication courses that have improved your writing and speaking skills, or foreign language courses that have prepared you for international assignments).

If you have pursued a more general curriculum, such as one in general business or liberal arts, you will need to look at your studies closely to see what they have prepared

---

[1]National Association of Colleges and Employers, "Paid Internships Key to Job-Search Success for New College Grads," *NACE*, NACE, 6 Oct. 2011, Web, 1 July 2012.

[2]*NACE.*

[3]Jean Chatzky, "Why Students Shouldn't Take Unpaid Internships," *Newsweek/The Daily Beast,* The Newsweek/Daily Beast Company, LLC, 21 Nov. 2011, Web, 1 July 2012.

COMMUNICATION MATTERS

The Where, What, and Whys of Hiring

Surveying 225 employers from a population of 10,000 U.S. companies, Millennial Branding and Experience Inc. examined the role of internships in securing an entry-level position, qualities employees look for, and where employers find their new hires. Highlights of the study include the following:

- **Internships:** Even though employers are split 50/50 on whether they hire interns, 91 percent say students should have one or two internships before graduating; 87 percent say that the internships should last at least 3 months.

- **Key Skills:** Communication skills (98 percent), a positive attitude (97 percent), and teamwork skills (92 percent) were rated by employers as "important" or "very important" in people hired for entry-level positions.

- **Employers' Hiring Resources:** Employers use social networks to varying degrees to find employees. Few use social networking all or most of the time (16 percent). Instead, many use job boards (48 percent) and employee referrals (44 percent),

a more traditional form of networking. However, many more do use social networks for background checks (35 percent). Within that 35 percent, LinkedIn (42 percent) and Facebook (40 percent) are the most popular, while Google+ (15 percent) and Twitter (2 percent) are less popular.

- **How to Stand Out:** Managers rank the following as "important" or "very important" when they review a candidate's qualifications: relevant course work (69 percent); referrals from a boss or professor (65 percent); leadership positions in campus organizations (50 percent); and entrepreneurship (29 percent).

- **How to Fail:** Respondents rank unpreparedness for an interview (42 percent) and a bad attitude (26 percent) as major turn-offs in potential or new employees.

SOURCE: Dan Schwabel, "Student Employment Gap Study," *Millennial Branding*, Millennial Branding and Experience, Inc., 14 May 2012, Web, 1 July 2012.

---

you to do. Perhaps you will find an emphasis on computers, written communication, human relations, or foreign languages—all of which are highly valued by some businesses. Or perhaps you will conclude that your training has given you a strong general base from which to learn specific business skills.

In analyzing your education, you should look at the quality of your record—grades, projects honors, special recognitions. If your record is good, you can emphasize it. But what if your work was only mediocre? As we will point out later, you will need to shift the emphasis to your stronger sales points—your willingness to work, your personality, your experience. Or perhaps you can explain—for example, by noting that while working your way through school may have limited your academic performance, it gave you valuable business qualities such as initiative, the ability to work as part of a team, and a willingness to take risks.

Personal Qualities. Your self-analysis also should cover your personal qualities. Employers often use **personality tests** such as the Myers-Briggs to screen new hires, and you can take them online as well as at most campus career centers. Qualities that relate to working with people are especially important. Qualities that indicate an aptitude for leadership or teamwork ability are also important.

Of course, you may not be the best judge of your personal qualities, so you may need to check with friends to see whether they agree with your assessments. You also may need to check your record for concrete evidence supporting your assessments. For example, organization membership and participation in community activities are evidence of people and teamwork skills. Holding office in an organization is evidence of leadership ability. Participation on a debate team, college bowl, or collegiate business policy team is evidence of communication skills.

Work Experience. Of course, work experience in your major field deserves the most emphasis, but work experience not related to the job you seek also can tell something important about you.

Your part-time server job or summer construction job may not seem like a big deal to you, but these jobs provide you with assets that any employer in any company can use, such as attention to detail, initiative, team skills, communication skills, and the ability to work well under pressure. You don't want to undersell this experience.

Special Interests. As we've mentioned, your self-analysis should include special qualifications that might be valuable to an employer. Your analysis can also include personal interests that may be relevant to types of positions you are seeking. To illustrate, athletic experience might be helpful for work for a sporting goods distributor, a hobby of automobile mechanics might be helpful for work with an automotive service company, and an interest in music might be helpful for work with a piano manufacturer or an online music website.

You also might take an **interest inventory** such as the Strong Campbell Interest Inventory or the Minnesota Vocational Interest Inventory. These tests help match your interests to those of others successful in their careers. Most college counseling and career centers make these tests available to their students, and some are available online. Getting good help in interpreting the results is critical to providing you with valuable information.

Analyzing Outside Factors. After you have analyzed yourself, you need to combine this information with the work needs of business and other external influences. Your goal in this process is to give realistic direction to your search for employment. Where is the kind of work you are seeking available? Are you willing to move? Is such a move compatible with others in your life—your partner, your children, your parents? Does the location meet your lifestyle needs? Although the availability of work may drive the answer to some of these questions, you should answer them as well as you can on the basis of what you know now and then conduct your job search accordingly. Finding just the right job should be one of your most important goals.

Career fairs and job boards are good places to look for announcements of job openings.

Finding Your Employer

LO3 Identify the sources that can lead you to an employer.

You can use a number of sources in your search for an employer with whom you will begin or continue your career. Your choice of sources will probably be influenced by the stage of your career.

Career Centers. If you are seeking an internship or just beginning your career, one good possibility is the career center at your school. Most large schools have career centers, and these attract employers who are looking for suitable applicants. Many centers offer excellent **job-search counseling** and maintain databases on registrants' school records, résumés, and recommendations that prospective employers can review. Most have directories listing major companies with contact names and addresses. And most provide interviewing opportunities. Campus career centers often hold **career fairs**, which are an excellent place to find employers who are looking for new graduates as well as to gather information about the kinds of jobs different companies offer. By attending them early, you often find out about internships and summer jobs as well as gather ideas for selecting courses that might give you an advantage when you do begin your career search.

Network of Personal Contacts. As we have noted, the personal contacts you make can be extremely helpful in your job search. In fact, according to some employment reports, personal contacts are the leading means of finding employees. Obviously, personal contacts are more likely to be a source of employment opportunities later in your career when you may need to change jobs. Business acquaintances may provide job leads outside those known to your friends.

Classified Advertisements. Help-wanted advertisements in newspapers and professional journals, whether online or in print, provide good sources of employment opportunities for many kinds of work. The opportunities they provide for new college graduates, however, may be limited. Classified ads are good sources for experienced workers who want to improve their positions, and they are especially good sources for people who are conducting a major search for high-level positions. Keep in mind that they provide only a partial list of jobs available. Many jobs are snapped up before they reach the classifieds, so be sure you are part of the professional grapevine in your field.

Online Sources. In addition to finding opportunities in classifieds, you also will find them in online databases. Monster.com, for example, lists jobs available throughout the United States and beyond, with new opportunities posted regularly. Many companies even post job openings on the Web, some with areas dedicated to new college graduates. If you are working now, you may want to check the company's intranet or portal for positions there, too. And professional associations often maintain job databanks. Furthermore, you could use blogs to post queries about job openings that readers might know of. All these online systems are sources for job opportunities. See the textbook website for links to these and more.

Employment Agencies. Companies that specialize in finding jobs for employees can be useful. Of course, such companies charge for their services. The employer sometimes pays the charges, usually if qualified applicants are scarce. **Executive search consultants** (headhunters) are commonly used to place experienced people in executive positions.

Employment agencies can also help job seekers gain temporary employment. Do not discount the value of such placements. Temping can lead to permanent employment. It allows the worker to get a feel for the company and the company to observe the worker before making a job commitment. You can also gain valuable on-the-job training in a temporary assignment.

Make Your LinkedIn Profile Work for You

By one study's estimate, of the 45 percent of companies using social media to recruit employees, nearly 90 percent use LinkedIn to find and screen potential applicants—far more than they use Facebook (46 percent) or Twitter (22 percent). Whether you're new to LinkedIn or a LinkedIn veteran, Victor Reklaitis provides tips from industry experts for creating a personal brand that employers will respond well to:

1. Include a photo. A LinkedIn study shows that profiles with photos are seven times more likely to get responses.

2. Have at least 50 connections. You'll be 12 times more likely to get information about opportunities.

3. Provide a complete work history.

4. Customize your account settings so that the URL for your profile is www.linkedin.com/YourName. It's easier to remember than the longer default URL, and you can easily include it on a business card.

5. Tell an interesting and unique story in the summary that lets an employer learn more about you.

6. Avoid buzzwords to describe yourself; they don't allow you to stand out. According to LinkedIn, words in the list of top ten overused words of 2011 included *creative, effective, innovative, dynamic, motivated,* and *extensive experience.*

7. Make sure you give as well as receive. That is, in addition to using LinkedIn to get attention from employers, share your expertise (e.g., post an article you found on an industry trend).

8. Write a headline for your profile that accurately and precisely describes who you are.

SOURCES: Derek Thompson, "Here Come the Raises," *The Atlantic,* The Atlantic Monthly Group, 1 Mar. 2012, Web, 1 July 2012; Victor Reklaitis, "Manage Your Personal Brand Online: Tips for LinkedIn," *Investors.com,* Investor's Business Daily, Inc., 29 June 2012, Web, 1 July 2012.

The *Occupational Outlook Handbook* is one of the best resources for finding out about a wide variety of jobs, including their education requirements, expected earnings, job duties and conditions, and more.

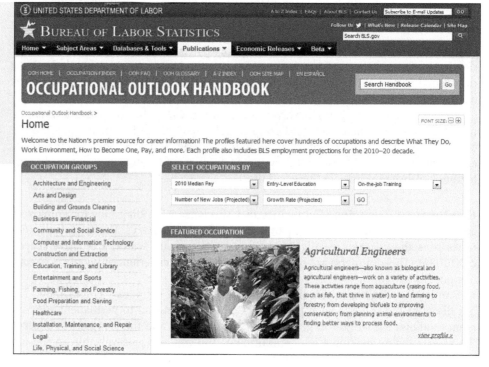

Personal Search Agents. In addition to searching online sources, you can request that job notices be sent to you automatically by websites. These sites use tools called **personal search agents** or **job agents.** Using a filter based on a confidential profile you have completed for the site, these tools find jobs that match your profile and send you email messages about these jobs. Starting with a very precise or narrow profile first is wise. You can always broaden your profile later if you find the number or nature of the job leads isn't what you expected. If you learn of a job listing that interests you for a company recruiting at your school, you should ask the recruiter about it. Not only will it show the employer you have done your homework, but it will also show that you have a sincere interest in working for the company.

Webpage Profiles. To make yourself more visible to potential employers, you may want to consider posting your résumé to the Web or using a social media site such as LinkedIn (see the Technology in Brief box on page 290). Today's word processors let you save your documents in hypertext markup language (HTML), creating a basic webpage for you. Additionally, easy-to-use webpage building and generating tools such as Weebly, Yola, SeaMonkey, and Google sites are available on the Web to help novices create personal Web profiles. Once posted, it is a good idea to link your webpage to your major department or to a business student club, allowing more potential employers to find it. With a little extra effort, you can create a webpage that greatly expands and enhances the printed résumé. You will want to put your webpage address on your printed résumé.

Prospecting. Some job seekers approach prospective employers directly, by either personal visit, mail, or email. Personal visits are effective if the company has an employment office or if a personal contact can set up a visit. Mail contacts typically include a résumé and a cover letter. An email contact can include a variety of documents and be sent in various forms. The construction of these messages is covered later in the chapter.

The websites of universities' career centers, like the one shown here, can be a great place for students to start their job search.

SOURCE: Used by permission from the University of Cincinnati.

PREPARING THE APPLICATION DOCUMENTS

How you pursue the employment opportunities that your research yields depends on your circumstances. When it is convenient and appropriate to do so, you make contact in person. It is convenient when the distance is not great, and it is appropriate when the employer has invited such a contact. When a personal visit is not convenient and appropriate, you may have to apply online or by mail, email, or fax.

Whether or not you apply in person, you are likely to need some written material about yourself. If you apply in person, probably you will take a résumé with you to leave as a record of your qualifications. If you do not apply in person, of course, the application is completely in writing. Typically, it consists of a résumé and a cover message. At some point in your employment efforts, you are likely to use each of these documents.

Approach preparing these documents as you would when preparing a sales campaign. Begin your work by studying what you are selling, and what you are selling is you. Take personal inventory, performing the self-analysis discussed earlier in the chapter, and list all the information about you that you believe an employer would want to know. Then learn as much as you can about the company—its plans, its policies, its operations. You can study the company's website, read its annual report and other publications, find any recent news articles about the company, and consult a variety of business databases. (See Chapter 13 for a more detailed list of resources for company information.) You can also learn the requirements of the work the company wants done. Today, campus career centers and student organizations often invite employers to give information sessions. Reading about various careers in the *Opportunity Outlook Handbook* at www.bls.gov/ooh/ will tell you about the nature of the work as well as salary range and demand.

With this preliminary information assembled, you are ready to plan the application. First, you need to decide what your application will consist of. Will it be just a cover message; a cover message and a résumé (also called a *vita, curriculum vita, qualifications brief,* or *data sheet*); or a cover message, résumé, and reference sheet? Though most select the combination of cover message and résumé, some people prefer to use a detailed cover message alone, while others include all three documents. You should use whatever will best support your case.

LO4 Compile résumés for print and electronic environments that are strong, complete, and organized.

CONSTRUCTING THE RÉSUMÉ

Writing a résumé requires you to use many of the same strategies we've discussed in previous chapters for writing business documents. To plan your résumé, you'll analyze your *goals, purpose, and audience.* Then you will draft your résumé and revise and edit it until it represents your best professional work. As with any other business document, you also need to consider your *channel of communication*—whether your audience will read your résumé as a printed (hard copy) document or an electronic document. Constructing the content for each type is similar, but because you are likely to need both printed and electronic copies of your résumé, you will need to be familiar with the special considerations for each type. In this section, we first present common content and organizational models for résumés in general. This is followed by a discussion of special considerations for formatting résumés to be read in print versus formatting résumés to be read in an electronic environment as email attachments and web pages. Lastly, we present guidelines for developing scannable résumés, which may be either print or electronic documents.

Résumé Content

Your résumé should include all the information that your cover letter reviews plus supporting and incidental details. Designed for quick reading, the résumé lists facts that have been arranged for the best possible appearance. It should also be tailored to the position for which you are applying.

The arrangements of résumés differ widely, but the following process generally represents how most are written:

- Logically arrange information on education (institutions, dates, degrees, major field); information on employment (dates, places, firms, job titles, and accomplishments); personal details (memberships, interests, and achievements—but not religion, race, and gender); and skills or specialized knowledge.

- Place your name and contact information at the top of the résumé and create subheadings for the main parts (e.g., objective, education, employment, extracurricular activities).

- Arrange the data for best visual appeal, making the résumé look balanced—without too much white space or too much text.

Selecting the Background Facts. Your first step in preparing the résumé is to review the facts you have assembled about yourself and then select the ones you think will help your reader evaluate you. You should include the information covered in the accompanying cover message, because this is the most important information. In addition, you should include significant supporting details not covered in the accompanying cover message to avoid making that message too cluttered.

Arranging the Facts into Groups. After selecting the facts you want to include, you should sort them into logical groups. Many grouping arrangements are possible. The most conventional is the three-part grouping of *Education*, *Experience*, and *Skills* or *Interests*. Another possibility is a grouping by job functions or skills, such as *Selling*, *Communicating*, and *Managing*. You may be able to think of other logical groups.

You also can derive additional groups from the three conventional groups mentioned above. For example, you can have a group of *Achievements*. Such a group would consist of special accomplishments taken from your experience and education. Another possibility is to have a group consisting of information highlighting your major *Qualifications*. Here you would include information drawn from the areas of experience, education, and skills or personal qualities. Illustrations of and instructions for constructing groups such as these appear later in the chapter.

Constructing the Headings. With your information organized, a logical next step is to construct the headings for the résumé. Figure 10–1 provides a list of category headings to consider.

In a way, your name could be considered the main heading. It should be presented in type that is larger and bother than that in the rest of the document so that your name stands out. If an employer remembers only one fact from your résumé, that fact should be your name, as in this example:

Julia M. Alvarez

The next level of headings might be *Objective, Education, Experience*, and *Skills*. These headings can be placed to the left or centered above the text that follows.

Consider using more descriptive headings that tell the nature of what follows. For example, instead of using the head, *Education*, you might use *Computer Skills*. These heads better indicate the information covered, and they help the reader interpret the facts that follow.

As you can see from the illustrations in the chapter, the headings are distinguished from the other information in the résumé by the use of different sizes and styles of type. The main head should appear to be the most important of all (larger and heavier). Your goal is to choose forms that properly show the relative importance of the information and are pleasing to the eye.

Including Contact Information. Your address, telephone number, and email address are the most likely means of contacting you. Most authorities recommend that you display them prominently somewhere in the résumé. You also may want to display your cell number, website address, or addresses for your social networking sites. The most common location for displaying contact information is at the top, under your name.

Figure 10–1

Résumé Headings & Titles

Academic Achievements	Credentials	Professional Affiliations
Academic History	Degree(s)	Professional Affiliations & Awards
Academic Honors	Designations	Professional Employment
Academic Training	Dissertation	Professional Experience
Accomplishments	Education	Professional Leadership
Activities	Education Highlights	Professional Memberships
Additional Experience	Education & Training	Professional Organizations
Additional Professional Training	Educational Background	Professional Objective
Additional Training	Employment	Professional Qualifications
Affiliations	Employment History	Professional Seminars
Appointments	Employment Objective	Professional Summary
Areas of Expertise	Exhibitions & Awards	Publications
Associations	Experience(s)	Published Works
Athletic Involvement	Experience Highlights	Qualifications
Awards	Extracurricular Involvement	References
Awards & Distinctions	Field Placement	Related Course Work
Background and Interests	Foreign Language	Related Experience
Business Experience	Graduate School	Relevant Course Work
Career Goal	Graduate School Activities	Research Experience
Career Highlights	Graduate School Employment	Seminars
Career History	Hardware/Software	Skill(s) Summary
Career Objective	Highlights of Qualifications	Skills & Attributes
Career Profile	Honors	Skills & Qualifications
Career-Related Experience	Honors, Activities, & Organizations	Special Abilities
Career-Related Fieldwork	Honors and Awards	Special Awards
Career-Related Workshops	International Experience	Special Awards & Recognitions
Career-Related Training	International Travel	Special Courses
Career Skills & Experience	Internship Experience	Special Interests
Career Summary	Internship(s)	Special Licenses & Awards
Certificate(s)	Job History	Special Projects or Studies
Certifications	Languages	Special Skills
Classroom Experience	Leadership Roles	Special Training
Coaching Experience	License(s)	Strengths
Coaching Skills	Major Accomplishments	Student Teaching
College Activities	Management Experience	Student Teaching Experience
Communication Experience	Memberships	Study Abroad
Community Involvement	Memberships & Activities	Summary
Computer Background	Military Experience	Summary of Experience
Computer Experience	Military Service	Summary of Qualifications
Computer Knowledge	Military Training	Teaching Experience
Computer Languages	Objective	Teaching & Coaching Experience
Computer Proficiencies	Occupational History	Teaching & Related Experience
Computer Skills	Other Experience	Thesis
Computer Systems	Other Skills	Travel Abroad
Consulting Experience	Overseas Employment	Travel Experience
Cooperative Education	Overseas Experience	Volunteer Experience
Cooperative Education Experience	Planning & Problem Solving	Work Experience
Course Highlights	Portfolio	Work History
Course Work Included	Position Objective	Workshops & Seminars
Courses of Interest	Practicum Experience	

SOURCE: College of Business, *The Job Campaign Workbook* (Eau Claire, WI: University of Wisconsin–Eau Claire, 2010) 17, *Student Professional Development Programs,* University of Wisconsin-Eau Claire, Web, 6 July 2012.

When it is likely that your address or telephone number will change before the job search ends, you would be wise to include two addresses and numbers: one current and the other permanent.

The logic of making the contact information prominent and inclusive is to make it easy for the employer to reach you. However, recently, in the interest of privacy, some schools have begun advising their students to include only their names, phone numbers, and an innocuous email address created specifically for job searches. For business use, a professional email address is always preferable to an informal one such as surferchick@hotmail.com. However, you will likely still need to include complete information on application forms provided by employers.

Including a Statement of Objective. Although not a category of background information, a **statement of your objective** is appropriate in the résumé. Headings such as *Career Objective, Job Objective,* or just *Objective* usually appear at the beginning after your name.

Not all authorities agree on the value of including the objective, however. Some argue that the objective includes only obvious information that is clearly suggested by the remainder of the résumé. Moreover, they point out that an objective limits the applicant to a single position and eliminates consideration for other jobs that may be available.

Those favoring the use of a statement of objective reason that it helps the recruiter see quickly where the applicant might fit into the company. Since this argument appears to have greater support, at least for the moment, you should include the objective. When your career goal is unclear, you may use broad, general terms. And when you are considering a variety of employment possibilities, you may want to have different versions of your résumé for each possibility.

Primarily, your statement of objective should describe the work you seek. When you know the exact job title of a position you want at the targeted company, use it.

> Objective: To obtain a marketing research internship in the arts and entertainment industry.

Another technique includes using words that convey a long-term interest in the targeted company, as in the following example. However, using this form may limit you if the company does not have the career path you specify.

> Objective: To secure a full-time sales representative position for McGraw-Hill leading to sales management.

Also, wording the objective to point out your major strengths can be very effective. It also can help set up the organization of the résumé.

> Objective: To apply three years of successful ecommerce accounting experience to a larger company with a need for careful attention to transaction management and analysis.

Presenting the Information. After crafting your job objective, you need to determine what information to present under the rest of your headings. Though the order of the headings will largely depend on your organizational strategy (see "Organizing for Strength," page 301), the information under each heading generally appears as follows.

Work Experience. The description of your work experience should contain your job title/position, company name, location, and dates of employment. You should also include your job duties and the skills you acquired, especially those that relate to the position for which you are applying. Consider the following example:

Marketing and Public Relations Intern

Alliant Health Plans, Incorporated, Boston, MA

Jan. 2013–May 2013

- Created a webpage, brochure, and press release for a community wellness program
- Interviewed and wrote about physicians, customers, and community leaders for newsletter articles

- Worked with a team of interns in other departments to analyze and update the company's website

Note in the above example that in addition to the basic information regarding the job, the writer lists *duties* that anyone in a marketing or public relations field would likely use in a related position. The duties are represented with **action-oriented, past tense verbs** because the position has ended. If the intern were still in the position, he or she would have used **simple present tense verbs** for duties he or she currently performs (e.g., *interview, write*). The use of these action verbs strengthens a job description because verbs are the strongest of all words. If you choose them well, you will do much to sell your ability to do the jobs you are targeting. A list of the more widely used action verbs appears in Figure 10–2.

Note also that the writer uses both *months and dates*. This is especially important when you consider that simply saying "2012" doesn't let the reader know how long the internship was. In another example, if a reader sees dates of employment as 2011–2012, he or she does not know if that included a full year of employment or if the writer started on December 31, 2011, and quit on January 1, 2012. Including the months along with the dates is the clearest and most ethical way to represent your employment timeline.

Education. Because your education is likely to be your strongest selling point for your first job after college, you will probably cover it in some detail. (Unless it adds something unique, you usually do not include your high school education once you have finished a college degree. Similarly, you also minimize the emphasis on all your education as you gain experience.) At a minimum, your coverage of education should include *institutions, dates, degrees, and areas of study*. For some jobs, you may want to list and even describe specific courses, especially if you have little other information to present or if your course work has uniquely prepared you for those jobs. In particular, if you are applying for an internship, you may want to list your course work as an indication of your current level of academic preparation as it relates to the requirements of the position. If your grade-point average (GPA) is good, you may want to include it. Remember, for your résumé, you can compute your GPA in a way that works best for you

---

Figure 10–2

A List of Action Verbs That Add Strength to Your Résumé

Communication/ People Skills				
	Conveyed	Incorporated	Participated	Suggested	Designed
Addressed	Convinced	Influenced	Persuaded	Summarized	Developed
Advertised	Corresponded	Interacted	Presented	Synthesized	Directed
Arbitrated	Debated	Interpreted	Promoted	Translated	Displayed
Arranged	Defined	Interviewed	Proposed	Wrote	Drew
Articulated	Developed	Involved	Publicized		Entertained
Authored	Directed	Joined	Reconciled	**Creative Skills**	Established
Clarified	Discussed	Judged	Recruited	Acted	Fashioned
Collaborated	Drafted	Lectured	Referred	Adapted	Formulated
Communicated	Edited	Listened	Reinforced	Began	Founded
Composed	Elicited	Marketed	Reported	Combined	Illustrated
Condensed	Enlisted	Mediated	Resolved	Composed	Initiated
Conferred	Explained	Moderated	Responded	Conceptualized	Instituted
Consulted	Expressed	Negotiated	Solicited	Condensed	Integrated
Consulted	Formulated	Observed	Specified	Created	Introduced
Contacted	Furnished	Outlined	Spoke	Customized	Invented

Figure 10–2

(continued)

Modeled
Modified
Originated
Performed
Photographed
Planned
Revised
Revitalized
Shaped
Solved

Data/Financial Skills
Adjusted
Administered
Allocated
Analyzed
Appraised
Assessed
Audited
Balanced
Budgeted
Calculated
Computed
Conserved
Corrected
Determined
Developed
Estimated
Forecasted
Managed
Marketed
Measured
Netted
Planned
Prepared
Programmed
Projected
Qualified
Reconciled
Reduced
Researched
Retrieved

Helping Skills
Adapted
Advocated
Aided
Answered

Arranged
Assessed
Assisted
Clarified
Coached
Collaborated
Contributed
Cooperated
Counseled
Demonstrated
Diagnosed
Educated
Encouraged
Ensured
Expedited
Facilitated
Familiarized
Furthered
Guided
Helped
Insured
Intervened
Motivated
Prevented
Provided
Referred
Rehabilitated
Represented
Resolved
Simplified
Supplied
Supported
Volunteered

Management/ Leadership Skills
Administered
Analyzed
Appointed
Approved
Assigned
Attained
Authorized
Chaired
Considered
Consolidated
Contracted
Controlled

Converted
Coordinated
Decided
Delegated
Developed
Directed
Eliminated
Emphasized
Enforced
Enhanced
Established
Executed
Generated
Handled
Headed
Hired
Hosted
Improved
Incorporated
Increased
Initiated
Inspected
Instituted
Led
Managed
Merged
Motivated
Navigated
Organized
Originated
Overhauled
Oversaw
Planned
Presided
Prioritized
Produced
Recommended
Reorganized
Replaced
Restored
Reviewed
Scheduled
Secured
Selected
Streamlined
Strengthened
Supervised
Terminated

Organizational Skills
Approved
Arranged
Catalogued
Categorized
Charted
Classified
Coded
Collected
Compiled
Corrected
Corresponded
Distributed
Executed
Filed
Generated
Incorporated
Inspected
Logged
Maintained
Monitored
Obtained
Operated
Ordered
Organized
Prepared
Processed
Provided
Purchased
Recorded
Registered
Reserved
Responded
Reviewed
Routed
Scheduled
Screened
Submitted
Supplied
Standardized
Systematized
Updated
Validated
Verified

Research Skills
Analyzed
Clarified

Collected
Compared
Conducted
Critiqued
Detected
Determined
Diagnosed
Evaluated
Examined
Experimented
Explored
Extracted
Formulated
Gathered
Inspected
Interviewed
Invented
Investigated
Located
Measured
Organized
Researched
Reviewed
Searched
Solved
Summarized
Surveyed
Systematized
Tested

Teaching Skills
Adapted
Advised
Clarified
Coached
Communicated
Conducted
Coordinated
Developed
Enabled
Encouraged
Evaluated
Explained
Facilitated
Focused
Guided
Individualized
Informed

Instilled
Instructed
Motivated
Persuaded
Simulated
Stimulated
Taught
Tested
Trained
Transmitted
Tutored

Technical Skills
Adapted
Applied
Assembled
Built
Calculated
Computed
Conserved
Constructed
Converted
Debugged
Designed
Determined
Developed
Engineered
Fabricated
Fortified
Installed
Maintained
Operated
Overhauled
Printed
Programmed
Rectified
Regulated
Remodeled
Repaired
Replaced
Restored
Solved
Specialized
Standardized
Studied
Upgraded
Utilized

SOURCE: "Job-Seeker Action Verbs—By Skills Sets," *Quintessential Careers,* Quintessential Careers, 2012, Web, 6 July 2012. Reprinted with permission of Quintessential Careers, http://www.quintcareers.com.

as long as you label it accurately. For example, you may want to select just those courses in your major, labeling it Major GPA. Or if your last few years were your best ones, you may want to present your GPA for just that period. In any case, include a GPA when it works favorably for you.

Personal Information. What personal information to list is a matter for your best judgment. In fact, the trend appears to be toward eliminating such information. If you do include personal information, you should *omit race, religion, gender, age, and marital status* because current laws prohibit hiring based on them. Interestingly, not everyone agrees on this matter. Some authorities believe that at least some of these items should be included. They argue that the law only prohibits employers from considering such information in hiring—that it does not prohibit applicants from presenting the information. They reason that if such information helps you, you should use it. The illustrations shown in this chapter support both viewpoints.

Personal information that is generally appropriate includes all items that tell about your personal assets. Information on your *organization memberships, civic involvement, and social activities* is evidence of experience and interest in working with people. Such information can be quite useful to some employers, especially when personal qualities are important to the work involved. Figure 10–3 presents a résumé that emphasizes education and experience.

References. Even though employers can (and do) check your social media sites, they are also likely to check specific references that you provide. Generally, you do not need to include references on or with your résumé unless the job posting asks you to. If the job posting does not require references, you can simply have a list of references ready for the point in the interview process when the employer requires it. Primary reasons for not including your references unless asked are that (1) references added to a résumé take up space that you could use to sell your skills, and (2) references included on a separate sheet, while not harmful, are not likely necessary if the employer has not asked for them. However, if you have a particularly impressive reference or a reference whom your audience might know, including your references can be a good idea. If you do include your references, it is usually best to put them on a separate **reference sheet**.

The type size and style of the main heading of this sheet should match that used in your résumé. It may say something like "References for [*your name*]." Below this heading is a listing of your references, beginning with the strongest one. In addition to solving the reference dilemma, use of this separate reference sheet allows you to change both the references and their order for each job. A sample reference sheet is shown in the example in Figure 10–4 on page 300.

How many and what kinds of references to include will depend on your background. If you have an employment record, you should include one for every major job you have held—at least for recent years. You should include references related to the work you seek. If you base your application heavily on your education or your personal qualities, or both, you should include references who can vouch for these areas: professors, clergy, community leaders, and the like. Your goal is to list those people who can verify the points on which your appeal for the job is based. At a minimum, you should list three references. Five is a good maximum.

Your list of references should include accurate mailing addresses with appropriate job titles. Also useful are telephone and fax numbers as well as email addresses. Job titles (officer, manager, president, supervisor) are helpful because they show what the references are able to tell about you. It is appropriate to include forms of address: Mr., Mrs., Ms., Dr., and so on.

Some résumé writers may be tempted to put "references available upon request" at the bottom of their résumés. However, this expression is outdated and serves no purpose. When you think about it, of course you would always make your references available at the employer's request, which means you're stating the obvious. Though some may argue that including this statement shows a willingness to provide the information, you can show your willingness by including a separate references sheet. You may

Figure 10–3

Traditional Print Résumé Emphasizing Education and Relevant Experience

Derek Masters
4321 Oak Street • Eau Claire, WI 54701
Home phone: (715) 555-5555 • Email: dlmasters@gmail.com

OBJECTIVE	A full-time position in the automotive maintenance field	*States type of position and field*
EDUCATION	Chippewa Valley Technical College Eau Claire, WI Diploma: Automotive Maintenance Technician program, July 2012 • Received President's List status for the 2010 fall semester and 2011 summer semester • Obtained all data certification • Earned certification to work with Freon • Completed a basic welding course with arc, oxyacetylene, and wire feed welding	*Lists honors and course work other graduates may not have*
RELEVANT EXPERIENCE	**Intern—Cooperative Education Capstone** January 2012 – May 2012 River Valley Motors 5555 Highway 93, Eau Claire, WI 54701 Phone: (715) 832-3859 • Provided excellent customer service • Learned and then trained co-workers how to use newly purchased tire balancer • Performed many fluid flushes and changes	*Uses a separate category heading to highlight internship*
EMPLOYMENT HISTORY	**Shift Supervisor** February 2010 – Present McDonald's Restaurant 4321 Hastings Way, Eau Claire, WI 54701 Phone: (715) 839-4444 • Train new employees • Motivate employees to be positive and friendly • Multi-task well in stressful situations • Trusted to work alone on many different projects **Night Stocker** December 2007 – January 2010 Sam's Club 4001 Gateway Avenue, Eau Claire, WI 54701 Phone: (715) 835-3333 • Worked alone and in teams to stock shelves • Took charge of my area to maintain and increase standards • Assembled and created displays to sell products	*As do many vocational résumés, this lists employers' contact information* *Uses action verbs to portray dependability, trustworthiness, and work ethic*
ACTIVITIES	• Meals on Wheels volunteer: Deliver 20 meals per week to the elderly and homebound • Church choir member	*Activities show a well-rounded individual*

Figure 10–4

Thoroughness and Good Arrangement for a Reference Sheet. This reference sheet presents Julia Alvarez's references completely.

References for Julia M. Alvarez

3177 North Hawthorne Boulevard
St. Louis, MO 63139
314.967.3117 (Voice/ Message)
jmalvarez358@hotmail.com

Heading format matches résumé

Mr. John Gibbs
Human Resources Director
Upton Industries
7114 East 71st Street
St. Louis, MO 63139
Telephone: 314.342.1171
Email: John.Gibbs@upton.com

Mr. Todd E. Frankle, Store Manager
The Gap, Inc.
Four Points Mall
St. Louis, MO 63139
Telephone: 314.466.9101
Email: tfrankle@gap.com

Professor Helen K. Robbins
Department of Management
Wilmont University
St. Louis, MO 63139
Telephone: 314.392.6673
Email: Helen.Robbins@wilmont.edu

Professor Carol A. Cueno
Department of Psychology
Wilmont University
St. Louis, MO 63139
Telephone: 314.392.0723
Email: Carol.Cueno@wilmont.edu

Complete information and balanced arrangement

want to use the space you would devote to this statement by adding another line to your job duties or other experience to sell your skills and abilities.

When you do list someone as a reference, good business etiquette requires that you ask for permission first. Although you will use only those who can speak highly of you, asking for your reference's permission beforehand helps that person prepare better. And, of course, it saves you from unexpected embarrassment such as a reference not remembering you, being caught by surprise, or, worse yet, not having anything to say.

Organizing for Strength. After you have identified the information you want to include on your résumé, you will want to organize or group items to present yourself in the best possible light. Three strategies for organizing this information are the reverse chronological approach, the functional or skills approach, and the accomplishments/ achievements or highlights approach.

The **reverse chronological organizational layout** (Figure 10–5) presents your education and work experience from the most recent to oldest. It emphasizes the order and time frame in which you have participated in these activities. It is particularly good for those who have progressed in an orderly and timely fashion through school and work. The reverse chronological format is the most common way of organizing a résumé; therefore, it is likely the best choice for most job seekers (including college students), as it provides a format familiar to employers.

A **functional or skills layout** (Figure 10–7) organizes the résumé's contents round three to five areas particularly important to the job you want. Rather than forcing an employer to determine that you developed one skill on one job and another skill on another job, this organizational plan groups related skills. It is particularly good for those who have had many jobs, have taken nontraditional career paths, or who are changing fields. Creating this kind of résumé takes much work and careful analysis of both jobs and skills to show the reader that you are a good match for the position. If you use a functional résumé, be sure that readers can see from the other sections— such as employment and education—where you likely developed the skills that you are emphasizing. Enabling your readers to make these connections lends credibility to your claims to have such skills.

An **accomplishments/achievements layout** (Figure 10–8) foregrounds the most impressive factors about you.

It features a *Highlights* or *Summary* section that includes key points from the three conventional information groups: education, experience, and personal qualities. This information comes near the beginning of the résumé, usually following the objective. Typically, this layout emphasizes the applicant's most impressive background facts that pertain to the work sought, as in this example:

Summary

- **Experienced:** Three years of full-time work as programmer/analyst in designing and developing financial databases for the banking industry.
- **Highly trained:** BS degree with honors in management information systems.
- **Self-motivated:** Proven record of successful completion of three online courses.

Keep in mind that this section should not repeat sections of the résumé; it should highlight strengths. If your résumé is short and your summary is just a repeat of other content, you may choose not to include this section. In the rest of the résumé, accomplishments should stand out. For example, rather than listing them within other categories, such as employment or education, you can put them in a separate section as illustrated by the example on p. 306.

Writing Impersonally and Consistently. Because the résumé is a listing of information, you should write without personal pronouns (no *I*'s, *we*'s, *you*'s). You should also write all equal-level headings and the parts under each heading in the same parallel

Figure 10–5

Traditional Print Résumé Organized in Reverse Chronological Format

Large size emphasizes name ————————

Manny Konedeng
5602 Montezuma Road • Apartment 413 • San Diego • California • 92115
Phone: (619) 578-8508 • Email: mkonedeng@yahoo.com

Includes complete contact information

Uses descriptive, specific statement

OBJECTIVE	A financial analyst internship with a brokerage firm
EDUCATION	**Bachelor of Science Degree in Business Administration**, May 2013, San Diego State University, Finance Major

Expands and emphasizes strongest points through precise detail

Dean's List
Current GPA: 3.32/4.00
Accomplishments:

- Published in *Fast Company Magazine* and the *San Diego Union Tribune*
- Won Greek Scholarship
- Finished in top five in mathematics competition

Related Courses:
- Business Communication
- Investments
- Tax Planning
- Estate Planning
- Risk Management
- Business Law

Computer Skills:
- Excel, Word, PowerPoint, Access, QuickBooks
- Statistical Software: SAS, SPSS
- Web-based Applications—Surveymonkey, Blogger, GoToMeeting
- Research Tools—Center for Research in Securities Prices (CRSP) stock price database and the Standard and Poor's Research Insight database of corporations' financial statements

WORK EXPERIENCE

Sales and Front Desk, Powerhouse Gym, Modesto, CA 95355   Summer 2012
- Sold memberships and facilitated tours for the fitness center
- Listened to, analyzed, and answered customers' inquires
- Accounted for membership payments and constructed sales reports
- Trained new employees to understand company procedures and safety policies

Emphasizes position held rather than place or date

Relay Operator, MCI, Riverbank, CA 95367   Summers 2010 & 2011
- Assisted over 100 callers daily who were deaf, hard of hearing, or speech disabled to place calls
- Exceeded the required data input of 60 wpm with accuracy
- Multitasked with typing and listening to phone conversations
- Was offered a promotion as a Lead Operator

Uses descriptive action verbs

Co-founder and Owner, Fo Sho Entertainment, Modesto, CA 95355   Aug. 2008–May 2010
- Led promotions for musical events in the Central Valley
- Managed and hosted live concerts
- Created and wrote proposals to work with local businesses
- Collaborated with team members to design advertisements

UNIVERSITY INVOLVEMENT

Communications Tutor, San Diego State University, San Diego, CA 92182   Spring 2013
- Critiqued and evaluated the written work for a business communication course
- Set up and maintained blog for business communication research

Includes items that will set him apart from other applicants

Recruitment Chair, Kappa Alpha Order Fraternity, San Diego, CA 92115
- Supervised the selection process for chapter membership   Fall 2012
- Individually raised nearly $1,000 for chapter finances
- Organized recruitment events with business sponsors, radio stations, and special guests

Figure 10-6

LinkedIn Profile. This Web-based profile presents not only the candidate's qualifications as they might appear on a printed résumé but also a personal summary and a recommendation from a previous employer. Links allow readers to access additional information regarding the candidate's education, employment, and skills.

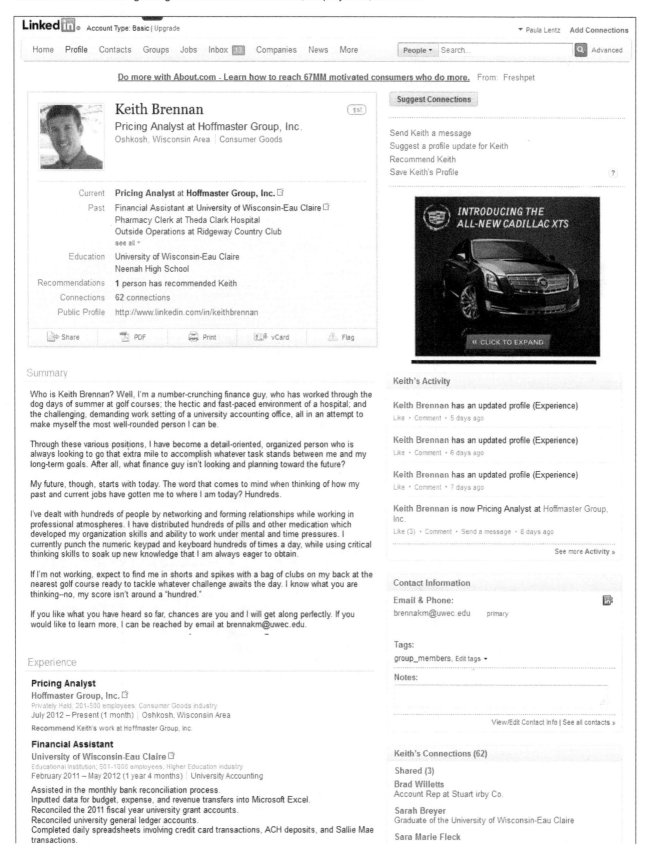

Figure 10–6

(continued)

Worked with thousands of student refund checks to ensure timely disbursement to students.

Keith has 1 recommendation (1 manager) including:

(2nd) Jackie Kriesel, *Controller, University of Wisconsin-Eau Claire*
Recommend Keith's work at University of Wisconsin-Eau Claire

Pharmacy Clerk

Theda Clark Hospital
December 2011 – January 2012 (2 months)

Delivered medication to patients on the following floors: Surgery, Rehabilitation, Intensive-Care, Birthing, Psych, and Outpatient.
Packaged medication to be sent out to the Appleton and New London campuses.
Heavily fast-paced and detail-oriented job required me to think and act quickly in stressful situations.
Responsible for making sure all medication was accurate and complete before delivery.
Adapted to change very fast and learned the entire clerk process in one day.
Recommend Keith's work at Theda Clark Hospital

Outside Operations

Ridgeway Country Club
May 2009 – August 2011 (2 years 4 months)

Worked in a dynamic, fast-paced environment.
Further developed customer service skills by assisting the 200+ members.
Gained valuable team-working experience with 15 other coworkers.
Set-up golf outings that were organized, top-notch, and professional.
Helped assistant golf professionals set-up new clothing and equipment in the golf shop to maximize selling potential.
Recommend Keith's work at Ridgeway Country Club

Golf Shop Attendant

Westridge Golf Club
June 2006 – August 2008 (2 years 3 months)

Developed customer service skills and proper business etiquette.
Became skilled with Fore! Reservations software and increased daily productivity.
Gained knowledge of orders, invoices, and bookkeeping procedures.
Set-up banquets, weddings, wedding receptions, private parties, and golf outings.
Recommend Keith's work at Westridge Golf Club

Skills & Expertise

Excel   PowerPoint   Access   Customer Service   Word   Outlook

Microsoft Office   General Ledger Reconciliation   Organization   Writing Skills

Time Management

Education

University of Wisconsin-Eau Claire

Bachelor of Business Administration (BBA), Finance; IS
2008 – 2012

Activities and Societies: Financial Management Association, Intramural Basketball, Intramural Volleyball, Intramural Soccer
Recommend Keith's work at University of Wisconsin-Eau Claire

Recommendations For Keith

Financial Assistant

University of Wisconsin-Eau Claire ☐

"Keith is a very good worker and is willing to take on any task asked of him. He is detail orientated and does not have any problem asking questions if he is not sure how to do something.

Keith is also very pleasant to have in the office and has a good sense of humor." *November 14, 2011*

(2nd) Jackie Kriesel, *Controller, University of Wisconsin-Eau Claire*
managed Keith at University of Wisconsin-Eau Claire

Intern at St. Gertrude's Health & Rehabilitation Center

Other (59)

Kristen Ellis
HR and Office Administration

Cheryl Stephenson
Owner at Paul Davis Emergency Services

Raelene Guenther
Executive Assistant at Hoffmaster

See all Connections »

How you're connected to Keith

You
⇓
(1st)
Keith Brennan

Groups you share with Keith:

 University of Wisconsin-Eau Claire
College of Business

Note: Groups shared with the viewer are shown here. Other groups, if visible, are shown under "Additional Information".

Viewers of this profile also viewed...

 Drew Christensen
Financial Representative Intern at...

 Sarah Breyer
Graduate of the University of...

 Erica Rasmussen
Marketing Intern at Bar106

 Kris Presler
Associate Professor at University of...

 Adam Schlecht
Actuarial Assistant at Assurant Health

 Dana Rasmussen
Human Resources Associate at...

 Paula Lentz
UW-Eau Claire Dept. of Business...

 Lauren Riensche
Marketing & Events Management Intern at...

 Greg Drusch
Marketing Manager & REALTOR at Cypress...

Carolynn W. Workman

12271 69th Terrace North
Seminole, FL 33772
727.399.2569 (Voice/Message)
cworkman@msn.com

Emphasizes tight organization through use of horizontal ruled lines

Objective	An entry-level tax accounting position with a CPA firm

Education

Layout emphasizes degree and GPA

Bachelor of Science: University of South Florida, December 2013
Major: Business Administration
Emphasis: Accounting
GPA: 3.42 with Honors

Uses internal bullets to increase readability

Accounting-Related Course Work:
Financial Accounting ❖ Cost Accounting and Control ❖ Accounting Information Systems ❖ Auditing ❖ Concepts of Federal Income Taxation ❖ Financial Policy ❖ Communications for Business and Professions

Activities:
Vice-President of Finance, Beta Alpha Psi
Editor, Student Newsletter for Beta Alpha Psi
Member, Golden Key National Honors Society

Emphasizes key skills relevant to objective

Skills

Computer

▶ Assisted in installation of small business computerized accounting system using QuickBooks Pro.
▶ Prepared tax returns for individuals in the VITA program using specialty tax software.
▶ Mastered Excel, designing data input forms, analyzing and interpreting results of most functions, generating graphs, and creating and using macros.

Accounting

▶ Reconciled accounts for center serving over 1,300 clients.
▶ Prepared income, gift, and estate tax returns.
▶ Processed expense reports for twenty professional staff.
▶ Generated financial statements and processed tax returns using Great Plains and Solomon IV.

Varies use of action verbs

Business Communication

▶ Conducted client interviews and researched tax issues.
▶ Communicated both in written and verbal form with clients.
▶ Delivered several individual and team presentations on business cases, projects, and reports to business students.

Work History

Administrative Assistant

Office of Student Disability Services, University of South Florida
Tampa, FL. Spring 2013.

Tax Assistant

Rosemary Lenaghan, Certified Public Accountant. Seminole, FL Jan. 2009–May 2013.

Kimberly M. VanLerBerghe

2411 27th Street
Moline, IL 61265
309.764.0017 (Mobile)
kmv@yahoo.com

JOB TARGET TRAINER/TRANSLATOR for a large, worldwide company

HIGHLIGHTS OF QUALIFICATIONS

Emphasizes those qualifications most relevant to position sought

- Experienced in creating and delivering multimedia PowerPoint presentations.
- Enthusiastic team member/leader whose participation brings out the best in others.
- Proficient in analytical ability.
- Skilled in gathering and interpreting data.
- Bilingual—English/Spanish.

EDUCATION

Presents the most important items here

DEGREE	B.A. English—June 2013—Western Illinois University	
EMPHASIS	Education and Spanish	MAJOR GPA—3.87/4.00
HONORS	Dean's List, four semesters	Chevron Scholarship, Fall 2010
MEMBER	Mortar Board, Women's Golf Team	

EMPLOYMENT

Identifies most significant places of work and de-emphasizes less important work

DEERE & COMPANY, INC.   CONGRESSMAN J. DENNIS HASTERT
Student Intern, Summer 2011   Volunteer in Computer Services, Fall 2011

Several years' experience in the restaurant business including supervisory positions.

ACCOMPLISHMENTS

Presents only selected accomplishments from various work and volunteer experience that relate to position sought

- ▶ Trained executives to create effective cross-cultural presentations.
- ▶ Developed online training program for executive use of GoToMeeting.
- ▶ Designed and developed a database to keep track of financial donations.
- ▶ Coded new screens and reports; debugged and revised screen forms for easier data entry.
- ▶ Provided computer support to virtual volunteers on election committee.
- ▶ Provided translation services for Hispanic employees.

grammatical form. For example, if one major heading in the résumé is a noun phrase, all the other major headings should be noun phrases. The following four job duties illustrate the point. All but the third are verb phrases. The error can be corrected by making the third a noun phrase, as in the examples to the right:

Not Parallel	**Parallel**
Greeted customers	Greeted customers
Processed transactions	Processed transactions
Data entry in Excel spreadsheets	Entered data in Excel spreadsheets
Balanced a cash drawer	Balanced a cash drawer

The following items illustrate grammatical inconsistency in the parts of a group:

Have fluency in Spanish
Active in sports
Ambitious

The understood word for the first item is *I* and for the second and third, the understood words are *I am*. Any changes that make all three items fit the same understood words would correct the error (e.g., fluent in Spanish, active in sports, ambitious).

Printed (Hardcopy) Résumés

As we've mentioned, one aspect of résumé writing you must consider is the environment in which your audience will read your document. Knowing whether your reader will read a printed or an electronic document helps you create résumés that are easily accessible to readers and ensure that you present a professional image.

A printed résumé is mean to be sent in hardcopy format through the mail and used in face-to-face interviews. Generally, a printed résumé is one or two pages. Whether a résumé is one or two pages is determined by the skills and other information that best demonstrate your qualifications for a position. A two-page résumé is not more impressive than a one-page résumé if the information on the second page is irrelevant. On the other hand, you should not feel pressured to have a one-page résumé and then cram two pages of content onto one page; doing so will crowd the page and make important information less obvious to your reader. Printed résumés should be formatted so that they are visually appealing and easily read. Be sure that your name, the word *résumé*, and the page number appear on page two.

The attractiveness of your résumé will say as much about you as the words. The appearance of the information that the reader sees plays a part in forming his or her judgment. While using a template is one solution, it will make you look like many other applicants. A layout designed with your reader and your unique data in mind will probably do a better job for you. Not only will your résumé have a distinctive appearance, but the design should sell you more effectively than one where you must fit your data to the design. A sloppy, poorly designed presentation, on the other hand, may even ruin your chances of getting the job. Thus, an attractive physical arrangement is a must.

There is no one best arrangement, but a good procedure is to approach the task as a graphic designer would. Your objective is to design an arrangement of type and space that appeals to the eye.

Margins look better if at least an inch of space is left at the top of the page and on the left and right sides of the page and if at least 1½ inches of space are left at the bottom of the page. Your listing of items by rows and columns appears best if the items are short and if they can be set up in two uncrowded columns, one on the left side of the page and one on the right side. Longer items of information are more appropriately set up in lines extending across the page. In any event, you would do well to avoid long and narrow columns of data with large sections of wasted space on either side. Arrangements that give a heavy crowded effect also offend the eye. Extra spacing between subdivisions and indented patterns for subparts are especially pleasing to the eye.

The Most Important Six Seconds in Your Job Search

TheLadders, a company that matches career-seeking professionals with recruiters, recently published a study that used eye-tracking technology to measure how long recruiters looked at résumés before determining whether a candidate was a "fit" or "no fit."

How long do you think they took? Five minutes? Ten minutes? They took just six seconds. Of that six seconds, they spent 80 percent of that time looking at the candidate's name; current title/company; previous title/company; previous position start and end dates; current position start and end dates; and education.

When you think about the volume of résumés an employer might review every day, it's not surprising that an initial review takes only seconds. This means that job seekers must organize their content and format their résumés so that key skills and qualifications stand out.

SOURCE: Will Evans, "Keeping an Eye on Recruiter Behavior," *TheLadders.com*, TheLadders, 2012, Web, 6 July 2012.

As you set up columns and bulleted lists, you will want to use tables rather than your space bar or tab key. This will allow you more control over your formatting and ensure that the alignment of the information in your columns is consistent and perfect.

While layout is important in showing your ability to organize and good spacing increases readability, other design considerations such as font and paper selection affect attractiveness almost as much. Commercial designers say that type size for headings should be at least 12 to 14 points and for body text, 10 to 12 points. They also recommend using no more than two font styles. Some word processing programs have a "shrink to fit" feature that allows the user to fit information on one page. It will automatically adjust font sizes to fit the page. Be sure the resulting type size is both appropriate and readable.

Another factor affecting the appearance of your application documents is the paper you select. The paper should be appropriate for the job you seek. In business, erring on the conservative side is usually better; you do not want to be eliminated from consideration simply because the reader did not like the quality or color of the paper. The most traditional choice is white, 100 percent cotton, 20- to 28-lb. paper. Of course, reasonable variations can be appropriate. When you mail your printed résumé, do not fold it; mail it in a 9 × 12 envelope and be sure to type (not handwrite) the mailing labels.

Contrasting Bad and Good Examples. The following two résumés are at opposing ends of the quality scale. The first one, scant in coverage and poorly arranged, does little to help the applicant. Clearly, the second one is more complete and better arranged.

Résumé with Poor Arrangement and Incomplete Information. Shortcomings in the first example are obvious. First, the form is not pleasing to the eye. The weight of the type is heavy on the left side of the page. Failure to indent wrapped lines makes reading difficult.

This résumé also contains numerous errors in wording. The headings are not parallel in grammatical form. All are in topic form except the first one. The items listed under *Personal* are not parallel either and contain irrelevant and inappropriate personal information. Throughout, the résumé coverage is scant, leaving out many of the details needed to present the best impression of the applicant. Under *Experience*, little is said about specific tasks and skills in each job; and under *Education*, high school

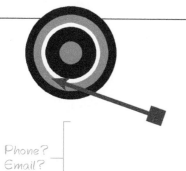

RÉSUMÉ

Julia M. Alvarez

3177 North Hawthorne Boulevard
St. Louis, MO 63139

Not needed

Name does not stand out

Bad form —Type heavily weighted to left

Phone? Email?

Personal

Age: 22
5 ft. 6 in. tall
Interests: tennis, fishing, reading
Active in sports
Weight: 140 lbs.
Memberships: Delta Sigma Pi, Sigma Iota Epsilon, Methodist Church, Olympia Community League

Not parallel and some unnecessary personal information

The font and other visual elements (e.g., underlining) are not inviting

Experience

2012—Intern, Upton Industries, St. Louis, MO
2011–Present—Team Lead, The GAP Inc., St. Louis, MO
2009–2011—Server, Applebee's, St. Louis, MO

Scant information on work done

Education

2008–2012—Wilmont University, Bachelor of Business Administration degree, major in human resources management, 16 semester hours in marketing and psychology courses, a 3.7 grade-point average, 3.9 in major field.
2004–2007—Roosevelt High School, St. Louis, MO

Facts run together

Not needed

References

Ms. June Rojas
Davidson Electric
St. Louis, MO

Prof. Helen K. Robbins
Wilmont University
St. Louis, MO 63139

Mr. Todd Frankle
Wayland Trucking Co.
47723 Beecher
St. Louis, MO

Prof. Carl Cueno
Wilmont University
St. Louis, MO 63139

References not needed; could use the space to describe skills and experience. Incomplete addresses— missing job titles, street addresses, and other contact information

Julia M. Alvarez

3177 North Hawthorne Boulevard
St. Louis, MO 63139
314.967.3117 (Voice/Message)
jmalvarez358@hotmail.com

Presents contact data clearly

Objective

To obtain a full-time position in human resources management specializing in safety and OSHA compliance.

Education

Bachelor of Business Administration
Wilmont University, St. Louis,
MO University—May 2013
GPA: 3.7/4.0

Major: Management:
    Human Resources Emphasis
Minor: Psychology
Certificate: Advanced Business
    Communication

Layout emphasizes key educational facts

Highlights most relevant courses and subjects

Related Coursework:
- Compensation Theory and Administration
- Organizational Change and Development
- Industrial Relations
- Advanced Human Resource Management

- Managerial Accounting
- Training and Human Resource Development

SHRM Certification

- Passed the Society for Human Resource Management (SHRM) Certification Examination

Internship

Human Resource Intern, Upton Industries, St. Louis, MO, June 2012–August 2012
- Consulted with management to ensure compliance with OSHA and state safety regulations
- Analyzed data from Upton's human resource database and created reports to guide management decisions
- Researched industry trends and reported them to management
- Participated in personnel-related tasks such as recruiting, reviewing candidates' resumes, conducting interviews, completing new hires' paperwork, training both new and current employees, determining compensation and benefits, and facilitating exit interviews
- Prepared timesheets for payroll

Special Project: Created and maintained an "HR News and Updates" page for the company intranet

Action verbs portray an image of a hard worker with good interpersonal skills

Employment

Team Lead, The Gap, Inc., St. Louis, MO, October 2011–Present
- Was promoted to Team Lead after two months of employment
- Was named top store sales associate four of eight quarters
- Create merchandise displays
- Train new sales associates
- Participate in interviews and hiring
- Set the weekly schedule

Host and Food Server, Applebee's, St. Louis, MO, September 2009 – September 2011
- Provided exceptional customer service
- Worked well as part of a team to seat and serve customers quickly and efficiently

Activities

Includes only most relevant information

Delta Sigma Pi (professional); Sigma Iota Epsilon (honorary), served as treasurer and president; Board of Stewards for church; Society for Human Resources Management (SHRM), served as chapter vice president

work is listed needlessly. The references are incomplete, omitting street addresses and job titles.

Traditional Print Résumé with Thoroughness and Good Arrangement. The revised résumé for Julia Alvarez (page 310) appears better at first glance, and it gets even better as you read it. It is attractively arranged. The information is neither crowded nor strung out. The balance is good. Its content is also superior to that of the other example. Additional words show the quality of Ms. Alvarez's work experience and education, and they emphasize points that make her suited for the work she seeks. This résumé excludes inappropriate personal information and has only the facts that tell something about Ms. Alvarez's personal qualities. A bulleted list of duties under each job describes the skills and qualities Ms. Alvarez brings to a human resources position. A separate references sheet (see Figure 10–4) with complete contact information permits the reader to contact the references easily. Job titles tell how each is qualified to evaluate the subject. Note that moving the references to a separate page frees space in the résumé for presenting Ms. Alvarez's qualifications.

Electronic Résumés

While some employers require printed résumés, others will require that you submit your résumé electronically via email or perhaps through an online application form or database. You might even want to create your own website to showcase your résumé or post a profile using sites such as LinkedIn (see Figure 10–6).

Preparing a résumé for electronic use requires more attention to software than it might if you were preparing a résumé to be read in printed form. For example, when you format your printed résumé, you can manipulate the software any way you wish to achieve the desired look or effect—and this is all right because all your reader needs is the final printed copy; he or she does not need to know what you did to get your document to look a particular way. However, if you send this formatted résumé to readers who will view it electronically, how you use software to format your résumé may affect how the document looks when the reader views it on a computer screen.

Creating an Unformatted Résumé. As you will learn in upcoming paragraphs, before you think about sending your résumé electronically, you'll want to have an **unformatted (plain-text) version** of your résumé to work with. A plain-text résumé contains no formatting (e.g., bold type, italics, tables, lists, bullets, centered text), which, as we discuss below, is useful when sending a résumé over email or submitting an application online. To create a plain-text résumé, just open your formatted résumé in Microsoft Word, select File > Save As > Save as Type dropdown list > "Plain text." You'll see that the file now has a .txt file extension. If you close the file and reopen it by clicking the file itself, the document will likely open in Notepad or WordPad. If you want to open the .txt file in Word, open Word first and then go to File > Open.

Sending Your Résumé via Email. If an employer requests that you send your résumé by email, he or she may specify how to submit it. Always follow those directions. In the absence of directions, you can place the résumé text in the body of the email, attach your formatted résumé to the email, or do both.

One reason to copy the text of your résumé into an email is that you will know your reader received the information. Another is that the reader may find it helpful to have the text in the body of the email—especially if he or she is using scanning software to screen candidates. If you're copying the text of your résumé into the body of the email, always copy from an unformatted résumé. You cannot be sure that your reader is able to read HTML or formatted messages; he or she may be only able to read plain-text messages. Copying from the unformatted document ensures that your text appears in plain format. It also saves you time from having to "unformat" anything you would have copied from your formatted résumé.

While copying the text of a résumé into the body of an email is functional, it does not leave you with a résumé as nice as the one you've formatted. For this reason, many job candidates will attach a copy of the **formatted résumé** to the email. It is especially important in formatted résumés sent as attachments that you do not format lists and blocks of text using the space bar or tab key. Many times when you do this, the attachment will look fine, but occasionally, the reader will open the file only to see text scattered across the page, as the tabs and the spacing were not preserved. To ensure that your text and lists stay aligned, use the ruler or a table (just be sure to turn off "View Gridlines" before emailing the document). Also be sure to use a **standard font** so that the font you use is the font the reader sees. For example, if you use Calibri but your reader is using an older version of Word that does not have Calibri, Word will substitute a new font. If you use Arial, a font all versions of Word have, you know your reader will see your document as you created it.

As a courtesy to your reader, be sure to use a **common file format** for attached documents. Because many people use Word, a .doc file or .docx file will work for most readers. In addition, include your name in the file name. Instead of a generic "résumé.doc," use "karen_jones_résumé.doc" so the reader can easily identify your résumé.

Lastly, always "test" your résumé by sending it and any attachments to yourself and a few others before sending it to an employer. One of the best ways to ensure that the résumé you create in Microsoft Word or other program looks the same to both your and your reader is to save the résumé as a PDF and attach it to your email. Word's "Save As" feature will let you save files as a PDF. If you are not using Word, free PDF converters are available online.

Submitting a Database or Online Job Application. If you're applying online, you may be asked to attach a résumé in the same way you would attach a file to an email. If this is the case, the same guidelines discussed above apply. However, applying online may require that you enter information into text boxes or fields. Because these fields are not likely to allow text formatting, you will want to copy the information from your unformatted résumé into the fields. Many times if you copy from a formatted résumé, you have to delete tabs or extra spaces, so copying from an unformatted résumé will save time. If you want to use any kind of formatting, you can always capitalize headings or use an asterisk (*) or hyphen (-) in place of a bullet.

Using a Webpage or Social Networking Site. Social networking sites such as LinkedIn provide an interface and design, making them a convenient way to present your professional qualifications. Figure 10–6 provides a sample of a well-designed LinkedIn page. Also, as we have mentioned, several free sites such as Weebly and Yola provide **professional templates** for creating personal webpages. All you need to do is input the content, following the guidelines presented earlier in this chapter. Whether you are creating your own webpage or using a template, you have a variety of options for creating a visually appealing, easily navigable Web résumé. The tips for Web writing presented in Chapter 6 can guide your design and presentation decisions; guidelines presented earlier in this chapter will help you develop the content.

Scannable Résumé

Some companies may require either in print or via email a résumé that can be scanned into a database and retrieved when a position is being filled. Since the objective is getting your résumé reviewed in order to be interviewed, you should use the following strategies to improve your chances of having it retrieved.

Include Keywords. One strategy, using **keywords**, is often recommended for use with **scannable résumés**. These keywords are usually nouns or concrete words that describe skills and accomplishments precisely. Instead of listing a course in comparative programming, you would list the precise languages compared, such as PHP, C++, and

Java. Instead of saying you would like a job in information systems, you would name specific job titles such as systems analyst, network specialist, or application specialist. Using industry-specific terminology is also persuasive.

Some ways to identify the keywords in your field are to read ads, listen to recruiters, and listen to your professors. Start building a list of words you find used repeatedly. From this list, choose those words most appropriate for the kind of work you want to do. Increase your use of abbreviations, acronyms, and jargon appropriate to the work you want to do.

Some experts recommend using a separate keyword section at the beginning of the résumé, loading it with all the relevant terms. If you use this technique, include the heading "Keywords" before your objective and follow it with 6 to 12 keywords. However, many résumé writers are well aware of the importance of using keywords and consciously work to integrate them into their résumés. Remember, though, to be ethical in your use of keywords from the job posting by using only those keywords that actually represent your qualifications.

Choose Words Carefully. Unlike the traditional résumé, the scannable résumé is strengthened not by the use of action verbs but rather by the use of nouns. Informal studies have shown that those retrieving résumés from such databases tend to use precise nouns when searching the database.

You may, however, prefer to combine the use of precise nouns with strong action verbs. The nouns will help ensure that the résumé gets pulled from the database, and if a recruiter pulls your résumé for further review, the verbs will help the recruiter see the link to the kind of work you want to do.

Present the Information. Since you want your résumé to be read accurately, you will use a font most scanners can read easily, such as Helvetica, Arial, and Times Roman. Most scanners can easily handle fonts between 10 and 14 points. Although many handle bold, when in doubt use all caps for emphasis rather than bold. Also, because italics often confuse scanners, avoid them. Underlining is best left out as well. It creates trouble with descending letters such as *g* or *y* when the line cuts through the letter. Also, avoid graphics and shading; they just confuse the software. Use white paper to maximize the contrast, and always print in the portrait mode. The Manny Konedeng résumé in Figure 10–9 is a scannable résumé employing these guidelines.

Today companies accept résumés by mail, fax, Web, and email. Be sure to choose the channel that serves you best. Some employers give the option to the sender. Obviously, when speed gives you a competitive advantage, you'll choose the fax, Web, or email options. If you elect to print and send a scannable résumé, do not fold it. Just mail it in a 9 × 12 envelope. For a little extra cost, you will help ensure that your résumé gets scanned accurately rather than wondering if your keywords were on a fold that a scanner might have had difficulty reading.

WRITING THE COVER MESSAGE

LO5 Write targeted cover messages that skillfully sell your abilities.

You should begin work on the cover message by fitting the facts from your background to the work you seek and arranging those facts in a logical order. Then you present them in much the same way that a sales writer would present the features of a product or service, carefully managing the appeal. Wherever possible, you adapt the points you make to the reader's needs.

Cover Letters

Cover letters come in two types: **solicited (invited)** and **unsolicited (prospecting)**. As their names suggest, a solicited letter is written in response to an actual job opening, and an unsolicited letter is written when you don't know whether a job exists but would

Figure 10–9

Scannable Résumé for Employers Who Use Scanning Software to Screen Résumés. Notice how the writer has expanded the length through some added text when no longer confined to one physical page.

Manny Konedeng
5602 Montezuma Road
Apartment 413
San Diego, California 92115
Phone: (619) 578-8058
Email: mkonedeng@yahoo.com

Avoids italics and underlines yet is arranged for both scanner and human readability

KEYWORDS

Finance major, bachelor's degree, leadership skills, ethics, communication, teamwork

OBJECTIVE

A financial analyst internship with a broker-dealer where both analytical and interpersonal communication skills and knowledge are valued

Uses all caps and spacing for enhanced human readability

EDUCATION

Bachelor of Science Degree in Business Administration, May 2012
San Diego State University, Finance Major

Dean's List
Current GPA: 3.32/4.00

Related Courses

Business Communication
Investments
Tax planning
Estate Planning
Risk Management
Business Law

All items are on one line and tabs avoided for improved comprehension

Computer Skills

Statistical Software: SAS, SPSS Excel, Word, PowerPoint, Access, QuickBooks
Web-based Applications: Surveymonkey, Blogger, GoToMeeting
Research Tools: Center for Research in Securities Prices (CRSP) stock price database and the Standard and Poor's Research Insight database of corporations' financial statements

Accomplishments

Published in Fast Company Magazine and the San Diego Union Tribune
Won Greek scholarship
Finished in top five mathematics competition

WORK EXPERIENCE

Powerhouse Gym, Sales and Front Desk, Summer 2012 Modesto, CA 95355

Sold memberships and facilitated tours for the fitness center
Listened to, analyzed, and answered customers' inquiries
Accounted for membership payments and constructed sales reports
Trained new employees to understand company procedures and safety policies

Integrates precise nouns and industry-specific jargon as keywords

MCI, Relay Operator, Summer 2010 & 2011, Riverbank, CA 95367

Assisted over 100 callers daily who were deaf, hard of hearing, or speech disabled to place calls
Exceeded the required data input of 60 wpm with accuracy
Multitasked with typing and listening to phone conversations
Was offered a promotion as a Lead Operator

Figure 10–9

(continued)

Fo Sho Entertainment, Co-founder and Owner, Aug. 2008–May 2010
Modesto, CA 95355

Led promotions for musical events in the Central Valley
Managed and hosted live concerts
Created and wrote proposals to work with local businesses
Collaborated with team members to design advertisements

UNIVERSITY EXPERIENCE

Information Decision Systems, Communications Tutor, Spring 2013,
San Diego, CA 92182
Critiqued and evaluated the written work for a business communica-
tion course

Set up and maintained blog for business communication research
Kappa Alpha Order Fraternity, Recruitment Chairman, Fall 2012,
San Diego, CA 92115
Supervised the selection process for chapter membership
Individually raised nearly $1,000 for chapter finances
Organized recruitment events with business sponsors, radio stations,
and special guests

Avoids graphics and extra lines

ACTIVITIES AND SERVICE

Campus Leadership

Recruitment Chair, Kappa Alpha Order Fraternity
Supervised all new member recruitment
Coordinated fundraisers for chapter finances
Organized recruitment events with business sponsors, radio stations,
and special guests
Advocated Greek Freshmen Summer Orientation and Greek life

Correspondent for External Chapter Affairs, Kappa Alpha Order
Fraternity
Communicated with chapter alumni and National Office to fulfill
chapter obligations

Upsilon Class Treasurer, Kappa Alpha Order Fraternity
Managed chapter budgets and expenditures
Held several Interfraternity Council Roles

Member, Fraternity Men against Negative Environments and Rape
Situations

Cochairman, Greek Week Fundraiser

Candidate, IFC Treasurer

Adds other relevant information since there is no physical page limit

Professional and Community Service

Member, Finance & Investment Society
Presenter, Peer Health Education
Marshal, SDSU New Student & Family Convocation
Volunteer, Muscular Dystrophy national philanthropy
Volunteer, Service for Sight philanthropy
Volunteer, Victims of Domestic Violence philanthropy
Volunteer, Camp Able philanthropy
Associated Students' Good Neighbor Program volunteer
Volunteer, Designated Driver Association
Volunteer, Beach Recovery Project

Uses black on white contrast for improved scanning accuracy

like to investigate the possibility of employment with a company. Generally, a cover letter is organized according to the following plan:

- An introduction that *gets the reader's attention* and *provides just a brief summary* of why you are interested or qualified or previews the information in the body of the letter. If you are writing a solicited letter, you will also mention where you learned of the position.
- A body that *matches your qualifications to the reader's needs*. You should also use good sales strategy, especially the you-viewpoint and positive language.
- A conclusion that *requests action* such as an interview and provides contact information that makes a response easy.

Figures 10–10 through 10–13 provide examples of effective cover letters.

Gaining Attention in the Opening. As in sales writing, the opening of the cover message has two requirements: It must gain attention and it must set up the information that follows.

Gaining attention is especially important in prospecting messages. Such letters are likely to reach busy executives who have many things to do other than read cover messages. Unless the résumé gains favorable attention right away, the potential employer probably will not read it. Even invited messages must gain attention because they will compete with other invited messages. Invited messages that stand out favorably from the beginning have a competitive advantage.

As the cover message is a creative effort, you should use your imagination in writing the opening, but the work you seek and your audience should guide your imagination. Take, for example, work that requires an outgoing personality and a vivid imagination such as sales or public relations. In such cases, you would do well to show these qualities in your opening words. At the opposite extreme is work of a conservative nature, such as accounting or banking. Openings in such cases should normally be more restrained.

In choosing the best opening for your case, you should consider whether you are writing a prospecting or an invited message. If the message has been invited, your opening words should refer to the job posting and begin qualifying you for the advertised work, as in these examples:

> Will an honors graduate in accounting, with experience in tax accounting, qualify for the work you listed in today's *Times*?

> Because of my specialized training in accounting at State University and my practical experience in cost-based accounting, I believe I have the qualifications you described in your *Journal* advertisement.

You can gain attention in the opening of an unsolicited letter in many ways. One way is to use a topic that shows understanding of the reader's operation or of the work to be

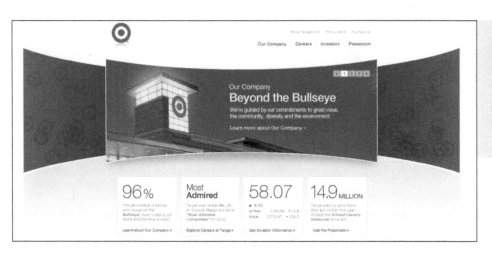

Companies often describe themselves and their career opportunities on their websites.

SOURCE: http://corporate.target.com/ Reprinted with permission of Target.

Figure 10–10

Sample Prospecting Email. Using a company executive's name to gain attention, this message is conservative in style and tone.

Molly H. Everson

From: Molly Everson
mheverson@creighton.edu

To: Marlene O'Daniel
modaniel@cic.org

SUBJECT: Application—Communications Specialist Position

Dear Ms. O'Daniel:

One of your employees, Victor Krause, suggested that I apply for the communications specialist position you have open. A summary and my résumé are attached for your review.

Gains attention with an associate's name

Presently, I am a communications intern for Atlas Insurance. My work consists primarily of writing a wide variety of documents for Atlas policyholders. This work has made me an advocate for well-crafted business communication, and it has sharpened my writing skills. More importantly, it has taught me how to get and keep customers for my company through writing well.

Employs a conservative style and tone

Shows the writer knows the skills needed for the job

Additional experience working with businesspeople has given me insight into the communication needs of business. This experience includes planning and presenting a communication improvement course for Atlas employees.

Uses subtle you-viewpoint—implied by the writer's understanding of the work

My college training provided a solid foundation for work in business communication. Advertising and public relations were my areas of concentration for my BS degree from Creighton University. As you will see on the enclosed résumé, I studied all available writing courses in my degree plan. I also studied writing through English and journalism courses.

References the résumé

Brings the review to a conclusion—fits the qualifications presented to the job

My education and experience have prepared me for work as your communication specialist. I know business writing, and I know how it can be used to your company's advantage. May we discuss this in an interview? You can reach me at 402-786-2575 to arrange a convenient time and place to meet.

Moves appropriately for action

Sincerely,

Molly H. Everson

Figure 10–11

An Interesting and Well-organized Cover Letter (Sent in Response to an Advertisement). Three job requirements listed in an advertisement determined the plan used in this letter.

4407 Sunland Avenue
Phoenix, AZ 85040-9321
July 8, 2013

Ms. Anita O. Alderson, Manager
Tompkins-Oderson Agency, Inc.
3901 Tampico Avenue
Los Angeles, CA 90032-1614

Dear Ms. Alderson:

Uses reader's words for good attention gainer

Sound background in advertising ... well trained ... works well with others....

Demonstrates ability to write advertising copy through writing style used

These keywords in your July 6 advertisement in the *Times* describe the person you want, and I believe I am that person.

Shows clearly what the writer can do on the job

I have gained experience in every area of retail advertising while working for the *Lancer*, our college newspaper. I sold advertising, planned layouts, and wrote copy. During the last two summers, I gained firsthand experience working in the advertising department of Wunder & Son. I wrote a lot of copy, some of which I am enclosing for your inspection; you will find numerous other examples on my blog at http://janekbits.blogspot.com. This experience will help me contribute to the work in your office.

Shows strong determination through good interpretation

In my major, I studied marketing with a specialization in advertising and integrated marketing communications. My honor grades show that I worked hard, especially on a project using a variety of media raising money for schools in Louisiana, Texas, and Mississippi's hurricane damaged areas. Understanding the importance of being able to get along well with people, I actively participated in Sigma Chi (social fraternity), the Race for the Cure (breast cancer fundraising event), and Pi Tau Pi (honorary business fraternity). The experience gained in these associations make me confident that I can fit in well at Tompkins-Oderson.

Provides good evidence of social skills

Leads smoothly to action

I ask that you review my qualifications and contact me for an interview. You can email me at janek@hotmail.com or call and text message me at 602-713-2199 to arrange a convenient time to talk about my joining your team.

Sincerely,

Michael S. Janek

Michael S. Janek

enclosures

Figure 10–12

Straightforward Prospecting Letter Sent as an Attached File to a Particular Receiver

12712 Sanchez Drive
San Bernadino, CA 92405
April 9, 2013

Mr. Conrad W. Butler
Office Manager
Darden, Inc.
14326 Butterfield Road
San Francisco, CA 94129

Dear Mr. Butler:

Gains attention with question

Can Darden, Inc., use a hardworking Grossmont College business administration major seeking an internship in management or office administration? My experience, education, and personal qualities have prepared me to contribute to your operations.

Sets up rest of letter

As the attached résumé indicates, I have worked as a receptionist for the past three summers. My duties have included managing a multi-line telephone system, using Excel and Access to monitor office traffic, and greeting visitors. I am excited about the possibility of developing more skills through an internship with Darden.

Brings out highlights with review of experience

Complementing my work experience are my studies at Grossmont College. In addition to studying the prescribed courses in my major field of business office technology, I have completed electives in Dreamweaver, QuickBooks, and professional speaking to help me in my career objective. In spite of full-time employment through most of my time in college, I was awarded the Associate of Arts degree last May with a 3.3 grade point average (4.0 basis). But most important, I am learning from my studies how office work can be done efficiently.

Interprets education facts for the reader

In addition, I have the personal qualities that would enable me to fit smoothly into your organization. I like people, and through work and academic experiences, I have learned how to work with them as both a team player and a leader.

Sets up action and uses adaptation in concluding statement

May I meet with you to talk about interning for Darden? Please call me at 714-399-2569 or email me at jgoetz@gmail.com to arrange an interview.

Requests action clearly and appropriately

Sincerely,

Jimmy I. Goetz

Jimmy I. Goetz

Enc.

Figure 10–13

A Form Prospecting Letter. Written by a recent college graduate seeking her first job, this letter was prepared for use with a number of different types of companies.

MARY O. MAHONEY

May 17, 2013

Mr. Nevil S. Shannon
Director of Personnel
Snowdon Industries, Inc.
1103 Boswell Circle
Baltimore, MD 21202

Dear Mr. Shannon:

Effective attention-getting question

Will you please review my qualifications for work in your management trainee program? My education, work attitude, and personal skills qualify me for this program.

Good organization plan setup

Good interpretation of education

My education for administration consists primarily of four years of business administration study at State University. The Bachelor of Business Administration degree I will receive in June has given me a broad foundation of business knowledge. As a general business major, I studied all the functional fields (management, marketing, information systems, finance, accounting) as well as the other core business subjects (communications, statistics, law, economics, production, and human resources). I have the knowledge base that will enable me to be productive now, and I can build upon this base through practical experience.

My grade point record at State is evidence that I took my studies seriously and that I worked hard. My 3.8 overall average (4.0 basis) placed me in the top 10 percent of the graduating class. I also worked diligently in student associations. My efforts were recognized by the special assignments and leadership roles you see listed on the enclosed résumé. I assure you that I would bring these work habits with me to Snowdon Industries.

Links qualifications to the company

Good use of fact to back up personal qualities

Throughout college, I developed my personal skills. As an active member of the student chapter of the Society for the Advancement of Management, I served as treasurer and program chairperson. I participated in intramural golf and volleyball, and I was an active worker in the Young Republicans, serving as publicity chairperson for three years. All this experience has helped me to have the balance you seek in your administrative trainees.

Good ending message

These highlights and the additional evidence presented in the enclosed résumé present my case for a career in management. May I have an interview to continue my presentation? You can reach me at 301.594.6942 or marymahoney@yahoo.com. Thank you for your consideration.

Clear request for action — flows logically from preceding presentation

Sincerely,

Mary O Mahoney

Mary O. Mahoney

Enclosure

1718 CRANFORD AVENUE • ROCKWELL, MD • 20854
VOICE/MESSAGE/FAX: 301.594.6942 • EMAIL: MARYMAHONEY@YAHOO.COM

Developing a Professional Portfolio

Imagine yourself in an interview. The interviewer says, "This position requires you to use PowerPoint extensively. How are your presentation and PowerPoint skills?" What do you say? Of course you say your skills are excellent. And so does everyone else who interviews.

One way you can set yourself apart from other applicants is to take a professional portfolio to an interview to demonstrate your qualifications. A portfolio may contain a title page, your résumé, references list, cover letter, a transcript, a program description, copies of licenses and certifications, work samples, letters of recommendation, personal mission statements—whatever creates your best

professional image. All you need to do is put your documents in sheet protectors in a professional looking three-ring binder for easy editing and updating and create tab dividers for the sections of the portfolio, and you're on your way. One note of advice, though: Protect your information by including a confidentiality statement; removing any student ID numbers, SSN numbers, or other private information from your documents; and using copies rather than originals of any licenses or certificates.

SOURCE: "Portfolios," *University of Wisconsin–Eau Claire Career Services*, University of Wisconsin–Eau Claire, 9 Mar. 2010, Web, 8 July 2012.

---

done. Employers are likely to be impressed by applicants who have made the effort to learn something about the company, as in this example:

> Now that Taggart, Inc., has expanded operations to Central America, can you use a broadly trained international business major who knows the language and culture of the region?

Another way is to make a statement or ask a question that focuses attention on a need of the reader that the writer seeks to fill. The following opening illustrates this approach:

> How would you like to hire a University of Cincinnati business major to fill in for your vacationing summer employees?

Sometimes one learns of a job possibility through a company employee. Mentioning the employee's name can gain attention, as in this opening sentence:

> At the suggestion of Mr. Michael McLaughlin of your staff, I am sending the following summary of my qualifications for work as your loan supervisor.

Many other possibilities exist. In the final analysis, you will have to use what you think will be best for the particular job you're seeking. But try to avoid the overworked beginnings that were popular a generation or two ago such as "This is to apply for . . ." or writer-centered beginings such as "I am writing to apply for . . ." or the tentative "I would like to apply for. . . ."

Selecting Content. Following the opening, you should present the information about your qualifications for the work. Begin this task by reviewing the job requirements. Then select the facts about you that qualify you for the job.

If your application has been invited, you may learn about the job requirements from the source of the invitation. If you are answering an advertisement, study it for the employer's requirements. If you are following up on an interview, review the interview for information about job requirements. If you are prospecting, your research and your logical analysis should guide you.

In any event, you are likely to present facts from three background areas: education, experience, and skills and/or personal details.

How much you include from each of these areas and how much you emphasize each area should depend on the job and on your background. Most of the jobs you will seek as a new college graduate will have strong educational requirements, and your education is likely to be your strongest selling point at this stage of your career. Thus, you should stress your education. When you apply for work after you have accumulated experience, you will probably need to stress experience. As the years go by, experience becomes more important and education less important. Your personal characteristics are of some importance for some jobs, especially jobs that involve working with people.

If a résumé accompanies the cover message, do not rely on it too much. Remember that the message does the selling, and the résumé summarizes the significant details. Thus, the message should contain the major points around which you build your case, and the résumé should include these points plus supporting details. As the two are parts of a team effort, somewhere in the message you should refer the reader to the résumé.

Organizing for Persuasion. You will want to present the information about yourself in the order that is best for you. In general, the plan you select is likely to follow one of three general orders. The most common order is a logical grouping of the information, such as education, experience, and skills and/or personal details. A second possibility is a time order. For example, you could present the information to show a year-by-year preparation for the work. A third possibility is an order based on the job requirements. For example, selling, communicating, and managing might be the requirements listed in an advertised job.

Merely presenting facts does not ensure conviction. You also will need to present the facts in words that make the most of your assets. Think of this as the difference between showing and telling. You could tell the reader, for example, that you "held a position" as sales manager, but it is much more convincing to say that you "supervised a sales force of 14," which actually shows your ability. Likewise, you do more for yourself by writing that you "earned a degree in business administration" than by writing that you "spent four years in college." And it is more effective to say that you "learned tax accounting" than to say that you "took a course in tax accounting."

You also can help your case by presenting your facts in reader-viewpoint language wherever this is practical. More specifically, you should work to interpret the facts based on their meaning for your reader. For example, you could present a cold recital like this one:

I am 21 years old and have an interest in mechanical operations and processes. Last summer I worked in the production department of a container plant.

Or you could interpret the facts, fitting them to the one job:

Last summer's experience working 10- and 12-hour days in the production department of Miller Container Company is evidence of my interest in mechanics and shows that I can and will work hard.

Since you will be writing about yourself, you may find it difficult to avoid overusing *I*-references, but an overuse of *I*'s sounds egotistical and places too much attention on the often repeated word. This creates the impression that you are more focused on yourself than you are on the reader's needs. Some *I*'s, however, should be used. The message is personal. Stripping it of all *I*-references would rob it of its personal warmth.

Overall, you are presenting your professional image, not only as a prospective employee but also as a person. Carefully shaping the character you are projecting is arguably just as important to the success of your cover message as using convincing logic.

Driving for Action in the Close. The presentation of your qualifications should lead logically to the action that the close proposes. You should drive for whatever action is appropriate in your case. It could be a request for an interview or an invitation to engage in further communication (perhaps to answer the reader's questions). Rarely would you want to ask for the job in a first message. You are concerned mainly with opening the door to further negotiations.

Websites Offer Valuable Interview Advice

The Web is a rich resource for help with interviewing. Your school's career center may have a website with interview advice, as well. Sites such as Monster.com and many of the other online job database sites offer tips on all aspects of interviewing. You can get ideas for questions to ask interviewers, techniques for staying calm, and methods of handling the telephone screening interview. They even include practice interactive virtual interviews with immediate feedback on your answers to questions as well as suggestions and strategies for handling difficult questions. The Monster site includes a planner listing a host of good commonsense tips from polishing your shoes to keeping an interview folder to keep track of all written and oral communication. Using these sites to help you prepare for interviews not only will help you feel more confident and interview more effectively but also will help you evaluate the company as well.

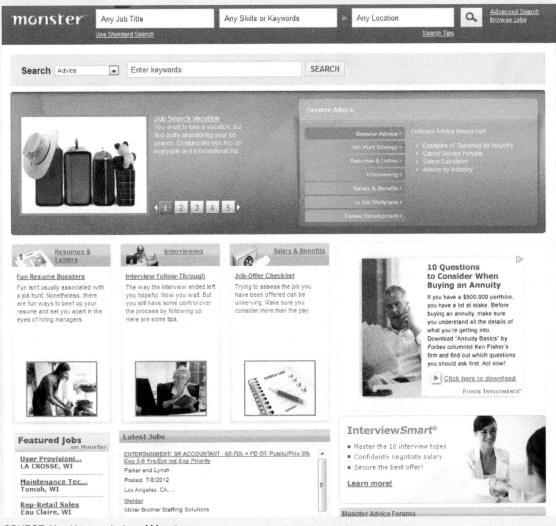

SOURCE: Used by permission of Monster.com.

Your action words should be clear and direct. As in the sales message, the request for action may be made more effective if it is followed by words recalling a benefit that the reader will get from taking the action. The following closes illustrate this technique:

> The highlights of my education and experience show that I have been preparing for a career in human resources. May I now discuss beginning this career with you? You can reach me at 727-921-4113 or by email at owensmith@att.com

I am very much interested in meeting for an interview to discuss with you how my skills can contribute to your company's mission.

Contrasting Cover Messages. Illustrating bad and good techniques, the following two prospecting messages present the qualifications of Julia M. Alvares, the job seeker described in the Introductory Challenge at the beginning of the chapter. The first message follows few of the suggestions given in the preceding pages, whereas the second message is in general accord with these suggestions.

A Bland and Artless Presentation of Information. The bad message begins with an old-style opening. The first words are of little interest. The presentation of qualifications that follows is a matter-of-fact, uninterpreted review of information. Little you-viewpoint is evident. In fact, most of the message emphasizes the writer (note the *I*'s), who comes across as bored and selfish. The information presented is scant. The closing action is little more than an I-viewpoint statement about the writer's availability.

This prospecting message is dull, selfish, and poorly written.

Dear Mr. Stark:

This is to apply for a position in marketing with your company.

At present, I am completing my studies in marketing at Wilmont University and will graduate with a Bachelor of Business Administration degree with an emphasis in human resource management this May. I have taken all the courses in marketing available to me as well as other helpful courses such as statistics, organizational psychology, and ecommerce.

I have had good working experience as a host and food server, a sales associate, and an HR intern. Please see details on the enclosed résumé. I believe that I am well qualified for a position in human resource management and am considering working for a company of your size and description.

Because I must make a decision on my career soon, I request that you write me soon. For your information, I will be available for an interview on March 17 and 18.

Sincerely,

Skillful Selling of One's Ability to Work. The better message begins with an interesting question that sets the stage for the rest of the contents. The review of experience is interpreted, showing how the experience would help the applicant perform the job. The review of education is similarly covered. Notice how the interpretations show that the writer knows what the job requires. Notice also that reader-viewpoint is stressed throughout. Even so, a moderate use of *I*'s gives the letter a personal quality, and the details show the writer to be a thoughtful, engaged person. The closing request for action is a clear, direct, and courteous question. The final words recall a main appeal of the letter.

This better prospecting message follows textbook instructions.

Dear Mr. Stark:

Is there a place in your Human Resource Department for someone who is well trained in the field and can talk easily and competently with employees? As a June graduate with a degree in human resource management and internship experience, I am well qualified to meet your needs.

My studies at Wilmont University were specially planned to prepare me for a career in human resource management. I have taken courses in compensation theory and administration, organizational change/development, and training and human resource development. As part of my degree requirements, I also passed the Society for Human Resource Management (SHRM) Certification Examination. In addition, I studied a wide assortment of supporting subjects: economics, business communication, information systems, psychology, interpersonal communication, and operations management. My studies have given me a solid foundation in HR work.

As my résumé shows, I have begun learning the practical side of HR through an internship, where I completed a variety of tasks from researching and reporting data on company and industry trends to participating in the hiring process. I would welcome the opportunity to continue working in HR with your company.

My work experiences have also prepared me for a career in human resource management. While in college I worked as a server at Applebee's, where I developed customer service and team skills, and I continued to develop my skills as a team lead for The Gap, where I was the top seller for four of eight quarters. From these experiences, I have learned to understand human resource management and listen carefully to people.

These brief facts and the information in my résumé describe my diligent efforts to prepare for a position in human resource management. May I now talk with you about beginning that position? You can reach me at 917.938.4449 to arrange an interview to discuss how I could fit in your Human Resource Department.

Sincerely,

Email Cover Messages

Like other email messages, an email cover message needs a clear subject line; like print cover messages, it needs a formal salutation and closing. And its purpose is still to highlight your qualifications for the particular job you are applying for. It can be identical to one you might create for print, or you may opt to introduce yourself and your purpose in a short email message and attach your full cover letter. The primary job of the email cover message is to identify the job, highlight the applicant's strengths, and invite the reader to review the résumé.

Notice how the solicited cover message below quickly gains the reader's attention in the opening, highlights the skills in the body, and calls for action in the close.

To: Kate Troy <kate_troy@thankyoutoo.com>
From: Jessica Franklin <jessica_franklin@yahoo.com>
Date: October 1, 2012
Subject: Web Design Intern Position

Dear Ms. Troy:

Yesterday my advisor here at Brown University, Dr. Payton Kubicek, suggested that I contact you about the summer intern position in Web design you recently announced.

At Brown I have taken courses that have given me a good understanding of both the design aspects and the marketing elements of that a good website needs. Additionally, several of my course projects involved working with successful Web-based businesses, analyzing the strengths and weaknesses of their business models.

I would enjoy applying some of these skills to help build a successful site targeted at the high-end retail customers that Thankyoutoo.com attracts. You will see from my webpage profile at www.jessicafranklin.com/ that my design preferences and styles complement those on your company's website, allowing me to contribute almost immediately. I can be available for an interview at any time the rest of this month.

Sincerely,

Jessica Franklin
jessica_franklin@yahoo.com

LO6 Explain how you can participate effectively in an interview.

HANDLING THE INTERVIEW

Your initial contact with a prospective employer can be by mail, email, phone, or a personal (face-to-face) visit. If all goes well, your application will eventually involve a personal visit—an interview. Sometimes, before inviting candidates to a formal interview session, recruiters use phone interviews for preliminary screening.

In a sense, the interview is the key to the success of the application—the "final examination." You should carefully prepare for the interview, as the job may be lost or won in it. The following review of employment interview highlights should help you do your best in your interviews. You will find additional information about interviewing on the textbook website.

Investigating the Company

Before arriving for an interview, you should learn what you can about the company: its products or services, its personnel, its business practices, its current activities, its management. Such knowledge will help you talk knowingly with the interviewer. And perhaps more important, the interviewer is likely to be impressed by the fact that you took the time to investigate the company. That effort can even give you an advantage.

Making a Good Appearance

How you look to the interviewer is a part of your message. Thus, you should work to present just the right image. Interviewers differ to some extent on what that image is, but you would be wise to present a conservative appearance. This means avoiding faddish, offbeat styles, preferring the conservative, conventional business colors such as black, brown, navy, and gray. Remember that the interviewer wants to know whether you fit into the role you are seeking. You should look like you are right for the job.

Answers to the 10 Toughest Interview Questions

Forbes recently published the following advice regarding common interview questions and their answers.

1. **Why should I hire you?** Know the job description and then tie your skills and knowledge to the employer's specific needs.

2. **Why is there a gap in your work history?** Explain the reason (employers understand that there are good reasons for being unemployed), but dwell on what you did during the gap, such as taking classes, taking care of family members, or volunteering.

3. **Tell me one thing you would change about your last job.** Be careful not to criticize your previous employer (no one likes a complainer), and be prepared to tell why you didn't change what you didn't like. Pick a safe topic such as updating the technology.

4. **Tell me about yourself.** Because this is a "warm-up" question for the rest of the interview, give yourself only a minute or two. Summarize your early experience, your education, your work history, and your current experience (with emphasis on the current experience). Do not talk about your "weekend activities."

5. **Explain a complicated database (or any other concept or procedure) to your eight-year-old nephew.** Your answer should show you know your industry so well that you could explain it even to an eight-year-old. Do your research and be able to talk about your field.

6. **What would the person who likes you least in the world say about you?** Pick a true fault that could be leveraged as a strength (e.g., impatience).

7. **Tell me about a time when old solutions didn't work.** The employer is testing your creativity and problem-solving ability. A good topic might be a time when you had to learn a new technology to accomplish a task.

8. **What's the biggest risk you've ever taken?** The employer is assessing your resiliency and your ability to make good decisions. Be sure you have examples of risks that paid off.

9. **Have you ever had a supervisor challenge a decision?** Your answer to this indicates your ability to take direction and remain humble. Focus on what you learned from the situation rather than the situation itself.

10. **Describe a time when your team did not agree.** The employer sees your answer as an indicator of how you will behave in the workplace. Make sure your answer focuses on the process—what happened, what you did, and what you learned. Concisely describe how your group came to consensus.

SOURCES: Meghan Casserly, "Why Are Manholes Round? The 10 Toughest Interview Questions," *Forbes*, Forbes.com, 27 July 2011, Web, 8 July 2012; Forbes, "10 Toughest Interview Questions: Answered," *Forbes*, Forbes.com, n.d., Web, 8 July 2012.

Some may argue that such an insistence on conformity in dress and grooming infringes on one's personal freedom. Perhaps it does, but if the people who can determine your future have fixed views on matters of dress and grooming, it is good business sense to respect those views.

Anticipating Questions and Preparing Answers

You should be able to anticipate some of the questions the interviewer will ask. Questions about your education (courses, grades, honors) are usually asked. So are questions about work experience, interests, career goals, location preferences, and activities in organizations. You should prepare answers to these questions in advance. Your answers will then be thorough and correct, and your words will display poise and confidence. Your preparation will also reflect your interest.

In addition to general questions, interviewers often ask more complicated ones. Some of these are designed to test you—to learn your views, your interests, and your ability to deal with difficult problems. Others seek more specific information about your ability to handle the job in question. Although such questions are difficult to anticipate, you should be aware that they are likely to be asked. Following are questions of this kind that one experienced interviewer asks:

What can you do for us?

Would you be willing to relocate? To travel?

Do you prefer to work with people or alone?

How well has your performance in the classroom prepared you for this job?

What do you expect to be doing in 10 years? In 20 years?

What income goals do you have for those years (10 and 20 years ahead)?

Why should I rank you above the others I am interviewing?

Why did you choose _____ for your career?

How do you feel about working overtime? Nights? Weekends?

Did you do the best work you are capable of in college?

Is your college record a good measure of how you will perform on the job?

What are the qualities of the ideal boss?

What have you done that shows leadership potential? Teamwork potential?

What are your beginning salary expectations?

Sometimes interviewers will throw in tough questions to test your poise. The Communication Matters box on page 327 provides some examples of these questions and provides tips for answering them.

Some questions, though, may not be legal regardless of the interviewer's intent, whether the interviewer is making small talk, is unaware the questions are illegal, plans to discriminate against you, or just wants to test whether you respond. How you respond is up to you; before you respond, you may want to ask how the question is relevant to the position, or you may politely decline to answer.

What religion do you practice?

How old are you?

Are you married?

Do you plan to have children?

Recently, the **behavioral interview style** has become popular with campus recruiters. Rather than just determining your qualifications for the job, interviewers are attempting to verify if you can do the work. They ask questions about what you would do in certain situations because how you behave now is likely to transfer to similar situations in another job. Here are a few examples of behavioral questions:

What major problem have you faced in group projects and how have you dealt with it?

Do you tend more toward following the rules or toward stretching them?

Describe a conflict you had with someone and how you resolved it.

Keep your answers concise. Briefly state the situation, describe the steps you took, and summarize the results. You can also share what you learned from the experience. For more practice preparing for questions, check the resource links on the textbook website.

Putting Yourself at Ease

Perhaps it is easier to say than to do, but you should be calm throughout the interview. Remember that you are being inspected and that the interviewer should see a calm and collected person. Appearing calm involves talking in a clear and strong voice. It also involves controlling your facial expressions and body movements. Developing such controls requires self-discipline and reassuring self-talk. You may find it helpful to convince yourself that the stress experienced during an interview is normal. Or you may find it helpful to look at the situation realistically—as merely a conversation between two human beings. Practicing your answers to common interview questions out loud may be helpful. You may even want to record one of these practice sessions and analyze your performance. Your school's career services office may be able to help

What's the Number One Interviewing Mistake?

According to Jessica Liebman, managing editor of the business-news site *Business Insider*, the number one interview mistake isn't wearing the wrong clothes, showing up with a cup of coffee, being late, having a limp handshake, or opening the interview by asking if you'll get a free iPad.

It's an action (or nonaction) that takes place after the interview—namely, failing to send a thank-you message. As Liebman says, even a brief email of thanks helps seal a positive impression, whereas no message indicates that

"you don't want the job" or "you're disorganized and forgot about following up."

So the next time you have an interview, be sure you get everyone's name. As soon as possible after the interview (preferably the same day), send your interviewers a thank-you email. It could mean the difference between getting your job and continuing your search.

SOURCE: Jessica Liebman, "The Number One Mistake People I Interview Are Making These Days," *Business Insider*, Business Insider, 24 Feb. 2012, Web, 8 July 2012.

---

with this. Other approaches may work better for you. Use whatever approaches work. Your goal is to control your emotions so that you present the best possible appearance to the interviewer.

Helping to Control the Dialogue

Just answering the questions asked is often not enough. Not only are you being evaluated, but you are evaluating others as well. The questions you ask and the comments you make should bring up what you want the interviewer to know about you. Your self-analysis revealed the strong points in your background. Now you should make certain that those points come out in the interview.

How to bring up points about you that the interviewer does not ask is a matter for your imagination. For example, a student seeking a job in advertising believed that her teamwork skills should be brought to the interviewer's attention. So at an appropriate time in the interview, she asked, "How important is the ability to collaborate in this company?" The anticipated answer—"very important"—allowed her to discuss her skills. To take another example, a student who wanted to bring out his knowledge of the prospective employer's operations did so with this question: "Will your company's expansion in the Madison area create new job opportunities there?" How many questions of this sort you should ask will depend on your need to supplement your interviewer's questioning. You might also want to ask questions to determine if the company is a good fit for you such as "How would you describe the work environment here?" Your goal should be to make certain that both the interviewer and you get all the information you consider important.

FOLLOWING UP AND ENDING THE APPLICATION

LO7 Write application follow-up messages that are appropriate, friendly, and positive.

The interview is only an early step in the application process. A variety of other steps can follow. Sending a brief thank-you message email is an essential follow-up step. Not only does it show courtesy, but it can also give you an advantage because some of your competitors will not do it. If you do not hear from the prospective employer within a reasonable time, it is appropriate to inquire by telephone, email, or letter about the status of your application. You should certainly do this if you are under a time limit on another employer's offer. The application process may end with no offer (frequently with no notification at all—a discourteous way of handling applicants), with a rejection notice, or with an offer. How to handle these situations is reviewed in the following paragraphs.

Other Job-Search Messages

Writing a Thank-You Message. After an interview it is courteous to write a thank-you message, whether or not you are interested in the job. If you are interested, the message can help your case. It singles you out from the competition and shows your interest in the job.

Such messages are usually short. They begin with an expression of gratefulness. They say something about the interview, the job, or the company. They take care of any additional business (such as submitting information requested). Then they end on a goodwill note—perhaps a hopeful look to the next step in the negotiations. While you can send your message by mail, an email will more quickly convey your thanks. The following message illustrates:

> Dear Mr. Woods:
>
> Thank you for talking with me yesterday about the finance internship. I enjoyed learning more about Sony Corporation of America and the financial analyst position.
>
> As you requested, I have enclosed samples of the financial analysis I developed as a class project. If you need anything more, please let me know.
>
> I look forward to the possibility of discussing employment with you soon.
>
> Sincerely,

Constructing a Follow-up to an Application. When a prospective employer is late in responding or you receive another offer with a time deadline, you may need to write a **follow-up message**. Employers are often just slow, but sometimes they lose the application. Whatever the explanation, a follow-up message may help to produce action.

Such a message is a form of routine inquiry. As a reason for writing, it can use the need to make a job decision or some other good explanation. The following message is an example:

> Dear Ms. Yang:
>
> Because the time is approaching when I must make a job decision, could you please tell me the status of my application with you?
>
> You may recall that you interviewed me in your office November 7. You wrote me November 12 indicating that I was among those you had selected for further consideration.
>
> SAIC remains one of the organizations I would like to consider in making my career decision. I will very much appreciate hearing from you by December 3.
>
> Sincerely,

Planning the Job Acceptance. Job acceptances in writing are merely favorable response messages with an extra amount of goodwill. Because the message should begin directly, a "yes" answer in the beginning is appropriate. The remainder of the message should contain a confirmation of the starting date and place and comments about the work, the company, the interview—whatever you would say if you were face to face with the reader. The message need not be long. This one does the job well:

> Dear Ms. Garcia:
>
> Yes, I accept your offer of employment as a junior analyst. After my first interview with you, I was convinced that Allison-Caldwell was the organization for me. I am delighted that you think I am right for Allison-Caldwell.
>
> Following your instructions, I will be in your Toronto headquarters on May 28 at 8:30 AM ready to work for you. Thank you for this opportunity.
>
> Sincerely,

Writing a Message Refusing a Job. Messages refusing a job offer follow the indirect refusal pattern. One good technique is to begin with a friendly comment—perhaps something about past relations with the company. Next, explain and present the refusal in clear yet positive words. Then end with a more friendly comment. This example illustrates the plan:

> Dear Mr. Chen:
>
> Meeting you and the other people at Northern was a genuine pleasure. Thank you for sharing so much information with me and for the generous job offer.
>
> I was impressed with all I learned about Northern, and as we discussed, a special interest of mine is to work abroad. After considerable thought, I have decided to accept an offer with a firm that has extensive opportunities along these lines.
>
> I appreciate the time and the courteous treatment you gave me.
>
> Sincerely,

Writing a Resignation. At some point in your career you are likely to resign from one job to take another. When this happens, you will probably inform your employer of your resignation orally. But when you find it more practical or comfortable, you may choose to resign in writing. In some cases, you may do it both ways. As a matter of policy, some companies require a written resignation even after an oral resignation has been made.

Your resignation should be as positive as the circumstances permit. Even if your work experiences have not been pleasant, you will be wise to depart without a final display of anger. As an anonymous philosopher once explained, "When you write a resignation in anger, you write the best letter you will ever regret."

The indirect order is usually the best strategy for negative messages like a resignation. But some are written in the direct order. They present the resignation right away, following it with expressions of gratitude or favorable comments about past working experiences. Either approach is acceptable. Even so, you would do well to use the indirect order because it is more likely to build the goodwill you want to leave behind you.

The example below illustrates the indirect order. It begins with a positive point— one that sets up the negative message. The negative message follows, clearly yet positively stated. The ending returns to positive words chosen to build goodwill and fit the case.

> Dear Ms. Shuster:
>
> Working as your assistant for the past five years has been a genuinely rewarding experience. Under your direction I have grown as an administrator, and I have learned a great deal from you about retailing.
>
> As you may recall from our past discussions, I have been pursuing the same career goals that you held early in your career, so you will understand why I am now resigning to accept a store management position with Lawson's in Belle River. I would like my employment to end on the 31st, but I could stay a week or two longer if needed to help train my replacement.
>
> I leave with only good memories of you and the other people with whom I worked. Thanks to all of you for a valuable contribution to my career.
>
> Sincerely,

Continuing Job-Search Activities

LO8 Maintain your job-search activities.

Continuously keeping your finger on the pulse of the job market is a good idea. Not only does it provide you with information about changes occurring in your field, but it also keeps you alert to better job opportunities as soon as they are announced.

Maintaining Your Résumé. While many people intend to keep their résumés up to date, they just do not make it a priority. Some others make it easy by updating as changes occur. And a few update their résumés at regularly designated times such as a birthday, New Year's Day, or even the anniversary of their employment. No matter what works best for you, updating your résumé as you gain new accomplishments and skills is important. Otherwise, you will be surprised to find how easily you can lose track of important details.

Reading Job Ads/Professional Journals. Nearly as important as keeping your résumé updated is keeping up on your professional reading. Most trade or professional journals have job notices or bulletin boards you should check regularly. These ads give you insight into what skills are in demand, perhaps helping you choose assignments where you get the opportunity to develop new skills. Staying up to date in your field can be stimulating; it can provide both challenges and opportunities.

THERE'S MORE . . .

Would you like to learn more about impressing an interviewer? Do you need tips for developing your LinkedIn profile? Are you interested in taking a personality inventory to see what careers you might be suited for? Scan the QR code with your smartphone or use your Web browser to visit www.mhhe.com/lesikar13e. Choose Chapter 10 > Bizcom Tools & Tips.

SUMMARY BY LEARNING OBJECTIVES

Develop and use a network of contacts in your job search.

1. A good first step in your job search is to build a network of contacts.
   - Get to know people who might help you later: classmates, professors, and businesspeople.
   - Use their knowledge to help you find a job.
   - Obtain an internship to develop your skills and build your network.

Assemble and evaluate information that will help you select a job.

2. When you are ready to find work, analyze yourself and outside factors.
   - Look at your education, personal qualities, and work experience.
   - From this review, determine what work you are qualified to do.
   - Then select the career that is right for you.

Identify the sources that can lead you to an employer.

3. When you are ready to find a job, use the contact sources available to you.
   - Check university career centers, personal contacts, advertisements, online sources, employment agencies, personal search agents, and webpage profiles.
   - If these do not produce results, prospect by mail.

Compile résumés for print and electronic environments that are strong, complete, and organized.

4. In your application efforts, you are likely to use résumés and cover messages. Prepare them as you would written sales material.
   - First, study your product—you.
   - Then study your prospect—the employer.
   - From the information gained, construct the résumé, cover message, and reference sheet.

   In preparing the traditional résumé, follow this procedure:
   - List all the facts about you that an employer might want to know.

- Sort these facts into logical groups: *experience, education, personal qualities, references, achievements, highlights.*
- If you include your references list them on a separate page. Use complete mailing addresses, and have a reference for each major job held.
- Include other helpful information: address, telephone number, email address, website address, and career objective.
- Write headings for the résumé and for each group of information; prefer descriptive headings.
- Organize for strength when choosing the reverse chronological, functional/ skills, or accomplishment/highlights approach.
- Write the résumé without personal pronouns, make the parts parallel grammatically, and use words that help sell your abilities.
- Present the information with good visual appeal, selecting font sizes that show the importance of the headings and the information.
- Present the facts. At a minimum, include job experience (dates, places, firms, duties) and education (degrees, dates, fields of study). Use some personal information, but omit race, religion, sex, marital status, and age.

In preparing the scannable résumé, follow these procedures:

- Include industry-specific keywords.
- Choose precise nouns over action verbs.
- Present the information in a form that can be read accurately by scanners.

Consider whether your reader will view the résumé in printed (hardcopy) or electronic format.

For printed résumés

- Keep printed résumés to one or two pages.
- Include a header on page two.
- Make sure the document is visually appealing and easy to read.

For résumés sent electronically

- Create an unformatted version of your text.
- Use the appropriate format when sending résumés by email:
  — Use unformatted text when sending the résumé in the body of an email.
  — Attach a formatted résumé that uses software properly to align text.
  — Use a common font.
  — Save your résumé as a .doc, .docx, or PDF file and include your name.
  — Send your résumé to yourself and others to test that it looks as you intend it to.
- Use unformatted text when copying and pasting résumé content into a database or online application.
- Use social networking sites or other free services to create an online résumé.

5. As the cover message is a form of sales message, plan it as you would a sales message.

Write targeted cover messages that skillfully sell your abilities.

- Study your product (you) and your prospect (the employer) and think out a strategy for persuasion.
- Begin with words that gain attention, indicate that you are applying for the job, and set up the presentation of your sales points (briefly describe your qualifications).
- Adapt the tone and content to the job you seek.
- Present your qualifications, fitting them to the job you seek.
- Choose words that enhance the information presented.
- Drive for an appropriate action—an interview, further communication, reference checks.

Explain how you can participate effectively in an interview.

6. Your major contact with a prospective employer is the interview. For best results, you should do the following:

- Research the employer in advance so you can adapt your communication to the audience.
- Present a good appearance through appropriate dress and grooming.
- Try to anticipate the interviewer's questions and to plan your answers.
- Make a good impression by being at ease.
- Help the interviewer establish a dialogue with questions and comments that enable you to present the best information about you.

Write application followup messages that are appropriate, friendly, and positive.

7. You may need to write other messages in your search for a job.

- Following the interview, a thank-you message is essential.
- Also appropriate is an inquiry about the status of an essential.
- You also may need to write messages accepting, rejecting, or resigning a job.
- Write these messages much as you would the messages reviewed in preceding chapters: direct order for good news, indirect order for bad.

Maintain your job-search skills

8. To learn information about the changes occurring in your field and to be aware of better job opportunities, you should

- Maintain your résumé.
- Read both job ads and professional journals.

KEY TERMS

job search, 285

network of contacts, 285

internships, 286

personal qualities, 286

personality tests, 287

interest inventory, 288

job-search counseling, 289

career fairs, 289

executive search consultants, 289

employment agencies, 289

personal search agents or job agents, 291

statement of your objective, 295

action-oriented, past tense verbs, 296

simple present tense verbs, 296

reference sheet, 298

reverse chronological organizational layout, 301

functional or skills layout, 301

accomplishments/achievements layout, 301

unformatted (plain-text) version, 311

formatted résumé, 312

standard font, 312

common file format, 312

professional templates, 312

keywords, 312

scannable résumés, 312

solicited (invited) and unsolicited (prospecting), 313

behavioral interview style, 328

follow-up message, 330

CRITICAL THINKING QUESTIONS

1 "Building a network of contacts to find jobs seems selfish. It involves acquiring friendships just to use them for one's personal benefit." Discuss this view. **LO1**

2 Do employers who offer unpaid internships take unfair advantage of students' knowledge and skills? Under what circumstances might it be a good idea to take an unpaid internship? When might it not be a good idea? **LO1**

3 Maryann Brennan followed a broad program of study in college and received a degree in general management.

She did her best work in English, especially in the writing courses. She also did well in history, managerial leadership, organizational behavior, and psychology. As much as she could, she avoided math and computer courses.

Her overall grade point average of 3.7 (4.0 basis) placed her in the top 10 percent of her class. What advice would you give her as she begins her search for a career job? **LO1, 2, 3**

4 Discuss the value of each of the sources for finding jobs (a) before an internship, (b) right after graduation, and (c) after 20 years of work in a specialty. **LO1, 2, 3**

5 Assume that, in an interview for the job you want, you are asked the questions listed in the text under the heading "Anticipating Questions and Preparing Answers." Answer these questions. **LO6**

6 The most popular arrangement of résumé information is the three-part grouping: education, experience, and personal details. Describe two other arrangements. When would each be used? **LO4**

7 Distinguish between the print résumé and the electronic résumé. When would each be most appropriate? **LO4**

8 What is meant by *parallelism of headings*? **LO4**

9 Describe the cover message and résumé you would write (a) immediately after graduation, (b) 10 years later, and (c) 25 years later. Point out similarities and differences, and defend your decisions. **LO2, 4, 5**

10 What differences would you suggest in writing cover messages for jobs in (a) accounting, (b) banking, (c) advertising copy writing, (d) management, (e) sales, (f) consulting, and (g) information systems? **LO5**

11 Discuss the appropriateness of beginning a cover message with these words: "This is to apply for . . ." and "I would like to. . . ." **LO5**

12 "In writing cover messages, just present the facts clearly and without analysis and interpretation. The facts alone will tell the employer whether he or she wants you." Discuss this viewpoint. **LO5**

13 When should the drive for action in a cover message (a) request the job, (b) request an interview, and (c) request a reference check? **LO5**

14 Discuss some of the advantages that writing a thank-you note to the interviewer gives the writer. **LO7**

15 Identify some of the benefits one gains from continuing to read professional journals for job information after one is employed. **LO8**

SKILLS BUILDING EXERCISES

1 Criticize the following excerpts from résumés. (They are not from the same résumé.) **LO4**

a. **Work Experience**

2009–2012 Employed as sales rep for Lloyd-Shanks Tool Company

2006–2009 Office manager, Drago Plumbing Supply, Toronto

2003–2006 Matson's Super Stores. I worked part time as sales clerk while attending college.

b. **References**

Mr. Carl T. Whitesides
Sunrise Insurance, Inc.
317 Forrest Lane
Dover, DE 19901-6452

Patricia Cullen
Cullen and Cullen Realtors
2001 Bowman Dr.
Wilmington, DE 19804

Rev. Troy A. Graham
Asbury Methodist Church
Hyattsville, MD 20783

D. W. Boozer
Boozer Industries
Baltimore, MD 21202

c. **Education**

2012   Graduated from Tippen H.S. (I was in top 10 percent of class.)

2012   BS from Bradley University with major in marketing

2012 to   Enrolled part time in MBA program at
present   the University of Phoenix

d. **Qualifications**

- Know how to motivate a sales force. I have done it.
- Experienced in screening applicants and selecting salespeople.
- Know the pharmaceutical business from 11 years of experience.
- Knowledgeable about realistic quota setting and incentives.
- Proven leadership ability.

2. Criticize these sentences from cover messages: **LO5**

Beginning Sentences

a. Please consider this my application for any position for which my training and experience qualify me.

b. Mr. Jerry Bono of your staff has told me about a vacancy in your loan department for which I would like to apply.

c. I am that accountant you described in your advertisement in today's *Times-Record*.

d. I want to work for you!

Sentences Presenting Selling Points

e. From 2009–2013 I attended Bradley University where I took courses leading to a BS degree with a major in finance.

f. I am highly skilled in trading corporate bonds as a result of three years spent in the New York office of Collins, Bragg, and Weaver.

g. For three years (2009–2012) I was in the loan department at Bank One.

h. My two strongest qualifications for this job are my personality and gift of conversation.

Sentences from Action Endings

i. I will call you on the 12th to arrange an interview.

j. If my qualifications meet your requirements, it would be greatly appreciated if you would schedule an interview for me.

k. Please call to set up an interview. Do it now—while it is on your mind.

PROBLEM-SOLVING CASES

1 You have successfully prepared yourself for the career of your choice, but the recruiters visiting your school have not yet offered you a job. Now you must look on your own. So by searching newspapers, online job databases, and company website announcements, find the best job for which you believe you are qualified. Write two cover messages that you might use to present your qualifications for this job: one for print presentation and one for email. Attach a copy of the job description to the messages. Write the résumé and reference sheet to accompany the message.

2 Project yourself three years past your graduation date. During those years, you have had good experience working for the company of your choice in the field of your choice. (Use your imagination to supply this information.)

Unfortunately, your progress hasn't been what you had expected. You think that you must look around for a better opportunity. Your search through the classified advertisements in your area newspapers, online, and in *The Wall Street Journal*, and you turn up one promising possibility (you find it). Write a cover message that skillfully presents your qualifications for this job. (You may make logical assumptions about your experience over the three-year period.) For class purposes, attach the advertisement to your message. Write the résumé and reference sheet to accompany the message.

3 Assume you are in your last term of school, and graduation is just around the corner. Your greatest interest is in finding work that you like and that would enable you to support yourself now and to support a family as you win promotions.

No job of your choice is revealed in the want ads of newspapers and trade magazines. No career center has provided anything to your liking. So you decide to do what any good salesperson does: survey the product (yourself) and the market (companies that could use a person who can do what you are prepared to do) and then advertise (send each of these companies a résumé with a cover message). This procedure sometimes creates a job where none existed before, and sometimes it establishes a basis for negotiations for the "big job" two, three, or five years after graduation. And very frequently, it puts you on the list for the good job that is not filled through advertising or from the company staff. Write the cover message. Write the résumé and reference sheet to accompany the message.

4 Move the calendar to your graduation date so that you are now ready to sell your working ability in the job market. Besides canvassing likely firms with the help of prospecting messages and diligently following up family contacts, you have decided to look into anything that appears especially good in the ads of newspapers, online sources, and magazines. The latest available issues of large city publications and online services yield the jobs listed below.

Concentrate on the ad describing the job you would like most or could do best—and then write a cover message that will get you that job. Your message will first have to survive the filtering that eliminates dozens (sometimes hundreds) of applicants who lack the expected qualifications. Toward the end you will be getting into strong competition in which small details give you the superiority that will get you an interview.

Study your chosen ad for what it says and even more for what it implies. Weigh your own preparation even more thoroughly than you weigh the ad. You may imagine far enough ahead to assume completion of all the courses that are planned for your degree. You may build up your case a bit beyond what you actually have. Sort the qualifications for the job, organize them strategically, and then present them in a cover letter. Write a résumé and reference sheet to accompany your message.

a. *Office manager.* Currently seeking an office manager with initiative and flexibility for work in a fast-paced environment. Must have an outgoing personality and excellent communication skills and be a team player. Must be a "power user" of Word and Excel and have excellent Internet search skills. Knowledge of PowerPoint a plus. Some overtime expected during crunch periods. Send application materials to Chris Eveland at ceveland@qconline.com.

b. *Assistant webmaster.* Outstanding information technology, organizational, and interpersonal skills are needed for work on a company portal. Mastery of HTML and PHP, experience with website design including graphic design, and knowledge of client/server technology are vital. Candidates should be able to communicate with international audiences.

Candidates also must possess excellent writing skills and the ability to effectively manage multiple projects while interfacing with company employees. A bachelor's degree with a background in information systems, marketing, or communications is required. Please send résumé to Megan Adami in Human Resources, 7165 North Main Street, (your city), or fax it to 1-888-444-5047, or email it to megan_adami@ cnet.com.

c. *Management trainee.* Named by *Fortune* magazine as one of the best places to work, this constantly expanding international company uses shared decision making and clear career paths so that employees can be productive and well rewarded. The challenging management training program requires candidates with good communications skills and high energy levels to be successful. Applicants must be computer literate and possess good interpersonal skills. Fax résumé to Don Zatyko at 1-888-399-2569.

d. *Staff accountant—payroll specialist.* We are looking for an accountant who desires to grow and move up the ladder. One should be motivated and willing to work in a fast-paced, multitasking environment. An associate's degree in accounting or finance is required. Additionally, the ideal candidate will be detail-oriented and able to meet deadlines. The job involves coordinating transfers of time worked data from time collection systems to payroll systems. Must have extended knowledge of Excel to compute withholdings and deductions, and must stay up-to-date on multiple state laws regarding payroll. Excellent compensation package and benefits. Apply to Carolynn Workman, accounting director, at carolynn_workman@adelphia.net.

e. *Staff accountant.* Successful candidate should have a BS in accounting and be proficient in QuickBooks and/or Excel. Would be responsible for performing account analysis for corporate accounts, assisting in consolidation of subsidiaries, and assisting in the preparation of annual and quarterly financial statements and financial reports for certain subsidiaries. Experience in the local environment of small business is desirable. If you are concerned with order, quality, and accuracy, please contact us by mail at Administrative Partner, Winship and Acord, P.C., 3013 Stonybrook Drive, (your city), or by email at CWA@msn .com, or by fax at 1-217-399-2569.

f. *Network specialist.* We seek someone who can help deliver reliable, secure, and integrated networks. Must be able to bring together data and voice, WAN and LAN, fiber optics and wireless. Opportunity to learn newest technologies. Must have network certification such as MCP, MCSE, CNA, or CNE as well as a college degree or the equivalent experience. Requires excellent interpersonal and problem-solving skills. Experience with multiplatform computing is preferred. Will be expected to develop technical documentation and help establish network policies, procedures, and standards to ensure conformance with information systems and client objectives and strategy. Qualified applicants should send application documents to Robert Edwards at redwards@tyt.com.

g. *Technology analyst/consultant.* A fast-growing, highly regarded information technology assessment/consulting firm has a position for someone with expertise in client/ server technology and Access. Must have excellent written communication and interpersonal skills. Vendor or user organization experience is highly desirable. Position is in the Bay Area. Send or fax your résumé to director of human resources at 500 Airport Road, Suite 100, (your city), or 415-579-1022.

h. *Financial analyst.* An eastern-based investment firm is seeking an analyst to help with the evaluation of potential private equity investments and marketing of an existing and a new leveraged buyout fund. Should have a bachelor's degree from a good school and some experience in banking. Ideal candidates will have strong analytical capabilities and excellent computer skills, particularly spreadsheet, statistics, and database. Please email your résumé to andrew-winston@fidelity.com.

i. *Trade show exhibits coordinator.* Position reports to the national sales manager and requires an individual who can work independently as well as part of a team. Professional telephone and computer skills are essential. Coordinator will maintain exhibitor contact databases, serve as an internal liaison to accounting and as an external liaison to vendors, and assist the on-site floor managers with various exhibitor-related responsibilities. Also must create exhibitor and attendee pre- and post-show surveys, collect data, and compile results. Trade show, association, or convention services experience is a plus. Some limited travel is expected. Send your résumé to lmiller@aol.com.

j. *Sales representative.* Major pharmaceutical company is expanding and looking for a sales representative in your area. Ideal candidate will have a successful record of sales experience, preferably in a business-to-business environment. Candidate must be well versed in science and willing to continually learn about new products. Good knowledge of your area is highly desirable. Send your résumé to Jane_Adami@pfizer.com.

k. *Internet programmer.* Seeking a professional individual with experience in complex HTML/DHTML, strong web development, and a thorough understanding of ajax and PHP. Will design, write, modify, test, and maintain programs and scripts for a suite of server applications. Must be comfortable in a UNIX environment and possess some competency in SQL. Any experience with data warehousing would be a plus. Additionally, a qualified candidate should be a team player and self-motivated and possess excellent speaking and writing skills. Send all application documents to James.Andrews@menshealth.com.

l. *Marketing professional.* An international, rapidly growing consumer and trade publisher is seeking a self-motivated individual to help us reach our goal of doubling revenues by the year 2015. Ideal candidate will be an innovative, results-oriented professional willing to take the challenge of developing new markets in Central and South America. Should be good at packaging and repackaging information products for a large and expanding customer base. We are looking for those with some experience, creative writing talent, leadership skills, good communication skills, and strong interpersonal skills. Sell yourself through your cover message and résumé. Send a rich media text to Thomas McLaughlin, corporate vice president, Blackhawk Publishing at tjmclaughlin@blackhawk.com.

m. *Executive administrative assistant.* Vice president of a Fortune 500 manufacturing company seeks a highly competent, personable, organized, and dependable executive assistant. College degree desired. Must have excellent communication skills and thorough command of Internet navigation as well as word processing and presentation programs. In addition to basic business knowledge in accounting, economics, computer systems, finance, marketing, and management, an understanding of manufacturing in a global market would be desirable. Apply to director of human resources, P.O. Box 3733, (your city).

n. *Graphic artist.* An employee-owned systems integration firm has an immediate need for a graphic artist. A bachelor's degree or an associate's degree with some experience desired. Must be proficient in PhotoShop and Illustrator, preferably in a Windows environment. Will prepare presentation and curriculum support graphics for government customer. Knowledge of project management software is a plus. Must have a work portfolio. Send résumé to the attention of KML, P.O. Box 900, (your city).

o. *MIS specialist.* A local medical clinic is seeking an individual to manage a multisite, multiplatform computer system. Will be responsible for troubleshooting and coordinating problems in a Windows Vista environment and writing reports for management. A background in the healthcare/medical field combined with a good knowledge of computing is highly desirable. Send résumé to (your city's name) Community Clinic, 1113 Henderson, (your city), or fax to 888-316-1026.

p. *Financial manager.* Multispecialty medical group (60 doctors) needs dedicated professional to work in providing financial planning and control in a growing organization. Join a team of financial specialists who bear responsibility for budgeting, general accounting, reimbursement, billing processes, and external reporting. Also responsible for development of long- and short-range financial goals and evaluation of their impact on strategic objectives and service mission. Degree in accounting/finance. Technical and team skills needed. Competitive salary and benefits package. Send letter and résumé to Mount Renault Medical Group, Box 14871, New York, NY 00146.

q. *Accountant.* A major real estate developer and property management company seeks an accountant. Must have a bachelor's degree in accounting. Will assist in financial reporting, tax preparation, cash flow projections, and year-end audit workpaper preparation. Mastery of Excel is required as are good communication skills. Some work experience in accounting is desirable; internship experience in an accounting or real estate environment is also desirable. Send your résumé and cover letter to TPL, P.O. Box 613, (your city) or email it to tpl@hotmail.com.

r. *Accounting majors.* Multinational consumer electronics firm seeks entry-level accountant for work in its controller's division. This person must be knowledgeable in financial and managerial accounting, internal auditing, budgeting, and capital investments. A multinational orientation, degree in accounting, and progress toward completion of CPA or CMA are a plus. Good communication skills (written and oral) and computer applications are required. Interested applicants should send letter and résumé to hrdirector@circuitcity.com.

s. *Bank examiner.* Federal Reserve Bank (nearest to your location) seeks career-oriented individuals. Persons hired will conduct on-site examinations of foreign banks operating in the U.S. in their lending activities, derivative products, bank operations, and financial information. Applicants must possess a bachelor's degree in accounting, finance, or economics. Evidence of cross-cultural sensitivity and foreign language proficiency is preferred. Travel 30–50 percent of the time. Excellent oral/written skills and U.S. citizenship required. Apply with letter, résumé, and reference sheets to Federal Reserve Board, Human Resources Department, (your region).

t. *Proposal writer.* Global leader in high-technology asset management needs individual to prepare proposals for clients. Person selected must be a team player, thrive on high-tech challenges in fast-paced environment, and possess a state-of-the-art solution orientation. Excellent writing skills essential, along with BBA degree and experience with various hardware/software technologies. Job includes coordinating appropriate persons to define solutions and preparing program plans with cost estimation for clients. Send letter, résumé, and writing sample to Department SAS, (your city).

u. *Assistant to operations manager.* Proven leader in the insurance industry seeks a highly motivated assistant to the operations manager of regional service center. Technical skills include proficiency in Internet use and Microsoft Word, Excel, PowerPoint, Access, and other database applications. College training preferred with good people skills. Person selected must be able to develop and maintain effective working relationships with internal and external customers.

Apply to HR Department, Box 7438, (your city) or email to hrdirector@statefarm.com.

v. *Environmental safety and health assistant.* World leader in battery manufacturing is looking for an individual to work in safety and health area of production plant and distribution center. The successful candidate will need to have a business or environmental engineering degree and possess excellent organizational and people skills. Job duties involve administering health/safety programs, conducting training, and working with governmental agencies and regulatory personnel. Excellent opportunity for results-oriented individual seeking to work for a safe, attractive, and sanitary environment. Send cover message and résumé to Box SH, (your city).

w. *Account executive for display advertising.* State business journal invites applications for career-oriented individuals. Qualified candidates must be college graduates (business preferred) and have work background to demonstrate reliability and commitment. Job scope involves selling display advertising in creative ways for specialized business print and online publications. Applicants should be of high energy, aggressive, and creative. Send applications to Drawer HBD, (your city), or salesmgr@busjrnl.com.

x. *Financial consultant.* Large communications services company needs qualified person to provide communication-based utility automation consulting to electric utilities. Must have comprehensive financial management knowledge. Perform economic analyses on current and proposed projects; assist in development of budgets; evaluate budget to actual performance; prepare monthly reports. Demonstrated knowledge of strategic planning, valuation techniques, accounting principles, and economic forecasts. Must communicate well orally and in writing. Email letter, résumé, and references to applications@alc.com.

y. *SEO Blogger.* New website is seeking a writer/intern for its search engine optimization (SEO) blog. This new site, which has free SEO tools, is attracting a growing worldwide interest. We are seeking two writers for three to five posts per week. Must have a background in SEO and be abreast of the field in order to write on current topics. Telecommuting is OK. Please send samples of your work or links to it along with your SEO credentials to jobs@nonbot.com.

z. *Corporate trainer.* Exciting opportunity is available for a professional with strong presentation skills, good organizational skills, and excellent written and oral communication skills. Successful trainer will be able to effectively communicate technical information to both technical and nontechnical users. Should be able to design classroom training modules and measure their effectiveness. Good time management and use of Outlook are required. Some travel to clients' sites may be required. Application documents including a sample PowerPoint presentation should be sent to Sharon Garbett, President, Sedona Training, P.O. Box 1308, Moline, Illinois 61266.

5 You are looking ahead to your graduation soon. You've decided to begin to look for jobs online. Tap into a system that you know posts jobs in your major or a corporate website that posts job openings. (See the textbook website for links to some of these sites.) Browse through the jobs until you see one that appeals to you and for which you will be qualified when you graduate. Print (or save) a copy of the ad so you will have it handy when you write your résumé and cover messages. Address the points covered in the ad and explain that you learned about the position from a particular online system. Plan to send your résumé electronically via email. Plan to send both a formatted and a scannable version of your résumé.

6 Using a tool of your choice such as LinkedIn, Weebly, or Yola, create a webpage profile complete with links that provide supporting details. Take care that your online portfolio is easy to navigate as well as pleasing to view.

7 You are seeking an internship in your field. Using your school's career services office, online internship sites, personal contacts, or other sources, find an internship in your field that you are currently qualified to hold. Write a résumé, references list, and cover letter for the position. Print a copy of the position description for your instructor. If you find the information through a personal contact or have no official job posting to print, write a brief paragraph describing the position. Be sure the description includes your personal contact's name, job title, company name, and contact information as well as a list of job duties and qualifications.

8 You are seeking an internship but have not yet found a job posting that fits your interests and abilities. However, you have always wanted to work for _____ (pick a real company), and even though the company has no positions advertised, you decide to send an unsolicited cover letter, résumé, and references to this company. Before you write the letter and résumé, though, you will want to analyze your purpose and goals; your audience; and the skills, experience, and qualifications you could bring to an internship with this company. Submit this analysis in a short memo to your instructor. Then prepare a résumé and cover letter targeted to the internship.

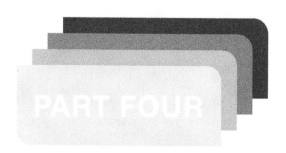
Fundamentals of Report Writing

Why is sound, well-presented research so important in business? Caroline Molina-Ray, MBA, PhD, and Executive Director of Research and Publications at Apollo Research Institute, explains:

"Business leaders must base their decisions on relevant facts—not just on intuition. Effective research provides leaders with facts they can use to plan, evaluate, and improve business performance. To be most useful, research must not only include pertinent data but also explain what the data mean and how a decision maker might act on this information. For example, if the data show that many competitors are entering the market, this may mean a potentially smaller market share for the business, and the company may need to re-evaluate its sales and marketing strategy to maintain a competitive advantage.

"Readers appreciate research that is clear and concise but with enough detail to answer their key questions. Visual elements such as charts, tables, and graphs can be efficient tools for illustrating data—but don't let the visuals speak for themselves. Always provide a brief explanation of any graphic, and synthesize the overall findings in a reader-friendly executive summary."

Caroline Molina-Ray, Executive Director of Research and Publications, Apollo Research Institute

CHAPTER ELEVEN

Preparing Informative and Influential Business Reports

Learning Objectives

Upon completing this chapter, you will be able to prepare well-organized, objective reports. To reach this goal, you should be able to

1 Write clear problem and purpose statements.

2 List the factors involved in a problem.

3 Explain the common errors in interpreting data and develop attitudes and practices conducive to good interpreting.

4 Organize information in outline form, using time, place, quantity, factor, or a combination of these as bases for division.

5 Turn an outline into a table of contents whose format and wording are logical and meaningful.

6 Write reports that are focused, objective, consistent in time viewpoint, smoothly connected, and interesting.

7 Prepare reports collaboratively.

Writing Reports to Solve Workplace Problems

Introduce yourself to the subject of report writing by assuming the role of an operations analyst at Technisoft, Inc. Much of your work at this large software company involves getting information for your boss, the president of the company. Yesterday, for example, you looked into the question of excessive time spent by office workers on the Internet. A few days earlier, you worked on an assignment to determine the causes of unrest in one of the local branches. Before that assignment you investigated a supervisor's recommendation to change an evaluation process. You could continue the list indefinitely because investigating problems is a part of your work.

You must write a report on each of your investigations. You write such reports for good reasons. Written reports make permanent records. Those who need the information contained in these reports can then review and study them at their convenience. Written reports also can be routed to a number of readers with a minimum of effort and for this reason are often a convenient and efficient means of transmitting information.

Your report-writing work is not unique to your job. In fact, report writing is common throughout the company. For example, the engineers often report on the technical problems they encounter. The accountants regularly report to management on the company's financial status and compliance with regulations. The salespeople regularly report on marketing matters. And so it is throughout the company. Such reporting is vital to your company's operations—as it is to the operations of all companies.

Writing to external audiences can also be critical to an organization's success. If the organization is a consulting firm, reports to the client may be its primary deliverable. If the company is publicly traded, it is required by law to submit financial reports to the government and to shareholders. Depending on the nature of its business, a company may have to write reports to various agencies about its impact on the environment, its hiring practices, or its compliance with quality standards.

Sometimes reports are written by individuals. Increasingly, however, they are prepared in collaboration with others. Even if one person has primary responsibility for a report, he or she will often need contributions from many people. Indeed, report writing draws on a wide variety of communication skills, from getting information to presenting it clearly.

This and the following chapter describe the structure and writing of this vital form of business communication.

REPORTS AND YOUR FUTURE

How often you write reports in the years ahead will depend on the size and nature of the organization you work for. If you work for a very small organization (say, one with fewer than 10 employees), you will probably write only a few. But if you work for a midsize or larger organization, you are likely to write many. The larger the organization, the greater its complexity; and the greater the complexity, the greater the need for information to manage the organization.

The nature of the business can also influence the number and type of reports you will write. The Securities and Exchange Commission requires all publicly traded businesses to write certain financial reports at regular intervals. A consulting firm's whole business effort may be directed toward informational and advisory reports to its clients. A business performing work under government contracts will also have special reporting needs. Though the frequency with which you will write reports and the kinds you will write will depend on your job and your employer, you can be fairly certain that report writing will figure significantly in your business career.

DEFINING REPORTS

You probably have a good idea of what reports are. Even so, you might have a hard time defining them. Some people define reports to include almost any presentation of information, while others use the term to refer only to the most formal presentations.

We use this middle-ground definition: *A business report is an orderly and objective communication of factual information that serves a business purpose.*

As an *orderly* communication, a report is prepared carefully. This care in their preparation distinguishes reports from casual exchanges of information. The *objective* quality of a report is its unbiased approach. Good reports present all the relevant facts and interpret them without personal bias. The word *communication* in our definition is broad in meaning. It covers all ways of transmitting meaning: speaking, writing, using visuals, or a combination of these. The basic ingredient of reports is *factual information*. Factual information is based on events, statistics, and other data. Finally, a business report must *serve a business purpose*. Research scientists, medical doctors, ministers, students, and many others write reports, but to be classified as a business report, a report must help a business solve its problems or meet its goals.

This definition is specific enough to be useful but broad enough to account for the variations in business reports. For example, some reports (information reports) do nothing more than present facts. Others (analytical reports) go a step further by including interpretations, sometimes accompanied by conclusions. Recommendation reports go further yet, presenting advice for future action. Some reports are highly formal both in writing style and in physical appearance, while some are highly informal. The situation will determine the specific qualities of any given report. However, all reports should help readers make informed business decisions.

DETERMINING THE REPORT PROBLEM AND PURPOSE

LO1 Write clear problem and purpose statements.

Your work on a report logically begins with a need, which we refer to in the following discussion as the **problem**. Someone or some group (usually your superiors) needs information for a business purpose. Perhaps the need is for information only; perhaps it is for information and analysis; or perhaps it is for information, analysis, and recommendations. Whatever the case, someone with a need will authorize you to do the work. How you define this need (problem) will determine your **report's purpose**.

The Preliminary Investigation

Your first task is to understand the problem. To do this well, you will almost surely have to gather additional information beyond what you've been given. You may need to study the company's files or query its databases, talk over the problem with experts, search through external sources, and/or discuss the problem with those who authorized the report. You should do enough preliminary research to be sure you understand the problem that your report is intended to address.

The Need for Clear Problem and Purpose Statements

Your next task is to clearly state your understanding of the *problem* and your report's *purpose*. Clear problem and purpose statements are important for you as you plan and write the report and for those who will read and use the report.

The **problem statement** provides a clear description of the situation that created the need for your report. Problem statements are generally written as declarative statements. For example, a simple one might read "Sales are decreasing at Company X."

You should then write a **purpose statement** (also called the report's *objective, aim,* or *goal*). This statement is often written in the form of a question or infinitive phrase. Thus, if your problem is that Company X wants to know why sales are decreasing, your purpose statement may be "to determine the causes of decreasing sales at Company X" or "What are the causes of decreasing sales at Company X?"

Sometimes, as in the preceding example, the purpose will be clearly implied in the problem statement. Other times, the problem will be so complex or general that you will need to put some thought into your report's purpose. For example, the purpose of a report intended to help a company reduce employee turnover could be "to find out why

Report-Writing Practices and the Sarbanes-Oxley Act

Changes in the regulatory environment can have a significant impact on the kinds of reporting that companies must do. One of the most major changes in recent history was the adoption of the Sarbanes-Oxley Act in 2002.* The law, which applies to all publicly traded companies, was intended to minimize financial scandals like those involving Enron, Arthur Andersen, Lehman Brothers, and Bernie and Peter Madoff and to maintain investor confidence. It requires companies to submit periodic reports on their financial practices to outside audit committees and assessments of those practices to the Securities and Exchange Commission (SEC), beyond the financial reports they were already submitting (such as their annual 10-K reports).

But chief financial officers are not the only ones writing more reports. Managers, office personnel, and information technology professionals also must do much more reporting on procedures and controls involving financial transactions and recordkeeping. And the process of bringing these companies into compliance has generated thousands of internal directives and reports.

You will not be able to predict all the kinds of reports you may be asked to write. At any moment, your company, its needs, or its environment may change. You must be ready to adapt with your problem-analysis, data-gathering, interpreting, and writing skills.

*For further information, see the Sarbanes-Oxley Beginner's Guide at http://beginnersguide.com/accounting/sarbanesoxley/.

employee turnover is so high," "to find out how other companies have addressed employee turnover," "to find out what makes loyal employees stay," a combination of these, or some other purpose. Consider carefully what approach your report will take to the problem.

These statements will help keep you on track as you continue through the project. In addition, they can be reviewed, approved, and evaluated by people whose assistance may be valuable. Most important, putting the problem and purpose in writing forces you to think them through. Keep in mind, though, that no matter how clearly you try to frame the problem and your research purpose, your conception of them may change as you continue your investigation. As in other types of business writing, report writing often involves revisiting earlier steps (recursivity), as discussed in Chapters 1 and 6.

In your completed report, the problem and purpose statements will be an essential component of the report's introduction and such front matter as the letter of transmittal and executive summary; they will orient your readers and let them know where your report is headed.

DETERMINING THE FACTORS

Once you've defined the problem and identified your purpose, you determine what **factors** you need to investigate. That is, you determine what subject areas you must look into to solve the problem.

LO2 List the factors involved in a problem.

What factors a problem involves can vary widely, but we can identify three common types. First, they may be subtopics of the overall topic about which the report is concerned. Second, they may be hypotheses that must be tested. Third, in problems that involve comparisons, they may be the bases on which the comparisons are made.

Use of Subtopics in Information Reports

If the problem concerns a need for information, you will need to figure out the areas about which information is needed. Illustrating this type of situation is the problem of preparing a report that reviews Company X's activities during the past quarter. This is an informational report problem—that is, it requires no analysis, no conclusion, no recommendation. It requires only that information be presented. The main effort in this case is to determine which subdivisions of the overall topic should be covered. After thoroughly evaluating the possibilities, you might come up with a plan like this:

Purpose statement: To review operations of Company X from January 1 through March 31.

Subtopics:

1. Production
2. Sales and promotion
3. Financial status
4. Computer systems
5. Product development
6. Human resources

Hypotheses for Problems Requiring Solution

Some problems concern why something bad is happening and perhaps how to correct it. In analyzing problems of this kind, you should seek explanations or solutions. Such explanations or solutions are termed **hypotheses**. Once formulated, hypotheses are tested, and their applicability to the problem is either proved or disproved.

To illustrate, assume that you have the problem of determining why sales at a certain store have declined. In preparing to investigate this problem, you would think of the possible explanations (hypotheses) for the decline. You might identify such possible reasons as these:

Purpose statement: To find out why sales at the Springfield store have declined.

Hypotheses:

1. Activities of the competition have caused the decline.
2. Changes in the economy of the area have caused the decline.
3. Merchandising deficiencies have caused the decline.
4. Changes in the environment (population shifts, political actions, etc.) have caused the decline.

You would then conduct the necessary research to test these hypotheses. You might find that one, two, or all apply. Or you might find that none is valid. If so, you would have to generate additional hypotheses for further evaluation.

Bases of Comparison in Evaluation Studies

When the problem concerns evaluating something, either singularly or in comparison with other things, you should look for the bases for the evaluation. That is, you should determine what characteristics you will evaluate and the criteria you will use to evaluate them.

Illustrating this technique is the problem of a company that seeks to determine which of three cities would be best for expansion. The bases for comparing the cities are the factors that would likely determine the success of the new branch. After considering such factors, you might come up with a plan like this:

Purpose statement: To determine whether Y Company's new location should be built in City A, City B, or City C.

Comparison bases:

1. Availability of skilled workers
2. Tax structure
3. Community attitude
4. Transportation facilities
5. Nearness to markets

Report writing requires hard work and clear thinking in every stage of the process. To understand the problem, identify your report's purpose, and prepare the report that will solve the problem, you may need to consult many sources of information.

Each of the factors selected for investigation may have factors of its own. In this illustration, for example, the comparison of transportation in the three cities may well include such subdivisions as water, rail, truck, and air. Workers may be compared by using such categories as skilled workers and unskilled workers. Subdivisions of this kind may go still further. Skilled workers may be broken down by specific skills: engineers, programmers, technical writers, graphic designers. Make as many subdivisions as you need in order to provide a thorough, useful comparison.

GATHERING THE INFORMATION NEEDED

For many business problems, you can conduct the investigation on your own. A production problem, for example, might require gathering and reviewing the company's production records. A sales problem might require collecting information through discussions with customers and sales personnel. A computer problem might require talking to both end users and programmers. A purchasing problem might require getting product information, finding prices, and compiling products' performance statistics. A problem involving adopting a new business practice might require searching business literature and relevant websites to learn about the practice's pros and cons and to gather advice about its implementation. An investigation that you do by yourself usually requires knowledge of your field of work, which is probably why you were assigned the problem.

Some business problems require a more formal type of research, such as an experiment, survey, or focus group. In such cases, you will almost surely require others' assistance. Chapter 13, as well as the collaborative writing section at the end of this chapter, can help you prepare for these projects.

As you conduct your research, follow these general guidelines:

- *Gather more information than you will use.* Busy college students are sometimes tempted to gather just enough information and no more or to exert the effort

Report-Writing Tools Help Businesses Succeed

To survive and thrive, businesses must have timely, accurate data about their operations. For many businesses, that means investing in software that will generate the informational reports they need.

The most powerful report-writing tools are those that are integrated with enterprise resource planning (ERP) systems, which allow managers real-time access to data about the different facets of the company. These products' report-writing tools make it easy to get a snapshot of any part of business operations, whether it be the current financial picture, the sales history of a certain product, or the status of customers' accounts.

But even small businesses can benefit from report-writing tools. Shown here is the title page of a sample home-inspection report created with Horizon software. The software enables home inspectors to create all the necessary components—from transmittal letter to contract to results and recommendations—and then generates a professional-looking report for the customer.

While you may not be able to find software to support your report writing to this extent, you will almost surely use electronically generated reports when preparing your own reports. Be sure to familiarize yourself with any report-writing tools your organization uses so that you do not overlook important data or leave out information that your reader expects to see in your report.

SOURCE: "Professional Reports," *CarsonDunlop*, Carson, Dunlop & Associates Ltd., 2012, Web, 8 July 2012. Reprinted with permission.

they think the research should require and then stop. But those are bad research practices. In business, your job is to help solve a problem, not just to show that you spent some time on it. Keep researching until you feel you have found the information that will allow you to generate the best solution.

- *Be resourceful.* As Chapter 13 explains, you'll have many research methods and resources at your disposal. Use good judgment when figuring out where you're likely to find the best information. And when you find information in one place (for example, a website about customers' preferences), check it against information in another place (the research literature or opinions of your own customers).

- *Keep accurate notes.* To make your research efficient, keep a record of where you've looked and what you've found there. For example, if you're searching the Internet or a database, jot down the different search terms and combinations of terms you've used so that you don't repeat the same search. As Chapter 13 advises, you should also keep careful records of your sources so that you can go back to them as needed and document them accurately in your report.

INTERPRETING THE FINDINGS

The next major stage of the report-writing process is to interpret the information you've gathered.

Actually, you will have done a good bit of interpreting already by the time you reach this stage. You had to interpret the elements of the situation to understand the problem and determine your research purpose. You also had to interpret your data as you were gathering them to make sure that you were getting appropriate and sufficient information. But when your research is finished, you will need to formulate the interpretations that will guide the shape and contents of your report.

LO3 Explain the common errors in interpreting data and develop attitudes and practices conducive to good interpreting.

Interpreting facts requires not only analytical skills and objective judgment but consideration for ethical issues as well.

To do this, keep both your problem and your readers in mind. Your findings will need to apply clearly to the given problem in order to be viewed as logical solutions. But they will also need to meet the readers' needs in order to be viewed as relevant and helpful. If you have kept your reader-based problem and purpose statements in mind while doing your research, making logical, reader-based analyses of your data should follow naturally.

How you interpret your data will vary from case to case, but the following general advice can help you with this process.

Advice for Avoiding Human Error

Certain human tendencies lead to error in interpretation. The following list explains how to minimize them:

1. *Report the facts as they are.* Do nothing to make them more or less exciting. Adding color to interpretations to make the report more interesting compromises objectivity.

2. *Do not think that conclusions are always necessary.* When the facts do not support a conclusion, you should just summarize your findings and conclude that there is no conclusion. All too often, report writers think that if they do not conclude, they have failed in their investigation.

3. *Do not interpret a lack of evidence as proof to the contrary.* The fact that you cannot prove something is true does not mean that it is false.

4. *Do not compare noncomparable data.* When you look for relationships between sets of data, make sure they have enough similarities to be comparable. For example, you might be able to draw conclusions about how two groups of employees differ at Company X, but you probably would not be justified in comparing Group A from Company X to Group B from Company Y.

5. *Do not draw illogical cause–effect conclusions.* The fact that two sets of data appear to affect each other does not mean they actually do. They may be only **correlated** (strongly associated for an undetermined reason). Use research and good logic to determine whether a cause–effect relationship is likely.

6. *Beware of unreliable and unrepresentative data.* Much of the information to be found in secondary sources is incorrect to some extent. The causes are many: collection error, biased research, recording mistakes. Beware especially of data collected by groups that advocate a position (political organizations, groups supporting social issues, and other special interest groups). Make sure your sources are reliable. And remember that the interpretations you make are no better than the data you interpret.

7. *Do not oversimplify.* Most business problems are complex, and it can be tempting to settle for easy answers. Avoid conclusions and recommendations that do not do justice to the problem.

You're right. This report does make you look like a fool.

SOURCE: © 1985 Dean Vietor. Used with permission.

8. *Tailor your claims to your data.* There's a tendency among inexperienced report writers to use too few facts to generalize far too much. If you have learned about a certain phenomenon, do not assume that your interpretations can automatically be applied to similar phenomena. Or if your research has revealed the source of a problem, do not assume that you can also propose solutions; finding solutions can be a separate research project altogether. Make only those claims that are well supported by your evidence, and when you are not sure how strong to make them, use such qualified language as "may be," "could be," and "suggest."

Appropriate Attitudes and Practices

In addition to being alert to the most likely causes of error, you can improve your interpretation of findings by adopting the following attitudes and practices:

1. *Maintain a judicial attitude.* Play the role of a judge as you interpret. Look at all sides of every issue without emotion or prejudice. Your primary objective is to form the most reliable interpretations of the situation.

2. *Consult with others.* It is rare indeed when one mind is better than two or more. You can usually profit by talking over your interpretations with others.

3. *Test your interpretations.* While the ultimate test of your interpretations' validity will be how well they hold up in their actual application to a company problem, you can perform two tests to help you make reasonable inferences from your data.

    First is the **test of experience**. In applying this test, you ponder each interpretation you make, asking yourself, "Does this appear reasonable in light of all I know or have experienced?"

    Second is the **negative test**, which is a critique of your own conclusions. Here, you consider what a skeptic or "devil's advocate" might say about your interpretations. By considering the opposing viewpoint, you can make your interpretations more reliable.

Statistical Tools for Data Analysis

In many cases, the information you gather is quantitative—that is, expressed in numbers. "You can't manage what you can't measure" is a common business expression, and while nonnumerical data, such as descriptions of customers' experiences or comments by employees, are also extremely valuable, the popularity of this expression rightly suggests that businesses need accurate numbers in order to succeed. As Chapter 1 points out, barcode systems and other "smart machines," which store statistics about their use, are generating huge amounts of numerical information. To use such data intelligently, you must find ways of simplifying them so that your reader can grasp their general meaning.

Statistical techniques provide many methods for analyzing data. By knowing them, you can improve your ability to interpret. Although a thorough review of statistical techniques is beyond the scope of this book, you should know the more commonly used methods, described in the following paragraphs.

Possibly of greatest use to you in writing reports are **descriptive statistics**—measures of central tendency, dispersion, ratios, and probability. Measures of central tendency—the mean, median, and mode—will help you find a value that roughly represents the whole. The measures of dispersion—ranges, variances, and standard deviations—help you describe how spread out the data are. Ratios (which express proportionate relationships) and probabilities (which determine how many times something will likely occur out of the total number of possibilities) can also help you give meaning to data. **Inferential statistics**, which enable you to generalize about a whole population based on the study of a sample, are also useful but go beyond these basic elements. You will find descriptions of these and other useful techniques in the help documentation of your spreadsheet and statistics software as well as in any standard statistics textbook.

A word of caution, however: Your job as a writer is to help your reader interpret the information. Sometimes unexplained statistical calculations—even if elementary to you—may confuse the reader. Thus, you must explain your statistical techniques and findings explicitly with words and appropriate visuals. You must remember that statistics are a help to interpretation, not a replacement for it. Whatever you do to turn numerical data into meaningful information deserves careful explanation.

LO4 Organize information in outline form, using time, place, quantity, factor, or a combination of these as bases for division.

ORGANIZING THE REPORT INFORMATION

When you have interpreted your information, you will know your report's main points. Now you are ready to organize this content for presentation. Your goal here is to arrange the information in a logical order that meets your reader's needs.

The Nature and Benefits of Outlining

An invaluable aid at this stage of the process is an **outline**. A good one will show what things go together (**grouping**), what order they should be in (**ordering**), and how the ideas relate in terms of levels of generality (**hierarchy**). Although you can outline mentally, a written plan is advisable for all but the shortest reports. Time spent on outlining at this stage is well spent because it will make your drafting process more efficient and orderly. For longer reports, your outline will also form the basis for the table of contents.

If you have proceeded methodically thus far, you probably already have a rough outline. It is the list of topics that you drew up when planning how to research your problem. You may also have added to this list the findings that you developed when interpreting your data. But when it's time to turn your research plan into a report plan, you need to outline more deliberately. Your goal is to create the most logical, helpful pattern of organization for your readers.

In constructing your outline, you can use any system of numbering or formatting that will help you see the logical structure of your planned contents. If it will help, you can use the conventional or the decimal symbol system to mark the levels. The **conventional outlining system** uses Roman numerals to show the major headings and letters of the alphabet and Arabic numbers to show the lesser headings, as illustrated here:

Conventional System

    I. First-level heading
        A. Second level, first part
        B. Second level, second part
            1. Third level, first part
            2. Third level, second part
                a. Fourth level, first part
                    (1) Fifth level, first part
                        (a) Sixth level, first part
    II. First-level heading
        A. Second level, first part
        B. Second level, second part
        etc.

The **decimal outlining system** uses whole numbers to show the major sections, with decimals and additional numbers added to show subsections. That is, the digits to the right of the decimal show each successive level in the outline, as shown here:

Decimal System

    1.0 First-level heading
        1.1 Second level, first part
        1.2 Second level, second part
            1.2.1 Third level, first part

Brainstorm and Outline with Visualization Tools

Inspiration is a concept mapping tool aimed at helping writers generate ideas and outline their documents. The example shown here demonstrates how individuals or groups can brainstorm the factors of a report that investigates which color laser printer a product design department should purchase. Using either the diagram or outline view (or both), a report writer would list as many ideas as possible. Later the items and relationships can be rearranged by dragging and moving pointers.

The software will update the outline symbols as changes are made. Users can toggle between the different views to work with the mode that works best for them. When ready to write, users can export the outline or diagram to Word or Google Docs.

You can download a free 30-day trial version from www.inspiration.com/freetrial. Or try the online version, WebspirationPro, available at www.mywebspiration.com/. Both forms are relatively inexpensive, and the Web-based version is particularly good for collaborative planning and report writing.

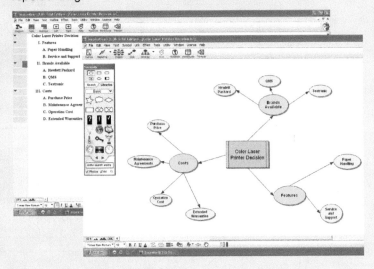

    1.2.2 Third level, second part
        1.2.2.1 Fourth level, first part
            1.2.2.1.1 Fifth level, first part
                1.2.2.1.1.1 Sixth level, first part

2.0 First-level heading
    2.1 Second level, first part
    2.2 Second level, second part
    etc.

Bear in mind that the outline is a tool for you, even though it is based on your readers' needs. Unless others will want to see an updated outline as you work, spend minimal time on its appearance. Allow yourself to change it, scribble on it, depart from it—whatever seems appropriate as your report develops. For example, you might want to note on your outline which sections will contain visuals, or to jot down a particularly good transition between sections that comes to mind. The time to labor over the outline's format and exact wording will be when you use it to create the headings and the table of contents for your finished report.

Organization by Division

One methodical way to create an outline is to use the process of dividing the contents into smaller and smaller sections. With this method, you begin by looking over all your information. You then identify its major parts. This first level of division gives you the major outline parts indicated in Figure 11–1 by the Roman numerals (I, II, III, and so on).

Next, you find ways to subdivide the contents in each major section, yielding the second-level information (indicated by A, B, C). If practical, you keep dividing the contents, generating more levels. This method helps you divide your report into manageable chunks while also creating a logical and clear structural hierarchy.

Figure 11–1

Procedure for Constructing an Outline by Process of Division

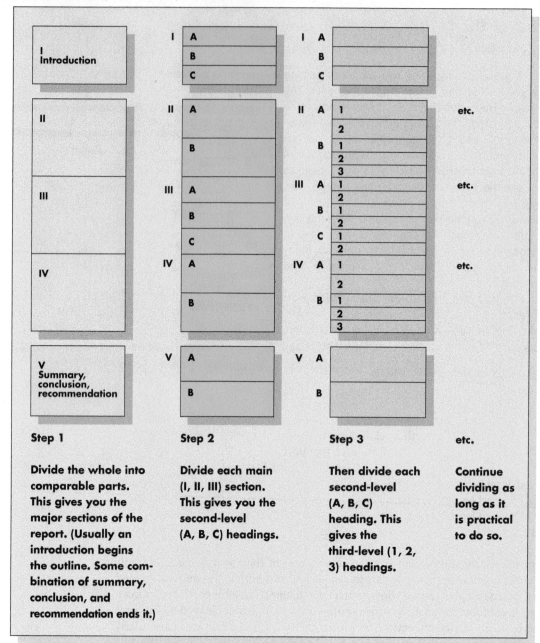

Step 1

Divide the whole into comparable parts. This gives you the major sections of the report. (Usually an introduction begins the outline. Some combination of summary, conclusion, and recommendation ends it.)

Step 2

Divide each main (I, II, III) section. This gives you the second-level (A, B, C) headings.

Step 3

Then divide each second-level (A, B, C) heading. This gives the third-level (1, 2, 3) headings.

etc.

Continue dividing as long as it is practical to do so.

Division by Conventional Relationships

In dividing your information into subparts, you have to find a way of dividing that will produce approximately equal parts. Time, place, quantity, and factor are the general bases for these divisions.

Whenever the information you have to present has some time aspect, consider organizing it by **time division**. In such an organization, the divisions are periods of time. These time periods usually follow a logical sequence, such as past to present or present to past. The periods you select need not be equal in duration, but they should be about equal in importance.

A report on the progress of a research committee illustrates this possibility. The period covered by this report might be divided into the following comparable subperiods:

Orientation, May–July

Project planning, August

Implementation, September–November

The happenings within each period might next be arranged in order of occurrence, and additional subdivisions might even be possible.

If the information you have collected has some relation to geographic location, you may use a **place division**. Ideally, this division would be such that the areas are nearly equal in importance.

A report on the U.S. sales program of a national manufacturer illustrates division by place. The information in this problem might be broken down by these major geographic areas:

New England

Atlantic Seaboard

South

Southwest

Midwest

Rocky Mountains

Pacific Coast

Another illustration of organization by place would be a report on the productivity of a company with a number of customer service branches. A major division of the report might be devoted to each of the branches. The information for each branch might be broken down further, this time by sections, departments, or divisions.

Quantity divisions are possible for information that has quantitative values. To illustrate, an analysis of the buying habits of potential customers could be divided by such income groups as the following:

Under $30,000

$30,000 to under $45,000

$45,000 to under $60,000

$60,000 to under $85,000

$85,000 to under $100,000

$100,000 and over

Problems often have few or no time, place, or quantity aspects. Instead, they require that certain factors, or information areas, be investigated. You might identify these areas by figuring out what questions must be answered in order to have complete information pertaining to the problem. Sometimes the problem you're investigating will naturally suggest certain subtopics.

An example of **division by factors** is a report that seeks to determine which of three locations is the best for a new office for property management. In arriving at this decision, one would need to compare the three locations based on the factors affecting the office location. Thus, the following organization of this problem would be a possibility:

Location accessibility

Rent

Parking

Convenience to current and new customers

Facilities

Another illustration of organization by factors is a report advising a manufacturer whether to begin production of a new product. The solution of this problem will be reached through careful consideration of the factors involved. Among the more likely factors are these:

Production feasibility

Financial considerations

Strength of competition

Consumer demand

Marketing considerations

Combination and Multiple Division Possibilities

In some instances, combinations of two or more bases of division are possible. In a report on a company's sales, for example, the information collected could be arranged by a combination of quantity and place:

> Areas of high sales activity
> Areas of moderate sales activity
> Areas of low sales activity

A report on sales of cyclical products might use the following combination of time and quantity:

> Periods of low sales
> Periods of moderate sales
> Periods of high sales

Some contents can be organized in more than one way. For example, take a report that addresses the problem of determining the best of three locations for an annual sales meeting. It could be organized by site or by the bases of comparison. Organized by sites, the bases of comparison would probably be the second-level headings:

> Site A
>> Airport accessibility
>> Hotel accommodations
>> Meeting facilities
>> Favorable weather
>> Costs
>> Restaurant/entertainment options
>
> Site B
>> Airport accessibility
>> [and so on]
>
> Site C
>> Airport accessibility
>> [and so on]

Organized by bases of comparison, cities would probably be the second-level headings:

> Airport accessibility
>> Site A
>> Site B
>> Site C
>
> Hotel accommodations
>> Site A
>> Site B
>> Site C
>
> Meeting facilities
>> Site A
>> Site B
>> Site C
> [and so on]

Both plans would be logical. However, the organization by cities separates information that has to be compared, thus making it difficult to see which city has the best hotel accommodations. In the second outline, the information that has to be compared is close together. You can determine which city has the best hotel accommodations after reading only one section of the report. In this example, then, the second way would be preferable.

Nevertheless, the two plans show that some problems can be organized in more than one way. In such cases, you must compare the possibilities carefully to find the one that most helpfully presents the report information.

From Outline to Table of Contents

LO5 Turn an outline into a table of contents whose format and wording are logical and meaningful.

When you are ready to prepare the table of contents for your report, you will be, in essence, turning the outline that helped you write into an aid for the reader. Because it will be your public outline, the table of contents needs to be carefully formatted and worded.

True, you will probably design the table of contents late in the report-writing process. We discuss it here as a logical conclusion to our discussion of outlining. But if others involved in the project want to see a well-prepared outline before your report is done, you can use the following advice to prepare that outline.

Note also that what we say about preparing the headings for the table of contents also applies to writing the headings for the report sections. The two sets of headings, those in the table of contents and those in the report itself, should match exactly. Using Word's Styles to format your headings and its Table of Contents generator to create your table of contents will ensure this consistency.

Formatting Decisions. Whatever format you used for your personal outline, you now need to choose one that your reader will find instructive, readable, and appropriate. You create an *instructive* format by clearly indicating the hierarchy of the information. You should use form (font selection, size, style, and color) and placement (location and indentation) to distinguish among the levels of your contents, as illustrated by the table of contents of Chapter 12's sample long report (page 418). You make the format *readable* by using ample vertical white space between topics and enabling readers to see at a glance how the report is organized. Using leaders (dots with intervening spaces) between your topics and your page numbers can also enhance readability.

An *appropriate* format is one that your reader expects. Some business readers view the conventional outlining system (Roman numerals, letters, and Arabic numbers) and the decimal system (as in 1.2.1) as adding unnecessary clutter to the table of contents. Instead, they prefer the use of form and placement to show them how the parts relate to each other. However, in the military and some technical environments, the decimal system is expected, and in other contexts, your readers may want the full numerals and letters of the conventional system. In our examples, we use format rather than numbering to indicate levels of information, but be sure to use whatever format your readers will prefer.

Topic or Talking Headings. In selecting the wording for your table of contents headings, you have a choice of two general forms: topic headings and talking headings. **Topic headings** are short constructions, frequently consisting of one or two words. They merely identify the topic of discussion, as in "Cost" or "Space Requirements." **Talking headings** also identify the subject matter to be covered, but they go a step further: They also indicate what is said about the subject. In other words, talking headings summarize the material they cover, as in "Increase in Cost of Operation" or "Less Space Required."

The following table of contents is for a longer report recommending the site for a new food-processing plant. It uses headings that talk:

Introduction to the problem
    Authorization by Board Action
    Selection of the Potential Sites
    Reliance on Government Data
    Factors to Be Discussed

Community Attitudes Toward a New Plant
    Favorable Reaction of All Towns to a New Employer
    Mixed Attitudes of All Towns Toward Our Labor Policies

Labor Supply and Prevailing Wage Rates
    Prevalence of Unskilled Labor in San Marcos

> Concentration of Skilled Workers in San Marcos
> Mixed Pattern of Wage Rates

> Nearness to Suppliers
>> Location of Ballinger, Coleman, and San Marcos in Farming Areas
>> Relatively Low Production Near Big Spring and Littlefield

> Availability of Utilities
>> Inadequate Water Supply for All Towns but San Marcos
>> Unlimited Supply of Natural Gas for All Towns
>> Electric Rate Advantage of San Marcos and Coleman
>> General Adequacy of All Towns for Waste Disposal

> Adequacy of Existing Transportation Systems
>> Surface Transportation Advantages of San Marcos and Ballinger
>> General Equality of Airway Connections

> A Final Weighting of the Factors
>> Selection of San Marcos as First Choice
>> Recommendation of Ballinger as Second Choice
>> Lack of Advantages in Big Spring, Coleman, and Littlefield

This contrasting version uses topic headings:

> Introduction
>> Authorization
>> Purpose
>> Sources
>> Preview

> Community Attitudes
>> New Plant
>> Labor Policy

> Labor Factors
>> Unskilled Workers
>> Skilled Workers
>> Wage Rates

> Available Suppliers
>> Adequate Areas
>> Inadequate Areas

> Utilities
>> Water
>> Natural Gas
>> Electricity
>> Waste Disposal

> Transportation
>> Surface
>> Air

> Conclusions
>> First Choice
>> Alternative Choice
>> Other Possibilities

Which of these versions is better? The answer depends on the situation. Talking heads would be appropriate if your readers are extremely busy, trust your judgment, and are likely to skim the supporting facts. Topic headings, because they do not announce the point of the section, are better for readers who want to see the facts before being told what to think about them.

Parallelism of Construction. As a general rule, you should write headings at each level of the table of contents in the same grammatical form. In other words, equal-level headings should be *parallel* in structure. For example, if the first major heading is a noun phrase, the rest of the major heads should be noun phrases. If the first second-level heading under a major head is an *-ing* phrase, all second-level headings in the section should be *-ing* phrases.

This rule is not just an exercise in grammar; its purpose is to show similarity. As you will recall from Chapter 4, parallelism helps your readers understand which topics are alike and go together. If you state similar topics in different forms, your logic will become blurry, and your reader will have trouble following you. It is usually considered permissible to vary the form from one section and level to another; that is, the second-level heads in one section need to match, but they do not need to match the second-level heads in the other sections, and the third-level heads do not need to match the second-level heads. Just be sure that the headings on each level of each section are parallel.

The following headings illustrate violations of parallelism:

Programmer Output Is Lagging (sentence).
Increase in Cost of Labor (noun phrase)
Unable to Deliver Necessary Results (adjective phrase)

Making the headings all noun phrases would fix the problem:

Lag in Programmer Output
Increase in Cost of Labor
Inability to Deliver Necessary Results

Or you could make all the headings sentences, like this:

Programmer Output Is Lagging.
Cost of Labor Is Increasing.
Information Systems Cannot Deliver Necessary Results.

Here's a different kind of faulty parallelism:

Managers Prefer an Intranet
U.S. Employees Prefer a Social Media Site
A Newsletter Is Preferred by Overseas Employees

The third heading is "off." Can you see why? If you answered that it switches from active to passive voice, you're right.

Concise Wording. Your headings should be as concise as possible while still being clear and informative. Although the following headings are informative, their excessive length obviously hinders their communication effectiveness:

Personal appearance enhancement is the most desirable feature of contact lenses that wearers report.
The drawback of contacts mentioned by most people who can't wear them is that they are difficult to put in.
More comfort is the most desired improvement suggested by wearers and nonwearers of contact lenses.

Obviously, the headings contain too much information. Just what should be left out depends on your judgment. Here is one possible revision:

Most Desirable Feature: Personal Appearance
Prime Criticism: Difficulty of Insertion
Most Desired Improvement: Comfort

In your effort to be concise, should your headings omit *a*, *an*, and *the*, as some of the examples above do? Authorities on readability recommend including these words in body text, but there appears to be no consensus on whether to use or omit them in headings and titles. See what your teacher or boss prefers, and whichever way you choose, be consistent throughout your report.

Variety of Expression. In the wording of headings, as in all other forms of writing, you should use some variety of expression. Repeating words too frequently makes for monotonous writing. The following outline excerpt illustrates this point:

> Oil Production in Texas
> Oil Production in California
> Oil Production in Louisiana

As a rule, if you make the headings talk well, there is little chance of monotonous repetition. The headings in the preceding example can be improved simply by making them talk:

> Texas Leads in Oil Production.
> California Holds the Runner-up Position.
> Rapidly Gaining Louisiana Ranks Third.

The table of contents is an important preview of your report. Your goal is to use headings that will make it interesting, precise, and logically structured.

WRITING THE REPORT

LO6 Write reports that are focused, objective, consistent in time viewpoint, smoothly connected, and interesting.

By the time you write your report, you will have already done a good deal of writing. You will have written—and probably rewritten—problem and purpose statements to guide you through your research. You will have collected written data or recorded your findings in notes, and you will have organized your interpretations of the data into a logical, reader-centered structure. Now it is time to flesh out your outline with clearly expressed facts and observations.

When you draft your report, your first priority is to get the right things said in the right order. As Chapter 6 advises, you should not strive for a perfect draft the first time around. Understand that some pieces will seem to write themselves, while others will be much more difficult. Allow yourself to move along, stitching together the pieces. Once you have a draft to work with, you can perfect it.

When revising, let the advice in the previous chapters be your guide. As with all the business messages previously discussed, reports should communicate as clearly and quickly as possible. Your readers' time is valuable, and you risk having your report misread or even ignored if you do not keep this fact in mind. Use both words and formatting to get your contents across efficiently.

You can help your reader receive the report's message clearly by giving your report some specific qualities of well-written reports. Two critical ingredients are a reader-centered beginning and ending. Such characteristics as objectivity, consistency in time viewpoint, coherence, and interest can also enhance the reception of your report. We review these topics next.

Beginning and Ending

Arguably the most critical parts of your report will be the beginning and ending. In fact, researchers agree that these are the most frequently read parts of a report. Chapter 12 goes into detail about report beginnings and endings, but some general advice is in order here.

Whatever other goals it may achieve, the opening of your report should convey what problem you studied, how you studied it, and (at least generally) what you found out. Why? Because these are the facts that the reader most wants to know when he or she first looks at your report.

Here is a simple introduction that follows this pattern:

> In order to find out why sales were down at the Salisbury store, I interviewed the manager, observed the operations, and assessed the environment. A high rate of employee turnover appears to have resulted in a loss of customers, though the deteriorating neighborhood also seems to be a contributing factor.

In a formal report, some brief sections may precede this statement of purpose (for example, facts about the authorization of the study), and there might be extensive front matter (for example, a title page, letter of transmittal, table of contents, and executive summary). What follows the purpose statement can also vary depending on the size and complexity of the report (for example, it may or may not be appropriate to go into more detail about the research methods and limitations or to announce specifically how the following sections will be organized). But whatever kind of report you are writing, make sure that the beginning gets across the subject of the report, what kind of data it is based upon, and its likely significance to the reader.

Your ending will provide a concise statement of the report's main payoff—whether facts, interpretations, or recommendations. In a short report, you may simply summarize your findings with a brief paragraph, since the specific findings will be easy to see in the body of the report. In a longer report, you should make this section a more thorough restatement of your main findings, formatted in an easy-to-read way. Both the gist ("so what did you find out?") and the significance ("why should I care?") of your report should be clear.

Being Objective

As we have said, a good report is objective; it presents all relevant facts and interprets them logically, without bias. Your objectivity should be evident in both your content and your writing style.

Objectivity as a Basis for Believability. An objective report has an ingredient that is essential to good report writing—**believability**. Powerful assertions made in emotionally charged language may at first glance appear to strengthen your report. But if bias is evident at any point in a report, the reader will question the credibility of the entire report. Maintaining objectivity is, therefore, the only sure way to make report writing believable.

The Question of Impersonal versus Personal Writing. Recognizing the need for objectivity, early report writers worked to develop an objective style of writing. Since the source of bias in reports was people, they reasoned that objectivity was best attained by emphasizing facts rather than the people involved in writing and reading reports. So they tried to take the human beings out of their reports. The result was **impersonal writing**—that is, writing in the third person, without *I, we,* or *you* perspectives.

In recent years, some writers have opposed this approach. They argue that **personal writing** is more forceful and direct than impersonal writing. They point out that writing is more conversational and therefore more interesting if it brings both the reader and the writer into the picture. They contend that objectivity is an attitude—not a matter of pronoun use—and that a report written in the personal style can be just as objective as a report written in the impersonal style. These writers argue that impersonal writing frequently leads to an overuse of the passive voice and a dull writing style. (While this last claim may be true, impersonal writing need not be boring. One has only to look at the lively style of many newspaper articles to see that impersonal writing can be interesting.)

As with most controversies, the arguments on both sides have merit. In some situations, personal writing is better. In other situations, impersonal writing is better. And in still other situations, either type of writing is good.

Your decision should be based on the facts of each report situation. First, you should consider the expectations of those for whom you are preparing the report. If your readers prefer an impersonal style, use it—and vice versa. Then you should consider the

Formal, Informal, or Somewhere in Between?

As the next chapter points out, the format and makeup of your report will signal its level of formality. But you will also need to decide how formal your report will be on the stylistic level. Compare the following three versions of the same point:

- The study revealed that 20 percent of the participants were unaware of Jacob's Foods.

- Our study revealed that 20 percent of the participants were unaware of your store.

- We found out that 20 percent of your market had never heard of your store.

Did you notice the decreasing level of formality? What accounts for the differences? Be sure to choose a style that matches the relationship you have with your readers and their preferences. But whatever style you choose, write clearly and readably.

---

formality of the situation. In general, personal writing is appropriate for informal situations and impersonal writing for most formal situations.

Here are contrasting examples of the personal and impersonal style:

Personal

Having studied the advantages and disadvantages of using coupons, I recommend that your company not adopt this practice. If you used coupons, you would have to absorb their cost. You would also have to hire additional employees to take care of the increase in sales volume.

Impersonal

A study of the advantages and disadvantages of using coupons supports the conclusion that the Mills Company should not adopt this practice. The coupons themselves would cost extra money. Also, use of coupons would require additional personnel to take care of the increase in sales volume.

Notice that both versions are active, clear, and interesting. Strive for these effects no matter which style you choose.

Being Consistent with Time

A report that has illogical time shifts—for example, one that says "The managers responded . . . " (past tense) in one place but "The employees say . . . " (present tense) in another place—confuses the reader. Thus, it is important that you maintain a **consistent time viewpoint**.

You have two main choices of time viewpoint: past or present. Although some authorities favor one or the other, either viewpoint can produce a good report. The important thing is to be consistent—to select one time viewpoint and stay with it. In other words, you should view all similar information in the report from the same position in time.

If you adopt the **past-time viewpoint**, you treat the research, the findings, and the writing of the report as past. Thus, you would report the results of a recent survey in past tense: "Twenty-two percent of the managers *favored* a change." You would write a reference to another part of the report this way: "As Part II *indicated*, . . ." Your use of the past-time viewpoint would have no effect on references to current and future happenings. It would still be proper to write a sentence like this: "If the current trend *continues*, 30 percent *will favor* a change by 2015." Prevailing concepts and proven conclusions are also exceptions. You would present them in present tense. For example, you would write "Solar energy *is* a major potential source of energy" and "The findings *indicate* that managers are not adequately trained."

Writing in the **present-time viewpoint** presents as current all information that can logically be assumed to be current at the time of writing. All other information is presented in its proper place in the past or future. Thus, you would report the results of a recent survey in these words: "Twenty-two percent of the managers *favor* a change." You would refer to another part of the text like this: As Part II *indicates, ...*" But in referring to an earlier survey, you would write: "In 2009 only 12 percent *held* this opinion." And in making a future reference, you would write: "If this trend continues, 30 percent *will hold* this opinion by 2015."

Including Transitions

A well-written report reads as one continuous story, with the parts smoothly connected. Much of this flow is the result of good, logical organization. But more than logical order is needed in long reports. As you will see in Chapter 12, a special coherence plan may be needed as well. In all reports, however, lesser transitional techniques are useful to connect information.

As Chapter 4 explains, transitions are words or sentences that show the relationships between parts of a sentence, paragraph, or document. In reports, they may appear at the beginning of a part as a way of relating this part to the preceding part. They may appear at the end of a part as a forward look. Or they may appear within a part as words or phrases that help move the flow of information.

Sentence Transitions. Throughout the report you can improve the connecting network of thought by using sentence transitions. They are especially helpful between parts of the report.

In the following example, the report parts are connected by sentences that make a forward-looking reference and thus set up the next subject. As a result, the shift of subject matter is smooth and logical.

> These data show clearly that alternative fuel cars are the most economical. Unquestionably, their operation by gas and hydrogen and their record for low-cost maintenance give them a decided edge over gas-fueled cars. *Before a definite conclusion about their merit can be reached, however, one more vital comparison should be made.*

The final sentence above clearly introduces the subsequent discussion of an additional comparison. Here is another example of a forecasting sentence:

> *. . . At first glance the data appear convincing, but a closer observation reveals a number of discrepancies.*

The reader knows to expect a discussion of the discrepancies next.

Placing topic sentences at key points of emphasis is another way of using sentences to link the various parts of the report. Usually the topic sentence is best placed at the paragraph beginning. Note in the following example how topic sentences maintain the flow of thought by emphasizing key information.

> *The Acura accelerates faster than the other two brands, both on a level road and on a 9 percent grade.* According to a test conducted by *Consumer Reports*, Acura reaches a speed of 60 miles per hour in 13.2 seconds. To reach the same speed, Toyota requires 13.6 seconds, and Volkswagen requires 14.4 seconds. On a 9 percent grade, Acura reaches the 60-miles-per-hour speed in 29.4 seconds, and Toyota reaches it in 43.3 seconds. Volkswagen is unable to reach this speed.

> *Because it carries more weight on its rear wheels than the others, Acura has the best traction of the three.* Traction, which means a minimum of sliding on wet or icy roads, is important to safe driving, particularly during the cold, wet winter months. Since traction is directly related to the weight carried by the rear wheels, a comparison of these weights should give some measure of the safety of the three cars. According to data released by the Automobile Bureau of Standards, Acura carries 47 percent of its weight on its rear wheels. Nissan and Toyota carry 44 and 42 percent, respectively.

Choice Lines Gleaned from Accident Reports Submitted to Insurance Companies

- Coming home, I drove into the wrong house and collided with a tree I don't have.
- The other car collided with mine without giving warning of its intentions.
- I thought my window was down, but found it was up when I put my hand through it.
- I collided with a stationary truck coming the other way.
- A pedestrian hit me and went under my car.
- The guy was all over the road. I had to swerve a number of times before I hit him.
- I pulled away from the side of the road, glanced at my mother-in-law, and headed over the embankment.
- I was having rear-end trouble when my universal joint gave way, causing me to have this accident.

- My car was legally parked as it backed into the other car.
- I told police that I was not injured, but on removing my hat, I found that I had a fractured skull.
- I was sure the old fellow would never make it to the other side of the road when I struck him.
- The pedestrian had no idea which direction to run, so I ran over him.
- The indirect cause of this accident was a little guy in a small car with a big mouth.
- The telephone pole was approaching. I was attempting to swerve out of the way when it struck my front end.

Transitional Words. Although the most important function of transitions is to connect the major parts of the report, transitions are also needed between the lesser parts. If the writing is to flow smoothly, you will need to connect clause to clause, sentence to sentence, and paragraph to paragraph, as Chapter 4 advises.

Numerous transitional words are available. The following list shows such words and how you can use them.

Relationship	Word Examples
Listing or enumeration of subjects	In addition
	First, second,. . .
	Besides
	Moreover
Contrast	On the contrary
	In spite of
	On the other hand
	In contrast
	However
Likeness	Also
	Likewise
	Similarly
Cause–effect	Thus
	Because of
	Therefore
	Consequently
	For this reason

Relationship	Word Examples
Explanation or elaboration	For example
	To illustrate
	For instance
	Also
	Too

Helpful as transitions are, you should use them only when they are needed—when including them would provide a useful preview or leaving them out would produce abruptness. For example, avoid such boring, unnecessary transitions as "This concludes the discussion of Topic X. In the next section, Y will be analyzed."

Maintaining Interest

Like any other form of writing, report writing should be interesting. Actually, interest is as important as the facts of the report because communication is not likely to occur without it. Readers cannot help missing parts of the message if their attention is allowed to stray. (If you have ever tried to read dull writing when studying for an exam, you know the truth of this statement.)

To write interestingly, avoid business clichés and unnecessarily abstract language. Remember that behind every fact and figure there is life—people doing things, machines operating, a commodity being marketed. A technique of good report writing is to bring that life to the surface by using concrete words and active-voice verbs as much as possible. Keeping your wording efficient also helps maintain the reader's interest.

But you can overdo efforts to make report writing interesting. Such is the case whenever your reader's attention is attracted to how something has been said rather than to what has been said. Effective report writing simply presents information in a clear, concise, and interesting manner. Report-writing style is at its best when the readers are prompted to say "Here are some interesting facts" rather than "Here is some interesting writing."

COLLABORATIVE REPORT WRITING

LO7 Prepare reports collaboratively.

In your business career, you are likely to participate in numerous collaborative writing projects, and the end product of many of them is likely to be a report. Group involvement in report preparation is becoming increasingly significant for a number of reasons. For one, the specialized knowledge of different people can improve the quality of the work. For another, the combined talents of the members are likely to produce a document better than any one of the members could produce alone. A third reason is that dividing the work can reduce the time needed for the project. And fourth, many different software tools allow groups to collaborate easily and well from different places.

Determining the Group Makeup

The first step is to decide who will be in the group. The availability and competencies of the people in the work situation involved are likely to be the major factors. At a minimum, the group will consist of two. The maximum will depend on the number actually needed to do the project. As a practical matter, however, a maximum of five is a good rule since larger groups tend to lose efficiency. All major areas of specialization needed to investigate the problem should be represented by the team members.

In most business situations the highest ranking administrator in the group serves as leader. In groups made up of equals, a leader usually is appointed or elected. When no leader is so designated, the group works together informally. In such cases, however, an informal leader usually emerges. Especially with group writing projects, it is a good idea to have one person in charge of overseeing the entire process.

Does Your Group Have Emotional Intelligence?

Ever since the publication of Daniel Goleman's *Emotional Intelligence: Why It Can Matter More Than IQ* in 1995, companies have been looking for ways to cultivate the emotional intelligence (EI) of its members.

But groups can enhance their collective EI, too. According to Vanessa Urch Druskat and Steven B. Wolff of the *Harvard Business Review*, "Group EI norms build the foundation for true collaboration and cooperation—helping otherwise skilled teams fulfill their highest potential."

What kinds of things should a group do to channel its members' insights and emotions into positive results? Here's a partial list from Druskat and Wolff:

- Encourage all members to share their perspectives before making key decisions.

- Handle confrontation constructively. If team members fall short, call them on it by letting them know the group needs them.

- Regularly assess the group's strengths, weaknesses, and modes of interaction.

- Create structures that let the group express its emotions.

- Cultivate an affirmative environment.

- Encourage proactive problem solving.

And try to keep things fun. In one company, the industrial-design firm IDEO, participants throw stuffed toys at anyone who prematurely judges ideas during brainstorming sessions.

SOURCE: "Building the Emotional Intelligence of Groups," *Harvard Business Review* 1 Mar. 2001, *HarvardBusiness.org*, Harvard Business Publishing, Web, 8 July 2012.

Creating the Ground Rules

In organizations where teamwork is common, the ground rules for participation in a group may be understood. But students and working professionals alike may find it helpful to establish explicit guidelines for the participants.

Some rules may govern the members' interactions. For example, a rule might be "Listen respectfully and actively to what others are saying, without interrupting." Or it might instruct members to use "I" language ("I think . . .") rather than "you" language ("The problem with your idea is . . .") when disagreeing. Others might cover more logistical issues, such as conscientiously doing one's share of the work, keeping the group informed if problems arise, and being on time with one's contributions.

Ideally, the group will generate its own ground rules to which all members will agree. Some instructors find that actually drawing up a contract and having each member sign it is a good way to get group work off to a good start and prevent problems down the line.

Choosing the Means of Collaboration

Not that many years ago, groups needed numerous face-to-face meetings in order to get their work done. Today there are many other venues for group interactions. Your group should put careful thought into the choice of media that will enable effective collaboration while taking into account members' time constraints, distance from each other, and technological preferences.

If possible, you should have at least two face-to-face meetings—one at the start of the project and another near the end (for example, when doing the final revisions). But the bulk of the collaborating may take place by email, by discussion board, or through such online collaborative authoring tools as Google Docs or wikis (see Chapter 17).

Many reports written in business are produced in collaboration with others. Although you will do some work individually, you can expect to plan, organize, and revise the report as a group.

You might even use a live-meeting application or Skype to converse with each other. Whatever tools you use, it is vitally important that you choose them consciously and create any ground rules that will apply to their use.

Making a Project Plan

Especially when the desired outcome is a coherent, effective report, the group should structure its tasks to meet the project's goals. Using the steps discussed in the next section and any additional considerations, the group should prepare a timeline that clearly states or shows the deadline for each task. A Gantt chart can be very useful along these lines (see Chapters 14 and 17), but even a simple list or table can suffice. In addition, your plan should make clear who is responsible for what. If your group has taken an inventory of its strengths before its planning, you can match members up with what they do best (for example, doing research or revising a document).

Your plan can also describe in some detail the desired form and style of the final document (such as which template it will use or whether or not it will use "you"). The more the group determines such matters up front, the less scrambling it will need to do at the end to generate a coherent, consistent-looking report.

Researching and Writing the Report

However the group decides to operate, the following activities typically occur, usually in the sequence shown.

1. *Determine the Problem and Purpose.* As in all report projects, the participants must determine just what the report must do. Thus, the group should follow the preliminary steps of determining the problem and purpose of the project as discussed previously. They also need to develop a coherent, shared sense of the report's intended readers and their needs.

TECHNOLOGY IN BRIEF

Comment and Review Tools Help Writers Track Changes to Their Documents

The commenting and reviewing tools in most word processors help people work together on documents asynchronously. When others review content and edit your document digitally, the commenting tool allows them to express opinions and concerns while the tracking tool makes their editing changes clearly visible. The tools allow you to accept or reject their suggestions individually or en masse.

In the example shown here, the reviewer clicked Word 2010's Review tab, circled in red, to reveal the commenting and reviewing tools. By clicking "Track Changes" (highlighted on the toolbar), the reviewer had Word keep track of all changes being made to the document as well as any comments being added. Word's tracking system allows reviewers to use a variety of colors so that others can easily determine whom the changes belong to. The commenting tool identifies each reviewer, too. Clicking on "Reviewers" in the dropdown menu will show which people have reviewed the document.

When the writer opens the reviewed document, he or she will see all the comments and edits. The "Accept" and "Reject" options (circled in dark blue), which also appear when you right-click on a given edit, enable the writer to keep the desired changes and remove the rest.

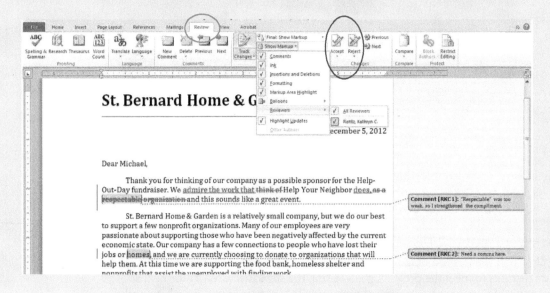

2. *Identify the Factors.* The group next determines what needs to be studied in order to achieve the report's purpose. This step involves determining the factors of the problem, as described earlier in the chapter. An advantage of collaboration is that several minds are available for the critical thinking that is so necessary for identifying the factors of the problem.

3. *Gather the Needed Information.* Before the group can begin writing the report, it must get the information needed. This activity can include any of the types of research discussed in Chapter 13. In some cases, however, group work begins after the information has already been assembled, thus eliminating this step.

4. *Interpret the Information.* Determining the meaning of the information gathered is the next logical step for the group. In this step, the participants apply the findings to the problem and select the appropriate information for the report. In doing so, they also give meaning to the facts collected. The facts do not speak for themselves. Rather, group participants must think through the facts, identify their significance, and interpret them from the readers' points of view.

368   PART 4   Fundamentals of Report Writing

5. *Organize the Material.* Just as in any other report-writing project, the group next organizes the material selected for presentation. They will base the report's structure on time, place, quantity, factor, or other relationships in the data.

6. *Plan the Report's Components and Style.* A next logical step is planning the makeup of the report. In this step the formality of the situation, the anticipated length of the report, and the intended audience need to be considered (see Chapter 12). In addition, the team needs to agree on such matters as the report's style, the kinds of headings to use, and whether to use the present- or past-time viewpoint.

7. *Assign Parts to Be Written.* After the planning has been done, the group next turns its attention to the writing. The usual practice is to assign each person a part of the report.

8. *Write Parts Assigned.* Following comes a period of individual work. Each participant writes his or her part. Each should apply the ideas in Chapters 3–5 about word selection, sentence design, paragraph construction, and tone.

9. *Revise Collaboratively.* The group meets and reviews each person's contribution and the full report. This should be a give-and-take session with each person actively participating. It requires courteous but meaningful criticisms. It also requires that the participants be open minded, remembering that the goal is to construct the best possible document.

10. *Edit the Final Draft.* After the group has done its work, one member is usually assigned the task of editing the final draft. This editor gives the document a consistent style and serves as the major proofreader. However, since the document reflects on all members, they should assist with the final proofreading.

If all the work has been done with care and diligence, this final draft should be a report better than anyone in the group could have prepared alone.

THERE'S MORE ...

How can you find out if your reader read your report? What are six team personality types? Scan the QR code with your smartphone or use your Web browser to find out at www.mhhe .com/lesikar13e. Choose Chapter 11 > Bizcom Tools & Tips.

SUMMARY BY LEARNING OBJECTIVES

1. Your work on a report begins with a business problem, which will determine your report's purpose.

   Write clear problem and purpose statements.

   - Get the problem in mind by gathering all the information you need about it.
   - Develop a problem statement from the information.
   - Then write a purpose statement that will capture the goal of your research and your report.
   - Understand that you may need to revise your problem and purpose statements as you proceed with your research.

2. From the problem statement, determine the factors involved.

   List the factors involved in a problem.

   - These may be subtopics in information reports.
   - They may be hypotheses (possible explanations) in problems requiring a solution.
   - They may be bases of comparison in problems requiring evaluations.

3. After you have gathered the information you need, interpret it as it applies to the problem.

Explain the common errors in interpreting data and develop attitudes and practices conducive to good interpreting.

- Interpret the information in light of the problem and your readers' needs.
- Heed this advice for avoiding human error:
  — Report the facts as they are.
  — Do not think that conclusions are always necessary.
  — Do not interpret a lack of evidence as proof to the contrary.
  — Do not compare noncomparable data.
  — Do not draw illogical cause–effect conclusions.
  — Beware of unreliable and unrepresentative data.
  — Do not oversimplify.
  — Tailor your claims to your data.
- Adopt these attitudes and practices:
  — Maintain a judicial attitude.
  — Consult with others.
  — Test your interpretations by applying the test of experience (using reason) and the negative test (challenging them).
  — Use statistical analysis to help you interpret numerical data.

4. Next, organize the information by constructing an outline.

Organize information in outline form, using time, place, quantity, factor, or a combination of these as bases for division.

- An outline helps you group and order the information and create an information hierarchy.
  — Your research plan and interpretation notes can help you make your report outline.
  — You may choose to use conventional outline symbols (I, A, 1, a) or numeric symbols (1, 1.1, 1.1.1), but any outline format is fine if it helps you write a well-organized draft.
  — The outline is a tool to help you—feel free to mark it up and revise it.
- Organize the report body (the part between the introduction and the ending section) by a process of division.
  — Look for ways to divide the findings on the basis of time, place, quantity, factor, or a combination.
  — Then divide them to form the major parts of the report.
  — Next, look at these divisions for ways of dividing them.
  — Continue to subdivide as far as necessary.
  — The end result is your outline.

5. Turn your outline into a table of contents.

Turn an outline into a table of contents whose format and wording are logical and meaningful.

- Use a format that your reader will find instructive, readable, and appropriate.
- You may use topic headings (which identify each topic being discussed).
- Or you may use talking headings (which identify each topic and also say something about it).
- Make the wording of comparable parts grammatically parallel.
- Edit each heading for conciseness.
- Avoid excessive repetition of words.

6. From the outline, write the report.

Write reports that are focused, objective, consistent in time viewpoint, smoothly connected, and interesting.

- Draft to get the right information in the right order; then revise for perfection.
- Make your beginning and ending reader centered.
  — Write a beginning that tells what problem you studied, how you studied it, and what you found out.

- Write an ending that summarizes the main findings and their significance to the readers.
- Maintain objectivity in both content and style.
  - To achieve believability, avoid bias in your presentation of facts and in your tone.
  - Whether using the impersonal or personal style, be sure your attitude is objective.
  - For most formal reports, use the impersonal style.
- Be consistent in time viewpoint—either past or present.
  - Past-time viewpoint views the research and findings as past and prevailing concepts and conclusions as present.
  - Present-time viewpoint presents as current all that is current at the time of writing.
- Use transitions to make the report parts flow smoothly.
  - Between large parts, you may need to use full sentences to make connections.
  - Topic sentences also can help the flow of thought.
  - Use transitional words and phrases to connect the lesser parts.
- Work to make the writing interesting.
  - Select words carefully for the best effect.
  - Use the techniques of good writing (e.g., correctness, rhythmic flow of words, vigorous words).
  - Do not overdo these efforts by drawing attention to how you write rather than what you say.

7. Expect that you will sometimes prepare reports collaboratively.

Prepare reports collaboratively.

- Groups (two to five members) may produce better reports than individuals if all things go well.
- Members of groups (leaders and participants) should have clear roles.
- Groups should establish their ground rules, choose their means of collaboration, and make a project plan.
- Groups should follow this procedure in writing reports collaboratively:
  - Determine the report's problem and purpose.
  - Identify the factors of the problem.
  - Collect facts for the report.
  - Interpret the facts.
  - Organize the material.
  - Plan the report's components and style.
  - Assign parts to members.
  - Write the assigned parts.
  - Revise members' contributions collaboratively.
  - Edit the final draft.

KEY TERMS

report problem, 344

report purpose, 344

problem statement, 344

purpose statement, 344

problem factors, 345

hypotheses, 346

correlated, 350

test of experience, 351

negative test, 351

CRITICAL THINKING QUESTIONS

1 What kinds of reports do you expect to write in your chosen profession? Why? **LO1**

2 Explain the concept of outlining as a process of division. **LO4**

3 What formatting devices in a table of contents can aid reader comprehension? Find some examples of helpfully formatted tables of contents and discuss what makes them effective. **LO5**

4 You are writing a report on the progress of your local cable company's efforts to increase sales of five of its products through extensive advertising in print and online newspapers and magazines and on television and radio. Discuss the possibilities for major headings. Evaluate each possibility. **LO2, LO4**

5 Find a sample short report online on a topic of interest to you and evaluate it using the advice in this chapter. Is it a good report? Why or why not? **LO3, LO6**

6 Explain the difference between personal and impersonal writing. Which is "better"? Argue both sides. **LO6**

7 Explain the differences between the present-time viewpoint and the past-time viewpoint. **LO6**

8 Is it incorrect to have present, past, and future tense in the same report? In the same paragraph? In the same sentence? Explain. **LO6**

9 "Transitional sentences are unnecessary. They merely add length to a report and thus run contrary to the goal of conciseness." Discuss. **LO6**

10 "Reports are written for business executives who want them. Thus, you don't have to be concerned about holding your reader's interest." Discuss. **LO6**

11 "Collaborative reports are better than reports written by an individual because they use many minds rather than one." Discuss. **LO7**

12 "Disagreements in groups are counterproductive." Discuss. **LO7**

SKILLS BUILDING EXERCISES

1 For each of the following problem situations, write a clear purpose statement and list the factors you would probably need to investigate. When necessary, you may use your imagination to supply any additional information needed. **LO1, LO2**

   a. A manufacturer of breakfast cereals wants to attract a new demographic of customers.

   b. The manufacturer of a toothpaste wants a bigger share of the toothpaste market.

   c. Wal-Mart wants to give its stockholders a summary of its operations for the past calendar year.

   d. A building contractor engaged to build a new office for Company X needs to submit a progress report.

   e. Able Wholesale Company wants to find out how much cash it should have in reserve.

   f. The supervisor of Department X must prepare a report evaluating the performance of an administrative assistant.

   g. Baker, Inc., is experiencing higher than normal employee turnover.

   h. An executive must rank three subordinates on the basis of their suitability for promotion to a particular job.

   i. The supervisor of production must compare three competing machines that are being considered for use in a particular production job.

   j. An investment consultant must advise a client on whether to invest in the development of a lake resort.

   k. A consultant needs to hep a restaurant improve its profits.

2 Select a hypothetical problem with a time division possibility. What other division possibilities does it have? Compare the two possibilities as the main bases for organizing the report. **LO2**

3 Assume that you are writing the results of a survey conducted to determine what kinds of groceries are purchased by female college students in the United States. What division possibilities exist here? Which would you recommend? **LO4**

4 For the problem described in the preceding exercise, use your imagination to construct topic headings for the outline. **LO4**

5 Point out any error in grammatical parallelism in these headings: **LO4**

  a. Region I sales lagging.

  b. Moderate increase seen for Region II.

  c. Sales in Region III.

6 Point out any error in grammatical parallelism in these headings: **LO4**

  a. High cost of operation.

  b. Slight improvement in production efficiency.

  c. Maintenance cost is low.

7 Which of the following headings is inconsistent with the others? **LO4**

  a. Agricultural production continues to increase.

  b. Slight increase is made by manufacturing.

  c. Salaries remain high.

  d. Service industries show no change.

8 Select an editorial, feature article, book chapter, or other document that has no headings. Write talking headings for it. **LO4**

9 Assume that you are reporting the results of a survey you have conducted. Write a paragraph of the report using the present-time viewpoint; then write the paragraph using the past-time viewpoint. The paragraph needs to convey the following information: **LO6**

Answers to the question about how students view the proposed Aid to Education Bill in this survey and in a survey taken a year earlier (last year's results are in parentheses):

For, 39 percent (21); Against, 17 percent (43).

No answer, undecided, etc., 44 percent (36).

10 List the advantages and disadvantages of each of these different media for writing collaboratively.

  a. Face-to-face meetings

  b. Email

  c. Discussion boards

  d. Online editing tool (e.g., Google Docs)

  e. Website (e.g., blog or wiki)

  f. Live online interaction (e.g., Skyping or IM-ing) **LO7**

CHAPTER TWELVE

Choosing the Right Type of Report

Learning Objectives

Upon completing this chapter, you will be able to write well-structured business reports. To reach this goal, you should be able to

1 Explain the makeup of reports relative to length and formality.

2 Discuss the four main ways that the writing in short reports differs from the writing in long reports.

3 Choose an appropriate form for short reports.

4 Adapt the procedures for writing short reports to routine operational reports, progress reports, and problem-solving reports as well as to minutes of meetings.

5 Write longer reports that include the appropriate components, meet the readers' needs, and are easy to follow.

Preparing Different Types of Business Reports

Assume again the position of an operations manager at Technisoft (as introduced in Chapter 11). Writing reports is a significant part of your job. Most of the time, these reports concern routine, everyday problems: human resource policies, administrative procedures, work flow, and the like. Following what appears to be established company practice, you write the reports on these problems in simple email form.

Occasionally, however, you have a more involved assignment. Last week, for example, you investigated a union charge that the company showed favoritism to nonunion workers on certain production jobs. Because your report on this formal investigation was written for the benefit of ranking company administrators as well as union leaders, you used a more formal style and format.

Then there was the report you helped prepare for the board of directors last fall. That report summarized pressing needs for capital improvements. A number of executives contributed to this project, but you were the coordinator. Because the report was important and was written for the board, you made it as formal as possible.

Clearly, reports vary widely. This chapter will help you determine your reports' makeup, style, form, and contents. It will then focus on the types of reports that are likely to figure in your business-writing future.

AN OVERVIEW OF REPORT COMPONENTS

LO1 Explain the makeup of reports relative to length and formality.

As you prepare to write any report, you will need to decide on its makeup. Will it be a simple email? Will it be a long, complex, and formal report? Or will it fall between these extremes?

To a great extent, your decisions will be based on the report's anticipated length and formality. The more complex the problem and the more formal the situation, the more elaborate the report is likely to be. Conversely, less complex problems and less formal situations will require less elaborate reports. Adjusting your report's form and contents based on its likely length and formality will help you meet the reader's needs in each situation.

In the subsections that follow, we first explain how to decide which components to use for a given report. We then briefly review the purpose and contents of each of these components.

The Report Classification Plan

The diagram in Figure 12–1 can help you construct reports that fit your specific need. At the top of the "stairway" are the most **formal reports**. Such reports have a number of pages that come before the report itself, just as this book has pages that come before the first chapter. Typically, these **prefatory pages**, as they are called, are included when the situation is formal and the report is long. The exact makeup of the prefatory pages may vary, but the most common parts, in this order, are title fly, title page, letter of transmittal, table of contents, and executive summary. Flyleaves (blank pages at the beginning and end that protect the report) also may be included.

As the need for formality decreases and the problem becomes smaller, the makeup of the report changes. Although the changes that occur are far from standardized, they follow a general order. First, the title fly drops out. This page contains only the report title, which also appears on the next page. Since the title fly is used primarily for reasons of formality, it is the first component to go.

On the next level of formality, the executive summary and the letter of transmittal are combined. When this stage is reached, the report problem is simple enough to be summarized in a short space. As shown in Figure 12–1, the report at this stage has

Figure 12–1

Progression of Change in Report Makeup as Formality Requirements and Length Decrease

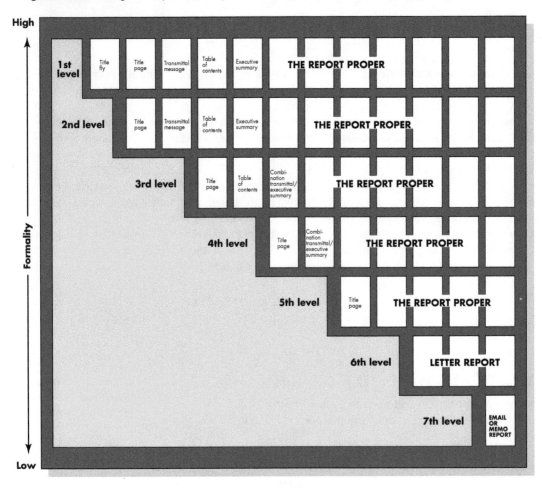

three prefatory parts: title page, table of contents, and combined transmittal letter and executive summary.

At the fourth step, the table of contents drops out. Another step down, as formality and length requirements continue to decrease, the combined letter of transmittal and executive summary drops out. Thus, the report commonly called the **short report** now has only a title page and the report text. The title page remains to the last because it serves as a useful cover page. In addition, it contains the most important identifying information.

Below the short-report form is a form that presents the information as a **letter report**. And finally, for short problems of less formality, the **email** or **memo** form is used.

This is a general analysis of how reports are adapted to the problem and situation. While it won't cover every report, it can be relied upon for most reports you will write.

The Report Components

To be able to decide which parts of a long, formal report to include in your reports, you need a basic understanding of each part. This section describes the different report components represented in Figure 12–1.

Title Pages. The first two pages of a long, formal report—the **title fly** and **title page**—contain identification information. As we have said, the title fly contains only the report

Creating a Report Title with the 5 Ws and 1 H

As this chapter says, the five Ws (*who, what, where, when, why*) and one H (*how*) can help you craft a report title that is precise and informative.

For example, to generate a title for a recommendation report about sales training at Nokia, you might ask yourself . . .

Who?	Nokia
What?	Sales training recommendations
Where?	Implied (Nokia regional offices)
When?	2014
Why?	Implied (to improve sales training)
How?	Studied the company's sales activities

From this analysis would come the title "Sales Training Recommendations for Nokia," with the subtitle "Based on a 2014 Study of Company Sales Activities."

title; it is included simply to give a report the most formal appearance. The title page, as illustrated on pages 386 and 416, is more informative. It typically contains the title, identification of the writer and reader, and the date.

Although constructing title pages is easy, composing the title is not. In fact, on a per-word basis, the title requires more time than any other part of the report. A good title efficiently and precisely covers the contents. Consider building your title around the five Ws: *who, what, where, when,* and *why*. Sometimes *how* may be important as well. You may not need to use all the Ws, but they can help you check the completeness of your title. Remember that a good title is concise as well as complete, so be careful not to make your title so long that it is hard to understand. A subtitle can help you be both concise and complete, as in this example: "Employee Morale at Florida Human Resource Offices: Results from a 2013 Survey."

In addition to displaying the report title, the title page identifies the recipient and the writer (and usually their titles and company names). The title page also contains the date unless it is already in the title of the report. Your word-processing program likely includes some attractive templates for title pages, like those used in the sample reports in this chapter. You can also download report templates from the Internet.

Transmittal Message. As the label implies, the **transmittal message** is a message that transmits the report to the reader. In formal situations, it usually takes letter form. In less formal situations (e.g., when delivering a report to internal readers whom you know fairly well), the report can be transmitted orally or by email. Whatever the case, you should think of the transmittal as a personal message from the writer to the reader, with much the same contents you would use if you were handing the report over in a face-to-face meeting with the recipient. Except in cases of extreme formality, you should use personal pronouns (*you, I, we*) and conversational language.

The transmittal letters on pages 387 and 417 illustrate the usual structure for this component. Begin with a brief paragraph that says, essentially, "Here is the report." Briefly identify the report's contents and purpose and, if appropriate, its authorization (who assigned the report, when, and why). Focus the body of the message on the key points of the report or on facts about the report that could be useful for your readers to know. If you are combining the transmittal message with the executive summary, as represented by the third and fourth levels of Figure 12–1, here is where you will include that summary. At the end of the message, you should provide a pleasant and/or forward-looking comment. You might express gratitude for the assignment, for example, or offer to do additional research.

Figure 12–2

Diagram of the Executive Summary in Indirect and Direct Order

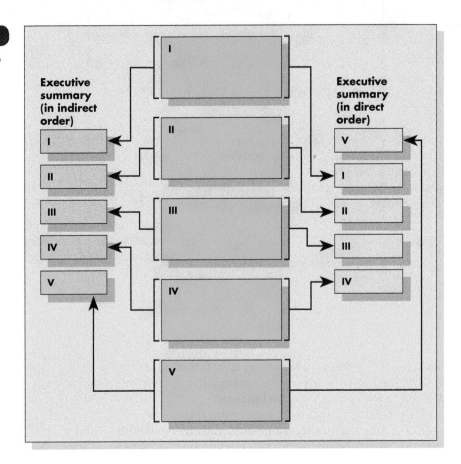

Table of Contents. If your short report goes much over five pages (or 1,500 words), you might consider including a brief **table of contents**. This part, of course, is a listing of the report's contents. As Chapter 11 points out, it is the report outline in finished form, with page numbers to indicate where the parts begin. The formatting should reflect the report's structure, with main headings clearly differentiated from subheadings. The section titles should state each part's contents clearly and match the report's headings exactly. The table of contents may also include a list of illustrations (or, if long, this list can stand alone). If a separate table of contents would be too formal, you can just list the topics that your report will cover in its introductory section.

Executive Summary. The **executive summary** is the report in miniature. For some readers it serves as a preview to the report, but for others—such as busy executives who may not have time to read the whole report—it's the only part of the report they will read. Because of this latter group of readers, the summary should be self-explanatory; that is, readers shouldn't have to read other parts of the report in order to make sense of the summary. As pointed out previously, whether the executive summary is one of the prefatory parts, is included in the transmittal message, or is part of the report proper depends on how long and how formal the report is.

You construct the executive summary by reducing the parts of the report in order and in proportion. You should clearly identify the topic, purpose, and origin of the report; state at least briefly what kind of research was conducted; present the key facts, findings, and analysis; and state the main conclusions and recommendations. If you include these parts in this order, which usually matches the order of the report contents, your summary will be written in the indirect order. But sometimes writers use the direct order by starting with the conclusions and recommendations and then continuing with the other information. Figure 12–2 shows the difference between these two structures, and Figures 12–3 and 12–4 give examples. Whichever order you choose, the executive summary will need to be a masterpiece of economical writing.

Figure 12–3

An Executive Summary in Indirect Order

EXECUTIVE SUMMARY

Midwestern Research Associates was contracted to study the performance of Nokia's salespeople. A team of two researchers observed 20 productive and 20 underperforming salespeople over five working days. The study also included an exit interview and a test of each salesperson's product knowledge.

Productive Use of Time

The data show that the productive salespeople used their time more effectively than did the underperforming salespeople. Compared with the latter, the productive salespeople spent less time in idleness (28% vs. 53%). They also spent more time in contact with prospects (31.3% vs. 19.8%) and more time developing prospects (10.4% vs. 4.4%).

Quality of Sales Presentations

Observations of sales presentations revealed that productive salespeople displayed higher integrity, used pressure more reasonably, and knew the product better than underperforming salespeople.

- Of the 20 productive salespeople, 16 displayed at least "moderately high integrity." Members of the underperforming group ranged widely on the integrity scale, with 7 in the "questionable" group and 5 each in the "moderately high integrity" and "deceitful" groups.
- Most (15) of the productive salespeople used moderate pressure, whereas the underperforming salespeople tended toward extremes (10 high pressure, 7 low pressure).
- On the product knowledge test, 17 of the productive salespeople scored excellent and 3 fair. In the other group, 5 scored excellent, 6 fair, and 9 inadequate.

Recommendations

On the basis of these findings, this report recommends adding the following topics to Nokia's sales training program:

- Negative effects of idle time
- Projection of integrity
- Use of moderate persuasion
- Value of product knowledge

Coverage of these topics will help bring the underperforming salespeople up to the level of Nokia's high-performing sales staff.

Figure 12-4

An Executive Summary in Direct Order

EXECUTIVE SUMMARY

To enhance the performance of Nokia's salespeople, this report recommends adding the following topics to Nokia's sales training program:

- Negative effects of idle time
- Projection of integrity
- Use of moderate persuasion
- Value of product knowledge

Supporting these recommendations are the findings and conclusions drawn from a five-day observational study of 20 productive and 20 underperforming salespeople. The study also included an exit interview and a test of each salesperson's product knowledge.

Productive Use of Time

The data show that the productive salespeople used their time more effectively than did the underperforming salespeople. Compared with the latter, the productive salespeople spent less time being idle (28% vs. 53%). They also spent more time in contact with prospects (31.3% vs. 19.8%) and more time developing prospects (10.4% vs. 4.4%).

Quality of Sales Presentations

Observations of sales presentations revealed that productive salespeople displayed higher integrity, used pressure more reasonably, and knew the product better than underperforming salespeople.

- Of the 20 productive salespeople, 16 displayed at least "moderately high integrity." Underperforming group members ranged widely on the integrity scale, with 7 in the "questionable" group and 5 each in the "moderately high integrity" and "deceitful" groups.
- Most (15) of the productive salespeople used moderate pressure, whereas the underperforming salespeople tended toward extremes (10 high pressure, 7 low pressure).
- On the product knowledge test, 17 of the productive salespeople scored excellent and 3 fair. In the other group, 5 scored excellent, 6 fair, and 9 inadequate.

These findings support a training program that covers productive use of time and the importance of integrity, moderate sales pressure, and product knowledge.

It may be desirable to include other report components not discussed here—for example, a copy of the message that authorized the report, various appendices containing supplementary material, a glossary, or a bibliography. As with any writing task, you will need to decide what parts to provide given the facts of the situation and your readers' preferences.

CHARACTERISTICS OF THE SHORTER REPORTS

LO2 Discuss the four main ways that the writing in short reports differs from the writing in long reports.

The shorter report forms (those at the bottom of the stairway) are by far the most common in business. These are the everyday working reports—those used for the routine information reporting that is vital to an organization's communication. Because these reports are so common, our study of report types begins with them.

Little Need for Introductory Information

Most of the shorter, more informal reports require little or no introductory material. These reports typically concern day-to-day problems. Their lives are short; they are not likely to be kept on file very long. They are intended for only a few readers, and these readers are likely to understand their context and purpose. If readers do need an introduction, that need is likely to be small.

Determining what introductory material to provide is simply a matter of answering one question: What does my reader need to know before reading the information in this report? In very short reports, an incidental reference to the problem or to the authorization of the investigation will be sufficient. In extreme cases, however, you may need a detailed introduction comparable to that of the more formal reports.

Reports need no introductory material if their very nature explains their purpose. This holds true for personnel actions, weekly sales reports, inventory reports, and some progress reports.

Predominance of the Direct Order

Because shorter reports usually solve routine problems, they are likely to be written in the direct order. That is, the report will begin with its most important information—usually the conclusion and perhaps a recommendation. Business writers use this order because they know that busy readers typically want the key point quickly.

The form that the direct order takes in longer reports is somewhat different. The main findings will be somewhere up front—either in the letter of transmittal, executive summary, or both—but the report itself may be organized indirectly. The introduction will present the topic and purpose of the report, but the actual findings will be brought out in the body sections, and their fullest statement will usually appear in the conclusions or recommendations section.

As you move down the structural ladder toward the more informal and shorter reports, however, the need for the direct order in the report itself increases. At the bottom of the ladder, the direct order is more the rule than the exception.

Many routine reports are submitted on hand-held devices.

Illustrating the direct arrangement is the following beginning of a report on a personnel issue:

The hiring committee recommends appointing Sue Breen as our new Corporate Communications Officer.

We interviewed three candidates for the position . . . [*The rest of this paragraph describes the candidates.*]

While all three candidates had strengths, Ms. Breen emerged as the top candidate, for these reasons:

- She was the most experienced of the three candidates, with 27 years' experience in corporate communication.
- She had the most expertise with the widest variety of communication media, from annual reports to blog posts to intranets and social networking, and she understood the advantages and disadvantages of each.
- She has an impressive track record. At Gemini Web Conferencing, she launched a corporate communications program that . . . [*The report continues to make the case and then reiterates its recommendation at the end.*]

As you can see, this report states its main point first and then supplies the supporting information.

In contrast, a report written in the indirect order presents the supporting information before stating its main conclusion or recommendation.

Using the personnel issue from the last example, the indirect arrangement would appear like this:

The hiring committee interviewed three candidates for the position of Corporate Communications Officer: . . . [*The opening paragraph briefly describes the candidates.*]

While all three candidates had strengths, Ms. Breen emerged as the top candidate, for these reasons:

- She was the most experienced of the three candidates, with 27 years' experience in corporate communication.
- She had the most expertise with the widest variety of communication media, from annual reports to blog posts to intranets and social networking, and she understood the advantages and disadvantages of each.
- She has an impressive track record. At Gemini Web Conferencing, she launched a corporate communications program that . . . [*The list continues to make the case.*]

In light of these assets, we recommend that Sue Breen be appointed as our new Corporate Communications Officer.

Deciding whether to use the direct order is best based on a consideration of your readers' likely use of the report. If your readers need the report conclusion or recommendation as a basis for an action that they must take, directness will speed their effort by enabling them to quickly receive the most important information. If they have confidence in your work, they may choose to skim or not even read the rest of the report before acting on your information. Should they desire to question any part of the report, however, the material is there for their inspection.

On the other hand, if there is reason to believe that it would be better for your readers to arrive at the conclusion or recommendation only after a logical review of the analysis, you should organize your report in the indirect order. This arrangement is especially preferable when you will be recommending something that you know your readers will not favor or want to hear. For example, in the illustration above, if you suspect that one of the executives to whom you're making your hiring recommendation prefers another candidate to Sue Breen, you'll want to make your case before stating the committee's decision. Presenting the supporting data before the recommendation prepares resistant readers to accept your solution to the report problem.

Tips from a Professional Explainer

City planners have to write proposals and reports that make sense to both experts and ordinary citizens. Consider incorporating these 10 recommendations from a San Francisco-based planner into your proposals and reports:

1. **Summarize**. Most people don't have time to read a long plan. Write a clear executive summary, and make it a stand-alone document that can be reproduced and distributed separately.

2. **Hit the facts**. Consider writing a one- or two-page fact sheet or flyer for your plan or project for such secondary audiences as reporters and others who just want the key details.

3. **Unclutter**. Move lengthy supplementary information into appendices.

4. **Break it up**. Put such information as definitions, examples, and lists into margin notes, textboxes, or sidebars.

5. **Add on**. If some readers might want additional information, tell them where to find it.

6. **Help navigate**. Use "signposting" tools—such as a table of contents, section previews, and section-specific headers and footers—to help readers find what they need and know where they are in your document.

7. **Add headings**. Break up the text visually with informative headings and subheadings—and use form and placement rather than numbering to indicate the different levels.

8. **Don't overdo acronyms**. Spell out acronyms the first time you use them, and consider including them in a glossary, along with technical terms.

9. **Experiment**. Perhaps black and white text in portrait orientation on 8½ × 11-inch paper is not the most effective format to use. Consider adding color, using landscape orientation, and incorporating other kinds of visual interest.

10. **Why not video?** Or other kinds of electronic media? If you will be delivering your document electronically, consider including dynamic content for interest and persuasiveness.

SOURCE: Niko Letunic, "Beyond Plain English," *Planning* 73.9 (2007): 40–44, *ProQuest*, Web, 20 July 2012.

A More Personal Writing Style

The writing in shorter reports tends to be more personal than in long reports. That is, the shorter reports are likely to use the personal pronouns *I*, *we*, and *you* rather than only the third person.

Several factors account for this tendency toward personal writing in shorter reports. In the first place, short-report situations usually involve personal relationships. Such reports tend to be from and to people who know each other and who normally address each other informally when they meet. In addition, shorter reports are apt to involve personal investigations and to represent the observations, evaluations, and analyses of their writers. Finally, shorter reports tend to deal with day-to-day problems. These problems are informal by their very nature. It is logical to report them informally, and personal writing tends to produce this informal effect.

TECHNOLOGY IN BRIEF

Using a Report Template for a Polished Look

When preparing a report, consider using a pre-designed template to give your report a professional, consistent design.

In Word 2010, you can access the available report templates by clicking File > New and entering *report* in the "Search Office.com for templates" field. When you find a template you like, such as the one shown here, you can download it to your computer for your current and future use.

If you're not pleased with the color scheme, you can click File > Themes to select a different palette of colors, as shown. If you like, you can also change the fonts and margins.

For most business reports, you'll want to choose a relatively conservative design like the one shown here. The more visually elaborate designs are better for special publications, such as annual reports and sales proposals.

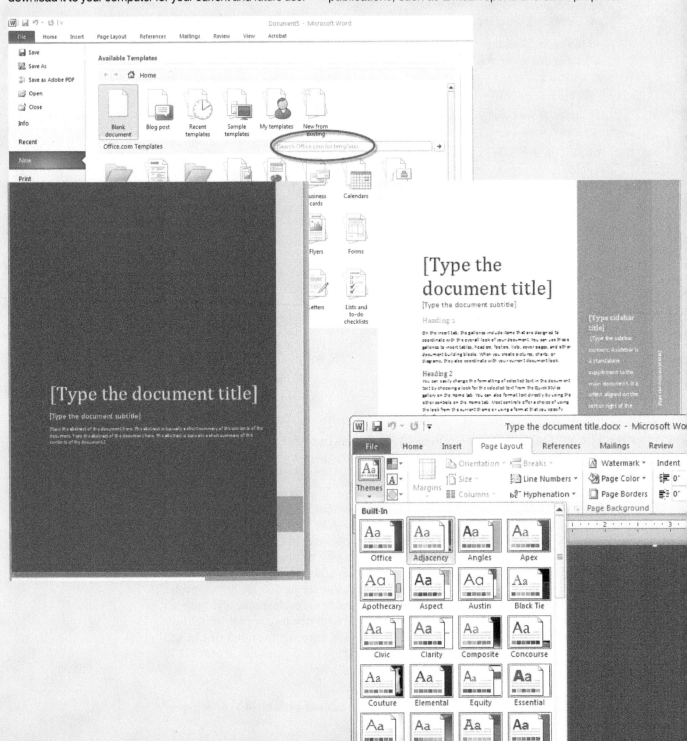

As explained in Chapter 11, your decision about whether to write a report in personal or impersonal style should be based on the situation. Convention favors using impersonal writing for the most formal situations. For most short reports, personal writing is likely to be preferable because of their relatively routine nature.

Less Need for a Structured Coherence Plan

A long, formal report usually needs what we call a "structured coherence plan"— a network of introductions, conclusions, and transitions that guides the reader through the report. Creating such a plan means giving the report an overview and a conclusion, providing the same for the individual sections, and incorporating transitions that bridge each section to the next. Such devices enable the reader to know at every point where he or she is in the report and how the current section is related to the overall goal of the report.

Short reports, because they are short, generally do not need an elaborate coherence plan. Readers will not need many reminders of what they just read or previews of what they're about to read. The report introduction (which should contain an overview), clear headings, and brief transitional devices (such as "Second," "next," and quick references to previous points) will usually be sufficient to keep readers on track.

FORMS FOR SHORT TO MID-LENGTH REPORTS

LO3 Choose an appropriate form for short reports.

As noted earlier, the shorter report forms are by far the most numerous and important in business. In fact, the three forms represented by the bottom three steps of the stairway in Figure 12–1—short reports, letter reports, and email or memo reports—make up the bulk of written reports.

The Short Report

One of the more popular of the less formal report forms is the short report. Representing the fourth and fifth steps in the formality stairway, this report consists of only a title page and text or a title page, combined transmittal message/summary, and text, respectively. Its popularity may be explained by the middle-ground impression of formality that it conveys. The short report is ideally suited for the short but somewhat formal problem.

Like most of the less formal report forms, the short report may be organized in either the direct or indirect order. If the report is addressed to an internal audience, it will likely use the direct order unless there is reason to believe that readers will resist the conclusions or recommendations. Reports written to external audiences may or may not state the main conclusions or recommendations in the opening paragraphs, but it is customary to include these in the transmittal message since it doubles as an executive summary.

When you open your short report with the main results of your investigation, the next section usually provides background on the report problem and what you did to investigate it. In other words, it provides your problem and purpose statements, as described in the previous chapter. When your report uses the indirect order, a coherent statement of your problem and purpose open the report, as illustrated by the sample long report that appears later in this chapter.

Even if you have provided your recommendations up front, you should reiterate and perhaps expand on them at the end of your report. Readers do not mind this kind of redundancy as long as the recommendations are helpfully restated, not just copied and pasted from the front of the report. Plus, stopping short of your main points at the end of your report would end it too abruptly.

A Mid-Length Recommendation Report. This report, with its title page and combined letter of transmittal and executive summary, would fall on the fourth level of Figure 12–1. It is organized indirectly in order to prepare the reader for the students' recommendations.

Increasing Student Patronage at Kirby's Grocery

*Title makes the topic and purpose
of the report clear*

May 28, 2013

Prepared for:

Mr. Claude Douglas, Owner
Kirby's Grocery
38 Lance Avenue
Crestview, IN 45771

*Page uses an
attractive but
simple template*

Prepared by:

Kirsten Brantley, Business Communication Student
College of Business
P. O. Box 236
Metropolitan University
Crestview, IN 45770-0236

(continued)

METROPOLITAN UNIVERSITY

College of Business, P. O. Box 236, Crestview, IN 45770-0236
Phone: (421) 555-5555, Fax: (421) 555-5566

May 28, 2013

Mr. Claude Douglas
Kirby's Grocery
38 Lance Avenue
Crestview, IN 45771

Dear Mr. Douglas:

As you requested, our Business Communication class conducted a study to determine ways to increase Metropolitan University students' awareness of Kirby's Grocery and to attract more students to your store. This report presents the results.

Identifies the project and "hands over" the report

To gather our information, we first interviewed assistant manager Bradley Vostick, who leads the store's marketing efforts. To get a veteran customer's perspective, we also interviewed our professor, Beth Rawson, a long-time Kirby's customer. Next we researched MU campus events, publications, transportation issues, demographics, and the Lance Avenue area surrounding Kirby's. Finally, the class did walkthroughs of Kirby's to gain firsthand reactions to the store as well as quantified data in the form of an exit survey on overall reactions to Kirby's.

We found that Kirby's is part of a niche market that offers a wide variety in a small space, much like the surrounding Lance Avenue area. Given these findings, we recommend the following:

Combines letter of transmittal and executive summary

- Targeting health-conscious, older MU students who enjoy shopping.
- Adding Facebook to your current promotional strategies.
- Focusing on your strengths to make these shoppers aware of the experience that is Kirby's Grocery.

Thank you for allowing us the opportunity to do this real-world project. We enjoyed learning about your store and hope that our research will bring many more MU students to Kirby's Grocery.

Ends with goodwill comments

Sincerely,

Kirsten Brantley

Kirsten Brantley
For Professor Beth Rawson's Business Communication Class

(continued)

Increasing Student Patronage at Kirby's Grocery

Introduction

Kirby's Grocery is a full-service neighborhood grocery store in the vicinity of Metropolitan University. With its appealing range of products and proximity to the university, its potential to attract student customers is great. Yet according to a survey conducted by Professor Beth Rawson's Fall 2012 Business Communication class, only one in three MU students has ever shopped at Kirby's. As a follow-up to this study, our Business Communication class conducted research to determine how Kirby's might attract more MU student shoppers. This report presents our results and recommendations.

Opening gives the context and purpose in a nutshell

Research Methods

The research for this study was conducted in three phases:

- Phase One: As preparation for the observational part of the study, the class gathered supplemental information about a variety of topics related to Kirby's. It was carried out by groups of three to four students, with each group focusing on one of seven particular "beats." These beats included MU campus events and publications, MU's demographic information, and interviews with Kirby's customers and Bradley Vostick of Kirby's.

- Phase Two: This was the main phase of our research. For this phase, 13 pairs of students visited Kirby's during the week of March 7–14, 2013, to gather observational data. Each pair consisted of an observer, who made oral comments about any and all aspects of the store, and a recorder, who recorded these observations. On average, each pair spent approximately 40 minutes in the store, and each pair was required to make a small purchase. At the end of their visits, the observers all completed exit surveys to quantify their overall reactions to Kirby's and to provide some demographic information about themselves.

- Phase Three: Given our findings, we gathered information to develop our recommendations for marketing Kirby's to MU students.

Detailed description of research builds confidence in the validity of the findings

The following sections describe the study participants, present the observational data, and offer our recommendations.

Preview adds to report's coherence

CASE ILLUSTRATION

Demographics of the Participants

Previews table

While our observer number of 13 was very small in comparison to the entire MU population of 33,000, it was actually a fairly representative sample in terms of student diversity, gender, and age. The following table shows how these observers compared to the general MU population.

Demographics of Store Observers		
	Study Participants	**MU Population**
Diversity	77% (11) European American 23% (2) African American 77% (11) US citizens	71.5% European American 12% African American 83% US citizens
Gender	47% (6) female, 54% (7) male	54.2% female, 45.8% male
Average Age	24	23

Lone table in nonacademic report does not need to be numbered

Report includes a special section to further support the validity of the findings

Paragraphs interpret and elaborate on the table

Compared to the MU population, our sample of 13 was relatively diverse. In addition to including 2 African American participants, it included 2 non-U.S. participants, one from Russia and one from Sweden.

The gender ratios were also relatively close. The MU population is 54.2% female to 45.8% male. Again, our observers came very close to this ratio, with 47% female and 54% male.

The average age for full-time students at Metropolitan University is 23. The average age of our observers was 24. This included a student who is 41 years old, but even without this outlier, our group closely represented the average MU student in terms of age.

In addition, all students in our class (26) were juniors and seniors at MU, and most were business students with some background in marketing. Through class discussion, we were able to bring our collective perspective as MU students to bear on our observations.

Qualitative Findings

Section preview adds coherence

This section presents the qualitative results from our observational research, broken down into two categories: perceived strengths and perceived weaknesses.

2

CASE ILLUSTRATION

Perceived Areas of Strength

Three main positive reactions came out of this research:

- Students were impressed with the wide product variety.
- Students were happy to see organic and health food products.
- Kirby's employees provided excellent service to their customers.

Section starts with a helpful summary

Product variety was seen as the strongest asset of Kirby's. Of the 13 observation surveys, 11 mentioned the large variety of products offered by Kirby's as a positive aspect of the store. Overall, the consensus was that the selection offered by Kirby's in such a small space was impressive. This was especially apparent in the beer aisle, which received the most praise of any section in Kirby's for a selection that rivals that of specialty stores.

Organic and health food products also received a large positive reaction, being mentioned by almost two-thirds of the observers. While health may not be the main concern of the stereotypical college student, it is certainly appealing to older students. Since the average age of an MU student is 23, it is likely that Kirby's organic and health food selection can also be a strong selling point for getting more students into the store.

Paragraphs present and interpret data

Customer service was the third most mentioned positive aspect of Kirby's. During observations, employees at Kirby's were consistently happy and helpful. The long-time customer we interviewed, Professor Rawson, cited Kirby's excellent customer service as one of the reasons she continues to shop there. She commented that the employees of Kirby's care more about their customers' shopping experiences than employees of other stores, and the data compiled by the class supported this claim.

Not only were students asked if they needed help, but they also observed that employees knew their customers, which makes the customer feel more like family than just another person wanting groceries. When observers made their small purchases, they noted that they were treated in the same friendly manner as customers who were checking out with filled carts.

Perceived Areas of Weakness

Two main negative reactions came out of this research:

- Students observed a number of dirty shelves and floors.
- The placement of some products was confusing.

Another helpful summary

About half of the observers made note of areas of Kirby's that seemed to need a good cleaning, with specific remarks about stained floor tiles, produce on the floor

3

(continued)

that hadn't been swept up, and dusty shelves. This was a significant negative for several student shoppers, as dirty floors and shelves don't shed the kindest light on the products for sale, especially when compared to the seeming sterility of larger grocery stores like Kroger and Biggs.

More helpful data and interpretation

But the largest negative reaction to Kirby's concerned the random-seeming placement of a variety of products. Examples included cakes next to whole turkeys, freezers next to greeting cards, and hot peppers next to candies. This confused student shoppers because the placement of some of these products did not fall in line with the aisle signs. While Kirby's is a smaller grocery store and is certainly impacted by the limits of space, the class as a whole felt that more could be done to eliminate this random product layout.

Quantitative Findings

Introduces the figure

The following figure contains the composite results of the 13 exit surveys. Students were asked to rate their Kirby's experience on a variety of topics on a scale of one to five, with one being the worst and five being the best. The observers took the survey immediately after completing their walkthroughs of the store.

Lone figure in a nonacademic report does not need to be numbered

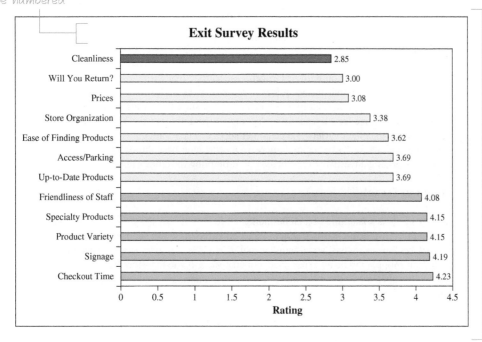

Visual, textual, and numerical elements work together to present specific findings clearly

4

(continued)

Paragraphs help the reader interpret the findings

These results simply quantify what was discovered in the qualitative phase of the observation. Checkout time, friendliness, variety, and specialty products were the highest scorers, while cleanliness received the lowest rating. Still, Kirby's scored above average in all categories, which is an important positive result.

Along these lines, the "Will You Return?" score is encouraging. Though it may seem negative when compared to the other reactions, a score of 3.00 is actually above average. This means that with only one trip through Kirby's, there is a better than average chance that students will return to purchase groceries.

Prices ranked just above "Will You Return?" at 3.08. Again, its comparative rating is low, but it is still above average. Price is an important consideration for student shoppers, and Kirby's has a tough time competing with prices offered by the nearby Kroger store, its main competitor. Even given these two facts, though, observers felt that Kirby's had slightly better than average prices, which is another important positive result.

Interesting to note are the scores for Signage, Ease of Finding Products, and Store Organization. Signage was rated high at 4.19, while Ease of Finding Products was rated lower (3.62), and Store Organization even lower (3.38). These numbers correlate with the student shopper reactions. While Kirby's has excellent signs, some of the aisles are difficult to find because of displays blocking them, and the placement of certain products adjacent to other unrelated products only increases this confusion.

Recommendations

Summarizes the main impression and leads into recommendations

From our compiled data on Kirby's Grocery, we learned that Kirby's is not a large, faceless grocery chain that slashes prices in order to make up for poor customer service and variety. Rather, Kirby's is a niche-market store that offers wide variety and excellent service for a decent price. Yet only about a third of the MU population is aware of its excellent variety and customer service. The following recommendations for Kirby's aim to increase its customer base through targeted awareness-raising advertising that focuses on promoting the store's uniqueness.

Whom to Target

Since Kirby's is something of a niche-market store, it will only truly appeal to a niche market of MU students. Kirby's should focus on attracting those shoppers who want variety, healthy selections, and a familiar feel. Kirby's is a grocery store for people who want shopping to be an experience, not an errand. It can therefore be especially appealing to the more mature, somewhat alternative segment of the MU population.

5

(continued)

How to Reach Them

While Kirby's has been using the MU Coupon Book for campus ads and participating in campus events such as Welcome Week, the store's marketing efforts do not take advantage of a key fact about modern students: They are heavy users of the social networking site Facebook. According to a poll conducted by researchers at Harvard University, 80% of all 18- to 29-year-olds and 90% of four-year college students now have a Facebook account. Facebook thus represents a huge opportunity for Kirby's to reach its student market.

You can take advantage of this site in two main ways: creating a page and advertising.

Creating a Free Online Profile

Kirby's currently has an attractive website, but it is unlikely to receive many student visitors. Creating an appealing presence on Facebook (*www.facebook.com*) can help you build a student fan base and generate a buzz about your store. Once you register at the site, Facebook makes it easy to create your "page." Here you can feature major selling points, photos, directions, a link to your website, and other static material. The page can also feature such dynamic material as posts to your "wall" (an interactive message board), polls, quizzes, and special promotions.

Once the page is posted, users can learn about your site using Facebook's search engine or any other search engine. If they like what they see and want to be kept updated about special offerings, they can click a link to include Kirby's in their network. This will place your logo and name on their own Facebook pages, where all their friends will see it and perhaps consider becoming "fans" of Kirby's themselves. In this way, your store can take advantage of "viral marketing."

Using Paid Advertising

It is also possible to advertise on Facebook. You can go to *www.facebook.com/*Ads to get advice on creating ads and to create your ads. Facebook allows you to target your ads to certain readers, so you could target your ads to MU students with particular interests. You can also track the success of several ads to see which are the most successful.

The cost for these ads varies depending on whether you choose to pay per view (how many times users see your ad) or per click (how many times users click on your Facebook page), as well as on what other advertisers targeting the same market are offering to pay. Using the Facebook help page "Campaign Cost and Pricing," you can indicate how much you are willing to spend each day, and Facebook will calculate a "cost per click" estimate for you. If few other businesses are competing for the same users, the cost may actually be lower than this, whereas it will be higher if many businesses are trying to reach the same demographic.

Recent research supports the claim

Link makes it easy to learn more

Shows knowledge of the store's current efforts

Informal citation of sources is acceptable in an informal report

Paragraphs adapt research to reader's needs

6

(concluded)

What to Say

Kirby's advertisements need to focus on promoting the store's variety and uniqueness to the MU student body. It has to dispel the idea that it is simply another grocery store and emphasize that it encompasses a wide variety in a small space, just like the eclectic Lance Avenue area in which it is located.

Promotions for students should focus on its wide beer selection (perhaps mentioning the exact number of domestic and imported brands offered), on its organic and health food selection, and on its unique products such as sushi and fresh peanut butter. These advertisements will not appeal to the entire MU student body, but it will make the students who are likely to value Kirby's strengths aware of these and give them a desirable, convenient alternative to shopping at a giant superstore.

Paragraphs use the main findings to suggest a marketing strategy

Conclusion

We found that Kirby's Grocery offers a shopping experience that simply cannot be found at larger grocery stores. The variety and customer service are top notch, and this makes a trip to Kirby's an experience rather than an errand (perhaps this could be a slogan?). By taking advantage of the large-scale marketing opportunities offered by Facebook, Kirby's can raise awareness of its many positive qualities among the MU student body well beyond what it currently achieves with its current outreach efforts. This strategy is also appealing because it can greatly increase Kirby's visibility at no to very little cost.

Ending wraps up the report in a positive way

7

The mechanics of constructing the short report are much the same as the mechanics of constructing the more formal, longer types. The short report uses the same form of title page and page layout. Like the longer reports, it uses headings, though usually only one or two levels because of its brevity. Like any other report, the short report uses visuals, an appendix, and a bibliography when these are needed.

Letter Reports

The second of the more common shorter report forms is the letter report—that is, a report in letter form. Letter reports are used primarily to present information to people outside the organization. For example, a company's written evaluation of its experience with a particular product may be presented in letter form and sent to the person who requested it. An outside consultant may deliver his or her analyses and recommendations in letter form. Or the officer of an organization may report certain information to the membership in a letter.

Typically, the length of letter reports is three to four pages or less, but they may be longer or shorter.

As a general rule, letter reports are written personally, using *I, you,* and *we* references. Exceptions exist, of course, such as letter reports for very important readers—for example, a company's board of directors. But since letters are traditionally a personal form of communication, letter reports tend to use the personal style.

Letter reports may use either the direct order or the indirect order. Those in the direct order begin with the main finding or recommendation. Sometimes they use a subject line to announce the topic of the report so the first paragraph of the letter can get right to the main point. The subject line usually appears after the salutation. It commonly begins with the word *subject* followed by a description of the report's contents, as the following example illustrates:

Subject: Review of Travel Expenditures of Association Members, Authorized by
Board of Directors, January 2014

Association members spent 11 percent more on travel to asssociation meetings in 2013 than they did in 2012, and they expect another increase in travel expenses this year.

Indirect-order letters tend not to use a subject line, and they open with brief background information, such as who authorized the report and the topic. A letter report written to the executives of an organization, for example, might use the following indirect opening:

As authorized by your board of directors January 6, this report reviews member expenditures for travel for 2012 and 2013. It is based on . . . [whatever research was performed].

Following the introduction would be a logical presentation and analysis of the information gathered. After this presentation would come the conclusion or recommendation that the facts were leading to.

With either the direct or indirect order, a letter report may close with whatever friendly goodwill comment fits the occasion.

Email and Memo Reports

As we noted in Chapter 6, email is a heavily used form of written communication in business. It has largely eclipsed memoranda, but memos are still written, especially in cases where computers aren't easily accessible or the writer prefers to deliver a print message. Both email and memos can be used for internal reports—that is, for reports written by and to people in an organization.

Because email and memos are primarily communication between people who know each other, they are usually informal. Some, however, are formal, especially reports directed to readers high in the administration of the organization. In fact, some email and memo reports rival the longer forms in formality. Like the longer forms, they may

A Letter Report. This direct-order letter report compares two hotels for a meeting site. It starts with the recommendation, followed by well-organized supporting facts. The personal style is appropriate in this situation. To make the letter easy to share with the other board members, the writer might send it to the reader as an email attachment.

INTERNATIONAL COMMUNICATION ASSOCIATION

314 N. Capitol St. NW • Washington, DC 20001 • 202.624.2411

October 26, 2013

Professor Helen Toohey
Board of Directors
International Communication Association
Thunderbird American Graduate School of International Management
15249 N. 59th Ave.
Glendale, AZ 85306-6000

Dear Professor Toohey:

Subject: Recommendation of Convention Hotel for the 2014 Meeting

The Hyatt Hotel is my recommendation for the International Communication Association meeting next October. The Hyatt has significant advantages over the Marriott, the other potential site for the meeting.

One of the Hyatt's main advantages is its downtown location, which will appeal to convention goers and their spouses. The accommodations, including meeting rooms, are adequate in both places, although the Marriott does have a more contemporary decor. But the Hyatt room costs are approximately 15 percent lower than those at the Marriott. Thus, although both hotels are adequate, the Hyatt appears to be the better choice because of its location and cost advantages.

Recommendation and key facts are up front

Bases of comparison (factors) permit hotels (units) to be compared logically

The Hyatt's Favorable Downtown Location

The older of the two hotels, the Hyatt, is located in the heart of the downtown business district, making it convenient to the area's major mall as well as the other downtown shops. The Marriott, on the other hand, is approximately nine blocks from the major shopping area. Located in the periphery of the business and residential area, it provides little location advantage for those wanting to shop. It does, however, have shops within its walls that provide for virtually all of the guests' normal needs. Because many members will bring spouses, however, the downtown location does give the Hyatt an advantage.

Short sentences and transitional words increase readability and move ideas forward

(continued)

Alternate placement of topic sentences offers variety

Board of Directors   -2-   October 26, 2013

Adequate Accommodations at Both Hotels

Talking headings (all noun phrases) make the key points stand out

Both hotels can guarantee the 600 rooms we will require. Because the Marriott is newer (built in 2006), its furnishings are more modern. The 16-year-old Hyatt, however, is well preserved, and its guest rooms are elegant and comfortable.

The Marriott has 11 small meeting rooms, and the Hyatt has 13. All are adequate for our purposes. Both hotels can provide the nine we need. For our opening session, the Hyatt would make available its Capri Ballroom, which can easily seat our membership. It would also serve as the site of our presidential luncheon. The assembly facilities at the Marriott appear to be somewhat crowded, although the management assures me that their largest meeting room can hold 600. Pillars in the room, however, would make some seats undesirable. In spite of the limitations mentioned, both hotels appear to have adequate facilities for our meeting.

Logical paragraphing helps the different points stand out

Lower Costs at the Hyatt

Both the Hyatt and the Marriott would provide nine rooms for meetings on a complimentary basis. Both would provide complimentary suites for our president and our executive director. The Hyatt, however, would charge $500 for use of the room for the opening session. The Marriott would provide this room without charge.

Analysis is adapted to the readers' needs

Convention rates at the Hyatt are $169 for singles, $179 for double-bedded rooms, and $229 for suites. Comparable rates at the Marriott are $189, $199, and $350. Thus, the savings at the Hyatt would be approximately 15 percent per member.

Cost of the dinner selected would be $35 per person, including gratuities, at the Hyatt. The Marriott would meet this price if we would guarantee 600 plates. Otherwise, they would charge $38. Considering all of these figures, the total cost picture at the Hyatt is the more favorable one.

In conclusion, while both hotels would meet our needs, the significant location and cost advantages of the Hyatt make it the more desirable site for next year's conference.

Repetition of the key point provides a sense of closure

Sincerely,

Willard K. Mitchell

Willard K. Mitchell
Executive Secretary

Knowledge Management Gives Companies the Competitive Edge

As the pace of business increases, flexibility and responsiveness become more and more important. Hence the use of *knowledge management*—the "strategies and processes of identifying, capturing, and leveraging knowledge to enhance competitiveness"—is growing.

In a study of 71 manufacturing companies in India, executives identified six kinds of knowledge as "critical for the success of the organization":

- Knowledge obtained from customers.
- Knowledge about core competencies (that is, knowledge to do one's job).
- Knowledge about products and services.
- Knowledge about emerging trends.
- Knowledge about best practices (in the industry).
- Knowledge about the competition.

How is such vital information shared in a business? While much is still distributed through email and conventional reports, companies are increasingly using intranets, smart documents (templates that enable the contents to go into searchable databases), enterprise systems, and other communication technologies to make its most precious commodity—knowledge—more readily available across the organization.

The benefits? Participants in the India study cited better strategic planning, better attention to the customer, better-quality products and services, better learning from disasters and failures, and better management of resources as the main payoffs—all of which add up to a sharper competitive edge.

SOURCE: M. D. Singh, Ravi Shankar, Rakesh Narian, and Adish Kumar, "Survey of Knowledge Management Practices in Indian Manufacturing Industries," *Journal of Knowledge Management* 10.6 (2006): 110–28, *ProQuest*, Web, 21 July 2012.

use headings to display content and visuals to support the text. For the longer email reports, writers will often choose to make the report itself an attached document and use the email message as a transmittal message.

Because they are largely internal, email reports tend to be problem-solving reports. They are intended to help improve operations, lay the groundwork for an innovation, solve a problem, or otherwise assist decision makers in the organization.

Written Reports in Other Forms

While most written reports in business will take the form of short reports, letter reports, or email or memo reports, they can take a variety of other forms as well. The report featured in Figure 12–5 appeared in an online newsletter by the John Deere company. It used objectively gathered and reported evidence to persuade readers of the value of a John Deere product. Research can also be reported in pamphlets, white papers, and other publications, and many reports are uploaded to the Web as stand-alone documents in PDF format. You can apply your report-writing knowledge to all these forms and more. Just be sure to choose the appropriate form for your readers and purpose.

LO4 Adapt the procedures for writing short reports to routine operational reports, progress reports, and problem-solving reports as well as to minutes of meetings.

COMMON TYPES OF SHORT REPORTS

Because organizations depend heavily on short reports, there are many varieties, written for many different purposes. We cover some of the most common types here, categorized on the basis of their main purpose, but the form they take will vary from company to company. Also, most companies will have developed unique types of reports to accomplish particular goals. Always consider your company's typical ways of reporting when deciding what to report and how.

Figure 12.5

A Report from a Company Newsletter.

Guess Row Study

Introduction

Producers are becoming increasingly interested in using GPS-based guidance systems as either an enhancement to or in replacement of mechanical markers in planting operations. Recently, a study was conducted to assess the accuracy of mechanical markers for planting operations, and compare this to manual GPS guidance and GreenStar™ AutoTrac. While the pass-to-pass accuracy of the StarFire receiver has been determined to be +/- 4 inches by the University of Illinois, the measurements taken in this study are more indicative of what producers are achieving in the field.

The guess row is the distance between the outside rows of two side-by-side passes made in the field (Figure 1). If the planter is set up to plant 30-inch rows, the perfect guess row width would be 30-inches. Significant guess row variability causes difficulty in using mismatched row equipment (i.e. 16 row planter harvested with a 12 row corn head). In addition, wide guess rows may allow weed escapes that decrease yields.

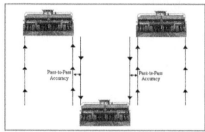

Figure 1: Pass-to-pass accuracy

Methods

Servi-Tech, a crop consulting company offering services primarily in Kansas, Nebraska, and Iowa, measured the guess row width on a number of fields in these three states. Twenty consecutive guess row measurements were taken in each field. The data presented in this discussion are from corn and soybean fields planted in 30-inch rows only. The distribution of fields is shown in Table 1.

Table 1 Distribution of Fields Measured

	Mechanical Markers	Manual GPS Guidance	AutoTrac	All Data
Number of Fields Measured	70	9	19	98

Note: all planting using AutoTrac was done with JD8000T tractors.

SOURCE: Reprinted with permission of John Deere Intelligent Solutions Group.

In addition to guess row width and guidance type, additional information was recorded for each field, including:

- Crop
- Tillage system
- Field topography
- Tractor and planter model
- Planter width
- Approximate planting speed
- Time of day planted

After preliminary analysis of the data, it was determined that in some fields consistent planter draft to one direction (often caused by improper set up) resulted in guess row variability over and above that attributable to the guidance system used. In order to remove these fields from the analysis, odd and even passes were analyzed and 35 fields were removed.

Results

While the average guess row width for all marker systems was similar (Figure 2), both the manual GPS

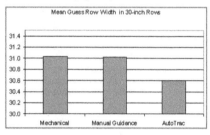

Figure 2: Mean Guess Row Width for all guidance systems

guidance and AutoTrac systems exhibited much less variability than that of mechanical markers (Figure 3; Table 2). Range in guess row width for manual GPS guidance and AutoTrac was nearly half that of mechanical marker systems. The standard deviation for manual GPS guidance and AutoTrac planted guess rows was 2.1 inches compared to 3.3 inches for the mechanical marker planted fields.

Conclusions

Guess row width in fields planted with GPS-based guidance systems was less variable than those planted with mechanical marker systems. On average, GPS-based guidance systems were as accurate as those fields planted with mechanical marker systems. The test

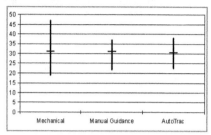

Figure 3: Mean Guess Row Width and Range

data showed many row crop planters were not set up properly (unit spacing or marker arm mis adjustment), causing them to pull one direction consistently or resulting in varied pass-to pass 'guess row' width. Experienced operators may compensate for this automatically when using mechanical marker systems, so proper planter setup is more important with automatic steering systems.

While the guess row widths for both the manual GPS guidance system and AutoTrac were similar, AutoTrac would be expected to deliver this accuracy over a wide range of conditions consistently. Manual GPS guidance system accuracy depends on how well the operator can follow the steering cues. As time progresses, the operator may become fatigued, resulting in a reduced accuracy. This is not a factor with GreenStar AutoTrac.

Table 2

	All Data	Mechanical	Manual Guidance	AutoTrac
Maximum	50	47	37	38
Minimum	19	19	22	22.5
Mean	31.3	31.0	31.0	30.6
Range	31	28	15	15.5
Standard Deviation	3.4	3.3	2.1	2.1
Coefficient of Variation	0.11	0.11	0.07	0.07

The bottom line is that GreenStar AutoTrac was found to be capable of delivering the same to slightly better accuracy than producers achieve using mechanical markers in the fields used for the study. Coupled with the fact that AutoTrac users will be less fatigued at the end of the day, GreenStar AutoTrac may be able to help your operation during one of the most important times of the growing season, planting. For more information about GreenStar Parallel Tracking or AutoTrac, visit your local John Deere dealer.

Routine Operational Reports

The majority of the reports written within companies are **routine operational reports** that keep supervisors, managers, and team members informed about the company's operations. These can be daily, weekly, monthly, or quarterly reports on the work of each department or even each employee. They can relate production data, information on visits to customers, issues that have arisen, or any kind of information that others in the organization need on a routine basis.

The form and contents of these reports will vary from company to company and manager to manager. Many will be submitted on predesigned forms. Others may not

A Progress Report in Email Form. This email report summarizes a sales manager's progress in opening a new district. It begins with the highlights—all a busy reader may need to know. Organized by three categories of activity, the factual information follows. The writer–reader relationship justifies a personal style.

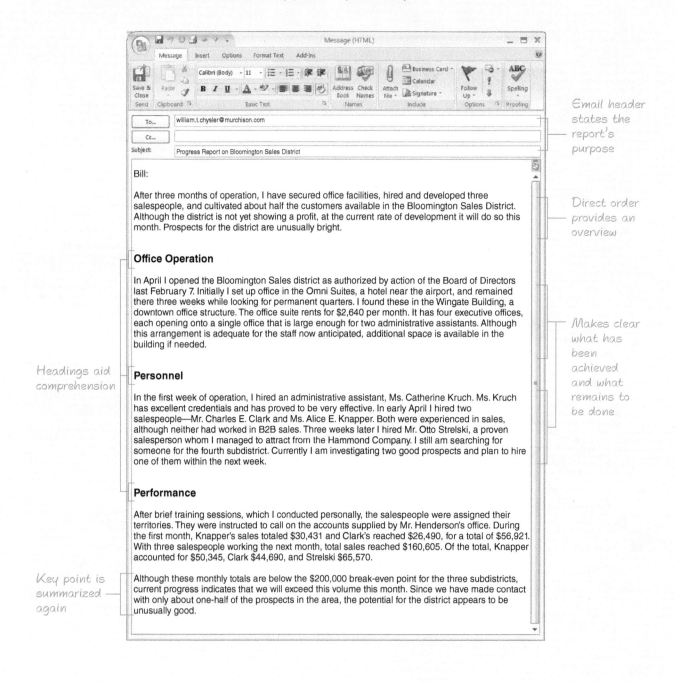

Email header states the report's purpose

To... william.t.chysler@murchison.com

Cc...

Subject: Progress Report on Bloomington Sales District

Bill:

Direct order provides an overview

After three months of operation, I have secured office facilities, hired and developed three salespeople, and cultivated about half the customers available in the Bloomington Sales District. Although the district is not yet showing a profit, at the current rate of development it will do so this month. Prospects for the district are unusually bright.

Office Operation

In April I opened the Bloomington Sales district as authorized by action of the Board of Directors last February 7. Initially I set up office in the Omni Suites, a hotel near the airport, and remained there three weeks while looking for permanent quarters. I found these in the Wingate Building, a downtown office structure. The office suite rents for $2,640 per month. It has four executive offices, each opening onto a single office that is large enough for two administrative assistants. Although this arrangement is adequate for the staff now anticipated, additional space is available in the building if needed.

Makes clear what has been achieved and what remains to be done

Headings aid comprehension

Personnel

In the first week of operation, I hired an administrative assistant, Ms. Catherine Kruch. Ms. Kruch has excellent credentials and has proved to be very effective. In early April I hired two salespeople—Mr. Charles E. Clark and Ms. Alice E. Knapper. Both were experienced in sales, although neither had worked in B2B sales. Three weeks later I hired Mr. Otto Strelski, a proven salesperson whom I managed to attract from the Hammond Company. I still am searching for someone for the fourth subdistrict. Currently I am investigating two good prospects and plan to hire one of them within the next week.

Performance

After brief training sessions, which I conducted personally, the salespeople were assigned their territories. They were instructed to call on the accounts supplied by Mr. Henderson's office. During the first month, Knapper's sales totaled $30,431 and Clark's reached $26,490, for a total of $56,921. With three salespeople working the next month, total sales reached $160,605. Of the total, Knapper accounted for $50,345, Clark $44,690, and Strelski $65,570.

Key point is summarized again

Although these monthly totals are below the $200,000 break-even point for the three subdistricts, current progress indicates that we will exceed this volume this month. Since we have made contact with only about one-half of the prospects in the area, the potential for the district appears to be unusually good.

A Memo Progress Report on a Class Project. As a student, you will sometimes need to submit a progress report on a complex project, such as a group project. In such cases, the same goals apply here as to workplace progress reports—to show that you understand the project's purpose, that you have made good progress, that you have a good sense of what remains to be done, and that you're headed toward a successful conclusion.

Memo Report

Date: May 12, 2013

To: Professor Rodriguez

From: Sam Ellis SE

Subject: Group Four's Progress on the Report for Ms. Herbert

Direct opening orients the reader and announces good progress on the project

Our group consists of Bo Riddle, Ina Ward, Tiffany Paine, and me. We have made good progress on gathering information to help Ms. Herbert decide whether to include personality testing in her hiring process for Fashion Sense.

Research Topics and Methods

In our first group meeting, on May 3, we decided to investigate the following topics, assigned as shown:

List shows that the group is well organized

- Types of personality testing available (Tiffany)
- Use of personality testing in the retail industry (Ina)
- Cost of personality testing (Bo)
- Possible legal risks of personality testing (me)

Discussion of research methods builds credibility

To research the types of testing available, we conducted mostly Internet research. We did both Internet and library research to investigate the remaining topics. We also interviewed Amy Loehmann, a professor in the law school, about possible legal issues.

Findings So Far

Informative headings and bulleted lists make the contents easy to digest

In the first week of work, we have gathered these main findings:

- Companies use many different kinds of personality tests, such as the Big Five personality test (see queendom.com) and tests based on four personality types (see MaximumAdvantage.com). But the most popular is the Myers-Briggs Type Indicator. Given its proven track record, Ms. Herbert is likely to want to use some version of this test if she adopts personality testing.
- Large retail stores such as Macy's do use personality testing, but we have not yet found much use of such testing for smaller businesses like Ms. Herbert's.
- Personality testing can be extremely expensive if the company hires a trained consultant to conduct the testing. For large-scale testing, these consultants charge thousands of dollars. However, there are many small testing outfits that provide relatively simple, yet valid, tests. For example, for about $500, ProvenResults will test a company's high-performing employees and develop a personality test based on those employees' traits (ProvenResults.com). This test can then be given to job applicants to determine their suitability for the work.
- There are definitely legal risks to personality testing. Mainly, one must be sure not to ask questions that discriminate against the test takers on the basis of religion, race, or gender. If a company hires a consultant or firm like ProvenResults to do the testing, that person or firm will be the responsible legal party. If one doesn't hire a third party, it is advisable to have an attorney review the testing procedure before it is used.

Convincing details attest to the group's hard work

Next Steps

A good plan for completing the work builds the instructor's confidence in the group

We will continue to explore the kinds of tests that might be suitable for Ms. Herbert. Specifically, we will try to find out what kinds of personality tests the smaller retail companies use and which of these might be appropriate for Fashion Sense.

We will also try to determine the most cost-effective method for Ms. Herbert to adopt and acquire contact information for any testing services that look promising.

Conclusion shows good awareness of the next major deadline and of the end goal

We are on track to have a complete draft of our report prepared by the May 22 deadline. This is an interesting project, and we believe we will be able to help Ms. Herbert make a well-informed decision.

use forms but will follow a prescribed format. Still others will be shaped by the writer's own judgment about what to include and how to present it.

The nature and culture of the organization can heavily influence the forms taken by these reports. For example, one innovative format for weekly reporting is the 5-15 report.[1] The name comes from the fact that it is intended to be read in 5 minutes and written in 15 minutes. Its typical three-part contents are a description of what the employee did that week, a statement about the employee's morale and that of others he or she worked with, and one idea for how to improve operations. Clearly, this format would work best in an organization where employees have nonroutinized jobs and the management values the employees' opinions.

Whatever the form, the routine operational report should convey clearly and quickly what readers most need and want to know about the time period in question. It is also an opportunity for you, the writer, to showcase your ability to provide needed information on deadline.

When using standardized forms for periodic reports, you should consider developing a template macro or merge document with your word-processing software. A macro would fill in all the standard parts for you, pausing to let you fill in the variable information. A template merge document would prompt you for the variables first, merging them with the primary document later. However standardized the process, you will still need to be careful to gather accurate information and state it clearly.

Progress Reports

You can think of an internal **progress report** as a routine operational report except that it tends to be submitted on an as-needed basis, and, as its name implies, it focuses on progress toward a specific goal. If you are working on a project for an external client, you may also need to submit progress reports to show that your work is on track. For example, a fundraising organization might prepare weekly summaries of its efforts to achieve its goal. Or a building contractor might prepare a report on progress toward completing a building for a customer. Typically, the contents of these reports concern progress made, but they also may include such related topics as problems encountered or anticipated and projections of future progress.

Progress reports follow no set form. They can be quite formal, as when a contractor building a large manufacturing plant reports to the company for whom the plant is being built. Or they can be very informal, as in the case of a worker reporting by email to his or her supervisor on the progress of a task being performed. Some progress reports are quite routine and structured, sometimes involving filling in blanks on forms devised for the purpose. Most, however, are informal, narrative reports, illustrated by the examples on pages 400 and 401. As these examples show, you should organize and format the "story" of your progress for easy comprehension.

As with most reports, you have some choice about the tone to use when presenting your information. With progress reports, you want to emphasize the positive if possible. The overall message should be "I (or we) have made progress." The best way to convey this message confidently, of course, is to be sure that you or your team has in fact made progress on the task at hand.

Problem-Solving Reports

Many short reports are **problem-solving reports**. These reports help decision makers figure out what to do any time a problem arises within an organization—which is often. For example, a piece of equipment may have broken down, causing mayhem on the production line. Or employees may have gotten hurt on the job. Or, less

---

[1] For a fuller description and history, see Joyce Wycoff, "5-15 Reports: Communication for Dispersed Organizations," *Innovation Network,* InnovationNetwork, 2001, Web, 21 July 2012.

"I suggest we take a look at the floating, glowing incident report first."

SOURCE: Copyright © 2009 Ted Goff.

dramatically, a company procedure may have become outdated, or a client company may want to know why it's losing money. If we define *problem* as an issue facing the company, we could include many other scenarios as well—for example, whether or not a company should adopt flextime scheduling or what location it should choose for a new store. Whatever the context, the writer of a problem-solving report needs to gather facts about the problem or issue, define it clearly, research solutions, and recommend a course of action.

Like progress reports, problem-solving reports can be internal or external. Internal problem-solving reports are usually assigned, but sometimes employees may need to write unsolicited problem-solving reports—for example, if they must recommend that a subordinate be fired or if they feel that a change in procedure is necessary. External problem-solving reports are most often written by consulting companies for their clients. In these cases, the report is the main product that the client is paying for.

A type of problem-solving report that deserves special attention is a **feasibility study**. For these reports, writers study several courses of action and then propose the most feasible, desirable one. For instance, you might be asked to compare Internet service providers and recommend the one that suits the company's needs and budget best. Or you might investigate what type of onsite childcare center, if any, is feasible for your organization. Sometimes feasibility studies are not full-blown problem-solving reports. They may offer detailed analysis but stop short of making a recommendation. The analysis they provide nevertheless helps decision makers decide what to do.

In fact, many short reports that help solve company problems may not be complete problem-solving reports. Decision makers who assign research reports may not want recommendations. They may want only good data and careful analysis so that they can formulate a course of action themselves. Whether you are preparing an internal or external report, it is important to understand how far your readers want you to go toward proposing solutions.

You have some latitude when deciding how direct to make your opening in a problem-solving report. If you believe that your readers will be open to any reasonable findings or recommendations, you should state those up front. If you think your conclusions will be unexpected or your readers will be skeptical, you should still state your report's purpose and topic clearly at the beginning but save the conclusions and recommendations until the end, after leading your readers through the details. Figure 12–6, a pattern for a problem-solving report used by the U.S. military, follows this more indirect route. As always, try to find out which method of organization your readers prefer.

While they usually propose action, problem-solving reports are not true persuasive messages. Because they have either been assigned or fall within an employee's assigned duties, the writer already has a willing reader. Furthermore, the writer has no obvious personal stake in the outcome the way he or she does with a persuasive message. However, when writing a problem-solving report, especially one that makes recommendations, you do need to show that your study was thorough and your reasoning sound. The decision makers may not choose to follow your advice, but your work, if it is carefully performed, still helps them decide what to do and reflects positively on you.

Meeting Minutes

Many short reports in business, especially internal ones, do not recommend or even analyze. Instead, they describe. Trip reports, incident reports, and other such reports are meant to provide a written record of something that happened. Whatever their type and specific purpose, they all share the need to be well organized, easy to read, and factual. Perhaps the most common of these reports is **minutes** for meetings. We thus single them out for special emphasis.

Figure 12–6

Military Form For Problem-Solving Report

DEPARTMENT OF THE AIR FORCE
HEADQUARTERS UNITED STATES AIR FORCE
WASHINGTON, DC 20330

REPLY TO
ATTN OF   AFODC/Colonel Jones

SUBJECT   Staff Study Report

TO:

PROBLEM

1. --
--.

FACTORS BEARING ON THE PROBLEM

2. Facts.

a.--
--.
b---.

3. Assumptions.

4. Criteria.

5. Definitions.

DISCUSSION

6. --.

7. --.

8. --.

CONCLUSION

9. --.

ACTION RECOMMENDED

10. --.

11. --.

JOHN J. JONES, Colonel, USAF   2 Atch
Deputy Chief of Staff, Operations   1. ---------------------
                                      2. ---------------------

Minutes provide a written record of a group's activities, which can include announcements, reports, significant discussions, and decisions. They include important details, but they are primarily a summary that reports the gist of what happened, not a verbatim transcript. Minutes include only objective data; their writer carefully avoids using such judgmental words as *excellent* or *impractical* or such descriptive words as *angrily* or *calmly*. However, if the group passes a resolution that specific wording be officially recorded, a writer should include it. Accurate minutes are important because they can sometimes have legal significance, such as when shareholders or boards vote to approve certain corporate activities.

The expected format varies across organizations, but any format you use should enable the reader to easily review what happened and retrieve particular information. Headings in bold or italics are usually appropriate, and some writers find that numbering items in the minutes to agree with the numbering of a meeting's agenda is helpful. Additional advice on writing minutes can be found on pages 531–532 in Chapter 15.

The sample on the next page illustrates typical minutes. The following preliminary, body, and closing items may be included.

Preliminary Items

- Name of the group.
- Name of the document.
- Type of meeting (monthly, emergency, special).
- Place, date, and time called to order.
- Names of those attending including guests (used to determine if a quorum is present).
- Names of those absent and the reasons for absence.

Body Items

- Approval of the minutes of previous meeting.
- Meeting announcements.
- Old business—Reports on matters previously presented.
- New business—Reports on matters presented to the group.

Closing Items

- Place and time of the next meeting.
- Notation of the meeting's ending time.
- Name and signature of the person responsible for preparing the minutes.

When you are responsible for preparing the minutes of a meeting, you can take several steps to make the task easier. First, get an agenda in advance. Use it to complete as much of the preliminary information as possible, including the names of those expected to attend. If someone is not present, you can easily move that person's name to the absentee list. You might even set up a table in advance with the following column headings to facilitate your note taking:

Topic	Summary of Discussion	Action/Resolution

Bear in mind that meeting minutes, while they look objective, almost always have political implications. Because minutes are the only tangible record of what happened, meeting participants will want their contributions included and cast in a positive light. Since you will not be able to record every comment made, you will need to decide which ones to include, whether or not to credit a particular speaker, how to capture the group's reaction, and so forth. Use your good judgment when translating a rich oral event into a written summary.

Illustration of Meeting Minutes. Good minutes, like these, include the expected components and are objective, easy to read, and efficient.

Minutes of the Policy Committee
Semiannual Meeting
November 21, 2013, 9:30–11:30 A.M., Conference Room A

Present: Elaine Horn (chair), D'Marie Simon, DeAnne Overholt, Michelle Lum, Joel Zwanziger, Rebecca Shuster, Jeff Merrill, Donna Wingler, Chris Woods, Tim Lebold (corporate attorney, guest).

Absent: Joan Marian, Jeff Horen (excused), Leonna Plummer (excused)

Complete preliminary information provides a good record

Approval of Minutes

Minutes from the May 5, 2013, meeting were read and approved.

Subheads help readers retrieve information

Announcements

Chris Woods invited the committee to a reception for Milton Chen, director in our Asia region. It will be held in the executive dining room at 3:00 P.M. tomorrow. Chris reminded us that Asia is ahead of the United States in its use of wireless technology. He suggested that perhaps we can get an idea of good policies to implement now.

Old Business—Email Policy

Joel Zwanziger reported the results of his survey on the proposed email policy. While 16 percent of the employees were against the policy, 84 percent favored it. A January 1, 2014, implementation is planned, subject to its distribution to all employees before the Christmas break.

Discussions are summarized and actions taken are included

Web-Surfing Policy

D'Marie Simon reported on her study of similar companies' Web-surfing policies. Most have informal guides but no official policies. The guidelines generally are that all surfing must be related to the job and that personal surfing should be done on breaks. The committee discussed the issue at length. It approved a policy that reflects the current general guidelines.

Temp Policy

Tim Lebold presented the legal steps we need to take to get our old and new temporary employees to sign a nondisclosure agreement prior to working here, as we've been discussing in relation to a new temp policy. The committee directed Tim to begin the process so that the policy could be put in force as soon as possible.

New Business—Resolution

Michelle Lum proposed that a resolution of thanks be added to the record recognizing Megan for her terrific attention to detail as well her clear focus on keeping the committee abreast of policy issues. It was unanimously approved.

Resolutions often include descriptive language

Next Meeting

The next meeting of the committee will be May 3, 2013, from 9:30–11:30 A.M. in Conference Room A.

Closing gives reader complete needed facts

Adjournment

The meeting was adjourned at 11:25 A.M.

Respectfully submitted,

Elaine Horn

Elaine Horn

Signing signifies the minutes are an official record

It takes both skill and judgment to prepare accurate, neutral minutes for an important meeting.

COMPONENTS OF LONG, FORMAL REPORTS

LO5 Write longer reports that include the appropriate components, meet the readers' needs, and are easy to follow.

Although not as common as short reports, long, formal reports are highly important in business. They are usually the result of major investigations, which explains their length. And they are usually prepared for high-level executives, which explains their formality.

Our main advice for preparing such reports is presented in Chapter 11. Here we will focus on the special components of formal reports, emphasizing their purpose and design. For any given case, you will need to decide which of these components to use and whether or not your report needs different special elements. As always, the facts of the situation and your readers' preferences should be your guide.

The first parts of a formal report are the prefatory pages described on pages 376–378. As noted in Figure 12–1, the longest, most formal reports contain all of these. As the length of the report and the formality of the situation decrease, certain changes occur. As the report architect, you must decide which prefatory parts meet the length and formality requirements of your situation.

Since these elements have already been discussed, the rest of this section will focus on other components.

The Report Introduction

The introduction is the first section of the report itself. Its purpose is to prepare the readers to receive the report's findings. Whatever will help achieve this goal is appropriate content.

In determining what to include, consider all the likely readers of your report. As we noted earlier, the readers of many shorter reports are likely to know the problem well and have little or no need for an introduction. But such is not often the case for longer

A long report can be daunting to readers. Be sure to provide prefatory material that invites them in and makes the key information easy to find.

reports. Many of these reports are prepared for a large number of readers, some of whom know little about the problem. These reports often have long lives and are kept on file to be read in future years. Your introductory material will need to prepare both immediate and later readers.

Ask yourself what you would need or want to know about the problem if you were in your readers' shoes. As the report's author, you know more about the report than anyone else, so you will need to work hard not to assume that readers have the same knowledge of the problem that you do. In selecting the appropriate information, you would do well to use the following checklist of likely introduction contents. Remember, though, that it is only a checklist. Only on rare occasions, such as for the longest, most complex reports, would you include all the items.

Origin of the Report. The first part of your introduction might be a review of the **facts of authorization**. Some writers, however, leave this part out. If you decide to include it, you should present such facts as when, how, and by whom the report was authorized; who wrote the report; and when the report was submitted. Information of this kind is particularly useful in reports that have no transmittal message.

Problem and Purpose. As Chapter 11 explains, a vital part of almost every report's introduction is a statement of its problem and purpose.

The problem statement is a description of the problem or situation that prompted the investigation. The complexity of the problem and the readers' familiarity with it will determine how much description you need to provide. In cases where the problem is very complex, you may need to provide a short description of the problem here and then go into further detail in a later section of your report.

The purpose statement conveys the goal of your investigation. In essense, it says, "given the problem or situation that needed addressing, this is what I tried to find out." For example, if your company needs an Internet-use policy, your purpose statement might say that you analyzed other companies' policies to determine guidelines for your company's policy. You will need to weave the what and why of the report together for a smooth flow of thoughts. See the first two paragraphs of the sample formal report for an example (page 420).

Scope. If the **scope** of your report is not clearly covered in any of the other introductory parts, you may need to include it in a separate part. By *scope* we mean the boundaries of your investigation. In this part of the introduction—in plain, clear language—you should describe what parts of the problem you studied and what parts you didn't.

Limitations. In some reports, you will need to explain **limitations**. By *limitations* we mean anything that keeps your report from being an ideal treatment of the problem. No real-world problem can be completely explored, and because different writers will approach the same problem differently, what seems complete to one person may not seem complete to another. But in certain cases, you will want to state explicitly what forms of research were not employed so your readers will know how to evaluate your information.

For example, if time constraints permitted only a quick email survey rather than in-depth interviews of your sources, you would say so. Or if a major source of information was unavailable (perhaps a key expert had left the company or relevant industry reports were too expensive), you would note this limitation in your report. You might also indicate the extent to which your findings can be applied to similar situations.

Be frank in this section but not too negative. State clearly what was not done and why, but do so without apology or such negative wording as "impair" or "compromised the validity of our findings." If you have done a good job with the resources at your disposal, this section of the report can use a directness that shows confidence in the report's usefulness despite its limitations.

Historical Background. Knowledge of the history of the problem is sometimes essential to understanding the report. Thus, you may need to cover that history in your introduction. Your general aim in this part is to acquaint the readers with how the problem developed and what has been done about it. Your discussion here should bring out the main issues. It should review what past investigations have determined about the problem, and it should lead to what still needs to be done.

Sources and Methods of Collecting Information. You usually need to tell the readers how you collected the information in the report. You specify whether you used published research, surveys, experiments, qualitative research, or a combination of methods, and you describe the steps you followed. In general, you describe your research in enough detail to allow your readers to judge it. You also want to convince them that your work was done competently.

In reports based on published research, this section can be short. If most of your findings came from a few sources, you can name the sources. If you used a large number of sources, you can just describe the types of sources you used and then refer to the report's bibliography.

More complex research requires a more detailed description. If you conducted a survey, for example, you probably would need to explain all parts of the investigation. You would cover how you chose your sample, how you developed the survey, and how you administered it. If you conducted an experiment, you would describe it carefully. Whatever your method, include enough detail so that readers will be able to judge the reliability and validity of your findings.

Definitions, Initialisms, and Acronyms. If you use terms, initialisms, or acronyms that are likely to be unfamiliar to readers of the report, you should define these. You can define each term in the text or as a footnote when it is first used in the report, or you can define all unfamiliar terms in a separate part of the introduction. If you use the latter method, begin this part with an introductory statement and then list the terms with their definitions. If the list is long, you may choose to arrange the terms alphabetically.

Report Preview. In very long reports, the final part of the introduction should preview the report structure. In this part you tell the readers how the body of the

TECHNOLOGY IN BRIEF

Using a Table of Contents Generator for Speed and Accuracy

The table of contents generator tool in today's word-processing software frees writers from both the physical formatting and the accuracy tasks. Just a few clicks produce and format the table of contents, along with leaders and page numbers. Additionally, today's generators add links so that those reading the report on the screen rather than on paper can easily navigate to a particular section or page by simply clicking it in the table of contents.

The table of contents generator works with Word's built-in styles, which you use as tags to mark the different levels of headings that will be included in the table of contents. If you are using a standard report template, styles are already

incorporated in it. If you are creating your own report from a blank document, you could use predefined styles or define your own styles to create titles, headings, and subheads. Styles provide consistency so that headings at certain levels always appear the same, helping the reader see the relationship of the parts of your report.

Furthermore, if you decide to change the material in your report after you have generated the table of contents, you simply regenerate it to update page numbers with only a few clicks.

Shown here is a sample table of contents automatically created in Word 2010.

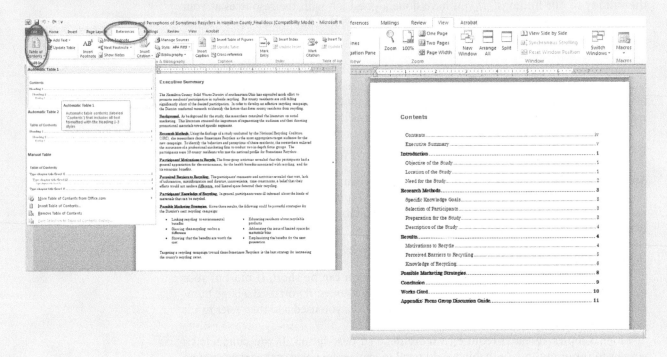

report is organized—what topics will be taken up first, second, third, and so on. In short, you give your readers a clear picture of the road ahead. As you will see later in the chapter, this part of the introduction is a basic ingredient of the coherence plan of the long report.

The Report Body

In the report body, the information collected is presented and related to the problem. Normally, this part of the report comprises most of its content. In a sense, the report body is the report. With the exception of the conclusion or recommendation part, the other parts of the report are attached parts.

Advice presented throughout this book will help you prepare this part of the report. You should organize it according to the instructions presented in the preceding

"This has so many different fonts in it,
I thought it was a ransom note."

SOURCE: www.CartoonStock.com. Reprinted with permission.

chapter. As that chapter also advises, you may choose the personal or impersonal style, but whichever you choose should be interesting and clear. You should format this part of the report for easy comprehension, and any visuals you include should follow the guidelines discussed in Chapter 14. If you've used outside sources, these should be noted and documented as illustrated in Appendix E. In short, writing this major section of the long, formal report will require virtually all your organizing, writing, and formatting skills.

The Ending of the Report

You can end your report in any number of ways: with a **summary**, a **conclusions section,** a **recommendations section,** or a combination of the three. Your choice depends on the purpose of your report. You should choose the way that enables you to satisfy that purpose.

Ending Summary. When the purpose of the report is to present information, the ending is logically a summary of the major findings. There is usually no attempt to interpret at this point. Informational reports often have minor summaries at the ends of the major sections. When this arrangement is followed, the ending summary basically justs restates these summaries.

You should not confuse the ending summary with the executive summary. The executive summary is a prefatory part of the report; the ending summary is a part of the report text. Also, the executive summary is more complete than the ending summary. The executive summary reviews the entire report, usually from the beginning to the end. The ending summary reviews only the major findings of the report.

Conclusions. Some reports must do more than just present information. They must analyze the information in light of the problem, and from this analysis, they must reach a conclusion or conclusions.

The makeup of the conclusions section varies from case to case. In investigations for which a single answer is sought (e.g., "Has our new schedule reduced our utility costs?"), this section normally reviews the preceding information and analyses and, from this review, arrives at the answer. For more complex investigations (e.g., "How do employees feel about the new schedule?"), the report may treat each topic in a separate section and draw conclusions in each section. The conclusions section of such a report would then summarize these previous conclusions.

On the other hand, you should avoid mechanically repeating the findings you've already stated in earlier sections. Some interpretation is appropriate here. Put the findings back into the context of the overall problem and help the reader see what they mean in terms of the problem (e.g., why employees may have responded as they did).

Recommendations. When the goal of the report is not only to draw conclusions but also to present a course of action, a recommendation or recommendations are in order. You may provide them in a separate section following the conclusions section, or you may include them in the conclusions section. Regardless, if you have several recommendations, you may want to bullet them for easy reading. Whether you include recommendations should be determined by whether the readers want or expect them.

Appended Parts

Sometimes you will need to include an **appendix**, a **bibliography**, or both at the end of the report. Whether you include these parts should be determined by need.

Appendix. The appendix, as its name implies, is a something appended (attached) to the main report. You use it for supplementary information that supports the body of the report. Possible appendix contents are questionnaires, working papers, summary tables, additional references, and other reports.

As a rule, the appendix should not include the charts, graphs, and tables that directly support the report. These should be placed in the body of the report where they can support the findings. Because it is not convenient for readers to have to flip to the appendix to find the data they need, put in the appendix only those visuals that are too large or complex to insert into the body of the report.

Bibliography. When your investigation makes heavy use of published sources, you normally include either footnotes, a bibliography, or both. The construction of these is described in Appendix E of this book.

THE STRUCTURAL COHERENCE PLAN

Because of its length, a long report runs the risk of losing readers' attention or causing them to lose track of the report's logical structure. For this reason, a long report can benefit from a **structural coherence plan**.

By *structural coherence plan* we mean a network of explanations, introductions, summaries, and conclusions that guide the reader through the report. Of course, you will also employ the devices for coherent writing discussed in Chapters 4 and 5. But because of the formal report's length, your reader will probably need additional help relating the parts of the report to each other and remembering where he or she is in the report. A structural coherence plan provides this extra help. Although you should not use its components mechanically, it is likely to follow the general plan illustrated in Figure 12–7.

The coherence plan begins with the report preview at the end of the introduction. The preview covers the topics to be discussed, their order, and the logic behind that order. With this information in mind, the readers know how the parts of the report will relate to one another. The following paragraphs do a good job of previewing a report comparing four automobiles to determine which is the best for a company's sales fleet.

> To identify which light car Allied Distributors should buy, this report compares the cars under consideration on the basis of three factors: cost, safety, and performance. Each of these factors is broken down into its component parts, which are applied to the specific models being considered.

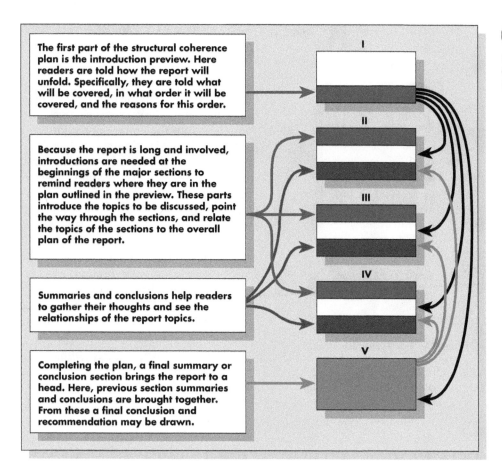

The first part of the structural coherence plan is the introduction preview. Here readers are told how the report will unfold. Specifically, they are told what will be covered, in what order it will be covered, and the reasons for this order.

Because the report is long and involved, introductions are needed at the beginnings of the major sections to remind readers where they are in the plan outlined in the preview. These parts introduce the topics to be discussed, point the way through the sections, and relate the topics of the sections to the overall plan of the report.

Summaries and conclusions help readers to gather their thoughts and see the relationships of the report topics.

Completing the plan, a final summary or conclusion section brings the report to a head. Here, previous section summaries and conclusions are brought together. From these a final conclusion and recommendation may be drawn.

Figure 12–7

Diagram of the Structural Coherence Plan of a Long, Formal Report

Because cost is the most tangible factor, it is examined in the first major section. In this section, the four automobiles are compared for initial and trade-in values and for operating costs, as determined by mileage, oil use, and repair expense. In the second major section, the safety of the four makes is compared. Driver visibility, special safety features, brakes, steering quality, acceleration rate, and traction are the main considerations here. In the third major section, the dependability of the four makes is compared on the basis of repair records and salespersons' time lost because of automobile failure. In the final major section, weights are assigned to the foregoing comparisons, and the automobile that is best suited to the company's needs is recommended.

In addition to the preview in the introduction, the plan uses introductory and summary sections at convenient places throughout the report. Typically, these sections are at the beginning and end of major divisions, but you should use them wherever they are needed. Such sections remind the readers where they are in the report. They tell the readers where they have been, where they are going, and perhaps why they are going there.

Illustrating this technique is the following paragraph, which introduces a major section of a report. Note how the paragraph ties in with the preceding discussion, which concerned industrial activity in three geographic areas. Note also how it justifies covering secondary areas in the next section of the report.

Although the great bulk of industry is concentrated in three areas (Grand City, Milltown, and Port Starr), a thorough industrial survey needs to consider the secondary, but nevertheless important, areas of the state. In the rank of their current industrial potential, these areas are the Southeast, with Hartsburg as its center; the Central

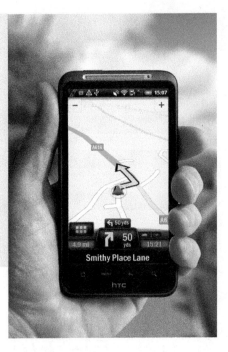

Structural coherence helpers guide readers through the report. Helpers are similar to today's GPS applications. Readers can clearly see where they have been, where they are, and where they will go next. With transitional paragraphs, sentences, and words at important positions throughout the report, you can guide readers skillfully to the report's ending.

West, dominated by Parrington; and the North Central, where Pineview is the center of activities.

Completing the coherence plan is the final major section of the report. In this section, you achieve the goal of the report. Here you recall from the preceding section summaries all the major findings and analyses. Then you apply them to the problem, draw conclusions, and make recommendations if appropriate. With this section, you thus complete the plan that your introduction previewed.

Wisely used coherence helpers can form a network of connections throughout the report. You should keep in mind, however, that these helpers should be used only when they are needed. That is, you should use them when your readers need help seeing relationships and remembering where they have been and where they are going. If you use such aids well, they will appear as natural parts of the report story. When paragraphs are combined with sentence and word transitions, as discussed in Chapters 4, 5, and 11, the total plan should guide your readers smoothly and naturally through the report.

THE FORMAL REPORT ILLUSTRATED

The formal report that begins on the next page was written by a communications professional in a waste-management agency and addressed to her boss. The report illustrates many of the components and strategies described in the preceding pages.

THERE'S MORE . . .

What are mistakes to avoid in executive summaries? What are some effective headings for different types of reports? How should you tell your organization's "story" in an annual report? Scan the QR code with your smartphone or use your Web browser to find out at www.mhhe.com/lesikar13e. Choose Chapter 12 > Bizcom Tools & Tips.

A Long, Formal Report. This report, with its many prefatory parts, exemplifies the top level of Figure 12–1. It is intended not only for the writer's boss but also for those in other recycling agencies and organizations.

Behaviors and Perceptions of Sometimes Recyclers in Hamilton County, Ohio

Title fly–for the most formal reports

(continued)

Behaviors and Perceptions of Sometimes Recyclers in Hamilton County, Ohio

Title page repeats the title...

Prepared for:

Jeanine Smart
Solid Waste Manager
Hamilton County Solid Waste Management District

...and adds additional information

Prepared by:

Michelle Tonney
Community Outreach Coordinator
Hamilton County Solid Waste Management District

March 7, 2013

(continued)

HAMILTON COUNTY
ENVIRONMENTAL
S E R V I C E S

250 William Howard Taft Road, First Floor, Cincinnati, OH 45219
Ph: 513-946-7777 | Fax: 513-946-7778
Ph: Toll Free in Ohio 1-800-889-0474

March 7, 2013

Ms. Jeanine Smart
Solid Waste Manager
Hamilton County Solid Waste District

Dear Jeanine:

Here is the in-depth qualitative study of Hamilton County residents' attitudes
toward recycling that you authorized on December 3, 2012.

We contracted the services of Advanced Marketing, a Cincinnati marketing firm, to
conduct the study in collaboration with four representatives from the District. The
study revealed positive and negative attitudes that Sometimes Recyclers in
Hamilton County have toward recycling. This report describes their attitudes in
detail.

In light of these findings, the report identifies several strategies that can be
implemented to make our next recycling campaign a success.

Thank you for authorizing this research. I look forward to working with you to
create our most effective campaign ever.

Sincerely yours,

Michelle Tonney

Michelle Tonney
Community Outreach Coordinator

*Letter of
transmittal
"hands over"
the report*

Contents

Entries match the report headings

Table of contents previews the report structure

CASE ILLUSTRATION

Executive Summary

The Hamilton County Solid Waste District of southwestern Ohio has expended much effort to promote residents' participation in curbside recycling. But county residents are still falling significantly short of the desired participation. In order to develop an effective recycling campaign, the District conducted research to identify the factors that deter county residents from recycling.

Background. As background for the study, the researchers consulted the literature on social marketing. This literature stressed the importance of segmenting the audience and then directing promotional materials toward specific segments.

Research Methods. Using the findings of a study conducted by the National Recycling Coalition (NRC), the researchers chose Sometimes Recyclers as the most appropriate target audience for the new campaign. To identify the behaviors and perceptions of these residents, the researchers enlisted the assistance of a professional marketing firm to conduct two in-depth focus groups. The participants were 18 county residents who met the national profile for Sometimes Recyclers.

Participants' Motivations to Recycle. The focus-group activities revealed that the participants had a general appreciation for the environment, for the health benefits associated with recycling, and for its economic benefits.

Perceived Barriers to Recycling. The participants' comments and activities revealed that cost, lack of information, misinformation and distrust, inconvenience, time constraints, a belief that their efforts would not make a difference, and limited space deterred their recycling.

Participants' Knowledge of Recycling. In general, participants were ill informed about the kinds of materials that can be recycled.

Possible Marketing Strategies. Given these results, the following could be powerful strategies for the District's next recycling campaign:

- Linking recycling to environmental benefits.
- Showing that recycling makes a difference.
- Showing that the benefits are worth the cost.
- Educating residents about recyclable products.
- Addressing the issue of limited space for materials/bins.
- Emphasizing the benefits for the next generation.

Targeting a recycling campaign toward these Sometimes Recyclers is the best strategy for increasing the county's recycling rates.

v

419

(continued)

Introduction

Local governments have numerous motivations to increase recycling rates. Some want to reach state-mandated recycling goals, while others wish to improve the bottom line and reduce landfill-tipping fees. Still other communities want to add a few more years to the life of their landfill. Almost all local governments recognize the societal benefits of recycling: reduced pollution, saved energy, and a stronger economy. However, local governments have struggled to increase recycling rates in communities since curbside-recycling collection began in the early 1990s.

To identify deterrents to recycling, the Hamilton County Solid Waste District studied county residents participating in two focus groups. The results, presented here, can be used to develop a more effective recycling campaign.

Objective of the Study

Promotional materials designed to increase recycling rates can be described as a type of social marketing, the use of marketing techniques to persuade an audience to change their behavior in a way that benefits society as a whole. In their study of social marketing methods, Kotler, Roberto, and Lee stress the importance of segmenting the intended audience and understanding the different segments' behaviors. "This important and often-skipped step explores current knowledge, beliefs, and behaviors of target audiences."[1] Traditional local government advertising, however, directs promotional materials to all residents, failing to segment the audience. By leaving the target audience broad and undefined, local government advertising loses its potential to influence specific segments of the population.

The need to segment the population is especially true in recycling outreach. Portions of the population have different attitudes toward recycling and clearly have different recycling behaviors. This research project thus aimed to build on previous knowledge about one specific segment—Sometimes Recyclers. Understanding the recycling knowledge, beliefs, and behaviors of this significant portion of the population will enable the district to do more effective social marketing.

Location of the Study

The research took place in Hamilton County, Ohio, located in the southwestern corner of the state. According to the U.S. Census, Hamilton County has an estimated 346,790 households in 49 different political jurisdictions, including the City of Cincinnati. The Hamilton County Solid Waste Management District is a county organization, established by state law, responsible for ensuring that the county achieves state-mandated goals for recycling and waste reduction. The Solid Waste District includes 48 of the 49 political jurisdictions.

Each of the 48 political jurisdictions decides what type of recycling program to offer its residents. Approximately half of the municipalities contract for recycling services with a private waste hauler, making recycling no additional cost to the residents. Residents in communities with a recycling contract can receive weekly curbside recycling collection without having to pay a monthly fee. However, the other half of the municipalities, mostly townships, has a subscription-based recycling program.

---

[1]Philip Kotler and Nancy R. Lee, *Social Marketing: Improving Behaviors for Good*, 3rd ed. (Thousand Oaks, CA: Sage, 2007) 116, print.

Identifies the context and the report problem

States the report's purpose

Explains and justifies the study's specific purpose

Clearly states the scope of the study

Provides helpful background for secondary readers

Citation footnotes are convenient for readers

(continued)

Residents in subscription communities have to subscribe for curbside recycling and trash services by calling their waste hauler and paying an additional fee of approximately $3.00 a month.

Need for the Study

Several prior studies have gathered information on local recycling habits:

- Sixty-one percent of Hamilton County residents say they participate in some sort of recycling.[2]
- In 2011, Hamilton County communities recycled 35,116 tons of material.[3]
- Approximately 60% of the material entering the landfill is recyclable.[4]

Although 61% of residents claim to recycle, the volume of recyclables collected shows that residents fall short of recycling everything possible. Communities with strong, established recycling programs in Hamilton County regularly average 500 to 600 pounds of material set out for recycling per household per year. If 61% of the households recycled at this high volume, the county would recycle 52,885 tons of material a year—or 17,769 tons more than it currently does. The shortfall becomes even more significant considering that 60% of what enters the landfill could be easily recycled through a curbside recycling program.

So why are household recycling rates so low? The National Recycling Coalition (NRC) may have identified the cause. NRC separates people who claim to participate in recycling into two categories: Always Recyclers and Sometimes Recyclers. Always Recyclers consistently recycle everything possible and have difficulty throwing an item away if they know it is recyclable. A Sometimes Recycler, however, recycles only certain materials and has little difficulty throwing an item away if it is inconvenient to recycle. These residents do not see themselves as typical recyclers and recycle only when it is convenient.

Uses research and good logic to justify the study

Sometimes Recyclers care about health and environmental issues and support charitable causes. According to the NRC research, these residents want to feel connected to others and need to believe that their efforts make a difference. But they are stuck between trial recycling and consistent recycling. They often do not connect the dots between recycling and benefits and therefore do not see the relevance of recycling to them.[5]

Sometimes Recyclers outnumber Always Recyclers by two and half times. Using a national survey estimate,[6] Hamilton County has roughly 257,000 Sometimes Recyclers compared to roughly 107,000 Always Recyclers, making them an ideal audience for an outreach campaign.

Past outreach campaigns of the District did not define a clear target audience but tried to reach all residents of Hamilton County. By choosing a target audience, the District will be able to profile the behaviors of the audience and shape the message to match their behaviors.

---

[2]Dan Stevens, *Greater Cincinnati Survey 62, Fall 2011* (Cincinnati, OH: University of Cincinnati Institute for Policy Research, 2012), print.

[3]Data collected through the Residential Recycling Incentive program for the Hamilton County Solid Waste Management District.

[4]Ohio Department of Natural Resources, *State of Ohio Waste Characterization Study* (Columbus, OH: Engineering Solutions and Designs, Inc., 21 April 2012), print.

[5]Jane Leigh, "Uncovering the Drivers of Consumer Recycling Behavior," National Recycling Coalition Annual Congress and Expo, Washington, DC, June 2012, presentation.

[6]Leigh.

(continued)

Research Methods

The NRC data on Sometimes Recyclers did not provide specific information that could be applied to a local context. To better understand the target audience, the researchers conducted two focus groups with local Sometimes Recyclers. Conducting focus groups allowed the researchers to gather in-depth data about local Sometimes Recyclers' recycling behaviors and motivations.

Specific Knowledge Goals

The specific objectives of the study were to

- Identify motivations to recycling.
- Understand perceived barriers to recycling.
- Understand what would encourage participants to recycle.
- Learn where and when the participants find current information about recycling and where they would like to find it in the future.

Selection of Participants

Using NRC identifiers for Sometimes Recyclers,[7] the researchers recruited participant groups within the following parameters:

- Homeowners.
- Between 30–55 years of age.
- Equal number of male and female participants.
- Supporters of charitable causes through donation or volunteering.
- Participants in some type of recycling but not avid recyclers.
- Hamilton County, Ohio, residents.
- Married.
- Voters.
- College educated (at least partially).

Although these identifiers are by no means descriptive of all residents falling into the Sometimes Recyclers group, they enabled researchers to choose residents who met the national profile. Approximately three-fourths (14) of the participants came from townships where residents are charged for recycling services.

Preparation for the Study

Since the District has a limited staff and limited resources, it contracted out the service of finding participants to a professional marketing firm in Cincinnati, Advanced Marketing. By reading past surveys conducted locally as well as national research on recycling behavior, the researchers prepared a list of questions for the focus groups and organized the questions in a logical manner. A volunteer moderator not related to the project moderated the focus group so the researchers would

Well-organized research specifics build confidence in the study and help with interpretation of results

---

[7]Leigh.

(continued)

4

not influence the answers of the participants.[8,9] The researchers met with the moderator beforehand to further refine the questions and tailor them to the objectives of the study. The appendix to this report shows the final draft of the discussion guide for the focus groups.

Description of the Study

On January 30, 2013, the researchers conducted two focus groups, with 10 participants in the first group and 8 participants in the second. The contractor provided a space with one-sided glass for observation, as well as a recorded DVD of the session for later review.[10]

Each focus group was questioned for approximately one hour and participated in exercises that followed the predetermined outline. The moderator had experience with the level of questioning to ask and with drawing out participants who were not contributing.[11]

After asking general questions, the moderator asked participants to take part in these exercises:

- Clipping pictures from magazines to express the primary barriers they perceive to recycling.
- Drawing their recycling process.
- Writing down all the materials they know are recyclable.
- Reviewing a preprinted list of recyclables to mark items they did not know were recyclable.

Participants were also asked to evaluate a series of slogans related to recycling.

Four staff members from Hamilton County Environmental Services attended the focus group: two from the Solid Waste District and two from the Public Affairs Department. In addition, two staff members of Keep Cincinnati Beautiful also attended because the two organizations coordinate their recycling outreach efforts. All staff members took notes and recorded their observations from behind one-way glass.

Afterward, all the observers met to discuss their impressions, share notes, and reach consensus on the key findings. The next section presents the results.

Results

This section groups the main findings into three categories: participants' motivations to recycle, their perceived barriers to recycling, and their knowledge of recyclable materials.

Section preview adds coherence

Motivations to Recycle

When asked why they recycle, participants responded, "Recycling is good for the environment" and "I want to take responsibility." Some said they want to save resources. Two participants said that recycling spared their families trash bags and time taking out the trash. Several parents expressed concern about "leaving a better place for their kids" or said "I do it for my children's future."

---

[8]Richard A. Krueger and Mary Anne Casey, *Focus Groups: A Practical Guide for Applied Research*, 4th ed. (Thousand Oaks, CA: Sage, 2009) 87, print.

[9]Frank I. Luntz, "Voices of Victory, Part II: The Makings of a Good Focus Group," *The Polling Report*, 30 May 1994, Web, 18 Feb. 2012.

[10]Krueger and Casey 144, 96.

[11]Luntz.

Most participants saw the environmental and health benefits as the biggest motivators to recycle. Several participants commented that they were not "tree-huggers" but that they did have a general concern for the environment. One mentioned that he wanted an "opportunity to give back to the environment." Several said recycling is "good for everyone" or "I want to make a difference." Some responded that they didn't want to add to the landfill.

Specific quotes add authenticity

Several participants mentioned that they collect recyclables for local charities. Their charitable recycling included removing the tabs from aluminum cans and then donating the cans to Children's Hospital and collecting paper for local school and church paper drives.

Many of the participants collect their metal cans to bring to a metal scrap dealer. Almost all participants who described doing this explained that they rinsed and crushed the cans before driving them to the drop-off and receiving compensation for the cans.

Participants were asked to identify the primary benefit of recycling. Figure 1 provides a numerical summary of the benefits identified by the two groups.

Previews the visual

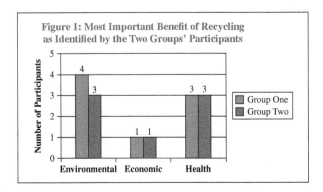

Figure 1: Most Important Benefit of Recycling as Identified by the Two Groups' Participants

At the chart shows, many participants listed environmental and health benefits as the most important. (Two participants in group one and one participant in group two did not respond.) In both groups, participants said that environmental and health benefits were connected.

Interprets and adds to figure data

Perceived Barriers to Recycling

Much of the discussion in the focus groups related to barriers to recycling. Participants identified several of these, both in the magazine activity and in response to the question "Is recycling an easy or difficult thing to do? Tell me why."

- **Cost.** One of the most often talked about barriers was the cost of recycling. Participants said, "Why do they charge when they make money?"; "I don't recycle because of the charge"; and "Why does the hauler make you pay?" The perception of recycling is that it is expensive. Several participants used drop-off recycling centers or used their neighbor's recycling bin to avoid paying for curbside recycling. Additionally, the participants felt that waste management companies were profiting from residents' recycling efforts.

- **Lack of Information.** Participants mentioned that they were confused about what is recyclable. One woman said the recycling symbol was hard to locate on the product. Even when she found it, the symbol confused her; she asked "What does PET mean?" Several people also mentioned

(continued)

6

confusion over the number system, saying "I don't know all the stuff that can be recycled" and "I don't know how much you have to pay for recycling."

- **Myths.** One participant commented that "products made out of recycled materials are not as good," to which several others nodded in response. Another participant expressed disbelief that the material was going to be recycled, saying, "It all ends up in the landfill."

- **Perception That It Is Not Convenient.** This perception was revealed through such comments as "I don't like separating my waste," "I don't like rinsing my cans," "The recycling container is too far away," and "I don't have enough space in my kitchen." Several participants admitted that they were just too lazy. Many also mentioned that it was inconvenient and even "gross" to have to rinse the containers. Another woman mentioned it was too cold to recycle; she didn't want to go to her garage.

- **Time Constraints.** Many participants talked about being too busy to recycle. This was especially true when the participant had children with many activities to attend. They did not think recycling fit easily into their daily routine. Some participants responded by saying, "I have too many things on my plate."

- **Perception That It Is Not Important.** Participants made such statements as "I have other things to do," "Sometimes I just don't care," or "I guess I should care more about it." They did not think their effort really made a difference. Participants also wanted a reward for recycling; one said "Make it worth my while," and another said "What's in it for us?"

- **Space Constraints.** Another barrier mentioned was limited space. Comments along these lines were "Why don't they give you an extra bin?" and "The bin is too small."

Helpful, well-organized qualitative data

Participants made collages from magazines to express what they felt were the biggest barriers to recycling for them. By far the most popular images were of a watch or busy people. Table 1 summarizes the results of this activity.

Tables are numbered consecutively throughout the report

Table 1: Barriers to Recycling Shown in Collages			
	Group One	Group Two	Total
Not enough time	4	7	11
Not enough information	2		2
Materials not recyclable	2	1	3
Materials attract animals	1		1
Cost	1	1	2
Laziness		1	1

Knowledge of Recycling

The moderator asked participants to list what materials they knew were recyclable on a sheet of paper. After they completed their lists, the moderator then gave them a list of the materials that can currently be recycled in a curbside bin. The moderator asked the participants to circle the materials

Adds helpful procedural details

425

(continued)

7

Lead-in prepares readers to interpret the table

they did not know were recyclable and place a star by the materials they will start recycling after becoming aware that the item is recyclable. Table 2 shows the results of this exercise broken down according to group. The list of items in the leftmost column is the list that the moderator gave the participants.

Table 2: Participants' Responses to List of Items You Can Recycle				
	Focus Group One		Focus Group Two	
Item	Surprised	Will start recycling	Surprised	Will start recycling
Plastic bottles and jugs				
Glass bottles and jars				
Empty aerosol cans	4	5	8	2
Aluminum cans				
Steel cans			1	1
Tin cans				
Paperboard	1	1	1	1
Junk mail	6	2		1
Envelopes	1			
Magazines	2	2		1
Newspaper				
Cardboard				
Office paper				
Brown grocery bags				
Writing paper				
File folders	2	1		
Post-it notes	3	1		2
Index cards	1	1		2
Phone books		1		3

In both groups, most participants were surprised to learn that aerosol cans are recyclable, and in the first group, 6 of 10 participants were surprised that junk mail is recyclable. Some of the other

Helps readers identify the noteworthy data

(continued)

8

paper items also elicited surprise for being recyclable. This is likely because several years ago these items were not recyclable and the participants remembered those rules.

In general, the "will start recycling" responses were positive; most people who were surprised that something could be recycled said they would start recycling it. But in the second group, only 2 of the 8 people who were surprised that aerosol cans are recyclable said that they would start recycling the cans.

Possible Marketing Strategies

With the information from the focus group, the researchers were able to generate ideas for an outreach campaign targeted toward Sometimes Recyclers. First, the barriers should be addressed and, if possible, broken down. Then the campaign needs to appeal to Sometimes Recyclers' motivations for recycling and extend that motivation into further involvement.

■ **Linking Recycling to Important Environmental Benefits**
One of the most significant barriers that the focus group participants discussed was the lack of time for and the inconvenience of recycling. They feel their lives are hectic and that recycling is just one more thing to add to their list of things to do. But do Always Recyclers have less hectic lives than Sometimes Recyclers? What helps Always Recyclers transcend this barrier is the relative importance they place on recycling. A related barrier the participants discussed was not feeling recycling was important or not feeling they were making a difference. Sometimes Recyclers do not make the connection between recycling and the environmental benefits.

The barrier of not completely believing the importance of recycling ties into one of the chief motivations for recycling that the Sometimes Recyclers expressed: the opportunity to give back to the environment and make a difference. Sometimes Recyclers seem to have a surface belief that recycling betters the environment, but they cannot explain exactly how or why. The outreach campaign needs to overcome these barriers to recycling by connecting recycling to the environmental benefits in ways that Sometimes Recyclers can understand.

Recommendations are closely tied to research findings

■ **Showing That Individual Recycling Makes a Difference**
The moderator asked participants what message would most motivate them to start recycling. Participants responded that they wanted to see results. They wanted to see numbers that expressed the tangible benefits of recycling. They wanted to know that little things do make a difference. They wanted to know what immediate impact their actions made, not just how it would benefit the future of the planet. Including actual numbers on the immediate environmental benefits of recycling could address this need. Making the numbers personally relevant by using a per-household or per-item scale could also help residents understand that their actions can make a difference.

■ **Showing That the Benefits Are Worth the Cost**
Although cost was a major barrier discussed by participants, addressing this issue is difficult on the level of recycling outreach. Individual communities can make the decision to contract the recycling service and lower the cost to help overcome this barrier. Similarly, myths about and distrust of the hauler are difficult barriers to address with an outreach campaign. These barriers would make for interesting future research. How can a community build trust for recycling and

the processes involved? What type of message is needed to convey the idea that while recycling is not free, the benefits outweigh the cost? The answers could help recyclers transcend this barrier.

■ **Educating Residents about Recyclable Products**

Lack of information pertaining to what is recyclable arose as a barrier in several of the collages. The lack of knowledge about what can be recycled was also apparent in the activities involving the list of recyclables. Communities wishing to address this barrier should examine the method by which the message is delivered. For example, would a magnet with a list of recyclables be more effective than a radio advertisement?

■ **Addressing the Space Issue**

Another barrier the participants addressed was lack of space. The 14- or 18-gallon recycling bin provided in local curbside recycling programs seems to be inadequate to contain all of the materials participants could recycle. This concept could explain why many Sometimes Recyclers do not create the volume of recycling that one would expect with an Always Recycler. Once the bin is full, the Sometimes Recycler simply throws the item in the trash while the Always Recycler finds creative solutions for recycling more, such as purchasing an additional container to store recyclables. Communities can address this issue by providing an additional recycling bin at no charge or by providing larger recycling containers, such as 64-gallon wheeled carts.

■ **Emphasizing the Benefits for the Next Generation**

Many participants also mentioned that their children were their primary mode of receiving information about recycling. This is good news for all the environmental educators working so hard to teach children about the importance of recycling. Motivating children to recycle and educating them on what materials can be recycled seems to have permeated their home life. Targeting the participants' motivation to leave a better place for their children combined with continuing environmental education in the schools could be a powerful strategy.

Conclusion

While this study involved a small number of people representing a small portion of the Sometimes Recyclers in Hamilton County, the 18 participants all met the NRC's profile of Sometimes Recyclers, and the research methods used enabled them to express their opinions in depth. The perceptual data collected can be immensely helpful in shaping and directing an outreach campaign.

Research limitations are briefly acknowledged

The ultimate goal of the outreach campaign is to motivate Sometimes Recyclers to adopt consistent recycling behaviors and beliefs that elevate them to the Always Recyclers status. They should want to recycle every piece of waste they generate that is recyclable, whether through a curbside program or a community drop-off.

In order to reach the Sometimes Recyclers, a campaign needs to make the connection between their daily recycling actions and benefits to the environment, both immediately and in the future. By identifying the target audience of Sometimes Recyclers and directing outreach efforts specifically toward them, local governments can come one step closer to converting Sometimes Recyclers to Always Recyclers and increasing residential recycling rates.

Ending reiterates the main point of the report and uses motivational language to spark action

(continued)

10

Works Cited

Kotler, Philip, and Nancy R. Lee. *Social Marketing: Improving Behaviors for Good*. 3rd ed. Thousand Oaks, CA: Sage, 2007. Print.

Krueger, Richard A., and Mary Anne Casey. *Focus Groups: A Practical Guide for Applied Research*. 4th ed. Thousand Oaks, CA: Sage, 2009. Print.

Leigh, Jane. "Uncovering the Drivers of Consumer Recycling Behavior." National Recycling Coalition Annual Congress and Expo. Washington, DC. June 2012. Presentation.

Luntz, Frank I. "Voices of Victory, Part II: The Makings of a Good Focus Group." *The Polling Report* 30 May 1994: n. pag. Web. 18 Feb. 2012.

Ohio Department of Natural Resources. *State of Ohio Waste Characterization Study*. Columbus, OH: Engineering Solutions and Designs, Inc., 21 Apr. 2012. Print.

Stevens, Dan. *Greater Cincinnati Survey 62, Fall 2011*. Cincinnati, OH: University of Cincinnati Institute for Policy Research, 2012. Print.

Though not necessary with citation footnotes, a bibliography is included as a convenience to readers

(continued)

Appendix: Focus Group Discussion Guide

Introduction (10 minutes)

Have participant make introductions (name, # in household, where you live).
Ask participants to name an idea they have seen that helps the environment.
Transition to recycling; ask them what they know about recycling and its benefits.
First activity: Have participants draw their recycling process using any item as an example. Use very basic pictures to draw cycle from when they are finished with the item to when the recyclables leave their hands.

Current Perception (20 minutes)

"Why is recycling important to you?"
"How long have you been recycling and what influenced you to start?"
"Is recycling an easy or difficult thing to do? Tell me why."
Second activity: "Cut out pictures from a magazine that describe your biggest barrier to recycling. Discuss the pictures."

Current Process (20 minutes)

Third Activity: "On a piece a paper write everything that you know you can recycle."
Pass out list of recyclable material (in normal curbside program) and have participants flag what they are surprised about and what they will start doing now that they know.
"What determines if something goes into your recycling bin?"
"How do you feel when you throw something in the trash that you know is recyclable? Does it invoke any emotions?"
"Where do you keep your recycling bin?"
"How do you go about getting a bin?"
"Do you know where a drop-off is that is close to you?"
"What type of schedule do you have for recycling (weekly, monthly, etc.)?"
"Does anyone recycle at work?"
"What do you know about materials that use recycled content? What do you feel about the quality of those products?"
"What is your impression of how much profit companies make on recycling?"

Recycling Motivation (20 minutes)

Fourth Activity: "Write down the benefit you feel is the most important benefit of recycling—economic, environmental, health."
"Raise your hand if you knew recycling had economic benefits. Can you explain them?"
"Raise your hand if you knew recycling had environmental benefits. Can you explain them?"
"Raise your hand if you knew recycling had health benefits. Can you explain them?"
"What could someone tell you to influence you to start recycling? What would make the message more persuasive?"
"How can recycling be made more relevant to you?"
"Where do you look for recycling information?"

Slogans (5 minutes)

Read slogans and ask them their reaction. Ask what they like and don't like.
Have them write their top two favorite slogans on their paper.

Appendix includes helpful supplementary material

1. Length and formality largely determine the makeup of reports.
   - The very long ones have prefatory pages.
     - Title fly—a page displaying only the title.
     - Title page—a page displaying the title, writer and reader's names and their titles/organizations, and date.
     - Authorization message—included only when a written message authorized the report.
     - Transmittal message—a personal message "handing the report over" to the reader.
     - Table of contents, list of illustrations—a listing of the report parts and illustrations with page numbers.
     - Executive summary—the report in miniature, written in direct or indirect order.
   - As reports become shorter and less formal, the composition of the prefatory pages changes, generally in this order:
     - First, the title fly drops out.
     - Then, the executive summary and letter of transmittal are combined.
     - The table of contents is omitted.
     - The combined letter of transmittal and executive summary is dropped.
   - Even less elaborate are letter, email, and memo reports.

   Explain the makeup of reports relative to length and formality.

2. Apart from their makeup, short reports differ from long reports in four main ways:
   - They have less need for introductory material.
   - They are more likely to begin directly (conclusion or recommendation first).
   - They are more likely to use a personal style.
   - They have less need for a formal coherence plan.

   Discus the four main ways that the writing in short reports differs from the writing in long reports.

3. The shorter reports come in three main forms.
   - The short report form can be for any situation of mid-level formality and complexity.
     - It consists of a title page and report text, or a title page, combined transmittal message/summary, and report text.
     - It can be written in the direct or indirect order.
     - Internal reports usually use the direct order. External reports that use the indirect order often state the main findings in the transmittal message.
   - Letter reports tend to be written to those outside the company.
     - They tend to use a personal style.
     - They can be written in the direct or indirect order. A direct-order letter often uses a subject line.
   - Email and memo reports are usually written to those within the organization.
     - They are usually informal but can also be formal.
     - They tend to be problem-solving reports.

   Choose an appropriate form for short reports.

4. Among the varieties of short reports, four types stand out.
   - Routine operational reports keep others informed about company operations.
     - Their form and content will vary, depending on the organization.
     - They should deliver the required information efficiently, clearly, and on time.
     - Special word-processing features can assist you with standardized reports.

   Adapt the procedures for writing short reports to routine operational reports, progress reports, and problem-solving reports as well as to minutes of meetings.

- Progress reports review progress on an activity.
  - Most are informal and in narrative form, but some are formal.
  - They should emphasize the positive.
- Problem-solving reports help decision makers choose a course of action.
  - They can be internal or external.
  - You will need to decide whether or not to make recommendations.
  - You will need to decide whether to take a direct or indirect approach.
  - Though not persuasive per se, these reports do need to convince with their good data and analysis.
- Meeting minutes, a type of descriptive report, provide a written record of a group's activities and decisions.
  - They should avoid judgmental and emotional language.
  - Their format varies from organization to organization.
  - Typical minutes include common preliminary, body, and closing items.
  - Minutes have political implications. Use good judgment when preparing them.

Write longer reports that include the appropriate components, meet the readers' needs, and are easy to follow.

5. Longer reports need to include the appropriate elements, meet the readers' needs, and facilitate easy reading.
   - They include the prefatory parts that are appropriate for the report's length, formality, and readers.
   - The report introduction prepares the readers to follow and interpret the report.
     - Include whatever helps with this goal.
     - Use these items as a checklist for content: facts of authorization, problem and purpose, scope, limitations, problem history, research methodology, definitions, preview.
   - Preparing the body of a long, formal report will require virtually all your organizing, writing, and formatting skills.
   - The ending of the report achieves the report's purpose.
     - Use a summary if the purpose is to review information.
     - Use a conclusions section if the purpose is to reach an answer.
     - Use a recommendations section if the purpose is to determine a desirable action.
   - An appendix and/or bibliography can follow the report text.
     - The appendix contains items that support the text but have no specific place in the text (such as questionnaires, large visuals, and tabulations of data).
     - The bibliography is a descriptive list of the secondary sources that were used in the investigation.
   - The longer reports need various structural devices to give them coherence.
     - These devices consist of a network of explanations, introductions, summaries, and conclusions that guide the reader through the report.
     - Begin the coherence plan with the introduction preview, which tells the structure of the report.
     - Then use the introductions and summaries in following parts to tell readers where they are in this structure.

formal reports, 375

prefatory pages, 375

short report, 376

letter report, 376

email (or memo) report, 376

title fly, 376

title page, 376

transmittal message, 377

table of contents, 378

executive summary, 378

routine operational reports, 399

progress report, 402

problem-solving reports, 402

feasibility study, 403

meeting minutes, 404

facts of authorization, 408

scope, 409

limitations, 409

summary, 411

conclusions section, 411

recommendations section, 411

appendix, 412

bibliography, 412

structural coherence plan, 412

CRITICAL THINKING QUESTIONS

1 Discuss the effects of formality and likely length on report makeup as described in the chapter. **LO1**

2 Which of the prefatory pages of reports appear to be related primarily to the length of the report? Which to the need for formality? **LO1**

3 Describe the role and content of a transmittal message. **LO1**

4 Why is the personal style typically used in the transmittal message? **LO1**

5 Explain how to write the executive summary of a report. **LO1**

6 Why does the executive summary include key facts and figures in addition to the analyses and conclusions drawn from them? **LO1**

7 Explain why some routine report problems require little or no introduction. **LO2**

8 Why is the direct order generally used in the shorter reports? When is the indirect order desirable for such reports? **LO2**

9 Describe a situation in which you would use short-report format rather than email format for an internal report. Why would you choose the short-report format? **LO3**

10 Describe a situation in which you would prepare a memo report rather than an email report for an internal report. Why would you choose the memo format? **LO3**

11 What kinds of information might go into routine operational reports for different kinds of organizations? Why would these organizations need this information regularly? **LO4**

12 Given what you've learned about progress reports, suggest a general structure for these reports. What might go into the beginning? What might the middle parts be? What would the conclusion do? **LO4**

13 How might an internal problem-solving report that has been assigned differ from one on the same subject that an employee generated on his or her own? **LO4**

14 Discuss the pros and cons of including a list of absentees in meeting minutes. **LO4**

15 Give examples of long-report problems whose introduction could require historical background or a discussion of the report's limitations. **LO5**

16 Explain how the advice in Chapter 11 can help you prepare a long report. **LO5**

17 Give examples of report problems that would require, respectively, (*a*) an ending summary, (*b*) an ending conclusion or conclusions, and (*c*) an ending recommendation or recommendations. **LO5**

18 Find a sample report or white paper and analyze its coherence plan. Does it have enough coherence helpers? Does it have any that don't seem necesssary? **LO5**

SKILLS BUILDING EXERCISES

1 Review the following report situations and determine for each the makeup of the report you would recommend for it. **LO1**

a. A professional research organization has completed a survey of consumer attitudes toward BankOne. The survey results will be presented to the bank president in a 28-page report, including seven charts and three tables.

b. Joan Marion was asked by her department head to inspect the work area and report on safety conditions. Her report is two pages long and written in personal style.

c. Bill Wingler has an idea for improving a work procedure in his department at McLaughlin Body Company. His department head suggested that Bill present his idea in a report to the production superintendent. The report is almost five pages long, including a full-page diagram. It is written in the personal style.

d. Karen Canady, a worker in the corporate library of Accenture, was asked by Doug Edmunds, its president, for current inventory information on a number of subscriptions. Her report is less than a full page and consists mostly of a list of items and numbers.

e. Bryan Toups, a sales manager for Johnson and Johnson, was asked by the vice president of marketing to prepare an analysis of the results of a promotional campaign conducted in Toups's district. The report is six pages long (including one chart) and is written in the personal style.

2 Following is a report that was written for the manager of a large furniture retail store by the manager's assistant. The manager was concerned about customer complaints of late deliveries of furniture purchased and wanted to know the cause of the delays. Critique this report. **LO2, LO4**

11-17-04

TO: Martina Kalavoda

FROM: Anthony Dudrow

SUBJECT: Investigation requested 11-17-04

This morning at staff meeting it was requested that an investigation be made of the status of home deliveries and of the causes of the delays that have occurred. The investigation has been made with findings as follows.

Now that a new driver's helper, Morris Tunney, has been hired, there should be no more delays. This was the cause of the problem.

Over the past two weeks (10 working days), a total of 143 deliveries were made; and of these, 107 were made on or before the date promised. But some of the deliveries were late because of the departure two weeks ago of the driver's helper, Sean Toulouse, who had to be fired because of dishonesty and could not be replaced quickly with a permanent, qualified helper. Now that a permanent, qualified helper has been hired, there should be no more delays in delivery as this was the cause of the problem.

The driver was able to find a temporary helper, a man by the name of Rusty Sellers, for some help in the unloading work, but he got behind and couldn't seem to catch up. He could have caught up by working overtime, in the opinion of the writer, but he refused to do so. Of the 36 deliveries that were late, all were completed within two days. The problem is over now that the driver has a helper, so there should be no additional delays.

3 Making any assumptions needed, construct complete yet concise titles for the reports described below. **LO5**

a. A report writer reviewed records of exit interviews of employees at Marvel-Floyd Manufacturing Company who left their jobs voluntarily. The objective of the investigation was to determine the reasons for their leaving.

b. A researcher studied data from employee personnel records at Magna-Tech, Inc., to determine whether permanent (long-term) employees differ from short-term employees. Some of the differences found would be used in hiring employees in the future. The data studied included age, education, experience, and scores on pre-employment tests.

c. A report writer compared historical financial records (1995 to the present) of Super Saver Foods to determine whether this grocery chain should own or rent store buildings. In the past it has done both.

4 Criticize the following beginning sentences of transmittal messages. **LO5**

a. "In your hands is the report you requested January 7 concerning . . . "

b. "As you will recall, last January 7 you requested a report on . . . "

c. "That we should open a new outlet in Bragg City is the conclusion of this report, which you authorized January 7."

5 In a report comparing four automobiles (Alpha, Beta, Gamma, and Delta) to determine which one is the best buy for a company, Section II of the report body will cover these cost data: (*a*) initial costs, (*b*) trade-in values, and (*c*) operating expenses. Section III will present a comparison of these safety features of the automobiles: (*a*) standard safety features, (*b*) acceleration data, (*c*) weight distribution, and (*d*) braking quality. **LO5**

a. Bearing in mind that your readers will probably view cost as the main criterion but that the company salespeople spend almost half their work week driving, write the introductory paragraph for Section III.

b. The next section of the report (Section IV) will cover these topics: (*a*) handling, (*b*) quality of ride, and (*c*) durability. Write an introductory paragraph for this section.

c. Criticize this final paragraph (a preview) in the introduction of the report described above:

This report compares the automobiles on three factors. These are costs, safety, and comfort and construction, in that order. Costs include initial expenditure, trade-in value, and operating expense. Safety covers safety devices, acceleration, weight distribution, and braking. Comfort and construction includes handling, ride quality, and durability. A ranking is derived from this comparison.

Shorter Reports

1 You started working for a local car dealership as an office clerk when you were in high school. You're in college now, but you still work there part time, and you've noticed that the management of the company seems to respect your opinion and judgment a little more each day.

Today you and some others were hanging around the coffeemaker with one of the owners, who mentioned that he'd seen a new electronic sign at one of his competitor's sites. "I wonder how much it costs to buy one of those things?" he asks.

"People can see us from the highway, so an electronic sign with changing messages might be a good investment." After a moment of thought, he turns to you. "Will you find out what kind of electronic sign businesses usually use, and what they cost?" he asks. "And see how you change the content on the sign. Is it hard to learn how to use it once it's set up?"

You tell him you'll look into the matter and send him an email about it. Do the appropriate research and tell your boss everything he needs to know to decide whether to pursue this idea.

2 Take advantage of the many career resources to research what the career outlook is in your field. Research the employment prospects, typical jobs, advancement opportunity, salary range, career advantages/disadvantages, typical responsibilities—whatever you can find. You might start with the U.S. Government's *Occupational Outlook Handbook* (www.bls.gov/ooh/). Professional societies also sometimes have excellent statistics on salaries and working conditions in their fields. And don't neglect such job-search sites as Monster.com. If your instructor directs, interview someone in your field who can give you an insider's view. Write up your findings as a well-organized short report, and be sure to interpret your findings in terms of their likely significance to you.

3 The insurance company where you work as assistant to the information technology (IT) manager is doing well. Just last year, the company hired 9 customer service representatives and a receptionist, bringing the total number of employees to 54. But with growth come certain headaches—and one of them is figuring out how to regulate employees' Internet use.

The company's customer service representatives work largely on the phone to handle claims and field other questions. Although they need to use the Internet to do their work, during downtime they continue to use the Internet for personal reasons, including email, social networking, watching favorite television shows, viewing YouTube videos, and even downloading programs or files that have nothing to do with their jobs. Your boss is worried about three things: (1) security breaches resulting from these downloads and from other Internet activities, (2) inappropriate content being viewed or downloaded, and (3) computers running slowly or frequently locking up as a result of the Internet content being viewed or downloaded.

It's time for an Internet-use policy, and your boss thinks you're just the person to help write it. Your assignment is to study the current wisdom on workplace Internet policies and send your findings to your boss in an email report. She will use the report as the basis for a meeting with her boss next week.

4 It's almost time for the annual awards dinner for your city's chapter of the Leukemia and Lymphoma Society (LLS). The two most honored awardees will be the LLS's Man and Woman of the Year, the volunteers who have raised the most money for the cause during the society's 10-week competition. Your boss, who serves on the organization's board of directors, has been asked to announce the winners at the event and to present them each with a gift book.

Your boss has asked you to recommend some appropriate books for each winner. Learn more about the LLS and past Men and Women of the Year and then choose three appropriate books to propose for each. Send your recommendations to your boss in an email report.

5 You were recently hired as an intern at a Mayim's, a distributor of high-end cosmetics and skin care products. Kori Roberts, sales manager and your supervisor, drops by your office to chat one day and brings up a subject she's been wondering about. "Our sales staff have been communicating with each other and our retailers fairly effectively via phone and email, but I think it's time to look into an online meeting application to supplement these methods. Do you know what kind of tool I'm talking about?" she asks. You nod, having learned about online meeting tools in your Technology for Business Communication class. "I heard some of these options were totally free and really easy to use," she continues, "so I looked into a few. Skype and OpenMeetings seem to be pretty popular for businesses. I'm thinking about recommending that all the sales staff subscribe to one of these. Then maybe they could talk to each other and the retailers more easily. I wonder which of these tools is better for us. And is there any downside to online meetings? Maybe security issues?" You take the hint and offer to look into the matter for her.

Do the necessary research—and, if you haven't yet done so, try one or more of these services yourself—and then write Kori a report giving her the information she needs in order to decide whether or not to pursue this idea further. She may want to share your report with other managers in the company, so be sure you give it your best effort.

6 You work for the owner of three casual-apparel stores for young adults, both men and women. Business is pretty good, but your boss wonders if the atmosphere needs to be more "hip." She already plays "cool" music, but she's considering using video somehow in the stores. Since she knows you're an Internet whiz, she turns to you for help. "How do other stores use video?" she wants to know. "Is it worth the effort and expense? What are my options? Is this kind of marketing effective? How can I maximize the results?"

You research the Internet, the sales literature, and stores in your area, and you find a lot of great stuff about using video in retail stores—so much, in fact, that you decide to present your findings to your boss in writing. Tell her what she needs and wants to know in a clear, well-organized report. Having the information in writing will also be helpful if she wants to share it with other employees. Be sure she can go to your sources and learn more if she wants to.

7 You work in the marketing department of a company that manufactures clothing for outdoor sports enthusiasts (runners, hikers, skiers, snowboarders). Your company just expanded its market by acquiring a company that manufactures clothing for other outdoor interests (e.g., camping, hunting, and fishing). The clothing will be made under your brand.

You have successfully marketed your brand in such magazines as *Runners' World*, but you know you need to expand your advertising to accommodate your new market. Your boss wants to find out what publications would be good advertising opportunities. He also wants to know the options for advertising in the online publications for these same magazines or on the apps that these magazines may have for mobile devices. What sizes and types of ads are available for purchase, and at what cost?

Write a memo to your boss giving him the necessary details about placing an ad in a possible publication for your new market. Provide as much information as you believe is necessary to make a sound decision, covering circulation, rates, specifications, and demographics.

8 In an effort to cut down on waste and expenses, the campus food service company at your university implemented a new policy a month ago, in the middle of the fall semester: no more trays. Instead of going from station to station loading their trays up with food, students must now get their food carrying only a plate and/or bowl (but they can use as many plates and bowls and visit the stations as often as they like).

After a month has gone by, the director of the campus food service wants to know two things: Is there significantly less food waste, and how do the students feel about the new policy? He asks you, his trusty assistant, to find out and write up your findings in a report that he can share with university administrators.

You gather the information in two ways. First, you ask the managers of the three campus eateries how many 13-gallon bags of food waste (not including paper) they threw out during the last week before the policy was implemented and during the fourth week afterward. Since the managers have been asked to keep track of this information, they are ready for your question. The manager at the smallest dining hall reports 5.5 bags for the "before" week and 4 bags for the "after" week. At the midsized hall, the "before" figure is 9.5 bags and the "after" figure is 8. At the largest facility, the "before" figure is 15 bags and the "after" figure is 12. The total number of student meal card swipes for the "before" week was 42,363; for the "after" week it was 40,907.

Next, you send a brief online survey to the 2,440 students who are on a campus meal plan. In fact, you send it out twice to encourage as much participation as possible. Altogether, 1,003 students participate (though a few do not answer all the questions). In response to the question "I waste less food now that the trays are gone," 56 students pick "strongly disagree," 135 "disagree," 432 "agree," and 380 "strongly agree." In response to the question "I eat less now that the trays are gone," 176 pick "strongly disagree," 312 "disagree," 292 "agree," and 223 "strongly agree." In response to the question "I favor the new trayless policy," 131 students pick "strongly disagree," 63 "disagree," 418 "agree," and 380 "strongly agree." In response to the question "My attitude toward being on a meal plan is more positive now," 160 pick "strongly disagree," 315 "disagree," 390 "agree," and 120 "strongly agree." In response to the open-ended question inviting feedback on the new policy, you get many positive comments about the university's effort to reduce waste, to help the environment, and to keep up with the times. A few even praise the university's effort to help students not overeat. The negative comments are about the loss of convenience, the difficulty of getting enough food on one plate, and the awkwardness of carrying a stack of dishes to the dishwashing area. A few students comment that, for the high price they're paying, the food service should at least include trays.

Now that you have your data, organize and interpret it for your boss, being careful to use qualified language (e.g., "perhaps," "may be") where appropriate.

9 You're part-time assistant to the office manager of a successful veterinary clinic with four locations in the greater _____ area (you pick the city). For some time now, the practice's three owners have been discussing making its contributions to the community more extensive and better organized. Animal hospitals in other cities feature their community service efforts on their websites and in their print literature, but thus far your company's contributions have been random and relatively sparse. The owners think it's time to create a focused, well-organized, appealing philanthropy and/or employee volunteer program that will generate more positive publicity—and business—for the company.

They've asked your boss to review the literature on such programs and harvest useful information for them. They particularly want to know what kinds of programs other clinics have, the features of successful programs, and the business benefits of such programs.

Since you're a college student with good writing and research skills and free access to your university's extensive online resources, your boss asks if you'll tackle this task. You decide you'll start your research by consulting your library's resources on corporate philanthropy and on veterinary philanthropy in particular. You'll also look at the websites for the Boston College Center for Corporate Citizenship, ServiceLeader.org, and the Points of Light Corporate Institute. (If your instructor directs, you may also interview an appropriate employee in a relevant business.) Once you believe you've found everything useful, you'll digest it, interpret it, and present the results in a well-organized, well-written report to the owners. Keep your report to about four pages, but be sure to include your sources so your readers can consult them if they want.

---

10 It is common knowledge that today's college graduates are different from those who came before them. The distinctive traits of Gen Y (or Millennial) employees have been well documented. Your boss, the owner of a small but growing software development company (you can decide what type of software), thinks his managers and recruiters need a better understanding of this generation. He asks you, one of his more accomplished young employees, to review the literature on Gen Y employees and write him a report in which you describe the main traits of this segment of the workforce and recommend ways to recruit, manage, and retain them. He'll share this report, or parts of it, with his managers, who are Gen Xers and Baby Boomers.

---

11 Write a report to your instructor in which you argue for or against one of the following:

a. Business students should be required to take a business communications course as part of their degree program; business communication classes should not be optional.

b. Students graduating with business degrees should be required to pass a proficiency exam in the use of Microsoft Word, Excel, Outlook, PowerPoint, and Access.

c. Business writing/presentations/communications courses should have a minimum grade requirement of a B-.

d. All business students should be required to complete a professional internship to graduate.

e. To be prepared for today's global business environment, all business students should be required to speak a foreign language proficiently (the equivalent of four semesters of study) or complete a study abroad experience.

f. Business students learn as much and as well in online classes as they do in face-to-face classes.

---

12 Like many companies, Artemis Financial Services has had to address the increasing cost of employee health insurance. The company had been paying 100 percent of the premium ($1,200/month for the family plan; $600/month for the individual plan), as well as the $1,500 annual deductible for the family plan and a $750 deductible for the individual plan, but it recently had to reduce these benefits. Now the company pays 85 percent of the total premium, with employees paying the other 15 percent, and employees now pay the annual deductible.

Your boss is looking for some way to ease the burden of these additional costs to the employees and wonders whether a flexible spending account (FAS) could be a way to do so. Are FSAs a good idea for businesses and employees? Prepare a report to your boss in which you analyze the advantages and disadvantages of FSAs so that she can decide whether to offer FSAs to the employees.

---

13 You work in human resources for Henderson, Xiong, and Pirelli, LLC, an accounting and financial services firm. The company offers both single-person and family health insurance coverage to its 150 employees. Seventeen percent of the employees do not take the health insurance benefit. If an employee declines health insurance upon employment, he or she forfeits the benefit—no other benefits are offered in its place.

Last week you hired Mike Richards. You sent him the standard paperwork that all new hires complete. When Mike stopped by today to submit his paperwork, he said that he had turned down the health insurance, as he has health insurance coverage through his spouse. In telling you this, he mentions that his spouse's company offers an annuity the equivalent of a single-person premium as an alternative benefit for employees who decline the health insurance, and he wants to know if Henderson, Xiong, and Pirelli will do the same for him. The cost of a single-person premium per month is $435.

You present the idea to your boss, who initially says "absolutely not" but then decides that you should research the issue first. What are the advantages and disadvantages for the employee and for the company? How much will this potentially cost if other employees choose an annuity over health insurance? What if the cost of a single-person premium increases? Can you go back? That is, can you decide to discontinue this benefit at any time? Present your research in a report so your boss can make an informed decision.

---

14 You're a management major on co-op with a large robotics and automation company. Most of the employees are engineers, salespeople, customer support staff, and technicians. You've been assigned to various areas of the company, and you're currently reporting to Jack Kiley, the director of communications. One of Jack's duties is to write the president's monthly column for the employee newsletter, a column the president reviews before it is published. Jack has been coming across more and more articles and blog posts about the detrimental effects of multitasking and the benefits of focused, "mindful" work, so he thinks he'll write the president's next newsletter article about this topic. That's where you come in. "See what you can find out about mindfulness on the job," Jack asks you. "Find out what it means, how to have it, what its benefits are, who's practicing it."

Do the research and then write Jack an email report answering his likely questions and helping him see what approach to take with this topic in the newsletter article.

---

15 As the Student Senate's representative on the faculty's Academic Affairs Committee at your school, you make sure that students' concerns are heard on all academic matters. One of the committee members recently introduced a proposal to change the grading system from straight letter grades (A, B, C . . .) to plus/minus grading (A, A-, B+, B . . .), and the change seems appeal to the rest of the committee. As the representative of the students, you believe you'd better weigh in on this issue.

See what grading system other schools like yours in your state use, and see if you can find out how students in general feel about one system or the other. Then write the other committee members a short report for or against the plus/minus grading system. Explain why you feel one is better than the other for the students at your school. (And/or, if your instructor directs, design and conduct a student survey and prepare a longer, more formal report; or choose a different student-related issue.)

---

16 You are quite comfortable in your position as supervisor at a commercial printing office in your hometown, but you find some employees a bit more challenging than others. Laurie, your receptionist, is one of those challenges.

Laurie is a terrific receptionist—in fact, she is the best you have. She is a whiz on every computer program you use. Her organizational skills are exceptional. Losing her would have a detrimental impact on your customers and on the office in general. Besides, she's really a nice person. Unfortunately, she is frequently late to her shift, causing you to answer the phones or leave your office to greet customers. You have reminded Laurie of her hours, and she always indicates she will change her behavior, but she continues to be late. To make things worse, you've noticed recently that others in the office are arriving late to work because, you believe, Laurie has not suffered any consequences for her actions. Quite honestly, you're not sure what the consequences should be.

You don't want a negative work environment, but lately, it seems as though a practice that has always been taken for granted (employees being on time for work) is now one that you need a policy about.

You ask your boss for some guidance with this matter. She asks you to do some research and to present some options. She agrees that a policy is needed, but she does not want it to seem parental or patronizing, and she does not want to harm morale by making employees feel that they are being disciplined or punished. She just wants a policy that gives offenders the opportunity to improve their behavior while also giving her the flexibility to impose harsher sanctions if employees continue to be late. Write a report to your supervisor investigating the many options available to managers when dealing with tardy employees. Address in a general sense any legal challenges you may encounter. You may consider interviewing a human resources specialist regarding your options.

---

17 You're an assistant manager for Cougar Country, Inc., a mid-sized manufacturer of specialty agricultural equipment, in Morris, MN, population 5,096. Many of the company's employees commute a considerable distance to work each day or live in Morris during the week to cut down on commuting time and gas. The larger cities in the region are more than 30 miles away:

- Alexandria, MN, is 45 miles away,
- Fergus Falls, MN, is 55 miles away,
- Saint Cloud, MN, is 99 miles away, and
- The Fargo, ND/Moorhead, MN, area is 136 miles away.

Your firm is proud to compete on a national level and have top-notch employees working for it.

However, some employees are starting to feel the stress and pressure of years of commuting. A recent conference session you attended focused on work–life balance and alternative workplace configurations (i.e., telecommuting, online meetings, software options, etc.). During this session, it became clear to you that Cougar Country should investigate this topic, and when you mentioned this point to your boss, he agreed.

Do some preliminary research on distributed workspaces and related options for Cougar Country. To what extent is a distributed workforce even feasible for a manufacturing outfit like yours? Send your boss an email telling him what you found out and what next steps, if any, Cougar Country should take.

18 You were recently hired as the office manager for Stormbird Designs, an upscale fashion studio specializing in the design and manufacture of high-end women's clothing. The company is doing well, but it's a start-up, so money is tight and employees often have to serve multiple roles within the company.

A couple of weeks ago, the owner of the studio, Susan Wong, was having some computer difficulties. Being a technologically savvy person, you were able to identify the problem and fix it. Susan was very impressed and now views you as the person to contact when there is any IT issue in the office! Yesterday, you were having lunch with Susan, and she was mentioning the possibility of purchasing laptops for everyone in the office. This would enable employees to work remotely, and would also improve productivity, as some of the current desktop computers in the office are slow and in need of upgrades. Susan asks you if you currently own a laptop, and you respond that you've had a Toshiba laptop for the last two years and have been very pleased with it. Intrigued, Susan asks you to recommend a Toshiba laptop that would be suitable for designers in the studio. You respond that you will have to do some research but that you will get back to her in three days.

Research the different options and make a recommendation to Susan. You were told that the budget for the laptop purchases would be $8,000, and that you would need to purchase 6 laptops in total. Write your recommendation in the form of a report, highlighting the benefits of the option that you have chosen.

19 You serve as an assistant in the human resources department at Heckworth Holdings, a large manufacturer of machine tools. Three months ago, your company switched from a typical five-day work week to a four-day work week. Under the new arrangement, employees at Heckworth work 10-hour days, Monday through Thursday. The change was made to save money on utility expenses, specifically electricity. Under the new arrangement, the plant is completely closed on Friday, Saturday, and Sunday.

Your supervisor, Scott Morgan, the director of human resources, wants to know two things about the schedule change. First, have utility expenses actually decreased, and second, what do employees think about the schedule change? You make a visit to the accounting department, where you ask for the gas and electric bills for the previous six months. The total cost for utilities is displayed in Table 1 below:

Table 1	Previous 6 Months Gas and Electric Expenses for Heckworth Holdings
Month	**Total Expense**
March 2012	$21,364
April 2012	$24,567
May 2012	$28,526
June 2012	$33,426
July 2012	$39,217
August 2012 (current month)	$42,357

The accounting clerk, Shane Wang, suggests that you also look at the gas and electric bills for the same three months (June, July, and August) of last year. Total gas and electric expenses for those three months are displayed in Table 2:

Table 2	June–August 2011 Gas and Electric Expenses for Heckworth Holdings
Month	**Total Expense**
June 2011	$37,917
July 2011	$44,785
August 2011	$47,612

After collecting this information, you begin to analyze the data from a survey that Mr. Morgan recently sent to all 1,500 employees at Heckworth, which asked their opinions on the scheduling change. A total of 871 employees responded to the survey. The survey asked a series of questions, but three in particular are of most interest to Mr. Morgan.

The first question is, "Do you like the new four-day work week?" The breakdown in responses was as follows: 365 "Strongly Agree", 141 "Agree," 147 "Neutral," 128 "Disagree," and 90 "Strongly Disagree."

The second question is, "Do you think the new four-day work week has made you more productive?" The breakdown in responses to the second question was as follows: 143 "Strongly Agree," 165 "Agree," 201 "Neutral," 189 "Disagree," and 173 "Strongly Disagree."

The third question is "Do you recommend that we continue with the new four-day work week?" The breakdown in responses to the third question was as follows: 237 "Strongly Agree," 192 "Agree," 226 "Neutral," 153 "Disagree," and 63 "Strongly Disagree."

Finally, there was an open-ended question that asked employees for any other thoughts they had on the four-day work week. You got only a few responses, but they tended to be like these: "I like the three-day weekend!," "This is another example of why I like working for this company!," "I am very tired at the end of the 10-hour day," and "The lunch break is not long enough."

Longer Reports

20 Every year, Gutenberg Media prints a community calendar and distributes it to over 10,000 residential homes and businesses. Typically, you have sold calendar advertising to 16 different companies for 12-month ad spots.

While many of the advertisers are the same from year to year, you have noticed in the past three years that it has taken an increased effort to retain them.

The calendar runs from January to December. Historically, Gutenberg Media has contacted previous advertising businesses in early September, giving them a three-week deadline to respond. If you did not hear back from the company within two weeks, one of your associates contacted the company by phone or in person. Typically, by the end of the three-week deadline, approximately 80–90 percent of the companies had responded positively.

However, as shown in the table, compliance with the three-week deadline has decreased dramatically over the past three years. Further, the number of returning clients seems to be on the decline as well.

The Gutenberg Media administrative team is perplexed as to why this is happening. Three years ago, to increase efficiency, your company went to a completely online system for renewing advertising spots for the calendar. Rather than receiving a phone call or personal visit, your company sent a series of emails as reminders. Other data sets collected have

Using these data, write a report to Mr. Morgan about the impact that the schedule change has had on the plant's overall gas and electric costs, as well as the employees' perceptions of the new four-day work week.

proven that a calendar still remains an effective way to advertise and gain customers, so your team is baffled that so many of the advertisers are not jumping at the opportunity to participate.

It's mid-June, and Gutenberg Media is talking about starting the calendar process again. After seeing the trends over the past seven years, your boss has asked you to analyze the data and make some recommendations for increasing compliance and advertising sales for this year's calendar. Do you need to update your process? Collect more data? Utilize social media? Be sure to support your proposal with research, facts, and data.

Year	Compliance by Week 2	Compliance by Week 3	# of Returning Advertisers by Printing
2013	7	7	9/16
2012	5	6	8/16
2011	6	8	10/16
2010	9	14	15/16
2009	8	12	14/16
2008	9	13	14/16
2007	10	15	15/16

21 You were recently hired to be the assistant manager at Turn Back the Clock Sports, a sports memorabilia company based in Columbus, Ohio. Your company predominantly deals in historic baseball memorabilia, and due to your strong Internet presence, you have clients throughout the world. Every summer, you host a large memorabilia expo that attracts many of your largest customers to Columbus for the weekend.

This year, a group of three wealthy customers from Tokyo will be attending the expo. In addition to being great customers, these individuals are huge baseball fans and love to catch a couple of games any time they visit the United States. Your boss, the manager, suggests that the two of you treat them to a baseball game while they are in the United States. Since Columbus does not have a Major League baseball team, you will have to travel to see a game. Your boss

recommends that the five of you attend a game in one of the three closest cities to Columbus with a major league team: Cincinnati, Cleveland, or Detroit.

Since you are not a very large company, your budget for entertaining customers is not large. Your boss asks you to research ticket prices at the various stadiums in the three cities (assume that all three baseball teams will be "in town" when your guests are here). In addition, he suggests that you research the cost of parking, concessions, and hotel stays for two nights in the three cities (hotels that you recommend should be within walking distance of the stadiums). You will also want to factor in transportation costs (rental car) to the three cities. Make your recommendation for a city in the form of a report to the manager. The report should include an estimate of the total trip cost to the three cities, as well as your recommendation for which city to visit.

22 The University Career Center is a great place to begin your career in information systems, so you were thrilled to land a part-time position as an assistant to the lead counselor. Your boss selected you because she is concerned that

the office is a bit "old fashioned" and she expects you to help bring them into the digital age.

On your first day of work you were surprised to learn that little emphasis is placed on helping students create a Web presence. That is, students are not routinely advised on how to create an effective LinkedIn profile, nor are they informed about resources (e.g., Weebly) for creating Web versions of their résumés or portfolios of their work. Prepare a report for the lead counselor in which you discuss the benefits of students' having electronic versions of their résumés in LinkedIn and other Web-based formats. In addition to discussing LinkedIn, provide three options for creating and posting a résumé as a Web document on sites such as Weebly. Compare them based on several factors including cost, ease of use, effectiveness, compatibility, and any other factors you believe important. This report will be passed up to the head of the department, so it will need a certain amount of formality (as your instructor directs).

---

23 You've been invited by a married couple in your town to help them launch a business venture: a service that delivers organic and local produce to households and small businesses in town. You were recommended to them by your former entrepreneurship professor, for whom you'd written a great business plan when you took her class.

The couple is now preparing a business plan to attract investors. They have done the research to prove that there is sufficient demand for the business and that they will have sufficient and reliable suppliers. But they haven't yet figured out all the likely costs. One big cost yet to be determined is that of the vehicles they'll be using to deliver the produce.

They turn to you for help. They figure they'll need two large vans to start with, adding more as needed. Should they rent or buy? And if they buy, which makes and models might be best for their purposes?

Do the necessary research to find out what their options are and make a recommendation. Carefully consider all the criteria that would make one option better than another, and invent any additional realistic details that you need to be able to do so (perhaps information on the website of Green Bean Delivery, on which the company in this case was based, can help). Write a polished report so that these entrepreneurs can use appropriate parts of it in their business plan.

---

24 Every employee at Giffen Technologies needs to be current in his or her field. As a developer of medical practice management software for hospitals, clinics, and private practices, Giffen requires everyone from the programmers to the sales staff to the communications specialists be up to date on current practices, trends, and client needs so that the company can survive in an extremely competitive industry.

To ensure that its employees have the most current knowledge, Giffen invests a lot of money in employees' continuing education, which includes workshops, seminars, and continuing education courses at two-year colleges and four-year colleges and universities; the company has even paid for some employees' courses toward an MBA. Wherever the education is, Giffen sends its employees.

This practice for continuing education has become too costly. As a result, the company has decided that nearly all employees might be able to remain current in their fields by taking advantage of more cost-effective online opportunities.

Your boss sees two issues. The first is that he needs to know if online opportunities provide the same quality of training or education as face-to-face opportunities. The second is that, in talking with a few department heads and employees informally, your boss senses some resistance to online learning. Your boss wants to learn whether there really is widespread resistance to online learning and, if so, where the points of resistance are. Your boss also wants to know some best practices for promoting online training opportunities as valid options for continuing education. You have been assigned the task of gathering the information your boss requires and presenting both the information and recommendations for ensuring that employees see online education opportunities as useful.

Write a report that answers your boss's questions and provides direction to him for how to best proceed with the plan to use online continuing education in your workplace.

You will need to do secondary research to answer your boss's questions regarding issues surrounding the quality of online learning and how to promote it to employees, especially those who are resistant. Cite your sources in the style required by your instructor.

Your primary research, however, is complete. You surveyed your 1,500 employees and received 524 responses. The survey results (primary data) are provided below. The numbers represent frequency data (the number of respondents, not percentages).

Survey Questions and Reponses

Q1: In what department do you work?

- 79 Research and Development
- 200 Sales
- 19 Communications
- 59 Accounting
- 14 Training and Education
- 21 Marketing
- 14 Human Resources
- 46 Hardware and Software Support
- 51 Information Technology
- 21 Legal

Q2: What is the nature of your position?

- 80 Manager
- 87 Supervisor
- 283 Subject Matter Expert (accountants, technical writers, programmers, salespeople)
- 74 Clerical/Support

Q3: Have you ever participated in any of the following online education opportunities? Check all that apply.

10 Online workshop

69 Webinar (online seminar)

41 Online course

37 Other (please specify): 21 bachelor's degree from an online university or a face-to-face university with an online program; 16 technical/vocational degree through an online program

Q4: Do you participate in any of the following? Check all that apply.

247 Professionally related blog

412 Professionally related online social networking site (e.g., Twitter, LinkedIn, Facebook)

Q5: What is your perception of the workload in online seminars/workshops/courses?

150 More work than face-to-face opportunities

150 About the same work as face-to-face opportunities

224 Less work than face-to-face opportunities

Q6: What is your perception of the quality of online seminars/workshops/courses?

99 Better quality than of face-to-face opportunities

175 About the same quality as face-to-face opportunities

250 Less quality than face-to-face opportunities

Q7: Indicate your level of agreement with this statement: People can learn as much in an online environment as they can in a face-to-face environment.

62 Strongly agree

119 Agree

55 Neither agree nor disagree

257 Disagree

31 Strongly disagree

Q8: Indicate your level of agreement with this statement: If the following online continuing education opportunity presented itself, I would willingly take it.

An online seminar (1–2 hours)

72 Strongly agree

346 Agree

13 Neither agree nor disagree

63 Disagree

30 Strongly disagree

An online workshop (1–2 days)

37 Strongly agree

112 Agree

207 Neither agree nor disagree

149 Disagree

19 Strongly disagree

An online course (1–3 weeks)

92 Strongly agree

172 Agree

119 Neither agree nor disagree

83 Disagree

58 Strongly disagree

An online course (4–8 weeks)

30 Strongly agree

67 Agree

60 Neither agree nor disagree

208 Disagree

159 Strongly disagree

An online course (9–16 weeks)

38 Strongly agree

92 Agree

138 Neither agree nor disagree

151 Disagree

105 Strongly disagree

Q9: My general attitude toward online learning in any form is

75 Strongly positive

125 Positive

121 Neutral

110 Negative

93 Strongly negative

Cross tabulations for "Q 9: My general attitude toward online learning in any form is":

75 Strongly Positive (22 managers, 19 supervisors, 24 subject matter experts, 10 clerical/support staff)

125 Positive (33 managers, 35 supervisors, 44 subject matter experts, 15 clerical/support staff)

121 Neutral (14 managers, 18 supervisors, 74 subject matter experts, 15 clerical/support staff)

110 Negative (5 managers, 9 supervisors, 93 subject matter experts, 3 clerical support staff)

93 Strongly negative (6 managers, 7 supervisors, 48 subject matter experts, 32 clerical support staff)

Employee comments on the survey:

- "I enjoy the opportunity to meet others in my field and network. I can't do that online."
- "Getting away from the company for a few days of training is a nice break from the routine."
- "I can't imagine being able to learn when I can't see the instructor or other students."
- "This is just one more way for the company to cut costs and quality. I can't see online learning as having the same quality as the face-to-face seminars and courses I attend."
- "How can online learning use the hands-on activities we do in face-to-face workshops?"
- "I have taken an online course and several webinars. I like that I don't have to leave my family or my office for workshops and seminars."

- "Online seminars are great! Today's technology is so good that it's just like being in the same room with other participants."

- "I just finished a webinar and loved it! I've had face-to-face experiences that weren't as good. I think it depends on the quality of the course and the instructor, not whether the location is face-to-face or online."

---

25 You are the clinic manager for the Springville branch of Meridian Healthcare Systems. Meridian recently announced that it would be reducing the number of staff by 140, primarily by not replacing vacant positions but also by eliminating and combining positions. This requires you to lay off 15 people at your clinic; the rest of the positions would be eliminated at other clinics in the system.

Meridian's news release sent to local media outlets cites as reasons for the layoffs rising healthcare costs, a poor economy, and fewer patients seeking care due to high insurance deductibles.

You follow your local news television station on Facebook and notice that 80 people have commented on the news. You believe that the reasons for the layoffs are those stated by Meridian in the press release, so you are surprised to read the comments. Some of them are complimentary, but many of them cite billing errors, poor customer service, excess or unfair charges on their bills, long waits for appointments, and long waits to see a physician as reasons they have sought healthcare at a competitor's clinic in your town.

Even if Meridian's reasons for the layoffs are accurate, you worry that you are not providing the level of customer care your patients require, and you really cannot afford to have these negative perceptions continue. The Facebook post inspires you to survey patients at your branch to assess what you are doing well and what you can do better. Your survey data appear below.

Write a report in which you incorporate secondary research on markers of quality patient service/experiences/care with your primary data to provide a picture to clinic employees of what they are doing well, what they need to do to improve, and what steps they can take to improve patient satisfaction. Be sure your problem and purpose statement are clear. N = 1,188

Demographic Information

Q1: How many times have you visited the clinic in the past six months?

0:	209
1–5:	889
6–10:	71
11–15:	12
16 or more:	7

Q2: How would you rate your health?

Excellent:	398
Very good:	223
Good:	314
Fair:	178
Poor:	75

Customer Service

Q3: How would you rate the ease of getting through to the clinic on the phone?

Very good:	267
Good:	429
Fair:	312
Poor:	175
Very poor:	5

Comments: Generally very quick. I get why you have to go through all of the "If this is an emergency please hang up and dial 911," but to hear it every time you get transferred to another number gets annoying and wastes my time . . . once waited seven minutes to talk to someone. If the wait is longer than three minutes, you should have some way to let the caller know . . . If you say you're going to call back, give a time frame and follow through; physicians/nurses/staff are terrible at returning calls [mentioned by several respondents].

Q4: How would you rate the ease of scheduling an appointment?

Very good:	70
Good:	294
Fair:	400
Poor:	318
Very poor:	106

Comments: I read that you're laying off people because of lower patient demand. Really? If you have so few patients, how come I had to wait five months to see a dermatologist? . . . One time I had an appointment scheduled and the office called to ask me to reschedule. When I asked why, they said it wasn't an urgent appointment, and since I was the only patient that afternoon, the doctor wanted to take the afternoon off. The appointment was urgent to me. I thought they might have at least had the courtesy to say the doctor had an emergency. I felt completely disregarded and unimportant . . . I know a same-day appointment is not often possible, but it seems like the wait time for any appointment is at least three weeks . . . No complaints. I can usually get in right away . . . This clinic is not for sick people; you just have to hope that what you have can wait for a month until you can get an appointment . . . Have you ever calculated average wait times for an appointment? I bet you'd be surprised at the length.

Q5: How would you rate the courtesy of the staff in the registration area?

Very good:	301
Good:	492
Fair:	235
Poor:	100
Very poor:	60

Comments: Very helpful and friendly . . . The courtesy depends on the time of day. In the morning, they are very nice. When I have afternoon appointments, they are sometimes nice, sometimes really crabby . . . Overall, friendly and helpful, maybe a little mechanical and stiff sometimes.

Q6: Once you are in the waiting room, the amount of time you wait before seeing your provider is

Never longer than 25 minutes:	75
Occasionally longer than 25 minutes:	108
Regularly longer than 25 minutes:	300
Always longer than 25 minutes:	735

Comments: The wait time is absolutely ridiculous. If I didn't like my provider so much, I would go elsewhere [this comment was made by several people] . . . I have complained about this to anyone who will listen; if I don't see changes, I'll find another clinic . . . My last three visits? 45-, 60-, and 75-minute waits . . . You should calculate your average wait time; I bet you'd be surprised.

Q7: Are the bills sent from our billing office (not those you may receive from your insurer) accurate?

Always:	297
Usually:	372
Sometimes:	319
Almost never:	140
Never:	60

Comments: To be honest, I just pay the amount on the bill; your bills are really hard to understand . . . Usually, the bills are accurate; it's my insurer who disputes them [mentioned by several respondents] . . . How hard is it to calculate a bill? It seems like every bill is calculated wrong and requires six phone calls to get it fixed . . . The billing is ridiculous . . . Apparently, I spent too long during my annual exam talking about a particular health issue and I got billed for both the physical *and* an additional office visit . . . I get a lot of refund checks for overcharges. Wouldn't it be easier to just get the bill right in the first place? . . . Never had a problem; bills are always accurate.

Q8: Think about the times when you have had to contact our billing office (not your insurer) regarding questions about your bill. How would you rate the courtesy of the staff?

Always courteous:	50
Usually courteous:	278
Sometimes courteous:	642
Almost never courteous:	200
Never courteous:	10
I've never had to contact the billing office:	8

Comments: It's really hit or miss. You just have to hope you don't get any of them on a bad day . . . They get really defensive when you ask a question [mentioned by several respondents]. They have to know I'm not blaming them for the mistake; I just want an answer and a resolution . . . This is just a job to them. They don't care that the surprise $500 charge on my bill has a major impact on my life . . . Is this where all of your employees with a bad attitude work? ["Bad attitude" was mentioned by several respondents] . . . The billing office is outstanding! One person even called me at 8:30 on a Friday night to say that my billing error had been corrected so that I wouldn't have to worry about it over the weekend.

Q9: Think about the times when you have had to contact our billing office (not your insurer) regarding questions on your bill. How would you rate the helpfulness of the staff?

Always helpful:	190
Usually helpful:	482
Sometimes helpful:	67
Almost never helpful:	425
Never helpful:	16
I have never had to contact the billing office:	8

Comments: They are almost always helpful; you just have to expect the bad attitude that goes with it . . . I have to say my bill always gets corrected, though I don't get why they make so many mistakes in the first place [mentioned by several respondents] . . . They are helpful; just not friendly [mentioned by several respondents].

---

26 Universal Casualty Insurance, which insures your company, Hillsboro Assisted Living Village, has requested a copy of your emergency preparedness plan for protecting your facilities, employees, residents, and data in the event of a disaster or accident. Your boss knows your company has an evacuation plan for tornados or fires and that the IT department backs up the system every day, but the plan needs to be updated and made more thorough to specifically address the issues surrounding the evacuation of your residents who have special needs. For example, many residents are in wheel chairs, have Alzheimer's disease, or are otherwise limited in their ability to help themselves during an evacuation. Your boss has asked you to research an emergency preparedness plan for your company.

After you have done the research on what an emergency preparedness plan should contain for a company of your size and nature, write a report to your boss in which you report your findings. Based on your research, also present a policy and include it as an appendix.

---

27 You work for the Boys and Girls Club for your town. You and your boss know that many nonprofit organizations in your area make a lot of money through scrip fundraising. You have no idea what this is; you've just heard that Horizon Respite Services, another nonprofit in your town, earned $5,000 last year in scrip funds. Your job is to research scrip fundraising, describe what it is and how it raises funds for an organization, and provide options for scrip fundraising brokers. Recommend to your boss whether to pursue the idea.

28 Research three trends in your field using primary or secondary research as your instructor directs. Analyze what these trends mean for graduates in your field. What should students in your field do to prepare to be able to address these trends?

---

29 You're the new assistant to the director of marketing and sales at Ace Computer Services. One of your first tasks is to advise your boss, Becky Meece, on how the company's website should be enhanced. As Becky rightly points out, the current site looks amateurish. Its homepage has random-seeming contents in a random-looking layout, and since the structure of the site isn't clear, it's hard to tell what kind of information is here and where to find the specific information one is looking for. She has decided to contract out the redesign of the website, but she wants to be able to make clear to the designer what changes she is looking for.

Conduct research on what makes a website good in terms of content, design, navigation, and usability, and—putting that together with what you know about adaptation to the readers, effective writing, use of visuals, and readable formatting—advise your boss on the qualities and content the revised site should have. Prepare your report in such a way that she can hand it over to the Web designer without much revision. (*Helpful hint*: Find a computer services website that is not well designed and pretend that this is Ace Computer Services' current site. Then study some well-designed sites to get ideas for improvement. Let your instructor know what sites you consulted.)

---

30 You're a finance co-op working in the executive office of a successful public relations firm. The three partners who own the firm rely on an investment advisor to advise them on managing their assets, but sometimes they decide on their own to add or remove companies from their investment portfolio. They're interested in catching one of the current technology waves. In particular, they wonder if buying some shares in Google, Netflix, or Amazon would be a good investment.

One of the partners turns this research task over to you. You decide to start with the Internet since it provides a lot of investor news and advice, as well as some companies' annual reports (on their investor relations page) and financial reports (at www.sec.gov, the U.S. Securities and Exchange Commission's site). You'll also go to Hoover's Online (or some other company-information database), a great research tool you learned about in your classes. You'll compare the three companies on all factors that you think would be of interest to your employers.

Using your resourcefulness and great research skills, scout out the three companies and write a clear, well-organized, report that will help your readers decide whether or not to pursue this idea with their investment advisor.

---

31 The management of Goodnight Hotels, a regional chain of mid-priced hotels, wants to know why some of its hotels are doing much better than others. They have contracted the services of your company, LJR Research, to find out.

As a senior researcher for LJR, you and a team of four associates have been researching the problem for four weeks. As authorized by Dora Smitherman, VP of Operations for Goodnight, your team visited 20 hotels in the midwestern U.S., where Goodnight operates. The hotels, which Goodnight chose, were roughly equal in size, traffic flow past the hotel, and facilities. But they differed in one crucial way: 10 of the hotels were underperforming on sales, while the other 10 were thriving.

To find the reasons for high or low sales volumes, you worked out a detailed plan for collecting data. First you had your trained evaluators visit each hotel posing as customers and spend one night in the hotel. While they were there, they observed and recorded data on such features as the hotel's appearance, cleanliness, and service, as well as on the complimentary breakfast. The evaluations were based on a detailed assessment guide. Later, the researchers returned to interview the manager to gather pertinent information on the hotel's personnel.

The research is done, and you have the summary tabulations before you. Your next step is to put these data into a meaningful order. Then you will analyze them in light of the problem. From these analyses you hope to identify possible reasons for the different sales volumes of the two groups of hotels. Finally, you will prepare a report presenting the information to Ms. Smitherman. (You'll be careful to refrain from making specific recommendations for corrective action. Since your company does not specialize in hospitality research, it does not have the expertise to make such recommendations.)

The summary findings are presented in the table below. Use your logic and imagination to develop any additional details you may need to write a successful report. For example, in describing your research procedure, you may add specifics that your reader would find helpful, and you may generate some plausible specifics when discussing your findings. You can assume that the tabulations and notes for each of the 20 hotels are attached as an appendix. [Note that "S" = Satisfactory and "U" = Unsatisfactory in the table's column heads.]

Check-in experience	S	U
Courtesy/helpfulness of staff:		
Unusually courteous	3	1
Above average	7	6
Below average	0	3
Check-in wait time:		
No waiting	4	6
1-5 minutes	4	4
Over 5 minutes	2	-

Curb appeal

Visibility/condition of sign:		
Excellent	6	4
Average	4	5
Poor	-	1
Outdoor lighting:		
Excellent	8	4
Average	2	5
Poor	-	1
Cleanliness:		
Excellent	8	4
Average	2	3
Poor	-	3
Grounds:		
Excellent	8	5
Average	2	3
Poor	-	2

Breakfast area

Cleanliness:		
Excellent	8	5
Average	2	3
Poor	-	2
Food display:		
Appealing	6	2
Average	3	6
Unappealing	1	2
Food quality:		
Excellent	6	5
Average	3	3
Poor	1	2
Restocking of items:		
Excellent	6	4
Average	4	3
Poor	-	3

Preparation of room	S	U
Excellent	4	2
Above average	6	6
Below average	-	2

Qualifications of managers

Education:		
Some high school	-	-
High school graduate	2	3
Some college	2	4
College graduate	6	3
Experience:		
Less than 1 year	1	3
1–5 years	4	4
Over 5 years	5	3
Age:		
21–25	-	1
26–30	1	3
31–40	5	4
41–50	3	2
Over 50	1	-
Grades on Manager's Aptitude Test:		
Did not take test	-	3
Below 40 (poor)	-	-
40–59 (acceptable)	2	4
60–79 (good)	4	2
80–100 (outstanding)	4	2

Service staff

Appearance:		
Excellent	6	2
Average	4	5
Poor	-	3
Friendliness:		
Excellent	6	3
Average	3	4
Poor	1	2

Check out experience

	S	U
Excellent	7	5
Average	3	4
Poor	-	1

---

32 Last month your boss, HR director for the building supplies company where you work, got the executives' approval to launch an employee-volunteer program. As assistant HR director, you were tasked with conducting phase one of the plan: surveying the 420 employees to find out what kind of program they would be most likely to support. You designed an online survey to gather this information, and you got 300 complete replies. Here are the aggregate results:

Q1: Do you currently volunteer in the community?
Yes:190   No: 110

If yes,
About how many hours per week do you volunteer? 0.8

Where do you volunteer? Choose all that apply.

School: 32	National nonprofit organization: 14
Church: 67	Local nonprofit organization: 22
Neighborhood/ community: 45	Other: 10

What type(s) of activity do you do? Choose all that apply.

Tutoring /teaching: 35	Mentoring: 16
Construction/ maintenance: 62	Organizing/promoting a cause: 20
Help at food pantry/ homeless shelter: 20	Coaching: 31
Beautification work: 39	Other: 4

Why do you volunteer? Rate each reason on a scale from 1 (not important) to 7 (very important).

It's important to give: 5.5

I'm needed: 6.5

It broadens my world: 2

It makes me feel good to share what I'm good at: 5

I learn new things: 3.5

It feels good to work with others for a good cause: 4.5

I meet others and make friends: 2.5

Other: [Use your imagination to invent plausible write-ins.]

If no,

Why not? Rate each reason on a scale from 1 (strongly disagree) to 7 (strongly agree).

I'm too busy: 6

I feel I give enough to others already: 3

It's too hard to find the right volunteer opportunity for me: 4.5

It just sounds like more work: 5

Other: [Use your imagination to invent plausible write-ins.]

Q2: How appealing would you find the following incentives for volunteering? Rate each on a scale from 1 (not important) to 7 (very important).

Volunteers receive time off: 5

Volunteers receive paid time off: 6

Volunteers are recognized in the company: 3

Volunteers can win non-monetary awards: 2

Volunteers can win tangible rewards (e.g., bonus or time off): 5

Volunteers can earn company grants for the organizations where they volunteer: 4.5

Volunteers have advancement opportunities: 3.5

Others in the company, including management, are volunteering: 4.5

Volunteering counts in my performance review or toward my job security: 4

Q3: If the company were to create a volunteer program, how would you feel about each of the following types? Rate each on a scale from 1 (not very positive) to 7 (very positive).

Individuals volunteer on their own time: 3

Individuals volunteer for an hour or two of paid time off per month: 6.5

The company holds a special volunteer event (e.g., community fix-up day): 5.5

Individuals take a paid "service sabbatical" for an extended period (one to 12 months) for special projects: 2

Q4: My general attitude toward a company volunteer program in any form is:

Strongly positive:	52
Positive:	90
Neutral:	76
Negative:	56
Strongly negative:	26

Write your boss a report that helps him or her interpret these data and decide what kinds of parameters the new program should have.

---

33 Write a recommendation report to help solve a problem on your campus or at your workplace. Choose a problem that you can reasonably investigate in the time you have, and find out who the most appropriate recipient for your report will be. Then carefully study both the problem and possible solutions, using any and all appropriate forms of research (including consulting with your intended recipient). Finally, prepare your findings and recommendations in a formal report. (Your instructor may request a progress report midway through your project.)

---

34 Your father just called to tell you that his hours at work have been reduced, so you're going to have to find a summer job to help pay for next year's tuition. One of your LinkedIn friends from your Business Marketing group who knows of your passion for reading tells you about a part-time position available at a local used bookstore. You jump at the chance to combine the two things you love: business and books.

The job interview with the store manager was not quite what you had expected. Instead of shelving books and ringing up sales, she has a special project for you. Your online résumé, she said, was quite impressive. She especially appreciated the links to your most recent marketing research project dealing with online marketing. She says that sales at the store have been in a free fall for the past several years. As she sees it, they must move their sales to the Internet or they will be out of business by the end of the year. Your job is to investigate her options for creating an online version of her bookstore. What would be involved? What would she have to do? Investigate the logistics and costs associated with setting up and maintaining a company website for her store, online payment options, shipping policies and procedures, Internet security, and any other factors your boss should consider.

Write a memo report that provides information to help her start her online business.

Following are suggestions for additional report problems ranging from the simple to the highly complex. You can convert them into realistic business problems by supplying details and/or adapting them to real-life business situations. For most of these problems, you can obtain the needed information through secondary research. The topics are arranged by business field, although many of them cross fields.

Accounting

1 Report on current depreciation accounting practices, and recommend depreciation accounting procedures for Company X.

2 Recommend measures that Company X, which recently went public, should take to comply with the Sarbanes-Oxley Act.

3 What security measures should Company X take regarding access to its accounting data online?

4 Advise the managers of Company X on the accounting issues that they can anticipate when the company begins overseas operations.

5 Analyze break-even analysis as a decision-making tool for Company X.

6 Explain to potential investors which sections in Company X's most recent annual report they should review most carefully.

7 Analyze the relative effects on income of the first-in, first-out (FIFO) and last-in, first-out (LIFO) methods of inventory valuation during a prolonged period of inflation.

8 Write a report for the American Accounting Association on the demand for accountants with information systems training.

9 Develop information for accounting students at your school that will help them choose between careers in public accounting and careers in private accounting.

10 Advise the management of Company X on the validity of return on investment as a measure of performance.

11 Report on operations research as a decision-making tool for accountants and managers.

12 Report to an association of accountants the status of professional ethics in accounting.

13 Report to management of Company X on the communication skills important to accounting.

14 Report to the board of directors at Company X on whether the balance sheet fails to recognize important intangible assets.

15 Review for Company X whether disclosure could be an effective substitute for recognition in financial statements.

16 Report to the management of Company X on whether intangible assets have finite or infinite lives.

17 Advise the founders of new Company X on income tax considerations in the selection of a form of business organization.

18 Review for Company X the pros and cons of current methods of securities evaluation.

General Business

19 Evaluate the adequacy of current programs at your school for developing business leaders.

20 Which business skills should schools and colleges teach, and which should companies teach?

21 What should be the role of business leaders in developing courses and curricula for business schools?

22 Report on ways to build and use good teams in the workplace.

23 Identify the criteria Company X should use in selecting a public relations firm.

24 Investigate the impact of electronic signatures on the business community.

25 How does today's business community regard the master of business administration (MBA) degree?

26 Evaluate the contribution that campus business and professional clubs make to business education.

27 How effective is online training for business courses?

28 What can Company X do to improve the quality of its product or service?

29 Advise Company X on the problems and procedures involved in exporting its products ___ to (your choice of country).

30 Determine when and how one needs to get permission to use music, text, and visuals (online, audio, and print) in business presentations.

31 Determine which of three franchises (your instructor will select) offer the best opportunity for investment.

32 Recommend guidelines to supervisors, managers, and employees of Company X for avoiding sexual harassment cases.

33 Determine cultural issues likely to be encountered by employees going to work in (a foreign country).

34 Should Company X use the U.S. Postal Service or a private courier (Federal Express, United Parcel Service)?

35 For an instructor, answer the question of whether Twitter should be used as a class teaching tool. (Or substitute clickers for Twitter.)

36 Advise a client on whether to invest in a company producing renewable energy (wind, solar, etc.).

37 Recommend for Company X a city and hotel for its annual sales meeting.

Labor

38 For the executives of the National Association of Manufacturers (or a similar group), report on the outlook for labor–management relations in the next 12 months.

39 For the officers of a major labor union, research and report progress toward decreasing job discrimination against minorities.

40 For Union X, project the effects that a particular technology (you choose) will have on traditionally unionized industries by the year 2015.

41 Advise the management of Company X on how to deal with Union Y, which is attempting to organize the employees of Company X.

42 Interpret the change in the number of union members over the past _____ years.

43 Report on the status and effects of "right to work" laws.

44 Evaluate the effects of a particular strike (your choice) on the union, Company X, the stockholders, and the public. Write the report for your boss in Company Y.

45 For Union X, prepare an objective report on union leadership in the nation during the past decade.

46 Layoffs based on seniority are causing a disproportionate reduction in the number of women, minority, and older workers at Company X. Investigate alternatives that the company can present to the union.

47 Investigate recent trends relative to the older worker and the stands that unions have taken in this area.

48 Review the appropriateness of unionizing government workers, and recommend to a body of government leaders the stand they should take on this issue.

49 Report on the role of unions (or management) in politics, and recommend a course for them to follow.

50 Reevaluate _____ (unions or employment relations—your instructor will specify) for the management of Company X.

51 Analyze the changing nature of work for the leaders of _____ union (your instructor will designate).

52 Report on the blending of work and family issues for Union X.

Finance

53 As a financial consultant, evaluate a specific form of tax shelter for a client.

54 Review the customer-relations practices of banks and recommend customer-relations procedures for Bank X.

55 Review current employee loan practices and recommend whether Company X should make employee loans.

56 Report on what Company X needs to know about financial matters in doing business with _____ (foreign country).

57 Give estate planning advice to a client with a unique personal situation.

58 Advise Company X on whether it should lease capital equipment or buy it.

59 Advise Company X on whether it should engage in a joint venture with a company overseas.

60 Should Company X accept major credit cards or set up its own credit card system?

61 Advise Company X on how to avoid a hostile takeover.

62 Which will be the better investment in the next three years: stocks or bonds?

63 Advise Company X on whether it should list its stock on a major stock exchange.

64 Advise Company X, which is having problems with liquidity, on the pros and cons of factoring accounts receivable.

65 Recommend the most feasible way to finance a startup restaurant.

Management

66 Investigate the likely advantages and disadvantages of requiring workers to wear uniforms at Company X.

67 Develop for Company X a guide to ethical behavior in its highly competitive business situation.

68 After reviewing pertinent literature and experiences of other companies, develop a plan for selecting and training administrators for an overseas operation for Company X.

69 Survey the current literature and advise Company X on whether its management should become politically active.

70 After reviewing the pros and cons, advise Company X on whether it should begin a program of hiring individuals with disabilities or the disadvantaged.

71 Report on the potential costs and benefits of company.

72 The executives of Company X (a manufacturer of automobile and truck tires) want a report on recent court decisions relating to warranties. Include any recommendations that your report justifies.

73 Report on the issues involved in moving Company X headquarters from _____ (city) to _____ (city).

74 After reviewing current practices regarding employee participation in management, advise Company X on whether it should encourage such participation.

75 Should Company X outsource for _____ (service) or establish its own department?

76 Review the advantages and disadvantages of rotating executive jobs at Company X, and then make a recommendation.

77 What should be Company X's policy on office romances?

78 Develop an energy conservation or recycling plan for Company X.

79 Evaluate the effectiveness of a portal (intranet) for handling internal communications for Company X.

80 Recommend security measures for preventing computer espionage at Company X, a leader in the highly competitive _____ industry.

81 Evaluate the various methods for determining corporate performance and select the one most appropriate for Company X.

82 Advise Company X on the procedures for incorporating in _____ (state or province).

83 Report to Company X on the civil and criminal liabilities of its corporate executives.

84 Research the ways that companies in the X industry have enhanced their diversity.

85 Determine for a legislative committee the extent of minority recruiting, hiring, and training in the industry.

86 As a consultant for an association of farmers, evaluate the recent past and project the future of growing, raising, or bioengineering _____ (your choice—cattle, poultry, wheat, soybeans, or the like).

87 Develop a plan for reducing employee turnover for Company X.

88 Investigate the feasibility of hiring older workers for part-time work for Company X.

Personnel/Human Resource Administration

89 Report on and interpret for Company X the effects of recent court decisions on the testing and hiring of employees.

90 Survey company retirement practices and recommend retirement policies for Company X.

91 Report on practices in compensating key personnel in overseas assignments and recommend policies for the compensation of such personnel for Company X.

92 Report on what human resource executives look for in job applications.

93 Report on the advantages and disadvantages of Company X's providing on-site day care for children of employees.

94 After reviewing the legal and ethical questions involved, recommend whether Company X should use integrity tests in employee hiring.

95 Review what other companies are doing about employees suffering from drug or alcohol abuse, and recommend a policy on the matter for Company X.

96 Report on effective interviewing techniques used to identify the best people to hire.

97 Investigate the impact of the Family Leave Act on Company X.

98 Compare the pros and cons of alternative methods of dispute resolution.

99 What can Company X do to improve employee retention?

100 Review the literature on employee and executive burnout and recommend remedies for it.

101 Investigate the pros and cons of hiring physically and/or mentally challenged workers for Company X.

102 Report on ways Company X can link performance improvement plans to discipline and pay.

103 Investigate the impact of the legal aspects of human resource management (EEO, ADA, wrongful termination, harassment, family care and medical leave, workplace violence—your instructor will select one or several) on Company X.

104 Analyze the impact of changing work priorities in a culturally diverse workplace for Company X.

105 Report on recent issues in employee communication for Company X.

106 Investigate the problem of employee absenteeism at Company X and recommend ways to decrease it.

Marketing

107 Review the available literature and advise Company X on whether it should franchise its _____ business.

108 Select a recent national marketing program and analyze why it succeeded or failed.

109 Advise the advertising vice president of Company X on whether the company should respond to or ignore a competitor's direct attack on the quality of its product.

110 Review the ethical considerations involved in advertising to children and advise Company X on the matter.

111 Explore the possibilities of trade with _____ (a foreign country) for Company X.

112 Determine for a national department store chain changing trends in the services that customers expect when shopping online.

113 Prepare a report to help a contingent of your legislature decide whether current regulation of advertising should be changed.

114 Determine the problems Company X will encounter in introducing a new product.

115 Report on the success of rebates as a sales stimulator and advise Company X on whether it should use rebates.

116 Should Company X buy or lease minivans for distributing its products?

117 Determine the trends in packaging in the_____ industry.

118 Should Company X establish its own sales force, use manufacturer's agents, or use selling agents?

119 How should Company X evaluate the performance of its salespeople?

120 Determine for Company X how it can evaluate the effectiveness of its (online, print, or radio) advertising.

121 Select the best channel of distribution for new product Y and justify your choice.

122 Should Company X establish its own advertising department or use an advertising agency?

123 Conduct a market study of _____ (city) to determine whether it is a suitable location for _____ (a type of business).

124 Report to Company X on drip marketing and recommend whether it should use drip marketing to increase sales.

125 Investigate the factors to consider when marketing to those with mobile devices.

126 Compare the effectiveness of three different types of online advertising and recommend one for Company X.

127 Determine whether any of the products of Company X are good candidates for infomercials.

Computer Applications

128 Recommend the application and/or service that Company X should use for its webinars.

129 Determine whether Company X should purchase or lease its computer equipment.

130 Report to the president of Company X the copyright and contract laws that apply to the use of computer programs.

131 Investigate the possibility of using the majority of office applications from the Internet rather than continually purchasing and upgrading programs.

132 Determine which positions Company X should designate as possible telecommuting candidates.

133 Report on the future developments of robotics in the _____ industry.

134 Review and rank for possible adoption three software programs that Company X might use for its _____ work (name the field of operations).

135 Determine for Company X the factors it should consider in selecting computer insurance.

136 Compare three online programs/courses for training your employees on _____ (name the topic) and recommend one.

137 Your company is considering the purchase of smart-phones for its sales representatives. Evaluate three brands and recommend one for purchase.

138 Do a cost/benefit analysis of purchasing tablet PCs for use by sales representatives at Company X.

139 Explore the procedures and methods for measuring information system effectiveness and productivity for Company X.

140 Investigate how to improve information security and control for Company X.

141 Identify and recommend Web-based survey tools that would be appropriate for Company X.

Business Education

142 Evaluate the effect of remodeling your new office site using both ergonomic and feng shui principles.

143 Report on ways companies now use and plan to use online meeting tools.

144 Analyze the possibility of instituting company-wide training on etiquette, covering everything from handling telephone calls to sexual harassment to dining out.

145 Advise management on the importance of the air quality in its offices.

146 Investigate ways to complete and submit company forms on the Web or the company portal.

147 Report on ways to hire and keep the best employees in the computer support center.

148 Report on ways to improve literacy in the workplace.

149 Report on ways to improve the communication of cross-cultural work groups.

150 Analyze the possible uses of voice-recognition software by the office staff in Company X.

151 Determine for Company X whether it should replace the laptop computers of its sales reps with tablet PCs.

152 Evaluate at least three data visualization programs and recommend one for use at Company X.

CHAPTER THIRTEEN

Conducting Research for Decision Makers

Learning Objectives

Upon completing this chapter, you will be able to design and implement a plan for conducting research to help solve a business problem. To reach this goal, you should be able to

1 Explain why research is useful in business.

2 Explain the difference between secondary and primary research.

3 Explain the difference between quantitative and qualitative research.

4 Use Internet search engines to gather existing information.

5 Use other Web resources to gather existing information.

6 Evaluate websites for reliability.

7 Use social networking and social bookmarking sites to gather existing information.

8 Use the library to gather existing information.

9 Use sampling to conduct a survey.

10 Construct a questionnaire and conduct a survey.

11 Conduct an experiment for a business problem.

12 Design an observational study for a business problem.

13 Explain the uses of focus groups and personal interviews.

14 Discuss important ethical guidelines for research.

Using Research to Solve a Business Problem

Introduce yourself to this chapter by assuming the position of administrative assistant to Carmen Bergeron, the vice president for human resources for Pinnacle Industries. Today at a meeting of administrators, someone commented about the low morale among sales representatives since last year's merger with Price Corporation. The marketing vice president immediately came to the defense of her area, claiming that there was no proof of the statement—that in fact the opposite was true. Others joined in with their views, and in time a heated discussion developed. In an effort to ease tensions, Ms. Bergeron suggested that her office survey employees "to learn the truth of the matter." The administrators liked the idea.

After the meeting, Ms. Bergeron called you in to tell you that you would be the one to do the research. And she wants the findings in report form in time for next month's meeting. She didn't say much more. No doubt she thinks your college training equipped you to handle the assignment.

Now you must do the research. This means you will have to choose appropriate methods and develop a research plan. Specifically, you will have to find resources about how to design a survey questionnaire and conduct interviews as well as research the reasons for low morale in business organizations. Then, you will need to construct a questionnaire; devise an interview procedure; conduct interviews; and record, analyze, and report your findings. All these activities require much more than a casual approach to research. How to do methodical research effectively is the subject of this chapter.

WHY RESEARCH MATTERS

LO1 Explain why research is useful in business.

Business decisions are made using accurate, timely, and objective information. Let's say your company wants to see if a new line of environmentally friendly household products would be profitable. To help make this decision, you might read the business literature on this topic, email other business people, analyze the competition, or survey consumers to see if they are interested in buying these kinds of products. When writing up your findings, you might provide just well-organized information; both information and analysis; or information, analysis, and recommendations. You'd also need to choose an appropriate format for the situation, whether a business report, a proposal, or a shorter document such as a progress report or email correspondence.

The information used to help make a business decision or solve a business problem is gathered through research. As this chapter explains, many different research methods are available to help you acquire the data you need, but it is important to understand that **data** are not **information**. Data are factual bits and pieces, whereas information is interpreted data that ultimately allows you or the reader to take action. To consider this idea more concretely, let's consider the Introductory Challenge above. Carmen Bergeron, the vice president for human resources, has asked you to collect data about low morale at Pinnacle Industries. These data will include what you find out about morale at similar companies as well as the employee perceptions you uncover at your own company when you conduct an employee survey. In and of themselves, these pieces of data may be interesting, but they become useful only when you evaluate and analyze them as a whole to create knowledge about why the company is having a morale problem. This knowledge, in turn, can be used to take action to fix the problem. This process has been referred to as **DIKA,** which stands for *data, information, knowledge, and action.*[1]

To turn data into knowledge, you'll need to analyze the facts you've collected and interpret them in light of your context and purpose. In other words, you will need to

---

[1] Thanks go to Professor Fiona Barnes for sharing this model at the Southeast Regional Meeting of the Association for Business Communication, St. Petersburg, FL, Mar. 2012.

adapt your findings to the particular business situation at hand. We discussed the concept of adaptation in Chapters 3 and 4 in terms of choosing reader-focused words and writing easy-to-follow sentences and paragraphs. In this chapter, adaptation means turning the information you have obtained through research into usable knowledge that can result in action.

WHAT RESEARCH IS

When I saw Patty in the elevator yesterday, she said that she was upset when the company sent out the memo about ending the policy for Friday pizza lunches.

To continue with our fictitious research scenario, the comment above might shed some light on the morale issue at Pinnacle, but the report you'd prepare for Carmen Bergeron wouldn't contain such a statement. The reason is that investigation of serious, complex subjects requires more than **informal research** consisting of casual conversations and random observations. Important fact-finding projects need to be conducted through **formal research**. This is kind of research is methodically planned and executed, and it is the type discussed in this chapter.

When you have been assigned a problem to research, your first task should be to get the problem and your research purpose clearly in mind. Elementary as this task may appear, all too often it is done haphazardly, which prevents a research project from achieving its goal. As Chapter 11 explains, you may need to do preliminary research to understand what your formal research should accomplish.

You will then need to determine what research method or methods you will use to investigate the problem. Whatever method you choose needs to be the type that will generate sufficient data to support relevant and reliable conclusions. Each type also comes with procedural guidelines that you will need to follow. In your final document, you will need to show that you adhered to these guidelines in order for your findings to be trusted.

Understanding the distinctions between primary and secondary research and qualitative and quantitative methods will help you choose the best method for the job. Some research tasks will involve only one of these types, while others may involve a combination or even all of them.

Primary versus Secondary Research

You can collect information you need for a project by using two basic forms of research: **primary** and **secondary**. Secondary research uses material that someone else has published in resources such as periodicals, brochures, books, digital publications, and websites. This research is typically conducted before you engage in primary research. Primary research is research that uncovers information firsthand. It produces new information through the use of experiments, surveys, interviews, and other methods of direct observation. To be an effective researcher, you should be familiar with the techniques of both primary and secondary research.

Conducting Secondary Research. For complex and important projects, many businesses hire professionals to find secondary information for them. These professionals charge from $60 to $120 per hour in addition to any online charges they incur. But for the vast majority of business problems, companies expect their employees to gather the information.

If you need to collect secondary information for a work project, knowing too little about how material is arranged in a library or online will cause you to waste valuable time on fruitless searches. With the volume of material available, your challenge is to find the information most relevant to the project or problem you are working on. As a business researcher you should be familiar with certain basic types of resources, whether in print or online. You should also become familiar with the general arrangement of a library or other repositories of secondary materials and learn the techniques for finding those materials.

LO2 Explain the difference between secondary and primary research.

The reference section of your library is a good place to start. There, either on your own or with the assistance of a research librarian, you can discover any number of timely and comprehensive sources of facts and figures.

Before starting your search, however, it is a good idea to have a system developed for how you are going to store and access the information you are collecting. Computer systems in today's libraries can aid you. These systems often allow users to print, download, email, or transfer directly the citations provided by the databases they're using. Some researchers cut their printouts apart and tape them to a master sheet. Others enter these items in databases they build. And still others export items directly into specialty databases, letting the software organize and number them. Using an orderly system to collect information is essential so you can quickly access and analyze it efficiently. Once you have a system set up for storing and retrieving the information you are going to collect, you can move on to the actual search.

Conducting Primary Research. If you cannot find the information you need using secondary sources, you must get it firsthand. That is, you must use primary (also called *empirical*) research. Businesses tend to use four main methods: surveys, experiments, observations, and qualitative research.

Primary research is almost always more expensive and elaborate than secondary research because it involves careful set up and the participation of other people. For example, conducting an experiment will require that you understand exactly what hypothesis you are testing and that you design your experiment to get accurate results. To plan and conduct your experiment, you'll likely need the assistance of co-workers and those outside your organization, such as other businesspeople or potential customers. Because primary research is so costly and labor intensive, you need to choose your method or methods especially carefully.

The types of primary research you use will depend on the types of data you need to generate or gather to complete your study. The two main types, quantitative and qualitative, are discussed next.

LO3 Explain the difference between quantitative and qualitative research.

Quantitative versus Qualitative Strategies

When doing firsthand research, you need to determine if you need **quantitative** data, **qualitative** data, or both types to solve the business problem. Quantitative researchers generally begin by constructing a hypothesis to test or developing a very specific research question to answer. They then use primary research methods such as experimentation, questionnaires, and surveys to generate numerical data. They apply statistical tests to these data to see whether they support or refute the hypothesis or answer the question and also to determine how applicable the findings might be to a larger population.

Qualitative researchers take a more interpretive approach to research. They begin with a more general question about what they want to learn and then study natural phenomena to gather insights into the phenomena or even to learn to ask different questions. Accordingly, they are likely to use research tools that generate verbal data, such as company documents, personal interviews, and focus groups.

The rest of this chapter will introduce you to the most common and useful business research methods and conclude with advice about using them ethically.

HOW TO FIND EXISTING RESEARCH

One of the most accessible research tools we have is the Internet. Using search engines, other Web-based tools, and online library materials, we can often find all the secondary information we need.

Searching the Web

The Internet is a network of networks. It operates in a structure originally funded by the National Science Foundation. No one organization owns or runs this globally connected network, but an international community called the World Wide Web

Consortium (W3C), made up of experts and interested members of the public, has developed certain Web standards that are constantly evolving.

Because no one is officially in charge, finding information on the Internet can be difficult, but these days, many powerful search and retrieval tools are available. These tools can search for files as well as text on various topics, and they can search both titles and the documents themselves.

Using Search Engines. Internet search engines compile indexes of information about websites, such as the meta tags (hidden keywords) they use, how often they're visited, and other sites they link to. When you use a search engine, you are actually searching its index, not the Web itself. According to Experian Hitwise,[2] the top five search engines are Google, Bing, Yahoo! Search, Ask, and AOL Search, with Google being the most popular of the five. Google, whose simple, clean screens you see in Figures 13–1 and 13–2, provides the ability to do a simple search or a more advanced search. As you can see in Figure 13–1, even a simple search includes ways to filter the information you are searching. In this case the search phrase "morale in organizations"

LO4 Use Internet search engines to gather existing information.

Figure 13–1

A Simple Search Using Google
SOURCE: www.google.com

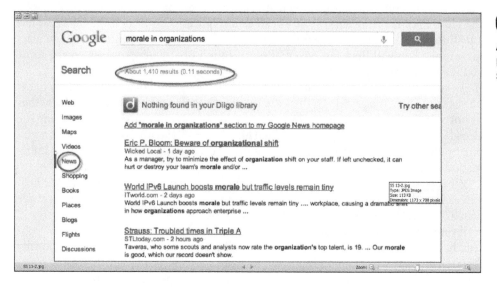

Figure 13–2

A Google Search Using a Filter to Narrow Results
SOURCE: www.google.com

---

[2]"Search Engine Trends," *Experian Hitwise*, Experian Information Solutions, Inc., 2012, Web, 7 July 2012.

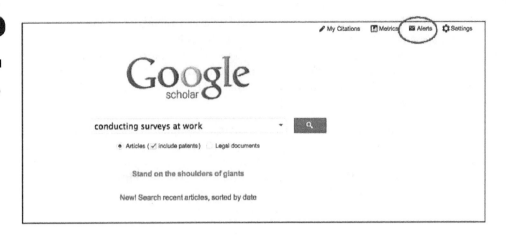

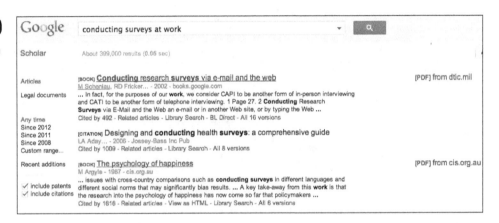

pulls up 11,900,000 results. If you use the categories on the left side of the screen (such as Videos, News, or Discussions), you can limit your results to those sources, as shown in Figure 13-2. In this case, when you filter for News, you receive 1,410 results.

You can use another Google tool, Google Scholar, to search scholarly literature, which includes journals from academic publishers, conference papers, dissertations, academic books, and technical reports. You can perform a simple search in Scholar much as you would in Google's regular search. For example, you could search with the phrase "conducting surveys at work," as in Figure 13-3. Google Scholar also has a feature called Alerts, as shown in Figure 13-3, which allows you to create an alert for a topic. You will then receive email notification of any new sources on the topic you are researching.

As you can see from the results in Figure 13-4, Google Scholar also provides filters on the left side of the screen. In this case the search tool can filter by date and whether or not to include patents and citations. You could also refine your research by using the Google Scholar Advanced Search option (Figures 13-5 and 13-6). Finally, when you pull up the results of a search, you can use the Related articles link to find more information on your research topic (Figure 13-7).

Whatever search engine you are using, a good command of Boolean logic will help you extract the information you need quickly and accurately. Boolean logic uses three primary operators: AND, OR, and NOT.

If your search yields too many citations, you can use the operator AND to narrow your search. When you link two search terms with AND, the search engine will retrieve only those citations that contain both terms. The operator NOT is another narrowing term, instructing the search engine to eliminate citations with a particular term. For example, if you were searching for articles on conducting surveys at work, you could search with the phrase "surveys at work NOT healthcare" to eliminate healthcare-related surveys.

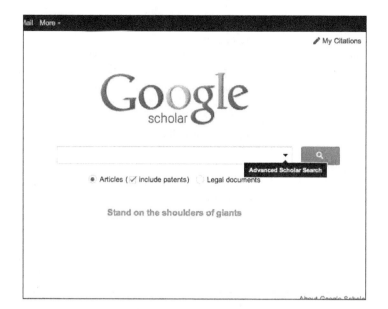

Figure 13–5

How to Access Google Scholar's Advanced Search
SOURCE: http://scholar.google .com/schhp?hl=en

Figure 13–6

Illustration of Google Scholar's Advanced Search Features
SOURCE: http://scholar.google .com/schhp?hl=en

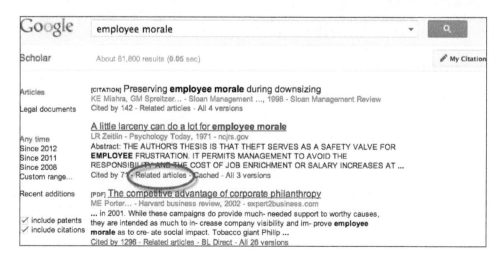

Figure 13–7

Illustration Showing the Related Article Link in a Google Scholar Search
SOURCE: http://scholar .google.com/scholar?as_ q=employee+morale&as_ epq=&as_oq=&as_eq=&as_ occt=any&as_sauthors=&as_ publication=&as_ylo=&as_ yhi=&btnG=&hl=en&as_ sdt=0%2C36

The OR operator can be used to expand the search by adding variations or synonyms to the basic search term. For example, to expand a search for articles on "surveys AND morale," you might add "productivity OR enthusiasm OR confidence." If you have difficulty thinking of terms to broaden your search, look at the keywords or descriptors of the items that have already been identified. Often these will give you ideas for additional terms to use. If the search still comes up short, you should check for spelling errors or variations. Becoming skilled at using Boolean logic will help you get the Internet-based information you need, and it will also help you search online databases (discussed in a later section) more efficiently.

Whether you are searching the Web or databases, you can add the full citation of a source you find to a bibliographic manager such as Endnote. You can also select your preferred citation format in Google Scholar by visiting the Scholar Settings page. Once you have saved your preferences, you can import a citation by clicking on the appropriate import link in your Google Scholar search results.

As search engines evolve to meet the changing needs of the Internet's content and its users, new forms of these tools have emerged as well. **Metasearch tools** allow you to enter the search terms once, run the search simultaneously with several search engines, and view a combined results page. Examples of such tools are Dogpile, Kartoo, Mamma, Metacrawler, and Search.com. You will find links to these and other search tools on the textbook website. Figures 13–8 and 13–9 illustrate how Dogpile searches various search

Figure 13–8

Illustration of the Metasearch Tool Dogpile
SOURCE: www.dogpile.com
Reprinted with permission of Blucora, Inc.

Figure 13–9

Illustration of a Search Using Dogpile
SOURCE: www.dogpile.com
Reprinted with permission of Blucora, Inc.

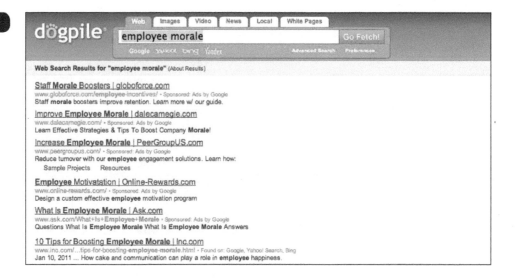

engines for the phrase "employee morale" and then combines the results and presents them in an easy-to-view form.

Another type of search tool that has emerged is the **specialized search engine**. Four popular examples are Yahoo!: People Search for finding people, Edgar for finding corporate information, FindLaw for gathering legal information, and Mediafinder for finding print items. In 2010 Mediafinder also launched an app for iPhone and iPad that provides access to data on more than 16,000 publications from the United States and Canada. The app allows users to search by title, keyword, and subject.

Another way to gather information from the Web is to use of electronic personal agents. These tools let you define the kind of information you want to find. The information can be waiting when you access your personal website, such as at my.yahoo.com or iGoogle, or it can be delivered by email or in the form of "push technology" broadcast directly to your computer. You are already using push technology if you have news/traffic/weather updates sent to you.

While these tools assist you in finding helpful Web documents, it is crucial to remember that the tools are limited. You must evaluate the source of the information critically. Also, you must recognize that not all of the documents published on the Web are indexed and that no search tool covers the entire Web. Skill in using the tools plays a role in finding good Web information, but judgment in evaluating the accuracy and completeness of the search plays just as significant a role.

Using Other Web-Based Resources. There are numerous other Web-based research sources in addition to the ones already mentioned. As technology changes, the list will continue to grow and change, but this section will introduce you to a number of current Web-based resources for research.

LO5 Use other Web resources to gather existing information.

You have probably been advised by many of your college instructors not to use **Wikipedia** as a reference when you write essays or other papers. The reason is that Wikipedia is written and maintained by volunteers, and virtually anyone can post and edit articles. Since its launch in 2001, though, Wikipedia has become a more credible and useful resource. And while we do not advise you to use it as your main resource, it can be a useful place to start to learn about a subject that is new to you.

WorldCat (Figure 13–10) is an online network of library content and services. You can use it to search the collections of local libraries and libraries around the world for books, CDs, videos, and digital content such as ebooks. You also can find article citations with links to their full text and historical documents and photos. If you have an active membership to the library that owns an item, you can check items out. You may also be able to access electronic databases if you have a valid login for the library that has access to these databases.

In Chapter 17 we talk about using **RSS (Really Simple Syndication) feeds** on websites and blogs, but RSS feeds can be useful research tools as well. News outlets such as *The New York Times* and *CNN* offer these feeds on their websites. Scholarly journals also offer RSS feeds for their tables of contents. Subscribing to these will allow you to keep up to date on the topics you are gathering information about.

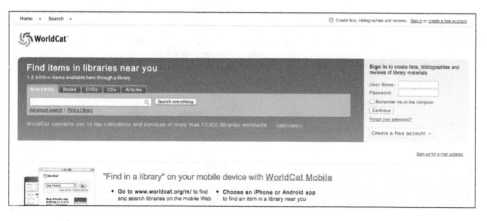

Figure 13–10

Illustration of the Online Library Collection WorldCat

SOURCE: www.worldcat.org Screenshot used with OCLC's permission; and WorldCat® is a registered trademark of OCLC Online Computer Library Center, Inc.

Managing Citations with Zotero

Zotero is a free citation manager tool you can use to help you collect and organize your research sources. It is an extension for the Firefox Web browser.

The left column of the Zotero screen includes My Library, which contains all the items you save. You can click the button above My Library to create a new collection, which is a folder you can use to help organize the information you add to Zotero.

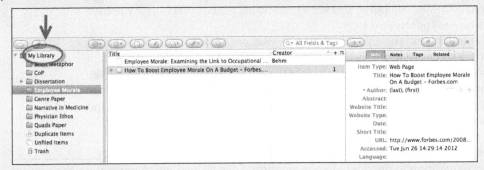

There are three main ways to add data to Zotero: attaching a webpage, capturing an item, and manually adding an item. You can attach a webpage as a snapshot by clicking the Create New Item from Current Page button. A snapshot keeps a locally stored copy of a webpage as it was when it was saved and makes it available without an Internet connection.

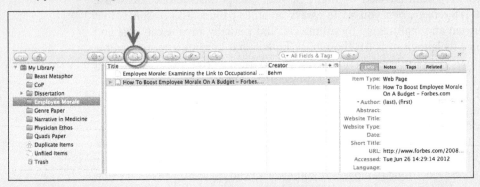

You can also add information from other sources such as books you find online through the Capture icon (the folder) that appears in the browser address bar once you have downloaded Zotero. This feature lets you automatically create an item. If a full-text PDF is available, it will be automatically attached to the item.

SOURCES: www.zotero.org/larduser/items

Finally, you can manually add resources to Zotero by clicking on the New Item button in the toolbar, selecting the appropriate item, and manually adding in information to the fields.

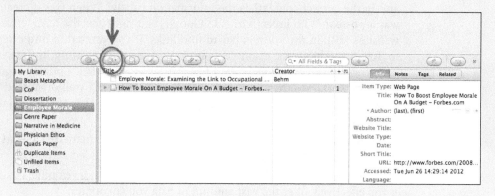

Once you have subscribed to an RSS feed, you will need an RSS reader (also known as a feed reader or aggregator) to access the content you subscribed to. Many options are available, including Newzcrawler, Google Reader, Feed Demon, and NewsGator. The difference between RSS readers is typically how the interface looks, so you can choose the one that best suits you.

Evaluating Websites

LO6 Evaluate websites for reliability.

Websites can be an invaluable source of useful information. But as you know, all are not equally credible. Some may be biased, while others may be inaccurate. So it is important to know how to evaluate websites for completeness, accuracy, and reliability.

Although most print sources include items such as author, title of publication, facts of publication, and date, websites do not have an established format that helps ensure their credibility. Most users of search engines also do not understand the extent or type of bias involved when search engines present and order their results. And even the best search engines index only a small fraction of the Internet content. So all Web findings must be carefully scrutinized, and many should be checked against other sources.

One experimental study found that users of website information were particularly susceptible to four types of misinformation: advertising claims, government misinformation, propaganda, and scam sites. Furthermore, the study found that users' confidence in their ability to gather reliable information was not related to their actual ability to judge the information appropriately. The results also revealed that level of education was not related to one's ability to evaluate website information accurately.[3]

One solution might be to use only those links posted on trustworthy sites (e.g., websites of professional organizations or of government agencies). However, these sites are not comprehensive and are often late in providing links to new sources. Therefore, developing the skill and habit of evaluating websites critically is probably a better choice. This skill can be honed by getting into the habit of looking at the purpose, qualifications, validity, and structure of the websites you use.

- **Purpose.** Why was the information provided? To explain? To inform? To persuade? To sell? To share? What are the provider's biases? Who is the intended audience? What point of view does the site take? Could it possibly be ironic, a satire, or a parody?

- **Qualifications.** What are the credentials of the information provider? What is the nature of any sponsorship? Is contact information provided? Is it accurate? Is it complete—name, email address, street address, and phone number? Is the information well written, clear, and organized?

---

[3]Leah Graham and Panagiotis Takis Metaxas, "'Course It's True; I Saw It on the Internet!': Critical Thinking in the Internet Era," *Communications of the AMC* 46.5 (2003): 73, print.

- **Validity**. Where else can the information provided be found? Is the information from the original source? Has the information been synthesized or abstracted accurately and in the correct context? Is the information timely? When was it created? When was it posted? Who links to it? (On Google, you can enter the term "link:" before a website's URL in the address bar to find links. If you wanted to find out who links to Toyota's website, for example, you would type the following in the search field: link: www.toyota.com.) How long has the site existed? Is it updated regularly? Do the links work? Do they represent other views? Are they well organized? Are they annotated? Has the site received any ratings or reviews? Is the cited information authentic?
- **Structure**. How is the site organized, designed, and formatted? Does its structure provide a particular emphasis? Does it appeal to its intended audience?

By critically evaluating the websites you use, you will be developing a skill that will help you effectively filter the vast amount of data you encounter.

Taking Advantage of Social Networks

Today's businesses take advantage of social media like Facebook and Twitter for marketing purposes, but such networks can also be useful for researching a business problem.

LO7 Use social networking and social bookmarking sites to gather existing information.

Facebook. Facebook was launched as a personal social networking service in 2004, but businesses large and small have adopted it as a key marketing venue. In fact, 70 percent of retail merchants now use Facebook to market their products.[4]

Because of its pervasiveness, Facebook also makes an excellent research tool. It is especially useful for surveys (which we discuss later in this chapter). You can also go to company Facebook pages like Ace Hardware's, shown in Figure 13–11, to research company-specific information.

Twitter. As Chapter 6 explains (and you probably already know), Twitter is a micro-blogging service that lets you send and read messages of up to 140 characters in length. Like blogs, Twitter started out as a personal communication tool, but organizations and

Figure 13–11

Illustration of Ace Hardware's Facebook Page
SOURCE: Illustration of Ace Hardware's Facebook Page, http://www.facebook.com/#!/acehardware.

---

[4]"Social Marketing Continues Meteoric Rise Among Local Businesses," *MerchantCircle*, Reply! Inc., 15 Feb. 2011, Web, 17 June 2012.

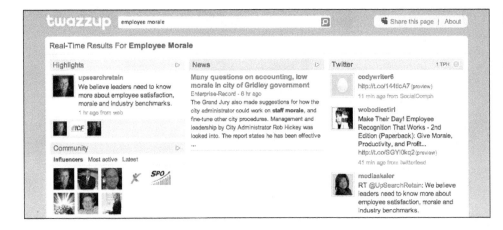

Figure 13–12

Illustration of a Real-Time Twitter Search Using the Tool Twazzup
SOURCE: www.twazzup
.com/?q=employee+morale&l=all

Figure 13–13

Illustration of a Real-Time Twitter Search Using the Tool Twinitor
SOURCE: www.twinitor.com/
#q=employeemorale&lang
=all&stop_spam=0&st
op_porn=1

companies now liberally populate the "Twitterverse." In fact, according to one study, 51 percent of active Twitter users follow companies, brands, or products on social networks.[5] While most tools that search "tweets" (the name for Twitter messages) are limited in terms of how far back in time they can search, two good real-time search services are Twazzup and Twinitor (Figures 13–12 and 13–13).

You can also "follow" people or topics on Twitter if you have a Twitter account. You can do a simple search for a topic with Twitter's search function, as shown in Figure 13–14. To get more information relevant to your particular business problem, you should consider following topics by following specific **hashtags**. Hashtags are created by using the symbol # to mark keywords or topics. These marked topics are then easier to find in Twitter Search. If you find a hashtag you want to follow to learn more about a certain topic, you can click on that link and be taken to all the other tweets in that category. In the example provided in Figure 13–15, @Evanish uses the hashtag #GreatTips. If you click on the link for the hashtag, you can see all the results for the discussion, as shown in Figure 13–16.

LinkedIn. LinkedIn is similar to Facebook in that it connects people, but whereas Facebook stresses social connections, LinkedIn focuses on professional contacts. People generally join LinkedIn to make these connections, but like Facebook, this network can be useful in researching a business problem.

To take full advantage of LinkedIn as a research tool, use the various Search options, particularly People, Companies, and Groups (Figure 13–17). If, for example, you wanted to see what types of employee morale issues other companies were having, you could search with the Companies search. You could use the Groups search function to research groups that focus on human resources, training, or motivation.

---

[5]Tom Webster, "Twitter Use in America: 2010," *Edison Research*, Edison Research, 29 Apr. 2010, Web, 17 June 2012.

Figure 13–14

Illustration of a Search Using Twitter's Search Function
SOURCE: https://twitter.com/search/employee%20morale

Figure 13–15

Illustration of a Twitter Hashtag in a Tweet
SOURCE: https://twitter.com/search/employee%20morale

Jason Evanish @Evanish   11 Jun
#GreatTips 7 Easy Ways to Improve **Employee Morale**
bit.ly/Mmu4Ps Yup, they're easy, but I bet you don't do all of them...
Expand

Figure 13–16

Illustration of the Results of Following a Hashtag
SOURCE: https://twitter.com/#!/search/%23GreatTips

Figure 13–17

Illustration of LinkedIn's News Webpage Showing the Various Search Functions Available on the Site
SOURCE: www.linkedin.com/today/?trk=hb_tab_news

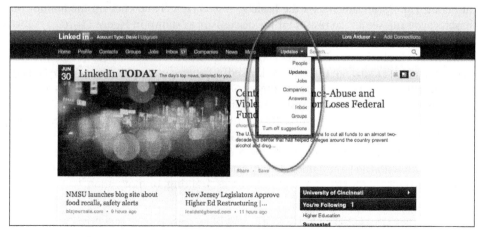

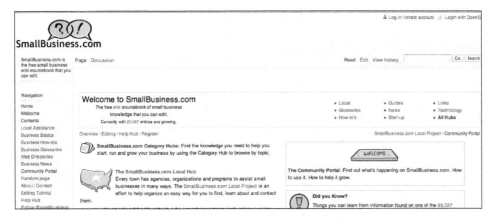

Figure 13–18

Illustration of a Business-Related Wiki
SOURCE: http://smallbusiness
.com/wiki/Main_Page

Figure 13–19

The Top Blogs About Finance According to the Technorati Authority Index
SOURCE: http://technorati.com/
business/finance/

Virtual contacts through LinkedIn, Facebook, and Twitter also have the advantage of giving you access to international data for your research.

Wikis. Wikis are basically collaborative collections of knowledge. You can find wikis on almost any business topic. One excellent business wiki resource is Smallbusiness.com, shown in Figure 13–18, which offers information on everything from tax preparation to time management. Along with using wikis as a research tool, you can create your own wiki for collaborative projects, such as team research projects. There are many free wiki-hosting sites to choose from, including Google Sites, PBworks, PmWiki, and Wikispaces.

Blogs. Blogs (short for "Web logs") started out as personal diaries or pages in 1994, but they soon became a journalism tool as well.[6] Today many companies maintain blogs, too. Like Facebook and LinkedIn, blogs can be a useful tool for finding information on a business problem.

Often, the challenge is to find blogs that are pertinent to the research you are pursuing. Google blog search (www.google.com/blogsearch) and Technorati are two useful blog search engines. Google's blog search works just like a typical Google search except that it limits the results to items posted on blogs. Technorati indexes over 1.3 million blogs, many of them authored by corporations and small businesses.[7] Technorati also helps you determine a blog's standing and influence with its feature Technorati Authority. Authority is calculated on the basis of a site's linking behavior, categorization, and other data over a short period of time. Therefore, a blog's rating will rise and fall rapidly depending on what is being discussed in cyberspace at the moment. Levels of authority range from 0–1,000, with 1,000 being the highest possible authority (Figure 13–19).[8]

---

[6]Clive Thompson, "The Early Years," *New York Magazine*, New York Media LLC, 12 Feb. 2006, Web, 17 June 2012.

[7]"Blog Directory," *Technorati*, Technorati, Inc., n.d., Web, 17 June 2012.

[8]"Technorati Authority FAQ," *Technorati*, Technorati, Inc., n.d., Web, 17 June 2012.

Listservs and Professional Organizations. Professional organizations are another good and sometimes overlooked research tool for business problems. Members of most professional organizations have benefits that often include access to a member directory, salary surveys, conferences, and educational opportunities. Most organizations today also have websites and listservs (electronic mailing lists). Because many of these listservs are very active, they can be useful for investigating business problems. You can send a question out to the membership and have responses the same day. You can also use the listserv to send out surveys.

There are any number of organizations to consider joining, including the Association for Financial Professionals, the Sales and Marketing Professional Association, the American Institute of CPAs, the Society for Human Resource Management, and the American Management Association.

Social Bookmarking Websites. Social bookmarking is a way for people to organize, store, manage, search, and share their favorite Web resources. Many online bookmark management services have been launched since 1996, including Delicious and Digg (Figures 13–20 and 13–21).

A major component of these sites is tagging, which lets users organize their bookmarks in flexible ways and develop shared vocabularies known as *folksonomies*, or *collaborative tagging*. Tagging works much like a keyword search. Let's say you are looking for information on companies' use of social media. You can search Delicious with this topic to see if anyone has tagged resources with related terms or phrases and then investigate those sources. This type of search can save you much of the time you would have spent conducting a search from scratch.

Figure 13–20

Illustration of the Social Bookmarking Site Delicious

SOURCE: http://delicious.com/

Figure 13–21

Illustration of the Social Bookmarking Site Digg
SOURCE: http://digg.com/ news/business/media/recent

Using the Library

LO8 Use the library to gather existing information.

With so much information available on the Web, it is tempting to think that libraries have become obsolete. But libraries contain a wealth of information that is unavailable anywhere else or available elsewhere only for a fee. You will often find your best information in a library—and probably save money in the process.

General libraries are the best known and the most accessible. General libraries, which include college, university, and most public libraries, are called *general* to the extent that they contain all kinds of materials. Many general libraries, however, have substantial collections in certain specialized areas.

Libraries that limit their collections to one type or just a few types of material are considered **special libraries**. Many such libraries are private and do not invite routine public use of their materials. Still, they will frequently cooperate on research projects that they consider relevant and worthwhile.

Among the special libraries are those libraries of private businesses. As a rule, such libraries are designed to serve the sponsoring company and provide excellent information in the specialized areas of its operations. Company libraries are less accessible than other specialized libraries, but a written inquiry explaining the nature and purpose of a project or providing an introduction from someone known to the company can help you gain access to them.

Special libraries are also maintained by various types of associations—for example, trade organizations, professional and technical groups, chambers of commerce, and labor unions. Like company libraries, association libraries may provide excellent coverage of highly specialized areas. Although such libraries develop collections principally for members or a research staff, they frequently make resources available to others engaged in reputable research.

A number of public and private research organizations also maintain specialized libraries. The research divisions of big-city chambers of commerce and the bureaus of research of major universities, for example, keep extensive collections of material containing statistical and general information on certain geographical areas. State agencies collect similar data. Again, though these materials are developed for a limited audience, they are often made available upon request.

No matter what type of library you use, you'll want to be familiar with how to consult such resources as online catalogs, databases, and reference materials.

Searching the Catalog. Today most libraries use online catalogs to list their holdings. You can locate sources in these catalogs by using the standard Keyword, Title, Author, and Subject options as well as a few other options. Becoming familiar with such catalogs is highly recommended, especially for the libraries you use frequently. Effective and efficient searching techniques can yield excellent information.

Two options you need to understand clearly are **Keyword** and **Subject**. When you select the Keyword option, the system will ask you to enter search terms and phrases. It will then search for only those exact words in several of each record's fields, missing all those records using slightly different wording (Figure 13–22). When you select Subject, the system will scan the Library of Congress subject heading for your search term (Figure 13–23). This means that for the most part you need to know the exact heading that the Library of Congress uses.

To find possible Library of Congress subject headings for your topic, visit the Library of Congress Authorities webpage at http://authorities.loc.gov and click "Search Authorities." Figure 13-24 shows possible headings for a search on "intercultural communication." Sometimes the search engine will cross-reference headings, such as suggesting that you "*See* Intercultural Communication" when you enter "cross-cultural communication." A Subject search will find all those holdings on the subject, including those with different wording such as "intercultural communication," "international communication," "global communication," and "diversity." If you were to run multiple searches under the Keyword option using these terms, you would have more complete information, though you would still miss those titles lacking the keywords.

Figure 13–22

Illustration of the Results from a Keyword Search in a Library Catalog

SOURCE: http://uclid.uc.edu/search/X

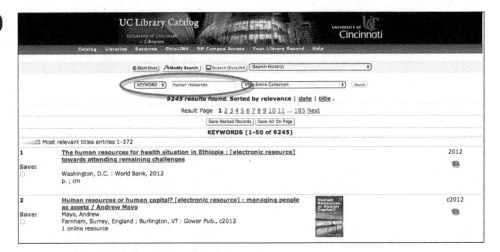

Figure 13–23

Illustration of Results from a Subject Search in a Library Catalog

SOURCE: http://uclid.uc.edu/search/X

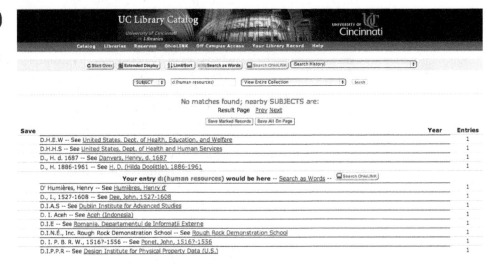

Figure 13–24

Illustration of the Library of Congress Authorities Subject Search Results

SOURCE: http://catalog.loc.gov/cgi-bin/Pwebrecon.cgi?DB=local&Search_Arg=human+resources&Search_Code=SUBJ%40&CNT=100&hist=1&type=quick

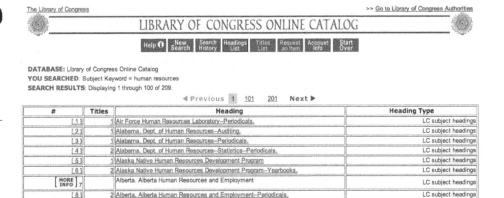

Searching Databases. The online catalog helps you identify books and other holdings in your library, and it may help you find some articles. But to do a good job of searching the periodical literature—that is, articles published in newspapers, magazines, and journals—you will need to use an online **database**, such as *ABI/Inform* (Figure 13–25). As the sophistication and capacity of computer technology have improved, much of the information that was once routinely recorded in print form and accessed through print

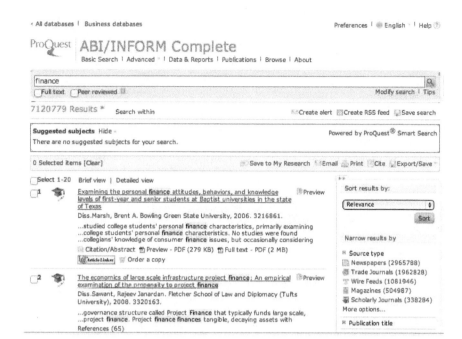

Figure 13–25

Illustration of a Search Using the *ABI/Inform* Database

SOURCE: http://search. proquest.com.proxy.libraries. uc.edu/abicomplete/ advanced?accountid=2909

directories, encyclopedias, and indexes is now stored digitally in computer files. These collections, called databases, are accessed through the use of search strategies much like those discussed for searching the Internet and the library catalog.

However, one first needs to identify which databases to use. Some of those most useful to business researchers are *ABI/Inform, Business Source Premiere, Factiva,* and *LexisNexis Academic. ABI/Inform* and *Business Source Premiere* are two of the most complete databases, providing access to hundreds of business research journals as well as important industry and trade publications. Most of the articles are included in full-text form or with lengthy summaries.

Factiva provides access to current business, general, and international news, including access to various editions of *The Wall Street Journal*. It also includes current information on U.S. public companies and industries. Similarly, *LexisNexis* offers access to current business and international articles, providing them in full text. Additionally, it includes legal and reference information.

If you need information on a particular company, you could use *LexisNexis®* *Company Dossier*. This database provides complete pictures of companies' financial health, brands, and competitors for both U.S. and international companies. *Hoover's Online* is also an excellent resource for company-specific information, and others include *Business & Company Resource Center, Business Source Complete,* and *D&B's Million Dollar Database*.

Consulting Reference Materials. Along with database sources, you may want to investigate other print and Web-based reference materials for information (Table 13–1). To gather research on a particular industry, for example, you could use *BizMiner*, which offers industry statistical reports and industry financial analysis benchmarks for over 5,000 lines of business and industries. Other industry-specific sources include *Plunkett Research Online* and *Standard & Poor's Industry Surveys*. To find out about international trade you can use the *(CIA) World Factbook*, which offers information on different countries' histories, governments, economies, geographical traits, and interactions with other countries. *Country Reports* from the Department of State also provides general information, region-specific information, and travel information.

The library materials you choose will be determined by your research question. Table 13–2 lists helpful resources for common research tasks in business. A reference librarian can recommend additional resources to help you with your research task.

Table 13–1

Useful Reference Materials

Type of Source	Description	Examples
Encyclopedias	Offer background material and other general information. Individual articles or sections of articles are written by experts in the field and frequently include a short bibliography.	*Encyclopedia Americana* *Encyclopaedia Britannica* *World Book* *Encyclopedia of Banking and Finance* *Encyclopedia of Business and Finance* *Encyclopedia of Small Business* *Encyclopedia of Advertising* *Encyclopedia of Emerging Industries*
Biographical Directories	Supply biographical information about leading figures of today or of the past.	*Who's Who in America* *Who's Who in the World* *Who's Who in the East* *Who's Who in the South and Southwest*
Almanacs	Offer factual and statistical information.	*The World Almanac and Book of Facts* *The Time Almanac* *The New York Times Almanac*
Trade Directories	Compile details in specific areas of interest. Variously referred to as *catalogs, listings, registers,* or *source books*.	*The Million Dollar Directory* *Thomas Register of American Manufacturers* *The Datapro Directory* *America's Corporate Families* *Who Owns Whom* *Directory of Corporate Affiliations* *Directories in Print*
Government Publications	Include surveys, catalogs, pamphlets, and periodicals from various governmental bureaus, departments, and agencies.	*Annual & Quarterly Services* (service-industry data) *Census of Wholesale Trade* *Census of Mineral Industries* *Statistical Abstract of the United States* *Survey of Current Business* *Monthly Labor Review* *Occupational Outlook Quarterly* *Federal Reserve Bulletin*
Dictionaries	Helpful for looking up meanings, spellings, and pronunciations of words or phrases. Electronic dictionaries add other options such as pronunciation in audio files.	*American Heritage Dictionary* *Funk & Wagnalls Standard Dictionary* *Random House Webster's College Dictionary* *Merriam-Webster's Collegiate Dictionary*
Additional Statistical Sources	Provide statistical data.	*Statistical Abstract of the United States* *Standard & Poor's Statistical Service* *Statistical Reference Index*
Business Information Services	Supply a variety of information to business practitioners.	*Corporation Records* *Moody's Investors' Advisory Service* *Value Line Investment Survey* *Gale Business Insights: Global* *Hoover's Online* *Factiva*
International Sources	Supply international corporate information.	*Principal International Businesses* *Major Companies of Europe* *Japan Company Handbook* *International Encyclopedia of the Social Sciences* *International Business Dictionary and References* *International Brands and Their Companies* *Foreign Commerce Handbook* *Index to International Statistics Statistical Yearbook*

Table 13-2

List of Resources by Research Question (Resources with Web links provided are available to the general public).

How do I find business news and trends?

ABI Inform Complete on ProQuest

Business Source Complete

Factiva (includes Dow Jones, Reuters Newswires and *The Wall Street Journal*, plus more than 8,000 other sources from around the world)

LexisNexis Academic, News and Business sections

Proquest Business Insights

Wilson OmniFile Full Text Mega

How do I find information about companies?

Business & Company Resource Center

Business Source Complete

Companies' own websites

Company Dossier (on Lexis/Nexis)

D&B's (Dunn & Bradstreet's) *Million Dollar Database*

Datamonitor 360

Factiva

Hoover's Online

Mergent Online

ORBIS

SEC Filings (on Edgar) at www.sec.gov/edgar/

Standard & Poor's NetAdvantage

Thomson One Banker

Value Line Research Center

How do I find information about particular industries?

ABI/INFORM Complete

Buzminer

Datamonitor 360

Freedonia Focus Market Research

Decision Support Database

Global Market Information Database

IBISWorld

ICON Group International

MarketLine

MarketResearch.com Academic

Mergent Industry Reports

Mintel Market Research Reports

Plunkett Research Online

Standard & Poor's Industry Surveys

How do I find biographical and contact information for businesspeople?

Biographical Dictionary of American Business Leaders

Biography in Context (Galegroup)

Biography Reference Bank (Wilson)

D&B's Million Dollar Database

LexisNexis Academic, Reference/Biographical Information section

Standard & Poor's NetAdvantage (Register of Executives)

How do I find information provided by the U.S. government?

American Community Survey (U.S. Census Bureau) at www.census.gov/acs/www/

American FactFinder at http://factfinder2.census.gov/

Business USA at http://business.usa.gov/

Fedstats at www.fedstats.gov/

FRED (Federal Reserve Economic Data) at http://research.stlouisfed.org/fred2/

Statistical Abstract of the United States at www.census.gov/compendia/statab/

Bureau of Labor Statistics Data at www.bls.gov/home.htm

How do I find out about other countries and international trade?

Country Studies at http://lcweb2.loc.gov/frd/cs/cshome.html

(CIA) World Factbook at www.cia.gov/library/publications/the-world-factbook/

Country Commercial Guides at www.buyusainfo.net/

Country Reports (From the Department of State) at www.state.gov/countries/

Europa World Yearbooks

Global Market Information Database

SourceOECD

WDI Online (World Bank's World Development Indicators)

Yahoo Country Links at http://dir.yahoo.com/Regional/Countries/

How do I find information about cities?

American FactFinder at http://factfinder2.census.gov/

Cities' own websites

Complete Economic and Demographic Data Source: CEDDS (Woods & Poole Economics)

County and City Data Book at www.census.gov/statab/www/ccdb.html

SimplyMap

SOURCE: Compiled with the assistance of Senior Business Librarian Wahib Nasrallah, University of Cincinnati.

HOW TO DO NEW RESEARCH

When you cannot find the information you need in secondary sources, you must get it firsthand through primary research. Primary research includes four basic methods:

1. Survey
2. Experimentation.
3. Observation.
4. Qualitative research.

Guidelines for each follow.

Conducting a Survey

The premise of the survey as a method of primary research is simple: You can best acquire certain types of information by asking questions. Such information includes personal data, opinions, behaviors, attitudes, and beliefs. It also includes information necessary to plan an experiment or an observation or to supplement or interpret the data that result.

Once you have decided to conduct a survey, you'll need to make a number of decisions, including what questions to ask and how to ask them. But none of these decisions will be more important than whom to survey. Except for situations in which a small number of people are involved in the problem under study, you won't be able to reach all the people involved. Thus, you'll need to select a **sample** of respondents who represent the group as a whole as accurately as possible. You can select that sample in several ways.

LO9 Use sampling to conduct a survey.

Choosing Your Sampling Technique. The type of sampling technique you use will be determined by the purpose of your research. While all samples have some degree of sampling error, you can reduce the error through techniques used to construct representative samples. These techniques fall into two groups: **probability** and **nonprobability sampling**.

Probability samples are based on chance selection procedures. Every element in the population has the same probability of being selected. These techniques include **simple random sampling**, **stratified random sampling**, **systematic sampling**, and **area** or **cluster sampling**.

- *Simple random sampling.* By definition, this sampling technique gives every member of the group under study an equal chance of being included. To ensure equal chances, you must identify every member of the group and then, using a list or some other convenient format, record all the identifications. Next, through some chance method, you select the members of your sample.

  For example, if you are studying the job attitudes of 200 employees and determine that 25 interviews will give you the information you need, you might put the names of all 200 workers in a container, mix them thoroughly, and draw out 25. Since each of the 200 workers has an equal chance of being selected, your sample will be random and can be presumed to be representative.

- *Stratified random sampling.* Stratified random sampling subdivides the group under study and makes random selections within each subgroup. The distribution of a particular group in the sample should closely replicate the distribution of that group in the entire population.

  Assume, for example, that you are attempting to determine the curriculum needs of 5,000 undergraduates at a certain college and that you have decided to survey 20 percent of the enrollment, or 1,000 students. To construct a sample for this problem, first divide the enrollment list by academic concentration: business, liberal arts, nursing, engineering, and so forth. Then draw a random sample from each of these groups, making sure that the number you select is proportionate to that group's percentage of the total undergraduate enrollment. Thus, if 30 percent

Researchers frequently survey a sample of the group that is being studied.

of the students are majoring in business, you will randomly select 300 business majors for your sample; if 40 percent of the students are liberal arts majors, you will randomly select 400 liberal arts majors for your sample; and so on.

- *Systematic sampling.* In systematic sampling you decide what percentage of a population you are interested in sampling, such as 10 percent of 10,000. Then, going down a list of the population's members, you select your participants at regular intervals (e.g, every 9th person).

  If you use this method, your sample will not really be random because by virtue of their designated place on the original list, items do not have an equal chance of being selected. Therefore, it is important to make sure your source list for the sample is not organized in a way that would create a biased sample.

- *Area* or *cluster sampling.* Researchers use area sampling when no master source list of a population is available. For example, if you want to survey employees in a given industry, it is unlikely there is a list of all these employees. An approach you may take in this situation is to randomly select a given number of companies from a list of all the companies in the industry. Then, using organization units and selecting randomly at each level, you break down each of these companies into divisions, departments, sections, and so on until you finally identify the workers you will survey.

Nonprobability samples are based on an unknown probability of any one member of a population being chosen. These techniques include **convenience sampling, purposeful sampling,** and **referral sampling**.

- *Convenience sampling.* A convenience sample is one whose members are convenient and economical to reach. When professors use their students as subjects for their research, they are using a convenience sample. Researchers generally use this sample to reach a large number quickly and economically. This kind of sampling is best used for exploratory research. A form of convenience sampling is *judgment* or *expert* sampling. This technique relies on the judgment of the researcher to identify appropriate members of the sample. Illustrating this technique is the common practice of predicting the outcome of an election based on the results in a bellwether district.

- *Purposeful sampling.* With purposeful sampling you look for a sample that has certain characteristics. Let's say you want to find out students' attitudes about a new tool to search the university's online library collections. It would be more logical to draw your sample from the students who use the system rather than from all the students at the university.

- *Referral sampling.* Referral samples are those whose members are identified by others. This technique is used to locate members when the population is small or hard to reach. For example, you might want to survey Six Sigma Black Belt certification holders. To get a sample large enough to make the study worthwhile, you could ask those from your town to give you the names of other Black Belt holders. Or perhaps you are trying to survey the users of a project management application. You could survey a user group and ask those members for names of other users. You might even post an announcement on a blog or online forum asking for names.

LO10 Construct a questionnaire and conduct a survey.

Constructing the Questionnaire. Once you have determined whom you will survey, you will need to construct a survey instrument, a **questionnaire**. A questionnaire is simply an orderly arrangement of the survey questions with appropriate spaces provided for the answers. But simple as the finished questionnaire may appear, it is the result of careful planning. You must word your questions so that the results will be **reliable**; a test of a questionnaire's reliability is its repeatability with similar results. You also want your questionnaire to be **valid**, measuring what it is supposed to measure.

Keeping these guidelines in mind will help you achieve reliable, valid results:

- *Avoid leading questions:* A **leading question** is one that in some way influences the answer. For example, the question "Is Dove your favorite bath soap?" may lead the respondent to favor Dove. Some people who would say "yes" would name another brand if they were asked, "What is your favorite brand of bath soap?"

- *Avoid absolute terms.* Try not to include words like *always* and *never* in your questions. Using these terms may make respondents unlikely to choose these answers, and the wording of the question could skew your data toward middle selections like *sometimes* or *frequently*.

- *Focus on one concept per question.* **Double-barreled questions** combine multiple questions and lead to inaccurate answers. An example of such a question is "To what extent do managers and co-workers affect your perception of the company?" This question asks a respondent two questions. If the respondent feels that managers do impact their perception but co-workers do not, the answer the respondent provides will not be an accurate reflection of his or her beliefs, and the question will not lead you to reliable data.

- *Make the questions easy to understand.* Questions that not all respondents will clearly understand will generate faulty data. Unfortunately, it is difficult to determine in advance just what respondents will not understand. As will be discussed later, the best means of detecting such questions in advance is to test the questions before using them, but you can be on the alert for a few common sources of confusion.

  One source of confusion is vagueness of expression, which is illustrated by the question, "How do you bank?" Who other than its author knows what the question means? Another source is using words respondents do not understand, as in the question, "Do you read your house organ regularly?" The words *house organ* have a specialized, not widely known meaning, and *regularly* means different things to different people.

- *Avoid questions that touch on personal prejudices or pride.* For reasons of pride or prejudice, people cannot be expected to answer accurately questions about certain areas of information. These areas include age, income status, morals, and some personal habits. How many people, for example, would answer "no" to the question "Do you brush your teeth daily?" How many people would give their ages correctly? How many citizens would admit to fudging a bit on their tax returns?

If such information is essential to the solution of the research problem, use a less direct means of inquiry. To ascertain age, for example, you could ask for dates of high school graduation. From this information, you could approximate age. Or you could provide an age range for a respondent to choose from, such as 20–24, 25–34, 35–44, 45–54, and 54 and older. This technique works well with income questions, too. People are generally more willing to answer questions that provide ranges instead of asking for specifics.

- *Ask only for information that can be remembered.* Since the memory of all human beings is limited, you should design your questionnaire to ask only for information that the respondents can be expected to remember. To be able to do this, you need to know certain fundamentals of memory. *Recency* is the most important principle of memory. People remember insignificant events that occurred within the past few hours. By the next day, however, they will forget some. A month later they may not remember any. You might well remember, for example, what you ate for lunch on the day of the survey, and perhaps you might remember what you ate for lunch a day, two days, or three days earlier. But you would be unlikely to remember what you ate for lunch a year earlier.

  The second principle regarding memory is *significance.* You may long remember minor details about the first day of school, your wedding, or an automobile accident. People readily remember events such as these because in each event there was an intense stimulus—a requisite for retention in memory.

  A third principle of memory is that fairly insignificant facts may be remembered over long time periods through *association* with something significant. Although you would not normally remember what you ate for lunch a year earlier, for example, you might remember if the day in question happened to be Christmas Day or your first day at college. Obviously, the memory is stimulated not by the meal itself but by the association of the meal with something more significant.

Designing the Questionnaire and Planning Its Delivery. Overall, the questionnaire should be designed to gather useful information that can be easily tabulated and meaningfully analyzed.

Be sure to enable the respondents to provide the demographic information you need. In some instances, such information as the age, sex, and income bracket of the respondent is vital to the analysis of the problem.

When practical, enable the respondents to check an answer. Easy-to-answer questions will encourage participation, and providing choices will make numerical analysis easier, too. Such questions must always provide for all possible answers, including conditional answers. For example, a direct question may provide for three possible answers: Yes _____, No _____, and Don't know _____ .

Consider using **scaling** when appropriate. It is sometimes desirable to measure the intensity of the respondents' feelings about a given topic, such as a product or company process. In such cases, some form of scaling is useful. The most common forms are ranking and rating. Though they are less sophisticated than some other forms,[9] they can nevertheless yield very helpful information.

The **ranking** technique consists simply of asking the respondent to rank a number of alternative answers to a question in order of preference (1, 2, 3, and so on). For example, in a survey to determine consumer preferences for toothpaste, the respondent might be asked to rank toothpastes A, B, C, D, and E in order of preference. The **rating** technique provides a scale showing the complete range of possible attitudes on a topic and assigns number values to the positions on the scale. The respondent

---

[9]Equivalent interval techniques, scalogram analysis, and the semantic differential are more complex techniques.

TECHNOLOGY IN BRIEF

Web-Based Survey Tools Help Writers Design, Analyze, and Report Results of Questionnaires

Web-based survey tools can help you design professional-looking questionnaires as well as compile and analyze the results. Some tools, such as those offered at Qualtrics.com and SurveyMonkey.com, are available in both free and for-purchase forms.

When preparing your questions, you can choose from several question types, and you can also select your preferred design (e.g., color and layout). You can move the questions to change the order, and you can enable respondents to skip parts of the survey based on their answers to certain questions. The tools also let you create open-ended questions. All these questions can be saved in a library for reuse. Some of the tools even include libraries of surveys that can be adapted for your particular use.

As shown below, these tools can provide helpful summary reports, even when the survey is still in progress. They also permit you to view the detailed raw data in various forms.

Businesses can use these tools in a variety of applications, including training program evaluations, employee feedback on policies and procedures, longitudinal studies of ongoing practices such as network advertising revenues, opinion surveys of customers and potential customers, and assessments of customer satisfaction.

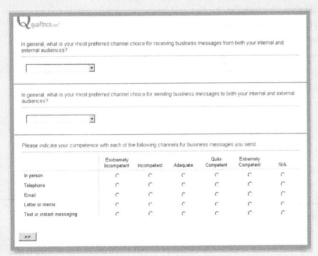

must then indicate the position on the scale that corresponds to his or her attitude. Typically, the numeral positions are described by words, as the example in Figure 13–26 illustrates. Because the rating technique deals with the subjective rather than the factual, it is sometimes desirable to use more than one question to cover the attitude being measured. Logically, the average of a person's answers to such questions gives a more reliable answer than does any single answer.

Use the best possible sequence of questions. In some instances, starting with a question of high interest may have psychological advantages. In other instances, it may be best to follow some other order of progression. Frequently, some questions must precede others because they help explain the others. Whatever the requirements of the individual case may be, you'll need to put careful thought into determining the sequence of questions.

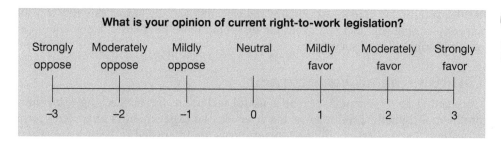

Figure 13–26

Illustration of a Rating Question

Fairly early in the planning process, you should choose your **survey channel**. You can get responses to your questions in four primary ways: by personal (face-to-face) contact, by phone, by mail (print or digital), or through websites (e.g., Facebook). You should select the way that in your unique case yields the best sample and the best results at the lowest cost.

All these decisions should be recorded in a **survey plan**. Your plan should include such logistics as when and where you'll conduct your survey, how many times it will be sent out, and when it will close. It should also include any additional materials you'll need. If you are conducting a mail or Web survey, for example, you'll need to develop an explanatory message that motivates the subjects to respond, tells them what to do, and answers all the questions they are likely to ask (see Figure 13–27). If you are conducting a personal or phone survey, you'll need to develop a script and/or instructions for the surveyors.

Conducting a Pilot Study. Before conducting the actual survey, it is advisable to conduct a **pilot study** on your questionnaire and survey plan. A pilot study is a small-scale version of your survey; in essence, it is a form of user testing (described on page 482). You select a few people to use as testers and have them take your survey to identify unclear questions, technological glitches, or other problems. Based on the

Figure 13–27

Illustration of a Cover Message for an Online Survey

results, you modify your questionnaire and working plan. Including this step in your survey planning will help you avoid the disappointment (and cost) that results from administering a flawed survey.

Conducting an Experiment

LO11 Conduct an experiment for a business problem.

Conducting an experiment can be a useful technique for researching a business problem. Originally developed in the sciences, the experiment is an orderly form of testing. Researchers conducting experiments are interested in testing the effects of a particular variable on some existing situation or activity. Therefore, to conduct an experiment, you systematically manipulate one factor of a problem while holding all the others constant. You then measure any changes resulting from your manipulations.

As an example, suppose you are conducting research to determine whether a new package design will lead to more sales. You might start by selecting two test cities, taking care that they are as alike as possible on all the characteristics that might affect the experiment. Then you would secure information on sales in the two cities for a specified time period before the study. Next, for a second specified time period, you would use the new package design in one of the cities and continue to use the old package in the other. During that period, you would keep careful sales records and check to make sure that advertising, economic conditions, competition, and other factors that might have some effect on the experiment remain unchanged. At the end of the study period, you could be relatively confident that any differences you found between the sales in the two cities were caused by the difference in package design.

Becoming familiar with two of the most common comparative study designs—the before–after and the controlled before–after—will give you a framework for understanding and applying this primary research technique.

The Before–After Design. The simplest experimental design is the **before–after design.** In this design, illustrated in Figure 13–28, you select a test group of subjects, measure the variable in which you are interested, and then introduce the experimental factor. After a specified time period, during which the experimental factor has presumably had its effect, you remeasure the variable in which you are interested. If there are any differences between the first and second measurements, you may assume that the experimental factor, plus any uncontrollable factors, is the cause.

Consider the following application. Assume you are conducting research for a retail store to determine the effect of point-of-sale advertising. Your first step is to select a product for the experiment. You choose Gillette razor blades. Second, you record sales of Gillette blades for one week, using no point-of-sale advertising. Then you introduce

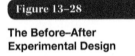

Figure 13–28

The Before–After Experimental Design

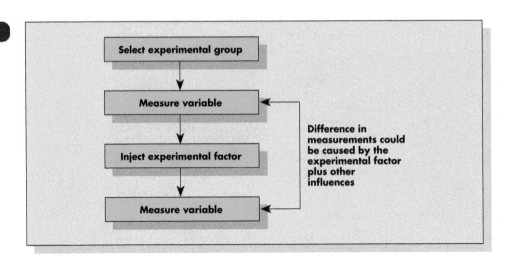

the experimental variable: the Gillette point-of-sale display. For the next week you again record sales of Gillette blades, and at the end of that week, you compare the results for the two weeks. Any increase in sales would presumably be explained by the introduction of the display. Thus, if 500 packages of Gillette blades were sold in the first week and 600 were sold in the second week, you would conclude that the 100 additional sales can be attributed to point-of-sale advertising.

You can probably recognize the major shortcoming of this research method: The experimental factor may not explain the entire difference in sales between the first week and the second. The sales of Gillette razor blades could have changed for a number of other reasons—e.g., changes in the weather, holiday or other seasonal influences on business activity, or advertising for other products. At best, you have determined only that point-of-sale advertising could influence sales.

The Controlled Before–After Design. To account for influences other than the experimental factors, you may use designs more complex than the before–after design. These designs attempt to measure the other influences by including some means of control. The simplest of these designs is the **controlled before–after design.**

In the controlled before–after design, you select not one group, but two: the experimental group and the control group. Before introducing the experimental factor, you measure the variable to be tested in each group. Then you introduce the experimental factor into the experimental group only. When the period allotted for the experiment is over, you again measure in each group the variable being tested. Any difference between the first and second measurements in the experimental group can be explained by two causes: the experimental factor and other influences. But the difference between the first and second measurements in the control group can be explained only by other influences because this group was not subjected to the experimental factor. Thus, comparing the "afters" of the two groups will give you a measure of the influence of the experimental factor (Figure 13–29).

In a controlled before–after experiment designed to test point-of-sale advertising, you might select Gillette razor blades and Schick razor blades and record the sales of both brands for one week. Next you introduce point-of-sale displays for Gillette only and you record sales for both Gillette and Schick for a second week. At the end of the second week, you compare the results for the two brands. Whatever difference you find in Gillette sales and Schick sales will be a fair measure of the experimental factor, independent of the changes that other influences may have brought about.

Figure 13–29

The Controlled Before–After Experimental Design

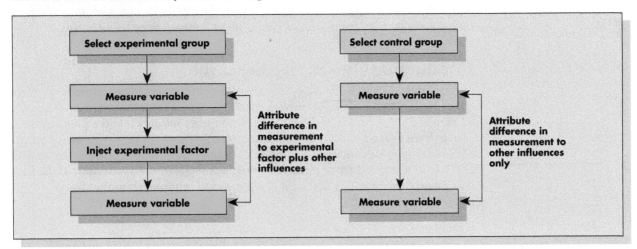

Using Observation

Like the experiment, **observation** is a technique perfected in the sciences that is also useful in business research. Simply stated, observation is seeing with a purpose. It consists of watching the events involved in a problem and systematically recording what you see. In observation, you do not manipulate the details of what you observe; you take note of situations exactly as you find them.

To see how observation works as a business technique, consider this situation. You work for a fast-food chain, such as McDonald's, that wants to check the quality and consistency of some menu items throughout the chain. By hiring observers, sometimes called mystery shoppers, you can gather information on the temperature, freshness, and speed of delivery of various menu items. This method may reveal important information that other data collection methods cannot.

The observation procedure can be any system that ensures the collection of complete and representative information. But every effective observation procedure includes a clear focus, well-defined steps, and provisions for ensuring the quality of the information collected. For example, an observation procedure for determining the courtesy of employees toward customers when answering the phone might include counting the number of times each employee used certain polite expressions, checking for the use of other courtesy techniques (e.g., offering further help), and recording how long it took for the employee to solve the customer's problem. In other words, you would have to identify observable courteous behaviors to be able to record them.

One particular observation technique that can be used in business research is **user testing.** User testing, also called **usability testing**, measures a person's experience when interacting with a product such as a document, a mobile device, a website, a piece of software, or any number of other consumer products.

In general, user testing measures how well users can learn and use a product and how satisfied they are with that process. When engaging in user testing, a researcher will measure the following factors:[10]

- Ease of learning.
- Efficiency of use.
- Memorability.
- Error frequency and severity.
- Subjective satisfaction.

There are many ways to perform a user test. The most common method is to select a small number of testers (5–15) representative of the people who would be using the product and have them perform a task. To set up a user test of a new tablet your company is developing, for example, you would create a situation (a scenario) in which a person performs a task using the product while observers watch and take notes. While the tester worked on this task, you would watch what he or she does to determine if the tester is having difficulty accomplishing the task or seems to like the device. After the testing session, you would administer a questionnaire to get feedback from the person as well.

Conducting Qualitative Research

As mentioned earlier in this chapter, qualitative researchers take a more interpretive approach to research. They begin with a more general question about what they want to learn and then study natural phenomena to gather insights into the phenomena or even to learn to ask different questions. Accordingly, they are likely to use such research tools as focus groups and personal interviews, and they will collect mostly verbal data. Qualitative research does not enable statistical analysis or the application of the findings to larger populations; rather, it enables you to interpret what the data mean at a more localized level.

---

[10]"Usability Basics," *Usability.gov*, U. S. Department of Health & Human Services, n.d., Web, 10 July 2012.

Whether you conduct a personal interview or convene a focus group, you need to decide how you will record the interactions. You cannot rely on your memory. Sometimes, simply taking notes is sufficient. Other times, you may want to videotape the session so that you can note nonverbal behaviors (e.g., tone, facial expressions, gestures) that influence the interpretation of a participant's response. Then transcribe the notes using a system for coding these nonverbal behaviors in the text of the transcript. You should always ask the participants for their permission to record focus groups or interviews.

Conducting Focus Groups. The purpose of a focus group is to bring together a group of people to find out their beliefs or attitudes about the topic of a research project. For instance, if you want to learn how one of your company's products could be improved, you might gather a group of people who currently use your product and have them discuss what they like or don't like about it.

As the moderator of the discussion, you can structure the conversation and ask questions that will elicit useful data from the participants, or you can simply allow participants to voice their ideas. As you may have experienced, when people discuss a topic in a group, they often generate more or better ideas than they would have working alone. The focus group thus becomes a sort of brainstorming session, which can yield rich data. Of course, as the moderator you also have to make sure that all participants can freely share their ideas. Some of the tips discussed in Chapters 11 and 15 for encouraging participation in writing projects and meetings may also help you facilitate focus groups. Because of advances in technology, focus groups can be conducted face to face, online with technologies like Skype, or even over the phone.

Conducting Personal Interviews. If you decide that talking with people one-on-one is the best way to gather data to answer your research question, you will likely conduct face-to-face interviews or phone interviews. People may be willing to share stories and opinions in a personal interview that they might not be comfortable sharing in a larger group.

Preparing for a personal interview is much like preparing for a survey. First, you need to decide whom to interview (your sample). Then you need to construct questions, as you would for a survey. However, the nature of the questions for a face-to-face interview will be a bit different. Researchers conducting surveys prefer to use **closed-ended questions**

Focus groups can help you learn not only what the target population prefers but why.

because these force the participants to give only one possible response (e.g., answering a yes/no question, choosing an age range from a list provided by the researcher, or selecting a rating on a scale) and allow for quick data analysis. However, when conducting interviews, many researchers favor **open-ended questions** because the conversational nature of the interview setting enables participants to provide detailed, rich, and varied responses. Furthermore, open-ended questions in personal interviews give researchers the opportunity to ask follow-up questions that they would not be able to ask participants taking a written survey.

LO14 Discuss important ethical guidelines for research.

CONDUCTING ETHICAL BUSINESS RESEARCH

Throughout the research process, you need to be sure you are conducting research in an ethical manner. In particular, you should adhere to guidelines for treating research participants ethically, and you should report your research accurately and honestly.

Treating Research Participants Ethically

Many companies, academic institutions, and medical facilities have guidelines for conducting research with human subjects and have institutional review boards (IRBs) that ensure employees comply with the laws and policies that govern research. Be sure that you are familiar with these policies before conducting research.

The main principle behind such policies is that participants in a research study have the right to informed consent. That is, they have the right to know the nature of their participation in the study and any associated risks. In addition, participation must be voluntary, and people have the right to discontinue their participation at any time during the study. Just because they agreed to participate at one point does not mean they are obligated to finish the project. Furthermore, participants need to know if their participation and the data associated with them in the study will be **confidential** (known only to the researcher and participant) or **anonymous** (known only to the participant). If protecting participants' rights will require you to develop a proposal to an IRB, an informed consent letter to the participants, and an informed consent form, be sure you build this process into the planning stage of your project.

Reporting Information Accurately and Honestly

When researching and writing business documents, do not ever lose sight of your main goal: to provide decision makers with reliable information. You will defeat this purpose if you misrepresent your findings.

As you interpret and present secondary information, assess its quality. Does the author draw conclusions that can be supported by the data presented? Are any sources used reliable? Are the data or interpretations biased in any way? Are there any gaps or holes in the data or interpretation? You need to be a good judge of the material, and if it has limitations, you should note them in your document.

Also, be sure to cite your sources. The whole point of including citations is to allow your readers to check your sources for themselves. Any mistakes in your citations may not only frustrate your readers but also make you look inept or dishonest. Be particularly careful to give credit where credit is due. **Plagiarism**, which is submitting another person's published work as your own without properly crediting it, is especially damaging to your credibility. Be sure to follow the guidelines in Appendix E for citing what you need to cite, and in the proper way.

As for primary research, once you have good data to work with, you must interpret them accurately and clearly for your reader. Here, too, you should acknowledge any limitations of your research. Be careful as well to avoid misleading visuals (see Chapter 14).

THERE'S MORE . . .

What are some expert resources on conducting an effective email sales campaign? What's the best way to find companies' annual reports? How do you conduct a research interview? Scan the QR code with your smartphone or use your Web browser to find out at www.mhhe.com/lesikar13e. Choose Chapter 13 > Bizcom Tools & Tips.

SUMMARY BY LEARNING OBJECTIVES

1. Business decisions are made using accurate, timely, and objective information.

   - To help make a business decision or solve a business problem, you may need to provide just information; both information and analysis; or information, analysis, and recommendations.

   - You may need to provide the information in the form of business reports, proposals, or shorter documents such as progress reports and email correspondence.

   - The information used to help make a business decision or solve a business problem is gathered through research.

   Explain why research is useful in business.

2. You can begin to collect information you need for a project by using two basic forms of research: secondary and primary.

   - Secondary research is the use of published information.

     — It is typically conducted before you engage in primary research.

     — To conduct skillful research, you need to understand how to find relevant print and online sources.

     — You should plan a system for storing the secondary information you gather.

   - Primary (or empirical) research is firsthand research. It can be quantitative, qualitative, or both. You can conduct primary research in four main ways:

     — Conducting a survey.

     — Conducting an experiment.

     — Recording observations.

     — Conducting qualitative research with focus groups or interviews.

   Explain the difference between secondary and primary research.

3. When doing firsthand research, you need to determine if you need quantitative data, qualitative data, or both types to solve the business problem at hand.

   - Quantitative researchers gather numerical data.

     — They generally begin by constructing a hypothesis to test or by developing a specific research question to answer.

     — They use primary research methods that generate numerical data, such as experimentation, questionnaires, reviews of company data, and surveys.

   - Qualitative researchers gather mostly verbal data.

     — They begin with a more general question about what they want to learn and then study natural phenomena to gather insights into the phenomena or even to learn to ask different questions.

     — They use research tools that generate verbal data, such as personal interviews and focus groups.

   Explain the difference between quantitative and qualitative research.

Use Internet search engines to gather existing information.	4. Internet search engines such as Google, Bing, Live Search, and Yahoo! can be used to search for secondary research sources. • You can use Google Scholar to search scholarly literature, which includes journals from academic publishers, conference papers, dissertations, academic books, and technical reports. • A good command of Boolean logic helps you extract the information you need quickly and accurately. Boolean logic uses three primary operators: AND, OR, and NOT. — The operator AND is a narrowing term. It instructs the computer to find only those citations with both terms. — The operator NOT instructs the computer to eliminate citations with a particular term. — The OR operator can be used to expand the search by adding variations or synonyms to the basic search term. • Metasearch tools allow you to enter the search terms once, run the search simultaneously with several individual search engines, and view a combined results page. • Specialized search engines are also useful. Examples of these are Yahoo!: People Search for finding people, Edgar for finding corporate information, FindLaw for gathering legal information, and Mediafinder for finding print items. • Personal agents allow users to define the kind of information they want to gather. The information gathered can be ready and waiting when users access their personal website, such as at my.yahoo.com or iGoogle, or it can be delivered by email or in the form of "push technology."
Use other Web resources to gather existing information.	5. Other useful Web-based research sources include Wikipedia, WorldCat, and RSS feeds. • Wikipedia can be a useful place to start to learn about a subject that is new to you. • WorldCat is an online network of library content and services. You can search the collections of both local libraries and libraries around the world for books, CDs, videos, and digital content such as ebooks. • RSS feeds on websites and blogs can be useful research tools as well. News outlets such as *The New York Times* and *CNN* offer these feeds on their websites. Scholarly journals also offer RSS feeds for their tables of contents. Subscribing to these will allow you to keep up to date on the research you are undertaking.
Evaluate websites for reliability.	6. Websites must be critically evaluated to ensure that the information is relevant and reliable. You should examine • The purpose of each site. • The qualifications of the information provider. • The validity of the content. • The site's structure and design.
Use social networking and social bookmarking sites to gather existing information.	7. Today's businesses take advantage of social media like Facebook, Twitter, and LinkedIn for marketing purposes, but such networks can also be useful for researching a business problem. • Because of its pervasiveness, Facebook is especially useful for surveys. You can also go to company Facebook pages to research company-specific information. • You can "follow" people or topics on Twitter if you have a Twitter account. To get more relevant information on your particular business problem, you should consider following certain hashtags. • To take full advantage of LinkedIn as a research tool, use the various Search options, particularly People, Companies, and Groups.

- Wikis—collaborative collections of knowledge—can help you can find information on almost any business topic.

- Many companies maintain blogs that can be a useful tool for finding information on a business problem.

- You can send a question about a business topic out to the membership of an organization's listserv to get feedback. You can also send out surveys on listservs.

- Social bookmarking sites allow people to organize, store, manage, search, and share their favorite Web resources.

8. You should also take advantage of your library's reference materials.

Use the library to gather existing information.

- Searching the library catalog gives you access to a library's holdings. You can locate sources by the standard Keyword, Title, Author, and Subject options as well as a few other options.

  — When you select the Keyword option, the system will search for only those exact words in several of each record's fields, missing all those records using slightly different wording.

  — When you select Subject, the system will scan the Library of Congress subject heading for your search term, and the search will find all those holdings on the subject, sometimes including those with related subject headings.

- Searching online databases gives you access to periodical literature such as articles published in newspapers, magazines, and journals.

  — *ABI/Inform* and *Business Source Premiere* are two of the most complete databases of business literature.

  — *Factiva* provides access to current business, general, and international news.

  — *LexisNexis* offers access to current business and international articles.

  — *LexisNexis® Company Dossier, Hoover's Online, Business & Company Resource Center, Business Source Complete,* and *D&B's Million Dollar Database* provide information on specific companies.

- Consulting reference materials can also be a useful way to find existing business research.

  — Encyclopedias offer background material and other general information.

  — Biographical directories supply biographical information about leading figures of today or of the past.

  — Almanacs offer factual and statistical information.

  — Trade directories compile details in specific areas of interest. They are variously referred to as catalogs, listings, registers, or source books.

  — Government publications include surveys, catalogs, pamphlets, and periodicals from various governmental bureaus, departments, and agencies.

  — Dictionaries are helpful for looking up meanings, spellings, and pronunciations of words or phrases.

  — Statistical sources provide a wide variety of statistical data.

  — Business information services supply specialized information to business practitioners.

  — International sources supply information on international corporations.

Use sampling to conduct a survey.

9. A sample is a group that is representative of the whole group. The procedure for selecting the group is called sampling. A good sample is controlled for sampling error. You may use any of a variety of sample designs. The two main types are probability and nonprobability sampling.

- Probability sampling is based on the principle that every member of a particular population of interest has an equal chance of being selected for a sample.

— Simple random sampling gives every member of the group under study an equal chance of being selected.

— Stratified random sampling involves proportionate and random selection from each major subgroup of the group under study.

— Systematic sampling involves taking selections at constant intervals (every fifth one, for example) from a complete list of the group under study.

— Area or cluster sampling involves dividing into parts the area that contains the sample, selecting from these parts randomly, and continuing to subdivide and select until you have your desired sample size.

- Nonprobability sampling is not random. In other words, there is no guarantee that each member of a population has the same chance of being selected for a sample group being studied.

— Convenience sampling involves selecting members who are convenient, easy to reach, and appropriate as judged by the researcher.

— Purposeful sampling requires that the people selected for the sample meet certain criteria or share a particular characteristic.

— Referral sampling involves building your sample from other participants' referrals.

10. When conducting a survey, you will need to construct a survey instrument or questionnaire.

Construct a questionnaire and conduct a survey.

- To ensure reliable and valid results, follow these guidelines:

— Avoid leading questions and questions with absolute terms (e.g., *always, never*).

— Focus on one concept per question (no double-barreled questions).

— Make the questions easy to understand (avoid vagueness, difficult words, and technical words).

— Avoid questions that touch on personal prejudices or pride.

— Ask only for what can be remembered (consider the laws of memory: recency, significance, and association).

- Plan the design and delivery of your survey with care.

— Don't forget to include the demographic questions you need.

— When possible, enable your respondents to check an answer (e.g., a range of years) rather than having to enter specific data.

— Consider using scaling (ranking or rating) in your questions to gather more specific information about respondents' attitudes.

— Put your questions in the order that will generate the most complete and accurate responses.

— Choose the survey channel that will yield the best sample and the best results at the lowest cost.

— Develop a survey plan that will include the logistics of delivering your survey and any additional materials you will need.

— Pilot test your survey so that you can catch any problems before you conduct the actual survey.

11. An experiment is an orderly form of testing. It can be designed using the before–after design or the controlled before–after design.

Conduct an experiment for a business problem.

- The simpler method is the before–after design. It involves selecting a group of subjects, measuring the variable, introducing the experimental factor, and measuring the variable again. The difference between the two measurements is assumed to be, at least partially, the result of the experimental factor.

- The controlled before–after design involves selecting two groups, measuring the variable in both groups, introducing the experimental factor in one group, and then measuring the variable again in both groups. The second measurement enables you to determine the effect of the experimental factor and of other factors that might have influenced the variable between the two measurements.

12. The observation method may be defined as seeing with a purpose.

   - It consists of watching events related to a problem and systematically recording what is seen. The events observed are not manipulated.

     > Design an observational study for a business problem.

   - One particular observation technique that can be used in business research is user testing. User testing measures a person's experience when interacting with a product such as a document, a mobile device, a website, a piece of software, or any number of other consumer products.

13. Qualitative researchers begin with a general question about what they want to learn and then study natural phenomena to gather insights into the phenomena or even to learn to ask different questions.

   > Explain the uses of focus groups and personal interviews.

   - Focus groups bring together a group of people to find out their beliefs or attitudes about the topic of a research project.
     - As the focus group moderator, make sure that all participants can freely share their ideas.
     - Consider using online technologies such as Skype.

   - Interviews encourage people to share stories and opinions that they might not be comfortable sharing in a larger group.
     - As with conducting a survey, you need to choose your respondents carefully and prepare the questions you will ask.
     - Interviewers tend to prefer open-ended questions because these can provide detailed, rich, and varied responses as well as the opportunity to ask follow-up questions.

14. Researchers must be ethical in their research. In particular, you should be aware of adhering to guidelines for treating participants in an ethical manner and reporting your results accurately and honestly.

   > Discuss important ethical guidelines for research.

   - Treat research participants ethically by following any company guidelines for conducting research with human subjects.
     - Be familiar with and follow any institutional guidelines for conducting research with human subjects.
     - Be sure that participants know of any risks the research presents, are participating voluntarily, and know whether their data will be anonymous or confidential.

   - Report the information you've reached accurately and honestly.
     - Do not lose sight of your main goal: to provide decision makers with reliable information.
     - As you interpret and present secondary information, assess its quality.
     - To avoid plagiarism, be sure to cite your sources and cite them accurately.
     - When using primary research, interpret data accurately and clearly for your reader.
     - Acknowledge any limitations of your research.
     - Avoid misleading graphics.

KEY TERMS

CRITICAL THINKING QUESTIONS

1 Which of the following are secondary research sources and which are primary research sources? Why? **LO2**

   a. Information from *The Wall Street Journal* about current foreclosure numbers.

   b. Information from a focus group with potential customers about a new online ordering system.

   c. Information about an industry's use of social media collected by following a hashtag on Twitter.

   d. Information about salaries collected from members of the listserv of a professional organization.

2 Explain the difference between quantitative and qualitative research. **LO3**

3 Develop two business scenarios, one in which a quantitative study would be more appropriate and one in which a qualitative study would be more appropriate. Be ready to defend your choices. **LO3**

4 Use Google, Bing, Yahoo! Search, Ask, and AOL Search to search a business-related topic. How do the results differ? Can you draw any conclusions about the different ways these search engines work? **LO4**

5 Visit a company's website and Facebook page. Compare the information. What does it tell you about the way the company is using each of these Internet forums? Who are the audiences? What types of information overlap? What types of information are unique to either the website or Facebook page? **LO5**

6 Use your critical skills to evaluate a website, identifying any problems you find (e.g., false advertising, misinformation, propaganda, scams). **LO6**

7 Follow a business-related topic on Twitter. What kinds of information can you find that might help solve a business problem? **LO7**

8 What specialized libraries are there in your community? What general libraries? **LO8**

9 Which databases or other sources would be good sources of information for each of the following subjects? **LO8**

   a. A certain company's market share.

   b. Viewpoints on the effect of deficit financing by governments.

   c. The top companies, by sales, in a certain industry.

   d. The job outlook in a certain industry.

   e. Recent trends in business-related technology.

   f. The potential world market for a certain product.

   g. The qualifications of a new CEO of a company.

10 Explain the difference between random sampling and convenience sampling. **LO9**

11 In what way is each of the following survey questions flawed? (The questions do not come from the same survey.) **LO10**

a. How many days on the average do you wear a pair of socks before changing them?

b. (The first question in a survey conducted by Coca-Cola:) Have you ever drunk a Diet Coke?

c. Do you consider the ideal pay plan to be one based on straight commission or straight salary?

d. What kind of gasoline did you purchase last time?

e. Do you think the management and employees affect your morale?

f. How much did you pay for clothing in the past 12 months?

g. Check the word below that best describes how often you eat dessert with your noon meal

Always

Usually

Sometimes

Never.

12 What is scaling? What is the difference between rating and ranking? **LO10**

13 Give an example of (*a*) a problem that can best be solved through a before–after design and (*b*) a problem that can best be solved through a controlled before–after design. Explain your choices. **LO11**

14 Explain the significance of keeping constant all factors other than the experimental variable of an experiment. **LO11**

15 Define *observation* as a research technique. **LO12**

16 Select an example of a business problem that can be solved best by observation. Explain your choice. **LO11**

17 When would you use a focus group or personal interview to gather information? What are the advantages and disadvantages of each? **LO13**

18 What are the basic ethical principles for working with human subjects in business research? Why are such guidelines important? **LO14**

19 Assume you are preparing a report to evaluate three possible sites for your company's next sales meeting. All three would work well, but you personally favor one location in particular. Is there any ethical way to sway the reader toward your choice? Discuss. **LO14**

SKILLS BUILDING EXERCISES

1 Visit a company website and evaluate it for completeness, accuracy, and reliability. What is the website's purpose? Are there biases? What are the qualifications of the organization providing the information on the website? Is the information accurate? Where else can this information be found? How is the website organized? Does it appeal to its intended audience? **LO6**

2 Using your critical thinking skills to supply any missing facts you may need, develop a survey for each of these problems. **LO10**

a. The American Restaurant Association wants information that will give its members a picture of its customers. The information will serve as a guide for a promotional campaign designed to increase restaurant eating. Specifically, it will seek such information as who eats out, how often, where they go, and how much they spend. Likewise, it will seek to determine who does not eat out and why.

b. The editor of your local newspaper wants to conduct a readership study to learn just who reads what in both print and online editions.

c. Your boss wants to hire an experienced computer webmaster for your company. Because you have not hired anyone in this category in five years, you were asked to survey experienced webmasters to gather salary figures.

d. A professional organization you belong to wants to find out how grammatical errors affect managers when they are evaluating the written work of their employees.

e. You work in the human resources department of a company. The director needs to make changes to the company's healthcare plan for the coming year and wants you to find out which of the three current plans employees are enrolled in and why they selected it.

3 Using your critical thinking skills to supply any missing facts you may need, develop a plan for the experiment you would use in the following situations. **LO11**

a. Golden Glow Baking Company has for many years manufactured and sold cookies packaged in attractive boxes. It is considering packaging the cookies in recyclable bags and wants to conduct an experiment to predict the likely consumer response to this change.

b. A national chain of drugstores wants to know whether using Quick Response (QR) codes could impact its profits on cosmetics. It is willing to pay the cost of an experiment in its research for an answer.

c. True Time Watch Company is considering the use of electronic sales displays ($49.50 each) instead of print displays ($24.50 each) in the 2,500 retail outlets that sell True Time watches. The company will conduct an experiment to determine the relative effects on sales of the two displays.

d. Marvel Soap Company has developed a new cleaning agent that is unlike current soaps and detergents. The product is well protected by patent. The company wants to determine the optimum price for the new product through experimentation.

e. National Cereals, Inc., wants to determine the effectiveness of advertising to the gluten-free market. The company will support an experiment to learn the answer.

4 Using your critical thinking skills to supply any missing facts you may need, develop a plan for research by observation for these problems. **LO12**

   a. The corporate sales managers for a chain of department stores want to know what causes differences in sales by departments within stores and by stores. They hope to get some of this information through research by observation.

   b. Your university wants to know the nature and extent of its parking problem.

   c. The management of an insurance company wants to determine the efficiency and productivity of its data-entry department.

   d. Owners of a shopping center want a study to determine the shopping patterns of their customers. They want information on such topics as what parts of town the customers come from, how they travel, and how many stores they visit.

e. The director of your library wants a detailed study of library use (what facilities are used, when, by whom, and so on).

f. The management of a restaurant wants a study of its workers' efficiency in the kitchen.

5 Using your critical thinking skills to supply any missing facts you may need, develop a plan for research by using focus groups for these problems. **LO13**

   a. Miller Brush Company, manufacturers of a line of household goods, has for years sold its products through conventional retail outlets. It now wants to examine the possibility of selling through print catalogs or online.

   b. The International Association of Publishers wants to gauge reader attitude toward ebooks.

   c. Sizemore Rental Car Company would like to add a line of hybrid cars for its business customers, but the CEO is not sure if customers would be willing to pay the higher rental price the company would have to charge.

6 Using your critical thinking skills to supply any missing facts you may need, develop a plan for research by using interviews for these problems. **LO13**

   a. Grow More Company sells children's clothes. The company has seen an increased rate of employee turnover this past year, and your supervisor wants you to find out why.

   b. Jacob's Hardware Store recently sent a survey out to get feedback on its customer service. The management would like to follow this up with some interviews to get a better sense of what happened on one particular Saturday that customers said they experienced very poor customer service.

CHAPTER FOURTEEN
Using Visuals to Make Your Point

Learning Objectives

Upon completing this chapter, you will be able to use visuals effectively in business reports. To reach this goal, you should be able to

1 Plan which parts of your report or other document should be communicated or supported by visuals.

2 Explain the factors that are important in the effective presentation of visuals: size, layout, type, rules and borders, color and cross-hatching, clip art, background, numbering, titles, title placement, and footnotes and acknowledgments.

3 Construct textual visuals such as tables, pull quotes, flowcharts, and process charts.

4 Construct and use visuals such as bar charts, pie charts, line charts, scatter diagrams, and maps.

5 Avoid common errors and ethical problems when constructing and using visuals.

6 Place and interpret visuals effectively.

Choosing the Right Visuals for Your Data and Your Audience

In your job as the sales manager for Green Living Industries, you are frequently called upon to gather sales data and market demographics. You share these data with your employees as well as your colleagues and corporate headquarters to support decisions that help achieve business goals.

In fact, you have just finished gathering data for a major report you will give orally and in writing to Green Living's upper management. These data include information on the makeup of your target markets, sales performance by division and geographic area, industry trends, and customer perceptions of your products. Although your primary audience is Green Living's upper management, you also know that these data will be used to inform decisions at various district offices and sales divisions. Essentially, you have a lot of information and several audiences who will use it. You need to think critically regarding how you will present this information so that your audiences quickly, clearly, and correctly understand what you are communicating.

In many of your reports and other business documents, you will need to use visuals to help convey information quickly and accurately. Visuals also grab attention and help the reader retain information. By **visuals** we mean any form of illustration (e.g., charts, pictures, diagrams, maps, tables, or bulleted lists). Although some situations call for decorative visuals, visuals in business tend to communicate data and information. Our focus is therefore on visuals that communicate.

PLANNING THE VISUALS

LO1 Plan which parts of your report or other document should be communicated or supported by visuals.

You should plan the visuals for a document soon after you organize your findings. Your planning for visuals should be guided largely by your communication purpose. Visuals can clarify complex or difficult information, emphasize facts, add coherence, summarize data, and provide interest. Of course, well-constructed visuals also enhance your document's appearance.

In selecting visuals, you should review the information that your document will contain, looking for any possibility of improving communication of the material through the use of visuals. Specifically, you should look for complex information that visual presentation can make clear, for information too detailed to be covered in words, and for information that deserves special emphasis.

Of course, you want to plan with your reader in mind and choose visuals appropriate to both the content and context where they are presented. You should construct visuals to help the intended reader understand the information more quickly, easily, and completely.

As you plan the visuals, remember that some visuals can stand alone, but others will supplement the writing or speaking—not take its place. Visuals in documents or oral reports should support your words by covering the more difficult parts, emphasizing the important points, and presenting details; however, the words should carry the main message.

DETERMINING THE GENERAL MECHANICS OF CONSTRUCTION

LO2 Explain the factors that are important in the effective presentation of visuals: size, layout, type, rules and borders, color and cross-hatching, clip art, background, numbering, titles, title placement, and footnotes and acknowledgments.

In constructing visuals, you will make decisions regarding the various conventions for presenting them to business audiences. The most common conventions are summarized in the following paragraphs.

Size

One of the first steps you must take to construct a visual is determining its **size**. The size of a visual is determined by its contents and importance. If a visual is simple (with only two or three quantities), a quarter page might be enough. But if a visual must display complex or detailed information, a full page might be justified.

With extremely complex, involved information, you may need to use more than a full page. When you do, make certain that this large page is inserted and folded so that the readers can open it easily. You may also consider including large or complex visuals in an appendix or attachment.

Orientation

You should determine the **orientation** of the visual by considering its size and contents. Sometimes a tall orientation (portrait) is the answer; sometimes the answer is a wide orientation (landscape). Simply consider the logical possibilities and select the one that is most easily read.

Type

The type used in visuals throughout a report should generally be consistent in terms of **style and font** (see Chapter 7, page 146, "Choosing the Right Font"). Style refers to the look of the type such as bold or italics; font refers to the look of the letters, such as those with or without feet (*serif* or *sans serif*, respectively). Be aware that even the design of the font you choose will convey a message, a message that should work with the text content and design.

Type size is another variable to watch. The size you choose should look appropriate in the context in which it is used. Your top priority when choosing type style, font, and size should always be readability.

Rules and Borders

You should use **rules (lines) and borders** when they improve the readability of the visual. Rules help distinguish one section or visual from another, while borders help separate visuals from the text. Keep in mind that rules can add clutter, so be sure to use

"This is where we added high-caffeine cappuccino in our office coffee machines."

Figure 14–1

Color versus Cross-Hatched Pie

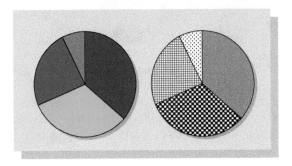

them only when they will enhance the audience's understanding of your visual. And when using borders, be sure to place borders around visuals that occupy less than a full page. You also can place borders around full-page visuals, but such borders serve mostly a decorative function. Except in cases in which visuals simply will not fit into the normal page layout, you should not extend the borders of visuals beyond the normal page margins.

Color and Cross-Hatching

Color and cross-hatching, appropriately used, help readers see comparisons and distinctions (see Figure 14–1). In fact, research has found that color in visuals improves the comprehension, retention, and ease of extracting information. Also, color and cross-hatching can add to the attractiveness of the report. Because color is especially effective for this purpose, you should use it whenever practical and appropriate.

Clip Art

Today you can get good-looking clip art easily—so easily, in fact, that some writers often overuse it. Although clip art can add interest and bring the reader into a visual effectively, it also can overpower and distract the reader. The general rule is to keep in mind the purpose your clip art is serving: to help the reader understand the content. It should be appropriate in both its nature and size; and it should be appropriate in its representation of gender, race, and age. Also, if the clip art is copyrighted, you may need permission to use it.

Background

Background colors, photos, and art for your visuals should be chosen carefully. The color should provide **high contrast** with the data and not distract from the main message. As with any photos or art, backgrounds should create a positive, professional impression. Additionally, when visuals are used cross-culturally, you will want to be sure the message your background sends is the one you intended by testing or reviewing it with your audience.

Numbering

Pull quotes, clip art, and other decorative visuals do not need to be numbered. Neither does a lone table or figure in a document. Otherwise, you should number all the visuals. Many schemes of numbering are available to you, depending on the types of visuals you have.

If you have many visuals that fall into two or three categories, you may number each of the categories consecutively. For example, if your document is illustrated by six tables, five charts, and six maps, you may number these visuals Table I, Table II, . . . Table VI; Chart 1, Chart 2, . . . Chart 5; and Map 1, Map 2, . . . Map 6.

However, if your visuals comprise a wide mixture of types, you may number them in two groups: tables and figures. Figures, a miscellaneous grouping, include all types

Infographics: Everything Old Is New Again

According to the folks at Visual.ly, the infographic has been around since humans used cave drawings. Even Florence Nightingale used an infographic (the Coxcomb chart) during the Crimean War to categorize diseases and causes of death. So while the infographic is nothing new, what is new is its popularity as a data visualization tool.

Though Visual.ly acknowledges that infographics serve much the same purpose as other visuals, infographics differ from other visuals in that they (1) "have a flow to them" that makes complex data more accessible to the reader, (2) present data so that the reader can engage with the story the data tell, and (3) are aesthetically engaging illustrations of data stories.

If you search the Internet for tools to create infographics, you'll find several at your disposal. You'll also see you can create beautiful data visualizations on widely varying topics—everything from survey results to résumés. The visual to the right illustrates how data regarding social media and Olympic viewers were captured clearly and concisely in an infographic. Should you incorporate infographics in your business writing or presentations? Like any type of visual, an infographic is only effective if it can tell a story more clearly than text alone. You'll also want to keep in mind that some infographics can look informal or cartoonish. As in any business communication, you must analyze your audience, communication goals, and context to know if an infographic is appropriate.

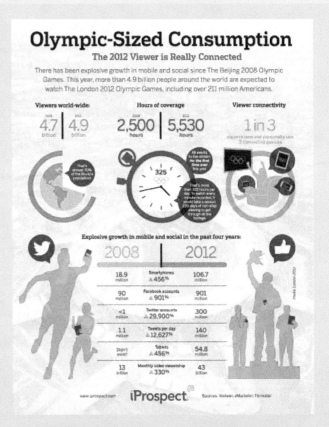

SOURCES: "History of infographics," *Visual.ly*, Visually, Inc., 2011, Web, 12 July 2012; "infographics Olympic-Sized Consumption," *Real Clear Technology*, Real Clear Technology, 12 July 2012, Web, 12 July 2012; "What Is an infographic?," *Visual.ly*, Visually, Inc., 2011, Web, 12 July 2012. Reprinted with permission of iProspect.

---

other than tables. To illustrate, consider a report containing three tables, two maps, three charts, one diagram, and one photograph. You would number these visuals Table I, Table II, and Table III and Figure 1, Figure 2, . . . Figure 7. Whatever your numbering scheme, remember that tables are numbered separately from other types of visuals.

Construction of Titles and Captions

The **title** is the name you give your visual; a **caption** is a brief description of the visual. All visuals generally have titles; captions may be used if the reader will need them to interpret or better understand the visual. Like the headings used in other parts of the report, the title or caption of the visual has the objective of concisely covering the contents. As a check of content coverage, you might well use the journalist's **five Ws:** *who, what, where, when,* and *why.* Sometimes you also might use *how.* But because conciseness is also important, it is not always necessary to include all the Ws in the title. For example, the title of a chart comparing the annual sales volume of the Texas and California territories of the Dell Company for the years 2010–2012 might be constructed as follows:

Who: Dell Company
What: Annual sales
Where: Texas and California branches
When: 2010–12
Why: For comparison

The title might read, "Comparative Annual Sales of Texas and California Territories of the Dell Company, 2010–12." For even more conciseness, you could use a major title and subtitle. The major title might read, "A Texas and California Sales Comparison"; the subtitle might read, "Dell Company 2010–12." Similarly, the caption might read "A Texas and California Sales Comparison: Dell Company 2010–12."

An alternative to this kind of topic heading is a talking heading. As you learned in Chapter 11, the talking heading tells the reader not only what topic will follow but also what the point of that topic is. The same holds true for a visual. In this case a talking heading might read, "Texas Leads California in Total Annual Sales for 2012." In a sense, it gives the reader the main message of the visual.

Placement of Titles and Captions

Titles are placed above tables, but they may be placed either above or below other visuals. However, most software programs automatically place titles at the top. Captions, on the other hand, are generally placed below tables and other visuals. When typing titles and captions, use **title case** (the kind of capitalization used for book titles). For long captions, you may opt to use sentence case (capitalization of the first word and any proper nouns).

Footnotes and Acknowledgments

Parts of a visual sometimes require special explanation or elaboration. When this happens, you should use **footnotes**. These footnotes are concise explanations placed below the illustration by means of a superscript (raised) number or symbol (asterisk, dagger, double dagger, and so on) (see Figure 14-2). Footnotes are placed immediately below a visual with no caption. If a visual contains a caption, the footnote is placed below the caption.

Figure 14-2

Good Arrangement of the Parts of a Typical Table

Table number and title → **Table I—U.S. Internet User Penetration by Race/Ethnicity 2008–2014 (% of population in each group)**							
Spanner heads → / *Column heads →*	**Actual**			**Projected**			
	2008	2009	2010	2011	2012	2013	2014
Non-Hispanic							
White alone	72.0%	74.0%	76.1%	77.5%	79.0%	80.1%	81.2%
Black alone	58.2%	60.5%	63.8%	66.9%	69.6%	71.7%	72.3%
Asian alone	70.0%	71.2%	73.4%	75.5%	77.5%	79.5%	81.0%
Other*	46.4%	50.0%	52.5%	55.0%	58.0%	62.0%	65.5%
Hispanic**	53.5%	56.5%	59.5%	62.9%	65.0%	67.6%	70.0%

Row heads bracket the row label column.

Footnote → *Includes native Americans, Alaska natives, Hawaiian and Pacific Islanders, and bi- and multiracial individuals.

**Could be of any race.

Source acknowledgment → SOURCE: Reprinted with permission of eMarketer.

SOURCE: "U.S. Internet User Penetration by Race/Ethnicity 2008–2014," *eMarketer Digital Intelligence*, eMarketer, Inc., March 2011, Web, 4 June 2012. Reprinted with permission of eMarketer, Inc.

Usually, a **source acknowledgment** is the bottom-most component of a visual. By *source acknowledgment* we mean a reference to the body or authority that deserves the credit for gathering the data used in the illustration. The entry consists of the word *Source* followed by a colon and the source information (in some cases, simply the source name will suffice). See Figure 14–2 for an illustration of source acknowledgment.

If you or your staff collected the data, you may either omit the source note or give the source as "Primary," in which case the note would read like this:

Source: Primary.

CONSTRUCTING TEXTUAL VISUALS

LO3 Construct textual visuals such as tables, pull quotes, flowcharts, and process charts.

Visuals for communicating report information fall into two general categories: those that communicate primarily through **textual content** (words and numerals) and those that communicate primarily through visual elements (charts and graphs). Included in the textual group are pull quotes and a variety of process charts (e.g., Gantt, flow, organization).

Tables

A *table* is an orderly arrangement of information in rows and columns. As we have noted, tables are textual visuals (not really pictures), but they communicate like visuals, and they have many of the characteristics of visuals.

Aside from the title, footnotes, and source designation previously discussed, a table contains heads, columns, and rows of data, as shown in Figure 14–2. Row heads are the titles of the rows of data, and column heads are the titles of the columns.

The construction of text tables is largely influenced by their purpose. Nevertheless, a few rules generally apply:

- If rows are long, the row heads may be repeated at the right.

- The em dash (—) or the abbreviation *n.a.* (or *N.A.* or *NA*), but not the zero, is used to indicate data not available.

- Since footnote numbers in a table full of numbers might be confusing, footnote references to numbers in the table should be keyed with asterisks (*), daggers (†), double daggers (‡), section marks ($), and so on. Small letters of the alphabet can be used when many references are made.

- Totals and subtotals should appear whenever they help readers interpret the table. The totals may be for each column and sometimes for each row. Row totals are usually placed at the right, but when they need emphasis, they may be placed at the left. Likewise, column totals are generally placed at the bottom of the column, but they may be placed at the top when the writer wants to emphasize them. A ruled line (usually a double one) separates the totals from their components.

- The units in which the data are recorded must be clear. Unit descriptions (e.g., bushels, acres, pounds, dollars, or percentages) appear above the columns, as part of the headings or subheadings. If the data are in dollars, however, placing the dollar mark ($) before the first entry in each column can be sufficient.

Tabular information need not always be presented in formal tables. In fact, short arrangements of data may be presented more effectively as parts of the text. Such arrangements are generally made as either leaderwork or text tabulations.

Leaderwork is the presentation of tabular material in the text without titles or rules. (*Leaders* are the repeated dots with intervening spaces.) Typically, a colon precedes the tabulation, as in this illustration:

The August sales of the representatives in the Western Region were as follows:

Charles B. Brown $33,517
Thelma Capp 39,703
Bill E. Knauth 38,198

Text tabulations are simple tables, usually with column heads and sometimes with rules and borders. But they are not numbered, and they have no titles. They are made to read with the text, as in this example:

In August the sales of the representatives in the Western Region increased sharply from those for the preceding month, as these figures show:

Representative	July Sales	August Sales	Increase
Charles B. Brown	$ 32,819	$33,517	$ 698
Thelma Capp	37,225	39,703	2,478
Bill E. Knauth	36,838	38,198	1,360

Pull Quotes

The **pull quote** is a textual visual that is often overlooked yet extremely useful for emphasizing key points. It is also useful when the text or content of the report does not lend itself naturally or easily to other visuals. By selecting a key sentence, copying it to a text box, enlarging it, and perhaps even enhancing it with a new font, style, or color, a writer can break up the visual boredom of a full page or screen of text. Software lets users easily wrap text around shapes as well as along curves and irregular lines. Figure 14–3 shows an example that is simple yet effective in both drawing the reader's attention to a key point and adding visual interest to a page.

Figure 14–3

Illustration of a Pull Quote

COVER STORY

It's a tragic tale — but not completely accurate, according to some tech-employment experts. The situation is more nuanced than what can be captured in a headline, and both workers and employers share responsibility for the gap, they say.

Most portentous, though, is that the gap, whatever its true nature, is rapidly becoming a yawning chasm — one that IT employees will have to cross sooner rather than later. Many hiring experts, IT managers and CIOs believe that the tech employment landscape will be radically different five years from now as more and more companies outsource IT operations to service providers, perhaps offshore, or move traditional IT jobs to other business units.

In the face of such rapid change, it's becoming clear that the one skill every member of the IT workforce needs is career management.

"Everybody is a free agent, navigating the corporate chaos," says Todd Weinman, president of The Weinman Group, an executive search firm headquartered in Oakland, Calif., that specializes in audit and corporate governance. In the IT job market, he says, "the people who are faring a little bit better are constantly cultivating their careers on a variety of fronts."

Tech employees log long hours, meaning they get a lot of hands-on experience, but they're not getting the training and other types of enrichment they need to develop their careers. "In addition to your 50-plus hours a week, you need in-depth coursework to refresh your skills, plus studying to sit for certifications," says Weinman. At many companies, employees used to be able to take time for those types of pursuits during the workday, but not anymore.

"Those who want to stay relevant have to work very hard" — at work and during off-hours, says Weinman, who is a member of the ISACA Leadership Development Committee. ISACA is an IT professional association that, among other things, provides security certifications.

services, concurs. "In today's marketplace, if you have good references and a strong technical skill set and can communicate how you'll provide ROI, four jobs will be waiting for you," he says.

What amazes, and to some degree frustrates, Cullen are those instances when clients choose not to hire a job applicant because they can't check every box on their wish lists. "We're seeing this huge pent-up demand, and the pool of labor isn't growing. And yet, what's perplexing is just how specific hiring managers still are," he says. "They want this skill, that particular work on the network side, certifications, this many years of experience. Companies are not willing to take a risk. Nobody's jumping out the window to hire the average employee."

Weinman blames the Great Recession for starting IT down the path that led to the skills gap, while cautioning that an improved economy won't much ease the crunch for many workers.

"Companies are getting leaner and leaner. Starting in 2008, they downsized and streamlined, and they haven't replaced those positions," he observes. "If you're the hiring director of one of these very lean teams, you want only A+ workers. In the past, someone could get away with being a solid middle-of-the-road employee. Not anymore."

> **Companies are not willing to take a risk. Nobody's jumping out the window to hire the average employee.**
> JACK CULLEN, PRESIDENT, MODIS

Charles Williams sees the situation from both sides. As manager of data systems at Georgia System Operations, an electric utility in Tucker, Ga., he wants and expects the people who report to him (currently there are seven) to keep their skills up to date. At the same time, he acknowledges that he is challenged to keep his own knowledge fresh when day-to-day duties take priority over opportunities to investigate up-and-coming technologies.

"In a way, it's natural for a manager to develop a technical skills gap. We're not able to sit down and play with things the way our employees might," he says. And that worries him. "I feel like I need

Bulleted Lists

Bulleted lists are listings of points arranged with bullets (•) to set them off. These lists can have a title that covers all the points, or they can appear without titles, as they appear in various places in this book. When you use this arrangement, make the points grammatically parallel. (See Chapters 4 and 18 for a description and examples of parallelism.) If the points have subparts, use **sub-bullets** for them. Make the sub-bullets different by color, size, shape, or weight. Darts, check marks, squares, or triangles can be used for the secondary bullets.

Flowcharts and Process Charts

Business professionals use a variety of specialized charts in their work. Often these charts are a part of the information presented in reports. Perhaps the most common of these is the **organization chart** (see Figure 14–4). This type of chart shows the hierarchy of levels and positions in an organization. A **flowchart** (see Figure 14–5), as the word implies, shows the sequence of activities in a process. Flowcharts use specific designs and symbols to show process paths. A variation of the organization and flowchart is the **decision tree**. This chart helps one follow a path to an appropriate decision. **Gantt charts** are visual presentations that show planning and scheduling activities (see Figure 14–6). You can easily construct these charts in a variety of applications.

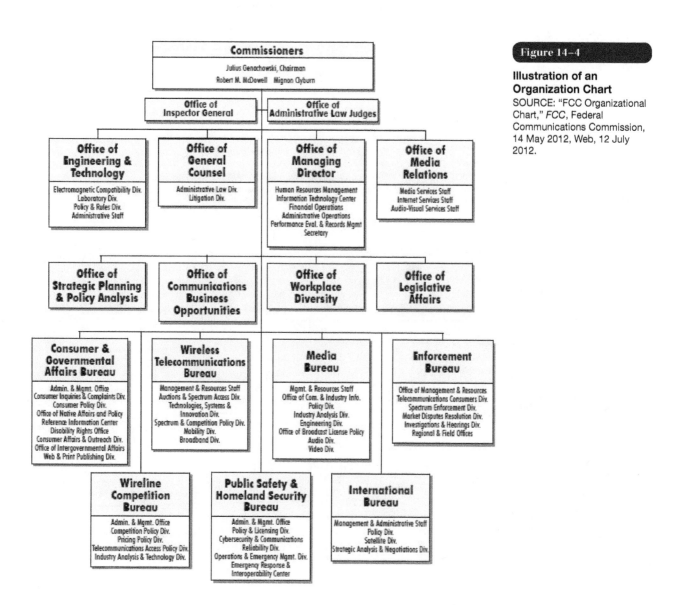

Figure 14–4

Illustration of an Organization Chart
SOURCE: "FCC Organizational Chart," *FCC*, Federal Communications Commission, 14 May 2012, Web, 12 July 2012.

Figure 14–5

Illustration of a Flowchart

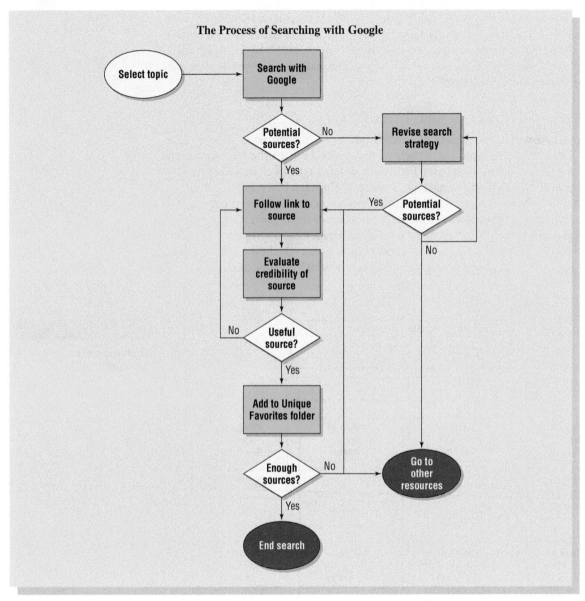

The Process of Searching with Google

SOURCE: Primary.

Figure 14–6

Illustration of a Gantt Chart

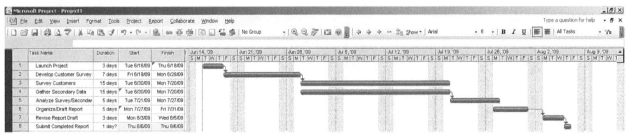

SOURCE: Primary.

CONSTRUCTING CHARTS, GRAPHS, AND OTHER VISUALS

LO4 Construct and use visuals such as bar charts, pie charts, line charts, scatter diagrams, and maps.

Visuals built with raw data include bar, pie, and line charts and all their variations and combinations. Illustrations include maps, diagrams, drawings, photos, and cartoons.

Bar and Column Charts

Simple bar and **column charts** compare differences in quantities using differences in the lengths of the bars to represent those quantities. You should use them primarily to **show comparisons** of qualities at a moment in time.

As shown in Figure 14–7, the main parts of the bar chart are the bars and the grid (the field on which the bars are placed). The bars, which may be arranged horizontally or vertically (then called a column chart), should be of equal width. You should identify each bar or column, usually with a caption at the left or bottom. The grid (field) on which the bars are placed is usually needed to show the magnitudes of the bars, and the units (e.g., dollars, pounds, miles) are identified by the scale caption below. It is often a good idea to include the numerical value represented by each bar for easy and precise comprehension, as shown in Figures 14–7 and 14–8.

When you need to compare quantities of two or three different values in one chart, you can use a **clustered** (or **multiple**) **bar chart**. Cross-hatching, colors, or other formatting on the bars distinguish the different kinds of information (see Figure 14–8). Somewhere within the chart, a **legend** (explanation) explains what the different bars mean. Because clustered bar charts can become cluttered, you should usually limit comparisons to three to five kinds of information in one of them.

When you need to show plus and minus differences, you can use **bilateral column charts**. The columns of these charts begin at a central point of reference and may go either up or down, as illustrated in Figure 14–9. Bar titles appear either within, above, or below the bars, depending on which placement works best. Bilateral column charts are especially good for showing percentage changes, but you may use them for any series that includes plus and minus quantities.

If you need to compare subdivisions of columns, you can use a **stacked (subdivided) column chart**. As shown in Figure 14–10, such a chart divides each column into its parts. It distinguishes these parts with color, cross-hatching, or other formatting; and it explains these differences in a legend. Subdivided columns may be difficult for your reader to interpret since both the beginning and ending points need to be found.

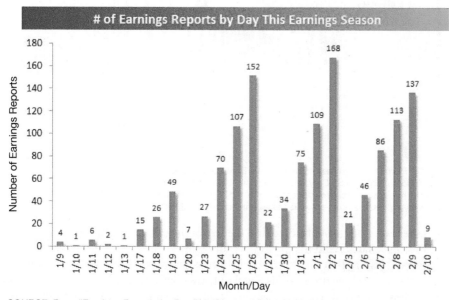

Figure 14–7

Illustration of a Bar Chart

SOURCE: From "Earnings Reports by Day This Season," *Think B.I.G,* Bespoke Investment Group, 9 Jan. 2012, Web, 12 July 2012. http://www.bespokeinvest.com/thinkbig/2012/1/9/earnings-reports-by-day-this-season.html.

Figure 14–8

Illustration of a Clustered Bar Chart

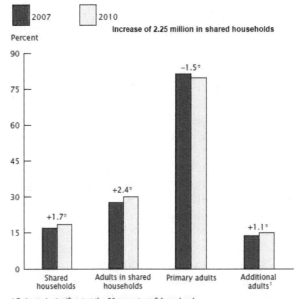

Percentage of Shared Households, All Adults in Shared Households, and Additional Adults[1]: 2007 and 2010

SOURCE: From "The Making of a Housing Market," *ZeroHedge*, ZeroHedge.com/ABC Media LTD., 13 July 2012, Web, 13 July 2012. http://www.zerohedge.com/contributed/2012-07-13/making-housing-market-%E2%80%93-hollywood-set-housing-inventory-looks-be-low-only-bec. Reprinted with permission.

Figure 14–9

Illustration of a Bilateral Column Chart

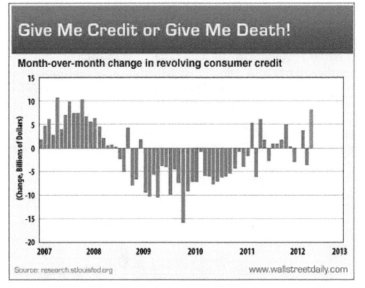

SOURCE: From Louis Basenese, "Friday Charts: Beer, Earnings, Recessions and Peak Oil Nonsense," *Wall St.* Daily, Wall Street Daily, LLC, 13 July 2012, Web, 13 July 2012. https://www.wallstreetdaily.com/2012/07/13/friday-charts-beer-earnings-recessions-and-peak-oil-nonsense/ Reprinted with permission of Wall Street Daily.

Then the reader has to subtract to find the size of the column component. Clustered bar charts or pie charts avoid this possibility for error.

Another feature that can lead to reader error in interpreting bar and column chart data is the use of three dimensions when only two variables are being compared. Therefore, unless more than two variables are used, choosing the two-dimensional presentation over the three-dimensional form is usually better. Figure 14–20 illustrates the appropriate use of a three-dimensional visual to compare three dimensions.

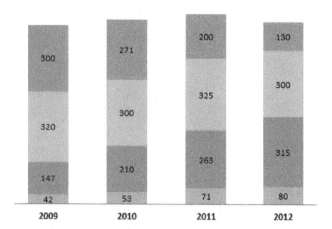

Number of Business Students Enrolled in Career Services' Professional Development Program 2009–2012

■ Freshman ■ Sophomore ■ Junior ■ Senior

Figure 14–10

Illustration of a Stacked Column Chart
SOURCE: Primary.

Figure 14–11

Illustration of a 100 Percent Stacked Column Chart

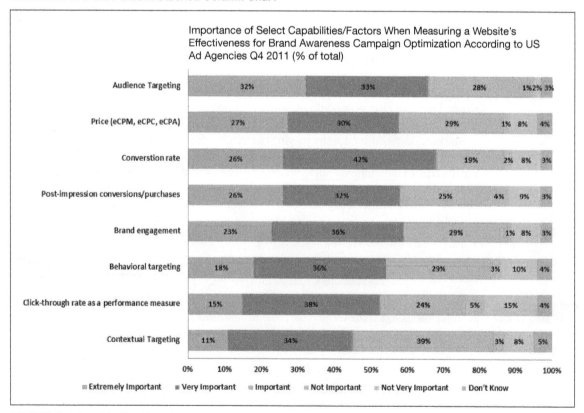

Importance of Select Capabilities/Factors When Measuring a Website's Effectiveness for Brand Awareness Campaign Optimization According to US Ad Agencies Q4 2011 (% of total)

SOURCE: Data from Maxifier, "Optimization Research," February 14, 2012. Reprinted with permission of eMarketer, Inc.

A special form of stacked (subdivided) column chart is used to compare the subdivisions of percentages. In this form, all the bars are equal in length because each represents 100 percent. Only the subdivisions within the bars vary. The objective of this form is to compare differences in how wholes are divided. The component parts may be labeled, as in Figure 14–11, or explained in a legend.

Figure 14–12

Illustration of a Pictograph
SOURCE: D. Morris,
"Sotomayor Approved for High
Court," *The Washington Post*,
The Washington Post
Company, 7 Aug. 2009, Web,
4 June 2012. Reprinted with
permission of AP Images.

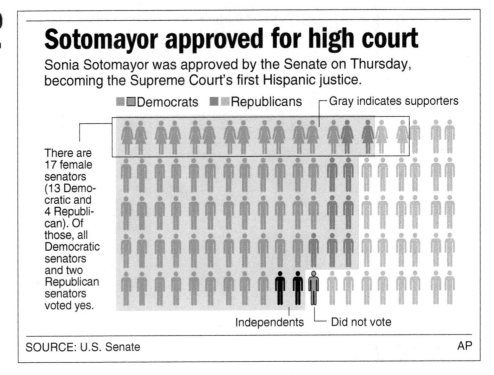

Sotomayor approved for high court

Sonia Sotomayor was approved by the Senate on Thursday,
becoming the Supreme Court's first Hispanic justice.

SOURCE: U.S. Senate   AP

Pictographs

A **pictograph** is a bar or column chart that uses bars made of pictures. The pictures are
typically drawings of the items being compared. For example, the number of senators
in Figure 14–12 is represented by the image of a single person for each senator instead
of by ordinary bars.

In constructing a pictograph, you should follow the procedures you used in constructing
bar and column charts. In addition, you must make all the picture units equal in size. The
human eye cannot accurately compare geometric designs that vary in more than one dimension, so show differences by varying the number, not the size, of the picture units. Also,
be sure you select pictures or symbols that fit the information to be illustrated. In comparing the cruise lines of the world, for example, you might use ships. In comparing computers
used in the world's major countries, you might use computers. The meaning of the drawings
you use must be immediately clear to the readers.

Pie Charts

The most frequently used chart in comparing the subdivisions of wholes is the **pie chart**
(see Figure 14–13). As the name implies, pie charts show the whole of the information

Figure 14–13

Illustration of a Pie Chart

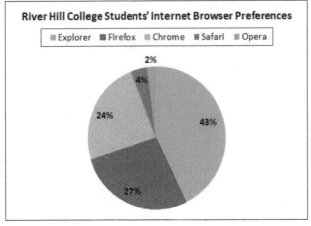

SOURCE: Primary.

being studied as a pie (circle) and the parts of this whole as slices of the pie. The slices may be distinguished by labeling and color or cross-hatching. A single slice can be emphasized by pulling it out from the pie or enlarging it. Because it is hard to judge the values of the slices with the naked eye, it is good to include the percentage values within or near each slice. Also, placing a label near each slice lets the reader more quickly understand the items being compared than using a legend to identify components. A good rule to follow for ordering the pieces of the pie is to begin by slicing the largest piece at the 12 o'clock position and then ordering the pieces largest to smallest; however, you should order the pieces in the way that will make the most visual sense to your audience.

Line Charts

Line charts are useful for showing changes of information over time. For example, changes in prices, sales totals, employment, or production over a period of years can be shown well in a line chart.

In constructing a line chart, draw the information to be illustrated as a continuous line on a grid that is scaled to show time changes from left to right (the X-axis) and quantity changes from bottom to top (the Y-axis). You should clearly mark the scale values and the time periods. They should be in equal increments.

You also may compare two or more series on the same line chart (see Figure 14–14). In such a comparison, you should clearly distinguish the lines by color or form (e.g., dots, dashes, dots and dashes). You should also label them on the chart or by a legend somewhere in the chart. But the number of series that you can effectively compare on one line chart is limited. As a practical guide, the maximum number is around five.

It is also possible to show parts of a series using an **area** chart. Such a chart, though, can show only one series. You should construct this type of chart, as shown in Figure 14–15, with a top line representing the total of the series. Then, starting from the base, you should cumulate the parts, beginning with the largest and ending with the smallest or beginning with the smallest and ending with the largest. You may use cross-hatching or coloring to distinguish the parts.

Line charts that show a range of data for particular times are called *variance* or *hi-lo* charts. Some variance charts show high and low points as well as the mean, median, or mode. When used to chart daily stock prices, they typically include closing price in addition to the high and low. When you use points other than high and low, be sure to make it clear what these points are.

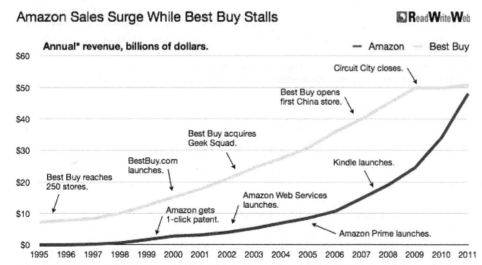

Amazon Sales Surge While Best Buy Stalls

ReadWriteWeb

*This isn't an exact, apples-to-apples comparison: Best Buy's fiscal year ends near February of the following year. For simplicity's sake, BBY's annual revenue is shown as the year in which *most* of it was reported. For example, BBY's "2011" revenue really represents the 12 months ending March 3, 2012. It's close enough for our purposes.

Figure 14–14

Illustration of a Line Chart
SOURCE: From Dan Frommer, "Amazon vs. Best Buy: A Tale of Two Retailers," *ReadWriteWeb*, SAY Media, Inc., 18 Apr. 2012, Web, 12 July 2012. http://www.readwriteweb.com/archives/amazon_vs_best_buy_a_tale_of_two_retailers.php

Figure 14–15

Illustration of an Area Chart

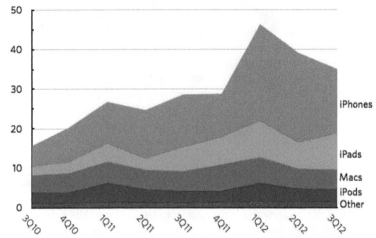

Apple Revenue Sources

$Billions

SOURCE: Jacqui Chen, "Apple CEO Tim Cook: Rumors Are a 'Great Thing about This Country,'" *Ars Technica: Infinite Loop/The Apple Ecosystem,* Condé Nast, 24 July 2012, Web, 25 July 2012.

Figure 14–16

Illustration of a Scatter Diagram

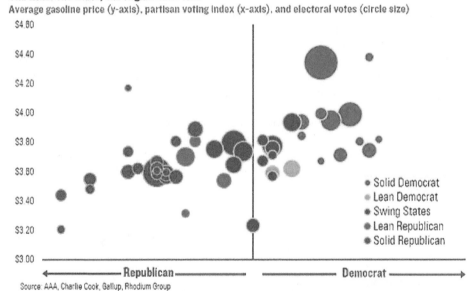

The Bluer the State, the Higher the Price

Average gasoline price (y-axis), partisan voting index (x-axis), and electoral votes (circle size)

Source: AAA, Charlie Cook, Gallup, Rhodium Group

SOURCE: From Trevor Houser, "Gasoline Prices and Electoral Politics in the Age of Unconventional Oil," *Notes,* Rhodium Group, LLC, 7 Mar. 2012, Web, 15 July 2012. Reprinted with permission.

Scatter Diagrams

Scatter diagrams are often considered another variation of the line chart. Although they do use X- and Y-axes to plot paired values, the points stand alone without a line drawn through them. For example, a writer might use a scatter diagram in a report on digital cameras to plot values for price and resolution of several cameras. While clustering the points allows users to validate hunches about cause and effect, they can only be interpreted for correlation—the direction and strength relationships. The points can reveal positive, negative, or no relationships. Additionally, by examining the tightness of the points, the user can see the strength of the relationship. The closer the points are to a straight line, the stronger the relationship. In Figure 14–16, the paired values are gas prices and political party affiliation.

Employed Down the Middle
Rural unemployment in January divides the nation

Figure 14–17

Illustration of a Map (Quantitative)
SOURCE: "International, U.S. and Local Economic Indicators for May 2012," *Scott Financial Group*, Scott Financial Group, 29 Apr. 2012, Web, July 12, 2012. http://www.samuelscottfg.com/domestic-and-international-economic-indicators-for-may-2012

Unemployment in rural and exurban counties in January 2012
National rate was 8.8%; rate in rural counties was 9.1%
(Blank areas above are metro regions.)

Low Unemployment. 6% or below (531 counties)

Below Average. 6.1% to 8.8% (824 counties)

Above Average. 8.9% to 10.9% (613 counties)

High Unemployment. Above 11% (590 counties)

Maps

You also may use maps to communicate quantitative as well as physical (or geographic) information. **Statistical maps** are useful primarily when quantitative information is to be compared by geographic areas. On such maps, the geographic areas are clearly outlined, and formatting techniques are used to show the differences between areas (see Figure 14–17). Statistical maps are particularly useful in illustrating and analyzing complex data. **Physical or geographic** maps (see Figure 14–18) can show **distributions**

Figure 14–18

Illustration of a Map (Physical)

SOURCE: "Google Maps," *Google.com*, Google, 15 July 2012, Web, 15 July 2012.

Figure 14-19

Illustration of a Combination Chart

as well as specific locations. Of the numerous formatting techniques available to you, these are the most common:

- Showing different areas with color, shading, or cross-hatching (see Figure 14–17). Maps using this technique must have a legend to explain the quantitative meanings of the various colors, or cross-hatchings.
- Placing visuals, symbols, or clip art within each geographic area to depict the quantity for that area or geographic location.
- Placing the quantities in numerical form within each geographic area.

Combination Charts

Combination charts often serve readers extremely well by allowing them to see relationships of different kinds of data. The example in Figure 14–19 shows the reader the price of stock over time (the trend), the volume of sales over time (comparisons), and the MACD (an indicator of trends in stock performance). It allows the reader to detect whether the change in volume affects the price of the stock. This kind of information would be difficult to get from raw data alone.

Three-Dimensional Visuals

Earlier we said that **three-dimensional graphs** are generally undesirable. However, we have mostly been referring to the three-dimensional presentation of visuals with two variables. But when you actually have three or more variables, presenting them in three dimensions is an option if doing so will help your readers see the data from multiple perspectives and gain additional information. In fact, Francis Crick, who won a Nobel prize for discovering the structure of DNA, once revealed that he and his collaborators understood the configuration of DNA only when they took a sheet of paper, cut it, and twisted it. Today we have sophisticated statistics, visuals, and data-mining tools to help us see our data from multiple perspectives.

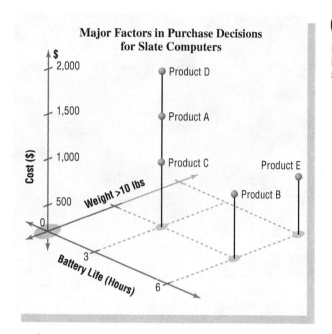

Major Factors in Purchase Decisions for Slate Computers

Figure 14–20

Illustration of a Three-Dimensional Visual
SOURCE: Primary.

These three-dimensional tools are making their way from science labs into business settings. Thanks to the increased use of data-gathering tools, businesses large and small are collecting and attempting to analyze extremely large amounts of detailed data. They are analyzing not only their own data but also data on their competitors. And advances in hardware, software, and Web-based applications are making it easier to visually represent both quantitative and qualitative data.

Although 3D visuals help writers display the results of their data analysis, they change how readers look at information and may take some time getting used to. These tools enable users both to see data from new perspectives and to interact with them. They allow users to free themselves from two dimensions and give them ways to stretch their insights and see new possibilities.

Figure 14–20 shows a three-dimensional visual plot of factors identified as the major ones consumers use when deciding which slate computer to purchase. Five products are plotted on three variables: cost, battery life, and slate weight. This visual could help a company identify its major competitors and help consumers identify those products that are best suited to their needs. The more products or data that are plotted, the more valuable the graph is at helping the reader extract meaning. If these data had been displayed on a two-dimensional graph, the lines would have overlapped too much to be distinguishable, thus requiring you to accompany this visual with a table, enable the reader to rotate the visual, or both in order to make the data clear.

In deciding whether to use a three-dimensional representation or a two-dimensional one, you need to consider your audience, the context, and goal of your communication. Overall, multidimensional presentation on paper is difficult; multiple representations can be made from separate two-dimensional views, but not always effectively. Moreover, if the 3D visual is being presented online or digitally where the reader can rotate it to see perspectives, it is likely to be much more effective.

Photographs

Cameras are everywhere today, enabling anyone to capture the images he or she needs. And royalty-free photos intended for commercial use are readily available on the Internet, too. Photos can serve useful communication purposes. They can be used to document events as well as show products, processes, or services. Figure 14–21 illustrates how a photo creates a message. What does the context created by the trees and sidewalk devoid of people suggest to you?

Figure 14–21

Illustration of a Photo

Today photos, like data-generated visuals, can easily be manipulated. A writer's job is to use them ethically, including getting permission when needed.

Other Visuals

The types of visuals discussed thus far are the ones most commonly used in business. Other types also may be helpful. **Diagrams** (see Figure 14–22) and drawings may help simplify a complicated explanation or description. **Icons** are another useful type of visual. You can create new icons, or you can select one from an existing body of icons with easily recognized meanings, such as ⊘. Even carefully selected **cartoons** can be used effectively. **Video clips** and **animation** are now used in many electronic documents. For all practical purposes, any visual is acceptable as long as it helps communicate the intended story.

LO5 Avoid common errors and ethical problems when constructing and using visuals.

Visual Integrity

In writing a business document, you are ethically bound to present data and visuals in ways that enable readers to interpret them easily and accurately. By being aware of some of the common errors made in presenting visuals, you learn how to avoid them and how to spot them in other documents. Keep in mind that any errors—deliberate or not—compromise your credibility, casting doubt on the document as well as on other work you have completed. Therefore, writers need to ensure that visuals accurately and honestly represent the data they contain.

Figure 14–22

Illustration of a Diagram

DIVERTING PLASTICS FROM LANDFILLS: A TWO-PRONGED APPROACH

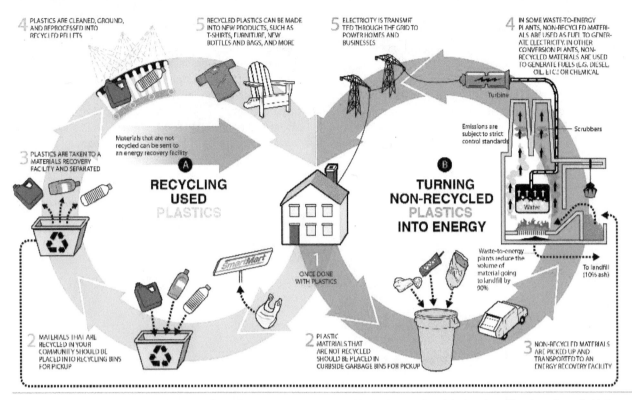

SOURCE: From "Diverting Plastics from Landfills: A Two-Pronged Approach," *Plastics Make It Possible,* American Chemistry Council, 21 Sept. 2012, Web, 15 July 2012. http://plasticsmakeitpossible.com/2011/09/diverting-plastics-from-landfills-a-two-pronged-approach/

Avoiding Errors in Graphing Data. Common graphing errors are errors of scale and errors of format. Another category of error is inaccurate or misleading presentation of context.

Errors of scale occur whenever the dimensions from left to right (X-axis) or bottom to top (Y-axis) are unequal. Three sources of scale errors include no uniform scale size, scale distortion, and violating the zero beginning.

No uniform scale size occurs when intervals in data points on the X or Y axis are not consistent. Note in the graphs below how the unequal intervals on the Y-axis in the graph on the right create a different presentation of the data.

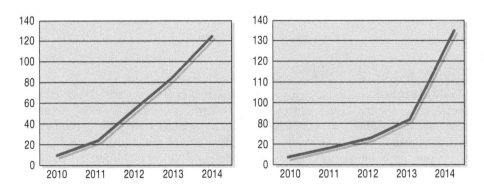

Avoiding Chartjunk

In 1983 Edward Tufte, a pioneer and leading expert in data visualization, invented the term *chartjunk* to refer to any elements in a visual that are either unnecessary or irrelevant to the reader's understanding of the data or that impede or distract from a reader's ability to understand the data.

Technology enables business communicators to incorporate many features (e.g., colors, lines, images) into their visuals—some that will enhance a visual's message and some that will not. Charley Kyd from the ExcelUsers blog explains that the distinction between visual elements that enhance a visual versus those that are chartjunk is the extent to which visual elements make the reader work to understand the information.

Kyd presents the following variations on the same visual from the April 24, 2012, edition of *The Wall Street Journal*. The one on the left contains chartjunk; the one on the right is Kyd's rendering of the visual minus the chartjunk.

SOURCE: Reprinted with permission of Charley Kyd, ExcelUser.com.

Kyd acknowledges that neither visual makes the data impossible to understand; what makes the elements chartjunk in the visual on the left is that the visual elements "act as noise where your readers need silence." That is, the shape of the bite in the apple appears to alter the shape of the bars in the chart, making the reader look twice to see that the bars, indeed, retain their shape. Is this a lot of work for the reader? No, but why make your reader work at all? When you create visuals, just as when you create text, all elements should enhance your reader's understanding of your message.

SOURCES: Charley Kyd, "Oh, No! Chart Junk from *The Wall Street Journal*," *ExcelUsers Blog: Insight for Business Users of Microsoft Excel*, 12 May 2012, Web, 12 July 2012; Jessica E. Vascellaro and Ian Sherr, "Apple Rides iPhone Frenzy: Quarterly Profit Nearly Doubles as Tech Giant Taps China, New Markets," *The Wall Street Journal*, Dow Jones & Company, Inc., 24 Apr. 2012, Web, 12 July 2012.

Scale distortion occurs when a visual is stretched excessively horizontally or vertically to change the meaning it conveys to the reader. Expanding a scale can change the appearance of the line. For example, if the values on a chart are plotted one-half unit apart, changes appear to be much more dramatic. Determining the distances that present the most accurate picture is a matter of judgment. Notice the different looks of the visuals at the top of the next page when they are stretched vertically and horizontally.

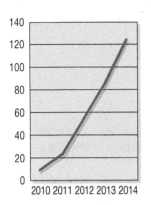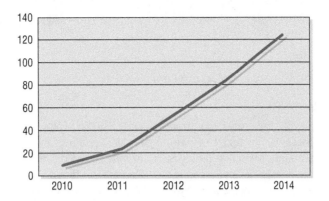

Finally, another type of scale error is the **missing zero beginning** of the series. For accuracy you should begin the scale at zero. But when all the information shown in the chart has high values, it is awkward to show the entire scale from zero to the highest value. For example, if the quantities compared range from 1,320 to 1,350 and the chart shows the entire area from zero to 1,350, the line showing these quantities would be almost straight and very high on the chart. Your solution in this case is not to begin the scale at a high number (say 1,300), which would distort the information, but to begin at zero and show a scale break. Realize, however, that while this makes the differences easier to see, it does exaggerate the differences. You can see this effect here.

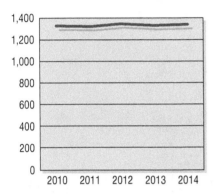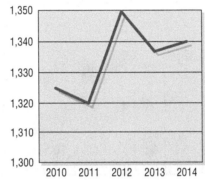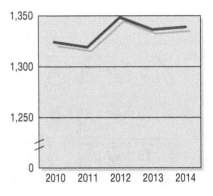

Occasionally, though, a writer needs to use his or her judgment when the guides for starting at the zero point are not practical. For example Figure 14–23 compares

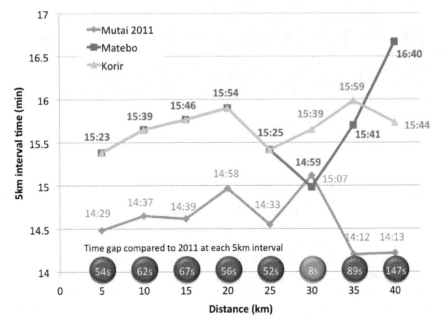

Figure 14–23

Illustration of a Line Graph That Considers Context
SOURCE: Ross Tucker, "Boston Strikes Back: The Boston 2012 Meltdown," *The Science of Sport,* Ross Tucker and Jonathan Dugas, 16 Apr. 2012, Web, 12 July 2012. http://www.sportsscientists. com/2012/04/boston-strikes-back-boston-2012.html

The Periodic Table of Visualization Methods

This chapter presents many of the most common options for using visuals to present your text and data. The Periodic Table of Visualization Methods provides an array of many other possibilities to help you choose the best visual as well. To see your options, just visit the website www.visual-literacy.org/periodic_table/periodic _table.html, move your mouse over any of the visual types, and view the example that appears. As you view the many creative options, you may be tempted to choose a visual format based on its novelty rather than its functionality. Remember, though, that the main purpose of any visual is to communicate. Choose wisely. You want your visuals to look good, but more importantly you want them to be appropriate for your message.

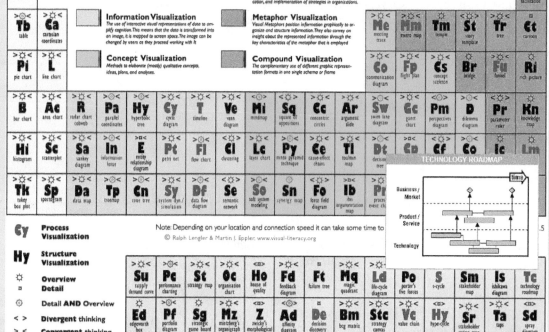

SOURCE: Ralph Lengler and Martin J. Eppler, www.visual-literacy.org. Reprinted with permission of Professor Dr. Martin Eppler.

race times of three runners, all of whom have times that cluster in the 14–17 second range. Beginning the time scale at 0 would hinder the reader's interpretation of the information. In this context, presenting the data at a scale that begins at 14 efficiently present the data while maintaining integrity.

Errors of format come in a wide variety. Some of the more common ones are choice of wrong chart type, distracting use of grids and shading, misuse of typeface, and problems with labels. For example, if a company used pie charts to compare expenses from one year to the next, readers might be tempted to draw conclusions that would be inappropriate because, although the pies would both represent 100 percent

of the expenses, the size of the business and the expenses may have grown or shrunk drastically in a year's time. If one piece of the pie is colored or shaded in such a way as to make it stand out from the others, it could mislead readers. And, of course, small type or unlabeled, inconsistently labeled, or inappropriately labeled visuals confuse readers.

Another ethical challenge is accurately representing the context. For example, as we have discussed, the number and size of visuals should be proportionate to the importance of the topic and appropriate for the emphasis a topic deserves.

Avoiding Other Ethical Problems. There are other ethical issues to consider. Writers need to be careful when choosing the information to represent and the visual elements to represent it. One area writers need to watch is appropriate **selection of the contents**. Are people or things over- or underrepresented? Are the numbers of men and women appropriate for the context? Are their ages appropriate? Is ethnicity represented appropriately? Have colors been used appropriately and not to evoke or manipulate emotions? Writers need to carefully select and design visuals to maintain integrity.

PLACING AND INTERPRETING THE VISUALS

LO6 Place and interpret visuals effectively.

For the best communication effect, you should place each visual near the place where it is discussed. Exactly where on the page you should place it, however, should be determined by its size. If the visual is small, you should place it within the text that discusses it. If it is a full page, you should place it on the page following the first reference to the information it covers.

Some writers like to place all visuals at the end of a document, usually in the appendix. This arrangement may save time in preparing the document, but it makes the readers' task more difficult because they have to flip through pages every time they want to see a visual. Therefore, place visuals where they are most helpful to the reader.

That said, sometimes you may have a visual that is necessary for completeness but is not discussed in the document (e.g., print out of an online survey or list of questions from an interview cited in a report). Or you may have summary charts or tables that apply to the entire document but to no specific place in it. When such visuals are appropriate, you should place them in an appendix, and you should refer to the appendix at an appropriate point in the document.

Visuals communicate most effectively when the readers view them at the right point in their reading. Thus, you should tell the readers when to look at a visual and what to see. Of the many wordings used for this purpose, these are the most common:

As Figure 4 shows, ...
. . . , indicated in Figure 4, ...
. . . , as a glance at Figure 4 reveals, ...
. . . (see Figure 4) . . . .

If your visual is carrying the primary message, as in a detailed table, you can just refer the reader to the information in the visual, as in "As Table 1 illustrates, our increased sales over the last three years. . . ." No further explanation or discussion may be necessary.

However, sometimes the visual is part of a more detailed discussion or presentation of your data. In these cases, you will start with a summary statement that reveals the big picture. If you were discussing Figure 14–17 (page 509), you might say, "As Figure 14–17 shows, areas of the country with the lowest unemployment rate are in the High, Central, and Southern Plains states." After presenting the figure, you would give one or more supporting examples that call your readers' attention to more specific points in the visual. Then you would give the exception to the general trend, if there is one.

Your readers will appreciate well-chosen, well-designed, and well-explained visuals, and you will achieve powerful communication results.

THERE'S MORE. . .

Would you like to create powerful graphics, view examples of creative visuals, or find unique visuals for your next report or presentation? Scan the QR code with your smartphone or use your Web browser to visit www.mhhe.com/lesikar13e. Choose Chapter 14 > Bizcom Tools & Tips.

SUMMARY BY LEARNING OBJECTIVES

Plan which parts of your report or other document should be communicated or supported by visuals.

1. Because visuals are a key part of communicating information, you should plan them when you plan your document.
   - Remember that they supplement the writing; they do not replace it.
   - Use them wherever they help communicate the report information.

Explain the factors that are important in the effective presentation of visuals: size, layout, type, rules and borders, color and cross-hatching, clip art, background, numbering, titles, title placement, and footnotes and acknowledgments.

2. Construct each visual carefully, following these general instructions:
   - Give each the size and arrangement that its contents and importance justify.
   - Use rules, borders, and color when they help.
   - Use clip art and background appropriately.
   - Number the visuals consecutively by type.
   - Construct topic titles for them using the five Ws (*who, what, where, when, why*) and one H (*how*) as a checklist. Alternatively, use the main message as a talking heading.
   - Use footnotes and acknowledgments when needed, placing them below the visual.

3. Choose textual visuals to display data that are largely text based.
   - Use an orderly arrangement of rows and columns to organize information in a table.
   - Use leaderwork or tabulations for short arrangement of data.
   - Use pull quotes to emphasize a key idea.
   - Use bulleted lists to set off points.
   - Use flowcharts and process charts to show activity sequences.

Construct textual visuals such as tables, pull quotes, flowcharts, and process charts.

4. In selecting charts, diagrams, and maps, consider these primary types:
   - Simple bar or column chart—shows quantity comparisons.
   - Clustered bar or column chart—shows two or three quantities on one chart.
   - Bilateral column chart—shows plus and minus differences and is especially good for showing percentage changes.
   - Stacked or subdivided bar chart—used to compare differences in the division of wholes.
   - Pictograph—shows quantitative differences in picture form.
   - Pie chart—shows how wholes are divided.
   - Line chart—useful in showing changes over time.
   - Scatter diagram—compares pairs of values.
   - Map—shows quantitative and physical differences by area.
   - Combination chart—shows relationships between separate data sets.
   - Three-dimensional visual—used to analyze and interpret large data sets with three or more variables.
   - Photograph—Documents events or shows products, processes, and services.
   - Visuals that serve special needs:
     - Diagrams and drawings.
     - Icons.
     - Cartoons.
     - Video clips and animation.

Construct and use visuals such as bar charts, pie charts, line charts, scatter diagrams, and maps.

5. Make sure that your visuals have integrity.
   - To present data objectively, avoid these common errors:
     — Errors of scale—no uniform scale size, scale distortion, missing zero point.
     — Errors of format—wrong chart type, distracting use of grids and shading, misuse of typeface, and problems with labels.
     — Errors in representing context.
   - Also consider the ethical use of the following:
     — Selection.
     — Color.
     — Volume and size.
     — Scale and format.

Avoid common errors and ethical problems when constructing and using visuals

6. Place and interpret visuals effectively.
   - Place visuals near to the text part they illustrate.
   - Place in the appendix those that you do not discuss in the text.
   - Invite readers to look at them at the appropriate place.
   - Interpret by introducing the visual, placing the visual, and offering any additional explanation or discussion.

Place and interpret visuals effectively.

CRITICAL THINKING QUESTIONS

1 For the past 20 years, Professor Clark Kupenheimer has required that his students include five visuals in the long, formal report he assigns. Evaluate this requirement. **LO1**

2 Because it was easier to do, a report writer prepared each of the visuals on a full page. Some of these visuals were extremely complex; some were very simple. Comment on this practice. **LO1, LO6**

3 A report has five maps, four tables, one chart, one diagram, and one photograph. How would you number these visuals? **LO2**

4 How would you number these visuals in a report: seven tables, six charts, nine maps? **LO2**

5 Discuss the techniques that may be used to show quantitative differences between areas on a statistical map. **LO4**

6 Give examples of data that are suited for presentation in three dimensions. **LO4**

7 Discuss the advantages and disadvantages of using pictographs. **LO4**

8 Find a graph that uses scale breaks. Discuss the possible effects of its use on the reader. **LO5**

9 Find a visual with errors in format. Tell how you would correct the errors to present the chart's data more clearly to the reader. **LO5**

10 "I have placed every visual near the place I write about it. The reader can see the visual without any *additional* help from me. It just doesn't make sense to direct the reader's attention to the visuals with words." Evaluate this comment. **LO6**

SKILLS BUILDING EXERCISES

1 Construct a complete, concise title for a line chart representing employment placement rates for graduates in your major at your school from 2006 to the present. **LO2**

2 The chart prepared in Exercise 1 requires an explanation for the years 2009–2011, to the present: In each of those years, data were collected in January (mid-academic year) rather than June (end of the academic year). Provide the necessary explanation. **LO6**

3 For each of the types of information described below, which form of visual would you use? Explain your decision. **LO1–4**

a. Record of annual sales for Kenyon Company for the past 20 years.

b. Comparison of Kenyon Company sales, by product, for this year and last year.

c. Monthly production of the automobile industry in units.

d. Breakdown of how the average middle-income family in your state (or province) disposes of its income dollar.

e. How middle-income families spend their income dollar as compared with how low-income families spend their income dollar.

f. Comparison of sales for the past two years for each of B&B Company's 14 sales districts. The districts cover all 50 states, Canada, and Puerto Rico.

g. National production of trucks from 1950 to present, broken down by manufacturer.

h. Relationship between list price and gas mileage of alternative and gasoline-fueled cars.

i. Home purchases by home value, geographic region, and income.

4 For each of the following sets of facts, (a) determine the visual (or visuals) that would be best, (b) defend your choice, and (c) construct the visual. **LO1–5**

a. Average (mean) amount of life insurance owned by Mutual Life Insurance Company policyholders. Classification is by annual income.

Income	Average Life Insurance
Under $30,000	$ 40,000
$30,000–34,999	97,500
$35,000–39,999	112,500
$40,000–44,999	129,000
$45,000–49,999	142,500
$50,000 and over	225,000

b. Profits and losses for Whole Foods Stores, by store, 2009–2013, in dollars.

	Store			
Year	Able City	Baker	Charleston	Total
2009	234,210	132,410	97,660	464,280
2010	229,110	–11,730	218,470	435,850
2011	238,430	–22,410	216,060	432,080
2012	226,730	68,650	235,510	530,890
2013	230,080	91,450	254,820	576,350

c. Share of real estate tax payments by ward for Bigg City, 2009 and 2013, in thousands of dollars.

	2009	2013
Ward 1	17.1	21.3
Ward 2	10.2	31.8
Ward 3	19.5	21.1
Ward 4	7.8	18.2
City total	54.6	92.4

d. Percentage change in sales by employee, 2012–2013, District IV, Abbott, Inc.

Employee	Percentage Change
Joan Abraham	+7.3
Helen Calmes	+2.1
Edward Sanchez	–7.5
Clifton Nevers	+41.6
Wilson Platt	+7.4
Clara Ruiz	+11.5
David Schlimmer	–4.8
Phil Wirks	3.6

5 Determine what percentage of each type of registered vehicle is owned in the U.S., including hybrid vehicles as appropriate. Choose an appropriate visual type and create it to convey the data. Consult the U.S. Department of Transportation for statistics. **LO1–5**

6 Through research, find the approximate milligrams of caffeine in the following items and create an appropriate visual for Affiliated Food Products, Inc., to illustrate your findings. **LO2–5**

5-oz. cup of coffee (drip brewed)

7-oz. glass of iced tea

6-oz. glass of soda with caffeine

1-oz. dark chocolate, semisweet

7 Choose five or six types of exercise. In a visual, identify the activity as a type of (1) cardiovascular training, (2) strength training, or (3) muscle stretching and toning. You can assume that some forms of exercise will incorporate all three types. You work for the Parks and Recreation Department of a city of your choosing. Provide an interpretation of your visual. **LO1, 2, 3, 4, 5, 6**

Oral Forms of Business Communication

Considered one of Fortune 500's "Most Powerful Black Executives" at age 39, Pamela Thomas-Graham was the first black woman to become a partner at management consulting firm McKinsey & Company. Between this position and her current one, she served as an executive vice president of NBC, president and CEO of CNBC, and Group President for Liz Claiborne, Inc. Thomas-Graham recognizes the importance of communicating informally to gather information and harvest good ideas.

"It's very important to have a lot of interaction with people at every level of the company. You should spend time walking around talking with people and have meetings that bring together different groups of people, either from different areas of the company or from different levels within the company. And my basic philosophy is, 'The best idea wins.' It doesn't matter where it comes from."

Pamela Thomas-Graham
Chief Talent, Branding, and Communications Officer, Member of the Executive
Board of Credit Suisse Group AG and Credit Suisse AG

CHAPTER FIFTEEN

Communicating Effectively in Meetings and Conversations

Learning Objectives

Upon completing this chapter, you will be able to understand and use good talking techniques, lead and participate in meetings, communicate effectively by telephone, listen well, and understand professional nonverbal communication. To reach these goals, you should be able to

1 Discuss talking and its key elements.

2 Explain the techniques for conducting and participating in meetings.

3 Describe good phone and voice mail techniques.

4 Explain the barriers to good listening and describe how to overcome them.

5 Describe the nature and types of nonverbal communication.

Speaking and Listening like a Professional Businessperson

You are a college senior who is four weeks into a semester-long accounting internship at Timon, David, and McGee, a public accounting firm. You expected that you would have to interact with other staff and interns, but you are amazed at the amount of interpersonal communication you engage in each day.

Take today, for example. This morning you had to meet with your supervisor regarding the research you did on a newly passed U.S. tax law. You thought you were thorough and quite clear in answering the questions your supervisor asked you to research, but the look on her face and her numerous questions indicated she either didn't understand you or hadn't been listening to you. Regardless, you felt your report would have been received better had your oral communication skills been more polished.

Then, you returned from lunch to find seven voice mails. You needed to return five of the seven calls because the caller left incomplete or vague messages. Not having to return those phone calls would have saved you 45 minutes. You feel pretty comfortable communicating over the phone, but you do wish your coworkers had better phone skills.

In the evening you returned to campus to lead a meeting of the Student Accounting Association. It was a disaster—everyone talking at once, arguing, interrupting. Everyone wanted to talk; no one wanted to listen. Fortunately, you were able to accomplish most of your agenda items, but you know your group needs to improve its dynamic.

You are fast realizing just how much you will rely on good oral and interpersonal communication in your professional career and vow to learn strategies and techniques for improving your skill. This chapter will help you.

THE PREVALENCE OF ORAL COMMUNICATION ON THE JOB

As you know, your work will involve oral as well as written communication. Although you may find written communication more challenging and may spend a lot of time planning, drafting, and revising, you are likely to spend more time communicating orally than you are in any other work activity.

Much of the oral communication that goes on in business is the informal, person-to-person communication that occurs whenever people get together. We all have experience with this form of communication, and most of us do it reasonably well, but all of us can improve our informal speaking and listening with practice.

In addition to informal talking and listening, various other kinds of interpersonal oral communication take place in business. Business people often conduct and participate in committee meetings, conferences, and group discussions. Phone calls are a routine part of the workday. And professionals are called on frequently to give informal and formal oral reports. All these kinds of oral communication are a part of the work that businesspeople do.

This chapter and the one that follows cover these kinds of communication. This chapter reviews the more interpersonal types of oral communication: informal talking, participating in meetings, talking by phone, listening, and using nonverbal communication. The following chapter discusses the two most formal kinds: oral reporting and public speaking. Together, the two chapters should give you an understanding of the oral communication situations you will encounter in business. Remember, though, that whether you are in a less formal or more formal situation, your oral communication must meet your audience's needs and project a professional image.

Finding Your Professional Voice

This chapter recommends that you improve your talking voice with self-analysis and practice. The experts at the *Excellent Work* blog provide several tips for helping you cultivate a talking voice that serves you well in any professional setting. Here is a summary of those tips:

- *Breathing:* Breathe from your diaphragm. Doing so will give you better control over your talking because at the end of the exhale, you create pauses that give your listener a chance to process what you say.

  To breathe from your diaphragm, take a deep breath. As you exhale, talk. *Excellent Work* recommends counting to 10 or reciting the months of the year or days of the week. As you're talking, increase the volume by using your abdominal muscles rather than your throat for volume. How do you know if you're using your diaphragm? This comes from us, not from the folks at *Excellent Work:* If you're breathing from the diaphragm, your abdomen should extend when you inhale; if you're breathing from your throat, your chest will extend, your abdomen will cave in, and your shoulders will rise.

- *Pitch:* High-pitched or monotone voices can be annoying. Using a lower pitch and varying your pitch holds listeners' attention. One way to practice lower and varied pitch is by humming.

- *Volume:* When you speak, ask your audiences if your volume is too loud or too soft and regulate it appropriately.

- *Pace:* Speaking either too quickly or too slowly will cause your audience to tune out. Record yourself

to assess your pace or get feedback from your audience.

- *Articulation:* Have you been told that you mumble? Exaggerating lip movement, practicing difficult tongue twisters until you can say them as quickly and clearly as possible, and exaggerating vowel sounds are all ways to improve articulation.

- *Timing:* Marking points in your speech where you want to take a break lets you plan your pauses. To add emphasis to your point, take longer or more breaths after you make the point.

- *Anxiety:* Are there people you talk with who make you nervous or situations where you find yourself so nervous that you cannot speak well? Before engaging in conversation or speaking before a group, do some simple exercises to release tension: Look side to side, roll your head in half circles, roll your shoulders, shift your rib cage from side to side, yawn, or stretch. You can also touch your toes and then slowly roll up, raising your head last.

- *Posture:* Standing up straight (not slouching) will help you breathe better, and better breathing leads to a better talking voice.

- *Self-assessment:* Many people do not like to listen to their own voice, but even if it's painful, record your voice using different pitches, pacing, articulations, etc. When you find a voice you like, practice that voice until it becomes your habit.

SOURCE: "10 Tips to Improve Your Speaking Voice," *Excellent Work*, Excellent Work, 9 July 2012, Web, 22 July 2012.

LO1 Discuss talking and its key elements.

INFORMAL WORKPLACE TALKING

As noted previously, most of us do a reasonably good job of **informal talking**. In fact, we do such a good job that we often take talking for granted and overlook the need to improve our talking ability. To improve our talking, we need to be aware of its nature and qualities.

As a first step in improving your talking ability, think for a moment about the qualities you like in a good talker—one with whom you would enjoy talking in ordinary conversation. Then think about the opposite—the worst conversationalist you can imagine. With these two images in mind, you can form a good picture of the characteristics of good talking. The following section covers the most important of these.

Elements of Professional Talking

The techniques of good talking use four basic elements: (1) voice quality, (2) style, (3) word choice, and (4) adaptation to your audience.

The Art of Negotiation

One common type of interpersonal communication you'll engage in as a professional is that of negotiation. You might negotiate a raise, a contract with a client, or even a deal with co-workers over who gets the office with a window. Whatever you're negotiating, you'll present your best professional image, achieve your communication goals, and preserve your listener's goodwill by heeding the following advice from author and entrepreneur Kevin O'Leary:

1. *Know What You Want:* Be sure you know, exactly, the goals of the negotiation and how to make your point in a way that makes sense to your audience. Also anticipate your audience's questions and have answers ready to show you've thought through your points.

2. *Know That Your Audience Is Judging You:* Your audiences are judging you on everything from how you're dressed to your body language to how well you're using their time. If you do not look the part, are not confident, or don't get to your point immediately, you lose your credibility.

3. *Help Others Help You:* Focus on benefits to your audience. Your audiences are not likely to negotiate if they cannot see any outcomes that benefit them.

4. *Know Your Facts:* Know everything you can about the audience or audiences you're negotiating with (and about the issue you're negotiating). If you look like you haven't done your homework, you lose your advantage or give your audience little reason to continue negotiating.

5. *Know When to Walk Away:* The goal of negotiation should be that everyone leaves with something he or she is satisfied with. When this doesn't happen (or looks like it's not going to happen), it's all right to walk away.

6. *Remember the Bottom Line:* In business, the success of a negotiation may be the extent to which you show the audience how your idea helps the bottom line (making money). Depending on what you're negotiating, if the negotiation does not look financially advantageous, your audience may lose interest.

7. *Don't Get Greedy:* Once you've gotten what you want, be done. If you press the issue, you may quickly lose what you've just gotten.

SOURCE: Kevin O'Leary, "How to Win in Business Negotiations: Never Forget, It's All About the Money," *Huffington Post—Business: Canada,* The Huffington Post, Inc., 26 July 2012, Web, 26 July 2012.

Voice Quality. Voice quality primarily refers to the pitch and resonance of the sounds a speaker makes and the sounds an audience hears, but it also includes speed and volume. Because we cover these topics in Chapter 16, we need only say here that voices vary widely, but whatever the quality of your voice, you can cultivate a professional style.

Perhaps the best way of improving voice quality is first to refer to your life experiences. From these you have learned to know good and bad voice qualities when you hear them. You know the effect of talking that is too fast, too slow, monotone, high-pitched, low-pitched, harsh, or pleasant. With this knowledge in mind, you should analyze your own voice, perhaps with the assistance of a recorder. Listen carefully to yourself and then make a conscious effort to improve what you hear.

Style. Style refers to a set of voice behaviors that makes your voice unique. It is the way that pitch, speed, and volume combine to give personality to your oral expression.

From the self-analysis described in our review of voice quality, you should have a good idea of your talking style. What is the image your talking projects? Does it project sincerity? Is it polished? Smooth? Rough? Dull? After your honest assessment, you should be able to improve your style.

Word Choice. A third quality of talking is word choice. Of course, word choice is related to one's vocabulary. The larger your vocabulary, the more choices you have. Even so, you should keep in mind the need for the listener to understand the words you choose. In addition, the words you choose should convey courtesy and respect for the listener's knowledge of the subject matter—that is, they should not talk down to or above the listener. Consider, too, that the vocabulary you use with your friends outside the workplace may not be professionally appropriate for use in the workplace—no matter how friendly you are with your co-workers, superiors, or subordinates.

Adaptation. Adaptation is the fourth quality of good talking. As you learned in earlier chapters, adaptation means fitting the message to the intended listener. Primarily this means fitting the words to the listener's level of understanding, but it also can include varying your voice and style. To illustrate, the voice, style, and words in an oral message aimed at children would be different from the same message aimed at adults. Similarly, these qualities might vary in messages delivered in different cultures as well as different social situations, work situations, and classrooms.

Courtesy in Talking

Our review of talking would not be complete without a comment about the need for courtesy. We have all been frustrated by talkers who drown out others with their loud voices, who interrupt while others are talking, who attempt to dominate others in conversation. Good talkers encourage others to make their voices heard.

This emphasis on courtesy does not suggest that you should be submissive in your conversations—that you should not be aggressive in pressing your points. It means that you should accord others the courtesy that you expect of them.

LO2 Explain the techniques for conducting and participating in meetings.

CONDUCTING AND PARTICIPATING IN MEETINGS

From time to time, you will participate in **business meetings**. These will range from extreme formality to extreme informality. On the formal end will be conferences and committee meetings, while discussions with fellow workers will be at the informal end.

Good talking is the foundation for effective oral communication in the workplace.

Collaborative Tools Support Virtual Meetings

It used to be that long-distance meetings or other types of collaboration required sophisticated teleconferencing or videoconferencing equipment. Today, however, anyone with Internet access can use virtual meeting software to collaborate with anyone anywhere in the world. Businesses routinely take advantage of this technology to save time and money while enhancing productivity.

In fact, you may have already used some of these on-line meeting tools, such as Skype, to communicate with your friends, family, and classmates. If not, becoming familiar with these tools is a good idea if you plan to enter the business world.

What can you do with a virtual meeting tool? If you're using Skype, for example, depending on the type of account you have, you can send large files to your group members (free); hold conference calls (free for Skype members); call landlines, mobile phones, or online numbers; and use Skype Manager to create and manage accounts for your team.

So the next time you're working on a group project and need to meet, why not try a virtual meeting tool, save some travel time, and have the meeting from the comfort of your own office, home, or dorm?

SOURCE: Jennifer Caukin, "Workspace Blog: Tips and How-tos for Using Skype in the Workplace," *Skype*, Skype, 4 April 2012, Web, 26 July 2012.

Whether formal or informal, the meetings will obviously involve communication, and the quality of the communication will determine their success.

Your role in a meeting will be that of either leader or participant. Of course, the leader's role is the primary one, but good participation is also vital. The following paragraphs review the techniques of performing well in either role.

Techniques of Conducting Meetings

How you conduct a meeting depends on the formality of the occasion. Meetings of such groups as formal committees, boards of directors, and professional organizations usually follow generally accepted rules of conduct called **parliamentary procedure**. These very specific rules are too numerous and detailed for review here, but when you

Figure 15–1

Example of a Meeting Agenda

Agenda

International Association of Business Communicators (IABC)
Executive Board Meeting
February 23, 2013
Clearwater Room, 7 p.m.

I. **Officer Reports**
    A.   President
    B.   Vice president
    C.   Secretary
    D.   Treasurer

II. **Committee Reports**
    A.   Public Relations Committee
    B.   Web Development Committee
    C.   Social Committee

III. **Old Business**
    A.   Bake sale fundraisers
    B.   Community service project

IV. **New Business**
    A.   Election of new officers
    B.   Attendance at exec board meetings
    C.   Hot chocolate promo

V. **Adjournment**

are involved in a formal meeting, you can study one of the many books and websites covering parliamentary procedure before the meeting so that you know, for example, what it means to make a motion or call for a vote. For less formal meetings, you can depart somewhat from parliamentary procedure, but keep in mind that every meeting has goals, and some structure is needed to help participants meet them. The following practices will help you conduct a successful meeting.

Plan the Meeting. A key to conducting a successful meeting is to plan it thoroughly. For informal meetings, just knowing your plan may be sufficient, but before conducting formal or complex meetings, you may want to prepare an **agenda** (a list of topics to be covered). To prepare an agenda, select the items that need to be covered to achieve the goals of the meeting. Then arrange these items in the most logical order. Items that explain or lead to other items should come before the items that they explain or lead to. After preparing the agenda, make it available to those who will attend. Figure 15–1 shows an agenda created for a student organization meeting, but you can tailor an agenda to whatever will help you accomplish your goals. Word processing programs also have templates that may be helpful.

Follow the Plan. You should follow the plan for the meeting item by item. In most meetings the discussion tends to stray, and new items tend to come up. As the leader, you should keep the discussion on track. If new items come up during the meeting, you can take them up at the end or perhaps postpone them for a future meeting.

Move the Discussion Along. Another job you have as the leader is to control the agenda. After one item has been covered, bring up the next item. When the discussion moves off subject, move it back on subject. In general, do what is needed to proceed through the items efficiently, but do not cut off discussion before all the important points have been made. You will have to use your good judgment to permit complete discussion on the one hand and to avoid repetition, excessive details, and off-topic comments on the other.

Control Those Who Talk Too Much. Keeping certain people from talking too much is likely to be one of your harder tasks. A few people usually tend to dominate the discussion, and one of your tasks as the leader is to control them. Of course, you want the meeting to be democratic, so you will need to let these people talk as long as they are contributing to the goals of the meeting. However, when they begin to stray, duplicate what's already been said, or bring in irrelevant matter, you should step in. You can do this tactfully by asking for other viewpoints or by summarizing the discussion and moving on to the next topic.

Encourage Participation from Those Who Talk Too Little. Just as some people talk too much, some talk too little. In business groups, those who say little are often in positions lower than those of other group members. You should to encourage these people to participate by asking them for their viewpoints and by showing respect for the comments they make.

Control Time. When your meeting time is limited, you need to determine in advance how much time will be needed to cover each item. Then, at the appropriate times, you should end discussion of the items. You may find it helpful to announce the time goals at the beginning of the meeting and to help the group members keep track of the time during the meeting. You might also consider including the time limits next to each item on the agenda so that readers know the time constraints before they attend the meeting and can plan their contributions accordingly.

Summarize at Appropriate Places. After a key item has been discussed, you should summarize what the group has covered and concluded. If a group decision is needed, the group's vote will be the conclusion. In any event, you should formally conclude each point and then move on to the next one. At the end of the meeting, you can summarize the progress made. You also should summarize whenever a review will help the group members understand what they agreed upon.

Take Minutes. As we discussed in Chapter 12, what is said and what is heard in a meeting may not be remembered consistently by participants. People at meetings may hear or interpret what is said differently. In addition, you may need to refer to the discussions or to the decisions made at a meeting long after the meeting when people's memories are even less reliable. To ensure you have an accurate, objective account of the topics covered and decisions made at a meeting, assign the task of recording the meeting events (taking minutes) to someone. In particularly contentious or detailed discussions, it is important that everyone have a shared understanding of what has transpired.

The format of meeting minutes will depend on the nature of the meeting, group preferences, and company requirements. Some minutes are highly formal, with headings and complete sentences, while others might simply resemble casually written notes. As pointed out in Chapter 12 (pages 405–407), the minutes of a meeting usually list the date, time, and location along with those persons who attended and those who were supposed to attend but were absent; some minutes may also note excused or unexcused absences. If there is an agenda, the minutes will usually summarize the discussion of each agenda topic. Figure 15–2 provides an example of minutes based on the meeting agenda presented in Figure 15–1. (See page 406 for another example.) Generally, the person who takes minutes sends them to those who attended the meeting and requests corrections, or he or she presents the minutes at the next meeting and asks for changes or corrections at that time. Group members may also vote on whether to accept the minutes as they were recorded.

Minutes

International Association of Business Communicators (IABC)
Executive Board Meeting
February 23, 2013
Clearwater Room, 7 p.m.

Attended: Jim Solberg, Aaron Ross, Linda Yang, Tyler Baines, Sara Ryan
Absent: Jenna Kircher (excused), Rebecca Anderson (unexcused)

I. Officer Reports

A. *President:* Jim Solberg. Jim received a message from the director of university programs reminding him to view IABC's officer roster. He reviewed it on February 16 and signed the required forms.

B. *Vice president:* Linda Yang. Linda compiled job descriptions for all officer positions. Jenna put them on the IABC website. The link to the description of the secretary's position was not working. She is contacting Jenna to fix the link.

C. *Secretary:* Aaron Ross. Minutes of the last meeting were read and approved. He sent a thank-you note to Village Pizza for letting us have our last social there. Our average general meeting attendance is 15 even though we have 27 people who have paid dues. At the next exec board meeting, we should discuss ways to improve attendance.

D. *Treasurer:* Rebecca Anderson. No report.

II. Committee Reports

A. *Public Relations Committee:* Tyler Baines. The committee wants to have a public relations campaign in place for next fall. He will be asking for volunteers at the next general meeting.

B. *Web Development Committee:* Jenna Kircher. No report.

C. *Social Committee:* Sara Ryan. The next social will be at the campus bowling alley on March 12 at 7 p.m.

III. Old Business

A. *Bake sale fundraisers:* The $76 we earned this time is less than the $102 we earned at the last one. We will discuss creative fundraising ideas at the next general meeting.

B. *Community service project:* Linda has the forms for participating in IABC's Relay for Life team on April 26–27. She will present them at the next general meeting and ask for volunteers.

IV. New Business

A. *Election of new officers:* Linda. Officers will be elected at the April meeting. We need to encourage people to run.

B. *Attendance at exec board meetings:* Jim. Rebecca has missed every exec board meeting this semester without an excuse. The bylaws state that anyone with more than three unexcused absences in an academic year can be removed from the exec board and office. Jim sent Rebecca an email reminding her of the bylaws, but she did not respond. The Executive Board voted unanimously to remove Rebecca from the board and office. Jim will send her a letter thanking her for her service and telling her she is off the board and no longer treasurer.

C. *Hot chocolate promo:* Sara. Sara requested $20 to buy supplies to serve hot chocolate on the quad from 7:30–9:30 a.m. on Monday, March 9, to promote IABC. Linda moved to spend the $20. Jim seconded the motion. Motion carried unanimously.

V. Adjournment

The meeting adjourned at 8:30 p.m. The next general meeting will be Monday, March 2, at 7 p.m. in the Alumni Room. The next exec board meeting will be Monday, March 9, at 7 p.m. in the Clearwater Room.

Respectfully submitted,

Aaron Ross

Techniques for Participating in a Meeting

From the preceding discussion of the techniques that a leader should use, you can infer the expectations for participating in a meeting. The following section reviews these expectations.

Follow the Agenda. When an agenda exists, you should follow it. Specifically, you should not bring up items not on the agenda or comment on such items if others bring them up. When there is no agenda, you should stay within the general limits of the goals for the meeting.

Participate. The purpose of meetings is to get the input of everybody concerned. Your participation, however, should be meaningful. That is, you should participate when your input helps move the meeting toward its goals.

Do Not Talk Too Much. As you participate in the meeting, you should speak up whenever you have something to say, but do not get carried away. As in all matters of etiquette, always *respect the rights of others* to have the opportunity to speak, too. As you speak, ask yourself whether what you are saying really contributes to the discussion. Not only is the meeting costing you time, but it is costing other people's time and salaries, as well as the opportunity costs of other work they might be doing.

Cooperate. Respect the leader and her or his efforts to make progress. Respect the other participants, and work with them in every practical way. You can demonstrate your willingness to cooperate by attending all meetings, completing your assigned tasks, or volunteering to lead or serve on a committee—anything that outwardly show your desire to help your group achieve its objectives.

Be Courteous. Being courteous is a part of being cooperative. You should respect others' rights and opinions, and you should let them speak.

USING THE PHONE

LO3 Describe good phone and voice mail techniques.

At first thought, a discussion of business phone techniques may appear to be unnecessary. After all, most of us have had experience in using the phone and may feel that we have little to learn about it. However, using the phone in professional contexts differs in some ways from how we use the phone in social contexts with family and friends.

Professional Voice Quality

Keep in mind that a phone conversation is a unique form of oral communication because the speakers cannot see each other unless they have phones that allow face-to-face conversation. As a result, impressions are formed only from the words and the quality of the voices. Thus, when speaking by phone, you must work to make your voice sound pleasant and friendly.

One often-suggested way of improving your phone voice is to talk as if you were face-to-face with the other person—even smiling and gesturing as you talk if this helps you be more natural. In addition, you want to be aware of your voice quality, pitch, and speed, just as you would in a face-to-face setting. You may even want to record a phone conversation and then judge for yourself how you come across and what you need to do to improve.

Courtesy

As in written communication, your goal in oral communication is to build goodwill. One way to do this over the phone is to always be courteous to your listener.

When you *initiate the call*, introduce yourself immediately and then ask for the person with whom you want to talk:

"This is Tessa Werner of Altman Media. May I speak with Mr. José Martinez?"

If you are not certain with whom you should talk, explain the purpose of your call:

"This is Tessa Werner of Altman Media. We have a question about next week's photo shoot. May I speak with someone who can help me?"

If a call is *coming directly to you,* identify yourself.

"Bartosh Realty. Toby Bartosh speaking. May I help you?"

If you are *screening calls* for others, first identify the company or office and yourself and then offer assistance:

"Rowan Insurance Company. This is Audrey Peters. How may I help you?"

"Ms. Santo's office. Marco Alba speaking. May I help you?"

If the person whose calls you're screening is not available, be helpful by saying, "Ms. Santo is not in right now. May I ask her to return your call?" You could also ask "May I tell her who called?" or "Can someone else help you?"

Assistants to busy executives often screen incoming calls. In doing so, they should courteously ask the purpose of the calls. The response might prompt the assistant to refer the caller to a more appropriate person in the company. It also might reveal that the executive has no interest in the subject of the call, in which case the assistant should courteously yet clearly explain this to the caller. If the executive is busy at the moment, the assistant should explain this and either suggest a more appropriate time for a call or promise a callback by the executive. However, only promise a call back if one will be made. Doing so promotes a positive, professional image of you and your company and promotes goodwill between you and the caller.

If the person being called is on another line or involved in some other activity, it may be desirable to place the caller on hold or ask if the caller would like to leave a message. But good business etiquette dictates that the choice should be the caller's. However, if you have to put a caller on hold, be sure the hold time is reasonable. If the hold continues for a period longer than anticipated, the assistant should check with the caller periodically to show concern and offer assistance. Avoid the practice of having an assistant place a call for an executive and then put the person called on hold until

Whether in or out of the office, those using mobile phones should practice the same voice quality and courtesies as on landlines.

the executive is free to talk. Although it may be efficient to use assistants for such work, as a matter of courtesy and etiquette the executive should be ready to talk the moment the call goes through.

Effective Phone Procedures

At the beginning of a phone conversation that you have initiated, state the purpose of the call and then use your listener's time efficiently by sticking to your point. To stay on point, you may want to outline an agenda for your call beforehand.

Courteous procedure is much the same in a telephone conversation as in a face-to-face conversation. You listen when the other person is talking, refrain from interrupting, and avoid dominating the conversation.

Effective Voice Mail Techniques

Sometimes when the person you are calling is not available, you will be able to leave a **voice message** in an electronic voice mailbox. Not only does this save you the time involved in calling back the person you are trying to reach, but it also allows you to leave a more detailed message than you might leave with an assistant. However, you need to be prepared to leave a complete and concise message.

You begin the message nearly the same way you would a telephone call. Be as courteous as you would on the telephone and speak as clearly and distinctly as you can. Tell the listener your name and affiliation. Begin with an *overview* of the message and continue with details. If you want the listener to take *action*, call for it at the end. If you want the listener to *return* your call, state that precisely, including when you can be reached. Slowly give the number where your call can be returned. *Close* with a brief goodwill message. For example, as a program coordinator for a professional training organization, you might leave this message in the voice mailbox of one of your participants:

> This is Ron Ivy from Metroplex Development Institute. I'm calling to remind Ms. Melanie Wilson about the Chief Executive Round Table (CERT) meeting next week (Wednesday, July 20) at the Crescent Hotel in Dallas. Dr. Ken Cooper of the Dallas Aerobics Center will present the program on Executive Health in the 21st Century. We will begin with breakfast at 7:30 AM and conclude with lunch at noon. Some of the CERT members will play golf in the afternoon at Dallas Country Club. If Ms. Wilson would like to join them, I will be glad to make a tee time for her. She can contact me at 940-240-1003 before 5:00 PM this Friday. We look forward to seeing her at our Chief Executive Round Table meeting next Wednesday. Thank you.

Courteous Use of Cell Phones

According to the Pew Research Center, 88 percent of all Americans own a cell phone.[1] To say the least, the benefits of this technology have greatly expanded our ability to communicate. To ensure that you project your best professional image, you'll want to keep in mind these tips for using your cell phone—whether you're calling, texting, or using any of your phone's other features.

1. Turn off the ringer in meetings and other places where it would be disruptive.

2. Do not use the cell phone at social gatherings.

3. Do not place the phone on the table while eating.

4. Avoid talking whenever it will annoy others. Usually this means when within earshot of others.

---

[1]"Nearly Half of American Adults Are Smartphone Users," *Pew Internet*, Pew Internet and American Life Project, 1 Mar. 2012, Web, July 25, 2012.

5. Avoid discussing personal or confidential matters when others can hear you.

6. Do not talk in an excessively loud voice.

7. Preferably call from a quiet place, away from other people.

8. If you must talk while around people, be conscious of them. Don't hold up lines or get in the way of others.

9. Avoid using the phone while driving (the law in some states).

For more on the courteous use of mobile devices, see the Communication Matters box on page 105.

LO4 Explain the barriers to good listening and describe how to overcome them.

LISTENING

Up to this point, our review of oral communication has been about sending information (talking). Certainly, good business communicators must also ensure that they are good listeners.

The Nature of Listening

When listening is mentioned, we think primarily of the act of sensing sounds. Viewed from a communication standpoint, however, the listening process involves the addition of filtering and remembering.

Sensing. How well we sense the words around us is determined by two factors. One factor is our ability to sense sounds—how well our ears can pick them up.

The other factor is our attentiveness or concentration. Our concentration on the communication varies from moment to moment. It can range from almost totally blocking out sounds to concentrating on them very intensely. From your own experience, you can recall moments when you were oblivious to the words spoken around you and moments when you listened with intensity. Most of the time, your listening falls somewhere between these extremes.

Filtering. From your study of the communication process in Chapter 1, you know that interpretation enables you to give meanings to the sounds you hear. In this process, your personal context affects how you filter these sounds and give meaning to incoming messages. This filter is formed by the unique contents of your mind: your knowledge, emotions, beliefs, biases, experiences, and expectations. In addition, larger social or workplace cultures will affect how you filter sounds. Thus, you sometimes give messages meanings that are different from the meanings that others give them.

Remembering. Remembering what we hear is the third activity involved in listening. Unfortunately, we retain little of what we hear. We remember many of the comments we hear in casual conversation for only a short time—perhaps for only a few minutes or hours. Some we forget almost as soon as we hear them. According to authorities, we even quickly forget most of the message in formal oral communications (such as speeches), remembering only a fourth of the information after two days.

Improving Your Listening Ability

Improving your listening is largely a matter of mental discipline—of concentrating on the activity of sensing. If you are like most of us, you are often tempted not to listen, or you just find it easier not to listen. Listening may seem like a passive activity, but it can be hard work.

After you have decided that you want to listen better, you must make an effort to be alert and to pay attention to all the words spoken.

What's in a Handshake?

A handshake is a common part of the greeting in U.S. business culture, especially in formal situations, in situations where individuals have not seen each other in a long time, or when people are meeting for the first time.

In fact, your handshake may be among the most critical nonverbal behaviors in the initial stage of any business relationship, such as the job interview or a meeting with a potential client. The professional handshake requires more than simply extending your hand. It requires that you practice so that you are prepared for any situation. Here are the rules according to Innovative Training and Communication Solutions:

- *Know when to shake hands:* Shake hands when (1) you are introduced to someone, (2) someone introduces himself or herself, (3) you introduce yourself to someone, (4) the conversation is over.

- *Shake for no more than three "pumps":* Another rule is to shake for about three seconds. Any longer than that and you make the situation awkward for everyone.

- *Shake from the elbow, not your shoulder:* This allows you to have a smooth handshake that is not rough or too forceful for the other person.

- *Don't be a "dead fish" or "wet fish":* Just as you do not want to shake too roughly, you do not want a limp handshake either. If your hands are sweaty, have some way to wipe them off (on your slacks or in the bathroom) before meeting people.

- *Don't be a "bone crusher":* Don't grip the other person's hand too hard. Not only do you not want to inflict pain, you don't want to appear too aggressive. Use the same force you would use to turn a door handle.

- *Don't give the "little lady" handshake:* Extend your whole hand, not just your fingertips. Extending just your fingertips signals that you are weak (especially if you are a woman).

- *Shake with one hand, not two:* Using both hands is too personal for a business setting. It also makes you look like you're trying too hard.

SOURCE: Amy Castro, "7 Handshake Rules You Shouldn't Break," *Innovative Communication and Training Solutions*, ICTS, 3 July 2012, Web, 26 July 2012.

Active listening is one technique individuals can use successfully. It involves **focusing** on what is being said and reserving judgment. Other components include sitting forward and acknowledging with "um-hm" and nodding. **Back-channeling** (repeating what you think you heard) is an effective way to focus your attention, as is asking questions of a speaker. Communicators can use technologies such as chat and blogs to comment on and enhance presentations in real time, which helps keep people focused on what is being said.

In addition to working on the improvement of your sensing, you should work on the **accuracy** of your interpreting. To do this, you will need to think in terms of what words mean to the speakers who use them rather than what the dictionary says they mean or what they mean to you. You must try to think as the speaker thinks—judging the speaker's words by considering the speaker's knowledge, experiences, culture, and viewpoints. Like improving your sensing, improving your ability to hear what is intended requires conscious effort.

Remembering what you hear also requires conscious effort. Certainly, there are limits to what the mind can retain, but authorities agree that few of us come close to them. Taking notes can also help ensure the accuracy of your hearing. By taking care to hear what is said and by improving your ability to interpret messages, you increase your chance of accurately understanding what is said.

Improve your listening skills by focusing your attention on the speaker and listening actively.

In addition to following the advice on the preceding pages, you will also want to review these steps offered in "The Ten Commandments of Listening":[2]

1. *Stop talking.* Even when we are not talking, we are inclined to concentrate on what to say next rather than on listening to others. So you must stop talking (and thinking about talking) before you can listen.

2. *Put the talker at ease.* If you make the talker feel at ease, he or she will do a better job of talking. Then you will have better input to work with.

3. *Show the talker you want to listen.* If you can convince the talker that you are listening to understand rather than oppose, you will help create a climate for information exchange. You should look and act interested. Doing such things as reading, looking at your watch, checking your phone, and looking away is disrespectful to the talker.

4. *Remove distractions.* Other things you do also can distract the talker. So don't doodle, tap with your pencil, or shuffle papers.

5. *Empathize with the talker.* If you place yourself in the talker's position and look at things from the talker's point of view, you will help create a climate of understanding that can result in a true exchange of information.

6. *Be patient.* You will need to allow the talker plenty of time. Remember that not everyone can get to the point as quickly and clearly as you can. And do not interrupt. Interruptions are barriers to the exchange of information.

7. *Hold your temper.* Anger impedes communication. Angry people build walls between each other; they harden their positions and block their minds to the words of others.

8. *Go easy on argument and criticism.* Argument and criticism tend to put the talker on the defensive. He or she then tends to "clam up" or get angry. Thus, even if you win the argument, you lose. Rarely does either party benefit from argument and criticism.

---

[2] To some anonymous author goes a debt of gratitude for these classic comments about listening.

9. *Ask questions.* By asking questions, you display an open mind and show that you are listening. You also help the talker develop his or her message and improve the correctness of your interpretation.

10. *Stop talking!* The last commandment is to stop talking. It was also the first. All the other commandments depend on it.

From the preceding review it should be clear that to improve your listening ability, you must set your mind to the task. Poor listening habits are ingrained in our makeup. We can alter these habits only through conscious effort.

THE REINFORCING ROLE OF NONVERBAL COMMUNICATION

LO5 Describe the nature and types of nonverbal communication.

In your role of either speaker or listener in oral communication, you will need to be aware of the nonverbal—nonword—part of your communication. In face-to-face communication, nonverbal communication accounts for a larger part of the total message than do the words you send or receive. Usually, we use nonverbal communication to supplement and reinforce our words. Sometimes, nonverbal communication communicates by itself.

Research indicates that developing your nonverbal communication skills and reading others' nonverbal communication have never been more important. According to one study,[3] **digital natives**—Generation X (born 1964–1979), Generation Y and Generation Y-Millennials (born 1980–present)—are particularly susceptible to overreliance on computer-mediated communication. The result is that they are likely to miss important nonverbal cues, such as those indicating deception or insincerity, that make them successful in positions where the development of trusting relationships is essential (e.g., sales). If you are one of these digital natives, then you may need to be more aware of your nonverbal skills and take special effort to develop them.

The Nature of Nonverbal Communication

Nonverbal or **nonword communication** means all communication that occurs without words. The "vocabulary" for this type of "language" is broad and imprecise. For instance, a frown on someone's forehead is sometimes interpreted to mean worry. But could it be that the person has a headache? Or is the person in deep thought? No doubt, there could be numerous meanings given to the facial expression. A recent article in *Forbes* illustrates how one behavior can have opposite interpretations. Younger employees were using computers or other technology during meetings. Senior employees took the use of technology to mean that employees were not paying attention or were engaged in activities unrelated to the meeting. The employees, however, thought they were making a positive contribution as they used their technology to research topics related to the meeting and provide input.[4]

The number of possible meanings is multiplied even more when we consider the cross-cultural side of communication. As noted in Chapter 2, culture teaches us about body positions, movements, and various factors that affect human relationships (e.g., intimacy, space, time). Thus, the meanings we give to nonverbal symbols will vary depending on how our culture has conditioned us.

Because of these numerous meanings, you need to be sensitive to what others intend with nonverbal communication, and you need to make some allowance for error in the meanings you receive from nonverbal symbols. As a listener, you need to go beyond the

---

[3]John K. Mullen, "The Impact of Computer Use on Employee Performance in High-Trust Positions: Re-examining Selection Criteria in the Internet Age," *Journal of Applied Social Psychology*, 14.8: 2009–2043, print.
[4]Eric Savitz, "Generation Gap: How Technology Has Changed How We Talk About Work," *Forbes*, Forbes, 16 May 2012, Web, 27 July 2012.

obvious to determine what nonword symbols mean. Just as we have said about word symbols, you need to consider what people intend with their nonverbal symbols.

Think for a few moments about a sample gesture you might make. What do you mean by it? What could it mean to others? Could it be interpreted differently by various audiences? Could someone from a different culture give a different meaning to it? Only if you analyze your nonverbal communication and realize its multiple meanings can you get some idea of how it might be interpreted differently. And when you become aware of the many differences, you then can become sensitive to the effects your nonverbal communication has on others.

The following section examines four types of nonverbal communication.

Types of Nonverbal Communication

Although there are many ways to classify nonverbal communication, we will examine four of the more common types: **body language, use of space, use of time,** and **paralanguage**. These four types are especially relevant to our discussion of speaking and listening.

Body Language. Much of what we say to others without using words is sent through the physical movements of our bodies. When we wave our arms and fingers, wrinkle our foreheads, stand erect, smile, gaze at another, or wear a coat and tie, we convey certain meanings; and others convey meanings to us in return. In particular, we use the face and eyes, gestures, posture, and physical appearance.

The face and eyes are by far the most important means of body language. We look to the face and eyes to determine much of the meaning behind body language and nonverbal communication. For example, happiness, surprise, fear, anger, and sadness usually are accompanied by definite facial expressions and eye patterns. You should be aware of these two aspects of body language as you speak and listen to others.

Gestures are another way we send nonword messages through our body parts. Gestures are physical movements of our arms, legs, hands, torsos, and heads. Through the movement of each of these body parts, we can accent and reinforce our verbal messages. And we can observe how others punctuate their oral communication with gestures. For example, observe the hand movements of another person while he or she is talking. As you observe these gestures, you will get a good picture of the person's emotional state. Moreover, speaking and gestures appear to be linked. In general, the louder someone speaks, the more emphatic the gestures used, and vice versa.

Another type of body language is physical appearance—our clothing, hair, and accessories. The appearance of our bodies can affect how our body movements are seen. Consider, for example, how you might perceive a speaker at a formal banquet dressed in faded blue jeans. Everything the speaker said or did would be perceived in relation to this attire. Accordingly, you want to make sure that your appearance fits the situation. And you want to remember that appearance is an important part of the body messages that are sent and received in oral communication.

Use of Space. Another type of nonverbal communication involves space. How we use space and what we do in certain spaces we create tell much about us and our culture.

We create four different types of space: intimate (physical contact to 18 inches), personal (18 inches to 4 feet), social (4 to 12 feet), and public (12 feet to the outer range of seeing and hearing). In each of these spaces, our communication behaviors differ and convey different meanings. For example, consider the volume of your voice when someone is 18 inches from you. Do you shout? Whisper? Now contrast the tone of your voice when someone is 12 feet away. Unquestionably, there is a difference, just because of the distance involved.

You will need to be sensitive to the spaces of others—especially those from different cultures. As noted in Chapter 2, when people's attitudes toward space are different, the odds of miscommunication increase.

Use of Time. A third type of nonverbal communication involves time. Just as there are body language and space language, there is also a time language. That is, how we give meaning to time communicates to others. To illustrate, think about how you manage your daily schedule. Do you arrive early for most appointments? Do you prioritize phone calls? Do you prepare agendas for meetings? Your response to time in these ways communicates to others, and, of course, others' use of time communicates to you.

As we discussed in Chapter 2, various cultures approach time differently. For Americans, Canadians, and many others from English-speaking countries, time values are monochronic. Monochronic people tend to view time as linear and always moving ahead. They expect events to happen at scheduled times. Polychronic people—such as those from Asian, Arabic, and Spanish-speaking countries—have a more indefinite view of time. Unlike the monochronic person who expects a meeting to start precisely at 9:00 a.m., the polychronic person sees a 9:00 a.m. meeting as an objective to be accomplished if possible. Such time orientations are parts of the messages we send to and receive from one another.

Paralanguage. Paralanguage, meaning "along with language," is a fourth type of nonverbal communication. Of all the types, it is the most closely tied to communication with word symbols. It has to do with the sound of a speaker's voice—those hints and signals in the way words are delivered, such as emphasis, pitch, volume speed, and connectivity, that also give meaning to a speaker's message. Are words spoken quickly or slowly? Are they high pitched or deep? Are they loud and forceful or barely audible? Are they smooth or disjointed? These questions are examples of the types you would ask to analyze the nonverbal symbols of paralanguage. The symbols become a part of the meaning that is conveyed by a spoken message.

To illustrate, read the following series of statements, emphasizing the underscored word in each.

> <u>I</u> am a good communicator.
> I <u>am</u> a good communicator.
> I am <u>a</u> good communicator.
> I am a <u>good</u> communicator.
> I am a good <u>communicator</u>.

By emphasizing the underscored word in each statement, you change the meaning of that statement from the others even though you use the same words. You do so by the way in which the word sequence sounds. As another example, try counting from 1 to 10 a number of times, each time expressing a different emotional state—say anxiety, anger, or happiness. The way you state each sequence of numbers will show what you intend quite accurately.

Paralanguage meanings also are conveyed by *consistencies* and *inconsistencies* in what is said and how it is said. Depending on the circumstance, a person's voice may or may not be consistent with the intended word meanings. Consistency between the words you choose and how you deliver them to create clear meaning should be your goal. For example, if you are happy or angry, your voice will be loud; if you are sad or delivering bad news, you will likely speak in a quieter tone.

Keep in mind that all communicators have certain assumptions about how a message should sound. Whether real or imagined, people infer background factors (race, education, etc.); physical appearance (age, height, gender); and personality (introversion, social orientation, etc.) when they hear and interpret paralanguage. When you speak, you should do whatever you can to influence these assumptions positively. Many of the suggestions in this chapter and the following one should help you deliver a consistent and effective message. Active listeners will also want to listen between the lines of a spoken message to determine the true meaning a speaker is sending.

Other Types of Nonverbal Communication. The preceding four types are the primary forms of nonverbal communication, but others exist. For example, artists, interior decorators, and "image consultants" believe that different colors project different meanings. What meanings do you get from red, yellow, black, blue? The colors in visual aids (see Chapter 14), wardrobe, and office decor all send nonverbal messages. Thus, you should give more than casual attention to color as a type of nonverbal communication.

Still another type of nonverbal communication involves the structure of our physical context. In an office, the physical arrangements—furniture, carpeting, size, location, and decorations—all communicate meaning to us and to others. These elements provide the context for many of our speaking and listening activities. We should therefore consider them as part of the messages we send and receive as well.

THERE'S MORE . . .

Are you interested in taking a listening skills inventory, learning more about parliamentary procedure, or finding organizations for businesspeople that can help you improve your oral communication skills? Scan the QR code with your smartphone or use your Web browser to visit www.mhhe.com/lesikar13e. Choose Chapter 15 > Bizcom Tools & Tips.

SUMMARY BY LEARNING OBJECTIVES

Discuss talking and its key elements.

1. Good talking depends on four critical factors:
   - Voice quality—talking with variations in pitch, delivery, and volume.
   - Speaking style—blending voice quality and personality.
   - Word choice—finding the right vocabulary for the situation.
   - Adaptation—fitting a message to the listener.

Explain the techniques for conducting and participating in meetings.

2. In business, you are likely to participate in meetings, some formal and some informal.
   - If you are in charge of a meeting, follow these guidelines.
     — Know parliamentary procedure for formal meetings.
     — Plan the meeting; develop an agenda and circulate it in advance.
     — Follow the plan.
     — Keep the discussion moving.
     — Control those who talk too much.
     — Encourage participation from those who talk too little.
     — Control time, making sure the agenda is covered.
     — Summarize at appropriate times.
     — Take minutes.
   - If you are a participant at a meeting, follow these guidelines:
     — Stay with the agenda; do not stray.
     — Participate fully.
     — But do not talk too much.
     — Cooperate.
     — Be courteous.

3. To improve your phone and voice mail techniques, consider the following:

- Cultivate a pleasant voice.

- Talk as if in a face-to-face conversation.

- Follow courteous procedures.

  — When calling, introduce yourself and ask for the person you want.

  — State your purpose early.

  — Cover points systematically.

  — When receiving a call, identify your company or office and yourself and offer assistance.

  — When answering for the boss, do not offend by asking questions or making comments that might give a wrong impression; and do not neglect callers placed on hold.

  — When screening calls for the boss, be courteous and honest.

  — Listen when the other person is talking.

  — Do not interrupt or dominate.

  — Plan long conversations, and follow the plan.

- For good voice mail messages, follow these suggestions:

  — Identify yourself by name and affiliation.

  — Deliver a complete and accurate message.

  — Speak naturally and clearly.

  — Give important information slowly.

  — Close with a brief goodwill message.

- Demonstrate courtesy when using cell phones by following these general guidelines:

  — Turn off the ringer where it could disrupt others.

  — Avoid use at social gatherings.

  — Keep the phone off the table during meals.

  — Talk only in places where others won't be in earshot.

  — Avoid talking about confidential or private business.

  — Keep voice volume down.

  — Initiate calls in quiet places away from others.

  — Be conscious of others when you talk.

  — Avoid talking while driving, especially if it is against the law.

Describe good phone and voice mail techniques.

4. Listening is just as important as talking in oral communication.

- Listening involves how we sense, filter, and retain incoming messages.

- Most of us do not listen well because we tend to avoid the hard work that good listening requires.

- You can improve your listening with effort.

- Put your mind to it and discipline yourself to be attentive.

- Make a conscious effort to improve your interpretation of incoming messages; strive to retain what you hear.

- Follow the practical suggestions offered in "The Ten Commandments of Listening."

Explain the barriers to good listening and describe how to overcome them.

5. Nonverbal (nonword) communication is the communication that occurs without words.

- One major type is body language—the movements of our arms, fingers, facial muscles, and other physical components.

  — Our face and eyes are the most expressive means of body language.

Describe the nature and types of nonverbal communication.

— Gestures also send messages.

— Our physical appearance (clothing, cosmetics, jewelry, hairstyle) communicates about us.

- Space is a second major type of nonverbal communication.

  — We create four unique types of spaces: (1) intimate, (2) physical, (3) social, and (4) public.

  — We communicate differently in each space, as influenced by our culture.

- How we give meaning to time is a third type of nonverbal communication.

- The meanings that the sounds of our voices convey (paralanguage) are a fourth type.

- Color and physical context are also nonverbal forms of communication.

- In our speaking, we should use nonverbal communication to accent our words.

- In listening, we need to "hear" the nonverbal communication of others.

KEY TERMS

informal talking, 526

business meetings, 528

parliamentary procedure, 529

agenda, 530

voice message, 535

active listening, 537

focusing, 537

back-channeling, 537

accuracy, 537

digital natives, 539

nonverbal or nonword communication, 539

body language, 540

use of space, 540

use of time, 540

paralanguage, 540

CRITICAL THINKING QUESTIONS

1 Talking is something we do every day, so we can be confident that these everyday skills are ready for use in the workplace. Discuss. **LO1**

2 How can being conscious of the elements of talking help us communicate better? **LO1**

3 Being able to start a conversation is especially important when meeting clients in social settings. Discuss the types of topics that would and would not be appropriate. **LO1, 2**

4 The people attending a meeting—not the leader—should determine the agenda. Discuss. **LO2**

5 As meetings should be democratic, everyone present should be permitted to talk as much as he or she wants without interference from the leader. Discuss. **LO2**

6 Describe an annoying phone practice that you have experienced or know about (other than the ones discussed in the chapter). Explain and/or demonstrate how it should be corrected. **LO3**

7 Describe the strengths and weaknesses of voice mail systems with which you are familiar. **LO3**

8 Discuss why we have difficulty listening well. **LO4**

9 What can you do to improve your listening? **LO4**

10 Explain how each type of nonverbal communication relates to speaking and to listening. **LO5**

SKILLS BUILDING EXERCISES

Talking

1 Record yourself in conversation with three different audiences (e.g., a friend, your parents, a customer or client at work, an instructor). Conduct a SWOT (strengths, weaknesses, opportunities, threats) analysis of your talking using the four elements of good talking discussed in this chapter. What are your *strengths*?

What are your *weaknesses*? Identify *opportunities* for improving your talking. Discuss *threats* to improving your talking (e.g., nervousness, lack of interest). What will you do to address the threats? Present your analysis in a memo report to your instructor. Be sure to explain to your audiences why you're recording your conversation and seek permission as appropriate.

2 Find a video or recording of talking done by someone you think has good voice quality and someone you think has poor voice quality. Analyze the speaker's voice quality in terms of the features discussed in this chapter. As your instructor requests, present your analysis to your class or a small group or to your instructor in the form of a memo. Your instructor may also require that you assess each person's nonverbal communication skills.

Meetings

3 For one of the topics below, develop a specific problem that would warrant a group meeting. (*Example:* For student government, the problem might be "To determine the weaknesses of student government on this campus and what should be done to correct them.") Then lead the class (or participate) in a meeting on the topic. Class discussion following the meeting should reinforce the text material and bring out the effective and ineffective parts of the meeting.

   a. Student drinking

   b. Scholastic dishonesty

   c. Housing regulations

   d. Student–faculty relations

   e. Student government

   f. Library

   g. Grading standards

   h. Attendance policies

   i. Varsity athletics

   j. Intramural athletics

   k. Degree requirements

   l. Parking on campus

   m. Examination scheduling

   n. Administrative policies

   o. University calendar

   p. Homework requirements

   q. Tuition and fees

   r. Student evaluation of faculty

   s. Community–college relations

   t. Maintaining files of old examinations for students

   u. Wireless Internet availability

4 Using one of the topics in the above exercise (or another topic as your instructor directs), work in groups of four to present a solution to the problem you decide to address. You should meet at least four times. One person should be designated to establish an agenda for and lead each meeting and another to take minutes at each meeting. Each person in the group should take a turn leading a meeting and taking minutes. After each meeting, group members should evaluate the group leader's abilities. Let your leader know of at least one strength and one area needing improvement. Submit your agendas, minutes, and leader evaluations to your instructor as directed. Present your group's solution to your class as a short presentation or to your instructor in a memo.

5 Working in groups of four or five, debate the following statement. *As long as the information they provide is truthful, employers should be able to give a negative reference without fear of lawsuits or other negative effects for a former employee seeking employment with another company.* Examine arguments that might lead you to agree with the statement or disagree with it, and come to a consensus. Tape the meeting and analyze the group members' performances. You may analyze the recording as a group or individually as your instructor directs. Who emerged as the leader of the discussion? How could you tell this person was the leader? Did anyone dominate the discussion? Did anyone not participate or participate very little? Why do you think this person did not participate as much as he or she could have? What could people in the group do to improve their skills? What did they do well?

Talking on the Phone

6 Make a list of bad phone practices that you have experienced or heard about. With a classmate, first demonstrate the bad practice and then demonstrate how you would handle it. Some possibilities: rudely putting a caller on hold, using an unfriendly tone, unintentionally insulting the caller, sounding uninterested.

7 Think about your outgoing message on your cell phone or answering machine. For whom is your message appropriate? Are the voice quality, style, and word choice appropriate? Is it courteous? Is there anyone you would not want to hear this message (e.g., a potential employer)? Does the message contain sufficient detail? Is it too detailed or too long? In a memo to your instructor, include the text of your current outgoing message. If your message needs revision, include the text of your revised message. Explain why you are revising the message and describe the audience for which you are making the message more appropriate. If you do not believe your message needs revision, explain how your message meets the needs of your current audiences. If you do not have a cell phone or answering machine, borrow a friend's.

Listening

8 After the class has been divided into two or more teams, the instructor reads some factual information (newspaper article, short story, or the like) to only one member of each team. Each of these team members tells what he or she has heard to a second team member, who in turn tells it to a third team member and so on until the last member of each team has heard the information. The last person receiving the information reports what she or he has heard to the instructor, who checks it against the original message. The team able to report the information with the greatest accuracy wins.

9   This exercise is similar to exercise #2 under Talking, but in this exercise, you will analyze your listening skills. Reflect on a recent conversation with a friend, oral instructions you received from your boss, or a class lecture where you demonstrated what you believe is representative of your listening skills in general. Use a SWOT analysis to evaluate your listening skills. What are your *strengths* as a listener? What are your *weaknesses*? Identify some *opportunities* for improving your skills. Identify possible *threats* (e.g., physical limitations, lack of interest) that may hinder your ability to improve your skills. What can you do to address these threats? Present your analysis in a memo report to your instructor.

Nonverbal Communication

10 Find three to five pictures of men and women with different facial expressions (happiness, sadness, anger, etc.) or gestures. Ask those native to your area to identify the emotions or the meanings of the gestures the pictures convey. Then ask at least three others from different countries (preferably different continents) to identify the emotions. Report your results to the class.

11 Go to a public place (e.g., your school's cafeteria, the library, a park, or a mall). Observe the interaction between two people whom you can see but whom you cannot hear. In a short memo to your instructor, describe the setting, the participants, the interaction, and the nonverbal behaviors. Analyze their nonverbal communication and present two possible interpretations of these behaviors. Be sure to justify your interpretations with evidence from your observation.

12 Record yourself in some type of oral communication setting (e.g., the meetings described in previous exercises, a mock job interview with your school's career services office, your next presentation for this or another course). Watch the recording without the sound, and pay attention to your nonverbal behaviors. In a short memo to your instructor, describe what you saw and evaluate what you do well and what you will work to improve.

CHAPTER SIXTEEN

Delivering Oral Reports and Business Speeches

Learning Objectives

Upon completing this chapter, you will understand how to give effective oral reports and speeches, whether face to face or online. To reach this goal, you should be able to

1 Define oral reports and describe important differences between oral and written reports.

2 Determine an appropriate topic, purpose, and structure for a speech or presentation.

3 Describe the personal, physical, and vocal traits that contribute to an effective report or speech.

4 Plan visuals (graphics and slides) to support oral reports and speeches.

5 Plan and deliver effective Web-based presentations.

6 Work effectively with a group to prepare and deliver a team presentation.

Meeting the Challenge of Formal Speaking

You joined the Corporate Affairs team at Sunfield Cereals only a few months ago, but you can already see that your work will involve several kinds of oral presentations.

For example, at its monthly meeting last week Sunfield's executive committee assigned your department the task of preparing a special oral report. The report concerns the results of a survey that your department conducted to find out how a shipment of flawed products had affected the company's public image. Because you designed and conducted the survey, your boss has asked you to give this report. The audience will be not only the company executives but also the managers at all 10 Sunfield locations across the U.S. You must find a way to deliver your report to all these audiences simultaneously.

Then today, your boss asked you to do something very special for the company. It seems that each year Sunfield Chemicals awards a $5,000 scholarship to a deserving business student at State University. The award is presented at the business school's annual Honors Day Convocation, usually by your boss. To show the business school's appreciation for the award, its administration requested that your boss be the speaker at this year's convocation. But she has a conflicting engagement, so you got the assignment. You are excited but nervous about this challenge.

Such assignments will only become more frequent as you move up the ladder at Sunfield. The following review of oral presentations should help you do them well.

MASTERING FORMAL SPEAKING

Researchers consistently note the growing importance of oral communication skills even as technologies such as email, blogs, and other social networking opportunities demand more of our writing skills. According to some estimates, "speakers address audiences an astonishing 33 million times each day . . . and businesspeople give an average of 26 presentations a year."[1]

While Chapter 15 addressed the informal, interpersonal types of oral communication you might encounter in business, this chapter addresses the more formal types of oral communication—oral reports and speeches—that you will be likely to prepare in any professional setting. As with the written forms of communication discussed in this book, these presentations require careful preparation.

REPORTING ORALLY

Each day, thousands of internal oral reports are needed to keep boards of directors, executives, and those in other areas of the company informed. Oral reports often have external audiences, too, such as progress reports to clients and informational reports to community or government groups.

The following sections will help you master the art of the oral report in business.

LO1 Define oral reports and describe important differences between oral and written reports.

Defining Oral Reports

In its broadest sense, an **oral report** is any objective presentation of facts and their interpretation using the spoken word. Such reports can range from brief status reports delivered by employees or managers at weekly meetings to elaborate reports delivered to clients, potential clients, or company executives. In any reporting situation, the audience expects the presenter (1) to speak without interruption for a certain amount of time and (2) to deliver useful, timely information in an orderly way. An oral report, in other words, shows evidence of research and planning.

---

[1] Ronald B. Adler and Jeanne Marquardt Elmhorst, *Communicating at Work: Principles and Practices for Business and the Professions* (New York: McGraw-Hill, 2010) 303, print.

Understanding the Differences between Oral and Written Reports

While both oral and written reports present and interpret data, the two modes of delivery entail the following significant differences.

Visual and Verbal Cues. As you have learned, readers rely on visual cues to interpret written reports. To help them, you can use headings and paragraphing to show the structure of the message and to make the thought units stand out. In addition, you can use punctuation to help show relationships and typography to add emphasis.

When you deliver an oral report, these aids will be missing unless you have supporting visual material, and even then, much of your spoken content will have no visual component. However, you can use inflection, pauses, volume emphasis, and changes in the rate of delivery to help your listeners follow you. If appropriate, you can also provide key points on slides, a flip chart, or a whiteboard and refer to them at the appropriate time.

Degree of Reader Control. A significant difference between oral and written reports is that the readers of a written report, unlike the listeners of an oral report, control the pace of the communication. They can pause, reread, change their rate of reading, or stop as they choose. Since the readers set the pace, the writing can be complex and still communicate. However, since the listeners for an oral report cannot control the pace of the presentation, they must grasp the intended meaning as the speaker says the words. For this reason, good presenters monitor the audience's reaction, slow down or speed up as needed, and use handouts or other written material for detailed information that might need careful review.

Formality in Oral and Written Reports. As with written reports, your use of correct grammar in oral reports is a reflection of your competence. However, it is often acceptable to use a less formal style in oral reports. Colloquialisms, contractions, and even slang can be effective with certain audiences. If using such a style, be sure that your language still reflects your professionalism.

Considering the differences between writing and speaking in terms of verbal and visual cues, degree of reader control, and level of formality can help you identify which type of report—written or oral—to prepare.

Planning the Oral Report

As with written reports, planning is the logical first step in your work on oral reports. For short, informal oral reports, planning may be minimal. But for the more formal oral reports, particularly those involving powerful or external audiences, proper planning is likely to be as involved as that for a comparable written report.

Determining the Report Objective. Logically, your first task in planning an oral report is to determine your objective. As prescribed for the written report in Chapter 11, you should state the problem or topic your report will address and, in light of that topic, your report's purpose. Then you should determine the factors you'll need to investigate in order to achieve your goal. This procedure will help you decide what information to gather and what the main sections of the report will be.

In determining your report objective, you must think carefully about your audience's traits and interests. For example, a board of directors may need information to decide your company's direction in the next quarter, while a client may need information to determine whether your company's product meets his or her needs.

Organizing the Content. The procedure for organizing oral reports is similar to that for organizing written reports. You will choose either the direct or indirect order, depending on the situation.

In general, though, oral reports are more likely to be delivered indirectly than are written reports. Perhaps this is because listeners expect an oral report to be more or less like a story, with the beginning and middle leading up to the main point. Whatever the reason, oral reports usually begin with the purpose, provide any helpful background information, present the facts and analysis, and then give the conclusions or recommendations. On the other hand, the direct structure may be more appropriate for some oral reports. For example, if you've been asked to report on the impact of a new federal regulation on the company's operations, your listeners may grow impatient if you do not reveal the main findings up front and then fill in the details.

Both written and oral reports may end with a conclusion, a recommendation, a summary, or a combination of the three. But the oral report is likely to have a more extensive closing statement. In a sense, your ending will serve the purpose of an executive summary by bringing together all the important information, analyses, conclusions, and recommendations. Your listeners cannot flip back through the report the way they could with a written report, so this kind of close will help them pull all the parts of your report together and remember the key points.

Planning for Interaction. Almost all oral reports give the audience an opportunity to ask questions or offer opinions. You will need to decide how to manage this part of the presentation.

Some speakers state or clearly imply at the beginning of the report that they will take questions at the end. Others tell the audience up front to ask questions at any time, and still others build audience participation into the report at specific times. One expert asserts that saving the Q&A until the end is a "quick-fire way to ensure that no one will ask a question"[2] because the audience won't want to prolong the talk, but in some cases, listeners actually want to hear the whole report before asking questions. As always, your topic, purpose, and audience should be your guide. Whatever method you choose, be sure you anticipate the questions your listeners are likely to ask, and be prepared with good answers.

Before you present, you'll need to make a number of additional decisions, ranging from how to prepare the venue, how to design helpful supplementary materials, and what personality to project during your talk. Later sections of this chapter will advise you on these topics.

GIVING SPEECHES AND PRESENTATIONS

Many people find delivering speeches difficult and uncomfortable. Having to give the speech online or in front of a video camera can increase the risk of awkwardness. But you can improve your public speaking and reduce any anxiety associated with it by learning what good speaking techniques are and then putting those techniques into practice.

Determining the Topic and Purpose

LO2 Determine an appropriate topic, purpose, and structure for a speech or presentation.

Electronic means of communication have greatly expanded the types of speeches that businesspeople give. Sometimes face-to-face delivery is still the best choice, but other times a video or a live online presentation may be more appropriate.

Whatever the medium, your first step in formal speaking—as with the oral report—is to determine the topic and purpose of your presentation. In some cases, you will be assigned a topic, usually one within your area of specialization. In fact, when you are asked to make a speech on a specified topic, it is likely because of your knowledge of the topic. In some cases, your choice of topic will be determined by the purpose of your assignment, as when you are asked to welcome a group, introduce a speaker, demonstrate a product, or pitch a proposal.

---

[2] Joey Asher, president of the company Speechworks, as quoted by Tonya Layman in "Presentation Pitfall," *Atlanta Business Chronicle*, American City Business Journals, 3 June 2011, Web, 1 Aug. 2012.

In other cases, you'll be asked to speak on a topic of your choice. In your search for a suitable topic, you should be guided by four basic factors. The first is *your background and knowledge*. Any topic you select should be one with which you are comfortable—one within your areas of proficiency. The second basic factor is *the interests of your audience*. Selecting a topic that your audience can appreciate and understand is vital to the success of your speech. The third basic factor is *the occasion of the speech*. Is the occasion a meeting commemorating a historic event? A monthly meeting of an executives' club? The keynote address at a professional conference? Whatever topic you select should fit the occasion. And fourth, consider *the medium you'll be using*. Whether your speech is an in-person address, a video, or a virtual presentation with remote participants may well affect your topic, as well as the length and contents of your speech.

Preparing the Presentation

After you have decided what to talk about, why, and in what medium, you will gather the information you need. This step may involve recalling relevant experiences or generating ideas, conducting research in a library, searching through company data, gathering information online, or consulting people in your own company or other companies.

When you have your information, you are ready to begin organizing your talk. Although variations are sometimes appropriate, you should usually follow the basic pattern of *introduction, body,* and *conclusion*. This is the order described in the paragraphs below.

Although not really a part of the speech, your first words should be a greeting appropriate for the audience. A simple "good morning" or "good evening" may suffice. Some speakers eliminate the greeting and begin with the speech, especially in more informal and technical presentations. If you have not been introduced to your audience, be sure to introduce yourself.

Introduction. The introduction of a speech has much the same goal as the introduction of a written or oral report: to prepare the listeners (or readers) to receive the message. But the opening of a speech usually needs some kind of attention-gaining material as well. The situation is somewhat like that of the sales message; at least some of the people with whom you want to communicate won't initially be interested in your talk. You will need an appropriate strategy to engage the audience right away.

**"My presentation lacks power and it has no point.
I assumed the software would take care of that!"**

Have You Met TED?

To see great presenters in action, visit TED.com, where the world's top thinkers on a wide range of topics share their insights. Because each speaker is held to an 18-minute time limit, these speeches are often models of efficiency and clarity. And many of the talks are supported by stunning visuals, which the speakers skillfully integrate into their talks.

TED.com is sponsored by the organization TED—whose name is an acronym for technology, entertainment, and design. As the site explains, TED is a nonprofit organization "devoted to Ideas Worth Spreading." It began as the name of a conference organized by Richard Saul Wurman (the inventor of the term *information design*) and associates, which first took place in Silicon Valley in 1984. Since then, the U.S. conference has become an annual event, and there is a yearly global conference as well.

The talks are organized by themes—such as "The Rise of Collaboration," "Not Business as Usual," "What's Next in Tech," and "Bold Predictions, Stern Warnings." You can also search the site by topic.

Here's a sampling of the business-related videos you'll find:

- In "Presentation Innovation," Dr. Hans Rosling makes public-health statistics come alive in animated visuals.

- In "Why Work Doesn't Happen at Work," Jason Fried, software entrepreneur, explores the counterproductive qualities of office buildings.

- In "Evan Williams on Listening to Twitter Users," the cofounder of Twitter talks about the unexpected uses of Twitter that have fueled its astronomical growth.

- In "Why We Have Too Few Women Leaders," Sheryl Sandberg, COO of Facebook, analyzes the striking shortage of women in high places and offers advice for women seeking such roles.

If you haven't visited TED.com already, be sure to do so before your next speech to see how the best and brightest do it.

One possibility is a human-interest story. For example, a speaker presenting a message about the opportunities available to people with original ideas might open this way: "Nearly 150 years ago, an immigrant boy of 17 walked the streets of our town. He had no food, no money, no belongings except the shabby clothes he wore. He had only a strong will to work—and an idea."

Humor is another widely used technique. If you know that someone will be giving you a glowing introduction, you might say, "Wow, after that introduction, I can hardly wait to hear what I'm going to say."

One communications expert advises against using prepared jokes, though, especially if you are not a good joke teller. The better course, in his view, is to interject humor that is "spontaneous, related to the event, and self-directed."[3] Whichever way you choose, make sure your humor is relevant and inoffensive.

Other effective attention getters are quotations and questions. By quoting someone the audience would know and view as credible, you build interest in your topic. You also can ask questions. One kind of question is the rhetorical question—the one everyone answers the same, such as "Who wants to be free of burdensome financial responsibilities?" Another kind of question gives you background information on how much to talk about different aspects of your subject. With this kind of question, you must follow through by basing your presentation on the response. If you asked "How many of you have IRAs?" and nearly everyone raised a hand, you wouldn't want to talk about the importance of IRAs. You could skip that part of your presentation, spending more time on another aspect, such as managing an IRA effectively.

Yet another possibility is the startling statement. Illustrating this possibility is the beginning of a speech to an audience of merchants on a plan to reduce shoplifting: "Last year, right here in our city, in your stores, shoplifters stole over $3.5 million of your merchandise."

---

[3] Bill Lampton, "5 Reasons You Shouldn't Start Your Speech with a Joke," *Business Know-How*, Attard Communications, Inc., n.d., Web, 28 July 2012.

In addition to arousing interest, your opening should lead into the topic of your speech. In other words, it should set up your message as the examples above do.

Following the attention-gaining opening, it is appropriate to tell your audience what you'll be talking about. In fact, in cases where your audience will already have an interest in what you have to say, you can begin here and skip the attention-gaining opening. Presentations of technical topics to technical audiences typically begin this way.

If you have a particular, and perhaps not widely shared, opinion about your subject, you may prefer to move into your subject indirectly—to build up your case before revealing your position. This inductive pattern may be especially desirable for sales proposals and other persuasive speeches.[4] But in most business-related speeches you should indicate your attitude toward the topic early in the speech.

Body. Organizing the body of your speech is much like organizing the body of an oral or written report. You take the whole and divide it into comparable parts. Then you take those parts and divide them, and you continue to divide as far as it is practical to do so. In speeches, however, you are more likely to use factors (subtopics) rather than time, place, or quantity as the basis of division because in most speeches your presentation is likely to be built around issues and questions that pertain to the subject. Even so, time, place, and quantity subdivisions are possibilities.

You need to emphasize the transitions between the divisions because, unlike the reader who can see them in a written report, the listener may miss them if they are not stressed adequately. Without clear transitions, you may be talking about one point, and your listener may think you are still on the previous point.

Successful oral presentations to large audiences are the result of thorough preparation.

---

[4] "The Secret Structure of Great Talks," a popular TED video by Nancy Duarte, recommends using a structure that moves back and forth between "what is" and "what could be," ending with the "call to action" (*TED*, Ted Conferences, LLC, Feb. 2012, Web, 29 July 2012). This would be an appropriate structure for talks intended to inspire, sell, or change people's minds. Its indirectness would not be appropriate for instructional or informational talks.

Conclusion. Like most reports, the speech usually ends by drawing a conclusion or conclusions. The conclusion is the culmination of your report—the point at which you achieve your communication goal. You should consider including these three elements in your close: (1) a restatement of the subject, (2) a summary of the key points developed in the presentation, and (3) a statement of the conclusion (or main message).

Bringing the speech to a climactic close—that is, making the conclusion the high point of the speech—is usually effective. Present the concluding message in words that gain attention and will be remembered. In addition to concluding with a summary, you can give an appropriate quote, use humor, or call for action. The following close of a speech advocating a new marketing strategy illustrates this point: "In short, switching from print to email marketing will save money, generate more sales leads, and gain us a bigger share of the market."

Choosing the Presentation Method

In addition to determining the speech's content and structure, you need to decide on your method of presentation—that is, whether to present the speech extemporaneously, memorize it, or read it.

Presenting Extemporaneously. **Extemporaneous presentation** is by far the most popular and effective method. With this method, you first thoroughly prepare your speech, as outlined above. Then you prepare notes and present the speech from them. You usually rehearse, making sure you have all the parts clearly in mind, but you make no attempt to memorize. Extemporaneous presentations generally sound natural to the listeners, yet they are (or should be) the product of careful planning and practice.

Memorizing. The most difficult method is to present your speech from memory. If you are like most people, you find it hard to memorize a long succession of words. Also, if you memorize, you can get flustered if you miss a word or two during your talk. You may even become panic-stricken.

For this reason, few speakers who use this method memorize the entire speech. Instead, they memorize key passages and use notes to help them through the speech. A delivery of this kind is a cross between an extemporaneous presentation and a memorized presentation.

Reading. The third presentation method is reading. Unfortunately, most of us tend to read aloud in a monotone. We also miss punctuation marks, fumble over words, lose our place, and so on. But many speakers have learned to read a speech in an interesting, smooth way, and with effort you can, too. One effective way is to practice with a recorder and listen to yourself. Then you can be your own judge of what you must do to improve your delivery. You would be wise not to read speeches until you have mastered this presentation method.

In most business settings, it is considered inappropriate to read. Your audience will want more personal interaction than that. However, when you are acting as the official spokesperson for a company or organization—for example, when responding to a crisis or giving an important announcement—reading from a carefully prepared speech is appropriate and even expected. Many top executives today use teleprompters when delivering read speeches, and many of these speeches are well done.

Choosing the Means of Audience Feedback

Traditionally, formal speeches have been one-way communication, with the presenter delivering a well-prepared talk and restricting audience participation to applause or questions at the end. Today's audiences are likely to expect more two-way communication, even during the talk.

With webinars, or live presentations conducted via the Web, participants expect to be kept involved through polls, questions, and even live chat with the speaker. But even in real settings, audiences often expect to be invited to contribute as well—whether by raising their hands, asking questions, voting with a clicker,[5] or tweeting their answers or comments.[6]

Even if you decide not to use extensive back-channeling, or the use of audience feedback during your talk, you may want to incorporate audience participation at some points in your presentation to break up your speech and keep the attention level high. How you do so will depend on the media you will use to deliver your talk and your relationship with your audience.

Whether or not you invite audience feedback during your talk, consider inviting the audience to email you afterward with their questions and comments. Many webinar presenters follow up their online sessions with evaluation forms that they email to the participants. This kind of post-presentation interaction can help you improve your presentations, acquire positive statistics to show to your boss, and build productive relationships with those who heard you speak.

PREPARING YOURSELF TO SPEAK

Whatever type of oral report, speech, or presentation you will be giving, be sure you are prepared to deliver it well. Of course, the content of a message must be solid, but if your delivery is poor, people may ignore or simply miss your most important points. The following sections provide strategies for ensuring that your audience will understand and respond positively to your message.

LO3 Describe the personal, physical, and vocal traits that contribute to an effective report or speech.

Appealing Personal Traits

An important preliminary to good oral reports or speeches is to analyze yourself as a speaker. In oral presentations you, the speaker, are a very real part of the message. The members of your audience not only take in the words you communicate but also form an impression of you. And how they perceive you can significantly affect how they respond. You should thus do your best to project personal traits that will appeal to your audience. Those that follow are particularly important.

Confidence. A primary characteristic of effective oral reporting is confidence—your confidence in yourself and the confidence of your audience in you. The two are complementary: Your confidence in yourself tends to produce an image that gives your audience confidence in you, and your audience's confidence in you can give you a sense of security that increases your confidence in yourself.

Typically, you earn your audience's confidence through repeated contact with them. When you speak to a room full of strangers, you must find other ways to gain their confidence. Preparing your presentation diligently and practicing it thoroughly will give you confidence and help you project it. Another confidence-building technique is an appropriate physical appearance. Looking like those your audience respects gives you credibility and helps you get into your role as presenter. Yet another confidence-building technique is simply to talk in strong, clear tones. Speaking as though you are relaxed and self-assured will actually help you feel this way.

Competence. Audiences expect speakers to be knowledgeable on the topic they're discussing. Do your homework so that you'll have the knowledge your audience will require of you. Anticipate the listeners' likely questions—and if you're asked something you don't know, don't try to fake an answer. Instead, offer to find the information and share it with the audience later (e.g., by email). Besides gathering the necessary

---

[5] Jan Hoffman, "Speak Up? Raise Your Hand? That May No Longer Be Necessary," *The New York Times*, The New York Times Company, 30 Mar. 2012, Web, 29 July 2012.

[6] See Kathy Reiffenstein's blog *Professionally Speaking* for the research behind Twitter's growing popularity as a presentation-enhancing tool ("Twitter in Presentations—Love It or Leave It?," 28 May 2009, Web, 29 July 2012).

Presentation Delivery Tools Help You Convey Your Message Effectively

Have you ever used PowerPoint's Presenter View? It can really enhance the smoothness of a presentation. You can see its major tools in the screenshot below. While your slides are being displayed to the audience in Slide Show view, Presenter View lets you view not only the slides but also your notes. Additionally, you see the title to the upcoming slide as well as the elapsed time since the beginning of the presentation. Furthermore, a menu under the current slide allows you to start or end the show on one click, black out that screen to bring the attention back to you, and perform other actions. As the presenter, you have the flexibility to skip slides or change the ordering on the fly.

In PowerPoint 2010 you can access the presenter's view by going to the Slide Show tab > Monitors box > Use presenter view. *Note:* You need to have your computer connected to two monitors—usually a laptop and a projector—to be able to set up and use Presenter View. For set-up instructions, search "presenter view" in PowerPoint's Help feature.

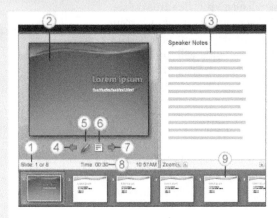

1 The slide number (for example, slide 1 of an 8-slide presentation)

2 The slide you are currently showing to the audience

3 The speaker's notes, which you can use as a script for your presentation

4 Click to go to the previous slide

5 The pen or highlighter

6 Click to display a menu that enables you to end the show, darken or lighten the audience screen, or go to a specific slide number

7 Click to go to the next slide

8 The elapsed time of your presentation, in hours and minutes

9 Slide thumbnails that you can click to skip a slide or to return to a slide that you already presented

SOURCE: Microsoft, "What Is Presenter View?" *Microsoft.com*, Microsoft Corporation, n.d., Web, 31 July 2012.

knowledge, spare no effort in making the presentation itself well designed and well written. Grammatical errors or poorly designed slides can sabotage an otherwise great speech.

Sincerity. Your listeners are quick to detect insincerity. And if they detect it, they are likely to give little weight to what you say. On the other hand, sincerity—when combined with competence—generates trust and conviction. The way to project an image of sincerity is clear and simple: You must *be* sincere. Be yourself, and acknowledge your

limits. If you can't answer a question, say so and invite others in attendance to offer their ideas. Graciously compliment those ideas and add what you do know. Show that your topic is of genuine interest to you and that it is more important than your ego.

Friendliness. A speaker who projects an image of friendliness has a significant advantage. Audiences simply like friendly people, and they are generally receptive to what such people say. To project friendliness, smile, make eye contact, and learn and use audience members' names. You can also watch yourself in a mirror as you practice speaking to improve your projection of friendliness.

Appropriate Appearance and Physical Actions

In face-to-face presentations and many videos and online presentations, your listeners will be looking at you and your surroundings. What they will see is a part of the message and can affect the success of your speech. Do your best to make these visual elements contribute to, not detract from, your talk.

The Communication Environment. Whenever you'll be visible, a background will be visible as well. For actual presentations, try to visit the room ahead of time to see what adjustments to the setting you might want to request. For example, you might want the podium moved or the lighting managed in a certain way. For virtual presentations, be sure to test how you'll actually look on camera so you can check the backdrop, the lighting, and how much of you will show. In both environments, ensure that your voice will be appropriately amplified and that extraneous noise will be kept to a minimum.

Personal Appearance. As Chapter 15 points out, your personal appearance is a part of the message your audience receives. Dress in a manner appropriate for the audience and the occasion. You should also be sure that nothing about your appearance (e.g., hairstyle or jewelry) is distracting.

Posture. Posture is likely to be the most obvious physical trait of yours that your audience will see. Even listeners not close enough to detect facial expressions and eye movements can see the general form of the body. Keep your body erect without appearing stiff and comfortable without appearing limp. Try to appear naturally poised and alert.

Walking. Your audience also forms an impression from the way you walk. A strong, sure walk to the speaker's position conveys an impression of confidence. Hesitant, awkward steps convey the opposite impression.

Walking during the presentation can be good or bad, depending on how you do it. Some speakers use steps forward and to the side to emphasize points. Too much walking, however, detracts from the message. You would be wise to walk only when you are reasonably sure that this will have the effect you want. And be sure not to walk away from the microphone.

Facial Expression. As noted in Chapter 15, probably the most communicative physical movements are facial expressions. When speaking, be sure to avoid those that convey unintended meanings. For example, if a speaker appears frightened, the image detracts from the entire communication effort. A smile, a grimace, and a puzzled frown may be appropriate or inappropriate, depending on the context. Choose those expressions that best convey your intended meaning.

Eye contact is important. The eyes, which have long been considered "mirrors of the soul," provide most listeners with information about the speaker's sincerity, goodwill, and flexibility. Making eye contact tends to show that you have a genuine interest in your audience.

Gestures. Like facial expressions, gestures are strong, natural aids to speaking. It is natural, for example, to emphasize a plea with palms up and to show disagreement by shaking one's head. Raising first one hand and then the other usually indicates contrasting points, while a shrug might mean "either way is fine" or "who knows?"

The appropriateness of physical movements is related to personality, physical makeup, and the size and nature of the audience. Also, a speaker appearing before a formal group tends to use more conservative gestures (e.g., slight head and hand movements) than one before an informal group. Which physical movements you should use on a given occasion is a matter for your best judgment.

Look Like a Pro with PowerPoint Keyboard Shortcuts

If you've ever attended a presentation during which the speaker had trouble finding the right view, going back to an earlier slide, or using other features of the software, you know how distracting that can be.

Familiarizing yourself with keyboard shortcuts can help you move around quickly and skillfully in your presentation. Here, for example, are some PowerPoint 2010 shortcuts for managing your slides like a pro:

To Do This	Press
Start your presentation in Slide Show view.	F5
Show or hide the arrow pointer.	A or =
Change the pointer to a pen (to draw on your slides while presenting).	CTRL + P
Change the pen back to an arrow.	CTRL + A
Show or hide the ink markup.	CTRL + M
Perform the next animation or advance to the next slide.	N, Enter, Page Down, Right Arrow, Down Arrow, or Spacebar

Perform the previous animation or advance to the next slide.	P, Page Up, Left Arrow, Up Arrow, or Backspace
Go to a certain slide.	*Slide number* + Enter
Return to the first slide.	Press and hold Right and Left Mouse buttons for 2 seconds
Display a blank black slide, or return to the last-viewed slide from a blank black slide.	B or Period
Display a blank white slide, or return to the last-viewed slide from a blank white slide.	W or Comma
Stop or restart an automatic presentation.	S
End a presentation.	Esc or Hyphen

To see all the PowerPoint shortcuts, press Shift + F10.

SOURCE: Microsoft, "Keyboard Shortcuts for Use While Delivering a Presentation in PowerPoint 2010," *Microsoft.com*, Microsoft Corporation, n.d., Web, 31 July 2012.

Pleasant Voice and Speaking Style

An interesting, pleasant voice is an obvious requirement of good speaking. Like physical movements, the voice should not hinder the listener's concentration on the message. Voices that cause such difficulties tend to have these flaws: (1) lack of pitch variation, (2) lack of variation in speed, (3) lack of vocal emphasis, and (4) unpleasant voice quality. Although these drawbacks are discussed in Chapter 15 in the context of interpersonal communication, we will review them here because of their significance to formal oral communication.

Lack of Pitch Variation. Speakers who talk in a monotone are not likely to hold the interest of their listeners for long. Listening to your voice and making a conscious effort to vary your pitch can help you develop a more interesting style.

Lack of Variation in Speaking Speed. As a general rule, you should present the easy parts of your message at a fairly fast rate and the hard parts and the parts you want to emphasize at a slower rate. A slow presentation of easy information is irritating; hard information presented fast may be difficult to understand. And no variation in the speaking speed can be boring.

A problem related to the pace of speaking is the incorrect use of pauses. Properly used, pauses emphasize upcoming subject matter and are an effective means of gaining attention. But frequent pauses for no reason are irritating and break the listeners' concentration. Pauses become even more irritating when the speaker uses fillers such as *uh, like, you know,* and *OK.*

Lack of Vocal Emphasis. A secret of good speaking is to give words their proper emphasis by varying the manner of speaking. You can do this by (1) varying the pitch of your voice, (2) varying the pace of your presentation, and (3) varying the volume of your voice.

You must talk loudly enough for your entire audience to hear you, but not too loudly. Obviously, your volume should be greater for a large audience than for a small audience, unless a microphone is provided. Regardless of audience size, however, variety in volume is good for interest and emphasis. It produces contrast, which is one way of emphasizing the more important points. Some speakers incorrectly believe that the only way to show emphasis is to get louder. But you can also show emphasis by decreasing volume. The contrast in volume provides the emphasis.

Unpleasant Voice Quality. It is a hard fact that some voices are more pleasant than others. Fortunately, most voices are reasonably pleasant, but some are raspy, nasal, or unpleasant in another way. To improve their voices, businesspeople sometimes do voice therapy. Short of that, concentrating on variations in pitch, speed of delivery, and volume can compensate considerably for a less-than-ideal speaking voice.

In this day of audio and video recorders, it is easy to hear and see yourself talk. Since you know good speaking when you hear it, you should be able to improve your vocal presentation if you analyze your current style.

Another good way to improve your presentation skills is to watch others. Watch your instructors, your peers, television personnel, professional speakers, and anyone else whom you might learn from. Today you can even watch top corporate executives on webcasts and video presentations. Analyze these speakers to determine what works for them and what does not, and then imitate those techniques that you think would help you. You may also want to refer to Chapter 15, page 526, for tips on improving your speaking voice.

LO4 Plan visuals (graphics and slides) to support oral reports and speeches.

SUPPORTING YOUR TALK WITH VISUALS

Audiences have become much more visually oriented than they used to be. They expect that most presentations will include a visual component to help them follow along and stay interested.

Plus, as professional trainers know, visuals also aid immensely in retention of the presented information. According to a U.S. government website that provides guidelines for safety and health training, an audience who has heard an oral presentation with no visuals recalls about 10 percent of what they've heard. If they've been given only a visual with no oral component, that number increases to 35 percent. Combining the two media to present the information raises the number to 65 percent.[7]

Planning the most effective visuals to go with your oral report or speech should thus be integral to planning the talk overall. Chapter 14 also provides tips for choosing the best visuals for the types of data you may need to present in your oral report or speech.

What Kinds of Information to Present Visually

The purpose and content of your talk will determine the points at which a visual might be appropriate, but the following guidelines can help.

- Most presenters who will be using supporting visuals in electronic form begin their talk with a *title slide* that conveys the point of the talk, the speaker's name, and the name and logo of the sponsoring company (if any).

- Providing an *outline* of what you will cover can help your listeners comprehend you better as you proceed through your talk.

- *Charts, tables,* and *line art* or *diagrams* will help your listeners understand statistical information or a process.

---

[7] United States, "Construction Safety and Health Outreach Program," Occupational Safety & Health Administration, Department of Labor, n.d., Web, 30 July 2012.

- *Photographs* help your listeners form a concrete image of something you're discussing, whether a happy customer, your products, or a vision of the future.

- If not overdone, *animation* (zooming in and out, bars or columns that grow, moving text or objects, photographs that change) can reinforce a point you're making or help you show a process.

- Most popular digital presentation tools make it easy to incorporate *multimedia* into your show. Consider embedding audio or video files in your slides to bring in an expert opinion, share a story, or show an example. If you know you will have an Internet connection, consider embedding hyperlinks to get audience feedback (e.g., via Twitter).

When your talk will not be electronically supported—and such talks still take place frequently—you should consider incorporating visuals (except animation and multimedia, of course) into a print handout for your listeners. Many of these types of visuals can also be adapted to a flip chart or whiteboard. Be sure to consult the advice in Chapter 14 when designing your visuals, including how to cite the sources for any copyrighted visuals you'll be using.

Techniques for Using Visuals

Any visuals you use will need to be skillfully incorporated into your talk. Here are some basic dos and don'ts:

- Make certain that everyone in the audience can see the visuals. Too many or too-faint lines on a chart, for example, can be hard to see. An illustration that is too small can be meaningless to people far from the speaker. Even fonts must be selected and sized for visibility.

- If necessary, explain the visual. Remember that the visual is there to help you communicate content, not just to add visual interest.
- When discussing a visual, refer to it with physical action and words. Use a laser pointer or slide animations to emphasize each point you're making.
- Talk to the audience—not to the visuals. Look at the visuals only when the audience should look at them. When you want the audience to look at you, you can regain their attention by covering the visual or making the screen white or black (in PowerPoint, toggle the W or B keys).
- Avoid blocking the listeners' views of the visuals, and make certain that the listeners' views are not blocked by lecterns, pillars, or furniture.

Use of Presentation Software

When most people think of designing visuals to go with a report or speech, they automatically think of PowerPoint—the first widely used, and still the most popular, presentation software. But cloud applications (those hosted by a service provider, not installed on your computer) and apps for mobile devices have really broadened your options.

For example, you may have tried Prezi, a cloud application (available in a free version) that enables you to zoom in and out as you move around an online canvas. SlideRocket is another popular PowerPoint alternative. Even its free version comes with design, timing, and multimedia options—such as adding a live Twitter feed to a slide—that PowerPoint doesn't offer. And of course there's Google Docs's presentation tool, which has almost as many features as PowerPoint, along with the added benefit of enabling online collaboration without the need for additional software.

Whichever tool you use, stay clear of the following pitfalls:

- *Putting too much on a slide.* This is one of the most common errors presenters make. Remember that your talk, not your slides, should convey most of your detailed information. Making a slide or Prezi object too crowded is a surefire way to make your audience stop looking at it. For PowerPoint, we recommend no more than six brief bullet points per slide and no more than two levels of bullet points (Figure 16–1).
- *Making the contents on the slide too small.* This is probably the second most common error. When you're designing your slides, you're looking at them on your computer, so small type and visuals are legible. But your audience for an in-person speech will be trying to read your slides from many feet away from the screen, and even those viewing webinar slides on their computers won't like tiny content.

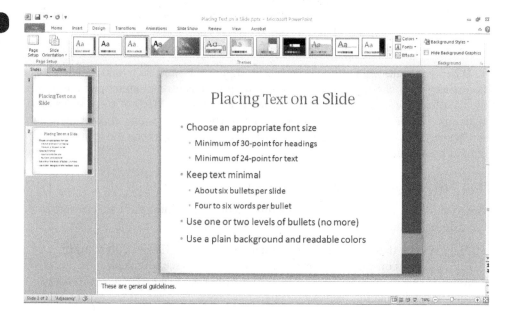

Figure 16–1

An Attractive, Readable Text Slide in PowerPoint 2010

We recommend 30-point type or larger for headings and 24-point type or larger for the text (Figure 16–1).

- *Using an inappropriate theme or unreadable color combinations.* Students tend to want to choose elaborate and flashy designs for their slides. But many templates included with the software are too busy for most presentation purposes, and certain text and background color combinations, such as red text on a blue background, make the slides difficult to look at, let alone read. Err on the side of conservatism. Black text on a white or pale background with the company logo discretely in the corner can make for easily readable slides as well as a clean, professional look.

- *Using too much animation.* Another tendency amateurs have is to go wild with the options for transitions between slides and with other dynamic features. Prezi is particularly susceptible to this problem; all of the zooming in and out can actually make viewers dizzy. Again, err on the side of conservatism. Remember that the goal is not to dazzle the audience with visual activity but to achieve your communication purpose.

- *Being inconsistent across slides.* Your whole presentation should have a consistent look. This means that similar slides should be formatted similarly (e.g., for text-based slides, use the same font throughout for the slide titles, as well as the same body font) and that no slide should look as though it belongs in a different presentation.

- *Reading vertatim what's on the slides (or, the opposite, not integrating what's on the slide into your talk).* Visuals should be included to help you present—not the other way around. Strike a good balance between helping the audience read what's on the screen and keeping the focus on you and what you have to say.

The checklist in Figure 16–2 can help you avoid these problems.

Figure 16–2

Tips for Effective Presentations

Checklist for Preparing/Editing Presentation Slides

Questions about the presentation as a whole:

- Is there an attractive, clearly worded, readable title slide?
- Does the writer make good use of an outline slide? Is it titled effectively, and are the items in the list of topics grammatically parallel?
- Do the slides seem to cover all the important information?
- Do the slides seem to be in the most logical order?
- Is there a final slide that sums things up or leaves people with a significant thought or finding?
- Does the whole presentation have a consistent look?

Questions about every slide:

- Is there a strong contrast between the background and the text color?
- Is there any type that is too small to be read? (Remember, no typeface should be smaller than 24 points.) Conversely, is any type too big (yelling)? Is any typeface hard to read (as with italics or too fancy a font)?
- Is there too much or too little information on any slide? Should any slides be combined or divided up? If a topic is covered in more than one slide, the title on the subsequent slides should include "(cont'd)."
- Is every slide accurately/informatively titled?
- Has the writer managed the hierarchy of the information well (not using more than two levels of information and making clear which is on the top level and which is on the secondary level)?
- Are all headings on the same level grammatically parallel? Are items in all lists grammatically parallel?
- Is the wording on each slide clear and grammatically correct?
- If there are borrowed facts or quotes, are the sources named clearly on the slides?
- Is each slide visually clean and attractive? Should/could the writer add visuals anywhere? Are all visuals appropriately used and clearly labeled?
- Are the dynamic elements (e.g., slide transitions) appropriate for the topic and audience? Should you use more or less animation at any point?

Use of Handouts

Should you supplement your presentation with handouts? If so, what kind? And at what point in the talk? These are good questions. You know from experience that some speakers provide no handouts, while others provide complete copies of their slides. If they have handouts, some speakers distribute them at the beginning of the talk, while others wait until the end.

Make your decisions given the purpose and occasion of your talk. If you're presenting information that your listeners will want to be able to review later, give them complete copies of your slides or even a complete copy of your report or proposal. If you think your listeners will want to take notes as you go, give a handout at the start of the talk that has room for notes; otherwise, save the handout until the end so that your speech can benefit from the element of surprise. If the information you're covering can be distilled into a useful quick-reference sheet or a list of resources, handing that out at the end of your talk is sufficient. As you can see, there is no overarching rule; what's best will depend on the situation.

If possible, always bring one complete print copy of your slides or a detailed outline of your talk to the presentation venue. Computers crash; projector bulbs go out; Internet connectivity sputters. If technological disaster strikes, it's likely that the venue will still have a copier, enabling you to deliver your talk with print support.

LO5 Plan and deliver effective Web-based presentations.

DELIVERING WEB-BASED PRESENTATIONS

Live Web presentations—commonly called *webinars* or *Web events*—have become a popular genre of business communication. They eliminate the speakers' and participants' travel expenses, and they can reach huge audiences. Plus, many powerful, easy-to-use applications for conducting such events are available. WebEx, once the undisputed leader in this area, now has competitors with such products as Citrix's Go-ToMeeting, Microsoft's Lync Online, Adobe's Acrobat ConnectPro, Dimdim, Wimba, and more. The affordable costs make this technology attractive to both large and small businesses for presentations to both large and small audiences.

Varieties of Web Presentations

While the terms *webcast*, *Web meeting*, and *webinar* are sometimes used interchangeably, and one Web-based application might support all three types of communication, the consensus of those in the industry seems to be that the terms have—or should have—different meanings.

A **webcast** typically consists of live video being "broadcast" to the audience. Like a television or radio show, it provides no means of audience participation. A **Web meeting** is a Web-based get-together, usually for a small group of people who have chosen to conduct their interactions online rather than in a conference room. Of the three terms, **webinar** is the most synonymous with *presentation*. Here, a main speaker or speakers present on their topic of expertise, but the audience almost always has an opportunity to participate.

Webinars can take many forms, depending on the technology being used and the preferences of the presenter. A simple and still very popular form of webinar uses PowerPoint slides and phone lines. At the appointed time, participants log into a website and dial the provided number on their phones. They then listen and watch as the presenter walks them through the slides that have been prepared for the occasion. A more sophisticated webinar might have an interface that provides a list of participants, allows them to "raise their hands" (by clicking an icon) and be called on, and enables them to comment via a chat field. At the most elaborate end of the spectrum are applications that also include live video of the presenter(s)—and if the participants have Web cameras, videos of them as well (see the screenshot in the Technology in Brief box on the next page). Many Web-presentation applications also

Virtual Presentations: The Next Best Thing to Being There

Web-based presentation tools offer many options for participant interaction. Featured here is the interface of Wimba, a popular application in academic environments. Its layout and capabilities are very similar to those of comparable tools in the business environment.

The Participant Area shows who is logged in. The buttons below the names (circled in red) let participants vote yes or no in a poll, raise their hands, and indicate their reactions with emoticons. The columns to the right of the names show the participants' choices and indicate who has speaking and/or video privileges. Using the chat window, participants can chat with the whole group or with particular participants.

Presenters have many options as well (circled in blue). They can display a website during the presentation; turn on a whiteboard in which all participants (with appropriate privileges) can draw, type text, or import graphics; share applications running on their desktops (which participants can be allowed to do as well); and move back and forth through imported slides. The presenter can also decide whether and when to enable various audio and video options.

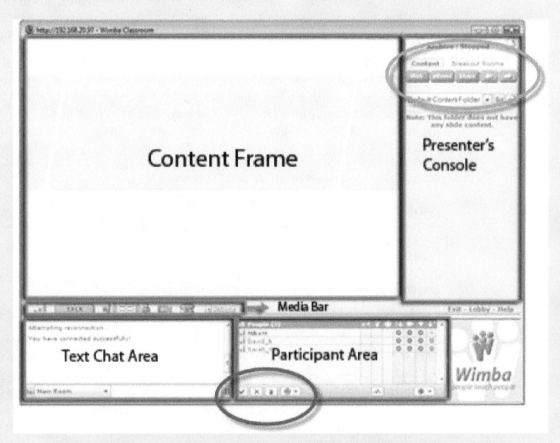

SOURCE: Wimba, Inc., *Wimba Classroom Version 6.0 Presenter Guide*, Wimba Classroom, Wimba, Inc., 2009, Web, 1 Aug. 2012.

make it easy for the presenter to record the webinar so that it can be viewed later and by other audiences.

Webinars are being used in business in many of the same ways that face-to-face presentations are used—to inform, educate, discuss, and persuade. They can improve productivity by giving remote employees up-to-date information and training, avoiding down time for travel and reducing travel costs. They can also allow sales people to reach broader audiences as well as highly targeted specialized audiences worldwide.

Special Guidelines for Web Presentations

To deliver a live virtual presentation effectively, you'll need to prepare for certain preliminary, delivery, and closing activities. Your first step is to choose a user-friendly technology that supports the type of webinar you want to give. Then you'll prepare and send out announcements of the presentation along with a note encouraging the audience to pretest their systems before the designated start time for the presentation. A day or two before and the day of the presentation, most presenters send email reminders of the event.

It is a good idea to line up a technical person to troubleshoot during the presentation, since, some participants will have trouble connecting, others will fall behind, and software or Internet glitches can occur. Also, you'll need to arrange ahead of time for an assistant if you need one. An assistant can help you keep track of time, take over if necessary, and provide other help to keep the presentation going smoothly.

You may want to create something for early arrivers to view in the first 5 to 10 minutes before you start. This could be an announcement, news of an upcoming presentation, or information about your products and services. At the end of the talk, you will want to tell participants where to access additional information, including your slides, video recording of the presentation, and other business links.

The delivery of your presentation will be much like that for other presentations, except you will be doing it from your desktop using a microphone and perhaps a Web camera (if the talk will include video). You may want to use the highlighter, drawing tools, or animation features of PowerPoint or the webinar application to help you emphasize key points that you would otherwise physically point to in a face-to-face presentation. You will want to plan breaks during which you will poll or quiz the audience or handle questions that have come in through the chat tool. If you use Presenter View in PowerPoint (see Technology in Brief, page 556), you can set the timer to help you do this at regular intervals.

In the closing, you will want to allow time to make any final points and answer any remaining questions. Watching your time is critical because some systems will drop you if you exceed your requested time.

Overall, presenting virtually requires the same keys to success as other presentations—careful planning, attentive delivery, and practice.

LO6 Work effectively with a group to prepare and deliver a team presentation.

GIVING TEAM (COLLABORATIVE) PRESENTATIONS

Team presentations are a common school assignment, and they're common in business as well. To give this type of presentation, you can apply all the preceding advice about giving individual reports and speeches. You can also use much of Chapter 11's advice on preparing written reports collaboratively. But you will need to adapt the ideas to an oral presentation setting.

First, you will need to take special care to plan the presentation—to determine the sequence of the presentation as well as the content of each team member's part. You also will need to select supporting examples and design any visual components carefully to build continuity from one part of the presentation to the next.

Groups should plan for the physical aspects of the presentation, too. You should coordinate the type of delivery, use of notes, and attire to present an impression of competence and professionalism. You should also plan the transitions from one presenter to the next so that the team will appear coordinated.

Another presentation aspect—physical staging—is important as well. For face-to-face presentations, team members should decide where they will sit or stand, how

visuals will be presented, how to change or adjust microphones, and how to enter and leave the speaking area. For videotaped and virtual presentations that will show the speakers and their settings, you will need to determine what kind of background to have and what distance the presenter will sit from the camera.

Attention to the close of the presentation is especially important because you'll need to ensure that all the pieces delivered by the team members are brought together into a coherent, complete conclusion. Teams need to decide who will present the close and what will be said. If a summary will conclude the talk, the member who presents it should attribute key points to appropriate team members. If there is to be a question-and-answer session, the team should plan how to conduct it. For example, will one member take the questions and direct them to a specific team member? Or will the audience be permitted to direct questions to specific members? Some type of final note of appreciation or thanks needs to be planned, with all the team nodding in agreement or acknowledging the final comment in some way.

Teams should also allow for plenty of rehearsal time. They should practice the presentation in its entirety several times as a group before the actual presentation. During these rehearsals, individual members should critique each other's contributions, offering specific ways to improve. After first rehearsal sessions, outsiders (nonteam members) might be asked to view the team's presentation and critique the group. Moreover, the team might consider videotaping a rehearsal of the presentation so that all members can evaluate it.

As you can see, an effective report or speech takes knowledge, preparation, and skill. But the rewards justify the effort. By following this chapter's advice (summarized in Figure 16–3) and using good judgment, you can give a successful talk in any medium or situation. This ability will make you a valued asset to your employer and further your professional success.

Oral Presentation Basics

- Be sure your report or speech has a clear, audience-adapted objective.
- Organize the talk so that it leads the listeners logically to your conclusion. The situation may call for either the direct or indirect order.
- Plan an engaging beginning.
- Plan for appropriate audience participation.
- Plan the visuals, if any, that will support your talk.
- Choose your speaking method (extemporaneous, memorization, reading, or a hybrid).
- Choose your presentation tools (if any), and be sure the venue is optimized for your talk. Manage any other visual elements of your talk (e.g., your appearance, the background) to your advantage.
- Project confidence, competence, sincerity, and friendliness.
- Employ body language to your advantage. Be relaxed and natural, and use appropriate gestures and facial expressions.
- Articulate clearly, pleasantly, and with proper emphasis. Avoid mumbling and the use of such fillers as *ah*, *er*, *like*, and *OK*.
- Punctuate the presentation with references to well-designed, non-distracting visuals.
- Field audience questions and comments with honesty, interest, and professionalism.
- End your presentation with a striking quote, statistic, or other comment that will reinforce your communication purpose.
- Provide handouts as needed to enable the audience to follow and use the information.

THERE'S MORE . . .

Where can you find cool PowerPoint add-ons, catchy quotes for a speech, or additional tips on giving Web-based presentations? Scan the QR code with your smartphone or use your Web browser to find out at www.mhhe.com/lesikar13e. Choose Chapter 16 > Bizcom Tools & Tips.

SUMMARY BY LEARNING OBJECTIVES

Define oral reports and describe important differences between oral and written reports.

1. Business oral reports are objective presentations of factual business information and its interpretation.
   - Written and oral reports have the following differences:
     — Written reports permit the use of such visual cues as paragraphing and punctuation; in oral reports, voice inflection, pauses, and other aural devices must replace many of these visual cues.
     — Oral reports permit the speaker to exercise greater control over the pace of the presentation; readers of a written report control the pace.
     — Both oral and written reports should be correct, but oral reports may be less formal.
   - Plan oral reports just as you do written ones.
     — First, analyze your audience, determine your topic and purpose, and identify the factors you'll need to investigate.
     — Next, gather the content and decide on either the indirect or the direct order.
     — Plan a logical order for the body sections of the report as well as introductory/concluding paragraphs.
     — End the report with a final summary—a sort of ending executive summary.
     — Plan the timing and type of audience interaction you will have.

2. Consider the following suggestions for preparing a speech or presentation.

- Begin by selecting an appropriate topic—one in your area of specialization and of interest to your audience.
- Organize the message (introduction, body, conclusion).
- Consider an appropriate greeting ("Good morning").
- Design the introduction to meet these goals:
  — Arouse interest, perhaps with a story, humor, quotation, or question.
  — Introduce the subject (topic).
- For persuasive speeches and those on potentially controversial topics, you may want to reveal your position late in the talk. Otherwise, state your position or purpose early.
- Organize the speech as you would an oral or written report: Divide and subdivide, usually by factors (subtopics).
- Select the most appropriate ending, usually restating your main point and making its significance to the audience clear.
- Consider using a climactic close.
- Choose the best manner of presentation.
  — Extemporaneous presentation is usually best.
  — Memorizing is risky.
  — Reading is difficult to do well unless you are skilled.
- Choose the means of audience feedback.
  — Today's audiences are likely to expect two-way communication.
  — Both in-person and virtual presentations can use back-channeling (gathering of feedback during the talk).
  — Post-presentation interaction (Q&A, email messaging) can also be used.

Determine an appropriate topic, purpose, and structure for a speech or presentation.

3. Prepare yourself and your environment for an effective talk.

- Work on these characteristics of a good speaker:
  — Confidence.
  — Competence.
  — Sincerity.
  — Friendliness.
- Manage the physical environment (stage, lighting, background), your personal appearance, and your body language (posture, walking, facial expressions, gestures) for a positive effect.
- Use a pleasant, interesting speaking voice.
  — For best effect, vary the pitch and speed.
  — Give appropriate vocal emphasis.
  — Cultivate a pleasant voice quality.

Describe the personal, physical, and vocal traits that contribute to an effective report or speech.

4. Use visuals whenever they help communicate.

- Organize your visuals as a part of your message.
- Select the most appropriate types for your contents.
- Blend the visuals into your speech, making certain that the audience sees and understands them.
- Talk to the audience, not to the visuals.
- Do not block your audience's view of the visuals.
- Use presentation software to enhance content, being careful to avoid common slide-design problems.
- Prepare and deliver handouts as appropriate.

Plan visuals (graphics and slides) to support oral reports and speeches.

Plan and deliver
effective Web-based
presentations.

5. Live Web presentations, called *webinars* (or *Web events*), have become popular in business.

- Webinars differ from webcasts and Web meetings in that webinars are the most like oral presentations.
- Webinars can take many forms, from those using slides and phone lines to those with integrated audio and video.
- Before delivering a virtual presentation, you'll need to choose the delivery technology, prepare and send announcements, test the system, arrange for technical assistance, and prepare material for early arrivers to view.
- During the delivery, you should have planned interactive activities (e.g., polling or quizzing), take regular breaks for feedback and questions, and be attentive to all feedback from the audience.
- In closing, you should allow ample time for final points and questions.
- Overall, the virtual presentation, like the face-to-face presentation, requires planning, attentive delivery, and practice.

6. Group presentations present special challenges.

- They require all the skills of individual presentation.
- In addition, they require extra planning to
  - Reduce overlap and provide continuity between the parts.
  - Provide a smooth transition to each presenter.
  - Deliver an effective conclusion and/or conduct a smooth question-and-answer session.

Work effectively with
a group to prepare
and deliver a team
presentation.

KEY TERMS

oral report, 548

extemporaneous presentation, 554

webcast, 564

Web meeting, 564

webinar, 564

CRITICAL THINKING QUESTIONS

1 As you consider your future career, think of three scenarios in which you might need to present an oral report. What would be the purpose of these reports, and who would be their audiences? In light of these factors, what kinds of information would you need to include? **LO1**

2 Explain the principal differences between oral and written reports. What do these differences mean in terms of how you'd need to adapt a written report for presentation to an audience? **LO1**

3 Give an example of a scenario in which you'd be wise to organize your report indirectly. Then give one in which the direct order would be preferable. **LO1**

4 Assume that your boss, the director of marketing, has asked you to prepare an oral report for the marketing team on the status of the current sales campaign. The sales messages being "pushed" to potential customers have been designed for viewing on three different technologies: PCs, tablets, and smartphones.

List, in order of presentation, the content you might include, along with any visuals that would go with it. **LO1, LO4**

5 Assume that you must prepare a speech on the importance of community service for an audience of business majors. Develop two attention-gaining openings for this speech. **LO2**

6 Assume that as a successful young _____ [fill in an appropriate job title] you've been asked to give a speech to a college honorary society or club in your area of professional expertise. Generate two good topics for your speech, and be ready to explain the reasoning behind your choices. **LO2**

7 Assume that in the scenario described in question #6 you invite questions at the end of your talk, and an arrogant-seeming student in the audience contradicts something you said. How would you handle this situation? **LO4**

8 Recall an effective speech you heard or viewed in which the speaker read his or her remarks. What made the speech effective even though it was read? **LO2**

9 View a TED talk (TED.com) and evaluate the projected personal qualities, use of body language, and speaking style/voice of the presenter. What techniques might your emulate? Which, if any, would be ones you'd want to avoid? **LO3**

10 Go to YouTube.com and examine a video in which a business professional is giving advice about making oral presentations. Evaluate the advice, and also evaluate the speaker's own presentation skills. **LO3**

11 View a TED talk (TED.com) and evaluate both the visuals the speaker uses and how he or she integrates them into the talk. What techniques might your emulate? Which, if any, would be ones you'd want to avoid? **LO4**

12 Find an online video or tutorial about designing effective presentation slides. Evaluate the advice being given. **LO4**

13 Recall a presentation you attended that effectively used supporting visual material. Then recall one that didn't. What were the differences? **LO4**

14 Find a videotaped webinar (e.g., Apollo Research Institute's complimentary Future of Work webinar or those available at www.webex.com/webinars), and evaluate it. What were its strengths? How might it have been improved? **LO5**

15 If you've taken any online courses, make a list of the presentation features (e.g., use of media, types of audience participation) that you liked about them. Then list the drawbacks that these courses had. **LO5**

16 Assume that you and some classmates have been asked to prepare a team presentation that will be videotaped. What logistics do you need to work out before you tape the presentation? **LO6**

17 Recall the team presentations that you've seen in your classes. What qualities made some team presentations better than others? **LO6**

SKILLS BUILDING EXERCISES

Topics for Oral Reports and Public Presentations

(*Note*: Many of the Problem-Solving Cases at the end of Chapter 12 can also serve as oral presentation topics.)

1 Survey the major business publications for information about the outlook for the national (or world) economy for the coming year. Then present a summary report to your entrepreneurship class.

2 Select a current technological innovation for business use and report it to a company's top administrators (you select the company). You will describe the innovation and point out how it will benefit the company. If appropriate, you may recommend its purchase.

3 Report to a meeting of a wildlife-protection organization on the status of an endangered species. You will need to gather the facts through research, probably in wildlife publications.

4 A national chain of _____ (your choice) is opening an outlet in your city. You have been assigned the task of reviewing site possibilities. Gather the pertinent information and make an oral recommendation to the board of directors.

5 The Future Business Leaders Club at your old high school has asked you to give a talk on what it takes to succeed in business school. You will cover all the factors that you think high school students need to know. Include visuals in your presentation.

6 You're one of a group of students who have been selected to go to China (or pick another country) to represent your school at a conference. Prepare a report to give to the group that will prepare them to behave appropriately in this culture.

7 As a member of an investment club, report to the membership on whether the club should purchase shares of a certain high-tech company. Your report will cover past performance, current status, and future prospects for the short and long run.

8 Look through current newspapers, magazines, and the Web to find the best available information on the job outlook for this year's college graduates. You will want to look at each major field separately. You also may want to show variations by geographic area, degree, and schools. Present your findings in a well-organized and illustrated oral report.

9 Present a plan for improving some phase of operations on your campus (registration, academic honesty, housing, grade appeals, library, cafeteria, traffic, curricula, athletics, computer labs, or the like).

10 Present an objective report on some legislation of importance to business (e.g., right-to-work laws, ethics, environmental controls, taxes). Take care to present evidence and reasoning from all the major viewpoints. Support your presentation with appropriate visuals.

11 Assume that you are being considered by a company of your choice for a job of your choice. Your prospective employer has asked you to make a _____ -minute report (your instructor will specify) on your qualifications. You may project your education to the date you will be on the job market, making assumptions that are consistent with your record to date.

12 Prepare and present a report on how individuals may reduce their federal or state income tax payments. You probably will want to emphasize the most likely sources of tax savings, such as tax sheltering and avoiding common errors.

13 Make a presentation to a hypothetical group of investors that will get you the investment money you need for a purpose of your choice. Your purpose could be to begin a new business, to construct a building, to develop land—whatever interests you. Make your presentation as real (or realistic) as you can. And support your appeal with visuals.

14 As chairperson of the site-selection committee of the National Federation of Business Executives, present a report on your committee's recommendation. The committee has selected a city and a convention hotel (you may choose each). Your report will give your recommendation and the reasons that support it. For class purposes, you may make up whatever facts you may need about the organization and its convention requirements and about the hotel. But use real facts about the city.

15 As a buyer of men's (or women's) clothing, report to the sales personnel of your store on the fashions for the coming season. You may get the necessary information from publications in the field.

16 The top administrators of your company have asked you to look into the matter of whether the company should own automobiles, lease automobiles, or pay mileage costs on employee-owned automobiles. (Automobiles are used by sales personnel.) Gather the best available information on the matter and report it to the top administrators. You may make up any company facts you need, but make them realistic.

17 Your work for a professional speakers bureau (a company that hires out speakers). Your boss has asked you to prepare a report on incorporating Twitter into presentations. Your report will be videotaped and distributed to the bureau's speakers to advise them on the potential uses of this tool.

18 Assume again the role described in topic #17, but this time your topic is the comparative advantages of Prezi, PowerPoint, and SlideRocket. Prepare a report that will help the bureau's speakers choose the best tool for a given situation and type of speech.

19 The career services center at your school is conducting a series of brief presentations on companies both local and national/international that students might want to learn about as potential employees. Your business communication teacher has gotten wind of this initiative and has offered to have her class prepare and deliver some of these as their report assignments. The director of the center has enthusiastically agreed! In this pretend scenario, you'll be preparing an oral report about a company of your choice for students at your school who are entering the job market. Your instructor and the director of your career services center are your secondary audiences.

Carefully plan your report to be between 8 to 10 minutes long. Support your talk with PowerPoint slides that have the following:

- An introductory slide to identify your company.

- An overview slide, listing the topics your talk is going to cover.

- A slide for each main section of your talk.

- A closing slide with the main point you want to leave with people.

The following kinds of information might be appropriate to include in your talk:

- Company's outputs (products/services); the industry to which it belongs.

- Company's size (dollars in sales/revenue; number of employees), ownership, financial health.

- Company's plants/facilities/location.

- Company's history (how founded? When? By whom? Main achievements and/or crises in the company's history?).

- Company's structure (if possible, include an organizational chart at the end of the report and refer to it in your report).

- Company's employees (labor force, unionized or not, kinds of expertise, values).

- Company's position in its industry or main competitors; company's market/customers.

- Company's culture/missions/policies/management style/work environment.

- Current problems/challenges facing this company.

- Any unique traits of this company or industry that are important to mention to the prospective employee.

Include at least two Web and two non-Web references in your report (that is, material in a publication or database).

PART SIX

Elements of Professionalism: Technological Proficiency and Correctness

Norm Fjeldheim credits much of the success in his career to learning and developing his business writing and reporting skills. As a leader in a top company in the digital wireless communications industry, he relies heavily on these well-honed skills. In overseeing all aspects of Qualcomm's information technology, he interacts with people in a wide variety of positions including Qualcomm senior executives and board members, senior executives of customers and suppliers, and occasionally even the Department of Justice and the FBI. He also keeps his direct reports and customers informed and on track. By far the most important tools he uses daily for the majority of his work are email, PowerPoint, and Word.

When asked about the most important class to take, he definitively answers "Business Communication." He says, "Even if you have great technical skills, your career will get stalled without good communication skills. In fact, the better your communication skills, the further you will go. While technology changes over time, being able to communicate well will always be valuable."

Norm Fjeldheim, Senior Vice President and CIO, Qualcomm

CHAPTER SEVENTEEN
Leveraging Technology for Better Writing

Learning Objectives

Upon completing this chapter, you will be able to describe the various technologies that can help you be more efficient in various stages of the writing process. To reach this goal, you should be able to

1 Use appropriate tools for planning a writing project.

2 Use tools to help you find and organize information.

3 Use tools to help you interpret and present information.

4 Make good use of drafting tools, especially those in your word-processing program.

5 Use tools in your word-processing software to revise and edit your documents and send them in the appropriate format to your audience.

6 Take advantage of computer tools for online collaboration.

Using Technology to Enhance Your Writing Skills

In your new position as an assistant safety manager at Sawyer Industries, you do a lot of writing. Email correspondence with management and your employees, weekly safety reports, OSHA documentation, operations proposals, and performance evaluations are just a few of the many types of writing you routinely do in your work.

You know how important it is not only to have accurate information but also to write in such a way that you accomplish your business goals, present a professional image, and maintain goodwill with your readers. At the same time, you need to make your writing process more efficient so that you are not spending an hour on a single email or days on an OSHA report. You could write more quickly, but you know that would just result in sloppy work. As you look at the software on your computer, you notice several tools you never use and wonder whether you can use them to be a more efficient writer.

TECHNOLOGICAL SUPPORT FOR WRITING TASKS

Technological tools can enhance your writing. But as with any set of tools, how one uses them determines their degree of effectiveness.

Though many technologies enhance communication in general, this chapter focuses on technologies that facilitate the writing process, specifically. Communication technologies that facilitate oral communication are discussed in Chapters 15 and 16.

TOOLS FOR CONSTRUCTING MESSAGES

LO1 Use appropriate tools for planning a writing project.

Computer tools for constructing written messages can be associated with the different stages of the writing process: planning, gathering and organizing, presenting, drafting, and revising and editing. As you'll discover, some tools can help you in multiple areas of the writing process.

Computer Tools for Planning a Writing Project

Sometimes, a writing project is so large that the project itself requires planning. Other times, perhaps writing a document is part of a larger project, and you need to schedule the process for writing the document among the other tasks in the project. It could also be that you are writing short documents that have specific deadlines or time lines associated with them, and you want to make sure you have allotted enough time in your schedule to write them.

Whatever the case, you may find it helpful to use **project planning tools** such as Microsoft Project. Project planning tools are a great way to visualize the scope of a project and see how all of the pieces will come together to create a final product or achieve a business goal. They allow you to identify all the tasks needed to complete a project, to determine how much time each task might take, and to generate a time-and-task chart, commonly called a Gantt chart (Figure 17–1). Also, they help you keep track of your progress and determine how to reallocate your resources to complete the project on time or within budget.

Finding time for writing, of course, is one of the major challenges for businesspeople. By using an annotated **electronic calendar**, you can plan time for completing writing projects.

One such desktop tool is Microsoft Outlook. Figure 17–2 shows Outlook's calendar. The bell icon in the right margin of the task pane shows that this writer set an alarm to

Figure 17–1

Illustration of a Gantt Chart and Calendar Using Microsoft Project

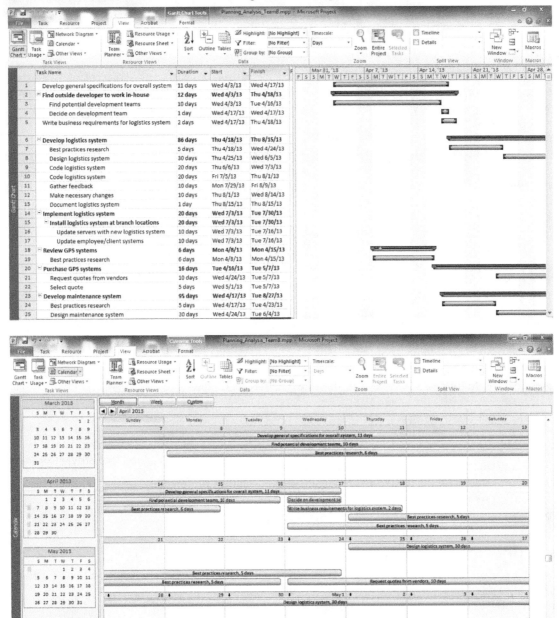

have the computer remind her when it was time to work. At the designated time, an alarm will sound, and a window will open with a precise message of what needs to be done.

Good business writers always take the time to plan, using whatever tool helps their planning process. Using the powerful features that both project management and electronic calendars provide will give you the potential to produce high-quality work in a timely fashion.

LO2 Use tools to help you find and organize information.

Computer Tools for Gathering and Organizing Information

As we've discussed in previous chapters, before you can write, you need to know what information you require to accomplish your business and communication goals. Gathering information, then, is one of the business writer's most important jobs.

Figure 17-2

Illustration of an Electronic Calendar Using Microsoft Outlook

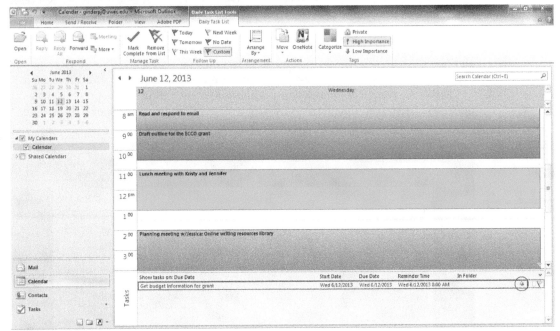

Figure 17-3

Illustration of Google's RSS Feed Reader

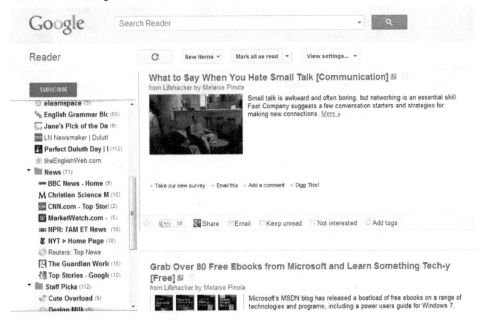

Chapter 13 introduced you to many resources for conducting secondary research—databases, reference materials, library catalogs, company webpages, listservs, professional organizations, social networking sites (e.g., Facebook, LinkedIn, and Twitter), and other helpful websites.

While these resources are great places to go for information, it's also convenient to have information come to you. An RSS (Really Simple Syndication) feed is one such way to gather information quickly and efficiently. When you go to a news site, blog, or other webpage and subscribe to its RSS feed, that site will push content through its RSS feed to a reader such as Google Reader (Figure 17-3), My Yahoo, or Outlook. By using RSS feeds, you can avoid having to go to multiple sites individually to access information; you just open your reader, and the information from all of the sites you subscribe to is there.

In addition, smartphones and tablets provide apps such as Zite that let you develop a custom news magazine by selecting topics that interest you (e.g., business, communication, world news). Unlike an RSS feed where you subscribe to sites and then receive content, Zite pulls news articles to your categories based on activity in your Twitter and Google Reader accounts and on your response to articles in your Zite categories. Figure 17–4 illustrates the variety of information that can appear in a Zite magazine.

Of course, some companies and organizations have individual apps that you can download to your mobile devices as well to receive the latest news or data you need.

Technology can help a writer create effective business messages.

Figure 17–5

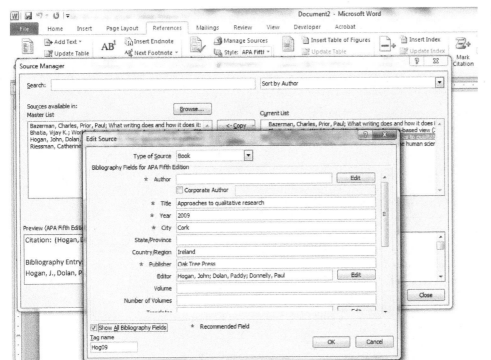

Illustration of the References Tool in Word 2010

Whatever method you choose, these options offer an opportunity to continually be updated on the latest trends, news, and research in your field and have ready information for your writing needs.

Organizing Your Information. Once you have gathered the facts, you will want to store them in some organized fashion so you can retrieve them readily when needed. **Database tools** will help you immensely here. For instance, if your company is interested in developing a product for a newly defined market niche, you may want to collect information about the targeted market, potential suppliers of components of your new product, sites for producing the product, projected labor costs, and so on. You could organize your information by entering your notes about target markets, names of suppliers, and other data in an individually designed form created with database tools. The information you have collected will be available whenever you need it. You can search and sort it on any of the categories (called fields) you set up on your data entry screen.

Variations of the generic database are specialty tools such as EndNote, ProCite, and RefWorks. These specialty programs allow you to transfer bibliographic information automatically from a wide variety of online databases. Microsoft Word 2010 also provides a database for managing sources (Figure 17–5). To use the database, click References > Citations & Bibliography tab > Insert Citation. After you have inserted your citations, you can organize them by clicking the Manage Sources icon. (An advisory, though: The bibliography of your sources is saved in a master list in an .xml file on the computer where you created the list. The list does not travel with your document if you save the document somewhere else, such as on a flash drive. To ensure that your document and sources travel together, you will need to copy and paste the sources.xml file from its location on the computer where you created it to the new device where your document is located.)

Organizing Your Ideas. Organizing your ideas is essential for writing a clear message. You may find it helpful to organize ideas using an **outlining** or **concept-mapping program** (Figure 17–6). Some, such as Edraw, have both free and at-cost programs available. Once you have captured your ideas and grouped related ideas, you can rearrange them into a meaningful order, organizing with the reader in mind.

Figure 17–6

Illustration of a Concept Mapping Tool for Organizing Ideas

SOURCE: http://www.edrawsoft.com/examples.php

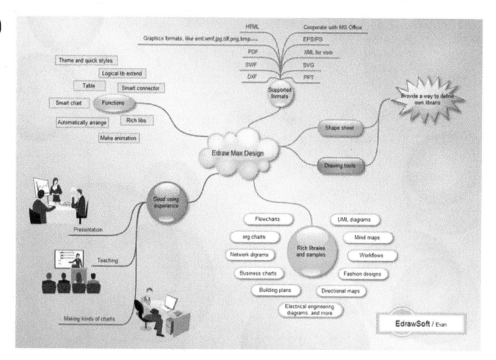

LO3 Use tools to help you interpret and present information.

Computer Tools for Presenting Information

Once you've gathered and organized your information, you need to think about how you will present the information to your audience. Deciding how to present your data requires that you think about how you will organize your data and content to best meet your audience's needs.

Statistical programs such as SPSS and SAS are now user friendly, allowing writers to organize raw numbers into meaningful pictures of their data. In addition, spreadsheet programs such as Excel will compute a broad range of statistics to help writers give meaningful interpretation to the data and to present the data to the reader in a visually accessible way (Figure 17–7).

In addition, as you think about presenting your information, you'll need to consider how different computer tools meet different needs. Picking the right tool makes your work as a writer easier and helps ensure that your message is communicated in ways appropriate for the genre or medium of communication.

- To develop **multimedia presentations**, consider programs such as Microsoft MovieMaker, Camtasia, PowerPoint, or Jing; you'll also want to consider programs such as Audacity to record and edit audio. All of these allow you to integrate video, music, still photos, screen captures, and narration into one presentation. Keep in mind, though, that with multimedia presentations you want to make them accessible to people of all abilities. For example, if you're creating a multimedia presentation that includes narration, you will want to accommodate listeners with hearing impairments by providing a transcription of your narration or include the text of the narration in the presentation. Likewise, if your presentation contains Flash elements, which are not recognized by screen readers used by people with visual impairments, you'll want to provide a transcript as well.

- To give your documents a professionally designed look, consider desktop publishing programs such as Microsoft Publisher or Adobe InDesign. Word-processing programs provide many layout and formatting options, but desktop publishing programs provide superior flexibility and precision for placing information on the page, formatting your text, and placing visual elements.

- To create documents for **online publication**, you can use programs such as Dreamweaver, Weebly, or SeaMonkey; however, programs such as Microsoft Word or Publisher let you save documents as .html files for Web publication. Word and Publisher also let you save documents as blog posts.

Figure 17–7

Illustration of Data Visualization Using Excel

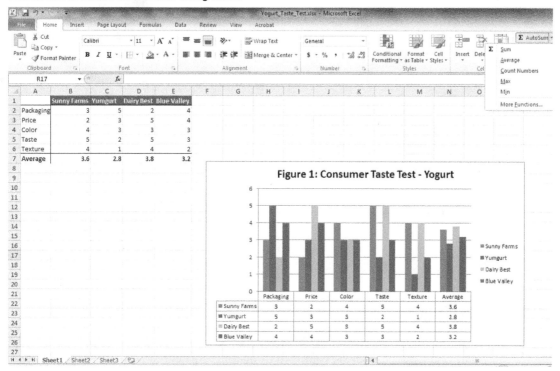

Choosing the right technology for a writing task makes at least part of your job easier. The following section describes some of the more common tools that can help you craft any business message.

Computer Tools for Drafting

You are likely familiar with Microsoft Word or another word-processing program as a technology for creating your documents. In addition to the basics of using the software to open files, draft, edit, cut and paste, change a font size and style, and print a document, this software offers many more options for helping you with the drafting process. Because of its popularity, we reference Microsoft Word, but many of the tools we discuss are readily available in other word-processing programs as well.

Use the *Help* Menu. When using your software, be sure that you control the software rather than letting it control you. That is, if you need your software to do something, look for a way to accomplish the task. "The computer wouldn't let me" is really not an issue anymore. For example, in Microsoft Word 2010, the default line spacing is 1.15 spaces, and the default paragraph spacing is 10 points. If you are not a proficient user of Word, you may think that you are stuck with this spacing. However, if you search the *Help* menu or think logically that the controls for line and paragraph spacing would be under *Paragraph*, you can quickly make changes.

Take Advantage of Built-in Styles and Themes. Word-processing programs also offer a variety of styles, document themes, and templates that you may use to ensure consistency in your documents. The built-in styles in Word 2010 are particularly useful not only to ensure consistency but also to create a table of contents. If you use the styles (or create your own using the *Styles* tool), Word can use them to automatically generate a table of contents. Styles also let you use Word's outline view (Figure 17–8) to move text just by clicking and dragging the heading to a new location in the outline. If you

LO4 Make good use of drafting tools, especially those in your word-processing program.

Figure 17–8

Illustration of Microsoft
Word's Outline View Using
Styles

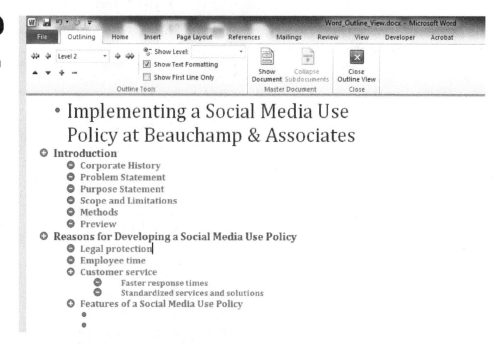

use the themes and templates, though, be aware that many of these have specially set formatting for line and paragraph spacing, bullets, and alignment. You can manipulate these settings to meet your preferences, but if you are not comfortable doing so, you may find it easier to create your own formatting. Again, the Help menu can help you make these changes.

Explore Other Interesting Features. Microsoft Word 2010 offers the following additional features (if you use other word-processing software, you may have access to similar features as well):

- Equation builder: lets you write equations.
- Quick Parts (also called Quick Words and AutoText in other software): lets you create a collection of information that you frequently use in documents so that you do not have to retype the information every time you create a document.
- Word count: allows you to keep track of your document's length.
- Collaboration: enables you to merge, view, or compare multiple documents.
- Digital signature: validates the authenticity of the writer much like the signature on a printed document.
- Smart Art, Clip Art, Charts: let you create appealing, informative visuals.
- Multiple *Save* options: allow you to save your document as a Word file, .PDF, or .html file. Word 2010 also enables users to create blog posts.

Figure 17–9 shows the various ribbons and their tools in Word 2010. Some people may find it useful to take courses to learn how to use word processing software, but many learn successfully by exploring the software and using the Help menu to accomplish their tasks.

Save Your Document Correctly. If your readers are getting printed copies of your document, you can save your file in whatever software format you are using. However, if your readers will view your document electronically, you need to save it in a format that your reader's software will recognize. For instance, Word 2010 files save as .docx files. If your reader has an earlier version of Word that recognizes only .doc files, he or she will not be able to open your file without first downloading a special utililty program. To accommodate this reader, you will need to do a *File > Save As* and save your document as a .doc file—though if you save your .docx file as a .doc, you may lose some

Illustration of the Many Tools in MS Word 2010

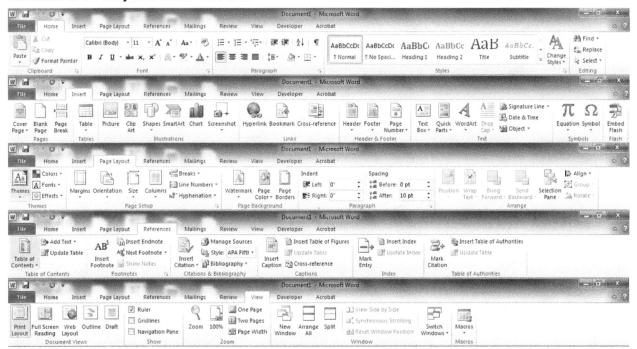

of the formatting from the themes or Smart Art that are not recognized by earlier versions of Word. If your reader's software is not compatible with your current version of Word, you may want to save your document as a .pdf (portable document format) file so that your reader can open it and so that you preserve the formatting. As with the actual composing process itself, saving your documents is an audience-centered effort. You don't want your reader to be angry and frustrated at not being able to open your documents, nor do you want to spend time (and the reader's time) backtracking to save the document in another format and then resending it.

Use Speech Recognition Tools. If you have mobility issues or find it easier to talk through your thoughts as you draft, you may want to consider using a speech recognition tool. You train the software to recognize your voice and speech patterns so that it can enter text in your document as you speak. Some programs, such as Dragon Naturally Speaking, are available at cost, while others, such as e-Speaking, are free.

Computer Tools for Revising and Editing

LO5 Use tools in your word-processing software to revise and edit your documents and send them in the appropriate format to your audience.

Word-processing software also offers several tools for proofing and editing your documents. If your editing consists of reading from the computer monitor or printing a document and simply reading it, you may be missing issues or errors that could be quickly fixed. Furthermore, although your software may help you identify some of the things you need to revise, you still need to be able to revise for issues your software does not detect. Again, we use Word 2010 as our reference, but the tools we address are readily available in other software as well.

The *Find* Feature. The *Find* feature (Ctrl+F, or Home > Editing > Find) can search for and highlight parts of the text you want to check. Let's say that you are writing a letter, and you know you have a problem with comma splices. You could have the software find and highlight every comma in the letter and then check to see whether you have two independent clauses on either side of the comma with no conjunction to link them. If you do, then you could replace the comma with a period or semicolon.

Figure 17–10

Illustration of the *Find and Replace* Feature

The *Find and Replace* Feature. This feature (Ctrl+H, or Home > Editing > Replace) allows you to make multiple changes simultaneously (see Figure 17–10). You can find and replace words or text formatting. If, for example, you spelled *internet* with a lowercase *i* and want to capitalize it instead, you would tell Word to search for all instances of *internet* and replace them with *Internet*. You can also find and replace line spacing, paragraph formatting, tabs, styles, and special characters much more efficiently than selecting all individual instances of a word, sentence, or paragraph and making changes one at a time.

The *Comments* and *Track Changes* Features. Though these features can be used separately, they are often used together when writers collaborate on documents, as Chapter 11 explains (see page 386). However, you may also want to use them to leave comments for yourself (e.g., "check the date of this source") or keep a record of your changes. Because you can accept or reject the changes, you are not committed to them, and because you still have a record of your earlier work, you can simply reject a change and revert to your original version.

***Auto Correct* Features.** As we discussed in Chapter 7, the *Auto Correct* feature lets you enable the software to recognize common errors you may make. For example, if you type quotation marks inside a period (e.g., ".), you can set the auto correct feature to always correct your text to read ." instead.

Spelling Checkers. Along with Quick Parts, AutoText, and QuickWords, spelling checkers are tools business writers rely on daily. However, they are only effective at identifying words that are not in their dictionary. Therefore, spell checkers will not identify as errors words that are spelled correctly but used in the wrong sense. For example, a spell checker will not identify wrong-word errors such as *compliment* for *complement* or *imply* for *infer*. A spelling checker also will miss errors such as *desert* for *dessert* or misused words such as *good* for *well*. Therefore, careful proofreading is still in order after a document has been checked with a spelling checker.

Thesaurus Software. Most word processors include a thesaurus; however, several good Web-based programs are available. For example, the Merriam-Webster website (www.m-w.com) includes a free online thesaurus, as well as a dictionary and

TECHNOLOGY IN BRIEF

Backing Up Frequently Is the Writer's Responsibility

Most writers know how difficult it is to create a document, much less recreate it, so they are willing to spend a little time to protect their investment. In the Save Options dialog box of Word (Microsoft Office Button > Word Options > Save in Office 2010), a writer can set up the program to have Word always create a backup file, to run these backups every 10 minutes, and to do it in the background. This writer could have also asked Word to allow fast saves, which saves only the changes but takes more disk space. This type of saving helps protect you from losing your work if your computer goes down unexpectedly whether from crashes, power outages, accidents, or viruses.

To protect your documents further, you might want to vary the backup media you use so that if your computer is damaged or becomes infected with a computer virus, you still have copies of your files. This media could range from simple backups on disks or USB drives to backups at off-site locations. Individuals can do this with subscriptions on Internet hosts, such as idrive, or on school networks or space provided by an Internet service provider. You might also back up your work by saving it to online services such as Dropbox or Google Docs.

Backing up is an easy, inexpensive form of insurance for a writer.

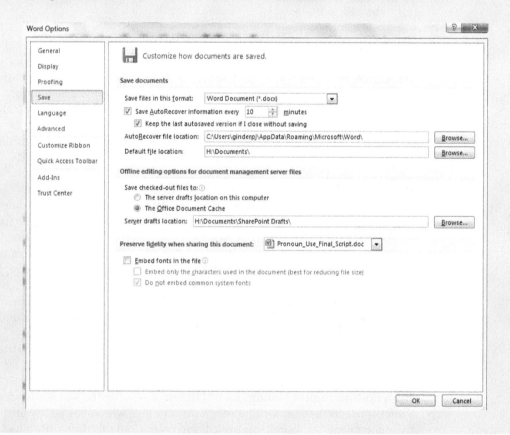

other tools. The thesaurus is a powerful writing aid, and the computer has made it easier to use.

Grammar and Style Checkers. Grammar and style checkers identify possible problems and give suggestions for revision. It is then your responsibility to decide whether the possible problem is a problem and whether the suggestion is the best solution. Making this decision requires that you have a good understanding of basic grammar (See Chapter 18).

Figure 17–11

Illustration of a Spelling and Grammar Checker

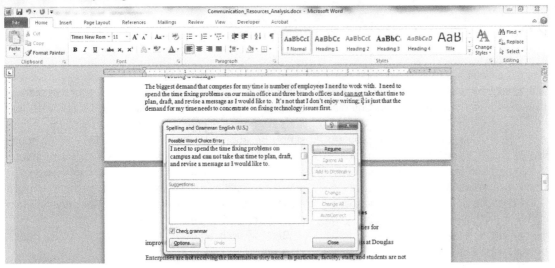

In addition to checking grammar, style, word usage, and punctuation, these programs now report readability indexes. They also perform sentence structure analysis, suggesting that you use simpler sentences, vary the sentence beginnings, use more or fewer prepositional phrases, and make various other changes. Grammar and style checkers also identify possible problems with specific words that might be slang, jargon, misspelled, misused, negative, or difficult for readers to understand. A complementary feature, Word Count, reports statistics for number of pages, words, characters, paragraphs, and lines. An example of the interactive use of one grammar checker is shown in Figure 17–11.

Recent versions of grammar and style checkers are much more flexible than older versions. In Word 2010 you can customize your grammar and style settings to fix common errors or to adapt your writing to your company's style preferences. For example, if you are writing in an environment where your boss finds beginning sentences with "And" and "But" acceptable, you can turn off the rule that would identify those beginnings as problems. Also, you can choose the level of writing your intended audience wants. To customize your settings in Word 2010, go to File > Options > Proofing and then click the Settings button. See Chapter 3, page 55, for more information on customizing your grammar and spell checker in Word 2010.

Grammar and style checkers are definitely important for the business writer. As with all tools, the more appropriately you use them, the better the job they do for you.

Information Rights Management (IRM). Following the lead of Microsoft's Office Professional 2003, many writing programs now give writers the ability to specify how their documents are shared, controlled, and used. Until this time writers had little control over a document once it was transmitted; one could password-protect a document or perhaps encrypt it, but both were awkward and a bit complicated to do. The new set of IRM tools is easy to use and much more powerful than these old methods. As you can see in Figure 17–12, Word 2010 offers several levels of security for a document.

Writers can determine how their documents are shared by specifying who can read, change, or have full control over them. Additionally, the writer can set an expiration date on these permissions. Not only do these features help businesses prevent sensitive information from getting into the wrong hands either accidentally or intentionally, but they also give writers control over documents once they leave their computers. If only certain people have permissions, forwarded and copied files will be protected from unauthorized use.

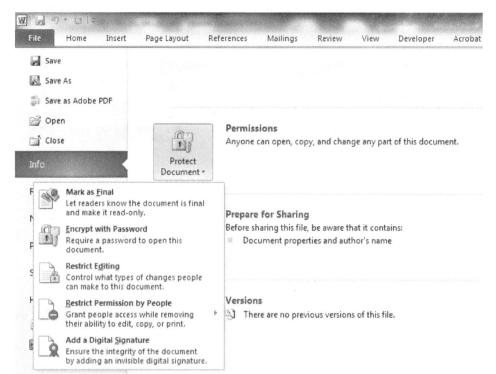

Figure 17–12

Illustration of Information Rights Management for Writing

IRM tools have prompted many businesses to establish practices or policies on the kinds of permissions required for various types of information to protect their intellectual property. These tools also help decrease in-box clutter because they force writers to think about who really needs the document and for how long.

Technology is certainly an important tool for constructing messages. While word processing is the writer's primary tool, a wide variety of other tools can help with the planning, gathering and organizing, presenting, drafting, and revising and editing. By using the tools discussed above, you will find that your writing process is more efficient and your writing more polished.

COMPUTER TOOLS FOR COLLABORATION

LO6 Take advantage of computer tools for online collaboration.

As discussed in Chapter 11, **collaborative writing** or **group writing** tasks occur regularly in business, and they vary widely in terms of the form and nature of the work. Fortunately, a variety of computer tools is available to support various aspects of the collaborative process. These tools for computer-supported collaborative writing may allow members to work in **asynchronous** or **synchronous** environments. Asynchronous tools are used for different-time/different-place collaboration; synchronous tools, are used for same-time/anyplace collaboration.

Many tools for collaborative writing have already been discussed in this text: blogs, other social networks, Word's Comments and Track Changes features, and virtual meeting programs such as Microsoft's Lync. The following tools may also be helpful.

Collaborative Writing Programs

Google Docs, Zoho Writer, Gobby, Socialtext, and Microsoft Groove are just a few of the free or at-cost collaborative writing tools that let you and your group members edit documents, spreadsheets, .html documents, and images. Other features may include simultaneous editing, chat, RSS feeds, privacy and security settings, and email updates. Programs such as Google Docs allow users to upload documents and edit them simultaneously only with other team members whom you have invited to edit the document.

Figure 17–13

Illustration of Google Docs, an Online Collaboration Tool

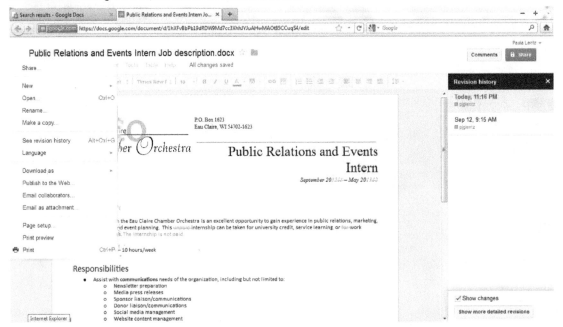

Some programs, such as Google Docs (see Figure 17–13), let you upload all documents associated with a project such as a schedule and to-do list. By locating all of your documents centrally, you and your team members will not have to deal with multiple versions of a document or multiple email attachments. Plus, everyone will have access to a common schedule, and contact among group members will be convenient. These collaborative programs can streamline your writing process, save time, and make the writing process more efficient.

Discussion Boards

Discussion boards such as those in blogs or online learning platforms (e.g., Blackboard, WebCT, or Desire2Learn) are also useful when groups have a difficult time meeting due to distance and time. To begin, the lead writer enters some text. Others then access the system, review the text, and enter their own comments that other group members can view.

Unlike blogs, which list posts chronologically, discussion boards generally list postings by threaded topics. If you are in a discussion board, it is helpful to coordinate with other group members to devise a strategy for threading and naming posts. For instance, if you and your group members are collaborating on a draft and every member names his or her part of the report "My Section," group members may become confused regarding which draft to view. Deciding on naming conventions in advance can prevent a lot of confusion.

A LOOK TO THE FUTURE

Given the recent explosion of communication-related technologies, you can anticipate further rapid advancements in how businesses use technology to support or enhance communication.

For example, innovative social media sites such as Pinterest and Instagram are continually being developed as businesses seek new and creative communication channels to help them achieve their business goals. And mobile applications such as those that

Do U Txt?

Odds are you've sent text messages using standard texting abbreviations. If you do this frequently, do you wonder whether your common use of text messaging has compromised your understanding of standard English conventions and usage? A recent study in *New Media and Society* indicates that tweens' use of texting language may affect their use of standard English. Though this is only one study, its implications are interesting in that it underscores the importance of not becoming so comfortable with one style of writing or one technology that we neglect to tailor our messages to our audiences and communication goals.

Texting is used in business every day—and rightly so given its speed and efficiency. Standard English usage and spelling, though, are still expected. If you don't know your audience or context well enough to know whether you can use a smiley face or text-message speak, you'll want to use a more standard writing style. Otherwise, the response you get might be "C U L8r."

SOURCE: Drew P. Cingel, and S. Shyam Sundar, "Texting, Techspeak, and Tweens: The Relationship between Text Messaging and English Grammar Skills" *New Media & Society* 14.8 (2012): 1304–1320. Print.

Smaller, smarter technology lets people be mobile in their work.

let people photograph checks and then use the photograph to deposit the funds into their bank accounts are changing how people access and use companies' products and services. In addition, **cloud computing** continues to change the way business communicators access and store their software and their work. For instance, because software and information are stored on websites—*in the cloud*—rather than on the computer nearly everyone has access to the software programs (e.g., Microsoft Word) used most frequently to communicate in business. Because cloud applications have no system requirements and require no software on the user's computer, be sure that you have a plan for backing up your data just as you would if you were working locally from your own computer.

Whatever technologies develop, human minds will still need to control communication using good judgment and skill. As Chapter 1 points out, the need for effective problem solving through skillful use of technology is dramatically increasing. Business-people who use technologies in ways that promote clear, professional communication will be assets to their companies and increase their odds of success in their careers.

THERE'S MORE . . .

Would you like tutorials on various software features discussed in this chapter? Would you like to learn more about collaborative work online? Scan the QR code with your smartphone or use your Web browser to visit www.mhhe.com/lesikar13e. Choose Chapter 17 > Bizcom Tools & Tips.

SUMMARY BY LEARNING OBJECTIVES

Use appropriate tools for planning a writing project.

1. Good business writers plan their writing projects using tools such as the following:
   - Gantt charts
   - Microsoft Outlook calendar

Use tools to help you find and organize information.

2. Writers have many tools at their disposal to help them find and organize information:
   - Databases, reference materials library catalogs, company webpages, listservs, professional organizations, social networking sites (e.g., Facebook, LinkedIn, and Twitter), and other websites
   - RSS feeds and mobile apps

Use tools to help you interpret and present information.

3. Information must be presented in ways that are visually appealing and in the right medium.
   - Statistical programs such as SPSS help writers manage statistical data.
   - Programs such as Jing or Dreamweaver allow writers to present information in a variety of media.

Make good use of drafting tools, especially those in your word-processing program.

4. Several drafting tools help writers do their work more efficiently:
   - Help
   - Styles and themes
   - Other tools such as Equation Builder, Quick Parts, and multiple options for saving a document

Use tools in your word-processing software to revise and edit your documents and send them in the appropriate format to your audience.

5. Writers will find the following tools helpful for revising, editing, and saving their documents:
   - Find and replace, comments and track changes, auto correct, and styles features
   - Spelling checker, Thesaurus, information rights management, speech recognition software.

Take advantage of computer tools for online collaboration.

6. A range of software tools assists groups of writers in asynchronous and synchronous writing environments.
   - Software such as Google Docs and Groove let writers collaborate asynchronously or simultaneously to compose, edit, and publish documents.
   - Discussion boards can also support collaborative writing efforts.

KEY TERMS

project planning tools, 575

electronic calendar, 575

database tools, 579

outlining *or* concept-mapping program, 579

statistical programs, 580

multimedia presentations, 580

online publication, 580

collaborative writing *or* group writing, 587

asynchronous *or* synchronous, 587

cloud computing, 589

CRITICAL THINKING QUESTIONS

1 Explain how technology can help the writer with both creative and tedious writing tasks. **LO1–LO6**

2 Identify specific software tools that assist with constructing written messages. Explain what each does. **LO1–LO4**

3 Word processing programs are the writer's primary tool. Identify five basic features and two advanced features useful to business writers. **LO4, LO5**

4 Discuss the advantages and disadvantages of spelling checkers and grammar and style checkers. **LO5**

5 Brainstorm some practices or policies that businesses might develop for using the Information Rights Management (IRM) tool effectively. **LO5**

6 How have text messaging or other technologies affected your writing? **LO1–LO6**

7 How can technology assist in collaboration? **LO3**

SKILLS BUILDING EXERCISES

1 Investigate your school and/or local libraries to determine what current (or future) computer sources will help you find information about businesses. Report your findings to the class.

2 Compile an annotated list of at least 10 websites with good links to business sources. Three of these links should be for local business information.

3 Locate six examples of video and audio clips you might use in a business document. Describe the examples along with a brief explanation of a good use in a business document.

4 Select a multimedia technology, and as your instructor directs, write a memo discussing considerations for accommodating audiences with special needs (e.g., those with visual, hearing, or mobility impairments).

5 Choose a feature from your word processor (such as index, table of contents, templates, or citation builder) that you have not used much. Learn how to use it and create an example of its use in a business document. Write a brief description of its application.

6 From a current computer magazine, find an article that relates to communication in business. Write a one-paragraph reaction to it and post it to a blog specified by your instructor.

CHAPTER EIGHTEEN

Conveying Professionalism Through Correctness

Learning Objectives

Upon completing this chapter, you will be able to use accepted standards of English in business writing and speaking. To reach this goal, you should be able to

1 Punctuate messages correctly.

2 Write complete, grammatically correct sentences, avoiding such problems as awkward construction, dangling modifiers, and misuse of words.

3 Determine when to spell out numbers and when to express them in numeral form.

4 Spell words correctly by applying spelling rules and using a dictionary or spelling checker.

5 Use capital letters for all proper names, first words of sentences, and first words of complimentary closes.

The Effects of Correctness on Communication

Play the role of Mike Rook, a purchasing agent for Hewlett-Packard, and read through today's mail. The first letter comes from Joe Spivey, sales manager, B and B Manufacturing Company. You have not met the writer, though you talked to him on the phone a few days ago. At that time, you were favorably impressed with Joe's enthusiasm and ability and with B and B. In fact, you assumed that, after he gave you the information you needed about B and B's products and services, you become one of its customers.

As you read Joe's letter, however, you are startled. "Could this be the same person I talked with?" you ask yourself. There in the first paragraph is *between Kyle and I*, a clear error in pronoun case. Farther down, *it's* is used to show possession rather than *its*. Joe apparently uses the sprinkle system for placing commas—that is, he sprinkles them wherever his whims direct. His commas often fall in strange places. For example, he writes, "Our salespeople,

say the Rabb Company engineers, will verify the durability of Ironskin protective coating," but you think he means "Our salespeople say the Rabb Company engineers will verify the durability of Ironskin protective coating." The two sentences, which differ only in their punctuation, have distinctly different meanings. Joe's message is filled with such errors.

In general, you now have a lower opinion of Joe and his company. Perhaps you'll have to take a long look at B and B's products and services. Are they careless about other things as well?

The problem just described is a very real one in business. Image does influence the success of both companies and people. And correctness in writing influences image. Thus, you will want to make certain that your writing is correct so that it helps form a favorable image both of you and of your company. The material presented in the pages that follow should help you in that effort.

THE IMPORTANCE OF CORRECTNESS

The correctness of your communication will be important to both you and your company. It will be important to you because people will judge you by it, and how they judge you will in part determine your professional success. It will also be important to your company because correctness in communication will help convey the image of competence that companies require. People judge a company by how its employees act, think, talk, and write, and company executives want such judgments to be favorable.

THE NATURE OF CORRECTNESS

While companies' styles and preferences for written communication will vary, businesspeople generally accept the **standards for correct usage** that educated people have developed and that you have studied in your English composition classes. Businesspeople expect you to follow them.

These standards of correctness have one basic purpose: to help you communicate clearly and professionally. Take, for example, the following two sentences. Their words are the same; only their punctuation differs. But what a difference the punctuation makes!

"The manager," said the employee, "is conscientious."
The manager said, "The employee is conscientious."

Can You Detect the Difference that Punctuation Makes?

Call me Karla.
Call me, Karla.

The groom was asked to call the guests names as they arrived.
The groom was asked to call the guests' names as they arrived.

A clever dog knows it's master.
A clever dog knows its master.

Everyone, I know, has a problem.
Everyone I know has a problem.

No matter what, I know I will graduate in June.
No matter what I know, I will graduate in June.

She ate a half-fried chicken.
She ate a half fried chicken.

I left him convinced he was a fool.
I left him, convinced he was a fool.

The play ended, happily.
The play ended happily.

Thirteen people knew the secret, all told.
Thirteen people knew the secret; all told.

Or what about the following pair of sentences? Who is rude, the clients or the customer service associates? The placement of commas determines the meaning of each sentence.

The clients, say the customer service associates, are rude.
The clients say the customer service associates are rude.

Because correctness is important to your communication in business, this chapter reviews the major standards for correct punctuation and grammar. The standards are coded with symbols (letters and numbers) so that your instructor can use them as grading marks to identify errors.

You probably already know many of the standards of correctness. To help you determine how much you know and do not know, you should take the self-analysis test or complete the review exercises at the end of the chapter. This will enable you to study the standards as you need to.

LO1 Punctuate messages correctly.

STANDARDS FOR PUNCTUATION

The following explanations cover the most important standards for correct punctuation.

Apostrophe: Apos 1

Use the apostrophe to show the **possessive case** of nouns and indefinite pronouns. Whether the apostrophe goes before or after the *s* depends on whether the possessive noun is singular or plural.

If the possessive noun is singular, just add an *'s*.

> one company's sales
> one employee's desk
> someone's pen
> one boss's policy
> Texas's state laws
> Sue Jones's car
> Joe's report

If the possessive noun is plural and already ends in an *s*, just add the apostrophe after the *s*.

Singular	Plural	Plural Possessive
company	companies	six companies' sales
employee	employees	three employees' desks
boss	bosses	two bosses' policies
Jones	Joneses	the Joneses' cars

If the plural noun does not end in an *s*, add an *'s*.

Singular	Plural	Plural Possessive
child	children	children's
person	people	people's

Note: A popular practice is to place only an apostrophe at the end of singular possessive nouns that end in *s* (e.g., one boss' policy). However, until you're comfortable distinguishing between singular and plural possessives, you may prefer to use the more standard punctuation. If a noun is singular, you don't have to think about putting the apostrophe inside or outside the *s*; just add the *'s* and move on because you'll know that your punctuation is correct.

Apos 2

Use an apostrophe to mark the place in a **contraction** where letters are omitted. Do not use it to make personal pronouns possessive (its, hers).

it is = it's
has not = hasn't
cannot = can't

Apos 3

Use the apostrophe to indicate **time, value, or measurement** of a noun. The placement of the apostrophe before or after the *s* depends on whether the possessive is singular or plural (see Apos 1).

- today's newspaper
- three weeks' vacation
- last year's sales
- 20 pounds' worth

Brackets: Bkts

Use brackets to set off words of your own that you wish to insert in another's quotation.

"The use of this type of mentor [the personal coach] may still be increasing."

"Direct supervision has diminished in importance during the past decade [the report was written in 2005], when 63 percent of the reporting business firms that started programs used teams."

You will project a professional image when you incorporate standards for correctness into your business messages.

Good Grammar: Your Ticket to Getting and Keeping a Job

In today's age of texting and other informal communication, you may wonder if standards for correctness really apply anymore. After all, if everybody is violating the standards in favor of less standard usage, then why not change the standards, right? If someone still understands your message regardless of whether you use *its* or *it's* correctly, then what's the big deal?

As it turns out, standards for business English are a big deal, and business leaders have become especially vocal recently about the need for employees to know them. As a result, pre-employment grammar tests are becoming popular. Kyle Wiens, CEO of iFixit, the world's largest online repair community, uses a pre-employment grammar exam as a "litmus test" for potential hires, saying, "If it takes someone more than 20 years to notice how to properly use *it's*, then that's not a learning curve I'm comfortable with." Further, he finds that applicants who do not value good grammar are less detail oriented and likely to place less value on other important workplace matters than those who do value good grammar.

In another article, columnist Sue Schellenbarger cites a survey indicating that "about 45 percent of 430 employers said they were increasing employee-training programs to improve employees' grammar and other skills." She further cites that many times it's not just a matter of people not knowing the rules; instead, it's a matter of people not knowing the contexts where texting or informal conversation is appropriate. Over time, it becomes habit for these employees to use more nonstandard English even when standard English is expected.

Fortunately, you do not need to be the applicant who cannot pass a grammar test or the employee who is known to need remedial training. You have a variety of resources available through this chapter that can help you be the applicant or employee who is admired for his or her skill.

SOURCES: Kyle Wiens, "I Won't Hire People Who Use Poor Grammar. Here's Why.," *Harvard Business Review Blog Network*, Harvard Business Publishing, 20 July 12, Web, 31 July 2012; and Sue Schellenbarger, "This Embarrasses You and I: Grammar Gaffes Invade the Office in an Age of Informal Email, Texting and Twitter," *The Wall Street Journal: Work and Family*, Dow Jones & Company, Inc., 19 June 2012, Web, 3 July 2012.

Colon: Cln 1

Use the colon to introduce an **enumeration**, a **formal quotation**, or a statement of **explanation**.

> *Enumeration:* Working in this department are three classes of support: clerical support, computer support, and customer support.
>
> *Formal quotation:* President Hartung had this to say about the proposal: "Any such movement that fails to get the support of the workers from all divisions fails to get my support."
>
> *Explanation:* At this time the company was pioneering a new marketing idea: It was attempting to sell customized products directly to consumers through its website.

Cln 2

An **independent clause** (complete sentence) should precede a colon. Do not use the colon when the thought of the sentence should continue without interruption. If you are introducing a list with a colon, precede the colon with a word that explains or identifies the list.

> *Not this:* Cities in which new sales offices are in operation are: Fort Smith, Texarkana, Lake Charles, Jackson, and Biloxi.
>
> *But this:* Cities in which new sales offices are in operation are Fort Smith, Texarkana, Lake Charles, Jackson, and Biloxi.
>
> *Or this:* Cities with new sales offices are as follows: Fort Smith, Texarkana, Lake Charles, Jackson, and Biloxi.

Comma: Cma 1

Use the comma to separate independent (main) clauses connected by a **coordinating conjunction**. Some coordinating conjunctions are *and, but, or,* and *nor.* (An independent clause has a subject and a verb and stands by itself as a sentence. A coordinating conjunction connects clauses, words, or phrases of equal rank.)

> Only two components of the index declined, and these two account for only 12 percent of the total weight of the index.
>
> New hybrid automobiles are moving at record volumes, but used-car sales are lagging behind the record pace set two years ago.

Make exceptions to this rule, however, in the case of compound sentences consisting of short and closely connected clauses.

> We sold and the price dropped.
>
> Sometimes we win and sometimes we lose.

Cma 2–1

Use commas to separate items in a **series**. To avoid misinterpretation of the instances in which some of the items listed have compound constructions, it is always good to include the comma between the last two items (before the final conjunction).

> Good copy must cover facts with accuracy, sincerity, honesty, and conviction.
>
> Direct advertising can be used to introduce salespeople, fill in between salespeople's calls, cover territory where salespeople cannot be maintained, and keep pertinent reference material in the hands of prospects.
>
> The DuPont Color Popularity Report conducted in 2005 indicated that silver, white, blue, and black were the top four car colors favored by the public.

Cma 2–2

Use a comma to separate **coordinate adjectives** in a series if they modify the same noun and if no *and* connects them. A good test to determine whether adjectives are coordinate is to insert an *and* between them. If the *and* does not change the meaning, the adjectives are coordinate.

> Miss Pratt has been a reliable, faithful, efficient employee for 20 years.
>
> We guarantee that this is a good, clean car.
>
> Blue office furniture is Mr. Orr's recommendation for the new conference room. (*Blue* and *office furniture* does not make sense.)
>
> A big crescent wrench proved to be best for the task. (The *and* won't fit between *big* and *crescent.*)

Cma 3

Set off **nonrestrictive clauses** with commas. By a *nonrestrictive clause* we mean a clause (a group of words with a subject and a verb) that could be omitted from the sentence without changing its meaning. **Restrictive clauses** (those that would change the meaning of a sentence if they were omitted) are not set off by commas.

> *Restrictive:* The salesperson *who sells the most* will get a bonus. (Not every salesperson will get a bonus. Only the person who sells the most will get a bonus. Therefore, the clause restricts the meaning of the sentence.)
>
> *Nonrestrictive:* Diana Chan, *who was the company's top salesperson for the year,* was awarded a bonus. (If the clause *who was the company's top salesperson for the year* is omitted, the meaning of the sentence is not changed.)
>
> *Restrictive:* J. Ward & Company is the firm *that employs most of the seasonal workers in this area.*
>
> *Nonrestrictive:* J. Ward & Company, *which employs most of the seasonal workers in this area,* has gained the admiration of the community.

Notice that some clauses can be either restrictive or nonrestrictive, depending on the writer's intended meaning.

> *Restrictive:* All the cars that were damaged in the flood were sold at a discount. (Not all cars were sold at a discount, only the cars damaged in the flood.)
>
> *Nonrestrictive:* All the cars, which were damaged by the flood, were sold at a discount. (Implies that the entire fleet of cars was damaged.)

Note: That usually indicates a restrictive clause that is not set off with commas. *Which* usually indicates a nonrestrictive clause that is set off with commas. *Who*, which should be used to refer to people, may indicate either a restrictive or nonrestrictive clause.

Cma 4–1

Use commas to set off **parenthetical expressions**. A parenthetical expression consists of words that interrupt the normal flow of the sentence. In a sense, they appear to be "stuck in." In many instances, they are simply words out of normal order. For example, the sentence "A full-page, black-and-white advertisement was run in the *Daily Bulletin*" contains a parenthetical expression when the word order is altered: "An advertisement, full-page and in black and white, was run in the *Daily Bulletin*."

> This practice, it is believed, will lead to financial ruin.
>
> Merck, as *The Wall Street Journal* reports, has sharply increased its alliance activity.

Although in such cases you may use dashes or parentheses in place of commas, the three marks differ in the degree to which they separate the enclosed words from the rest of the sentence. The comma is the weakest of the three, and it is best used when the material set off is closely related to the surrounding words. Parentheses and dashes are used to more obviously separate material from the rest of the sentence than would be indicated by commas. Parentheses are used when a writer wants to de-emphasize the material, while dashes are used when the writer wants to emphasize it.

Cma 4–2

Use commas to set off an **appositive** (a noun or a noun and its modifiers inserted to rename another noun) from the rest of the sentence. In a sense, appositives are parenthetical expressions because they interrupt the normal flow of the sentence.

> UPS, our primary shipper, is leasing a new distribution center in China.
>
> St. Louis, home office of our Midwest district, will be the permanent site of our annual sales meeting.
>
> President Cartwright, a self-educated woman, is the leading advocate of online training for employees.

But appositives that are required for the sentence meaning are not set off by commas.

> The word *liabilities* is not understood by most people.
>
> Our next shipment will come on the ship *Alberta*.

Cma 4–3

Set off parenthetical words including such transitional expressions as *however, in fact, of course, for example*, and *consequently* with commas.

> It is apparent, therefore, that the buyers' resistance was caused by an overvigorous sales campaign.
>
> After the first experiment, for example, the traffic flow increased 10 percent.
>
> The company, however, will be forced to adopt a more competitive pricing strategy.

Failing to observe standards for correctness in presentations and visuals projects a negative, unpolished image.

Included in this group of parenthetical words may be introductory interjections (*oh, wow*) and responsive expressions (*yes, no, surely, indeed, well*, and *and so on*). But if the words are strongly exclamatory or are not closely connected with the rest of the sentence, they may be punctuated as a sentence. (*No. Yes. Indeed.*)

Yes, the decision to increase product placement advertising has been made.

Oh, contribute whatever you think is appropriate.

Cma 4–4

When more than one unit appears in a **date or an address**, set off the units with commas.

One unit: December 30 is the date of our annual inventory.

One unit: The company has one outlet in Ohio.

More than one unit: December 30, 1906, is the date the Johnston Company first opened its doors.

More than one unit: Tuesday, June 30, is the project deadline.

More than one unit: Richmond, Virginia, is the headquarters of the new sales district.

Cma 5–1

Use the comma after a **subordinate clause** that precedes the main clause. A subordinate clause is a **dependent clause** (subordinating conjuntion + subject + verb). Examples of subordinating conjunctions are *although, since, because*, and *while*.

Although it is durable, this package does not have eye appeal.

Since there was little store traffic on aisle 13, the area was converted into storage space.

Cma 5–2

Place a comma after an **introductory phrase**. An introductory phrase may be a participial phrase, an infinitive phrase, or a prepositional phrase of five words or more.

Participial phrase: Realizing his mistake, Ron instructed his direct reports to keep a record of all salvaged equipment.

Infinitive phrase: To increase the turnover of automobile accessories, we must first improve their display area.

Prepositional phrase: Before the annual ABC board meeting, we met to discuss the agenda.

Cma 6–1

Use the comma only for good reason. As a rule, the use of commas should be justified by one of the standard practices previously noted.

In particular do not put a comma between the subject and the verb.

The thought that he could not afford to fail spurred him on. (No comma after *fail*.)

Cma 6–2

Take exception to the preceding standards wherever the insertion of a comma will help **clarity** of expression.

Not this: From the beginning inventory methods of Hill Company have been haphazard.

But this: From the beginning, inventory methods of Hill Company have been haphazard.

Not this: Ever since she has been a model worker.

But this: Ever since, she has been a model worker.

Dash: Dsh 1

Use the **em dash** to set off an element for **emphasis** or to show interrupted thought. In particular, use it with long parenthetical expressions or parenthetical expressions containing internal punctuation (see Cma 4–1).

Budgets for some past years—2006, for example—were prepared without consulting the department heads.

The test proved that the new process is simple, effective, accurate—and more expensive.

Only one person—the supervisor in charge—has authority to approve a policy exception.

If you want a voice in the government—vote.

Dsh 2

The **en dash** is longer than a hyphen but shorter than an em dash and is used to indicate ranges such as those that involve dates, times, or page numbers. Generally, if you can use the words *to* or *through* between dates, times, or page numbers, you can use the en dash.

The conference will be held Monday–Thursday.

Please read pages 1–50 before tomorrow's meeting.

See the Technology in Brief box, page 605, for tips on how to use Word to help you insert em dashes and en dashes correctly.

Exclamation Mark: Ex

Use the exclamation mark at the end of a sentence or an exclamatory fragment to show strong emotion. In business writing, the exclamation point is used sparingly, usually to convey good news or positive emotions.

We've done it again!

Congratulations! Your outstanding performance review qualifies you for merit pay.

Hyphen: Hpn 1

Use the hyphen to indicate the **division of a word** at the end of the line. You must divide between syllables. It is generally impractical to leave a one-letter syllable at the end of a line (*a-bove*) or to carry over a two-letter syllable to the next line (*expens-es*).

If you turn on the hyphenation feature of your word-processing software, you can let it automatically take care of hyphenating words and specify the amount of space after the hyphen at the end of a line. You also have the option of controlling the hyphenation you desire. That is, you can accept what the program recommends, suggest a different place to hyphenate, or tell it not to hyphenate.

Hpn 2–1

Place hyphens between the parts of some **compound words**. Generally, the hyphen is used whenever its absence would confuse the meaning of the words.

> *Compound nouns:* brother-in-law, cure-all, city-state
> *Compound numbers twenty-one through ninety-nine:* fifty-five, eighty-one
> *Compound adjectives* (two or more words used before a noun as a single adjective): *long-term* contract, *50-gallon* drum, *five-day* grace period, *end-of-month* clearance
> *Prefixes* (most have been absorbed into the word): co-organizer, ex-chairperson, anti-inflation, self-sufficient

Hpn 2–2

A **proper name** used as a compound adjective needs no hyphen or hyphens to hold it together as a visual unit for the reader. The capitals perform that function.

> *Correct:* a Lamar High School student
> *Correct:* a United Airlines pilot

Hpn 2–3

Two or more modifiers in normal grammatical form and order need no hyphens. Specifically, adverbs ending in *-ly* are not followed by a hyphen. But an adverb not ending in *ly* is joined to its adjective or participle by the hyphen.

> *No hyphen needed:* a poorly drawn chart
> *Use the hyphen:* a well-prepared chart

Italics: Ital 1

For the use of italics for book titles, see QM 4. Note that italics also are used for titles of periodicals, works of art, long musical compositions, and names of naval vessels and aircraft.

Ital 2

Italicize rarely used foreign words (*wunderbar, keiretsu, oobeya*). After a foreign word is widely accepted, however, it does not need to be italicized (carpe diem, faux pas). A current dictionary is a good source for information on which foreign words are italicized.

Ital 3

Italicize a word, letter, or figure used as its own name. Without this device, we could not write this set of rules. Note the use of italics throughout to label name words.

> The word *success* has many definitions.
> The pronoun *which* should always have a noun as a clear antecedent. (Without the italics, this one becomes a fragment.)

Using the Internet to Improve Your Grammar

Becoming an expert in grammar is much like becoming an expert in sports or music—it takes a lot of practice. Indeed, even experts seek opportunities to practice and keep their skills sharp. Technology certainly makes practice more convenient. Whenever you're online and have a few minutes, consider taking a quick quiz or listening to a short podcast on business writing. If you have more time, you may want to visit a business writing blog to learn from the answers to others' questions or even to share your expertise by responding to someone's post or discussing a topic. You could also get the RSS feeds available at many sites so that the topics come right to you. The websites here are only a few of the many available. Whether you use these or others, you'll likely find that your practice results in sharp, polished business documents that elicit a positive response from your audiences.

Online Quizzes

- Capital Community College: http://grammar.ccc .commnet.edu/GRAMMAR/quiz_list.htm
- Purdue Online Writing Lab: http://owl.english.purdue .edu/owl/
- GrammarBook.com www.grammarbook.com/ interactive_quizzes_exercises.asp

- Facebook Business Writing Daily Quiz: www.facebook .com/home.php?#/pages/Writing-for-Business-Daily-Grammar-Quiz/33633651366?ref=ts

Grammar Podcasts

- Grammar Girl: http://grammar.quickanddirtytips.com/. (See the screenshot below.)
- Grammar Grater (Minnesota Public Radio): http://minnesota.publicradio.org/radio/podcasts/ grammar_grater/

Business Writing Blogs

- Writing for Business: http://itknowledgeexchange .techtarget.com/writing-for-business/
- Business Writing: www.businesswritingblog.com/
- Society for the Promotion of Good Grammar: http://spogg.org/ (The blog is not specific to business writing, but many of the examples on the blog are from professional contexts.)

General Business Writing Tips:

- Business Writer's Free Library: http://managementhelp .org/commskls/cmm_writ.htm

SOURCE: Screenshot of Grammar Girl from www.grammar.quickanddirtytips.com. Reprinted by permission of Quick and Dirty Tips™. Quick & Dirty Tips™ and related trademarks appearing on this website are the property of Mignon Fogarty, Inc. and Macmillan Holdings, LLC.

Parentheses: Parens

Use parentheses to set off words that are inserted to explain or supplement the principal message (see Cma 4–1).

> David Rick's phenomenal illustrations (*Blunders in International Business*, 2006) show readers that even large corporations make disastrous mistakes.
>
> As soon as Owen Smith was elected chairperson (the vote was almost 2 to 1), he introduced his plan for reorganization.

Period: Pd 1

Use the period to indicate the end of a **declarative sentence** or an **imperative statement**.

> *Declarative sentence:* The survey will be completed and returned by October 26.
> *Imperative statement:* Complete and return the survey by October 26.

Pd 2

Use periods after abbreviations or initials.

> Co., Inc., a.m., etc.

But omit the periods and use all capitals in the initials or acronyms of agencies, networks, and associations: IRS, NBC, OPEC, EEC.

Pd 3

Use ellipses (a series of periods) to indicate the omission of words from a quoted passage. If the omitted part consists of something less than a sentence, three periods are customarily placed at the point of omission (a fourth period is added if the omission is a sentence or more). In all cases, the periods are separated by spaces.

> Logical explanations, however, have been given by authorities in the field. Some attribute the decline to recent changes in the state's economy. . . .
>
> . . . Added to the labor factor is the high cost of raw material, which has tended to eliminate many marginal producers. Moreover, the rising cost of electric power in recent years may have shifted the attention of many industry leaders to other forms of production.

Question Mark: Q

Place a question mark at the end of sentences that are **direct questions**.

> What are the latest quotations on Disney common stock?
> Will this campaign help sell Microsoft products?

But do not use the question mark with **indirect questions**.

> The president was asked whether this campaign would help sell Microsoft products.
> He asked me what the latest quotations on Disney common stock were.

Quotation Marks: QM 1

Use quotation marks to enclose the exact words of a speaker or, if the quotation is short, the exact words of a writer.

Short written quotations are quotations of four lines or less, although authorities do not agree on this point. Some suggest three lines; others, up to eight. Longer written quotations are best displayed without quotation marks and with an indented right and left margin.

> *Short written quotation:* Ben Bernanke sums up his presentation with this statement: "The central bank will remain vigilant to ensure that recent increases in inflation do not become chronic."
> *Oral quotation:* "This really should bring on a production slowdown," said Ms. Kuntz.

If a quotation is broken by explanation or reference words, each part of the quotation is enclosed in quotation marks.

"Will you be specific," he asked, "in recommending a course of action?"

QM 2

Enclose a quotation within a quotation with single quotation marks.

Professor Dalbey said, "It has been a long time since I have heard a student say, 'Prof, we need more writing assignments.'"

QM 3

Always place periods and commas *inside* quotation marks. Place semicolons and colons *outside* the quotation marks. Place question marks and exclamation points inside if they apply to the quoted passage only and outside if they apply to the whole sentence.

"If we are patient," he said, "we will reach this year's goals." (*The comma and the period are within the quotation marks.*)

"Is there a quorum?" he asked. (*The question mark belongs to the quoted passage.*)

Which of you said, "I know where the error lies"? (*The question mark applies to the entire sentence.*)

I conclude only this from the union's promise to "force the hand of management": A strike will be its trump card.

QM 4

Enclose in quotation marks the titles of parts of publications (articles in a magazine, chapters in a book). But italicize the titles of whole publications or underline them if you are handwriting.

The third chapter of the book *Elementary Statistical Procedure* is titled "Concepts of Sampling."

Anne Fisher's timely article, "Fatal Mistakes When Starting a New Job," appears in the current issue of *Fortune*.

Semicolon: SC 1

Use the semicolon to separate closely related independent clauses that are not connected by a conjunction. Although writers generally use periods to separate independent clauses, a semicolon can be used to indicate a smaller break in thought than a period would.

The new contract provides wage increases; the original contract emphasized shorter hours.

Covered by this standard are independent clauses connected by conjunctive adverbs (transitional expressions) such as *however, nevertheless, therefore, then, moreover,* and *besides.*

The survey findings indicated a need to revise the policy; nevertheless, the president did not approve the proposed revision.

Small-town buyers favor the old model; therefore, the board concluded that both models should be marketed.

SC 2

You may use the semicolon to separate independent clauses joined by *and, but, or,* or *nor* (coordinating conjunctions) if the clauses are long or if they have other punctuation

Hyphen, Small Dash, or Big Dash?

The hyphen, en dash, and em dash are regularly confused. Visually, the hyphen is the shortest. The em dash (the width of the letter *m* in the font you're using) is the longest, and the length of the en dash (the width of the letter *n* in the font you're using) is in between. This chapter discusses the use of the hyphen, em dash, and en dash (page 600), so if you know when to use them, the trick becomes how to insert them into your documents. Microsoft Word will occasionally help. In fact, you may have noticed that when you type two hyphens, Word sometimes automatically inserts the em dash. However, sometimes the software does not convert hyphens to a dash or may convert the hyphens to an en dash when you really need an em dash or vice versa. To ensure that you control the dash and use it correctly, use the *Symbols* list in Microsoft Word. Whether you are in Word 2010 or an earlier version, go to Insert > Symbol > More Symbols > Special Characters. You can then select the mark you need based on whether you're dividing a word or connecting adjectives (hyphen), emphasizing information (em dash), or indicating a range (en dash). Generally, when you insert the hyphen or dash, you do not need a space before or after the mark.

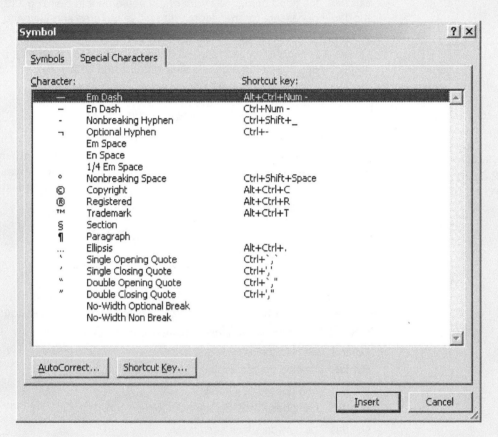

in them. In such situations, you may need the semicolon to make your message clear. If you visualize the example below with a comma instead of a semicolon, you can see that your message would be visually confusing.

> The OCAW and the NUPNG, rivals from the beginning of the new industry, have shared almost equally in the growth of membership; but the OCAW predominates among workers in the petroleum-products crafts, including pipeline construction and operation, and the NUPNG leads in memberships of chemical workers.

SC 3

Use a semicolon to separate items in a list that already have punctuation in them.

> The following gains were made in the February year-to-year comparison: Fort Worth, 7,300; Dallas, 4,705; Lubbock, 2,610; San Antonio, 2,350; Waco, 2,240; Port Arthur, 2,170; and Corpus Christi, 1,420.

> Elected for the new term were Anna T. Zelnak, attorney from Cincinnati; Wilbur T. Hoffmeister, stockbroker and president of Hoffmeister Associates of Baltimore; and William P. Peabody, a member of the faculty of the University of Georgia.

SC 4

Use the semicolon between equal (coordinate) units only. Do not use it to attach a dependent clause or phrase to an independent clause.

> *Not this:* The flood damaged much of the equipment in Building 113; making it necessary for management to close the area and suspend some employees.

> *But this:* The flood damaged much of the equipment in Building 113, making it necessary for management to close the area and suspend some employees.

> *Or this:* The flood damaged much of the equipment in Building 113; thus, management closed the area and suspended some employees.

LO2 Write complete, grammatically correct sentences, avoiding such problems as awkward construction, dangling modifiers, and misuse of words.

STANDARDS FOR GRAMMAR

Like the review of punctuation standards, the following summary of grammatical standards is not intended as a complete handbook on the subject. Rather, it is a summary of the major trouble spots that business writers encounter. If you learn these grammatical principles, you should be able to write with the correctness expected in business.

Adjective–Adverb Confusion: AA

Do not use adjectives for adverbs or adverbs for adjectives. *Adjectives modify only nouns and pronouns; and adverbs modify verbs, adjectives, or other adverbs.*

Possibly the chief source of this confusion occurs in statements in which the modifier follows the verb. If the modifier refers to the subject, an adjective should be used. If it refers to the verb, an adverb is needed.

> *Not this:* She filed the records *quick*.
> *But this:* She filed the records *quickly*. (Refers to the verb.)

> *Not this:* John doesn't feel *badly*.
> *But this:* John doesn't feel *bad*. (Refers to the noun.)

> *Not this:* The new cars look *beautifully*.
> *But this:* The new cars look *beautiful*. (Refers to the noun.)

It should be noted that many words are both adjective and adverb (*little, well, fast, much*).

> *Adverb:* The time went fast.
> *Adjective:* She drives a fast car.

Subject–Verb Agreement: Agmt SV

Subjects and their verbs must *agree in number*. A plural subject must be paired with a plural verb form; a singular subject must be paired with a singular verb form.

Nouns in *prepositional phrases* (i.e., phrases that begin with words such as *for, of, on, with, in, about,* and *between*) and nouns in phrases that are *separated from the sentence with commas* will not be the subjects of your sentences.

> *Not this:* **Expenditures** for miscellaneous equipment *was* expected to decline. (*Expenditures* is plural, so its verb must be plural.)
>
> *But this:* **Expenditures** for miscellaneous equipment *were* expected to decline.
>
> *Not this:* The *president*, as well as the staff, *were* not able to attend. (*President* is the singular subject, and the number is not changed by the modifying phrase.)
>
> *But this:* The *president*, as well as the staff, *was* not able to attend.

In a *there is* or *there are* sentence, the subject follows the verb.

> *Not this:* There is several reasons why we should act.
>
> *But this:* There are several reasons why we should act.

Compound subjects joined by *and* require plural verbs.

> *Not this:* The *salespeople* and their *manager is* in favor of the proposal. (*Salespeople* and *manager* make a compound subject, but *is* is singular.)
>
> *But this:* The *salespeople* and their *manager are* in favor of the proposal.
>
> *Not this:* Received in the morning delivery *was* an *ink cartridge* and two *reams* of copy paper. (*Ink cartridge* and *reams* are the subjects; the verb must be plural.)
>
> *But this:* Received in the morning delivery *were* an *ink cartridge* and two *reams* of copy paper.

When a sentence has a compound subject joined with *or*, the singular or plural nature of the verb is determined by the subject closest to the verb.

> *Not this:* Either the shift supervisors or the department's manager *are* allowed to alter a time card. (Even though there are two subjects, the verb *or* means that you need to look only at the subject closest to the verb.)
>
> *But this:* Either the shift supervisors or the department's manager *is* allowed to alter a time card. (*Manager* is closer to the verb and is singular, so the singular verb *is* is correct.)
>
> *Or this:* Either the department's manager or the shift supervisors *are* allowed to alter a time card. (The word *supervisors* is closer to the verb and is plural, so the plural verb *are* is correct.)

Collective nouns may be either singular or plural, depending on the meaning intended.

> The *committee have* carefully *studied* the proposal. (*Committee* is thought of as separate individuals.)
>
> The *committee has* carefully *studied* the proposal. (The *committee* is thought of as a unit.)

An **indefinite pronoun** does not refer specifically to another person or object or to groups of people and objects but to people, objects, or groups more generally. Some indefinite pronouns are always singular (e.g., *each, every, either, neither*), and any pronoun ending in *-body, -one,* or *-thing* (such as *anyone, anybody, anything, everyone, everybody, everything, someone, somebody, something, no one, nobody,* and *nothing*).

> *Either* of the campaigns *is* costly. (*Note:* If you have trouble finding the subject, remember that anything in a prepositional phrase can't be the subject of your sentence. *Campaigns* is in a prepositional phrase, so it cannot be the subject of your sentence.)
>
> *Nobody* who watches the clock *is* successful.

Other indefinite pronouns such as *both, few, many,* and *several* are always plural.

> Many *were* qualified for the job, but only three did well in the interview.

Some indefinite pronouns are either singular or plural (e.g., *all, any, most, none, some*), depending on what they refer to.

> *None* of the workers *were* ready for their assignments.
> *None* of the work *was* completed.

Adverbial Noun Clause: AN

Do not use an **adverbial clause** as a noun clause. Clauses beginning with *because, when, where, if,* and similar adverbial connections are not properly used as subjects, objects, or complements of verbs.

> *Not this:* The reason was *because* he did not submit a report.
> *But this:* The reason was *that* he did not submit a report.

> *Not this:* A time-series graph is *where* (or *when*) changes in an index such as wholesale prices are indicated.
> *But this:* A time-series graph is the picturing of . . .

Awkward: Awk

Avoid awkward writing. By **awkward writing** we mean word arrangements that are unconventional, uneconomical, or simply not the best for quick understanding.

Dangling Modifiers: Dng

Avoid the use of modifiers that do not clearly modify the right word in the sentence. Such modifiers are said to dangle. You can usually correct sentences containing dangling constructions by inserting the noun or pronoun that the modifier describes or by changing the dangling part to a complete clause.

> *Not this:* Believing that credit customers should have notice of the sale, special letters were mailed to them.
> *But this:* Believing that credit customers should have notice of the sale, we mailed special letters to them. (Inserting the pronoun *we* makes clear who did the believing.)
> *Or this:* Because we believed that credit customers should have notice of the sale, special letters were mailed to them. (Changing the dangling element to a complete clause makes clear who did the believing.)

Dangling modifiers are of four principal types: **participial phrases, elliptical clauses, gerund phrases,** and **infinitive phrases.**

> *Not this:* Believing that District 7 was not being thoroughly covered, an additional salesperson was assigned to the area. *(Dangling participial phrase.)*
> *But this:* Believing that District 7 was not being thoroughly covered, the sales manager assigned an additional salesperson to the area.

> *Not this:* By working hard, your goal can be reached. *(Dangling gerund phrase.)*
> *But this:* By working hard, you can reach your goal.

> *Not this:* To succeed at this job, long hours and hard work must not be shunned. *(Dangling infinitive phrase.)*
> *But this:* To succeed at this job, one must not shun long hours and hard work.

> *Not this:* While waiting on a customer, the watch was stolen. *(Dangling elliptical clause—a clause without a noun or verb.)*
> *But this:* While the salesperson was waiting on a customer, the watch was stolen.

However, several generally accepted introductory phrases are permitted to dangle. Included in this group are *generally speaking, confidentially speaking, taking all things into consideration,* and such expressions as *in boxing, in welding,* and *in farming.*

Generally speaking, business activity is at an all-time high.

In farming, the land must be prepared long before planting time.

Taking all things into consideration, this applicant is the best for the job.

Misplaced Modifiers: Mispl

Unlike dangling modifiers, which do not clearly modify anything, **misplaced modifiers** do have a clear referent but are placed in the sentence in such a way that the sentence reads awkwardly or is unclear. Frequently, misplaced modifiers are prepositional phrases (e.g., phrases that begin with prepositions such as *in, on, with, for, over, under, near,* or *by*) or are adverbs such as *only, just, almost,* or *often.*

> *Unclear:* New employees who demonstrate initiative *often* are promoted more quickly than those who don't.
>
> *Better:* New employees who *often* demonstrate initiative are promoted more quickly than those who don't.
>
> *Better:* New employees who demonstrate initiative are *often* promoted more quickly than those who don't.

Mixed Construction: MixCon

A **mixed construction** occurs when a writer inappropriately changes point of view, voice, tense, or sentence structure.

> *Mixed:* If one is often late for work, you may receive a poor performance review. (The sentence mixes third person, *one,* and second person, *you.*)
>
> *Consistent:* If you are often late for work, you may receive a poor performance review.

See Chapter 4, page 82, for additional examples.

Incomplete Constructions: IncCon

An **incomplete construction** occurs when a writer sets up a sentence that promises a certain kind of content but then does not deliver that content.

> *Incomplete:* More companies in the food and beverage industry are using viral marketing. (*More* than what?)
>
> *Better:* More companies in the food and beverage industry are using viral marketing than ever before.
>
> *Or:* More companies in the food and beverage industry are using viral marketing than those in the construction business.

See Chapter 4, page 83, for additional examples.

Sentence Fragment: Frag

Avoid the sentence fragment. Although the sentence fragment may sometimes be used to good effect, as in sales writing, business writers generally express their thoughts in complete sentences rather than in fragments. The **sentence fragment** consists of any group of words that are used as if they were a sentence but are not a sentence. Probably the most frequent cause of sentence fragments is the use of a subordinate clause as a sentence.

> *Not this:* Believing that you will want an analysis of sales for November. We have sent you the figures.
>
> *But this:* Believing that you will want an analysis of sales for November, we have sent you the figures.
>
> *Not this:* He declared that such a procedure would not be practical. And that it would be too expensive in the long run.
>
> *But this:* He declared that such a procedure would not be practical and that it would be too expensive in the long run.

Pronouns: Pn 1

Make certain that the word each pronoun refers to (its **antecedent**) is clear. Failure to conform to this standard causes confusion, particularly in sentences in which two or more nouns are possible antecedents or the antecedent is far away from the pronoun.

> *Not this:* When the president objected to Mr. Carter, he told him to mind his own business. (*Who* told *whom?*)
>
> *But this:* When the president objected to Mr. Carter, Mr. Carter told him to mind his own business.
>
> *Not this:* The mixture should not be allowed to boil; so when you do it, watch the temperature gauge. (*It* doesn't have an antecedent.)
>
> *But this:* The mixture should not be allowed to boil; so when conducting the experiment, watch the temperature gauge.
>
> *Not this:* The Model Q is being introduced this year. Ads in *USA Today, The Wall Street Journal*, and big-city newspapers throughout the country are designed to get sales off to a good start. It is especially designed for the businessperson who is not willing to pay a big price.
>
> *But this:* The Model Q is being introduced this year. Ads in *USA Today, The Wall Street Journal*, and big-city newspapers throughout the country are designed to get sales off to a good start. The new model is especially designed for the businessperson who is not willing to pay a big price.

Confusion may sometimes result from using a pronoun with an **implied antecedent**.

> *Not this:* Because of the disastrous freeze in the citrus belt, it is necessary that most of them be replanted.
>
> *But this:* Because of the disastrous freeze in the citrus belt, most of the citrus orchards must be replanted.

Except when the reference of *which, that,* and *this* is perfectly clear, avoid using these pronouns to refer to the whole idea of a preceding clause. Many times you can make the sentence clear by using a clarifying noun following the pronoun.

> *Not this* (following a detailed presentation of the writer's suggestion for improving the company suggestion plan): This should be put into effect without delay.
>
> *But this:* This suggested plan should be put into effect right away.

When a noun can be either singular or plural because it refers to a group of people, use a *singular pronoun if group members are acting as one* and a *plural pronoun if they are acting as individual group members.*

For reference to the group acting as one unit

> *Not this:* The committee gave their decision on the new proposal they reviewed.
>
> *But this:* The committee gave its decision on the new proposal it reviewed.

For reference to the group as individual units

> *Not this:* The presenter polled the audience for its interpretation of the data.
>
> *But this:* The presenter polled the audience for their interpretation of the data.

Pn 2

The *number of the pronoun should agree with the number of its antecedent* (the word it stands for). If the antecedent is singular, its pronoun must be singular. If the antecedent is plural, its pronoun must be plural.

> *Not this:* Taxes and insurance are expenses in any business, and it must be considered carefully in anticipating profits.

But this: Taxes and insurance are expenses in any business, and they must be considered carefully in anticipating profits.

Not this: Everybody should plan for their retirement. (Such words as *everyone, everybody,* and *anybody* are singular.)

But this: Everybody should plan for his or her retirement.

Pn 3

Take care to use the **correct case of the pronoun**. If the pronoun serves as the subject of the verb, or if it follows a form of the linking verb *be* (e.g., *is, are, was, were, being, have been*), use a pronoun in the nominative case. The nominative personal pronouns are *I, you, he, she, it, we, who, whoever,* and *they.*

He will record the minutes of the meeting.

I think it will be he who is promoted.

If the pronoun is the **object of a preposition or a verb**, use the objective case. The objective personal pronouns are *me, you, him, her, it, us, whom, whomever,* and *them.*

Not this: This transaction is between you and he. (*He* is nominative and cannot be the object of the preposition *between.*)

But this: This transaction is between you and *him.*

Not this: Because the investigator praised Ms. Smith and *I,* we were promoted.

But this: Because the investigator praised Ms. Smith and *me,* we were promoted.

Many writers are intimidated by the use of *who* and *whom.* However, their use is really no different from that of any other pronoun. As with all other pronouns, their use depends on whether they function as subjects or objects. *Who* and *Whoever* are **nominative pronouns** and are used as subjects or following a form of the linking verb *be* (e.g., *am, is, are, were, was, be, been, being*). *Whom* and *Whomever* are **objective pronouns** and are used as objects of verbs or prepositions. One trick for using who/whom is to substitute a common personal pronoun for the word and then choose who/whom based on which form of the substituted pronoun worked.

Example: George Cutler is the salesperson *who* won the award. (*He,* nominative, could be substituted for *who* because the pronoun is the subject of the verb *won.* You could say "*he* won the award"; therefore, *who* is the right choice.)

Example: Whom should we notify? (Turn the question into a statement: We should notify *whom. Him,* objective, could be substituted for *whom* because the pronoun is the object of the verb *should notify.* You could say "we should notify *him*"; therefore, *whom* is the right choice).

Sometimes, though, the choice is not as clear. What would you choose in the following case?

George is the person who/whom you recommended.

If you substitute *he/him* here, you might not know whether to choose *who* or *whom* because the substitution of *he* or *him* sounds equally awkward. The solution is to notice that who/whom is part of its own clause (*who/whom you recommended?*). To identify how who/whom is being used in the clause, see if it already has a subject. If it does, then you probably need *whom* because the clause won't need two subjects in a row. In the example above, *you* is the subject of the dependent clause, so the correct solution is *whom:*

George is the person whom you recommended.

Here is a contrasting example:

George is the person who recruited the most volunteers. (Here, the verb of the dependent clause, *recruited,* has no other possible subject, so *who* is the subject of the clause.)

And here is the exception:

> I can't remember who the president was. (Using the advice above, you might think the correct form would be *whom* since, otherwise, the clause would seem to have two subjects, *who* and *president*. But notice that the pronoun follows a verb that is a form of *be*. In such cases, you need the nominative [subject] form.)

The possessive case is used for pronouns that immediately precede a **gerund** (a verbal noun ending in *-ing*).

> *Our* selling of the stock frightened some of the conservative members of the board.
> *Her* accepting the money ended her legal claim to the property.
> I appreciate *your* offering to take my place on the committee.

Pn 4

Pronouns must agree in number with antecedents that are indefinite pronouns (see definition in Agmt SV section, page 606).

> *Neither* of the candidates released *his or her* tax returns. (*Note:* If you have trouble finding the antecedent, remember to disregard the preposition. *Candidates* is in a prepositional phrase, so it cannot be the antecedent of your pronoun.)

Other indefinite pronouns such as *both, few, many,* and *several* are always plural.

> Several candidates released *their* tax returns at the beginning of the campaign.

Some indefinite pronouns are either singular or plural (e.g., *all, any, most, none, some*), depending on what they refer to.

> *Most* of the student body spends *its* time studying.
> *Most* of the students spend *their* time studying.

Parallelism: Prl

Parts of a sentence that express equal thoughts should be **parallel (the same) in grammatical form**. Parallel constructions are logically connected by the coordinating conjunctions *and, but,* and *or*. Care should be taken to see that the sentence elements connected by these conjunctions are of the same grammatical type. That is, if one of the parts is a noun, the other parts also should be nouns. If one of the parts is an infinitive phrase, the other parts also should be infinitive phrases.

> *Not this:* The company objectives for the coming year are to match last year's sales volume, higher earnings, and improving customer relations.
> *But this:* The company objectives for the coming year are to match last year's sales volume, to increase earnings, and to improve customer relations.

> *Not this:* Writing copy may be more valuable experience than to make layouts.
> *But this:* Writing copy may be more valuable experience than making layouts.

> *Not this:* The questionnaire asks for this information: number of employees, what is our union status, and how much do we pay.
> *But this:* The questionnaire asks for this information: number of employees, union affiliation, and pay rate.

Tense: Tns

The **tense** of each verb, infinitive, and participle should reflect the logical time of happening of the statement. Every statement has its place in time. To communicate that place exactly, you must select your tenses carefully.

Tns 1

Use **present tense** for statements of fact that are true at the time of writing.

> *Not this:* Boston was not selected as a site for the headquarters because it *was* too near the coast. (Boston is still near the coast, isn't it?)
>
> *But this:* Boston was not selected as a site for the headquarters because it *is* too near the coast.

Tns 2

Use **past tense** in statements covering a definite past event or action.

> *Not this:* Mr. Burns *says* to me, "Bill, you'll never become an auditor."
>
> *But this:* Mr. Burns *said* to me, "Bill, you'll never become an auditor."

Tns 3

The time period reflected by the past participle (*having been . . .*) is earlier than that of its governing verb. The **present participle** (*being . . .*) reflects the same time period as that of its governing verb.

> *Not this:* These debentures are among the oldest on record, *being* issued in early 1937.
>
> *But this:* These debentures are among the oldest on record, *having been* issued in early 1937.
>
> *Not this:* Ms. Sloan, *having been* the top salesperson on the force, was made sales manager. (Possible but illogical.)
>
> *But this:* Ms. Sloan, *being* the top salesperson on the force, was made sales manager.

Tns 4

Verbs in **combined clauses** should be in the same tense. For instance, when the first verb is in the past tense, you should usually also place the second verb in a past tense (past, past perfect, or present perfect).

> I *noticed* [past tense] the discrepancy, and then I *remembered* [same time as main verb] the incidents that had caused it.

If the time of a subordinate clause is earlier than that of the main verb in past tense, use past perfect tense for the subordinate verb.

> *Not this:* In early July we *noticed* [past] that he *exceeded* [logically should be previous to main verb] his quota three times.
>
> *But this:* In early July we *noticed* that he *had exceeded* his quota three times.

The present perfect tense is used for the subordinate clause when the time of this clause is subsequent to the time of the main verb.

> *Not this:* Before the war we *contributed* [past] generously, but lately we *forget* [should be a time subsequent to the time of the main verb] our duties.
>
> *But this:* Before the war we *contributed* generously, but lately we *have forgotten* our duties.

Tns 5

The **present perfect tense** does not logically refer to a definite time in the past. Instead, it indicates time somewhere in the indefinite past.

> *Not this:* We *have audited* your records on July 31 of 2005 and 2006.
>
> *But this:* We *audited* your records on July 31 of 2005 and 2006.
>
> *Or this:* We *have audited* your records twice in the past.

Word Use: WU

Misused words call attention to themselves and detract from the writing. The possibilities of error in word use are infinite; the following list contains only a few of the common errors of this kind.

Don't Use	Use
a long ways	a long way
and etc.	etc.
anywheres	anywhere
continue on	continue
different than	different from
have got to	must
in back of	behind
in hopes of	in hope of
in regards to	in regard to *or* regarding
inside of	within
kind of satisfied	somewhat satisfied
nowhere near	not nearly
nowheres	nowhere
over with	over
seldom ever	seldom
try and come	try to come

Wrong Word: WW

Be careful not to use one word but mean another. Sometimes people confuse these words by their spelling and sometimes by their meanings. Since the *spell checker won't find these errors*, you need to proofread carefully to eliminate them. Here are a few examples:

affect	effect
among	between
bow	bough
capital	capitol
cite	sight, site
collision	collusion
complement	compliment
cooperation	corporation
deferential	differential
desert	dessert
except	accept
implicit	explicit
imply	infer
plane	plain
principal	principle
stationary	stationery

LO3 Determine when to spell out numbers and when to express them in numeral form according to standards of correctness.

STANDARDS FOR THE USE OF NUMBERS

Quantities may be spelled out or expressed as numerals. Whether to use one form or the other is often a perplexing question. It is especially perplexing to business writers, whose work often deals with quantitative subjects.

Numbers: No 1

A common guide for using numbers in business writing is to follow the **rule of nine.** By this rule, you spell out numbers nine and below. You use figures for numbers 10 and above.

> The auditor found 13 discrepancies in the stock records.
> The auditor found nine discrepancies in the stock records.

Apply the rule to both ordinal and cardinal numbers:

> She was the seventh applicant.
> She was the 31st applicant.

No 2

Make an exception to the rule of nine when a number begins a sentence. Spell out all numbers in this position.

> Seventy-three bonds and six debentures were destroyed.
> Eighty-nine strikers picketed the north entrance.

No 3

If you have numbers in a sentence or paragraph that refer to related items, be consistent. If one of the numbers is 10 or greater, use numbers for all of the related items even if the other items are 9 or fewer.

> We managed to salvage 3 printers, 1 scanner, and 13 monitors.

No 4

Use numerals for all **percentages**.

> Sales increases over last year were 9 percent on automotive parts, 14 percent on hardware, and 23 percent on appliances.

Authorities differ on whether to use the percent sign (%) or the word. One good rule to follow is to use the percentage sign in papers that are scientific or technical and the word in all others. Also, the convention is to use the sign following numbers in graphics and presentations. Consistent use of either is correct.

No 5

Present days of the month in number form when the month precedes the day or when the date precedes both month and year.

> June 29, 2008
> 29 June 2008

When days of the month appear alone or precede the month, they may be either spelled out or expressed in numeral form according to the rule of nine. The *th, rd,* and *st* follow the day only when the day is used by itself or precedes the month. These suffixes are never used when the month precedes the day.

> I will be there on the 13th.
> The union scheduled the strike vote for the eighth.
> Ms. Millican signed the contract on July 7.
> Sales have declined since the 14th of August.

No 6

Use either of two accepted orders for date information. One, preferred by *The Chicago Manual of Style,* is day, month, and year:

> On 29 June 2008 we introduced a new product line.

The other is the sequence of month, day, and year. This order requires that the year be set off by commas:

> On June 29, 2008, we introduced a new product line.

No 7

Present money amounts as you would other numbers. If you spell out the number, also spell out the unit of currency.

> Twenty-seven dollars

If you present the number as a figure, use the $ with U.S. currency and the appropriate abbreviation or symbol with other currencies.

U.S., Canada, and Mexico	US $27.33, Can $27.33, Mex $27.33
Euro countries	€202.61
Japan	¥2,178.61
Thailand	฿7,489.91

No 8

Usually spell out **indefinite numbers** and **amounts**.

> Over a million people live there.
> The current population is about four hundred thousand.
> Bill Gates's net worth is in the billions.

No 9

Spell out a **fraction** such as *one-half* that stands alone (without a whole number) or begins a sentence. Represent **mixed numbers** as figures.

> Two-thirds of all jobs in the United States are in the information industry.
> The median price of a home rose by 6½ percent this year.

No 10

Except in legal documents, do not express amounts in both *figures and words.*

> *For legal purposes:* 25 (twenty-five)
> *For business use: either the figure* or *the word, depending on circumstance*

No 11

Represent *times* as follows:

2:00, 2:30	two o'clock
2 p.m., 2:30 p.m.	*not:* 2:00 o'clock
2 o'clock	

LO4 Spell words correctly by applying spelling rules and using a dictionary or spelling checker.

SPELLING: SP

Misspelling is probably the most frequent error in writing. And it is the least excusable. It is inexcusable because all one needs to do to eliminate the error is to use a dictionary or a spell checker.

You can improve your spelling significantly with relatively little effort. Studies show that fewer than 100 words account for most spelling errors, so if you learn to spell these most troublesome words, you will go a long way toward solving your spelling problems. Eighty of these words appear in Figure 18–1.

Figure 18–1

Eighty of the Most
Frequently Misspelled
Words

absence	desirable	irritable	pursue
accessible	despair	leisure	questionnaire
accommodate	development	license	receive
achieve	disappear	misspelling	recommend
analyze	disappoint	necessary	repetition
argument	discriminate	ninety	ridiculous
assistant	drunkenness	noticeable	seize
balloon	embarrassment	occasionally	separate
benefited	equivalent	occurrence	sergeant
category	exceed	panicky	sheriff
cede	existence	parallel	succeed
changeable	forty	paralyze	suddenness
committee	grammar	pastime	superintendent
comparative	grievous	persistent	supersede
conscience	holiday	possesses	surprise
conscious	incidentally	predictable	truly
deductible	indispensable	privilege	until
definitely	insistent	proceed	vacuum
dependent	irrelevant	professor	vicious
description	irresistible	pronunciation	weird

Rules for Word Plurals

1. To form the plurals of most words, add *s*.

   price, prices
   quote, quotes

2. To form the plurals of words ending in *s, sh, ch,* and *x*, usually add *es* to the singular.

   boss, bosses
   relinquish, relinquishes
   glitch, glitches
   tax, taxes

3. To form the plural of words ending in *y*, if a consonant precedes the *y*, drop the *y* and add *ies*. But if the *y* is preceded by a vowel, add *s*.

   company, companies
   medley, medleys
   key, keys

Other Spelling Rules

1. Words ending in *ce* or *ge* do not drop the *e* when *ous* or *able* is added.

   charge, chargeable
   change, changeable
   notice, noticeable
   service, serviceable

2. Words ending in *l* do not drop the *l* when *ly* is added.

   final, finally
   principal, principally

3. Words ending in silent *e* usually drop the *e* when a suffix beginning with a vowel is added.

   have, having
   believe, believable

dine, dining
time, timing

4. Place *i* before *e* except after *c*.

relieve	conceive
believe	receive

Exception: when the word is sounded as a long *a*.

neighbor	weigh

Exceptions:

ancient	financier	seismograph
codeine	foreign	seize
counterfeit	forfeit	seizure
deficient	height	sovereign
efficient	leisure	sufficient
either	neither	surfeit
Fahrenheit	science	weird

LO5 Use capital letters for all proper names, first words of sentences, and first words of complimentary closes.

CAPITALIZATION: CAP

In text and instant messaging environments, writers may forego standard capitalization in informal circumstances. In all other communication situations, standard capitalization is expected. Always capitalize the *first word of a sentence, a person's name, and the pronoun I*. Generally, the more specific the noun, the more likely it is to require capitalization. The following table presents a guide for basic principles of capitalization; however, capitalization practices vary widely, so be sure to know your company's preferences.

Capitalize	Don't Capitalize
Proper names: • Richard Thompson	Common names: • the dean
Geographic places: • St. Paul, Minnesota, United States • Streets: 317 East Boyd Avenue • Chippewa River • Midwest, East Coast	General directions: • north side of town • travel east on Highway 29
Companies: • Qualcomm, Microsoft	Company names that intentionally begin with a lowercase letter: • eBay, iOmega
Titles *preceding* names when the title and name are not separated by commas: • President Watkins	Titles separated from the name by a comma: • Karen Watkins, president of the company, • company president, Karen Watkins
Important words in book, article, and poem titles: • *Getting Things Done: The Art of Stress-Free Productivity*	Conjunctions (*a, an, the*) and short prepositions (*in, on, to, for*) in book, article, and poem titles unless they are the first or last word of the title or the first word after a colon
Words *preceding* most numbers: • Room 418 • No. 10 envelopes • Figure 2	Words preceding page, verse, and paragraph numbers: • page 32 • paragraph three

Capitalize	Don't Capitalize
Official department names: • the Department of Human Resources	General references to a department: • the human resources department
Official degree names and course titles: • Bachelor of Business Administration • Principles of Accounting	Majors, minors, and general references to degrees or courses: • bachelor's degree • accounting class • marketing major
Races, nationalities, and ethnicities: • Caucasian, African American • German, Japanese	*White* and *black* when referring to people
Names of months • November	Names of seasons • winter, spring, fall, summer
First words of complimentary closes: • Sincerely yours,	Subsequent words of complimentary closes: • Yours truly

As noted earlier, other standards are useful in clear communication. But those covered in the preceding pages will help you through most of your writing problems. By using them, you can give your writing the precision that good communication requires.

THERE'S MORE . . .

Would you like to learn more about standard English grammar? Are you seeking opportunities to practice your grammar skills? Scan the QR code with your smartphone or use your Web browser to visit www.mhhe.com/lesikar13e. Select Chapter 18 > Bizcom Tools & Tips.

KEY TERMS

CRITICAL THINKING QUESTIONS

Correct any punctuation or grammar errors you can find in the following sentences. Explain your corrections. **LO1–LO5**

1. Charles E. Baskin, the new member of the advisory committee, has been an employee for seven years.

2. The auditor asked us, "If all members of the work group had access to the petty cash fund?"

3. Our January order consisted of the following items;: two dozen Post-it pads, cube size, one dozen desk blotters, 20 by 32 inches, and one dozen gel roller pens, permanent black.

4. The truth of the matter is, that the union representative had not informed the workers of the decision.

5. Sales for the first quarter were the highest in history, profits declined for the period.

6. We suggest that you use a mild soap for best results but detergents will not harm the product.

7. Employment for October totaled 12,741 an increase of 3.1 percent over September.

8. It would not be fair however to consider only this point.

9. It is the only shrink resistant antiwrinkle and inexpensive material available.

10. Todd Thatcher a supervisor in our company is accused of the crime.

11. Mr. Goodman made this statement, "Contrary to our expectations, Smith and Company will lose money this year."

12. I bought and he sold.

13. Soon we saw George Sweeney who is the auditor for the company.

14. Sold in light medium and heavy weight this paper has been widely accepted.

15. Because of a common belief that profits are too high we will have to cut our prices on most items.

16. Such has been the growth of the cities most prestigious firm, H.E. Klauss and Company.

17. In 2006 we were advised in fact we were instructed to accept this five year contract.

18. Henrys goofing off has gotten him into trouble.

19. Cyrus B. Henshaw who was our leading salesperson last month is the leading candidate for the position.

20. The sales representative who secures the most new accounts will receive a bonus.

21. The word phone which is short for telephone should be avoided in formal writing.

22. In last months issue of Fortune appeared Johnson's latest article Tiger! The Sky's the Limit for Golf.

23. Yes he replied this is exactly what we mean.

24. Why did he say John it's too late?

25. Place your order today, it is not too late.

26. We make our plans on a day to day basis.

27. There is little accuracy in the 60 day forecast.

28. The pre Christmas sale will extend over twenty six days.

29. We cannot tolerate any worker's failure to do their duty.

30. An assortment of guns, bombs, burglar tools, and ammunition were found in the seller.

31. If we can be certain that we have the facts we can make our decision soon.

32. This one is easy to make. If one reads the instructions carefully.

33. This is the gift he received from you and I.

34. A collection of short articles on the subject were printed.

35. If we can detect only a tenth of the errors it will make us realize the truth.

36. She takes criticism good.

37 There was plenty of surprises at the meeting.

38 It don't appear that we have made much progress.

39 The surface of these products are smooth.

40 Everybody is expected to do their best.

41 The brochures were delivered to John and I early Sunday morning.

42 Who did he recommend for the job.

43 We were given considerable money for the study.

44 He seen what could happen when administration breaks down.

45 One of his conclusions is that the climate of the region was not desirable for our purposes.

46 Smith and Rogers plans to buy the Moline plant.

47 The committee feels that no action should be taken.

48 Neither of the workers found their money.

49 While observing the employees, the work flow was operating at peak perfection.

50 The new building is three stories high, fifteen years old, solid brick construction, and occupies a corner lot.

51 They had promised to have completed the job by noon.

52 Jones has been employed by Kimberly Clark for twenty years.

53 Wilson and myself will handle the job.

54 Each man and woman are expected to abide by this rule.

55 The boiler has been inspected on April 1 and May 3.

56 To find problems and correcting them takes up most of my work time.

57 The case of canned goods were distributed to the homeless.

58 The motor ran uneven.

59 All are expected except John and she.

60 Everyone here has more ability than him.

SKILLS BUILDING EXERCISES

NOTE: See Chapter 3 for exercises on choosing the right word and Chapter 4 exercises related to awkward writing and misplaced modifiers.

Punctuation

Insert commas, colons, and semicolons as needed in the following sentences. As your instructor directs, cite punctuation standards from this chapter to support your choices. **LO1**

1 If your credit card is stolen call your bank credit union or other card carrier immediately.

2 We will develop the training course this fall but will not offer it until spring.

3 Our company specializes in management consulting employee development and leadership training.

4 Your payment is 15 days past due please make your payment immediately.

5 Rosa needs to submit her application immediately if she wants to be admitted for the fall semester.

6 Our goal is to have branch offices in the following cities Hayward Wisconsin Golden Colorado and Helena Montana.

7 New employees usually complete their hiring paperwork before they start however they have until the end of their first week at work to finish it.

8 In August 2014 we will begin the software conversion and we expect to complete it by October 1.

9 If we exceed our sales quota we receive a $1000 quarterly bonus but if we only meet our quota we receive a $500 bonus.

10 Because the bank approved our request for a loan we were able to purchase our dream house.

Apostrophes

Select the word that correctly completes the sentence. **LO1**

1 Many of the (businesses, business's, businesses') in town are closed for the holiday.

2 I share my (bosses, boss's, bosses') opinion that he and I should get the corner office suite.

3 Many (peoples, people's, peoples') lake homes are subject to high property taxes.

4 In two (weeks, week's, weeks') we leave for the conference.

5 Our (company's, companies, companies') policy is to let employees work from home one day per week.

6 Kyle frequently works evenings because (its, it's, its') not possible for him to finish his work during the day.

7 Carolyn's severance package included six (months, month's, months') salary and health insurance.

8 She worked her way up to the manager of the (womens, women's, womens') clothing department.

9 We were all impressed by (Joes, Joe's, Joes') presentation.

10 According to (todays, today's, todays') newspaper, gas prices are expected to rise in the coming weeks.

Pronouns

Select the pronoun that correctly completes the sentence. **LO2**

1 Our supervisor assigned the project to Jim and (I/me).

2 Do you know (who/whom) will lead today's meeting?

3 We want (she/her) to lead the meeting today.

4 (He/Him) and Rebecca are two of the hardest workers in our office.

5 The university told (we/us) students about the tuition increase.

6 (We/Us) employees are happy about the results of the union negotiations.

7 Lara said, "Because the agreement between (she/her) and (I/me) is confidential, I am not comfortable discussing the details of the contract."

8 I really appreciated (him/his) telling me about the job opening.

9 Matt is the type of employee (who/whom) we want to promote to management.

10 It was (she/her) who inquired about the open position.

Pronoun–Antecedent Agreement

First identify the antecedent. Then select the pronoun that agrees with its antecedent. **LO2**

1 Each employee received (his or her/their) performance review last week.

2 The staff gave (its/their) recommendations.

3 Joe and Sam shared (his/their) thoughts on Facebook.

4 All staff members should focus (its/their) energy on attracting new clients.

5 Whenever an employee signs up for one of the company intramural sports teams, (he or she/they) must sign a form releasing the company from any liability.

6 If every member of the committee votes "yes," (it/they) will be the first committee to have a unanimous vote.

7 The membership dues and maintenance fees are two separate assessments; (it/they) must be paid for your membership to be activated.

8 The condominium association publishes (its/their) bylaws in the January newsletter.

9 Rogers and Associates, Inc., offers health and dental insurance to (its/their) employees.

10 When a businessperson gives a professional presentation, (he or she/they) should speak clearly and use visuals to maintain the audience's interest.

Subject–Verb Agreement

First identify the subject. Then select the verb that agrees with the subject. **LO2**

1 A lot of time and energy (is/are) required for this project to succeed.

2 Sarah, along with several members of her staff, (support/supports) the policy change.

3 Neither the 20 vacation days nor the salary (was/were) enough to persuade Jorge to take the job.

4 The staff (has/have) considered all of the options and will give their opinions at the next meeting.

5 Each of the interns (receives/receive) a monthly stipend and a parking permit.

6 The cost and the timeline of the project (makes/make) it unlikely that we will proceed.

7 The report on the costs associated with the technology updates (is/are) due next Friday.

8 Either Marla or her associates (is/are) available to talk with you.

9 The jury (is/are) expected to return with a verdict this afternoon.

10 Barr, Douglass, and Company (is/are) going out of business.

A SELF-ADMINISTERED DIAGNOSTIC TEST OF CORRECTNESS

The following test is designed to give you a quick measure of your ability to handle some of the most troublesome punctuation and grammar situations. First, correct all the errors in each sentence. Then turn to Appendix A for the recommended corrections and the symbols for the punctuation and grammar standards involved. Next, review the relevant standards.

1 An important fact about this keyboard is, that it has the patented "ergonomic design".

2 Goods received on Invoice 2741 are as follows; 3 dozen blue denim shirts, sizes 15–33, 4 mens gortex gloves, brown, size large, and 5 dozen assorted socks.

3 James Silver President of the new union had the priviledge of introducing the speaker.

4 We do not expect to act on this matter however until we hear from you.

5 Shipments through September 20, 2013 totaled 69,485 pounds an increase of 17 percent over the year ago total.

6 Brick is recommended as the building material but the board is giving serious consideration to a substitute.

7 Markdowns for the sale total $34,000, never before has the company done anything like this.

8 After long experimentation a wear resistant high grade and beautiful stocking has been perfected.

9 Available in white green and blue this paint is sold by dealers all over the country.

10 Julie Jahn who won the trip is our most energetic salesperson.

11 Good he replied, sales are sure to increase.

12 Hogan's article Retirement? Never!, printed in the current issue of Management Review, is really a part of his book A Report on Worker Security.

13 Formal announcement of our Labor Day sale will be made in thirty-two days.

14 Each day we encounter new problems. Although they are solved easily.

15 A list of models, sizes, and prices of both competing lines are being sent to you.

16 The manager could not tolerate any employee's failure to do their best.

17 A series of tests were completed only yesterday.

18 There should be no misunderstanding between you and I.

19 He run the accounting department for five years.

20 This report is considerable long.

21 Who did you interview for the position?

22 The report concluded that the natural resources of the Southwest was ideal for the chemical industry.

23 This applicant is six feet in height, 28 years old, weighs 165 pounds, and has had eight years' experience.

24 While reading the report, a gust of wind came through the window, blowing papers all over the room.

25 The sprinkler system has been checked on July 1 and September 3.

26 Our meeting is at 9:00 o'clock a.m. tomorrow.

Corrections for the Self-Administered Diagnostic Test of Correctness

Following are the corrected sentences for the diagnostic test at the end of Chapter 18. The errors are underscored, and the symbols for the standards explaining the correction follow the sentences.

1. An important fact about this keyboard is, that it has the patented "ergonomic design".

   An important fact about this keyboard is that it has the patented "ergonomic design." *Cma 6–1, QM 3*

2. Goods received on Invoice 2741 are as follows; 3 dozen blue denim shirts, sizes 15–33, 4 men's gortex gloves, brown, size large and 5 dozen assorted socks.

   Goods received on Invoice 2741 are as follows: three dozen blue denim shirts, sizes 15–33; four men's gortex gloves, brown, size large; and five dozen assorted socks. *Cln 1, Apos 1, SC 3, No 1*

3. James Silver President of the new union_had the priviledge of introducing the speaker.

   James Silver, president of the new union, had the privilege of introducing the speaker. *Cma 4–2, Cap, SP*

4. We do not expect to act on this matter_however_until we hear from you.

   We do not expect to act on this matter, however, until we hear from you. *Cma 4–3*

5. Shipments through September 20, 2013_totaled 69,485 pounds_an increase of 17 percent over the year_ago total.

   Shipments through September 20, 2013, totaled 69,485 pounds, an increase of 17 percent over the year-ago total. *Cma 4–4, Cma 4–1, Hpn 2–1*

6. Brick is recommended as the building material_but the board is giving serious consideration to a substitute.

   Brick is recommended as the building material, but the board is giving serious consideration to a substitute. *Cma 1*

7. Markdowns for the sale total $34,000, never before has the company done anything like this.

   Markdowns for the sale total $34,000; never before has the company done anything like this. *SC 1*

8. After long experimentation a wear_resistant_high_grade_and beautiful stocking has been perfected.

   After long experimentation a wear-resistant, high-grade, and beautiful stocking has been perfected. *Hpn 2–1, Cma 2–2*

9. Available in white_green_and blue_this paint is sold by dealers all over the country.
   Available in white, green, and blue, this paint is sold by dealers all over the country. *Cma 2–1, Cma 3*

10. Julie Jahn_who won the trip_is our most energetic salesperson_
    Julie Jahn, who won the trip, is our most energetic salesperson. *Cma 3*

11. _Good_he replied, sales are sure to increase_
    "Good," he replied. "Sales are sure to increase." *QM 1, Pd 1, Cap*

12. Hogan's article_Retirement? Never!,_printed in the current issue of Management Review, is really a part of his book A Report on Worker Security.
    Hogan's article, "Retirement? Never!," printed in the current issue of *Management Review,* is really a part of his book, *A Report on Worker Security. Cma 4–2, QM 4, Ital 1*

13. Formal announcement of our Labor Day sale will be made in thirty-two days.
    Formal announcement of our Labor Day sale will be made in 32 days. *No 1*

14. Each day we encounter new problems. Although they are solved easily.
    Each day we encounter new problems, although they are solved easily. *Cma 5–1, Frag*

15. A list of models, sizes, and prices of both competing lines are being sent to you.
    A list of models, sizes, and prices of both competing lines is being sent to you. *Agmt SV*

16. The manager could not tolerate any employee's failure to do their best.
    The manager could not tolerate any employee's failure to do his or her best. *Pn 2*

17. A series of tests were completed only yesterday.
    A series of tests was completed only yesterday. *Agmt SV*

18. There should be no misunderstanding between you and I.
    There should be no misunderstanding between you and me. *Pn 3*

19. He run the accounting department for five years.
    He ran the accounting department for five years. *Tns 2*

20. This report is considerable long.
    This report is considerably long. *AA*

21. Who did you interview for the position?
    Whom did you interview for the position? *Pn 3*

22. The report concluded that the natural resources of the Southwest was ideal for the chemical industry.
    The report concluded that the natural resources of the Southwest are ideal for the chemical industry. *Agmt SV, Tns 1*

23. This applicant is six feet in height, _28 years old, weighs 165 pounds, and has had eight years' experience.
    This applicant is six feet in height, is 28 years old, weighs 165 pounds, and has had eight years' experience. *Prl*

24. While _ reading the report, a gust of wind came through the window, blowing papers all over the room.
    While she was reading the report, a gust of wind came through the window, blowing papers all over the room. *Dng*

25. The sprinkler system has been checked on July 1 and September 3.
    The sprinkler system was checked on July 1 and September 3. *Tns 5*

26. Our meeting is at 9:00 o'clock a.m. tomorrow.
    Our meeting is at 9:00 a.m. (or 9 a.m.) tomorrow. *No 11*

Physical Presentation of Letters, Memos, and Reports

The appearance of a letter, memo, or report plays a significant role in communicating a message. Attractively presented messages reflect favorably on the writer and the writer's company. They give an impression of competence and care, and they build credibility for the writer. The material presented here will help you present your documents attractively and appropriately in whatever medium you choose.

Today's word processors include automated formatting for a full range of documents and templates that can be customized to serve the precise needs of a business. A word of warning, though: Features such as templates and styles that are intended to make your work easier will do so only if you know how to control them. Many writers find these templates and styles helpful, but others become frustrated if they are not familiar enough with the software to tweak the templates and styles to their needs. A word-processing software's Help menu can help you learn the advanced features, as can written and video tutorials you can easily find on the Internet. Remember, too, that company styles and preferences will also influence the format of your document. See Chapter 17 for more information on how you can use technology to aid your writing process.

Learning the features of your software will help you use the font, layout, visuals, and document design most appropriate for your document and audience.

LAYOUT DECISIONS

Common layout decisions involve grids, spacing, and margins. Grids are the non-printed horizontal and vertical lines that help you place elements of your document precisely on the page. The examples shown in Figure B–1 illustrate the placement of text on two-, three-, and six-column grids. You can readily see how important it is to plan for this element. While it's true that much of the time you'll be writing correspondence or reports that do not require multiple columns, when you place information on a page, you'll want to consider whether multiple columns (such as in a newsletter or brochure) will better present information to your audience. Programs such as Microsoft Publisher let you view gridlines as you work so that you can easily map and align your text.

In addition, to make your document look its best, you must consider both external and internal spacing. External spacing is the white space on a page. Just as the amount of text denotes importance in writing, so, too, does white space. Surrounding text or a graphic with white spaces sets it apart, emphasizing it to the reader. Used effectively, white space also has been shown to increase the readability of your documents. Ideally, white space should be a careful part of the design of your document.

Layouts Using Different Grids

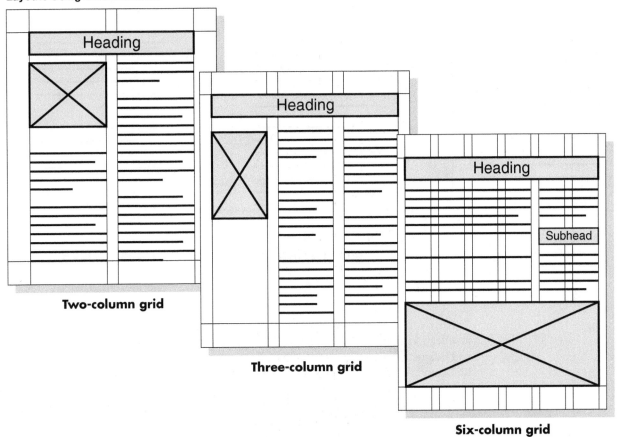

Two-column grid

Three-column grid

Six-column grid

Internal spacing refers to both vertical and horizontal spacing. The spacing between letters on a line is called *kerning*. With word-processing programs, you can adjust how close the letters are to each other. These programs also allow you to adjust how close the lines are to each other vertically, which is called *leading*. Currently, many still refer to spacing in business documents as single or double spacing. However, this is a carryover from the typewriter era when a vertical line space was always ⅙ inch or when six lines equaled an inch. Today's software and hardware allow you to control this aspect of your document much more exactly. Deciding on the best spacing to use depends on the typeface you decide to use. In any case, you need to make a conscious decision about the spacing of the text in your documents.

Another aspect of layout is your margin settings. Ideally, you want your document to look like a framed picture. This arrangement calls for all margins to be equal. However, some businesses use a fixed margin on all documents regardless of their length. Some do this to line up with design features on their letterhead; others believe it increases productivity. In either case, the side margins will be equal. And with today's word processors, you can easily make your top and bottom margins equal by telling the program to center the document vertically on the page. Although all margins will not be exactly equal, the page will still have horizontal and vertical balance. And some word processors have a "make it fit" feature. With this feature, the writer tells the program the number of pages, allowing it to select such aspects as margins, font size, and spacing to fit the message to the desired space.

Different Forms of Justification

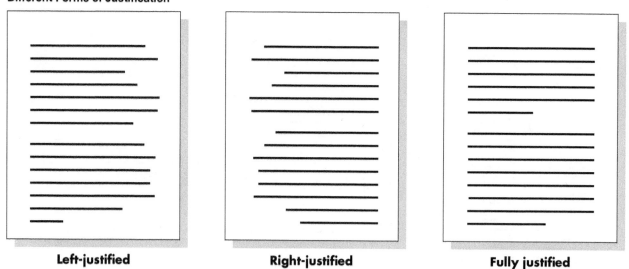

| Left-justified | Right-justified | Fully justified |

How you align your type at the margins or in the center is called *justification*. Left justification aligns every line at the left, right justification aligns every line at the right, and full justification aligns every line at both the left and the right (Figure B–2). Full justification takes the extra spaces between the last word and the right margin and distributes them across the line. This justification increases the amount of white space between words across the line, stopping most readers' eyes a bit. Therefore, it is usually best to set a left-justified margin with a ragged right margin.

CHOICE OF MEDIUM

The media you choose to transmit your documents also communicate. For example, text and instant messaging are perceived as informal media, but at the same time convey that you are a user of current technology. Or, assuming you know your audience will be able to read it, using the html option rather than plain text option to format an email shows that you know how to use technology to make information visually appealing. And using a formatted attachment shows consideration for your reader's need to have a formatted message—especially if you think your audience has only a plain text view of his or her email. Also, sending a formatted document, an rtf file, or a pdf document as an attached file both conveys your message while giving you some control over your document's display.

Today, paper is still a common choice of medium. In the United States, standard business paper size is 8½ by 11 inches; international business A4 (210 × 297 mm) results in paper sized slightly narrower than 8½ inches and slightly longer than 11 inches. Occasionally, half-size (5½ × 8½) or executive size (7¼ × 10½) is used for short messages. Other than these standards, you have a variety of choices to make regarding color, weight, and texture.

The most conservative color choice is white. Of course, you will find that there are numerous variations of white. In addition, there are all the colors of the palette and many tints of these colors. You want your paper to represent you, your business, and its brand but not to distract your reader from the message. The color you choose for the first page of your document should also be the color you use for the second and continuing pages. This is the color you would usually use for envelopes, too.

The weight and texture of your paper also communicate. While "cheap" paper may denote control of expenses to one reader, it may denote cost cutting to another. Usually businesses use paper with a weight of 16 to 20 pounds and a rag or cotton content of 25 to 100 percent. The higher the numbers, the higher the quality. And, of course, many readers often associate a high-quality paper with a high-quality product or service.

The choice of medium to use for your documents is important because it, too, sends a message. By being aware of these subtle messages, you will be able to choose the most appropriate medium for your situation.

FORM OF BUSINESS LETTERS

The layout of a letter (its shape on the page) accounts for a major part of the impression that the appearance of the letter makes. A layout that is too wide, too narrow, too high, too low, or off-center may impress the reader unfavorably. The ideal letter layout is one that fits that space much as a picture fits a frame. That is, a rectangle drawn around the processed letter has the same shape as the space under the letterhead. The top border of the rectangle is the dateline, the left border is the line beginnings, the right border is the average line length, and the bottom border is the last line of the notations.

As to the format of the layout, any generally recognized one is acceptable. Automated formatting allows you to choose your own format preferences. Generally, the most popular formats are block, modified block, and simplified. These are illustrated in Figure B–3. In all formats, single-spacing in paragraphs and double-spacing between paragraphs is the general rule.

The following suggestions represent common practice; however, you can expect some variation according to company or industry styles and preferences.

Return Address. The return address is the writer's address. In business letters, the return address appears in your company letterhead. In personal letters, the return address goes at the top of the page. It does not contain your name, just your street address, city, state, and zip code.

Dateline. You should use the conventional date form, with month, day, and year (September 7, 2014). When you are using a word processor's date feature, be sure to select the appropriate one. If you choose to insert a date code, decide whether you want it to record when the document was created (CreateDate), last printed (PrintDate), or last saved (SaveDate). Also, recognize that abbreviated date forms such as 9-7-14 or Sept. 7, '14 are informal and leave unfavorable impressions on some people. Further, 9-7-14 in the United States is September 7; in other cultures, it's July 9. Spelling out the date is the surest way to be clear. Most word processors allow you to set up your preference and will use that preference when you use the date feature.

Inside Address. The mailing address, complete with the courtesy title of the person being addressed, makes up the inside address. Preferably, form it without abbreviations, except for commonly abbreviated words (*Dr., Mr., Ms.*). In Word, you can use its smart tag feature to quickly and easily enter addresses stored in Outlook.

Attention Line. Some executives prefer to emphasize the company address rather than the individual. Thus, they address the letter to the company in the inside address and then use an attention line to direct the letter to a specific officer or department. The attention line is placed two lines below the inside address and two lines above the salutation. When used, the typical form of the attention line is

Attention: Mr. Donovan Price, Vice President

Salutation. The salutation you choose should be based on your familiarity with the reader and on the formality of the situation. As a general rule, remember that if

Standard Letter Formats

Full Block

Letterhead

Vary spacing to lengthen or shorten

April 9, 20–

Vary spacing to lengthen or shorten

Ms. Mary A. Smitherman, President
Smitherman and Sons, Inc.
3107 Western Avenue
New London, CT 04320-4133

Double Space

Dear Ms. Smitherman:

Subject: Your April 14 inquiry about Mr. H.O. Abel

Double Space

Single Space

Sincerely,

3 Blank Lines

Double Space

Calvin C. DeWitte
Secretary-Treasurer

apc

Modified Block, Blocked Paragraphs

Letterhead

Vary spacing to lengthen or shorten

September 17, 20–

Vary spacing to lengthen or shorten

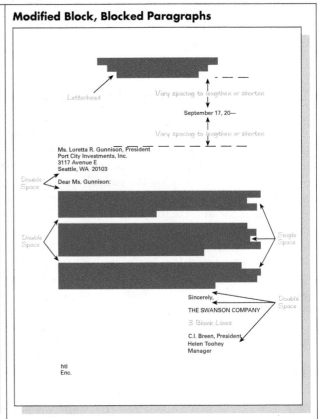

Ms. Loretta R. Gunnison, President
Port City Investments, Inc.
3117 Avenue E
Seattle, WA 20103

Double Space

Dear Ms. Gunnison:

Double Space

Single Space

Sincerely,

THE SWANSON COMPANY

Double Space

3 Blank Lines

C.I. Breen, President
Helen Toohey
Manager

htl
Enc.

Modified Block, Indented Paragraphs

Letterhead

Vary spacing to lengthen or shorten

September 28, 20–

Vary spacing to lengthen or shorten

Sales Manager
Midwest Novelty Distributors, Inc.
4171 North 41st Street
Chicago, IL 60602

Double Space

Dear Sales Manager:

Double Space

Single Space

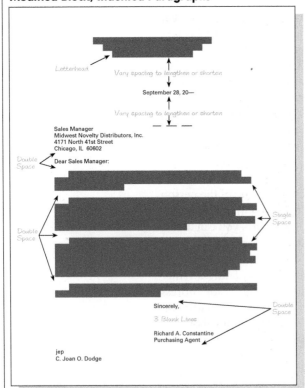

Sincerely,

3 Blank Lines

Double Space

Richard A. Constantine
Purchasing Agent

jep
C. Joan O. Dodge

Simplified

Vary spacing to lengthen or shorten

Letterhead

November 17, 20––

Vary spacing to lengthen or shorten

Ms. Stephanie Palmore, President
Palmore Management Services
4110 Black Forest Road
Cincinnati, OH 48519-5539

Triple Space

ILLUSTRATION OF AMS SIMPLIFIED STYLE

Double Space

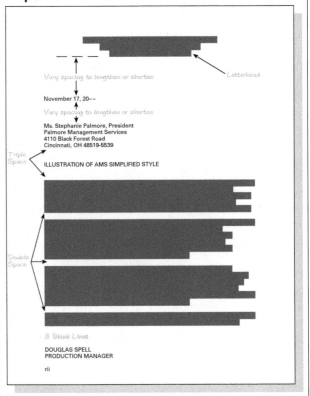

3 Blank Lines

DOUGLAS SPELL
PRODUCTION MANAGER

rii

the writer and the reader know each other well, the salutation may be by first name, as in *Dear Joan*. A salutation by last name, *Dear Mr. Baskin*, is appropriate in most cases.

If you do not know and cannot find out the name of the person to whom you are sending the letter, use a position title. By directing your letter to *Director of Human Resources* or *Public Relations Manager*, you are helping your letter reach the appropriate person.

Women's preferences have sharply reduced the use of *Mrs.* and *Miss.* Many writers ask why we distinguish between married and single women when we make no such distinction between married and single men. The logical solution is to use *Ms.* for all women, just as *Mr.* is used for all men. If you know that the woman you are writing has another preference, however, you should adhere to that preference.

Mixed or Open Punctuation. The punctuation following the salutation and the closing is either mixed or open. Mixed punctuation employs a colon after the salutation and a comma after the complimentary close. Open punctuation, on the other hand, uses no punctuation after the salutation and none after the complimentary close. These two forms are used in domestic communication. In international communication, you may see letters with closed punctuation—punctuation distinguished by commas after the lines in the return and inside addresses and a period at the end of the complimentary close.

Subject Line. So that both the sender and the receiver may quickly identify the subject of the correspondence, many writers use the subject line in their letters. The subject line tells what the letter is about. In addition, it contains any specific identifying material that may be helpful: date of previous correspondence, invoice number, order number, and the like. It is usually placed two lines below the salutation.

Subject lines are generally written as fragments. They may be capitalized as book titles (every important word capitalized), or they may be capitalized as sentences (the first word and proper nouns capitalized). Remember that using all capital letters in a subject line may create the impression that you are shouting at your reader.

The block may be headed in a number of ways, of which the following are representative:

Subject: Your July 2 inquiry about . . .
RE: Please Refer to Invoice H-320.

Second Page Heading. When the length of a letter must exceed one page, you should set up the following page or pages for quick identification. Always print such pages on plain paper (no letterhead). These two forms are the most common:

Ms. Helen E. Mann   2   May 7, 2012

Ms. Helen E. Mann
May 7, 2012
Page 2

Most standard templates automatically insert this information—name of addressee, date, and page number—on the second and following pages of your letter.

Closing. By far the most commonly used complimentary close is *Sincerely*. *Sincerely yours* is also used, but in recent years the *yours* has been used less frequently, as some see it as too personal. *Truly* (with and without the *yours*) is also used, but it also has lost popularity for the same reason. Such closes as *Cordially* and *Respectfully* are appropriate when their meanings fit the writer–reader relationship. A long-standing friendship, for example, would justify *Cordially*; the writer's respect for the position, prestige, or accomplishments of the reader would justify *Respectfully*.

Signature Block. The printed signature conventionally appears on the fourth line below the closing, beginning directly under the first letter for the block form. Most templates will insert the closing. A short name and title may appear on the same line, separated by a comma. If either the name or title is long, the title appears on the following line, blocked under the name. The writer's signature appears in the space between the closing and the printed signature.

Some people prefer to have the firm name appear in the signature block—especially when the letter continues on a second page without the company letterhead. The conventional form for this arrangement places the firm name in solid capitals and blocked on the second line below the closing phrase. The typed name of the person signing the letter is on the fourth line below the firm name.

Information Notations. Below the signature block and aligned at the left are notes for the reader regarding the document. *Enclosure, Enc., Enc.—3,* and so on indicate materials enclosed with the letter. If the writer and the typist are not the same person, the initials of the writer and the typist may be noted (e.g., *WEH:ga*). Indications of copies prepared for other readers also may be included: *cc:* (or *bcc:*) *Sharon Garbett, copy to* (or *blind copy:*) *Sharon Garbett.*

Postscripts. Postscripts, commonly referred to as the PS, are placed after any notations. While rarely used in most business letters because they look like afterthoughts, they can be very effective as added punch in sales letters.

Folding. The carelessly folded letter creates a bad first impression with the reader. Neat folding will complete the planned effect by (1) making the letter fit snugly in its cover, (2) making the letter easy for the reader to remove, and (3) making the letter appear neat when opened.

The two-fold pattern is the easiest. It fits the standard sheet for the long (Number 10) envelope as well as some other envelope sizes. As shown in Figure B–4, the first fold of the two-fold pattern is from the bottom up, taking a little less than a third of the sheet. The second fold goes from the top down, making exactly the same panel as the bottom segment. (This measurement will leave the recipient a quarter-inch thumbhold for easy

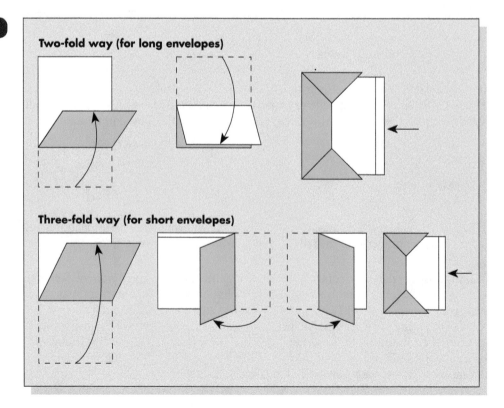

Figure B–4

Two Ways of Folding and Inserting Letters (See Text Descriptions for Dimensions)

Two-fold way (for long envelopes)

Three-fold way (for short envelopes)

Figure B–5

Form for Addressing Envelopes Recommended by the U.S. Postal Service, Publication 28

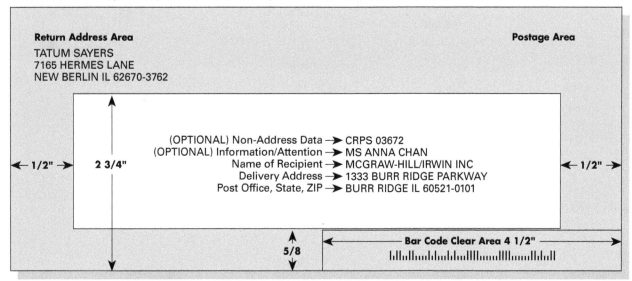

Return Address Area

TATUM SAYERS
7165 HERMES LANE
NEW BERLIN IL 62670-3762

Postage Area

← 1/2" →　　2 3/4"

(OPTIONAL) Non-Address Data ➤ CRPS 03672
(OPTIONAL) Information/Attention ➤ MS ANNA CHAN
Name of Recipient ➤ MCGRAW-HILL/IRWIN INC
Delivery Address ➤ 1333 BURR RIDGE PARKWAY
Post Office, State, ZIP ➤ BURR RIDGE IL 60521-0101

← 1/2" →

5/8

──── Bar Code Clear Area 4 1/2" ────

unfolding of the letter.) Thus folded, the letter should be slipped into its envelope with the second crease toward the bottom and the center panel at the front of the envelope.

The three-fold pattern is necessary to fit the standard sheet into the commonly used small (Number 6¾) envelope. Its first fold is from the bottom up, with the bottom edge of the sheet riding about a quarter inch under the top edge to allow the thumbhold. (If the edges are exactly even, they are harder to separate.) The second fold is from the right side of the sheet toward the left, taking a little less than a third of the width. The third fold matches the second: from the left side toward the right, with a panel of exactly the same width. (This fold will leave a quarter-inch thumbhold at the right, for the user's convenience.) So that the letter will appear neat when unfolded, the creases should be neatly parallel with the top and sides, not at angles that produce "dog-ears" and irregular shapes. In the three-fold form, it is especially important for the side panels produced by the second and third folds to be exactly the same width; otherwise, the vertical creases are off-center and tend to throw the whole carefully planned layout off-center.

The three-fold letter is inserted into its cover with the third crease toward the bottom of the envelope and the loose edges toward the stamp end of the envelope. From habit, most recipients of business letters slit envelopes at the top and turn them facedown to extract the letter. The three-fold letter inserted as described thus gives its reader an easy thumbhold at the top of the envelope to pull it out by and a second one at the top of the sheet for easy unfolding of the whole.

Envelope Address. So that optical character recognition (OCR) equipment may be used in sorting mail, the U.S. Postal Service requests that all envelopes be typed as follows (Figure B–5).

1. Place the address in the scannable area as shown in the white box in Figure B–5. It is best to use a sans serif font in 10 to 12 points.

2. Use a block address format.

3. Single-space.

4. Use all uppercase letters (capitals). While today's OCR equipment can read lowercase, the post office prefers uppercase.

5. Do not use punctuation, except for the hyphen in the nine-digit zip code.

6. Use the two-letter abbreviations for the U.S. states and territories and the Canadian provinces.

Use other address abbreviations as shown in the most recent edition of the *Post Office Directory* (see www.usps.com). When sending to a foreign country, include only the country name in uppercase on the bottom line.

States and Possessions of the United States

Alabama	AL	Kansas	KS	Northern Mariana Islands	
Alaska	AK	Kentucky	KY		MP
American Samoa	AS	Louisiana	LA	Ohio	OH
Arizona	AZ	Maine	ME	Oklahoma	OK
Arkansas	AR	Marshall Islands	MH	Oregon	OR
California	CA	Maryland	MD	Palau	PW
Colorado	CO	Massachusetts	MA	Pennsylvania	PA
Connecticut	CT	Michigan	MI	Puerto Rico	PR
Delaware	DE	Minnesota	MN	Rhode Island	RI
District of Columbia	DC	Mississippi	MS	South Carolina	SC
Federated States		Missouri	MO	South Dakota	SD
of Micronesia	FM	Montana	MT	Tennessee	TN
Florida	FL	Nebraska	NE	Texas	TX
Georgia	GA	Nevada	NV	Utah	UT
Guam	GU	New Hampshire	NH	Vermont	VT
Hawaii	HI	New Jersey	NJ	Virginia	VA
Idaho	ID	New Mexico	NM	Virgin Islands	VI
Illinois	IL	New York	NY	Washington	WA
Indiana	IN	North Carolina	NC	West Virginia	WV
Iowa	IA	North Dakota	ND	Wisconsin	WI
				Wyoming	WY

Canadian Provinces and Territories

Alberta	AB	Newfoundland	NF	Prince Edward Island	PE
British Columbia	BC	Northwest Territories	NT	Quebec	PQ
Manitoba	MB	Nova Scotia	NS	Saskatchewan	SK
New Brunswick	NB	Ontario	ON	Yukon Territory	YT

7. Type the return address in the left corner, beginning on the second line from the top of the envelope and three spaces from the left edge of the envelope.

8. Print any on-arrival instructions (Confidential, Personal) four lines below the return address.

9. Place all notations for the post office (Special Delivery) below the stamp and at least three lines above the mailing address.

FORM OF MEMORANDUMS

Memorandums (memos) have basic components in common, but their form varies widely from organization to organization. The basic components are the heading and body. The heading has four elements: *To, From, Date,* and *Subject.* These elements are arranged in various placements, but all are present.

The body of the memo is usually single-spaced with double-spacing between paragraphs. First-level headings are frequently used in long memos. And notations for typist and enclosures are included just as they are in letters but they are noted differently: *Attachment* or *Att.* rather than *Enclosure* is used to indicate items attached to the memo, and the *cc:* or *bcc:* notation is included as a heading element. Chapter 6 provides examples of memo formats.

First-Level Head

Second-Level Head

Third-Level Head.

Fourth-Level head.

Levels of Headings.
Use the placement and form of headings to indicate the structure of your report's contents. One way to do so is shown. You can modify your word processor's heading styles to suit your preferences and then easily format your different headings with these styles.

FORM OF LETTER AND MEMORANDUM REPORTS

Informal business reports may be written in letter or memo format, depending on the audience. The letter report contains the return address or company letterhead, date, inside address, and salutation; it may also contain a subject line. The memo report contains the standard *To, From, Date,* and *Subject* lines.

Beginning with the second page, letter and memo reports must have a header that contains the reader's name, the date, and a page number. Use your word-processing software's heading feature. In Word 2010 you can find the heading feature by going to Insert > Header. From here type the text of your header and insert a page number. Because you do not want this information on the first page of your report, also check "Different First Page."

Both letter and memorandum reports may use headings to display the topics covered. The headings are usually displayed in the margins, on separate lines, and in a different style (Figure B–6). Memorandum and letter reports also may differ from ordinary letters and memos by having illustrations (charts, tables), an appendix, and/or a bibliography.

FORM OF FORMAL REPORTS

Like letters, formal reports should be pleasing to the eye. Well-arranged reports give an impression of competence—of work professionally done.

General Information on Report Presentation

Since your formal reports are likely to be prepared with word-processing programs, you will not need to know the general mechanics of manuscript preparation if you use automated formatting, as shown in the Word 2010 template in Figure B–7. However, even if you do not have to format your own reports, you should know enough about report presentation to be sure your work is done right.

Conventional Page Layout. For the typical text page in a report, a conventional layout appears to fit the page as a picture fits a frame (Figure B–8). This eye-pleasing

Illustration of an MLA Report Template for Word 2010

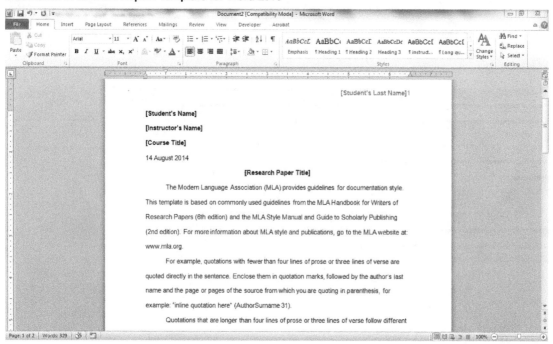

Recommended Page Layouts

Double-Spaced Page

Single-Spaced Page

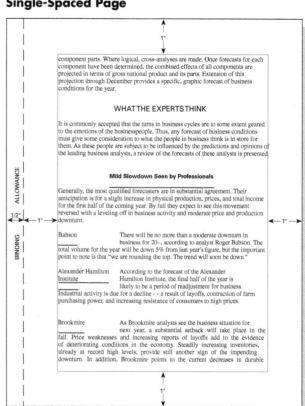

Word 2010 Provides Report Templates Available Online

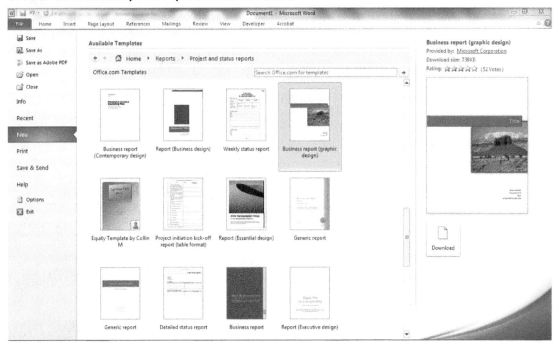

layout, however, is arranged to fit the page space not covered by the binding of the report. Thus, you must allow an extra half inch or so on the left margins of the pages of a single-sided left-bound report and at the top of the pages of a top-bound report.

Special Page Layouts. Certain text pages may have individual layouts. Pages displaying major titles (first pages of chapters, tables of contents, executive summaries, and the like) conventionally have an extra half inch or so of space at the top. Figure B–9 illustrates that some special pages can be created with templates.

Letters or memos of transmittal and authorization also may have individual layouts. They are arranged in any conventional letter or memos form. In the more formal reports, they may be carefully arranged to have the same general shape as the space in which they appear using the "make-it-fit" feature.

Choice of Spacing. The convention of double-spacing reports is becoming less popular. This procedure stems from the old practice of double-spacing to make typed manuscripts more readable for the proofreader and printer. The practice has been carried over into work that is not to be reproduced. The remaining advocates of double-spacing claim that it is easier to read than single-spacing.

In recent years, single-spacing has gained in popularity. The general practice is to single-space within paragraphs, double-space between paragraphs, and triple-space above all centered heads. Supporters of single-spacing contend that it saves space and facilitates reading, as it is like the printing that most people are accustomed to reading.

Patterns of Indentation. You should indent the paragraph beginnings of double-spaced typing. On the other hand, you should block single-spaced material because its paragraph headings are clearly marked by the blank lines between paragraphs.

No generally accepted distance of indentation exists. Some sources suggest ½ inch, and others 1 inch and more. Any decision as to the best distance to use is up to you, though you should follow the practice established in the office, group, or school for which you write the report. Whatever your selection, you should be consistent.

Numbering of Pages. Two systems of numbers are used in numbering the pages of the written report. Small Roman numerals are standard for the front matter of the report. Although these prefatory pages are all counted in the numbering sequence, the numbers generally do not appear on the pages before the table of contents. Arabic numerals are conventional for the main part of the report, normally beginning with the first page of the introduction and continuing through the appendix. See the text website for specific instructions on how to number pages in Word.

Placement of the numbers on the page varies with the binding used for the report. In reports bound at the top of the page, you should center all page numbers at the bottom of the page, two or three lines below the body and usually in a footer.

For left-sided binding, you should place the numbers in the upper-right corner, two or three lines above the top line, usually in the header, and right justified. Exception to this placement is customarily made for special-layout pages that have major titles and an additional amount of space displayed at the top. Such pages may include the first page of the report text; the executive summary; the table of contents; and, in very long and formal works, the first page of each major division or chapter. Numbers for these pages are centered two or three lines below the imaginary line marking the bottom of the layout.

In documents printed back-to-back, page numbers are usually placed at the top of the page even with the outside margin. Not only are word-processing programs capable of automatically placing page numbers this way if directed, but many printers are also capable of two-sided printing.

Display of Headings. Headings are the titles of the parts of the report. Designed to lead the readers through the report, they must show at a glance the importance of the information they cover.

In showing heading importance by position, you have many choices. If your software and printer make available a variety of typefaces, you can select various progressions of font sizes and styles to fit your needs. Your goal, of course, should be to select forms that show differences in importance at first.

You can use any combination of form and placement that clearly shows the relative importance of the heading (Figure B–6 demonstrates one way). One important rule for using headings is that all headings of the same level (e.g., First-level Heading) must have the same placement on the page and the same formatting. In addition, each heading level must have a format that is distinct from other heading levels.

When you create your headings, use your word-processing program's built in automatic styles feature to generate your table of contents. You can also create your own automatic heading formats using your software's styles feature and still automatically generate the table, but if you manually format your text (e.g., select the text and click the "B" icon to make it bold), you will have to manually type the table, which is not efficient. In Word 2010 you can also create a table of contents by marking individual headings that you have formatted in your text and then using the marked headings to generate the table. You will find the feature in References > Table of Contents > Add Text.

Mechanics and Format of the Report Parts

The advice above on physical appearance applies generally to all parts of the report. But as Chapter 12 illustrates, the prefatory sections and appended material of formal reports have special formatting considerations. Below we elaborate on the formatting advice in that chapter.

Title Fly. The title fly contains only the report title. Print the title in the highest-ranking form used in the report, and double-space it if you need more than one line. If your report cover has a window for the title, make sure you place the title in the window.

Title Page. The title page normally contains four main areas of identification. In the typical title page, the first area of identification contains the report title. Preferably, use the highest-ranking form used in the report.

The second area of identification names the individual (or group) for whom the report has been prepared. Precede it with an identifying phrase indicating that individual's role in the report, such as "Prepared for" or "Submitted to." In addition to the recipient's name, include the identification of the recipient by title or role, company, and address, particularly if you and the recipient are from different companies.

The third area of identification names you, the writer of the report. It is also preceded by an identifying phrase—"Prepared by," "Written by," or similar wording describing your role in the report—and it also may identify title or role, company, and address. The fourth and final part of this area of information is the date of presentation or publication. Placement of the four areas of identification on the page should make for an eye-pleasing arrangement. Most word processors will help you align the text vertically on the page.

Letters or Memos of Transmittal and Authorization. As their names imply, the letters or memos of transmittal and authorization are actual letters or memos. The authorization message should be included in its original form.

Acknowledgments. When you are indebted to the assistance of others, it is fitting that you acknowledge the indebtedness somewhere in the report. If you have only a few people to acknowledge, you may acknowledge them in the introduction of the report or in the letter of transmittal. If you need to make numerous acknowledgments, you may construct a special section for this purpose. This section, bearing the simple title "Acknowledgments," has the same layout as any other text page on which a title is displayed.

Table of Contents. The table of contents is the report outline in its polished, finished form. It lists the major report headings with the page numbers on which those headings appear. Although not all reports require a table of contents, one should be a part of any report long enough to make such a guide helpful to the readers. Most word processors are capable of generating a table of contents—complete with page numbers. See the textbook website for a short tutorial on how to create one in Word.

The table of contents is appropriately titled "Contents" or "Table of Contents." The layout of the table of contents is the same as that used for any other report page with a title display. Below the title, set up two columns. One contains the outline headings, generally beginning with the first report part following the table of contents; the other contains the page numbers. You have the option of including or leaving out the outline letters and numbers.

In the table of contents, as in the body of the report, you may vary the form to distinguish different heading levels. But the form variations of the table of contents need not be the same as those used in the text of the report. The highest level of headings is usually distinguished from the other levels, and sometimes typeface differences are used to distinguish second-level headings from lower-level headings. If you use indentation to show the levels of headings, it is acceptable to use plain capitals and lowercase for all levels of headings.

As mentioned in "Display of Headings," if you have used your word-processing program's styles feature to create automatic headings, you can automatically generate the table of contents quickly.

Table of Illustrations. The table (list) of illustrations may be either a continuation of the table of contents or a separate table. Such a table lists the graphics presented in the report in much the same way as the table of contents lists the report parts.

In constructing this table, head it with an appropriately descriptive title, such as "Table of Charts and Illustrations," or "List of Tables and Charts," or "Table of Figures." If you place the table of illustrations on a separate page, layout for this page is the same as that for any other text page with a displayed title. And if you place it as a continued part of the table of contents, you should begin it after the last contents entry.

The table consists of two columns, the first for the graphics titles and the second for the pages on which the graphics appear. The look of the table should match the format and layout of the table of contents. Preceding the title of each entry, place that entry's number; and should these numbers be Roman or otherwise require more than one digit, align the digits at the right. If your report contains two or more illustration types (tables, charts, maps, and the like) and you have given each type its own numbering sequence, you should list each type separately.

As with your table of contents, you can use your word-processing program's automatic features to create the titles for your illustrations, figures, and charts. If you do so, you can automatically generate a list of figures.

References (or Bibliography).   Anytime you use another's idea, you need to give credit to the source. Sometimes business writers interweave this credit into the narrative of their text, and often they use footnotes to convey their source information. But often these sources are listed in a reference or bibliography section at the end of the report. Typically, these sections are organized alphabetically, but they also can be organized by date, subject, or type of source.

As Appendix E illustrates, the format and content of citations vary depending on which citation method you use. Among the widely used formats are Chicago, MLA (Modern Language Association), and APA (American Psychological Association). The content for most items on the list of references is similar to that of the footnote. Word 2010's Reference ribbon includes a reference management tool that will help you generate a bibliography in these standard formats—but see Appendix E for cautionary advice about such tools.

General Grading Symbols: Punctuation, Grammar, Numbers, Spelling, Proofreading, Technique, Strategy, and Formatting

Listed below are general grading symbols and their descriptions. These symbols give you a general idea of how to improve your writing. You will find more detailed information in your text, particularly in Chapter 18, which provides guides for punctuation, grammar, spelling, numbers, and capitalization.

Punctuation

Symbol	Explanation	Description
Apos	Apostrophe	Use the apostrophe to show the possessive case of nouns and indefinite pronouns.
		Use an apostrophe to mark the place in a contraction where letters are omitted.
Bkts	Brackets	Set off in brackets words that you wish to insert in a quotation.
Cln	Colon	Use the colon to introduce a statement of explanation, an enumeration, or a formal quotation.
		But only use a colon before a list if the colon follows an independent clause.
Cma	Comma	
Dsh	Dash	Use the dash to set off an element for emphasis or to show interrupted thought.
Ex	Exclamation mark	Use the exclamation mark at the end of a sentence or exclamatory fragment to show strong emotion.
Hpn	Hyphen	
Ital	Italics	
Parens	Parentheses	
Pd	Period	
Q	Question mark	Place a question mark at the end of sentences that are direct questions.
QM	Quotation marks	Use quotation marks to enclose the exact words of a speaker or, if the quotation is short, the exact words of a writer.
SC	Semicolon	

Grammar

Symbol	Explanation	Description
AA	Adjective–adverb confusion	Do not use adjectives for adverbs or adverbs for adjectives. Adjectives modify only nouns and pronouns; adverbs modify verbs, adjectives, or other adverbs.
Agmt SV	Subject–verb agreement	Make nouns and their verbs agree in number.
AN	Adverbial noun clause	
Awk	Awkward	Avoid awkward writing where word arrangements are unconventional, uneconomical, or not quickly understandable.
Dng	Dangling modifier	Avoid the use of modifiers that do not logically modify a word in the sentence.
Frag	Sentence fragment	Avoid words used as a sentence that are not a sentence.
Pn	Pronoun	
Prl	Parallelism	Express equal thoughts in parallel grammatical form.
Tns	Tense	

Number

Symbol	Explanation
No	Number

Spelling

Symbol	Explanation	Description
SP	Spelling	Spell words correctly.
Cap	Capitalization	Capitalize all proper names and the beginning words of sentences.

Proofreading

Symbol		Explanation	Description
Align	═══	Align	Line up text or visual elements horizontally or vertically.
Stet	stet	Let original stand	Don't delete.
Close	◡	Close up	Close up space.
Del	℧	Delete	Delete.
Ins	∧	Insert	Insert space, punctuation, text, or graphic.
Keep		Keep together	Keep text and/or graphic together.
LC	lc /	Lowercase	Use lowercase.
Caps	cap ≡	Capitalize	Make all caps.
Mv L	[	Move left	Move left.
Mv R	]	Move right	Move right.
Cntr	] [	Center	Center.
Nl	nl	New line	Start new line.
Run	⌐⌐	Run together	Run text together.
Par	#	Paragraph	Start new paragraph.
Sp O	sp ⬭	Spell out	Spell out.
Trp	tr ◡	Transpose	Transpose.

Technique

Symbol	Explanation	Description
Adp	Adaptation	Adapt words to the one reader. These are (1) above or (2) below your reader.
Acc	Accuracy	Check for correct information.
Assign	Assignment	Follow the assignment instructions.
AV	Active voice	Use active voice.
Blky	Bulky arrangement	Make your paragraphs more inviting by breaking them into shorter units of thought.
Blame	Blaming	Avoid blaming or accusing the reader.
Chop	Choppy writing	Make writing smoother by varying sentence structures and styles and avoiding a succession of short sentences.
Coh	Coherence	Make the writing easier to follow by using clear, logical development.
Copy	Copying	Avoid copying or following examples too closely. Organize around the unique facts of the case.
CTone	Conversational tone	Be natural or less formal in your word choice.
Dis	Discriminatory	Avoid using words that discriminate unnecessarily against gender, age, race, disability, or sexual orientation.
DL	Dull writing	Bring your writing to life with vivid, concrete words.
Doc	Documentation	Cite the source of information.
Emp−	Emphasis too little	Give appropriate emphasis with placement, volume, words, or mechanical means.
Emp+	Emphasis too much	Give appropriate emphasis with placement, volume, words, or mechanical means.
GW	Goodwill	Build more goodwill.
Intp	Interpretation	Do more than just present facts. Make the data meaningful in terms of the reader's situation.
Jargon	Jargon	Avoid using jargon.
Los	Loose writing	Use words more economically. Write concisely.
Neg	Negative	Try wording more positively.
Ob	Obvious	Include only necessary information or detail.
Ord	Order of presentation	Use clear, logical order.
Org	Organization	Use clearer, tighter organization with setup and follow through.
Pomp	Pompous	Use more humble, sincere words.
Pre	Precise	Be more precise or concrete.
RB	Reader benefit	Incorporate more reader benefit.
Red	Redundant	Avoid unnecessary repetition.
Resale	Resale	Use more resale here.
RS	Rubber-stamp expression	Avoid overused phrases and timeworn words from the past.
Trans	Transition	Avoid abrupt shift of thought here.
Var	Variety	Vary the words and sentence patterns.
WU	Word use	Use words correctly. Misused words call attention to themselves and detract from the writing.
WW	Wrong word	Use the right words. Wrong words refer to meaning one word and using another.
YVP	You-viewpoint	Revise with the reader in mind.

Message Strategy

Symbol	Explanation	Description
O Dir	Directness needed	The opening is too slow in getting to the goal.
O Ind	Indirectness needed	The opening gets to the goal too fast.
O Qual	Quality	The opening could be improved by making it more on subject, logical, or interesting. It should also set up the rest of the message.
C Ex	Excess information	You have included too much information or irrelevant information.
C Exp	Explanation	You need to provide more or better explanation.
C Id	Identification	You need to completely identify the situation this message addresses.
C Inc	Incomplete	You need to cover the information more completely. Discussion of some topics is missing.
E AC	Action close	A drive for action is appropriate in this situation.
E AC S	Action strong	This action drive is too strong.
E AC W	Action weak	This action drive is too weak.
E IT	Individually tailored	The ending needs to be specific to this case.
E OS	Off subject	These words recall unpleasant things in the reader's mind.

Formatting

Symbol	Explanation	Description
Lay	Layout	Use standard or specified format.
T	Type	Select a readable font for size and style.
Media	Media	Use a medium appropriate for the reader and the context.

Grading Codes and Checklists: Messages and Reports

MESSAGES

The Opening

O Dir *Directness needed.* This opening is too slow in getting to the goal.

O Ind *Indirectness needed.* This opening gets to the goal too fast.

O Qual *Quality.* This opening could be improved by making it more (1) on subject, (2) logical, or (3) interesting.

Coverage

C Ex *Excess information.* You have included too much information or irrelevant information.

C Exp *Explanation.* Provide more or better explanation.

C Id *Identification.* Completely identify the situation this message addresses.

C Inc *Incomplete.* Cover the information more completely. Discussion of some topics is missing.

Ending

E AC *Action close.* A drive for action is appropriate in this situation.

E AC S *Action strong.* This action drive is too strong.

E AC W *Action weak.* This action drive is too weak.

E IT *Individually tailored.* The ending needs to be specific to this case.

E OS *Off subject.* These words recall unpleasant things in the reader's mind.

Technique

Adp *Adaptation.* Adapt words to the one reader. These are (1) above or (2) below your reader.

Awk *Awkward word arrangement.*

Blky *Bulky arrangement.* Make your paragraphs more inviting by breaking them into shorter units of thought.

Chop *Choppy writing.* Make your writing smoother by varying sentence structures and styles and avoiding a succession of short sentences.

DL *Dull writing.* Bring your writing to life with vivid, concrete words.

Emp + *Emphasis, too much.*

Emp − *Emphasis, too little.*   You give too much or too little (as marked) emphasis by (1) placement, (2) volume, or (3) words or mechanical means.

Intp *Interpretation.*   Do more than just present facts. Make the data meaningful in terms of the reader's situation.

Los *Loose writing.*   Use words more economically. Write concisely.

Ord *Order of presentation.*   Use clear, logical order.

RS *Rubber-stamp expression.*   Avoid overused phrases and outdated words.

Trans *Transition.*   Avoid the abrupt shift of thought here.

Effect

Conv *Conviction.*   This is less convincing than it should be. More fact or a more skillful use of words is needed.

GW *Goodwill.*   The message needs more goodwill. Try to make your words convey friendliness. Here you tend to be too dull and matter-of-fact.

Hur *Hurried treatment.*   Your coverage of the problem appears to be hurried. Thus, it tends to leave an effect of routine or brusque treatment. Conciseness is wanted, of course, but you must not sacrifice your objectives for it.

Log *Logic.*   Is this really logical? Would you do it this way in business?

Neg *Negative effect.*   By word or implication, this part is more negative than it should be.

Pers + *Too persuasive.*   Your words are too high-pressure for this situation.

Pers − *Not persuasive enough.*   More persuasion, by either words or facts, would help your message.

Ton *Tone of the words.*   Your words create a bad impression on the reader. Words work against the success of your message if they talk down, lecture, argue, accuse, and the like.

YVP *You-viewpoint.*   More you-viewpoint wording and adaptation would help the overall effect of your message.

REPORTS

Title

T 1   Complete? The title should tell what the report contains. Use the five Ws and 1 H as a check for completeness (*who, what, where, when, why*—sometimes *how*).

T 2   Too long. This title is longer than it needs to be. Check it for uneconomical wording or unnecessary information.

Transmittal

LT 1   More directness is needed in the opening. The message should present the report right away.

LT 2   Content of the message needs improvement. Comments that help the readers understand or appreciate the report are appropriate.

LT 3   Do not include findings unless the report has no executive summary.

LT 4   A warm statement of your attitude toward the assignment is appropriate— often expected. You either do not make one, or the one you make is weak.

LT 5   A friendlier, more conversational style would improve the transmittal.

Executive Summary

ES 1 *(If the direct order is assigned)* Begin directly—with a statement of findings, conclusion, or recommendation.

ES 2 *(If the indirect order is assigned)* Begin with a brief review of introductory information.

ES 3 The summary of highlights should be in proportion and should include major findings, analyses, and conclusions. Your coverage here is (1) scant or (2) too detailed.

ES 4 Work for a more interesting and concise summary.

Organization—Outline/Table of Contents

O 1 This organization plan is not the best for this problem. The main sections should form a logical solution to the problem.

O 2 The order of the parts of this organizational plan is not logical. The parts should form a step-by-step route to the goal.

O 3 One major section should not account for the entire body of the report.

O 4 One-item subdivisions are illogical. You cannot divide an area without coming up with at least two parts.

O 5 These parts overlap. Each part should be independent of the other parts. Although some repetition and relating of parts may be desirable, outright overlap is a sign of bad organization.

O 6 More subparts are needed here. The subparts should cover all the information in the major part.

O 7 This subpart does not fit logically under this major part.

O 8 These parts are not equal in importance. Do not give them equal status in the outline.

O 9 *(If talking headings are assigned)* These headings do not talk well.

O 10 Coordinate headings should be parallel in grammatical structure.

O 11 This (these) heading(s) is (are) too long.

O 12 Wording of the headings should vary to avoid monotonous repetition.

O 13 The structure of the heading levels is incorrect (e.g., some headings formatted as Level 1 headings should be formatted as Level 2 headings).

Introduction

I 1 This introduction does not cover exactly what the readers need to know. Although the readers' needs vary by problem, these topics are usually important: (1) origin of the problem, (2) statement of the problem, (3) scope and limitations, (4) methods used in researching the problem, and (5) preview of the presentation.

I 2 Coverage of this part is (1) scant or (2) too detailed.

I 3 Important information has been left out.

I 4 Findings, conclusions, and other items of information are not a part of the introduction.

Coverage

C 1 The coverage here is (1) scant or (2) too detailed.

C 2 More analysis is needed here.

C 3 Here you rely too heavily on a graphic. The text should cover the important information.

C 4 Information needs to be related to the goals of the report.

C 5   Facts should be distinguished from opinions; opinions should be identified as your opinions.

C 6   Your analyses and conclusions need the support of more fact and authoritative opinion.

Writing

W 1   Adapt your writing to the reader. It appears to be (1) too heavy or (2) too light for your readers.

W 2   Avoid the overuse of passive voice.

W 3   Work for more conciseness. Try to cut down on words without sacrificing meaning.

W 4   Use a more formal writing style for this report. You should write consistently in impersonal (third-person) style.

W 5   Use a more personal style for this report. That is, you should use more personal pronouns (*I*'s, *we*'s, *you*'s).

W 6   Do not abruptly change the thought.

> (1)   Between major parts, use introductions, summaries, and conclusions to guide the readers' thinking.
>
> (2)   Use transitional words, phrases, or sentences to relate minor parts.

W 7   Check the paragraphs for unity. Look for topic sentences.

Visuals

VI 1   You have (1) not used enough visuals or (2) used too many visuals.

VI 2   For the information presented, this visual is (1) too large or (2) too small.

VI 3   This type of visual is not the best for presenting the information.

VI 4   The visual needs to be placed near the place where its contents are discussed.

VI 5   The text must tell the story, so don't just refer the reader to a visual and let it go at that.

VI 6   The appearance of this visual needs improvement.

VI 7   Readers should be referred to the visual at the times that the readers should look at them.

VI 8   Interpretation is needed for patterns in the visual. Note central tendencies, exceptions, ranges, and trends.

VI 9   Visuals should be referred to incidentally, in subordinate parts of sentences that comment on their content (for example, ". . . as shown in Figure 5" or "see Figure 5").

Layout and Mechanics

LM 1   The margins are (1) too wide, (2) too narrow, or (3) too low, high, or off-center (as marked).

LM 2   Make the margins straighter. The raggedness here is visually distracting.

LM 3   Neat? Smudges and light type detract from the message or the print quality is poor.

LM 4   The spacing here needs improvement. (1) Too much space here. (2) Not enough space here.

LM 5   The page numbering is incorrect or incorrectly formatted. See the text for specific instructions.

LM 6   The text and white space are not balanced. (1) Too much white space. (2) Too much text.

LM 7   The selection of type placement and style for the headings is not the best.

LM 8   This item or form is not generally acceptable.

Documentation and the Bibliography

When writing reports and other business documents, you will frequently use information from other sources. Because this material is not your own, you may need to acknowledge it. Whether and how you should acknowledge it are the subject of this brief review.

WHEN TO ACKNOWLEDGE

Your decision to acknowledge or not acknowledge a source should be determined mainly on the basis of giving credit where credit is due. If you are quoting verbatim (in the original author's exact words), you must give credit. If you are paraphrasing (using someone else's ideas in your own words), you should give credit unless the material covered is general knowledge.

Today many colleges have academic honesty or academic integrity policies. Businesses, too, have similar ethics policies and codes. Following the policies not only ensures that you get full credit for your own work; it also helps you build an ethical character. This character leads others to trust you, serving you well both professionally and personally.

Plagiarism and falsifying data are two unethical practices plaguing schools and businesses alike. These practices range from carefully planned, intentional acts to careless, unintentional acts. Whether intentional or not, such mispresentations can have damaging results. Plagiarism, or presenting others' work as your own, steals from the real authors, depriving them of credit for their work and sometimes of the financial rewards they have earned. Additionally, being caught for or even accused of plagiarism affects your reputation as well as the reputation of your company or your school. Falsifying data is equally harmful, especially when others rely on the information you present to make decisions. Worse yet, if you are successful in passing off falsified or plagiarized work as your own, it tempts you to behave unethically in the future. Being sloppy or deceitful is a slippery slope toward potential disgrace and loss of your job.

In your writing tasks, you can eliminate such problems by following these guidelines.

Write Your Own Papers. Do not buy, beg, or borrow papers from others. Not only are instructors adept at spotting plagiarism, they now have powerful search engines and access to large databases of student papers. These databases even contain papers submitted recently. Tweaking these papers to fit your assignment does not get past these tools, which report percentages of similarity to other works. If you are going to go to all this work to copy a paper, you might as well do the work yourself and gain the benefits.

Quotation Marks, Citation, Both, or Neither?

For both ethical and complete communication, you should make clear where your words and content come from. To decide whether to use quotation marks, a citation (naming the source of the material), both, or neither, follow these rules of thumb:

- When the content is general knowledge and you use your own words, you need neither quotation marks nor a citation.

  Example: Microsoft is a developer of computer technology.

  You have not borrowed any special words, so you do not need quotation marks. And since anyone would agree with this general claim, you do not need to cite a source.

- When the content is specialized knowledge but you use either your own words or the only words that can be used, you need to cite but do not need quotation marks.

Example: Microsoft was founded in 1975 ("Microsoft at 30").

This is not a generally known fact, so you need a citation, but your words are a common way to state this plain fact, so you do not need quotation marks.

- When you use striking or biased language from a source, whether about a well-known fact or not, you need both a citation and quotation marks.

  Example: Microsoft "was founded upon an ambitious dream" in 1975 ("Microsoft at 30").

  Here, you are using Microsoft's own evocative language, so you need quotation marks—and whenever you have a quote, you need to cite the source.

The chart below summarizes this advice:

You . . .	Use Quotation Marks	Cite the Source	Do Neither
Used a **well-known fact** and **your own or ordinary language**			✓
Used a **special fact** from a source; used **your own language**		✓	
Used **the source's unique wording** (whether for a well-known or special fact)	✓	✓	

Give Credit to All Ideas That Are Not Your Own. Not only do you need to cite exact quotes, but you also need to cite paraphrased material when the ideas come from someplace else. Changing a few words does not make an idea either original or paraphrased. Also be sure to cite charts, tables, photos, and graphics. Give credit to adapted material as well. When in doubt, cite the source.

Keep Accurate Records of Your Sources Some unintentional problems arise when writers cannot retrieve the information they know they have collected, leading them to cite inaccurately or falsely. While making the information-gathering phase of research easier, the Internet has made managing the vast amount of information one finds a major task. By disciplining yourself to follow strict organizing practices, you will find retrieving the information easier when you need it. Tools such as EndNote or RefWorks (discussed here and in Chapter 17) help tremendously, but only if you use the tools faithfully and with a good style guide as a reference.

Ask Your Instructor or School's Librarian When You Need Help. Both these people want to help you learn how to document appropriately. They will probably be more approachable if you have shown you have tried to find the answer to your question and if you are asking well before the final hour.

HOW TO ACKNOWLEDGE

In brief, informal documents, it is often acceptable to cite your sources informally in the text. For example, you might simply include a phrase like "according to a recent article in *eMarketer*" in the sentence that conveys the information you found there. But in longer, more formal documents based on more extensive research, you will need to cite your sources more formally.

You can choose one of a number of citation styles to acknowledge your sources. Three of the most commonly used systems are Chicago (*The Chicago Manual of Style*), MLA (Modern Language Association), and APA (American Psychological Association) styles. Although their citations contain similar information, they differ in format. Because students tend to be most familiar with MLA format, we will review it in detail.[1] At the end of this appendix, we briefly compare the three systems.

After you have selected a citation style, you must choose a method of acknowledgment. Two methods are commonly used in business: (1) parenthetical references within the text and (2) footnote references. A third method, endnote references, is sometimes used, although it appears to be losing favor. Only the first two are discussed here.

The Parenthetical Citation Method

The parenthetical method of citing sources is widely used in both academia and business. It is called "parenthetical" because it involves putting the author's last name or other identifying information in parentheses immediately following the cited material. This reference is keyed to an alphabetical reference list—variously labeled "Works Cited," "References," or "Bibliography," or given a custom-made title—that appears at the end of the document. Readers thus see a brief reference to your sources as they read your text, and, if and when they are interested in the full reference information, they go to the list of references and use your citation to find that information in the alphabetical list.

The following examples in MLA format show how in-text citations and reference-list entries work together. (For a fuller discussion of how to prepare the reference list, see "The Reference List or Bibliography" on pages 662–666.)

A work with one author:

In-text citation: (Jensen 25)

If you are citing the whole work, omit the page number. If you are citing more than one work by the same author, provide a short form of the title as well, as in "(Jensen, *Winning* 25)."

Reference-list entry:

Jensen, Peter. *The Winning Factor: Inspire Gold Medal Performance in Your Employees.* New York: AMACOM, 2012. Print.

A work with two or three authors or editors:

In-text citation: (Kimmel, Weygandt, and Kieso 22)

Reference-list entry:

Kimmel, Paul D., Jerry J. Weygandt, and Donald E. Kieso. *Financial Accounting: Tools for Business Decision Making.* Hoboken, NJ: John Wiley & Sons, 2011. Print.

---

[1] Examples included here have been adapted to business communication from the *MLA Handbook for Writers of Research Papers*, 7th ed. (New York: MLA, 2009), print; Diana Hacker, and Barbara Fister, *Research and Documentation Online*, 5th ed., Bedford/St. Martin's, n.d., Web, 19 July 2012; and Linn-Benton Community College, "MLA Citation Guide," *Scribd*, Scribd Inc., 2012, Web, 24 July 2012. When these sources did not agree, we used the model that seemed to fit best with the logic used for other entries.

A work with more than three authors or editors:

In-text citation: (Bjelland et al. 497)

Reference-list entry:

Bjelland, Melissa, et al. "Employer-to-Employer Flows in the United States: Estimates Using Linked Employer–Employee Data." *Journal of Business & Economic Statistics* 29.4 (2011): 493–505. Print.

A work by a government or corporate author:

In-text citation: (United States 1)

Reference-list entry:

United States. Small Business Administration. *How to Write a Business Plan. U.S. Small Business Administration.* US SBA, n.d. Web. 18 July 2012.

In-text citation: (Janus 3)

Reference-list entry:

Janus. *U.S. Equities: Focus on Fundamentals. Janus.* Janus, 20 June 2012. Web. 18 July 2012. [authored by the company]

In-text citation: (Sant 2)

Reference-list entry:

Sant, Tom. *The Seven Deadly Sins of Proposal Writing. Qvidian.* Qvidian, 2011. Web. 25 July 2012. [authored by a specific person on behalf of a company]

A work with no author identified (and here, with no page numbers provided in the source):

In-text citation: ("Total Quality Management")

Reference-list entry:

"Total Quality Management (TQM)." *Encyclopædia Britannica Online.* Encyclopædia Britannica Inc., 2012. Web. 18 July 2012.

If citing more than one work in one parenthetical reference:

In-text citation: (Aigrain 140; Jeon and Ryoo)

Notice that the authors for the different works are put in alphabetical order, separated by a semicolon (multiple authors for one work stay in their original order).

Reference-list entries:

Aigrain, Phillippe. *Sharing: Culture and the Economy in the Internet Age.* Amsterdam: Amsterdam University Press, 2012. Print.

Jeon, Jin Q., and Juyoun Ryoo. "How Do Foreign Investors Affect Corporate Policy?: Evidence from Korea." *International Review of Economics & Finance*, 25 (2012): 52–65. Print.

In practice, you may find that it feels more natural to work your sources of information into your sentences rather than naming them in parentheses. For example, rather than write "E-learning has become a multibillion-dollar industry (Jacobs 8)," you might write "According to Jeff Jacobs, e-learning has become a multibillion-dollar industry (8)." Or, if you were citing the whole work rather than a particular page, you would not even need the parenthetical citation. The reader could still find the corresponding entry in the reference list by using the source information in the sentence—in this case, the author's name. Use your sense of good style and readability to decide whether to work the source into the sentence or to name it in parentheses.

Remember that the goal of this, or any, citation method is to enable your readers to identify, verify, and evaluate the sources of your information. At every point in your document, your reader should be able to tell exactly where the information came from. Include citations whenever you believe that the source isn't understood. If you are providing lengthy information from one source, you usually need to cite it only once per paragraph. When you move to a new paragraph, though, you should cite it again, just to confirm for your reader that you are still basing your discussion on that source.

When placing parenthetical references in your text, put them at the end of a sentence or in some other logical break in your text, and put them before any mark of punctuation that occurs there. Here are two examples:

> Palmeri observes that particular organizational contexts "will often both hinder and support the organization's writing goals" (60).

> Collaborative writing is pervasive in the workplace (Couture and Rymer; Ede and Lunsford), and it can be particularly difficult when the collaborators come from different organizational cultures (Spilka).

The Footnote Method

Footnotes are a second means used to acknowledge sources. Two types of footnotes are used in business documents: citation footnotes and discussion footnotes. The emphasis here is on the citation footnote, but the uses of the discussion footnote also will be briefly discussed.

Citation Footnotes. A common way to acknowledge sources is by footnotes; that is, the references are placed at the bottom of the page, and Arabic numbers in superscript (small raised type) indicate which part of the text they go with. The sequence of the numbers is consecutive throughout the document. The footnotes are placed above the bottom margin and single-spaced, with commas between their components.

If your footnotes include the complete facts about the cited sources, then you do not need to include a bibliography unless you believe that your reader would appreciate one. Thus, in addition to saving time and trouble for the writer, footnotes can be a convenience to business readers, keeping them from having to flip back and forth from the text to a bibliography as they read. While the latest version of MLA style excludes citation footnotes, we still recommend their use for business readers. Today's word-processing programs feature easy-to-use tools for creating superscripts and placing the footnotes at the bottom of the page.

The following lists show how you would use MLA style to create footnotes for different kinds of sources.

Note: Figure E–1 helps you identify what footnote form you need. To see the following examples in bibliographic form, consult the sample "Works Cited" list on pages 662–666.

Print Book (Hard Copy or Accessed Online)

1. *Name of the author, in normal order.* If a source has two or three authors, all are named. If a source has more than three authors, the name of the first author followed by the Latin *et al.* or its English equivalent "and others" may be used.

2. *Capacity of the author.* Needed only when the person named is actually not the author of the book but an editor, compiler, or the like.

3. *Chapter name* (italicized). Necessary only in the rare instances in which the chapter title helps the reader find the source.

4. *Book title* (italicized).

5. *Edition.*

6. *Location of publisher.* If more than one city is listed on the title page, the one listed first should be used. If the population exceeds half a million, the name of the city is sufficient; otherwise, include both the city and the state.

Flowchart for Citing Sources in MLA Style. Start at the top and work your way down to figure out what kind of source you have and which format to use.

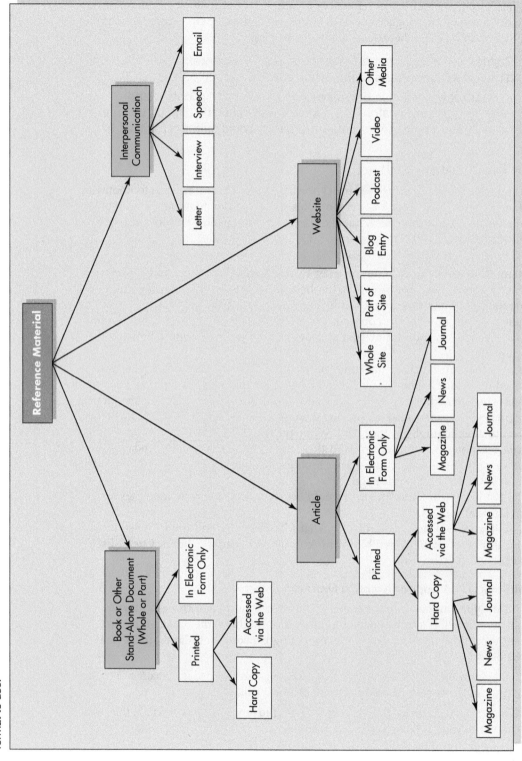

7. *Publishing company.*

8. *Date.* Year of publication. If revised, year of latest revision.

9. *Page or pages.* Specific page or inclusive pages on which the cited material is found.

If citing a hard copy, add

10. *The word* "print."

If citing a print book or document accessed online, add

10. *Title of the website* (italicized).

11. *The word* "Web."

12. *The date accessed.*

The following are examples of book entries:

Book by one to three authors:

[1]Peter Jensen, *The Winning Factor: Inspire Gold Medal Performance in Your Employees* (New York: AMACOM, 2012) 25, print.

[1]Ford Saeks, *Superpower: How to Think, Act, and Perform with Less Effort and Better Results* (Hoboken, NJ: John Wiley & Sons, 2012) 47, *Safari Books Online,* Web, 20 July 2012.

[1]Paul D. Kimmel, Jerry J. Weygandt, and Donald E. Kieso, *Financial Accounting: Tools for Business Decision Making* (Hoboken, NJ: John Wiley & Sons, 2011) 14, print.

Book by four or more authors or editors:

[1]Hiroyuki Odagiri et al., eds., *Intellectual Property Rights, Development, and Catch Up: An International Comparative Study* (Oxford, UK: Oxford UP, 2010) 421, print.

Edited collection (if citing the whole work):

[1]Greg N. Gregoriou and Nigel Finch, eds., *Best Practices in Management Accounting* (New York: Palgrave Macmillan, 2012), print.

A page or pages from a specific article or chapter in an edited work:

[1]Michael O'Brochta, "Proven Business-Leader Actions for Project Success," *Organizational Project Management,* ed. Rosemary Hossenlopp (Vienna, VA: Management Concepts, 2010) 60, print.

[1]Hanane Fathi, "Security and Privacy Challenges in Globalized Wireless Communications," *Globalization of Mobile and Wireless Communications: Today and in 2020,* ed. Ramjee Prasad, Sudhir Dixit, Richard van Nee, and Tero Ojanpera (Netherlands: Springer, 2011) 91, *OhioLink Scholarly & Reference E-Book Collection,* Web, 19 July 2012.

Electronic Book or Document

When citing books or documents (whole works, chapters, or sections) from the Web for which no print publication information is provided, include the first four items as you would for a print book (*author, capacity of the author, chapter name in quote marks, book/document title italicized*) and then provide the following:

5. *Page or pages* (if provided).

6. *Title of the website* (italicized).

7. Site sponsor or publisher. Use "n.p." if not evident.

8. *Date on the document.* Use "n.d." if no date is provided.

9. *The word* "Web."

10. *The date accessed.*

Here are some examples:

[1]Janus, *U.S. Equities: Focus on Fundamentals, Janus,* Janus, 20 June 2012, Web, 18 July 2012.

[1]Tom Sant, *The Seven Deadly Sins of Proposal Writing, Qvidian,* Qvidian, 2011, Web, 19 July 2012.

[1]United States, Small Business Administration, *How to Write a Business Plan,* U.S. Small Business Administration, US SBA, n.d., Web, 18 July 2012.

[1]"Total Quality Management (TQM)," *Encyclopædia Britannica Online,* Encyclopædia Britannica Inc., 2012, Web, 18 July 2012.

Print Magazine, Journal, or Newspaper Article (Hard Copy or Accessed Online)

When citing a periodical article for which print publication information exists, include these elements (when available) in this order:

1. *Author name.* If no author is given, the entry may be skipped.
2. *Article title* (within quotation marks).
3. *Periodical title* (italicized).
4. *Publication identification.* Complete date for magazines. For newspapers, complete date and edition (such as *Nat'l ed.*) For journals, volume number and issue number, followed by the year in parentheses.
5. *Page or pages* (if applicable).

If using a hard copy, add

6. *The word* "print."

If using a version accessed online, add

6. *Title of database or website* (italicized).
7. *The word* "Web."
8. *The date accessed.*

Examples of magazine, journal, and newspaper entries are shown below:

Print magazine article:

[1]Gerald Richards, "If Training Is Expensive, What's the Cost of Ignorance?" *Training + Development* Apr. 2012: 17, print.

[1]Wayne Rash, "AT&T's Bid for T-Mobile Suffers Another Setback," *eWeek* 5 Dec. 2011: 12, *Academic Search Complete,* Web, 18 July 2012.

Print journal article:

[1]Christopher Jones, "Written and Computer-Mediated Accounting Communication Skills: An Employer Perspective," *Business Communication Quarterly* 74.3 (2011): 261, print.

[1]Kelly Martin, Jean Johnson, and Joseph French, "Institutional Pressures and Marketing Ethics Initiatives: The Focal Role of Organizational Identity," *Journal of the Academy of Marketing Science* 39.4 (2011): 574, *Communication & Mass Media Complete,* Web, 18 July 2012.

[1]Ephraim Okoro, rev. of *Outsourcing Technical Communication: Issues, Policies and Practices,* ed. Barry L. Thatcher and Carlos Evia, *Business Communication Quarterly* 75.1 (2012): 108, print.

Using Microsoft 2010 to Add Footnotes

Word 2010 makes it very easy to insert footnotes into your documents. You simply put your cursor where you want the footnote number to go in the text and click References > Insert Footnote, as shown.

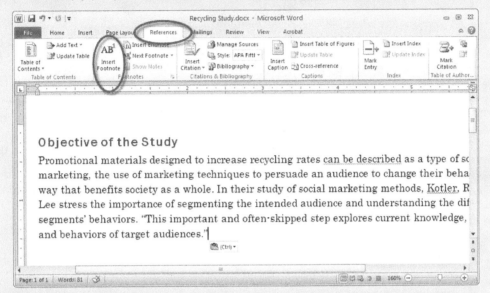

Word will enter the raised footnote number in superscript type in your text and also provide a corresponding place at the bottom of the page where you can enter your source information, as in this example:

When you enter more footnotes, Word will number them consecutively for you—and if you decide to delete one or insert a new one in an earlier part of your text, it will renumber them automatically.

Footnotes are a great convenience to your reader, and they give your research documents a professional appearance. Use them whenever they're appropriate.

Print newspaper article:

[1]"Cash-Strapped States Cut College Financial Aid," *The Wall Street Journal* 29 Jan. 2012, Sunday ed.: 2, print.

[1]Jean Eaglesham, "Regulators Serve Up Alphabet Soup," *The Wall Street Journal* 21 Apr. 2011, Eastern ed.: C1, *ProQuest,* Web, 18 July 2012.

When citing a full-text article from a database (rather than an exact visual copy of the article) that does not show where the page breaks are, just cite the full page range, as in the following example.

Full-text article from a database:

Jason Childs, "Demonstrating the Need for Effective Business Ethics: An Alternative Approach," *Business and Society Review* 117.2 (Summer 2012): 221, *ProQuest Research Library,* Web, 20 July 2012.

Online Periodical Articles

When citing a magazine or news article for which no print publication information is provided, include the first three items as you would for a print article (*author, article title in quotation marks, periodical or website title in italics*) and then provide the following:

4. *Publisher or sponsor of the database or website.* If not evident, use "n.p."

5. *Date of publication* (day, month, and year if available). If no date is provided, use "n.d."

6. *The word* "Web."

7. *The date accessed.*

Here are some examples.

Article from an online magazine:

[1]Howard Kurtz, "USA Today's Digital Gamble," *The Daily Beast,* The Newsweek/Daily Beast Company LLC, 16 July 2012, Web, 20 July 2012.

Article from the companion website for a print magazine:

[1]Victor Luckerson, "How LinkedIn Makes Money Off Your Résumé—And Why That's Good For You," *TIME Business,* Time Inc., 20 July 2012, Web, 24 July 2012.

Article from an online news source:

[1]John D. Sutter, "Can Skype 'Wiretap' Video Calls?," *CNN Tech,* Cable News Network, 24 July 2012, Web, 25 July 2012.

Article from the companion website for a print newspaper:

[1]Catherine Rampell, "Report Details Woes of Student Loan Debt," *The New York Times,* The New York Times Company, 20 July 2012, Web, 20 July 2012.

When citing an article in a scholarly journal for which there is no print counterpart (that is, the resource exists solely online), format as you would a print article but replace "print" with "Web" and add the date accessed. If there are no page numbers, put "n. pag." (no pagination) in place of the page number or numbers. Here is an example:

Journal article for which there is no print version:

[1]Stefanie Quade, "Improving Collaborative Learning and Global Project Management in Small and Medium Enterprise," *International Journal of Advanced Corporate Learning* 5.2 (2011): n. pag., Web, 20 July 2012.

When citing material from a database that has no print counterpart, use the same form as you would for an online periodical article, as in the example below.

Database material with no print counterpart:

"Starbucks: Earnings Estimates and Forecast," *Hoover's Online,* Hoover's, 2012, Web, 20 July 2012.

A Website or Part of a Website

As you may have already noticed, the current MLA citation guidelines for citing electronic sources no longer include URLs (Internet addresses). One reason is that many URLs for the Web either change quickly or are password protected, which means that providing the URL often doesn't really help the reader get to the Web source. Another is that today's search engines make it quite easy to find documented sources without using the URL. If you're used to typing or copying and pasting the extremely long URLs of some online sources into your documents, this will be a welcome change.

If your instructor directs you to include the URLs for your Web sources, though, include them at the end of each entry, in angle brackets, as in the example below. Otherwise, include just the following items in a citation for a website or other Web-based material:

1. *Author's name* (if available).
2. *Title of the specific page or element in quotation marks* (if applicable).
3. *Title of the site* (italicized).
4. *Sponsor of the site.*
5. *Date of publication or last update* (if no date, use "n.d.").
6. *The word* "Web" (or, if downloaded, the medium, such as "MP3 file").
7. *The date accessed.*

Here are various examples:

A corporate website:

[1]*TQL,* home page, Total Quality Logistics, n.d., Web, 18 July 2012.

Part of a website:

[1]"Careers with TQL," *TQL,* Total Quality Logistics, n.d., Web, 18 July 2012.

A part of a website for which the reader requests the URL:

[1]"Careers with TQL," *TQL,* Total Quality Logistics, n.d., Web, 18 July 2012 <http://jobs.tql.com/>.

A blog entry:

[1]Bruce Mayhew, "Tone. Do You Proofread for Email Tone?," *Bruce Mayhew Blog: Business Communication,* Bruce Mayhew, 11 Apr. 2011, Web, 19 July 2012.

A Facebook post:

[1]Jacqueline Rodriguez. "Have you nominated Starbucks for the 2012 NSHMBA Brillante Awards yet? Nominate today! www.nshmba.org/brillante," *Facebook.com,* 19 July 2012, Web, 20 July 2012.

A Twitter post:

[1]KimEl, "How to Manage Your Smartest, Strangest Employee: http://bit.ly/Nx3aGj," *Twitter.com,* 12 July 2012, Web, 20 July 2012.

An online map:

[1]"Damascus, Syria," map, *Google Maps,* Google, 18 July 2012, Web, 18 July 2012.

A podcast:

[1]Grammar Girl, "Tips for Editing and Revising," *Grammar Girl Podcasts, Quick and Dirty Tips,* MacMillian Holdings, LLC, 21 June 2012, Web, 20 July 2012. (If downloaded, put "MP3 file" instead of "Web.")

Online video:

[1]"The Welcome Party," *The Office, Hulu.com,* Hulu, 12 Apr. 2012, Web, 18 July 2012. (If seen on television instead, replace the items following title of the program with the network [e.g., NBC], the call letters for the local station on which the program was viewed [e.g. WNET], the city of the TV station, the date viewed, and the word "televison.")

[1]Best Buy, "The Company as Wiki," *You Tube,* You Tube, 27 Aug. 2008, Web, 19 July 2012.

A public wiki:

[1]"Copyrights and Trademarks," *SmallBusiness.com,* MediaWiki, 4 Jan. 2010, Web, 18 July 2012.

A posting to a listserv:

[1]Sarah Read, "Social Media Thread," *The Association of Teachers of Technical Writing Listserv,* ATTW, 1 Jan. 2012, Web, 18 July 2012.

An online radio program:

[1]Theo Francis, "Capital One's Credit Card Settlement, In Context," *NPR.org,* Natl. Public Radio, 18 July 2012, Web, 19 July 2012. (If downloaded, put "MP3 file" instead of "Web." If heard live, put "radio" after the date of broadcast and omit "Web" and the access date.)

Interpersonal Communications

Media for interpersonal communication abound in today's business environment. The following examples and those given above should enable you to create an acceptable citation for any type you wish to reference. (*Note:* Your reader may find it helpful if you include the author's title along with his or her name.)

A letter:

[1]Gregory H. Williams, President, University of Cincinnati, letter to the author, 5 Oct. 2012. TS. (*TS* stands for "typescript.")

An email message:

[1]Jim Dubinsky, Executive Director, Association for Business Communication, "Revised Operational Guidelines," message to the author, 15 July 2012, email.

An interview:

[1]Hans Bender, personal interview, 7 Aug. 2012.

A speech or presentation:

[1]Conan O'Brien, Commencement Address, Dartmouth College, Hanover, NH, 12 June 2011. (If there is an actual speech title, include it in quotation marks after the speaker's name. Add "speech" or "address" at the end of the note unless already obvious.)

[1]Deborah Roebuck, "Building Ethical Leaders from the Inside Out," Association for Business Communication Annual Meeting, Incline Village, NV, Nov. 2008, conference presentation.

The types of entries discussed in the preceding paragraphs are the ones you'll use most often. But so many different forms of communication are now available that you may need to prepare a citation for which no standard format is available (e.g., for a print or online ad, a photograph, or a computer program). When you do, you should adapt one of the more common citation formats to cite the unusual source. Label the item (e.g., *advertisement, abstract,* not italicized) if you think that will help.

Subsequent References. Writers used to use the Latin abbreviations *Ibid.* (which means "in the same place") and *Op. cit.* ("in the work cited") to refer back to earlier footnotes. These have largely been replaced by abbreviated forms of the original footnote entries. Usually the author's last name followed by the relevant page number is adequate for a previously cited work:

[4] Beehr and Glaser 34.

If you happen to have cited two or more works by the same author, simply add a short form of the title after the author's name to distinguish this source from the others:

⁴ Beehr and Glaser, "Organization" 34.

Discussion Footnotes. A second type of footnote is the discussion footnote. Through discussion footnotes, the writer strives to explain a part of the text, to amplify the discussion of a certain topic, to make cross-references to other parts of the report, or to add other commentary. The following examples illustrate some possibilities for this footnote type.

Cross-Reference:

¹ See the principle of inflection points on page 72.

Amplification of Discussion and Cross-Reference:

² Lyman Bryson says the same thing: "Every communication is different for every receiver even in the same context. No one can estimate the variation of understanding that there may be among receivers of the same message conveyed in the same vehicle when the receivers are separated in either space or time" (see *Communication of Ideas* 5).

Because discussion footnotes interrupt the reading of your document, you should use them sparingly. When possible, work such material into the text itself, or just omit it.

PRESENTATION OF QUOTED AND PARAPHRASED INFORMATION

You may use data obtained from secondary sources in two ways. You may paraphrase the information (cast it in your own words), or you may use it verbatim (exactly as the original author worded it). In typing paraphrased material, you need not distinguish it from the rest of the text. Material you use verbatim, however, must be clearly distinguished.

If the quoted passage is short (about 10 lines or less), place it within the text and with quotation marks before and after it. Set off longer quotations from the margins, without quotation marks, as shown in the example below. If the text is double-spaced, you may further distinguish the quoted passage by single-spacing it.

Professor Logan Wilson, an expert on academic assessment, makes this observation:

> It is a curious paradox that academicians display a scientific attitude toward every universe of inquiry except that which comprises their own profession. . . . Lacking precise qualitative criteria, administrators are prone to fall back upon rather crude quantitative measures as a partial substitute. For example, student evaluations of teachers often lack acceptable reliability and validity statistics. And when they are administered is quite illogical. Moreover, most statements on them relate to contextual factors—e.g., office hours, fairness of tests—and not to acquiring knowledge itself. Yet administrators use quantitative scores from these instruments to the minute fraction of a point to assess teaching quality. Multiple measures of teaching performance with an emphasis on student learning would bring a more rational approach to teaching as one dimension of academic responsibility. (201)

He then proposes a combination of methods for assessing student-learning outcomes.

Frequently, you will find it best to break up or use only fragments of the quoted author's work. Because omissions may distort the meaning of a passage, you must clearly indicate them, using ellipsis points (a series of three periods typed with intervening spaces) where material is left out. If an omission begins before or after a sentence, you must use four periods—one for the final punctuation plus three for the ellipsis points.

A passage with such omissions is the following excerpt from Jim Collins's bestselling book *Good to Great*:

> Perhaps your quest to be part of building something great will not fall in your business life. But find it somewhere. . . . For in the end, it is impossible to have a great life unless it is a meaningful life. (209–10)

THE REFERENCE LIST OR BIBLIOGRAPHY

A bibliography is an orderly list of resources on a particular subject. Usually it provides the full reference information for sources cited in parentheses in the text, as described in the section on parenthetical citation, and is labeled "References" or "List of Works Cited."

Sometimes the bibliography itself will be the main information product. For example, if someone asked you to compile a list of resources on e-learning, you would prepare your findings in the form of a bibliography, probably preceded by some introductory text. And if someone asked you to provide a brief description with each entry as well, you would prepare what is known as an annotated bibliography. If your bibliography is extensive, you might precede it with a fly page containing the title ("Bibliography" or a custom title such as "List of E-learning Sources"). You could also organize your entries by category, with subheadings (for example, "Books," "Periodicals," and "Internet Resources"). If your document has an appendix, the bibliography follows it.

As with footnotes, variations in bibliographic style are numerous, but in MLA style, the information for a bibliography entry follows the order described in this chapter's section on citation footnotes (pages 653–660). There are significant differences, however, between footnote and bibliography format. The latter uses periods rather than commas between the major components of an entry. Bibliographies also have these distinguishing traits:

1. The author's name is listed in reverse order—surname first—for the purpose of alphabetizing. If an entry has more than one author, however, only the name of the first author is reversed in MLA and Chicago format (in APA format, all the authors' names are inverted).

2. The entry is generally presented in hanging-indention form. That is, the second and subsequent lines of an entry begin some uniform distance (usually about one-half inch) to the right of the beginning point of the first line. The purpose of this indented pattern is to make the alphabetized first line stand out.

3. The entry gives the inclusive pages of articles, but not for books, and does not refer to any one page or passage.

4. Second and subsequent references to publications of the same author are indicated by a line formed by three hyphens. But this line may be used only if the entire authorship is the same in the consecutive publications. For example, the line could not be used if consecutive entries have one common author but different coauthors.

Below is a bibliography made up of the footnote citation examples presented in this chapter. (The material in brackets at the end of each entry should *not* be included in actual citations; it is included here to identify each type of entry.)

Works Cited

Aigrain, Phillippe. *Sharing: Culture and the Economy in the Internet Age.* Amsterdam: Amsterdam UP, 2012. Print. [Print book]

Bender, Hans. Personal interview. 7 Aug. 2012. [Interview]

Best Buy. "The Company as Wiki." *YouTube.* YouTube, 27 Aug. 2008. Web. 19 July 2012. [Online video]

Bjelland, Melissa, et al. "Employer-to-Employer Flows in the United States: Estimates Using Linked Employer–Employee Data." *Journal of Business & Economic Statistics* 29.4 (2011): 493–505. Print. [Print journal article]

Citation Management Tools: Use with Caution

As Chapter 17 points out, computerized tools for building citation lists (e.g., bibliography, list of works cited) abound. You can find such tools on the Internet, at computer stores, in your own word processing program, and even inside research databases. The top window below shows RefWorks, a widely used online citation-management program, which you may be able to access for free through your school library's website. You can import or create references here and then have RefWorks generate your bibliography from them, as shown. Below that is an illustration of the citation-creation function in *ABI/INFORM*, a ProQuest database. With this function, you can create citations in the desired citation style right from the record you're viewing (in this database, by

clicking the "Cite this" link at the bottom of the record) and then either export the citations to a program like RefWorks or copy and paste them into a document.

But a strong note of caution is in order: Such tools can be limited or misleading, and they can make mistakes. In the RefWorks example, the date of publication is correct only because the writer who entered the information in RefWorks knew to skip the *Pub year* field and enter the full date into the *Pub Date Free Form* field instead; otherwise, the year would have appeared twice in the entry. In the *ABI/INFORM* example, ProQuest's citation creator left off the pages covered by the article and mistakenly abbreviated *July*. But none of these tools is perfect. You will need to carefully check their output against a good citation handbook.

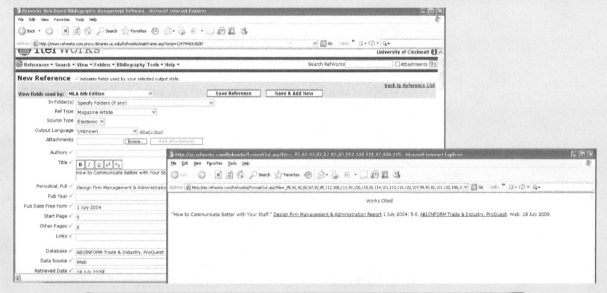

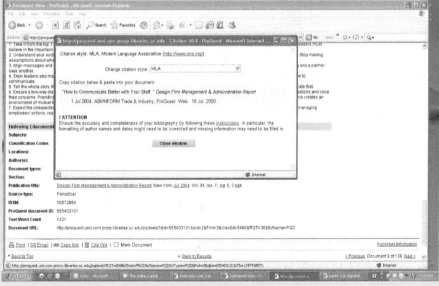

"Careers with TQL." *TQL.* Total Quality Logistics, n.d. Web. 18 July 2012. [Part of a website]

"Careers with TQL." *TQL.* Total Quality Logistics, n.d. Web. 18 July 2012 <http://jobs.tql.com/>. [Part of a website. In MLA format, provide the URL only at reader's request.]

"Cash-Strapped States Cut College Financial Aid." *The Wall Street Journal* 29 Jan. 2012, Sunday ed.: 2. Print. [Print newspaper article]

Childs, Jason. "Demonstrating the Need for Effective Business Ethics: An Alternative Approach." *Business and Society Review* 117.2 (Summer 2012): 221–32. *ProQuest Research Library.* Web. 20 July 2012. [Print journal article provided by a database]

"Copyrights and Trademarks." *SmallBusiness.com.* MediaWiki, 4 Jan. 2010. Web. 18 July 2012. [Public wiki]

"Damascus, Syria." Map. *Google Maps.* Google, 18 July 2012. Web. 18 July 2012. [Online map]

Dubinsky, Jim. "Revised Operational Guidelines." Message to author. 15 July 2012. Email. [Email message]

Eaglesham, Jean. "Regulators Serve Up Alphabet Soup." *The Wall Street Journal* 21 Apr. 2011, Eastern ed.: C1. *ProQuest.* Web. 18 July 2012. [Print newspaper article provided by a database]

Fathi, Hanane. "Security and Privacy Challenges in Globalized Wireless Communications." *Globalization of Mobile and Wireless Communications: Today and in 2020.* Ed. Ramjee Prasad, Sudhir Dixit, Richard van Nee, and Tero Ojanpera. Netherlands: Springer, 2011: 91–102. *OhioLink Scholarly & Reference E-Book Collection.* Web. 19 July 2012. [Chapter from a print collection accessed online]

Francis, Theo. "Capital One's Credit Card Settlement, In Context." *NPR.org.* National Public Radio, 18 July 2012. Web. 19 July 2012. [Online radio program]

Grammar Girl. "Tips for Editing and Revising." *Grammar Girl Podcasts, Quick and Dirty Tips.* MacMillian Holdings, LLC, 21 June 2012. Web. [If downloaded, put "MP3 file" instead] 20 July 2012. [Podcast]

Gregoriou, Greg N., and Nigel Finch, eds. *Best Practices in Management Accounting.* New York: Palgrave Macmillan, 2012. Print. [Print collection]

Janus. *U.S. Equities: Focus on Fundamentals. Janus.* Janus, 20 June 2012. Web. 18 July 2012. [Electronic document accessed via the Web]

Jensen, Peter. *The Winning Factor: Inspire Gold Medal Performance in Your Employees.* New York: AMACOM, 2012. Print. [Print book]

Jeon, Jin Q., and Juyoun Ryoo. "How Do Foreign Investors Affect Corporate Policy?: Evidence from Korea." *International Review of Economics & Finance* 25 (2012): 52–65. Print. [Print journal article]

Jones, Christopher. "Written and Computer-Mediated Accounting Communication Skills: An Employer Perspective." *Business Communication Quarterly* 74.3 (2011): 247–71. Print. [Print journal article]

KimEl. "How to Manage Your Smartest, Strangest Employee: http://bit.ly/Nx3zGj." *Twitter.com.* 12 July 2012. Web. 20 July 2012. [Twitter post]

Kimmel, Paul D., Jerry J. Weygandt, and Donald E. Kieso. *Financial Accounting: Tools for Business Decision Making.* Hoboken, NJ: John Wiley & Sons, 2011. Print. [Print book]

Kurtz, Howard. "USA Today's Digital Gamble." *The Daily Beast.* The Newsweek/Daily Beast Company LLC, 16 July 2012. Web. 20 July 2012. [Article from an online magazine]

Luckerson, Victor. "How LinkedIn Makes Money Off Your Résumé—And Why That's Good For You." *TIME Business*. Time Inc., 20 July 2012. Web. 24 July 2012. [Article from the companion website for a print magazine]

Martin, Kelly, Jean Johnson, and Joseph French. "Institutional Pressures and Marketing Ethics Initiatives: The Focal Role of Organizational Identity." *Journal of the Academy of Marketing Science* 39.4 (2011): 574–91. *Communication & Mass Media Complete*. Web. 18 July 2012. [Print journal article provided by a database]

Mayhew, Bruce. "Tone. Do You Proofread for Email Tone?" *Bruce Mayhew Blog: Business Communication*. Bruce Mayhew, 11 Apr. 2011. Web. 19 July 2012. [Blog entry]

O'Brien, Conan. Commencement Address. Dartmouth College, Hanover, NH. 12 June, 2011. [Speech]

O'Brochta, Michael. "Proven Business-Leader Actions for Project Success." *Organizational Project Management*. Ed. Rosemary Hossenlopp. Vienna, VA: Management Concepts, 2010. 57–72. Print. [Chapter from a print collection]

Odagiri, Hiroyuki et al., eds. *Intellectual Property Rights, Development, and Catch Up: An International Comparative Study*. Oxford, UK: Oxford UP, 2010. Print. [Print book, more than three editors]

Okoro, Ephraim. Rev. of *Outsourcing Technical Communication: Issues, Policies and Practices*. Ed. Barry L. Thatcher and Carlos Evia. *Business Communication Quarterly* 75.1 (2012): 108–13. Print. [Print book review]

Quade, Stefanie. "Improving Collaborative Learning and Global Project Management in Small and Medium Enterprise." *International Journal of Advanced Corporate Learning* 5.2 (2011): n. pag. Web. 20 July 2012. [Article in an online scholarly journal that has no print counterpart]

Rampell, Catherine. "Report Details Woes of Student Loan Debt." *The New York Times*. The New York Times Company, 20 July 2012. Web. 20 July 2012. [Article from the companion website for a print newspaper]

Rash, Wayne. "AT&T's Bid for T-Mobile Suffers Another Setback." *eWeek* 5 Dec. 2011: 12. *Academic Search Complete*. Web. 18 July 2012. [Print magazine article provided by a database]

Read, Sarah. "Social Media Thread." *The Association of Teachers of Technical Writing Listserv*. ATTW, 1 Jan. 2012. Web. 18 July 2012. [Posting to a listserv]

Richards, Gerald. "If Training Is Expensive, What's the Cost of Ignorance?" *Training + Development* Apr. 2012: 16–17. Print. [Print magazine article]

Rodriguez, Jacqueline. "Have you nominated Starbucks for the 2012 NSHMBA Brillante Awards yet? Nominate today! www.nshmba.org/brillante." *Facebook.com*. 19 July 2012. Web. 21 July 2012. [Facebook post]

Roebuck, Deborah. "Building Ethical Leaders from the Inside Out." Association for Business Communication Annual Meeting. Incline Village, NV. Nov. 2008. Conference presentation. [Presentation]

Saeks, Ford. *Superpower: How to Think, Act, and Perform with Less Effort and Better Results*. Hoboken, NJ: John Wiley & Sons, 2012. *Safari Books Online*. Web. 20 July 2012. [Print book accessed online]

Sant, Tom. *The Seven Deadly Sins of Proposal Writing*. Qvidian. Qvidian, 2011. Web. 25 July 2012. [Electronic document accessed via the Web]

"Starbucks: Earnings Estimates and Forecast." *Hoover's Online.* Hoover's, 2012. Web. 20 July 2012. [Material from a database with no print counterpart]

Sutter, John D. "Can Skype 'Wiretap' Video Calls?" *CNN Tech.* Cable News Network, 24 July 2012. Web. 25 July 2012. [Article from an online news source.]

"Total Quality Management (TQM)." *Encyclopædia Britannica Online.* Encyclopædia Britannica Inc., 2012. Web. 18 July 2012. [Article from an electronic reference work]

TQL. Home page. Total Quality Logistics, n.d. Web. 18 July 2012. [Corporate website]

United States. Small Business Administration. *How to Write a Business Plan. U.S. Small Business Administration.* US SBA, n.d. Web. 18 July 2012. [Electronic document accessed via the Web]

"The Welcome Party." *The Office. Hulu.com.* Hulu, 12 Apr. 2012. Web. 18 July 2012. [Online video]

Williams, Gregory H. Letter to the author. 5 Oct. 2012. TS. [Letter]

DIFFERENCES BETWEEN MLA, CHICAGO, AND APA FORMATS

As noted previously, the Chicago and APA systems differ somewhat from the MLA style presented in the preceding pages. The MLA style seems to be the most up to date on popular electronic media, and because it excludes URLs, it has the simplest format for citing online material. The APA favors current scholarly research, especially in the sciences, while the Chicago style gives the most formatting options.

The business field does not have its own citation style. Therefore, you should choose or even create one that will suit your purpose and audience best.

The primary differences among the MLA, Chicago, and APA formats are shown in the following illustrations.

Parenthetical Citation

MLA: (Kimmel, Weygandt, and Kieso 14)

Chicago: (Kimmel, Weygandt, and Kieso 2011, 14)

APA: (Kimmel, Weygandt, & Kieso, 2011, p. 14)

Footnote—Book

MLA:

[1]Paul D. Kimmel, Jerry J. Weygandt, and Donald E. Kieso, *Financial Accounting: Tools for Business Decision Making* (Hoboken, NJ: John Wiley & Sons, 2011) 14, print.

Note: As pointed out on page 653, MLA style no longer includes citation footnotes. Nevertheless, we recommend their use as a convenience to readers.

Chicago:

[1]Paul D. Kimmel, Jerry J. Weygandt, and Donald E. Kieso, *Financial Accounting: Tools for Business Decision Making* (Hoboken, NJ: John Wiley & Sons, 2011), 14.

APA:

(Does not use citation footnotes)

Footnote—Periodical:

MLA:

[1]Donovan A. McFarlane, "The Art of Connecting: How to Overcome Differences, Build Rapport, and Communicate Effectively with Anyone," *Journal of Applied Management and Entrepreneurship* 12.2 (2007): 114, print.

Chicago:

[1]Donovan A. McFarlane, "The Art of Connecting: How to Overcome Differences, Build Rapport, and Communicate Effectively with Anyone," *Journal of Applied Management and Entrepreneurship* 12, no. 2 (2007): 114.

APA:

(Does not use citation footnotes)

Bibliography Entry—Print Book

MLA:

Kimmel, Paul D., Jerry J. Weygandt, and Donald E. Kieso. *Financial Accounting: Tools for Business Decision Making.* Hoboken, NJ: John Wiley & Sons, 2011. Print.

Chicago:

Kimmel, Paul D., Jerry J. Weygandt, and Donald E. Kieso. *Financial Accounting: Tools for Business Decision Making.* Hoboken, NJ: John Wiley & Sons, 2011.

Note: In Chicago style, the footnotes–bibliography citation method and the parenthetical citations–reference list method put the publication date in different places. The entry above is for the former system (used with footnotes). With a parenthetical citation, the bibliography entry would look like this:

Kimmel, Paul D., Jerry J. Weygandt, and Donald E. Kieso. 2011. *Financial Accounting: Tools for Business Decision Making.* Hoboken, NJ: John Wiley & Sons.

APA:

Kimmel, P. D., Weygandt, J. J., & Kieso, D. E. (2011). *Financial accounting: Tools for business decision making.* Hoboken, NJ: John Wiley & Sons.

Bibliography Entry—Print Periodical Article Found Online:

MLA:

McFarlane, Donovan A. "The Art of Connecting: How to Overcome Differences, Build Rapport, and Communicate Effectively with Anyone." *Journal of Applied Management and Entrepreneurship* 12.2 (2007): 114–16. *ABI/INFORM Complete.* Web. 25 July 2012.

Chicago:

McFarlane, Donovan A. "The Art of Connecting: How to Overcome Differences, Build Rapport, and Communicate Effectively with Anyone." *Journal of Applied Management and Entrepreneurship* 12, no. 2 (2007): 114–116. http://search.proquest.com/docview/203918925?accountid=2909.

With the parenthetical citations–reference list method, the Chicago entry would look like this:

McFarlane, Donovan A. 2007. "The Art of Connecting: How to Overcome Differences, Build Rapport, and Communicate Effectively with Anyone." *Journal of Applied Management and Entrepreneurship* 12 (2): 114–116. http://search.proquest.com/docview/203918925?accountid=2909.

APA:

McFarlane, D. A. (2007). The art of connecting: How to overcome differences, build rapport, and communicate effectively with anyone. *Journal of Applied Management and Entrepreneurship*, 12(2), 114–116. Retrieved from http://search.proquest.com/docview/ 203918925?accountid=2909

Note: The Chicago and APA styles recommend using the Digital Object Identifier (DOI), if possible, when citing all electronic sources. The DOI is a long number that serves as a more stable identifier than a URL. If the source has a DOI, it will be on the electronic record for the source. Your readers can then use this number to find the source on the Internet and/or in research databases. If there is no DOI, provide the stable URL—the one provided by the database—as in the examples above.

Bibliography Entry—Online Reference Work:

MLA:

"Total Quality Management (TQM)." *Encyclopædia Britannica Online.* Encyclopædia Britannica Inc., 2012. Web. 18 July 2012.

Chicago:

Encyclopædia Britannica Online. 2012.

Note: In Chicago, in both the footnotes–bibliography and the parenthetical citations–reference list method, the article title ("Total Quality Management (TQM)"), the URL for the source, and the date accessed would be provided in the footnote or parenthetical citation, along with the encyclopedia title.

APA:

"Total quality management (TQM)." (2012). In Encyclopædia Britannica online. Retrieved from http://www.britannica.com/EBchecked/topic/ 1387320/Total-Quality-Management-TQM

Bibliography Entry—Blog Posting

MLA:

Mayhew, Bruce. "Tone. Do You Proofread for Email Tone?" *Bruce Mayhew Blog: Business Communication.* Bruce Mayhew, 11 Apr. 2011. Web. 19 July 2012.

Chicago:

(Not usually included in the bibliography. The footnote or parenthetical citation would include the author name, title of posting, title of blog, the date the entry was posted, the URL, and the access date.)

APA:

Mayhew, B. (2011, 11 April). Tone. Do you proofread for email tone? [Web log post]. Retrieved from http://brucemayhew.wordpress.com/2011/ 04/11/do-you-proofread-your-email-for-tone/

Whatever system you decide to use, use only one within a document, and always be complete, accurate, and consistent.

PHOTO CREDITS

Note: Page numbers followed by n refer to material found in notes.

C

Camouflaged verbs, 60–61
Capitalization, 618–619
Captions, in visuals, 497–498
Career centers, 289
Career fairs, 288
Cartoons, 512
Casserly, Meghan, 327n
Castro, Amy, 537n
Casual language, 128
Caukin, Jennifer, 529n
Cell phones, 105, 535–536
Change, openness to, 43–44
Character-based appeals, 228, 240
Chartjunk, 514
Charts. *See also* Visuals
    bar and column, 503–505
    combination, 510
    flowcharts, 501, 502
    line, 507, 508
    pie, 506–507
Chatzky, Jean, 286n
The Chicago Manual of Style, 615
Chicago style, 651, 666–668
Choi, Sejung Mariana, 36n
Chu, Shu-Chuan, 36n
Citations. *See also* Documentation
    APA style for, 651, 666–668
    Chicago style for, 651, 666–668
    footnote style of, 653–661, 666–667
    function of, 652–653
    MLA style for, 651, 654, 666–668
    parenthetical style of, 651–652, 666
    technological tools to manage, 663
Claims
    direct, 162–164
    indirect, 196–199
Clarke, Monica, 244
Classified advertisements, 289
Clauses
    adverbial, 608
    dependent, 79, 599
    elliptical, 608
    independent, 79, 596
    nonrestrictive, 597–598
    noun, 608
    restrictive, 597–598
Clichés, 52, 53
Clip art, 496
Closed-ended questions, 483–484
Closing, in letters, 631
Cloud computing, 588–589
Clustered bar charts, 503, 504
Cluster sampling, 475
Cluttering phrases, 74–75
Coherence, 88–89
Collaborative presentations, 566–567
Collaborative report writing
    computer tools for, 587–588
    ground rules for, 366
    group makeup for, 365–366
    process of, 366–368
    project plan for, 367
    steps in, 367–369
Collaborative tagging, 468
Collective nouns, 607
Collectivism, 34

Colloquialisms, 40
Colons, 596
Color
    of business paper, 628
    in visuals, 496
Combination charts, 510
Combined clauses, 613
Commas, 597–600
Common-ground persuasion technique, 230
Communication. *See also* Business
        communication; Cross-cultural
        communication; Nonverbal
        communication; Oral communication;
        Written communication
    business activity and variation in, 14–15
    channels of, 19
    contexts of, 16–18
    correctness in, 593–594
    external-operational, 9–10
    forms of, 119
    internal-organizational, 8–9
    personal, 10–12
    problem-solving approach to, 20
    process of, 18–19
Communication Matters
    active/passive voice, 59
    business etiquette, 96
    business report tips, 383
    channel choice, 19
    chartjunk, 514
    citation management tools, 663
    clichés, 52, 53
    cultural dimensions, 34
    documentation, 650
    email, 130, 162
    emotional intelligence, 366
    Facebook and Twitter messages, 244
    fonts, 146
    fundraisers, 232
    grammar, 596
    handshakes, 537
    high-context vs. low-context
        cultures, 33
    hiring practices, 287
    idioms, 58
    importance of business communication, 4
    infographics, 497
    interview mistakes, 329
    linear-actives, multi-actives, and
        reactives, 35
    lost in translation, 54
    misplaced modifiers, 83
    negative announcements, 209
    negotiation, 527
    Periodic Table of Visualization Methods, 516
    personal appearance, 63
    professional portfolios, 321
    proposals, 259
    sales message vividness, 247
    selling in white papers, 240
    stringy and see-saw sentences, 73
    surplus words, 75
    talking voice, 526
    TED.com, 552
    text messages, 589
    there is, there are, 77
    this, 87
    transactional analysis, 102

    visuals, 248
    workplace diversity, 65
Communication networks
    explanation of, 12
    formal, 12–13
    informal, 13–14
Communicators, relationship of, 17
Competence, 555–556
Compound subjects, 607
Compound words, 601
Compromise, in refused requests, 194
Computational thinking, 7
Computer tools. *See* Technological tools
Conclusions, for long reports, 411–412
Confidence, 555
Confidentiality, research practices and, 484
Conjunctions, coordinating, 598
Connotation, 56
Contractions, 595
Controlled before–after design, 481
Convenience sampling, 475
Conventional outlines, 352
Coordinated, 79
Coordinating conjunctions, 598
Corporate social responsibility, 8
Correct idioms, 57
Country Reports, 471
Courtesy
    avoiding blame and, 103
    avoiding preaching and, 104
    do more than is expected and, 104–105
    function of, 103
    mobile devices and, 105
    in phone use, 533–536
    sincerity and, 106
Cover letters. *See also* Business letters; Email
        cover messages
    bad and good illustrations of, 324–325
    closing for, 322–324
    content of, 321–322
    email, 325
    examples of, 317–320
    opening for, 316, 321
    organization of, 322
    types of, 313, 316
Crabb, Stuart, 1
Cross-cultural communication. *See also*
        Cultural diversity
    attitudes toward odors and, 32
    attitudes toward space and, 32
    body positions/movements and, 29–31
    cultural dimensions and, 34
    cultural diversity and, 27, 29
    effects of, 36
    emotional expression and, 35–36
    English-language use and, 38–40
    frankness and, 32
    high-context/low-context cultures and, 32, 33
    language issues and, 36–38
    overview of, 26–27
    persuasive strategies for, 250
    resources for, 42
    social hierarchy and, 32–34
    strategies for success in, 41–44
    views of time and, 31–32
    Web tools for, 28
    workplace values and, 34–35
Cross-cultural competency, 6